Economic Democracy

ECONOMIC DEMOCRACY

The Political Struggle Of the Twenty-first Century

3rd Edition
Expanded and Updated

J.W. Smith

Published jointly by: The Institute for Economic Democracy
& The Institute for Cooperative Capitalism
Group Discounts, Classroom/University Bookstore Discounts
www.ied.info/cc.html

Publisher's Cataloging-in-Publication
(Provided by Quality Books, Inc.)

Smith, J.W., 1930-
Economic democracy : the political struggle of the twenty-first century / J.W. Smith. – 3rd ed.
p. cm.
Includes bibliographical references and Index.
ISBN 0-9624423-4-8 (hbk)
ISBN 0-9624423-5-6 (pbk)

1. Free enterprise—History. 2. Free trade—History. 3. Capitalism—History. 4. Democracy—History. 5. International economic relations—History. I. Title

HB95.S587 2003 330.12'2
QB102-200997

Book cover designed by John Cole, www.johncolegrf.com

This book is printed on acid free paper.

Table of Contents

Acknowledgements

This treatise, like all knowledge and accomplishments, is the result of many people's thoughts and efforts. My special thanks go to the hundreds of authors and reporters who each had a special window on the world, knew that what they viewed was of importance, and had the talent and courage to express it. Their work was the hard part, and, in comparison, synthesizing their clear views of reality into a broad picture of the world economic and political landscape was easy.

Special thanks go to copy editor Barbara Chamberlain. William H. Kötke, author of the impressive *Final Empire*, took the pressure off the final manuscript preparation and his forthcoming books are something we will be watching for. Ralph McGehee and his 12-megabyte database on sources were indispensable. The support of William and Ann Furtick is greatly appreciated. Mr. Petru Dumitriu, United Nations Permanent Mission for Romania, provided important support. Professor Hillar D. Neuman, Jr. offered crucial advice while finalizing the manuscript.

Crucial statistics were provided by the work of Professor Seymour Melman of Columbia University (*Profits Without Production*), Greg Bishak of the National Commission for Economic Conversion and Disarmament, Professor David Gordon (Bowles, Gordon, and Weisskopf), and Arjun Makhijani of the Institute for Energy and Environmental Research.

The faith and advice of my doctoral committee (Professors Marvin Surkin, Stanley Aronowitz, and Tom O'Connell; Dr. Colin Greer, Mr. Richard Barnet, and Ms. Ingrid Lehmann) were greatly appreciated and this project would never have been completed without the credits and support of The Union Institute. Professors Ekema Manga, Nancy Owens, Sylvia Hill, and Rhoda Linton of The Union were especially helpful as was Bill Elison, social science librarian at the University of Montana's Mansfield Library.

The support of *Earth Island Journal* Senior Editor Gar Smith is sincerely appreciated as is the encouragement of Frances Moore Lappé and Professor Ismail Sharriff, Economics Chair at the University of Wisconsin. I thank Professor Richard Hienberg for suggesting this book's name. The support of Fred Rice will always be remembered. Bill Ellis, founding editor of TRANET, provided encouragement. The support of my friend Professor William Alexander of California Polytechnic (retired) is appreciated and the advice of author Michael Parenti was followed.

Bob Swann of The Schumacher Society, William F. Hixson, William Krehm, Cliff Cobb of Redefining Progress, and freelancer Robert Carroll provided crucial advice on money. Professor Tom Arysman, Joe Yarkin, and Clark Branch of Antioch College gave enormous support and advice.

Anup Shah's research and editing, Pofessor Mieczyslaw Dobija's research on money originating as an accounting unit of productive labor, John Bunzl's, Bernie Maopolski's, and Jeff & Diana Jewell were especially helpful.

Special mention must be made for the great help and advice of Feisal Mansoor and Jeanne Thwaites of Sri Lanka and Mochamad Effendi Aboed of Indonesia. Professor Andrej Grubacic of Yugoslavia, Professor Glen T. Martin of International Philosophers for Peace, Professor Radh Achuthan, Professor Michael Rivage-Seul and reporter Dmitry Yanovich from Belarus are valuable members of our team.

Before they took off for a new life in Australia, Jay and Sue McCadden were crucial in helping me understand the complexities of my computer. Ray Miklas and Pete Gannon (www.stuffguys.com) now do that job and do it well. Susan and Mark Coward and their Slonet group and Bob Banner of *Hopedance Magazine* were more helpful than they realize. Emanuel Wongibe of Cameroon and Franz Nahrada of Vienna, Austria have been consistent supporters.

I owe special thanks to Professor Robert Blain of the Southern Illinois University and Professor Walter Davis of Kent State University. Both have been using my research in their classes for years. Watch for their forthcoming books. And many thanks to all others, both known and unknown, who have alerted their students to my work.

The talents of editor Terri Dunivant were greatly appreciated. My first editor Michael Kriesberg was possibly the most crucial support of all.

Most important are the groups, both those internationally established and those who are regional, who have banded together to support this research. Marie Gunther, http://4thefixbooks.com, brought all this together.

Last, and most important, I wish to dedicate this book to my children, Betty, Ada, Patti, and Cynthia, and grandchildren Sam C., Will, Stephan, Mathew, Sam O, and Suzie. It is hoped that this work will contribute to their understanding of the world.

Foreword

At the pivotal point of each age, scholarship comes forward that becomes the defining template of the age to come. This is such a work of scholarship. It is a work that explains the creation of today's world, both its marvels and its violence and misery. Fortunately, it does not leave us with that analysis; it goes on to define what must be done in the future so we all may enjoy the fruits and comforts provided by the social productive capacity that is the property of us all.

History is written by the conquerors but there have always been the intellectual dissenters who have shaken the edifice erected by power and wealth. Jean Jacques Rousseau, Friedrich List, and Karl Marx were such voices, as were America's Thorstein Veblen and Henry George. At times these voices were muffled by the drumbeat of the cheerleaders for the dominant ideological explanation of reality. But, as Dr. Smith demonstrates, these unapproved philosophies are reexamined as each crisis returns to shatter the security and faith in the orthodox explanations.

Smith examines the economic basis of the history of Imperial Civilization. His examination of the precursor configuration of society just prior to the advent of the Industrial Revolution reveals the configuration that is with us even now. Cities in the Middle Ages monopolized the means of production to themselves and conquered and controlled the source of raw materials and the markets in the countryside. Through financial, technological, and military power, allied *imperial-centers-of-capital* control the present world, their countryside, by the same methods and for the same reasons. Smith laboriously outlines the changing verbal coloration of this chameleon through each age and documents that its configuration has not changed.

This serious academic study documents in detail the strategies and techniques whereby a small part of the world's population consumes the majority of the world's resources.

Fewer than 500 people now have more wealth than half of the earth's population. This is an astounding condition. That this is only known by scholars who study obscure statistics of economics attests to what Smith documents: the intense subtle monopolization of all structures of modern society, especially information, by those who own the bulk of it.

The masses of society have struggled for centuries to establish the rights that some of us now enjoy. Labor rights, political rights, women's rights, and human rights are now a popular item of interest in all countries, even though control of society by the masses is waning. Instructively, in the United States, through the sleight of hand of the money that finances politics, political control has moved toward the 1/2 of 1% of the population whose wealth in 1995 roughly equaled that of the lower 90% of society.

Those same people have guided the removal of political control from the level of the voters to more and more rarified levels, ultimately to what Smith refers to as the IMF/World Bank/GATT/NAFTA/WTO/MAI/GATS/FTAA/military colossus. As he describes, this is the legal and policing framework of a functioning, worldwide, corporate-controlled empire.

The value of Smith's scholarship is that he not only reveals the heretofore unrecognized forces that have created the present world, but he goes beyond that to paint a clear and concise picture of the future world. In a world in which we are told there is scarcity and therefore poverty, Smith documents the fact that only part of the money spent on military and economic warfare since the close of World War II could have developed the entire presently undeveloped world. In a time in which those who inhale the world's wealth for speculation, military hardware and economic warfare tell us there is no money for human needs, Smith documents there is an abundance of money and lays out specific and reasonable plans for providing for the world's human needs. Simply stated, one of the values of this work is that it demonstrates in reasonable terms that there are real and legitimate solutions to the problems of housing, food, environment, and peace.

All students who read this work will understand that the world does have a future. There are reasonable solutions. The way that those solutions will be achieved is that the people of the earth will take control of their collective destiny and that the activities of society will be directed toward our common goal of the care of all of human society and the earth. Thus, Smith brings into focus the urgent fact that economic democracy and a modern commons must be the next claim of the world's masses, in order to create full human rights and to institute policies beneficial to the collective destiny rather than profit and power for a few.

William H. Kötke
Author, *The Final Empire*

Acronyms

African Union (AU)
Asian Monetary Fund (AMF)
Associated Press (AP)
Association of Southeast Asian Nations (ASEAN)
Central Intelligence Agency (CIA)
Coordinating Committee for Multilateral Export Controls (Cocom)
European Community (EC)
FBI's Counterintelligence Program (COINTELPRO)
Federal Bureau of Investigation (FBI)
Free Trade Area of the Americas (FTAA)
General Agreement on Trades and Tariffs (GATT)
General Agreement on Trades in Services (GATS)
German Central Intelligence Agency (BND)
Gross National Product (GNP)
Indonesia's Special Forces Command (Kopassus)
International Monetary Fund (IMF)
International Workers of the World (IWW)
Iranian Secret Service (SAVAK)
Kosovo Liberation Army (KLA)
Military Professional Resources (MPRI)
Ministry of Finance (MOF)
Ministry of International Trade and Industry (MITI)
Most Favored Nation (MFN)
Multilateral Agreement on Investments (MAI)
Multilateral Trading Organization (MTO)
National Agreement on Free Trade of the Americas (NAFTA)
National Endowment for Democracy, (NED)
National Security Council Directive (NSC, NSD)
National Union for Total Independence (UNITA)
NATO Alliance High Representatives to Bosnia-Herzegovina (HR)
Newly Industrializing Countries (NIC)
North Atlantic Treaty Alliance (NATO)
Office of Strategic Services (OSS)
Organization for Economic Cooperation and Development (OECD)
Organization of Oil Exporting Countries (OPEC)
Partnership for Peace (PfP)
Popular Movement for the Liberation of Angola (MPLA)
Purchasing Power Parity (PPP)
Quadrilateral Group of Trade Ministers (QUAD)
Regional alliance of Eastern provinces of former Soviet Union (GUUAM)
Seven leading Western Countries (G7)
Socialist Workers Party (SWP)
Special Operations Command (SOCOM)
World Trade Organization (WTO)
Young Socialist Alliance (YSA)

Economic Democracy

Also by J.W. Smith

Cooperative Capitalism: A Blueprint for Global Peace and Prosperity

Why? A Deeper History Behind the September 11th Terrorist Attack on America Two editions

The World's Wasted Wealth 2

The World's Wasted Wealth

Introduction

Just a year after the first release of this book, terrorists hijacked four airliners and flew three of them into New York's World Trade Center and the Pentagon killing over 3,000 people. The attention of the world is now focused on the War on Terrorism and the occupation of Iraq triggered by that terrorist attack on America.

The United States of America, founded on the great ideals of freedom of speech, freedom of thought, freedom of movement, and freedom from oppression, is a great country. This author cherishes those values as much as anyone else and believes firmly that the war against terrorism must be waged. But that war cannot be permanently won without understanding and removing its rather straight forward cause—the most massive transfer of wealth in history from the periphery of empire to the imperial center.

Almost every book is written with a view on being *politically correct.* As we are attempting to look reality right in the eye, we do not worry about such niceties. Our research is simply finding honest history and there is much in history that does not square with justice, ethics, or doing what is right. Those unjust and unethical aspects of our history must be analyzed and understood; so it is capitalism's history we will be studying closely.

On this we wish to be clear. The unjust and unethical state policies we will be addressing were put in place by good people, no different than you and I. *Managers-of-state* are simply locked into a system of unequal trades which began in the Middle Ages. The very life-blood of powerful societies flow through those arteries of unequal trade and, until advancement to today's level of industrial technology and further advancement in social technology (truly democratic governments and a peaceful foreign policy of equal and fair trade), conscientious leaders could not disrupt that flow of commerce without creating a severe crisis.

The gains from efficiency of technology and from restructuring from *residual-feudal* subtle-monopoly capitalism to *democratic-cooperative-capitalism*, provides the opportunity for a historic shift to just and ethical state policies of equal and fair trade. That transition would quickly eliminate most poverty which, in turn, would eliminate terrorism and wars.

The elimination of the wastes of violence, if the benefits are shared, will wipe out most poverty. After all, only an additional $40-billion a year would provide clean water and sanitation, care for women's reproductive health, basic health and nutrition, and basic education for all the world's citizens. The money spent on arms annually is $800-billion, the wealth destroyed is surely an equal amount, and the wealth production forgone by these wasteful efforts is by far the greater waste.

Superior rights for the few and inferior rights for the many are structured into the subtle monopolization of land, technology, money, and information (Section B). The unearned wealth of the subtle monopolists of those enclosed commons both reduces the efficiency of an economy and lowers the share of wealth of others. Having been born and raised within the current legal structure and taught with sincerity—by those who learned those fables right in the university—that this is the most efficient economy, we are unaware that these highly inefficient subtle monopolies even exist.

An economy is a social machine to produce and distribute the needs of the people. People associate together in a society for mutual benefit; the basic civilizing impulse is the protection of the weak from the tyranny of the strong. Economic value is created by working, eating, drinking or, to put it simply, by 'living'. Through creating subtle-monopoly property rights structuring inequality into law, the cunning have convinced the unwitting to willingly hand a large share of this wealth to them.

That these subtle monopolies are necessary to accumulate capital is another fable (see subchapter The Tragedy of the Commons). Capital can accumulate much faster in an economy with full and equal rights for all. Removal of subtle monopolization and a return of the full and equal rights of a modern commons would not only increase your rights to land, your rights to the use of technology, your rights to finance capital, your rights to information, and your rights to your share of the returns from their productive use, it ensures those rights. A modern commons becomes *democratic-cooperative-capitalism*.

So long as all have access to land, technology, and finance capital, as outlined herein, those monopolies cannot reconstitute themselves and the huge overcharges which currently lay claim to the wealth produced by others will disappear. The managers of capital will be under such intense competition that the incompetent will quickly disappear, economic efficiency will rise steeply, and the competent will be held to a fair profit. That fair profit will then be recognized for what it really is; their fair wages.

It is unequal pay for equally-productive work which creates an extremely wealthy few and an impoverished many. Not only is unequal pay a cause of poverty, through failure to build buying power in step with productive capacity, it severely reduces economic efficiency, wastes industrial capacity, and creates wars. Those wars waste, and destroy, even more labor, capital, and resources.

Subtle-Monopolization is a Remnant of Feudal Property Rights

Social customs are a form of law. It is well recognized that these customs and laws are huge obstacles for societies to evolve efficiently. The fact that the debris of *residual-feudal exclusive* property rights to nature's wealth severely reduces the efficiency of capitalism is not even considered.

We are taught that monopolization has been eliminated by law. This is not true. Laws are designed by the powerful, for their protection, they have specifically designed subtle monopolization into laws of capitalism. Under *exclusive feudal* property rights a tiny minority totally monopolized wealth producing property and the wealth produced. Western societies evolved from Feudalism. Those who gained power and what appeared to be full rights were only being granted a share of *feudal monopoly rights.*

The basic principals of monopolization were never abandoned, that we are taught they were notwithstanding. We have full rights only in the sense that each have a chance at becoming a wealthy monopolist. But only a calculable few can attain those *residual-feudal* monopoly rights. This is not visible to Americans and Europeans because of the large percentage that have a high standard of living and thus appear to have full rights.

But, unrealized by the masses and most in academia, that high standard of living is only through the purchase of the wealth of weak nations for a fraction of its true value, and the distribution of that appropriated wealth through the massive expenditures on the military (the multiplier factor) which is the final arbiter to maintain the system of laying claim to the world's wealth. This translates to an economic system not viable in times of peace. The powerful today are fighting to retain their monopoly property rights just as the feudal powers fought to maintain the monopolization of wealth based on their *exclusive feudal property rights.*

All this will become visible as we demonstrate how, through abandoning those remnants of *feudal exclusive title* to nature's wealth and restructuring to *democratic-cooperative-capitalism*, economic efficiency will increase equal to the invention of money, the printing press, and electricity. As we describe today's internal economies and global trade, we ask the reader to take note of the close connection current subtle-monopoly laws have to the total monopoly laws of feudalism. Today's wars are protecting a monopolized *wealth-producing-process* just as aristocracy fought to retain their monopoly on power and wealth. Today's partial democracies are only stepping stones towards full freedom and full rights for all once the last remnant of *feudal exclusive property titles* to what is properly social wealth is converted to *conditional* property titles that recognize everyone's rights to their share of nature's bounty.

Accumulating capital through monopolization may have been unavoidable while evolving from up-front monopoly feudalism to subtle-monopoly capitalism. The unequal rights derived from that early history and firmly established in custom and law could not be quickly changed. But accumulating capital through subtle monopolization is not only unnecessary, it drastically lowers economic efficiency.

Proponents of the current excessive rights structured into law fail to understand that giving a few an excessive share of rights while restricting the rights of others (inequality structured in law, that remnant of feudalism) is a subtle form of monopolization. Our concluding chapters will demonstrate that, through relatively small changes in the legal structure, rights to the modern commons can be regained while expanding private property rights, individualism, and competition. *Democratic-cooperative-capitalism* is so efficient that each will be able to provide themselves a quality lifestyle working only 2-to-3 days per week.

Following the currency collapses in 1997-98 of the once-robust Asian tiger economies, equally-productive labor's pay in parts of the developing world dropped to 10% that of workers in the developed world. This is not just a 10-fold difference in buying power; wealth accumulates exponentially with the wage differential between equally-productive labor (Chapter 1). That 10-fold differential in wage rates for equally-productive labor translates into a 100-fold differential in wealth accumulation power and accumulated wealth (capital) is the engine of capitalism.

Current free trade is just as unequal as the mercantilist trade it supposedly replaced. Indeed, if unequal pay for the equally-productive work of weak nations were reduced to a 50% pay differential, the potential wealth accumulated by nations with high-paid labor in direct trades with low-paid labor nations would be reduced from a 100-times wealth accumulation advantage to an advantage of only four times.

Controlling technology in the outlying countryside so as to maintain access to resources and the *wealth-producing-process* originated in the city-states of Europe in the Middle Ages. As control of resources and trade determined who would be wealthy and powerful, those city-states battled over who would control the countryside and the *wealth-producing-process.*

Those city-states evolved into nations whose wealth was also determined by control of resources and trade beyond their borders. The need to control a vast countryside to maintain power and wealth led to the colonization of the world by the imperial nations of Europe. Control of vast territories meant immense wealth to the imperial centers and there were many wars as these empires fought over who would control these territories and that vast wealth.

When industrial technology became more refined and expensive, the British concluded they could monopolize the *wealth-producing-process* through a restructured mercantilism hiding under the cover of free trade. Certainly Adam Smith sought to discredit mercantilism and replace it with his vision of free trade. But he still envisioned the rest of the world as the countryside providing natural resources and Britain as the industrial center converting those resources into finished products.

So long as weak nations could be forced to accept those unequal trades, they would be handing their wealth to the powerful nations of their own free will. Through the monopolization of highly efficient industrial technology, control of the *wealth-producing-process* was to remain with the imperial center while the periphery was to provide the natural resources to feed those industries.

The American colonies rejected those rules of unequal trade, protected their industry and markets, and became wealthy. Other European imperial nations easily understood Britain's plan to establish an *imperial-center-of-capital.* Competition between the established and the emerging centers of capital for control of technology, resources, and markets eventually led to the two world wars that broke all the European *imperial-centers-of-capital* and the Japanese imperial center.

With the old imperial centers now too poor to finance the military forces necessary to maintain control, the colonial nations began breaking free. All wealth is processed from natural resources and without the natural wealth from the old colonial empires the shattered nations of Europe and Japan could not rebuild from WWII. The only intact center of capital left was the United States. The baton was passed to America to bring the periphery of empire back under control and retain those resources for the old imperial-centers. This is known in history as the Cold War.

The world looked up to America as a champion of freedom and rights. To admit to a suppression of freedom and rights under the rhetoric of free trade would be to lose the Cold War before it started. America solved its dilemma through demonizing as enemies any who had broken out from under, or were attempting to break out from under, the control of *imperial-centers-of-capital*. Unequal trades imposed by military power under colonialism were transformed to unequal trades imposed by financial and economic power supported by covert warfare. A few (Korea, Vietnam, Iraq, Yugoslavia) were brought to heel through open warfare.

Given opportunities and rights, people within all societies are equally capable. All wealth is processed from natural resources. With most of the world's natural resources within their borders, currently destitute regions of the world should be wealthy and strong. But those nations were impoverished by colonialism and they are further impoverished by current structural adjustment policies that lower their education and health levels, limit their access to technology, and force them into unequal trades. Thus resource-wealthy nations remain as impoverished providers of cheap resources and cheap labor to the resource-poor *imperial-centers-of-capital.*

Never did a Nation Develop under Adam Smith

That current free trade is just as unequal as the mercantilist trade it replaced is easily demonstrated. The structural adjustments imposed upon weak nations as necessary for free trade are the opposite policies under which every successful nation developed. Virtually every nation successfully developing did so under Friedrich List's philosophy of protection of tender new industries and markets. That they developed under the philosophies of Adam Smith is a myth designed to hide a continuation of plunder through unequal trades.

One cannot separate economics, political science, and history. Politics is the control of the economy and history, when accurately and fully recorded, is that story. In most textbooks and classrooms, not only are these three fields of study separated, they are further compartmentalized into separate subfields which hide the close interconnections between them.

To understand how the world's wealth is controlled and distributed we must study centuries of suppressed history. Eight-hundred years ago the powerful of the city-states of Europe learned to control the resources and markets of the countryside by raiding and destroying others' primitive industrial capital, thus openly monopolizing that capital and establishing and maintaining extreme inequality of pay. This low pay siphoned the wealth of the countryside to the *imperial-centers-of-capital* (Chapter 1). The powerful had learned to *plunder-by-trade* and have been refining those skills ever since (Chapters 2 through 9).

Two-hundred years ago, Britain's William Pitt (1759-1806) realized that Adam Smith's *Wealth of Nations* (if interpreted carefully and selectively), would be a great philosophy under which England could consolidate those unequal trades into customary practice and maintain dominance in world trade. As a cover under which England could maintain that dominance, British government, British intelligence, and British industry supported lecturers throughout the world promoting their interpretation of Adam Smith's philosophy.[1] That imposed belief successfully protected powerful nations' access to resources and markets and, for the same purpose, continues as the world's dominant philosophy today.

Every nation that successfully developed did so following the protectionist philosophy of German economist and naturalized American citizen Friedrich List (1789-1846) even as those same nations were mouthing the free-trade philosophy of Adam Smith. This includes Britain, America, Germany, Japan, the Asian tigers that were so essential for economically and philosophically containing the post WWII rapid expansion of socialism, and now China.

Friedrich List observed the collapse of European industry when Napoleon's continental system was dismantled after his defeat at Waterloo in 1815. From those observations, and after watching firsthand America's rapid development through ignoring Britain's imposition of Adam Smith's philosophy, List published his protectionist classic, *The National System of Political Economy*, in 1841.

When British power was shattered by World Wars I and II, America was the only remaining wealthy imperial nation. To protect herself and her historic allies, and against the interests of the economic liberation of the colonial world from the weakened imperial powers, America took over the job of maintaining the imposition of the neo-mercantilist/neo-liberal interpretation of Adam Smith upon the world (Chapters 6 through 11).

In *The Long Twentieth Century*, Giovanni Arrighi outlines "systemic cycles of accumulation" of capital that have occurred, starting with the trading empires of Genoa and Venice. Throughout those cycles of capital accumulation one spots the same financial warfare, economic warfare, and open warfare to control world trade and the *wealth-producing-process* that we address throughout this book. After building this solid base for understanding financial empires, Arrighi addresses the U.S. abandoning the historic monopolizations of the *wealth-producing-process* and describes America as championing the accumulation of capital and wealth for the once-colonized nations.[2]

We like Arrighi's optimism, wish it were true, and his analysis of the historic evolution of capitalism is crucial to understanding economic history. But the record proves that the West's financial empire is no different than all other financial empires in history. Those necessary as allies to control the *wealth-producing-process* are developed quickly and they rapidly become wealthy. Nations not needed for allies remain impoverished providers of cheap resources and cheap labor for the wealthy and powerful *imperial-centers-of-capital*. The allied financial, economic, and military might of the imperial centers maintain the continued siphoning of wealth from the weak to the powerful.

We all understand that dictatorships have secrets because they do vile and unjust things that they do not want known. But what could be so secret in democratic societies where governments are supposed to be employees of the people? Quite simply, most wealthy societies have very few resources and even the resource-wealthy American consumer society is dependent upon resources and markets throughout the world. The secret that cannot be told is that the wealth of an imperial center requires controlling the "countryside" to provide cheap resources: the minerals, timber, fuel, and fibers necessary for a comfortable society. Increasingly, that dependency extends to products manufactured with cheap labor on the periphery. Thus the terms "national security" and "national interests" and our acceptance of those spoken words as all we are entitled to know.

Although believing it is always other nations that are the aggressor, not their nation, most people understand that, if this continues, powerful nations battling and the wastes of mass production and mass consumption will eventually seriously degrade the world's ecosystem. To avoid that, we need only restructure from the violence of neo-mercantilism/neo-liberalism (metamorphosed to corporate imperialism) monopolizing the world's resources into all the world's people sharing those resources through *democratic-cooperative-capitalism*. Once that choice is made, all need for national secrets disappear and the goals of all—world peace, sustainable development, and elimination of poverty—can be attained, and all while rebuilding and protecting the world's soils and ecosystems.

The Legal Structure assuring the Imperial Centers access to the World's Resources

Denial of technology to the periphery by the cosmopolitan centers in the early centuries of capitalism is the cause of wealth concentration in the resource-poor, but powerful, regions of the world and impoverishment in the resource-rich, but weak, regions.

Inequality continues to be structured in law today. The powerful, developed world established the International Monetary Fund (IMF), the World Bank, the General Agreement on Trades and Tariffs (GATT), the North American Free Trade Agreement (NAFTA), the World Trade Organization (WTO), and is in the process of establishing the Multilateral Agreement on Investments (MAI [resurfacing under the General Agreement on Trade in Services {GATS}]) and FTAA (Free Trade Area of the Americas) as the financial and legal structure under which it retains access to the world's cheap resources:

> Final authority will rest with the Gats [MAI, WTO, FTAA] Disputes Panel to determine whether a law or regulation is, in the memo's language, 'more burdensome than necessary'. And Gats [MAI, WTO, FTAA], not Parliament, will decide what is 'necessary'. As a practical matter, this means nations will have to shape laws protecting the air you breathe, the trains you travel in and the food you chew by picking not the best or safest means for the nation, but the cheapest methods for foreign investors and merchants. … Under Gats [MAI, WTO, FTAA], as proposed in the memo, national laws and regulations will be struck down if they are 'more burdensome than necessary' to business. Notice the subtle change. Suddenly the Gats treaty is not about trade at all, but a sly means to wipe away restrictions on business and industry, foreign and local. … The WTO reports that, in the course of the secretive multilateral negotiations, trade ministers agreed that a Gats tribunal would not accept a defense of 'safeguarding the public interest'. In place of a public interest standard, the Secretariat proposes a deliciously Machiavellian 'efficiency principle': 'It may well be politically more acceptable to countries to accept international obligations which give primacy to economic efficiency.' This is an unsubtle invitation to load the Gats with requirements that rulers know their democratic parliaments could not otherwise accept. … Hearings are

> closed. Unions, as well as consumer, environmental and human rights groups, are barred from participating—or even knowing what is said before the panel.[3]

The wealthy world both creates and protects its wealth through processing those cheap resources into valuable products and powerful military weapons. Thus, the natural wealth of the impoverished regions finances the military of the wealthy world that protects the unequal trade structure and maintains the status quo. This wealth-confiscation process, ostensibly to accumulate capital, is not the efficient developer of the world we are taught to believe. That worldwide battle to maintain the dominance of imperial nations in world trade leads to nothing less than "capital destroying capital" (Chapter 18) and far more wealth is destroyed than is accumulated as capital. Yes subtle-monopoly capitalism is efficient when compared to any other form of monopolization but fair trade *democratic-cooperative-capitalism*, which eliminates all monopolization, is many times more efficient than free trade/subtle-monopoly capitalism.

Accumulated capital and consumer purchasing power are both derived from title to natural resources, title to industrial capital, title to distribution mechanisms, and adequately paid labor. Creating high capitalized values require mass markets, and mass markets develop only from well-paid labor. Therefore, whenever possible, developing nations should be trading with each other. If wages paid for production of the products traded are equal and each have their share of productive industry, neither appropriates the wealth of the other and trade functions efficiently and honestly.

Because much more wealth is retained when nations with low-paid labor trade with each other, emerging nations can develop their economies much more rapidly than when trading with a high-paid nation. Capital accumulation is not the limiting factor. Capital can be accumulated more easily, more equitably, and far more rapidly under *democratic-cooperative-capitalism* than through the current subtle monopolization of the world's land, technologies, money, resources, and markets.[4]

The subtle monopolization of world trade and internal commerce, having been hidden under imposed beliefs so long, makes it hard to conceptualize a world with true equality, true freedom, and full rights. All this thesis is saying is, "Be who we say we are. Do what we say we do. Have honest free trade and honest free enterprise." This requires equalizing wages worldwide for equally-productive work and thus eliminating the system of subtle monopolization of the world's resources and industries under which those inequalities of trade are maintained.

There are three foundations to production: natural resources (land), labor, and industrial capital. Freedom and rights cannot be obtained until there is equal sharing of the money creation process. Under conditions of full equality of rights for money creation, any region may create the money to combine surplus resources and labor to produce industrial capital and consumer products or services. Those industries, the products produced, and the increase in both money and production, through the multiplier factor as this money is spent again and again within the economy, become the wealth to back the created money.

The World Bank says it is moving toward these Suggestions

The underlying discussions at the 1999 World Bank meeting in Tokyo on the 1997-98 financial meltdowns of former healthy economies were: "American style free-market policies are seen as finished ... government should guide development, ... if necessary protecting key industries from competition and rely on bureaucratic wisdom instead rather than market forces, ... and expanding political rights and freedoms are the best means to development."[5] There is much more to do but that is a major shift by the World Bank, at least in words, towards what this book is recommending:

> "The World Bank … describes 'the full complement of core public goods and services' [for the developing nations] as consisting in 'a foundation of lawfulness, a stable macroeconomy, the rudiments of public health, universal primary education, adequate transport infrastructure, and a minimal safety net.' "[6]

But don't count on the World Bank living up to those words. Their chief economist, Joseph Stiglitz, suggested this change in policy and was summarily and immediately pushed out of the World Bank. In 2001 he was awarded the Nobel Prize for his efforts.[7]

Even if the full extent of the injustice of inequalities of trade were realized by enough people and change forced upon the world, adjusting to equal trade will be a slow and traumatic process. The world's arteries of commerce are built upon inequalities of trade, and severing those arteries will create extreme political crises. Whenever those arteries of commerce are threatened, the historic response has been to activate political, financial, economic, and military resources to re-impose the philosophies that have protected the beneficiaries of those unequal trades.

However, since the undeveloped world has yet to establish their production and distribution systems, they are not locked in. Our concluding chapters will demonstrate that, through utilizing the maximum efficiencies of technology and communication, the developing world can establish a production/distribution system in which, for the same standard of living, they work half as much as workers in the developed world.

Progressive philosophies that would equalize rights and wealth for all have been around for at least 120 years. However, the powerful have been able to avoid such threats to the status quo by cosmetic change, imposition of philosophies which protect their privilege and power, and suppression of all efforts to utilize the progressive philosophies. If we eliminate the waste of resources and the waste from capital battling over the world's wealth, extreme poverty can be eliminated in 10 years and the world can be industrialized to a sustainable level and poverty largely eliminated in two generations (Chapter 23).

It is impossible for the developing world to accumulate its own capital without—on the average—owning its own resources, building industries with created (debt free) money, owning and running its own factories, being paid equally for equally-productive labor, and having the right to sell through established markets. Regions cannot develop a healthy economy without broad-based local buying power. It is, after all, consumer purchasing power—adequate wages, adequate commodity prices, and profits from efficient industry and efficient traders—that determines who ends up with the world's wealth.

This book is an effort to show how simple it would be to restructure from the current subtle-monopoly capitalism (corporate imperialism) with all its violence and poverty to a caring *democratic-cooperative-capitalism* with a minimum level of violence and poverty.

The efficient economy we are describing can not happen until true democracy is established. At each point in the centuries-long march to full rights and full democracy, the powerful structured the laws for their protection (those *residual-feudal exclusive* property rights). The rights of the masses were only considered when a crisis threatened.

Full rights were not attained even after revolutions. There was simply too much debris of law and custom to clean away (those *residual-feudal exclusive* property rights again). But each gain in rights would be trumpeted as full rights and this hid the fact that full rights had not been attained.

Theoretically we have democracy today. But that is only theoretical. We only have partial democracies with the potential of full democracies. But we are getting closer. Once those subtle monopolies that evolved from feudal total monopolies are eliminated, a full democracy can emerge. Likewise if a crisis transposes today's partial democracies into full democracies simple legal changes can be made to eliminate those subtle *residual-feudal* monopolies and establish efficient *democratic-cooperative-capitalism.*

If we are so militarily secure, why does America have such a violent foreign policy as this book exposes? It is because students of foreign policy are not taught peace. Instead they are taught that no other nation can be trusted so give no quarter and take all they can get.[a]

The primary concept of a modern commons and *residual-feudal exclusive* property rights in *Cooperative Capitalism: A Blueprint for Global Peace and*

---

[a] Which is exactly what they do. All foreign policy planners are doing the opposite of what they are telling the masses. For that policy laid bare read Michel Chossodobsky's work. We chose to show the fictions of economics as taught today and to lay out an honest world development philosophy. He addresses foreign policy in much more depth.

Prosperity was so powerful that, to give all readers the benefit of these concepts, we inserted it into this book and that of *WHY? The Deeper History Behind the September 11, 2001 Terrorist Attack on America.* The central focus of each book gains strength from the others' primary concepts. We trust our readers will agree on the necessity of inserting these concepts into all three books.

We have referenced our work deeply. However, we highly recommend picking keywords and key people and countries off these pages and run Internet searches on Google. Try many combinations of those keywords and others that come to mind. One will be surprised at what news and history books have failed to tell us and each search only takes minutes. With those sources at the reader's fingertips on a Google search, in a few years authors will insert only a few citations. The really curious and motivated will make that Internet search at important points in all books and articles they read. A search for alternative views on subjects on the evening news will be a great education.

---

1 Friedrich List, *The National System of Political Economy* (Fairfield, NJ: Augustus M. Kelley, 1977), in Memoirs and Extracts.

2 Giovanni Arrighi, *The Long Twentieth Century* (New York: Verso, 2000).

3 "Necessity Test is Mother of GATS Intervention" *The Observer* (April 15, 2001). See also: John McMurtry, "The FTAA and the WTO: The Meta-Program for Global Corporate Rule," *Economic Reform* (April, 2001).

4 See subchapters "Accumulation of Capital through Cooperative Capitalism" and "A Banking System Structured to Protect the Rights of All" in Chapter 27, "Investment" in Chapter 27, and Chapter 23.

5 Cameron W. Barr, "Making the Financial Architecture More Crisis Proof," *The Christian Science Monitor.* March 3, 1999, pp. 1, 7. See also William H. Hatal and Richard J. Verey, "Recognizing the 'Third Way,'" *The Christian Science Monitor,* March 3, 1999, p. 9.

6 John Gray, *False Dawn* (New York: The Free Press, 1998), p. 202.

7 Lucy Komisar, "Taking on the Debt Collectors, Joseph Stiglitz" (*The Progressive,* June 2000), p. 34. Joseph E. Stiglitz, *Globalization and its Discontents* (New York: WW Norton, 2002).

Section A

External Trade

Part I

Security for Powerful Nations Entails Insecurity for Weak Nations

1. The Secret of Free Enterprise Capital Accumulation

Capitalism's capital accumulation has some studiously ignored secrets. That capital is properly owned and employed by labor is recognized by no less an authority than Adam Smith: "Produce is the natural wages of labor. Originally the whole belonged to the labourer. If this had continued all things would have become cheaper, though in appearance many things might have become dearer."[1] Of course, the production once claimed by labor and now lost is the ever-increasing share that is going to profits of subtle-monopoly landrent, subtle-monopoly patents, a subtly-monopolized banking system, and the enormous costs of running those monopolies.

What Smith means by all things being cheaper, though they appear dearer, is that if workers had been fully paid they would have retained full title to the value of what they produced. Things would be cheaper because fully-paid workers would be able to buy more from other well-paid workers, who in turn would both produce more and purchase more. Not only would purchasing power be advancing in step with productive capacity, those who lived off the labors of others would now have to find productive work.

Instead of workers being paid full value for their labor, much of history has been capital—through control of the law-making process—transferring a part of labor's rights to itself. As Adam Smith goes on to explain, this is a centuries-long process of the wealth produced by labor becoming a right of capital through subtly-monopolized title to land, technology, and finance capital.[2] The rights of labor have historically been ignored and an excessive share of the wealth produced by the increased efficiencies of labor has, under exclusive property rights of *residual feudalism*, accrued to capital.

Wealth Accumulation Expands or Contracts Exponentially with the Differential in Pay

> Technology and skill gaps, if initially large, tend to grow under free trade. This is an old Mercantilist insight that the modern economic analysis of innovation has reaffirmed and renamed the "learning-by-doing" requirement—that is,

> experience with the productive process is a *sine qua non* for building up productive skills and innovative prowess. —David Felix, "Latin America's Debt Crisis," *World Policy Journal*

The secret to siphoning away others' wealth is the low-paid labor in the poor nations and high profits and high wages in the rich societies that have dominated global trade for centuries. Arjun Makhijani calculates that, through an imbalance of currency values, equally-productive labor in the world's defeated, dependent nations were paid 20% that of the developed world, a 5-to-1 differential.[3] Later currency collapses in the developing world may have doubled that differential to 10-to-1.

Wealth accumulation advantage from unequally-paid but equally-productive labor is not a linear progression, it is exponential. Consider how long the underpaid nation must work to buy one unit of wealth from the high-paid nation and then *consider how many units of wealth the high-paid nation can purchase from the underpaid nation with the wages of their equally-productive labor working that same number of hours.*

Capital accumulation advantage increases or decreases exponentially with the differential in pay for equally-productive labor. The equally-productive worker in the poorly-paid nation produces a unique widget, is paid $1 an hour, and is producing one widget an hour. The equally-productive worker in the well-paid nation produces another unique widget, is paid $10 an hour, and also produces one widget per hour. Each equally-productive nation likes, and purchases, the other's widgets. All true costs are labor costs so we ignore monopoly capital costs, which go to the developed world and only increases the advantage anyway, and calculate the cost of those widgets at the labor cost of production, $1 an hour and $10 an hour. The $1 an hour country must work 10 hours to buy one of the widgets of the $10 an hour country but, with the money earned in the same 10 hours, the $10 an hour country can buy 100 of the widgets of the $1 an hour nation. In a homogenized market (a mixture of high-paid and underpaid equally-productive labor) there is a 10-times differential in wealth gained. *At that 10-times wage differential in a non-homogenized market (this example) there is an exponential 100-times differential in capital accumulation or buying power.*

The wealth accumulation advantage of the higher-paid nation over the lower-paid nation is equal to the high pay divided by the low pay squared: $(Wr/Wp)^2 = A$ (Wr is the wages paid to equally-productive labor in the rich country [$10 earned for every 1-hour time-unit of production]. Wp is the wages paid to equally-productive labor in the poor country [$1 earned for every 1-hour time-unit of production]. A is the capital accumulation advantage of the well-paid nation [100-to-1 in this example]). All wealth is processed from natural resources by labor utilizing industrial capital, most of those resources are in the weak, impoverished world, and that natural wealth is transferred to the powerful *imperial-centers-of-capital* through low commodity prices and unequal pay for equal work, as per this formula.

The scenario above is expressed *ã' priôri'* (assuming the labor cost to build industries in each country and the resources harvested in each country, and thus the value of those industries and resources and the profits produced, at the same differential). This math is only in trade between nations with a wage differential for equally-productive labor. It does not represent trade within homogenized multiple markets of many high-paid and low-paid equally-productive workers. It does, however, point the way towards complex formulas that will accurately describe those complex markets.

In reality, only a part of the workers in world trade are equally-productive but all could be relatively so if they had equal access to technology, training, and markets. Even now, grape pickers, strawberry pickers, janitors, et al.—any work which is not mechanized anywhere else in the world—and a share of the industrial labor of the developing world are just as productive as other workers anywhere.

It has been proven that labor everywhere can be trained to run industries just as efficiently and at times more efficiently, than developed world labor. Whenever the difference in pay is greater than the difference in productivity, a part of the production of the underpaid nation is transferred to the high-paid country. To maintain control of that *wealth-producing-process*, it has been the *Grand Strategy* of imperial nations for centuries to monopolize the production processes through denying other nations the use of technology and access to markets. Thus it has been imperial policies that have kept poor countries from learning industrial skills and building productive, affluent, economies—not their incapacity to learn.

Equal Pay for Equal Work is the Answer to World Poverty

As we have learned, in direct trades between countries, wealth accumulation advantage compounds in step with the pay differential for equally-productive labor. If the pay differential is 5, the difference in wealth accumulation advantage is 25-to-1. If the pay differential is 10, the wealth accumulation advantage is 100-to-1. If the pay differential is 20, the wealth accumulation advantage is 400-to-1. If the pay differential is 40, the wealth accumulation advantage is 1,600-to-1. If the pay differential is 60 (the pay differential between Russia and the victorious America [23-cents an hour against $14 an hour]), the wealth accumulation advantage is 3,600-to-1. And if the pay differential is 100, the pay differential between the collapsed Russia and the victorious Germany (23 cents and hour against $23 and hour), the wealth accumulation advantage is 10,000-to-1.[a] Place a trader

---

[a] Obviously the Russian worker's factory was at that time essentially shut down, they were still being paid their 23-cents an hour, nothing was produced, and the

between those two unequally-paid nations to claim all surplus value both through outright underpaying in hard currency or through paying in soft currency and selling in hard currency, capitalize those profits by 10-to-20 times, and you have accumulated capital through capitalized value.[4]

Inequality in pay creates *invisible borders* that guide the world's wealth to *imperial-centers-of-capital.* Equal pay for equally-productive labor instantly eliminates those borders and alleviates world poverty. If unequal pay for equally-productive work were reduced to a 50% pay differential (an equally-productive $5-an-hour nation trading with a $10-an-hour nation), the wealth accumulation advantage of the high-paid nation in direct trades with low-paid nations would be reduced to a 4-times advantage. A $3-an-hour labor nation trading with a $4-an-hour labor nation incurs a doubling (1.77 times) of wealth potentially accumulated (or consumed) for the better-paid nation. When all have access to technology and markets and pay is equal for equally-productive work, the wealth retained (and available for accumulation or consumption) by each nation is equal.

Underpay through unequal Currency Values

When the IMF/World Bank/GATT/NAFTA/WTO/MAI/GATS/ FTAA /military colossus forces other countries to devalue their currencies and reduce consumption to increase sales of their valuable natural resources to the developed world, this lowers the value of their labor and commodities, and raises the relative value of manufactured products from the developed world. The claim is made that this is due to the inefficiencies of developing world industry and labor, but this is hardly so:

> The low level of wages is intimately linked not to low productivity of labor-time, as classical economic theory would suggest, but to the undervalued exchange rates and the workings of the international monetary system.... The world's monetary system does not set values of the currencies on the basis of relative productivity of workers.... The present system is based on balance of payments considerations and on capital flows.... [*T*]*he Mexican currency is valued much lower than the relative productivity of Mexican workers collectively*.... [W]hile the average amount produced per unit of time by workers in Mexico, Brazil or

---

formula appears inaccurate. But it is the basis that is inaccurate, not the formula. Before its collapse, the Soviet Union was calculated to be within 8 years of equaling the West in technology (Rich Thomas, "From Russia, With Chips," *Newsweek* (Aug. 6, 1990). With its huge natural resources and its highly skilled workforce operating factories utilizing the latest technology, and assuming it had access to markets, Russia could theoretically produce just as efficiently as anyone else.

The billions of dollars poured into Russia were not building any *manufacturing* industry at all, let alone modern industries. A massive inflow of funds used for anything except building a technologically modern industrial capacity becomes a debt trap that lays claim to more and more of a dependent nation's wealth.

> Bangladesh is lower than in France, the United States or Japan, *the difference in wages at present exchange rates is much bigger than the difference in productivity.* This explains why the purchasing power of American dollars, French francs or Japanese yen is much bigger in Mexico, Bangladesh or Brazil than it is in their countries of origin.[5]

Arjun Makhijani explains further:

> The product that export platform countries in the developing world are selling is not merely cheap labor, but highly productive labor. In Singapore ... McGraw Hill produces in one year an encyclopedia that takes five years to produce in the U.S.... Mexican metal workers are 40 percent more productive than U.S. workers, electronics workers 10 to 15 percent more productive, and seamstresses produce 30 percent more sewing per hour than their U.S. counterparts.[6]

One study concluded developing world workers were paid as little as 8/10-of-1% of the product sales price in the industrial world and in all cases they were paid under 2% of the final sales price.[7]

Paying equally-productive developing world labor 20% the rate of developed world labor (since the currency collapses halved their wages, possibly under 10%), and the former Eastern bloc only a fraction of that, is a wealth confiscation rate far greater than at the origin of the monopolization of the tools of production and proto-mercantilist control of trade (*plunder-by-trade*) in the city-states and coalescing nations of Europe centuries ago (see next chapter).

There is "a continuing South-to-North resource flow on a scale far outstripping any the colonial period could command."[8] During Kennedy's presidency there were $3 flowing north for every $1 going south; in 1998 the ratio was 7-to-1 and, assuming the financial meltdown of the imperial centers is avoided, the rate of flow will increase. With their enormous reserves of wealth in the developed world, corporations and speculators are buying up properties in the financially collapsed world for 3-cents to 30-cents on the $1. Those titles to others' industries and natural resources will demand profits and those profits will flow to the imperial centers. That will further increase the flow of wealth to the financial centers.

Purchasing Power Parity, a Strategy of Deception

The farther one goes east from the borders of Western Europe, the lower the value of local currencies and thus the higher the rate of wealth confiscation. In each case, if labor values were calculated by the Purchasing Power Parity (PPP) system, one would find greater wealth in those countries.

Simply stated, PPP calculates commodity values in countries with undervalued currencies at their values in the *imperial-centers-of-capital.* Those values may have been calculated in all sincerity. But the low wages and prices received by the already impoverished when calculated in "hard" currency gave substantial moral power to impoverished countries when negotiating with the IMF and World Bank which chose PPP to offset such embarrassment. What was not addressed was that these low currency values denied full value to the soft currency nations when purchasing from the imperial center while simultaneously they were required to sell to the already wealthy world below value.

If the IMF, World Bank, and traders used these PPP equal values in purchase of commodities and payment of debts, the world's currently suppressed and oppressed people would be fully paid for their labors and would thus have gained their economic freedom. Of course, such calculations would immediately expose how powerful societies lay claim to others' wealth through unequal wages and low-priced commodities by imposed "soft" currency values.

Periphery of Empire Finances the Imperial Centers

Poor countries are financing the rich through the wealthy world underpaying equally-productive developing world labor, paying far less than full value for natural resources, and through primarily investing in commodity production for the wealthy world. In this process, between 1980 and 1990—when measured against the dollar (not internal [PPP] relative values)—"wage levels in Mexico declined by 60% [another 40% in 1994-95] ..., in Argentina by 50% and in Peru by 70%."[9] This appears as IMF/World Bank/GATT/NAFTA/WTO/MAI/GATS/FTAA failures. However, they are the successes of financial and economic warfare, not failures. The prices of developing world commodities are lowered while the prices of developed world products are retained, siphoning ever more wealth to corporate imperialists:

> Capital that has extended its influence over these new territories knows its own interests, works together in its common interests even while individual capitals compete, [and] coordinates its goals and its strategies in its common interest.... There will always be social inequality, because that increases profits; winners win more because losers lose more. Keeping the Third World in dependence and poverty is not an accident or a failure of the world capitalist system, but part of its formula for success.[10]

Holland consumes 14-times the natural resources within its borders as calculated in monetary units, which far undervalues developing world labor. Other European countries are more or less comparable, and the United States, with fewer than 5% of the world's population, consumes almost 30% of the world's natural resources.[11] That there is any intention of the developing world succeeding under a philosophy that siphons such enormous wealth from the impoverished to the wealthy is an oxymoron. For the world's poor to gain control of their destiny the wealthy world must pay them equally for equal work, pay full value for their natural resources, and permit them equal access to finance capital, technology, and markets.

Though the IMF/World Bank/GATT/NAFTA/WTO/MAI/GATS/FTAA purport to practice equal and honest trade, this is so only between developed *imperial-centers-of-capital* and then only partially so. Labor on the periphery of empire is being asked to take severe reductions in pay; the original advantages granted to Japan, South Korea and Taiwan (upon which China and other Southeast Asian nations were also riding) are being scaled back; and the needs of most impoverished nations for industrialization support (equal pay for equal work, access to technology, protection of home industry and markets, and access to world markets) are not even being addressed. Except for the currently emerging China and Southeast Asian countries (and their 1997-98 financial meltdown highlights that their success is not yet assured), the former colonial world is still the countryside providing cheap natural resources and cheap labor to *imperial-centers-of-capital.*

Trumpeting Partial Rights as Full Rights

The following scene is repeated over and over throughout history: Rights are taken away from the weak through violence and cunning. The excessive rights of power become excessive rights of capital formalized into law (primarily through the structure of *residual-feudal* property rights) and those excessive rights accumulate wealth. The greater share of that confiscated wealth is wasted (trade wars, cold wars, covert wars, hot wars, and high living) and a smaller share becomes accumulated capital. Historically, those rights were regained through revolutions. Once the rights of the Napoleonic Codes had been experienced, aristocracy could not nullify those political gains. Likewise with the economic rights given developing nations to gain allies in the Cold War, rescinding those rights will be very difficult.

A society becomes accustomed to whatever structure of rights through which it obtains food, clothes, and shelter. A change in the structure of rights will feel abnormal. If a gain of rights for the politically weak—and thus a loss of rights for the powerful—is imminent, political power (supported by true believers in academia, the media, and among the masses) will immediately be deployed to suppress those gains to the weak and re-impose a pattern of beliefs which protects that power.

After the initial appropriation of rights through violence or cunning, the further claiming or suppressing of rights is done by good people (it could be you or me) maximizing the gains to themselves within the law and customs of society. That self-interest typically takes the form of supporting the imposition of a set of beliefs and legal structures (inequality structured in law which is but a remnant of feudal law) to protect an interest group's newly gained rights.

Each partial gain of rights as society comes out from under the feudal system from which our legal system evolved is trumpeted as full rights (a *social-control-paradigm*). That incomplete gain in rights becomes customary; technology continues to gain in efficiency, producing ever-more wealth; the masses receive the smaller share, or none, of that increased wealth; the powerful receive the larger share or even all the increase plus a part of what once went to labor; the rich get richer; the poor get poorer; and eventually another revolution is born.

After a gain in rights through a successful revolution, new powerbrokers, or a coalition of old and new powerbrokers, continue the structuring of rights to lay claim to the greater share of the wealth produced by the ever-increasing efficiencies of technology (inequality structured in law). This cycle keeps repeating itself, normally giving more rights to more people each time. But full political rights cannot be won without full economic rights and full rights for all will never be attained so long as vestiges of *residual-feudal exclusive* property rights are structured into law.

Former Colonies do not have Economic Freedom

The former colonial societies furnishing most the world's natural resources were defeated centuries ago. We are taught that they are now free but that is not so, rhetoric that they are notwithstanding. Labor is too poorly paid in defeated, weak, and dependent nations to create buying power and those cheap resources are processed into useful products that become the wealth of the industrialized and militarily powerful imperial centers. A small share of those manufactured products is returned to the weak defeated nations to pay for the raw material from which those manufactured products (created wealth) were made.

To purchase a small share of manufactured products from the industrialized countries produced with developing world resources, defeated societies must sell even more of their resources. Manufactured product sales above the needs of payment for resources and money wasted on arms and corruption continually increase the debts of the dependent nations and servicing that continually increasing debt requires the sale of even more resources.

Heavy investment in extraction of the natural wealth of weak resource-wealthy nations while paying local labor subsistence wages assures a surplus of production and low prices for those natural resources while simultaneously denying both the accumulation of capital and buying power in the dependent nation. Of course, those debts cannot be paid off and that is the much spoken of, but little understood, debt trap.

Summary

Control of trade, and thus control of who becomes wealthy, has for centuries been through monopolization of technology and unequal currency values. The cooperative approach to Germany, Japan, and Southeast Asia we witnessed for 40 years as technology was shared and currency values equalized with allies was only to gain supporters for the battle to suppress the breaks for freedom worldwide that we will be addressing in depth. But those battles have been won by the *imperial-centers-of-capital* and the rules are changing.

If *developing centers of capital* were permitted to mature and true free trade developed this would be a crisis of the first order for the *imperial-centers-of-capital.* The high price of technology is a function of patent monopolies copied right off of feudal monopolies (Chapter 25). Honest capital is but stored labor and the proper cost of virtually every manufactured product, including industrial capital, is the price of labor to produce it. This includes a fair wage (not monopoly wage) for management and reasonable interest on capital (stored labor) for owners.

The fact that almost every region of the world has more natural resources than Japan attests that—once it has industrial capital, an efficient internal transportation system, and access to markets—the developing world can, on the average, produce more cheaply than Japan. Where are Hong Kong's resources? Where are South Korea's resources? Where are Taiwan's resources? Where are the resources of most of Europe? The answer, of course, is that those resources are primarily in the impoverished world and that natural wealth has been confiscated through inequalities of trade to become the wealth of the *imperial-centers-of-capital.*

The centuries-long process of embedding excessive rights in property (those *residue of feudal exclusive* property rights) and taking rights away from labor and those on the periphery of empire has created an economic monster. We grow up within that monstrosity, no other system for comparison is permitted to evolve, everything looks normal to us, and people are instinctively threatened by thoughts of major changes. After all, their livelihoods are tied to those same horrendously wasteful arteries of commerce.

But consider this: The greater share of low-paid labor we have been describing is essential work while over half the labor in the high-paid services in the industrialized world is, except as a method of distribution, totally unnecessary. The rights of property are so excessive and the rights of labor so inadequate that throughout the Industrial Revolution distribution by unnecessary labor has evolved to pull some of the unearned wealth back from property. It is the buying power of the masses from the wages of that unnecessary labor that created more demand, that created more industry, and that created today's developed world economy of income (wealth) distribution through unnecessary labor.[12]

When one realizes how distribution by unnecessary labor works within highly inefficient monopolies one can look up at the glass skyscrapers in the heart of any city, look at the plaques on the doors, and realize that the entire building is unnecessary as well as the business providing the fixtures and maintenance. Restructure the *residual-feudal exclusive* property rights under which those subtle monopolies are created into *conditional* property rights and those monopolies disappear even as use rights, competition, and efficiency increase. Instead of distribution through a *residual-feudal* monopoly structure there is efficient distribution through equal rights to nature's bounty, equal rights to a *productive* job (two to three days per week) and equal rights to leisure time (three to four days per week). There is no need for money to work its way through a monopoly for roughly half to be distributed to non-producers and those doing unnecessary work and half paid to those actually productively employed.

Wasted labor within what appeared to be an efficient economy has been outlined in classics by Benjamin Franklin 200 years ago, Charles Fourier 180 years ago, and Thorstein Veblen, Bertrand Russell, Lewis Mumford, Stuart Chase, Upton Sinclair, and Ralph Borsodi in the first half of the 20th-Century. Late 20th-Century writers describing the same phenomenon are Juliet Schor, Seymour Melman, Samuel Bowles, David Gordon, Thomas Weiskopf, Jeremy Rifkin, Andre Gorz, numerous European authors, and this author in *The World's Wasted Wealth 2* and *Cooperative Capitalism: A Blueprint for Global Peace and Prosperity.*

Notes

1 Adam Smith, *The Wealth of Nations*, Modern Library edition (New York: Random House, 1965), p. 64.

2 Ibid, pp. 64-67.

3 Arjun Makhijani, *From Global Capitalism to Economic Justice* (New York: Apex Press, 1992).

4 Doug Henwood, "Clinton and the Austerity Cops," *The Nation* (November 23, 1992): p. 628. Colin Hines and Tim Lang (Jerry Mander and Edward Goldsmith eds.) in *The Case Against the Global Economy and for A Turn Toward the Local* (San Francisco: Sierra Club, 1996), p. 487 say $24.90 an hour for the Germany and $16.40 for the U.S. When benefits are included German manufacturing wages rise to $30 and hour, America to $20 and hour and Britain to $15 (Richard C. Longworth, *Global Squeeze: The Coming Crisis of First-World Nations* (Chicago: Contemporary Books, 1999), p. 177. Russian wages will increase even greater when benefits are factored in.

5 Makhijani, *Economic Justice*, pp. xv, 80-81, 121-22, 162-65; see also pp. 159, 167-70.

6 Ibid, p. 163.

7 Jack Epstein, "Dickens Revisited," *The Christian Science Monitor*, August 24, 1995, pp. 1, 8; Amy Kaslow, "The Price of Low-Cost Clothes: U.S. Jobs," *The Christian Science Monitor,* August 20, 1995, p. 4; Christopher Scheer, "Illegals Made Slaves to Fashion," *The Nation,* September 11, 1995, pp. 237-38.

8 Susan George, *The Debt Boomerang* (San Francisco: Westview Press, 1992), p. xvii.

9 Susan George, Fabrizio Sabelli, *Faith and Credit* (San Francisco: Westview Press, 1994); Duncan Green, *Silent Revolution* (London: Cassel, 1995), especially pp. 95-96; Hancock, Graham, *Lords of Poverty* (New York: Atlantic Monthly Press, 1989); James Petras, "Latin America's Free Market Paves the Road to Recession," In These Times, February 13-19, 1991, p. 17.

10 Peter Marcuse, "Letter from the German Democratic Republic," *Monthly Review,* July/August 1990, p. 61.

11 David C. Korten, *When Corporations Rule the World* (West Hartford, CT, Kumarian Press, 1995), p. 33.

12 J.W. Smith, *World's Wasted Wealth 2* & *Cooperative Capitalism; A Blueprint for Global Peace and Prosperity* (ied.info/cc.html: The Institute for Economic Democracy, 2003).

2. The Violent Accumulation of Capital is Rooted in History

> The economic system [neo-mercantilism] we are now creating in [Adam] Smith's name bears a far greater resemblance to the monopolistic market system he condemned ... [and] opposed as inefficient and contrary to the public's interest ... than it does to the theoretical competitive market system he hypothesized would result in optimal allocation of a society's resources. –
> David C. Korten, *When Corporations Rule the World*

That unique historian of the Middle Ages, Petr Kropotkin, also recognized a "resemblance" in societies as they evolved towards modern times. At first glance, cities of different cultures may appear different and quaint but the basic structure was the same:

> The medieval cities ... [were] a natural growth in the full sense of the word.... Each one, taken separately, varies from century to century. And yet, when we cast a broad glance upon all the cities of Europe, the local and national unlikeness disappear, and we are struck to find among them a wonderful resemblance, although each has developed for itself, independently from the others, and in different conditions.... The leading lines of their organization, and the spirit which animates them, are imbued with a strong family likeness. Everywhere we see the same federations of small communities and guilds, the same "sub-towns" round the mother city, the same folkmote, and the same insigns of its independence.... Food supplies, labour and commerce are organized on closely similar lines [and] inner and outer struggles are fought with the same ambitions.[1]

The "wonderful resemblance" Kropotkin spotted as such a social positive had a dark side that went on to become a "resemblance to the monopolistic system" that David C. Korten observed in today's world economy. Monopolization through violence and economic warfare is with us today just as in the commerce of the Middle Ages. We will be following those common threads of *plunder-by-trade* through history, demonstrating that it is the foundation of today's world trade and the cause of immense wealth for the few and impoverishment for the many.

The Evolution of City-States and *Plunder-by-Trade*

Just as their predecessors fought to appropriate their neighbors' wealth through raids, the cities of the Middle Ages used their military superiority to monopolize the tools of production, control trade, and make the outlying societies dependent upon their commerce. They were learning to *plunder-by-trade.* Henri Pirenne and Eli F. Heckscher in their classics on the Middle Ages, and Immanuel Wallerstein in *The Origin of the Modern World System*, describe the birth of the modern market economy through the monopolization of the tools of production and proto-mercantilist trade imposed and controlled through violence:

> Up to and during the course of the fifteenth century the towns were the sole centers of commerce and industry to such an extent that none of it was allowed to escape into the open country.... The struggle against rural trading and against rural handicrafts lasted at least seven or eight hundred years.... The severity of these measures increased with the growth of 'democratic government.'.... All through the fourteenth century regular armed expeditions were sent out against all the villages in the neighborhood and looms and fulling-vats were broken or carried away.[2] The problem of the towns collectively was to control their own markets, that is, be able to reduce the cost of items purchased from the countryside and to minimize the role of stranger merchants. Two techniques were used. On the one hand, towns sought to obtain not only legal rights to tax market operations but also the right to regulate the trading operation (who should trade, when it should take place, what should be traded). Furthermore, they sought to restrict the possibilities of their countryside engaging in trade other than via their town. Over time, these various mechanisms shifted their terms of trade in favor of the townsmen, in favor thus of the urban commercial classes against both the landowning and peasant classes.[3]

Those simple looms and fulling vats were primitive industrial capital. With this primitive technology the cities could produce cheaper and better cloth and trade these commodities to the countryside for wool, timber, ore, and food. When the serfs came to town and looked at the simple looms and fulling vats it did not take them long to build their own tools and produce their own cloth, leather goods, metal tools, et al.

The loss of the city's markets for both raw material and manufactured products due to the comparative advantage of the countryside meant impoverishment and possibly even starvation for those in the city who formerly produced that cloth. The same loss of monopoly through increased technological knowledge of the countryside and its natural comparative advantage held true for other products and other cities. The comparative advantages of the outlying villages were eliminated by force to maintain dependency upon the city and lay claim to both the natural wealth of the countryside and the wealth produced by technology.

Obtaining raw material from the countryside cheap and selling their manufactured products high—through a legal system of *feudal* rights of their own creation—the powerful and crafty of the city transferred manufactured, monetized, and capitalized wealth within their trading region to themselves. These same powerful and crafty groups throughout history continually structured laws to protect property rights because monopoly property rights "entitled" them to all wealth (above labor and other costs) produced on, or with, that property. As an assured producer of wealth, privately-owned income-producing property developed value that could be capitalized and bought and sold.

Immanuel Wallerstein's phrase, "they sought to restrict the possibilities of their countryside engaging in trade in other than via their town"[4] describes the same problem facing the powerful today. To maintain their wealth and power and the standard of living their citizens now feel is normal the powerful maintain their monopolies and unequal trades.

To permit the countryside to utilize its natural comparative advantage would mean a drastic drop in living standards for both the established and the forming *imperial-centers-of-capital* and open revolt of their citizenry as they become poorer. Thus, the emergence of conscientious leaders in powerful *imperial-centers-of-capital*, with a sincere interest in the well-being of people in dependent societies providing their crucial resources, is a rare occurrence. Reality requires leaders to care for their own even as millions—or even billions—of people on the periphery are impoverished by leaders' *grand strategies* of *containments*, through economic, financial, diplomatic, covert, and overt warfare.[5]

To protect their access to crucial resources, powerful imperial cities of the Middle Ages used military power to eliminate the comparative advantage of the countryside and that of other cities. Power struggles between city-states had intrigues, alliances, balances of power, and preponderance of power foreign policies identical to, and for the same purpose as, modern nations and empires—control of resources and trade to maintain their security:

> The leading mercantile cities [of Europe] resorted to armed force in order to destroy rival economic power in other cities and to establish [a more complete] economic monopoly. These conflicts were more costly, destructive, and ultimately even more futile than those between the merchant classes and the feudal orders. Cities like Florence, which wantonly attacked other prosperous communities like Lucca and Siena, undermined both their productivity and their own relative freedom from such atrocious attacks. When capitalism spread overseas, its agents treated the natives they encountered in the same savage fashion that it treated their own nearer rivals.[6]

Title to industrial capital (the tools of production) and control of trade were the primary mechanisms for claiming the wealth of the countryside, of another city, of the weak within an empire, or of the weak on the periphery of empire. The destruction of another society's capital to protect markets substituted *plunder-by-trade* for plunder by raids. Instead of appropriating another's wealth directly, societies learned to accomplish this through the proto-mercantilist policies of making others dependent and laying claim to their wealth through unequal trades.

Thus evolved the foundation philosophy of mercantilism. The quote below describing British mercantilism is from Adam Smith's *The Wealth of Nations* but the origin of that trade philosophy in the 20th-Century can be traced to the free cities of Europe in the Middle Ages. Adam Smith's philosophical work was the result of studying world trade patterns that had been in force for centuries:

> [Mercantilism's] ultimate object ... is always the same, to enrich the country [city] by an advantageous balance of trade. It discourages the exportation of the materials of manufacture [tools and raw material], and the instruments of trade, in order to give our own workmen an advantage, and to enable them to undersell those of other nations [cities] in all foreign markets: and by restraining, in this manner, the exportation of a few commodities of no great price, it proposes to occasion a much greater and more valuable exportation of others. It encourages the importation of the materials of manufacture, in order that our own people may be enabled to work them up more cheaply, and thereby prevent a greater and more valuable importation of the manufactured commodities.[7]

Evolving from Imperial Cities to Nascent Imperial Nations

With the cities battling over the wealth of the countryside, the aristocracy and the Church reorganized and, while consolidating the first modern states, defeated the free cities of Europe. As those people's livelihoods were dependent upon control of their coveted wealth-producing resources, convincing them that their well-being should be entrusted to others controlling these resources went against all instinct and common sense. The masses wished to maintain control of their resources and retain their community support structures. "Only wholesale massacres by the thousand could put a stop to this widely spread popular movement, and it was by the sword, the fire, and the rack that the young states secured their first and decisive victory over the masses of the people."[8]

As the formation of the states overwhelmed the free cities of Europe and their communal ways, the 14th-Century saw the beginning of a 300-year-effort to erase all trace of community support structures and community ownership of social wealth. The process to individualize the masses to limit their power had begun:

> For the next three centuries the states ... systematically weeded out all institutions in which the mutual-aid tendency had formerly found its expression. The village communities were bereft of their folkmotes

> [community meetings], their courts and independent administration; their lands were confiscated. The guilds were spoliated of their possessions and liberties, and placed under the control, the fancy, and the bribery of the State's official. The cities were divested of their sovereignty, and the very springs of their inner life—the folkmote, the elected justices and administration, the sovereign parish and the sovereign guild—-were annihilated; the State's functionary took possession of every link of what formerly was an organic whole. Under that fatal policy and the wars it engendered, whole regions, once populous and wealthy, were laid bare; rich cities became insignificant boroughs; the very roads which connected them with other cities became impracticable. Industry, art, and knowledge fell into decay.... For the next three centuries the states, both on the Continent and in these islands [Great Britain], systematically weeded out all institutions in which the mutual-aid tendency had formerly found its expression. It was taught in the universities and from the pulpit that the institutions in which men formerly used to embody their needs of mutual support could not be tolerated in a properly organized State.[9]

Having gained control of the masses through the power of the state, those with power could safely concentrate on gaining control of the wealth-producing mechanisms of world trade:

> The problem of the towns collectively was to control their market, that is, be able to reduce the cost of items purchased from the countryside and to minimize the role of stranger merchants.... But the profits [in controlling the trade of the countryside], while important, were small by what might be earned in long-distance trade, especially colonial or semicolonial trade. Henri Sée estimates the profit margins of the early commercial operations as being very high: "Sometimes in excess of 200 or 300 percent from dealings that were little more than piracy.[10]

The raiders of the Middle Ages did not need to keep what they were doing secret; that it was for their survival was obvious. But, as soon as imperial cities evolved into imperial states, the connection between the traders who would lose business and those who would have to fight was broken. *Managers-of-state* cannot teach their citizens to be kind and just and then arm them and send them out to destroy the industries of peaceful neighbors.

The excuses used are those we read in history which have become so ingrained we accept them as the biological imperative of humankind. They are not biological imperatives. Humans are far more peaceful and cooperative than they are aggressive. Expose the real reason for these wars and suppressions, provide the world with a peaceful option for its "national interest" and "national security," establish a modest security force whose mission is everybody's security, and the world will be peaceful.

The Advantage of Cheap Water Transportation

While cities fought back and forth, those with timber for boats, with access to the sea, and with seafaring skills had a unique advantage. Dominance on the seas ensured they could move commodities much more cheaply than their competitors. Thus, the great trading and seafaring city state of Amalfi was destroyed by the sea power of Pisa. Pisa was then defeated by Genoa, which was later overwhelmed by Venice. Through naval power, Venice was able to enforce the rules of trade for centuries. However, along with the loss of the silk and spice trade through Muslim control of those routes, the Venetians slowly succumbed to the combined power of competing sister states and European powers.[11]

The battles between Italian city-states prevented a consolidation of wealth and power. It was now the turn of Western European cities. The Hanseatic League formed in the late 13th-Century and, within 100 years, 85-to-100 cities were cooperating to quell pirates, foster safe navigation with lighthouses and train pilots, import raw material and export manufactured goods (by agreement only in Hanseatic boats). They established navigation laws and custom duties with trading enclaves on foreign soil—the forerunner of today's duty-free ports and industrial enclaves ("Free trade zones where normal labor laws are suspended in deference to capital).

Having copied the principles of monopolization of trade practiced by the Venetian Empire, the Hansa dominated the trade of Western and Middle Europe for 300 years. With treaties between cooperating cities, this powerful league avoided most, but not all, of the pitched battles typical of Southeastern and Eastern European city-states. However, like those sister city-states, it was weakened by principalities and ruling families within its geographical area demanding tributes within their jurisdictions. This league lacked the power, cohesiveness, and coordination of a unified nation, and was overwhelmed by united national powers (Denmark, Sweden, Norway, Lithuania, Poland, the principality of Moscow, and Holland) in a replay of the unified coalitions which defeated Venice.[12] As the Hanseatic League's trade declined, nations with unique advantages of coastline, timber for building ships, and skilled seamen (Spain, Portugal, France, England, and Holland) spread across the world, overwhelming primitive cultures, and creating their colonial trading empires.

With the development of ships that carried many more tons of cargo, thus greatly reduced shipping costs, tiny Holland's trade blossomed. Out of 20,000 ships in world trade in the middle of the 17th-Century, 16,000 were Dutch. In James Buchan's *Frozen Desire,* 1997, Nouvelle Edition, 1768, Vol 1: Picador, quotes the *Siecle de Louis XIV,* "One day, when a French consul was telling the King of Persia that Louis XIV had conquered nearly the whole of Holland, that monarch replied, 'How can that be there are always twenty Dutch ships to one French in the Port of Ormuz.'"? But other imperial nations were continually studying the process of gaining wealth and power through control of trade and Holland's expanding trade monopoly would soon be overwhelmed by the English, who were slowly building a base for economic and military power.

Britain created enormous advantages for her industry through tariffs, support for industries, and other protectionist measures. But its primary advantage was rich beds of coal and iron ore only 15 miles apart. That was a favorable circumstance that, early in the industrial revolution, no other nation could match.

The British Empire and Control of Trade

The shortage of labor created by the Black Death of the 14th-Century and the wool market created by Hanseatic traders provided the impetus for English sheep farming (in the 15th-Century, 90% of English exports were wool). The greater wool profits triggered the English Enclosure Acts of the 15th, 16th, and 17th Centuries.

Skilled artisans were encouraged to emigrate from countries where they suffered religious persecution and declining economic fortunes, such as France after the revocation of the Edict of Nantes. This was quite the opposite of today's industry fleeing high-priced skilled labor and moving to cheap labor. During Britain's early industrial development, from virtually every country in Europe and as far away as Persia, India, and China, the technology and skilled labor to produce almost every product in world commerce were brought to England. English labor was trained in those productive skills, custom duties were enacted to protect those new industries, and bounties were given to promote exports of manufactures.[13]

The cornerstone of British control of trade was the Navigation Acts (1651-1847), copying Hanseatic and Venetian trade rules, which required British trade to be handled on British ships. England and Scotland peacefully forming into one nation in 1707 provided a cohesive government under which all industry could be nurtured and protected.

The Navigation Acts, economic warfare aimed directly at Dutch dominance of commercial trade, triggered a military war. English warships attacked Dutch shipping. English exports and imports—now produced and transported largely by English fishermen, manufacturers, and shippers—increased rapidly. The Methuen treaty of 1703 between Britain and Portugal, shutting the Dutch off from trade with the Portuguese empire, was a deadly blow to Holland. Suddenly-idled Dutch capital and skilled labor emigrated to the protective trade structure of England.

Take note that Britain developed under the yet-unwritten protection principles of Friedrich List, not under the principles of Adam Smith free trade as interpreted by neo-mercantilists. Britain becoming the wealthiest nation in the world for over 100 years is powerful evidence in favor of

Friedrich List's philosophy of protecting a nation's tender industries and markets. Past error has been, and still is, that protection is always for one selfish nation or bloc of nations. Weaker nations—which need even more protection—were at Britain's mercy:

> [Britain's Navigation Acts] became the fundamental basis for the Old Colonial System. According to this Act the colonies could send their most important products, the so-called Enumerated Commodities, only to the mother country. By an important law passed three years later, actually called the Staple Act, the same was ordered with regard to the export of European goods to the colonies, with the express purpose of "making this Kingdom a staple not only of the commodities of those plantations but also of the commodities of other countries and places for the supplying of them."[14]

Starting out more industrially and culturally advanced, the Spanish concentrated their labors on confiscating shiploads of gold and silver booty from their colonies. They did not produce consumer products for the elite, they imported them instead.[15] In 1593, an advisor explained the problem to King Philip II:

> The Cortes of Valladolid in the year 1586 petitioned Your Majesty not to allow the further importation into the kingdom of candles, glassware, jewelry, knives and similar articles; these things useless to human life come from abroad to be exchanged for gold, as though Spaniards were Indians.... The general remote cause of our want of money is the great excess of this Kingdom in consuming the commodities of foreign countries, which prove to us discommodities, in hindering us of so much treasure, which otherwise would be brought in, in lieu of those toys.[16]

Holland, Britain and France supplied these "toys" and Spain's wealth ended up in their vaults. Britain's First Earl of Shaftesbury (1621-83) was the primary promoter of the mercantilist plan to lay claim to Spain's wealth through trade. Shaftesbury explained, "If you will therein follow our directions we shall lay a way open to you to get all the Spanish riches in that country with their consent and without any hazard to yourselves."[17]

Wealth accumulated by Britain and the simultaneous impoverishment of Spain (its major rival), the eventual dominance of Britain in world trade for over 100 years, and the immense wealth this produced for the small nation of Britain, proved the validity of Shaftesbury's economic warfare plans. Although Spain was immensely wealthy, its riches and power were sapped by unnecessary purchases of other societies' labor and that British economic warfare, backed and enforced by superior sea power, overwhelmed other nations.

This book follows the two threads of *plunder-by-trade* that have been consistent through the last 800 years of history and are still fundamental in world trade in the 21st-Century: (1) Control of nations and resources on the periphery of empire through financial, economic, covert, and overt warfare to maintain control of resources and the *wealth-producing-process*, and (2) the imposition of *social-control-paradigms* (belief systems) to protect that power-structure and the wealth accumulated through those unequal trades. Any world trade thesis or formula is irrelevant if it does not take into account these two threads through history: the exponential gain or loss from unequal pay as outlined in Chapter 1 and powerful nations' imposing those unequal trades as addressed throughout this book.

Notes

[1] Petr Kropotkin, *Mutual Aid* (Boston: Porter Sargent, 1914), pp. 187-88.

[2] Karl Polanyi, *The Great Transformation* (Boston: Beacon Press, 1957), p. 277. Quoting the classics: Henri Pirenne's Economic and Social History and Eli F. Heckscher's Mercantilism.

[3] Immanuel Wallerstein, *The Origin of The Modern World System*, vol. 1 (New York: Academic Press, 1974), pp. 119-20. For "plunder-by-trade," see William H. McNeill, *The Pursuit of Power* (Chicago: University of Chicago Press, 1982).

[4] Wallerstein, *The Modern World System*, vol.1, pp. 119-20. For a fuller understanding of cities throughout history, read Paul Bairoch's, *Cities and Economic Development From the Dawn of History to the Present* (Chicago: University of Chicago Press, 1988).

[5] Christopher Layne, "Rethinking American Grand Strategy," *World Policy Journal*, (Summer 1998), pp. 8-28.

[6] Lewis Mumford, *Technics and Human Development* (New York: Harcourt Brace Jovanovich, 1967), p. 279; see also George Renard, *Guilds of the Middle Ages* (New York: Augustus M. Kelly, 1968), p. 35; Petr Kropotkin, *The State* (London: Freedom Press, 1987), p. 41; Kropotkin, *Mutual Aid*, Chapters 6-7; Dan Nadudere, *The Political Economy of Imperialism* (London: Zed Books, 1977), p. 186.

[7] Adam Smith, *The Wealth of Nations* (New York: Random House, 1965), p. 607.

[8] Kropotkin, *Mutual Aid*, Chapters 6-8, especially p. 225.

[9] Ibid, especially p. 226. See also Renard, *Guilds of the Middle Ages*, p. 66 and Chapters 7-8; Adam Smith, *Wealth of Nations*, pp. 523-626, 713; Wallerstein, *Modern World System*, vol. 2, pp. 5, 37, 245, vol. 3, p. 137.

[10] Wallerstein, *Modern World System*, vol. 1, pp. 119-20, emphasis added.

[11] Friedrich List, *The National System of Political Economy* (Fairfield, NJ: Auguatus M. Kelley, 1977), pp. 5-10.

[12] List, National System, pp. 9-10, 12-33, 40-45, 78-79.

[13] Ibid., pp. 71, 56, 345, Chapters 26, 27.

[14] Heckscher, *Mercantilism*, 1955, vol. 2, pp. 70-71; see also Adam Smith, *Wealth of Nations*, pp. 429-31, 544-65, 580.

[15] Michel Beaud, *A History of Capitalism, 1500 to 1980* (New York: Monthly Review Press, 1983), p. 19.

[16] Eric Williams, *From Columbus to Castro* (New York: Vintage Books, 1984), pp. 46-47. See also Paul Kennedy, *The Rise and Fall of Great Powers* (New York: Random House, 1987), p. 54, and Kevin Phillips, *Boiling Point* (New York: Random House, 1993), especially Chapter 8.

[17] List, *National System*, pp. 57-59, 66-68; William Appleman Williams, *The Contours of American History* (New York: W.W. Norton & Company, 1988), pp. 50-77, especially pp. 57, 77. See also Heckscher, *Mercantilism*, 2 vols.

3. The Unwitting hand Their Wealth to the Cunning

Classical Economists Sir William Petty (1623-87) down through Sir James Steuart (1712-80) built the philosophical foundation for Adam Smith free trade. In a replay of controlling the countryside to control resources and markets, each classical philosopher pointed out the necessity of using the powers of government to restrict self-provisioning in the countryside so as to provide labor for new industries and a market for those industries. "Classical political economy was, first and foremost, meant to be a formula for accelerating the overall accumulation process" and was meant to guide all wealth produced by the increased efficiencies of technology to the already wealthy.[1] The elimination of today's inequalities and injustices which have their foundation in those earlier classics addressed above is the inherent goal of this work.

Most the early classical philosophers were members of polite society writing a philosophy for, and publishers publishing for, other elites—a process still ongoing yet today. Speaking for the common people were Gerard Winstanley in the 16th-Century, Jean Jacques Rousseau in the 17th-Century, Johann Herder in the 18th-Century, and Karl Marx in the 19th-Century.[2] Friedrich List, in 1841, the primary source for this chapter, addressed the rights of European empires and the emerging United States but did not address rights of nations and people on the periphery of empire.

Borrowing heavily from Sir James Steuart (without acknowledgment) Adam Smith wrote his bible of capitalism, *The Wealth of Nations*, exposing mercantilism and promoting free trade. In-depth descriptions of 18th-Century mercantilist trade describe well the proto-mercantilist trade between the cities and countryside 600 years earlier and mirror the neo-mercantilist trade between developed and undeveloped nations for the next 227 years when the world was supposedly operating under Adam Smith philosophy. For neo-mercantilists to restructure their overt plunder of weak societies into covert plunder through inequalities of trade, it was necessary to ignore statements in *The Wealth of Nations* that contradicted neo-liberal trade philosophy. Free Trade was diplomatic code for continued mercantilist unequal trade. Adam Smith again:

> A small quantity of manufactured produce purchases a great quantity of rude produce. A trading and manufacturing country, therefore, naturally purchases with a small part of its manufactured produce a great part of the rude produce of other countries; while, on the contrary, a country without trade and manufactures is generally obliged to purchase, at the expense of a great part of its rude produce, a very small part of the manufactured produce of other countries. The one exports what can subsist and accommodate but a very few, and imports the subsistence and accommodation of a great number. The other exports the accommodation and subsistence of a great number, and imports that of a very few only. The inhabitants of the one must always enjoy a much greater quantity of subsistence than what their own lands, in the actual state of their cultivation, could afford. The inhabitants of the other must always enjoy a much smaller quantity.... Few countries ... produce much more rude produce than what is sufficient for the subsistence of their own inhabitants. To send abroad any great quantity of it, therefore, would be to send abroad a part of the necessary subsistence of the people. It is otherwise with the exportation of manufactures. The maintenance of the people employed in them is kept at home, and only the surplus part of their work is exported.... The commodities of Europe were almost all new to America, and many of those of America were new to Europe. A new set of exchanges, therefore, began to take place which had never been thought of before, and which should naturally have proved as advantageous to the new, as it certainly did to the old continent. The savage injustice of the Europeans rendered an event, which ought to have been beneficial to all, ruinous and destructive to several [most] of those unfortunate countries.[3]

John C. Miller, *Origins of the American Revolution*, points out that Britain's Navigation Acts were mercantilism translated into statute law, and that Britain's Staple Act completed the structure of British mercantilism.[4] Before Britain's near defeat by Napoleon and his continental system, these protectionist maxims later so vehemently denied under Adam Smith, were,

> plainly professed by all English ministers and parliamentary speakers: [1] Always to favour the importation of productive power, in preference to the importation of goods. [2] Carefully to cherish and to protect the development of the productive power. [3] To import only raw materials and agricultural products, and to export nothing but manufactured goods. [4] To direct any surplus of productive power to colonization, and to the subjection of barbarous nations. [5] To reserve exclusively to the mother country the supply of the colonies and subject countries with manufactured goods, but in return to receive on preferential terms their raw materials and especially their colonial produce. [6] To devote especial care to the coast navigation; to the trade between the mother country and the colonies; to encourage sea fisheries by means of bounties; and to take as active a part as possible in international navigation. [7] By these means to found a naval supremacy, and by means of it to extend foreign commerce, and continually increase her colonial possessions. [8] To grant freedom in trade with the colonies and in navigation only so far as she can gain more by it than she loses. [9] To grant reciprocal

> navigation privileges only if the advantage is on the side of England, or if foreign nations can by that means be restrained from introducing restrictions on navigation in their favor. [10] To grant concessions to foreign independent nations in respect of the import of agricultural products, only in case concessions in respect of her manufactured products can be gained thereby. [11] In cases where such concessions cannot be obtained by treaty, to attain the object of them by means of contraband trade. [12] To make wars and to contract alliances with exclusive regard to her manufacturing, commercial, maritime, and colonial interests. To gain by these alike from friends and foes; from the latter by interrupting their commerce at sea; from the former by ruining their manufactures through subsidies which are paid in the shape of English manufactured goods.[5]

As William Pitt refined the First Earl of Shaftesbury's formula for British trading supremacy, Britain seems to have decided that the protectionist policies through which she had become immensely wealthy had all been a mistake. In his classic, *The National System of Political Economy* (1977 edition), Friedrich List outlines how Britain, under the guidance of William Pitt, for the first time eulogized Adam Smith's doctrine of free trade. While secretly maintaining the old maxim of becoming wealthy by selling expensive manufactured goods and buying cheap commodities from weak dependent societies as outlined in the above 12 protectionist maxims, the British state department, British intelligence and British industry were funding think-tanks, correspondents, writers, and lecturers to impose their interpretation of Adam Smith's free-trade philosophy across the world.[6]

Friedrich List alerts us that, Adam Smith free trade—as interpreted, designed, and managed by neo-mercantilists—is a brer-rabbit/don't throw me in the brier patch scam designed to prevent the rest of the world from industrializing. This maintains their technological dependence and protects the flow of the world's resources cheaply to the imperial centers.

Friedrich List points out that the forces of production are the tree on which wealth grows and an individual may be better off purchasing something cheaper from another society but collectively everybody is better off if a society produces its own basic commodities, machine tools, and finished products.[7] For those who understand the multiplier factor this is obvious. However, note the relative equality that must be assumed and it is specifically that equality which is missing.

Napoleon knew well that any nation would be impoverished if their industry and trade were dominated by another: "Under the existing circumstances ... any state which adopted the principles of free trade must come to the ground ... [and] a nation which combines in itself the power of manufacturers with that of agriculture is an immeasurably more perfect and more wealthy nation than a purely agriculture one."[8]

And List tells us that both "Adam Smith and J.B. Say had laid it down that ... nature herself had singled out the people of the United States [and most of the rest of the world] exclusively for agriculture." *The Wealth of*

Nations had no allowance for industrial development beyond a few select nations and Friedrich List, who challenged the philosophy of Adam Smith because his native Germany could not develop under a philosophy designed to maintain the supremacy of Britain, allowed only for the industrialization of the temperate zones. Even List's staunchest supporters criticized his philosophy for not considering the rights of all people throughout the world.[9] An honest philosophy for world development, as we are advocating, must put rights for all as a first consideration.

Adam Smith recognized that by protection an undeveloped nation could "raise up artificers, manufacturers and merchants of its own" but claimed this would lower the price of their agriculture products.[10] Considering that agricultural production would be marketed to those employed in the new local industries and that dependency of others on British commodities markets and manufactures was the centerpiece for maintaining the wealth of his native Britain, this was a difficult logic. This tells us Adam Smith was considering only the rights of an imperial center and had relegated the periphery to providers of resources for that empire.

For the newly-free American colonies, France, and later Germany William Pitt's promotion of a philosophy for their dependency was easy to see through. "Such arguments did not obtain currency for very long [in France]. England's free trade wrought such havoc amongst the manufacturing industries (which had prospered and grown strong under the Continental Blockade system) that a prohibitive règime was speedily resorted to under the protecting aegis of which, according to Dupin's testimony, the producing power of French manufactories was doubled between the years 1815 and 1827."[11]

List's insights into the "distinction between the *theory of values* and the *theory of the powers of production*" and the "difference between *manufacturing power* and *agricultural power*" were gained through observing firsthand both the rapid development of the newly-free United States as they ignored Britain's promotion of Adam Smith [unequal] free trade and "the wonderfully favourable effects [to the continent] of Napoleon's Continental System and the destructive results of its abolition."[12]

Adam Smith pointed out that, "England had founded a great empire for the sole purpose of raising up a people of customers.... The maintenance of this monopoly has hitherto been the principal, or more properly perhaps the sole end and purpose of the dominion which Great Britain assumes over her colonies."[13] Historian Barbara Tuchman concurs:

> Trade was felt to be the bloodstream of British prosperity. To an island nation it represented the wealth of the world, the factor that made the difference between rich and poor nations. The economic philosophy of the time (later to be termed mercantilism) held that the colonial role in trade was to serve as the source of raw materials and the market for British manufacture, and *never* to usurp the manufacturing function.[14]

America's Freedom is based on Economic Freedom

The *Grand Strategy* of Britain to control the industry and markets of the American colonies was the primary reason for the American War of Independence. America's founding fathers recognized that the "consumption of foreign luxuries, [and] manufactured stuffs, was one of the chief causes of [the colonies'] economic distress":[15]

> In the harbor of New York there are now 60 ships of which 55 are British. The produce of South Carolina was shipped in 170 ships of which 150 were British.... Surely there is not any American who regards the interest of his country but must see the immediate necessity of an efficient federal government; without it the Northern states will soon be depopulated and dwindle into poverty, while the Southern ones will become silk worms to toil and labour for Europe.... In the present state of disunion the profits of trade are snatched from us; our commerce languishes; and poverty threatens to overspread a country which might outrival the world in riches.[16]

The famous Boston Tea Party, touted as one cause of the revolution, was only a particularly theatrical protest over a rather minor example of this systematic injustice. Not even a horseshoe nail was to be produced in America, and under no circumstances were manufactured products to be exported to countries within Britain's trade empire. The colonialists

> could import only goods produced in England or goods sent to the colonies by way of England. They were not allowed to export wool, yarn, and woolen cloth from one colony to another, "or to any place whatsoever," nor could they export hats and iron products. They could not erect slitting or rolling mills or forges and furnaces. After 1763, they were forbidden to settle west of the Appalachian Mountains. By the Currency Act of 1764, they were deprived of the right to use legal tender paper money and to establish colonial mints and land banks.[17]

After American independence England's Lord Brougham proposed destroying America's infant industries by selling manufactured goods to them below cost. "He thought it 'well worthwhile to incur a loss upon the first exportation [of English manufactures], in order, by the glut, TO STIFLE IN THE CRADLE THOSE RISING MANUFACTURES IN THE UNITED STATES.' " This experience (and the fact that Spain and France now blocked America's expansion) caused Americans to lay the foundation for their own *Grand Strategy*, copying Britain's neo-mercantilist trade policy. Gaining full freedom required military might and led to establishing the Naval War College and a powerful navy.[18]

U.S. statesman Henry Clay quotes a British leader: "[N]ations knew, as well as [we did], what we meant by 'free trade' was nothing more nor less than, by means of the great advantage we enjoyed, to get a monopoly of all their markets for our manufactures, and to prevent them, one and all, from ever becoming manufacturing nations."[19]

Lord Brougham's economic warfare plan was thwarted when, 36 years after gaining their political freedom and theoretical rights in the Revolutionary War and while Britain was busy battling Napoleon on the Continent, Americans fought the War of 1812 to remove Britain's iron grip from America's commerce. America was now both politically and economically free. It was by winning the War of 1812 that America truly gained its independence. Until then, the American economy, and thus the fundamental rights of Americans, was dependent upon the whims of British neo-mercantilists backed by British naval power.

America, Canada, New Zealand, and Australia were the only former colonies to eventually gain both their political and economic freedoms.[a] There is more to independence than the political freedom first gained by the American Revolution: the right to vote, free speech, and choice of religion. For example, the states could trade between themselves, but they

---

[a] The following books will lead you to primary sources on nations, especially America, successfully developing protecting their industries and markets. Though some—because they were needed as allies—developed under others protection, there are no nations which successfully developed without protection for their industries and markets. Friedrich List, *The National System of Political Economy* (Fairfield, NJ: Auguatus M. Kelley, 1977): Clarence Walworth Alvord, *The Mississippi Valley in British Politics: A Study of Trade, Land Speculation, and Experiments in Imperialism Culminating in the American Revolution* (New York: Russell & Russell, 1959); Paul Bairoch, *Economics and World History: Myths and Paradoxes* (Chicago: University of Chicago Press, 1993)*;* Correli Barnett, *The Collapse of British Power* (New York: Morrow, 1971); Oscar Theodore Barck, Jr. and Hugh Talmage Lefler, *Colonial America,* 2nd ed. (New York: Macmillan, 1968); Samuel Crowther, *America Self-Contained* (Garden City, N.Y.: Doubleday, Doran & Co., 1933); John M . Dobson, *Two Centuries of Tariffs: The Background and Emergence of the U.S. International Trade Commission* (Washington DC: U.S. International Trade Commission, 1976); Alfred E. Eckes, Jr., *Opening America's Markets: U.S. Foreign Trade Policy Since 1776* (Chapel Hill: University of North Carolina Press, 1995); James Thomas Flexner, *George Washington: The Forge of Experience* (Boston: Little Brown and Co., 1965); William J. Gill, *Trade Wars Against America: A History of United States Trade and Monetary Policy* (New York: Praeger, 1990); John Steele Gordon, *Hamilton's Blessing: The Extraordinary Life and Times of Our National Debt* (New York: Walker and Co., 1997); Irwin, *Against the Tide*; Emory R. Johnson, *History of Domestic and Foreign Commerce of the United States* (Washington DC: Carnegie Institute of Washington, 1915); Richard M. Ketchum, ed., *The American Heritage Book of the Revolution* (New York: American Heritage Publishing, 1971); Michael Kraus, *The United States to 1865* (Ann Arbor: University of Michigan Press, 1959); John A. Logan, *The Great Conspiracy: Its Origin and History, 1732-1775* (New York: A.R Hart & Co., 1886); William MacDonald, ed., *Documentary Source Book of American History, 1606-1926,* 3rd ed. (New York: MacMillan, 1926); John C. Miller, *Origins of the American Revolution* (Boston: Little Brown and Co., 1943); Samuel Eliot Morison and Henry Steele Commanger, *Growth of the American Republic*, 5th ed. (New York: W.W. Norton, 1959); Sir Lewis Namier and John Brooke, *Charles Townsend* (New York: St. Martin's Press, 1964; Gus Stelzer, *The Nightmare of Camelot: An Expose of the Free Trade Trojan Horse* (Seattle, Wash.: PB publishing, 1994); Peter D.J. Thomas, *The Townshend Duties Crisis: The Second Phase of the American Revolution, 1776-1773* (Oxford: Clarendon Press, 1987); Arthur Hendrick Vandenberg, *The Greatest American* (New York: G.P. Putman's and Sons, 1921).

could not trade freely with the rest of the world due to the British navy's denial of that basic right, which thus maintained colonial dependence upon British industry and shipping. A humiliating treaty (Peace of Versailles 1783) had been forced on the colonies that "permitted only the smallest American vessels to call at the island ports and prohibited all American vessels from carrying molasses, sugar, coffee, cocoa, and cotton to any port in the world outside the continental United States" and Britain's navy was there to ensure compliance.[20] But when Britain was fighting Napoleon on the Continent, the War of 1812 broke those trade barriers and gave the United States economic freedom.

With its great natural wealth, rapid industrialization, and rich gold and silver discoveries, America was able to break free from Britain's monopolization of finance capital.

Friedrich List Wrote His Classic observing America's Industrialization

Friedrich List, the German diplomat, writer, and promoter of a German state with no internal tariffs, observed 'the wonderful favourable effects of Napoleon's Continental System, and the destructive effects of its abolition" when France was defeated at Waterloo.[21]

Thirteen years after the American/British war of 1812, Friedrich List arrived in America, became an American citizen, and studied America's protectionist break for economic freedom. America's *Grand Strategy*, designed by America's founders and promoted through List's German language newspaper *Outlines of Political Economy*, provided the foundation for his 1841 protectionist classic, *The National System of Political Economy*.[22] America took the philosophical lead in protection of industry and markets, from 1816 to 1945 was one of the most protected nations, and virtually every nation which has ever successfully industrialized did so under the protection principals laid down by Friedrich List.

List analyzed how the British had industrialized; their strategy of technological monopolization and control of trade; noticed the collapse of European industry when sales of English products penetrated Europe after Napoleon's defeat; how America had ignored British free trade propaganda, protected its industry and markets, and became wealthy; and how Britain's promotion of free trade was a subterfuge to maintain control of markets. He then designed a philosophy under which his beloved native Germany, or any other nation, could industrialize, protect their tender industries and markets, and become powerful.

America's founding fathers, especially Alexander Hamilton, had made the same analysis. The prosperity Americans enjoyed once they had gained both their political and economic freedom exposes the *Grand Strategy* of the original promoters of Adam Smith to keep America's, and the world's, wealth going to British vaults. America's treasured *independence* is little more than breaking the chains of financial *dependence*. Financial independence depends on gaining control of industrial technology, access to raw material and fuel to process into more industrial tools and useful products, as well as access to markets to sell enough products to pay for necessary imports. Gaining their economic freedom to manufacture and trade is what most colonial nations were unable to do.

Adam Smith's philosophy, although quite just between equally developed nations and quite valuable as an analysis of trade between nations of equal power, is the industrial world's self-protective philosophy being forced upon the rest of the world under the guise of it being for their own good.

America Allies with the Old Imperial Nations

America's two *Grand Strategy* choices (championing the economic freedom of other colonized nations or joining the imperial nations in neo-mercantilist siphoning of their wealth) were complicated by its being forced to take sides in the battles between the old imperial nations (the two world wars) and by the almost certain post-WWII collapse of the American and European *imperial-centers-of-capital* if the entire world became nonaligned or if they allied with the emerging *socialist-centers-of-capital*.

The enormous industrial success of Germany's Bismarck and later Hitler's Third Reich following List's precepts proved the sound logic of that philosophy, as did America's protection for European industrial development under the Marshall Plan. That support was protection, even though it came from without. Under threat of the entire world gaining their economic freedom, and thus the loss of crucial resources and markets, the old imperial nations allied, informally, under one protective bloc.

Containing fast expanding socialism required the allied *imperial-centers-of-capital* to bring Japan, Taiwan, and South Korea under the umbrella of protected trade. Their success again proved the soundness of List's philosophy and that the *managers-of-state* knew exactly what they were doing; protecting crucial allies and maintaining—frequently imposing—the dependency status of others. When the leading threat to the allied *imperial-centers-of-capital* disappeared with the collapse of the Soviet Union and those protections were partially withdrawn, the financial meltdown of those once -allied nations on the periphery of empire again proved the validity of protecting tender emerging economies.

Those Asian Tigers still had full rights to sell their production but their industrial capacities, developed to feed the imperial center, were far overbuilt. Except for Japan, their populations were grossly underpaid, thus unable to purchase their own production, and their rights to capital to make that adjustment disappeared with the flight of capital in the 1997-98 financial meltdown. "That financial Meltdown was pure theft."

> Capital looks for a small stock market and injects liquidity into it. This little stock market starts rising and the locals who have been trading on it start making huge profits. They tell their friends and relations and soon all the savings that were in the local banks are sucked into the market. As soon as the market has taken more liquidity than it can withstand (sophisticated computer models can monitor just this) the foreign capital sells its portfolios. It then sells all the local currency it has acquired through the sales of shares thereby driving down the value of the local currency. In short it takes its dollar-profit and runs.[23]

The IMF/World Bank was imposing structural adjustments which reduced regional development and buying power. Private capital analyzed that overcapacity, knew that much of that industry must close down, fled, and then returned to buy up key industries for pennies on the dollar.

Removing protection was little more than turning loose the dogs of speculation through structural adjustments requiring access to Asian markets for speculative capital. Some leaders of the nations that underwent financial meltdowns complain that Federal Reserve Chairman Alan Greenspan, then Deputy Secretaries of the Treasury Robert Rubin and Larry Summers, and "their henchmen at the International Monetary Fund—have turned countries like Malaysia and Russia into leper colonies by isolating them from global capital and making life hellish in order to protect U.S. growth. The three admitted they had made hard choices—and they will even cop to some mistakes."[24] These same "usual suspects"—as Professor Stephen Gill, Professor of Political Science at York University in Toronto, calls those always paraded forward to justify such policies—derailed Japan's plan for an Asian Monetary Fund (AMF) which would not have required the massive structural adjustments that quickly collapsed those tiger economies.[25] The "hard choices" faced by these "usual suspects" can only be the taking care of one's own and letting others take care of themselves. Greenspan, Summers, and Rubin knew they had no reason to worry:

> As the crisis spread across the region, the US Treasury and the Federal Reserve were serene about its global consequences. They knew from a wealth of past experience that financial blow-outs in countries of the South provided a welcome boost for the US financial markets and through them the US domestic economy. Huge funds could be expected to flood into the US financial markets, cheapening the cost of credit there, boosting the stock market and boosting domestic growth. And there would be a rich harvest of assets to be reaped in East Asia when these countries fell to their knees before the IMF.[26]

We must remember that historically all *rising centers-of-capital* are a threat to *established centers-of-capital*. Such financial and economic warfare has been the latter's policy when threatened, and is the policy today even if unrealized by the second and third echelons of power:

> In any long and broad historical perspective the free market is a rare and short-lived aberration. Regulated markets are the norm, arising spontaneously in the life of every society.... The idea that free markets and minimum governments go together ... is an inversion of the truth.... The normal concomitant of free markets is not stable democratic government. It is the volatile politics of economic insecurity.... Since the natural tendency of society is to curb markets, free markets can only be created by the power of a centralized state.... A global free market is not an iron law of historical development but a political project.... Free markets are the creatures of government and cannot exist without them.... Democracy and free markets are competitors rather than partners.... [just as the disastrous British free market 100 years ago which culminated into two world wars, the current] global free market is an American project.... In the absence of reform, the world economy will fragment, as its imbalances become insupportable.... The world economy will fracture into blocs, each riven by struggles for regional hegemony.[27]

In financial warfare, currency markets become a weapon of mass destruction. The speculator

> takes out huge forward contracts to sell pounds for French francs at 9.50 to the pound in one month's time: say forward contracts totaling £10-billion. For these he must pay a fee to a bank. Then he waits until the month is nearly up. Then suddenly he starts buying pounds again in very large volumes and throws them against the exchange rate through selling them. So big is his first sale of pounds that the currency falls, say 3 percent against the franc. At this point other, smaller players see the pound going down and join the trend he has started, driving it down another 3 percent. Overnight he borrows another vast chunk of pounds and sells into francs again, and meanwhile the word is going around the market that none other than the master speculator is in action, so everyone joins the trend and the pound drops another ten percent. And on the day when the forward contract falls due for him to sell pounds for francs at 9.50 the pound in the spot market is down at 5 francs. He takes up his huge forward contract and makes a huge profit. Meanwhile there is a sterling crisis, etc. etc.[28]

John Gray, author of *False Dawn*, points out that the imperial centers are also at risk:

> A global free market ... no more works in the interests of the American economy than of any other. Indeed, in a large dislocation of the world markets the America economy would be more exposed than many others.... In this feverish atmosphere a soft landing is a near impossibility. Hubris is not corrected by twenty percent.... Economic collapse and another change of regime in Russia; further deflation and weakening of the financial system in Japan, compelling a repatriation of Japanese holdings of US government bonds; financial crisis in Brazil or Argentina; a Wall Street crash – any or all of these events, together with others that are unforeseeable, may in present circumstances act as the trigger of a global economic dislocation. If any of

> them come to pass, one of the first consequences will be a swift increase of protectionist sentiment in the United States, starting in Congress.[29]

With U.S. President George Bush's imposition of 30% tariffs on imported steel in 2002 may be the first signal of such a crisis.

Successful Protection of the "Free" World Validates Friedrich List

> Throughout the century the flood of 'foreign aid' grew and grew until in the half century preceding 1914 Western Europe, led by Great Britain, 'had invested abroad almost as much as the entire national wealth of Great Britain.... If the same proportion of American resources were devoted to foreign investment as Britain devoted ... in 1913, the flow of investment would require to be thirty times as great. The entire Marshall Plan would have to be carried out twice a year.'[30]

The economic miracle after WWII was the rebuilding of Europe in five years under the Marshall Plan. However, if the entire industrialized world today provided industry to the developing world at the relative rate that Britain exported capital at the height of her empire's expansion, the annual "*donation*" of capital from the currently developed world to the developing world would total over four-times that given Europe during the 5-year period of the Marshall Plan. Note we say "donation," not "export," of capital. If control of world trade is to be maintained as capital is "exported," developing world labor must remain underpaid and overcharged. This prevents development of purchasing power in the undeveloped world and—due to that lack of buying power—wealth will continue to flow from the impoverished world to the wealthy world. Europe and Japan were simultaneously granted the right to protect their industry and labor as well as access to American markets Thus they could simultaneously raise the pay to their workers and repay that "exported" capital where under current free trade rules it is typically unpayable.

Although Adam Smith free trade was being preached, Friedrich List protection was provided to Japan, Taiwan, and South Korea, and later, until the Soviet Union collapsed, all of Southeast Asia and China were allowed under that umbrella. Within that bloc, capital and access to markets was provided on easy terms, equality of trade was maintained, and labor was continually being better paid. Under those Friedrich List protection policies, buying power and prosperous economies were developing.

The rest of the undeveloped world were not afforded protection and their share of world trade dropped from 28% to 13% as their commodity prices dropped 60% and are still dropping.[31] That is Friedrich List protection of tender industries within a block of nations with need for group protection, not Adam Smith free trade as designed, preached, and managed by neo-mercantilists. Southeast Asia and China had only moved in under the protection provided Japan, Taiwan, and South Korea at the height of the Cold War and the rest of the undeveloped world remained the providers of raw material and markets.

The clincher that the *imperial-centers-of-capital* are practicing Friedrich List protection philosophy under the cover of Adam Smith free trade philosophy was the 1997-to-2003 economic collapse on the periphery of empire while the centers held firm. With the exception that China is still intact as this book goes to press, this is a perfect model of a successful neo-mercantilist policy laying claim to the wealth of weak nations under the cover of free trade.

To maintain credibility and thus protect the center, almost certainly structural adjustment rules—which are little more than the withdrawal, and forced elimination, of protections that brought on those collapses—will be relaxed. That event will also be an acknowledgment that Adam Smith (as interpreted and applied) was wrong and Friedrich List was right.

Secondary Industrial Powers are at Greatest Risk

Even the center collapsing will prove List and disprove Adam Smith. If there is another worldwide collapse such as that of the 1930s we must remember that world trade was in British pounds and Britain—with its ability to print and allocate the currency of world trade—suffered the least of all industrialized nations and that the nations on the periphery of empire defaulted on their debts and actually found life easier during the depression than before. It was the emerging industrial nations, especially the United States, which suffered the most.

We can analyze why. Money flees the periphery of empire for the safety of the center. That money is available both to push up the stock markets of the center and invest in the real economy. IMF loans to the financially troubled countries are made under the condition that those funds repay investors from the center. Typically those IMF funds never leave the center of empire. The worried investors of the center are credited, the IMF funds debited, and the collapsed nation now has the identical debt as before, only it is now owed to the IMF. While the center is still holding and with money seeking safety bloating its financial institutions, speculators and stock market "bottom fishers" borrow those funds, and purchase equities and property on the collapsed periphery. Prices and sales in the center hold due to the flight of capital back to the center, the cheapening of imports, and the purchase of industries on the periphery for pennies on the dollar. Resources, labor, and production costs in the peripheral nations drop by half or more as a factor of currency collapses and enormous wealth transfers from the periphery to the center. So long as that center holds, wealth is now (1998-2003) being transferred at a rate unheard of in modern times.

If the world economy collapses, the weakest and most impoverished nations can repudiate their debts and, just as they were in the Great Depression, be better off than before the crash. The emerging nations will be at greatest risk but, with the substantial technology and skilled labor they now have, they too have the option of repudiating unjust debts, creating their own trading currency, and reorganizing their economies to trade with the weaker nations now at least partially free of the old *imperial-centers-of-capital.*

The Dilemma of the Old *Imperial-Centers-of-Capital*

Choosing its ethnic, religious, and cultural European cousins, America took the helm of the imperial nations and led the battle to suppress the world's break for economic freedom. But, now that the Cold War is won, the questions facing the powerbrokers are:

(1) Do the wealthy nations develop the world and establish equality of trades?

(2) Do they include only China and Southeast Asia and form a subtle bloc of 40% of the world trading unequally with the other 60% (a trading empire feeding upon the remaining 60% of the world)?

(3) Will the corporate mercantilists decide (state department policies are, as is much domestic law, corporate decisions) to "contain" the once fast-emerging Chinese and Southeast Asians and return to the old standard of white, Western Christian, European-cultured, wealthy nations—an *allied imperial-center-of-capital*, 15% of the world's people—covertly and militarily controlling the world?

(4) Or will the world break into three competing trading blocs—the newly expanded and allied Europe, a Western hemisphere bloc, and an Asian bloc (three trading empires)?

This is a bigger dilemma than it first appears. Previous capital accumulations were little more than the world's wealth siphoned from defeated people of color to the winners of colonial wars, the white, Western Christian, European cultures. The need for allies to defeat fast-expanding socialism and the nonaligned movement for the first time brought non-white nations (Japan, Taiwan, and South Korea) into the fold.

As over 60% of the developed world (40% of the total world) become people of color to many of the powerful it will be the primary problem. But if these racial jealousies can be overcome, if the financial meltdown of the developing world is reversed, and if the waste of the world's wealth can be eliminated, there would be substantial capital and resources to develop the remaining 60% of the world.

Notes

[1] Michael Perelman, The Invention of Capitalism: Classical Political Economy and the Secret History of Primitive Accumulation (London: Duke University Press, 2000), especially p. 91: Thomas C. Patterson, Inventing Western Civilization (New York: Monthly Review Press, 1997).

[2] Perelman, The Invention of Capitalism, Chapter 3.

[3] Adam Smith, *The Wealth of Nations* (New York: Random House, 1965), pp. 413, 426, 642. For free trade philosophy before Adam Smith, see Perelman, *The Invention of Capitalism* and Douglas A. Irwin, *Against the Tide: An Intellectual History of Free Trade* (Princeton, N.J.: Princeton University Press, 1996), Chapter 3.

[4] John C. Miller, *Origins of the American Revolution* (Stanford: Stanford University Press, 1959), pp. 4-6.

[5] Friedrich List, *The National System of Political Economy* (Fairfield, NJ: Auguatus M. Kelley, 1977), pp. 366-370.

[6] Ibid, pp. xxvii-xxviii, 368-69.

[7] List, The National System summarized.

[8] Ibid, p. 73. Earlier theorists on protection against mercantilists were: Alexander Hamilton, 1791; Adam Muller, 1809; Jean-Antoine Chaptal, 1819 and Charles Dupin, 1827, see Paul Bairoch, *Economics and World History: Myths and Paradoxes* (Chicago: University of Chicago Press, 1993), p. 17.

[9] List, *National System*, Memoirs and p. 99.

[10] Smith, *Wealth of Nations*, pp. 66-67, 636-37; see especially List, *National System*, pp. xxvi, xxvii, 11, 73-75, 150-55, 99-100, 351.

[11] List, *National System*, pp. 73-75.

[12] Ibid, p. xxv.

[13] Quoted by Herbert Aptheker, *The Colonial Era* (New York: International Publishers, 1966), pp. 23-24; taken from Smith, *Wealth of Nations*, pp. 579-80, 626.

[14] Barbara Tuchman, *The March of Folly* (New York: Alfred A. Knopf, 1984), pp. 130-31 (emphasis added). For early mercantilist theory see Irwin, *Against the Tide*, Chapter 2.

[15] Charles A. Beard, *An Economic Interpretation of the Constitution* (New York: Macmillan Publishing Co., 1941), p. 46. See also Michael Barratt Brown, *Fair Trade* (London: Zed Books, 1993), p. 20.

[16] Beard, *Economic Interpretation*, pp. 46-47, 171, 173.

[17] Philip S. Foner, *From Colonial Times to the Founding of the American Federation of Labor* (New York: International Publishers, 1982), p. 32. See William Appleman Williams, *Contours of American History* (New York: W.W. Norton & Company, 1988), pp. 105-17; Smith, *Wealth of Nations*, pp. 548-49, Book IV, Chapters VII, VIII; James Fallows, "How the World Works," *Atlantic Monthly*. December 1993, p. 42 ; Frederic F. Clairmont, *Rise and Fall of Economic Liberalism* (Goa India: Other India Press, 1996), p. 100.

[18] Williams, *Contours of American History*, pp. 192-97, 339-40; Aptheker, *Colonial Era*, pp. 23-24; List, *National System*, especially pp. 59-65, 71-89, 92, 342, 421-22; Chapter *XI;* Dean Acheson, *Present at the Creation* (New York: W.W. Norton & Company, 1987), p. 7; Richard Barnet, *The Rockets' Red Glare: War, Politics and American Presidency* (New York: Simon and Schuster, 1983), pp. 40, 60, 68. 18 34.

[19] Williams, Contours of American History, p. 221.

[20] Barnet, Rockets' *Red Glare*, p. 40.

[21] List, *National System*, pp. xxv-xxvi.

[22] Ibid., in Memoirs. See also Irwin, *Against the Tide*, pp. 125-27, Chapter 14 and Eckes, *Opening America's Markets*, Chapter 1.

[23] Feisal Mansoor, "The Health of Nations," *Lanka Monthly Digest* (December 2000)

[24] "The Three Marketeers," *Time*. February 15, 1999, pp. 34-42.

[25] Stephen Gill, "The Geopolitics of the Asian Crisis," *Monthly Review* (March, 1999), pp. 1-9.

[26] Peter Gowan, The Global Gamble: Washington's Faustian Bid for World Dominance (New York: verso, 1999), pp. 104-05.

[27] John Gray, *False Dawn* (New York: The Free Press, 1998), pp. 210-13, 217-18; see also p. 199.

[28] Gowan, *The Global Gamble*, p. 96, see also pp. 95-138 and Richard C. Longworth, *Global Squeeze: The Coming Crisis of First-World Nations* (Chicago: Contemporary Books, 1999), pp. 225, 243.

[29] Gray, *False Dawn*, pp. 217, 224-25.

[30] Acheson, Present at the Creation, p. 7.

[31] Lester Thurow, The Future of Capitalism: How Today's Economic Forces Shape Tomorrow's World (England: Penguin Books, 1996), p.67.

4. The Historical Struggle for Dominance in World Trade

With Europe's discovery of the sea route to the East and America, the maximum control of natural resources as well as markets for manufactured products could be attained through gaining title to lands of easily conquerable people. The race was on to colonize the world. "By 1900 Great Britain had grabbed 4,500,000 square miles.... France had gobbled up 3,500,000; Germany, 1,000,000; Belgium 900,000; Russia, 500,000; Italy, 185,000; and the United States, 125,000."[1]

An imperial center must be careful about importation of manufactured products from either its colonies or from other great powers:

> "So it is now," explained the [British] Protectionist Act of 1562, "that by reason of the abundance of foreign wares brought into this realm from the parts of beyond the seas, the said artificers are not only less occupied, and thereby utterly impoverished ... [but] divers cities and towns within this realm greatly endangered, and other countries notably enriched."[2]

In the late 17th-Century, Jean Baptiste Colbert, French Naval Secretary of State and Finance Minister, recognized the threat if France became dependent upon British mercantilism—as was being established by Lord Shaftesbury. Therefore, Colbert duplicated Britain's industrial development efforts. France purchased the latest technology, encouraged skilled workers, protected the home markets, eliminated internal tariffs, and constructed canals and roads. France developed flourishing industries, a profitable shipping industry, and a powerful navy. However, wars, spendthrift governments, the revocation of the Edict of Nantes (which encouraged persecution of Protestants and forced 500,000 of France's most productive workers to flee) and the 1786 Eden Treaty with Britain (a replay of the Methuen Treaty's monopoly agreements which severely damaged Portugal, Holland, and Germany) impoverished the French economy.[3]

Napoleon understood Britain's economic warfare and in 1807 issued his Continental Decrees to establish manufacturing to protect France's market from Britain and to prevent the loss of continental wealth:

> Napoleon was forced to devise a new tactic to deal with his perpetual enemy [Britain]: the Continental System. Developed during 1806/1807, this policy called for economic warfare against the "nation of shopkeepers," whereby France, either through the cooperation of friends or by the use of force against enemies, would close the entire European continent to British trade and commerce. By weakening Britain's economy, Napoleon would destroy her ability to wage war, and also make it impossible for Great Britain to provide the huge subsidies to Continental allies which had characterized all the previous coalitions against France.[4]

Napoleon resurrection of Colbert's protective system started the rapid industrialization of Europe. This immense trading bloc would have meant the end of Britain's dominance of world trade. Britain, the European monarchies, and the Church (fearful of a revolution) quickly entered into a "Holy Alliance" and defeated Napoleon at Waterloo. The markets of Europe were breached and industries throughout the continent collapsed.[5] This collapse, along with the unequal trades imposed upon the fledgling United States alerted Friedrich List and Alexander Hamilton to the necessity of protecting regional industries and markets. One cannot miss the similarity between the industrial collapse on the Continent and its *dependency* upon Britain after the French defeat and the 1991-to-1999 collapse of the Russian economy and its *dependency* on the West.

At its peak Britain was manufacturing 54% of the finished products in world trade. The British "exulted at their *unique* state, being now (as the economist Jevons put it in 1865) the trading center of the universe." The world was Britain's "countryside," a huge plantation system feeding its *developed imperial-center-of-capital*:

> The plains of North America and Russia are our corn fields; Chicago and Odessa our granaries; Canada and the Baltic our timber forests; Australia contains our sheep farms, and in Argentina and on the Western prairies of North America are our herds of oxen; Peru sends her silver, and the gold of South Africa and Australia flows to London; the Hindus and the Chinese grow our tea for us, and our coffee, sugar and spice plantations are all in the Indies. Spain and France are our vineyards and the Mediterranean our fruit garden; and our cotton grounds, which for long have occupied the Southern United States, are being extended everywhere in the warm regions of the earth.[6]

To funnel this wealth to the mother countries, exclusive trading companies—East India Company (English, Dutch, and French), Africa Company, Hudson Bay Company, et al., were established.

Forcing the natives to work for nothing while providing their own subsistence created enormous profits. Thus Indians were enslaved in Spanish mines and Africans were enslaved to replace the Indians when over 95% of their population died off under such oppression. Wealth on the periphery—American, African, and Asian colonies—was claimed by Europe in trade for trinkets, knives and guns.

The wealth accumulation power of imperialists was bound only by the limits of their naval and military power which were used to prevent other societies from infringing on their control of trade and accumulation of capital and wealth.

India: Her Vast Wealth siphoned to Britain

In 1897, British statesman Neville Chamberlain wrote a Colonial Office report: "During the present century ... you will find that every war, great or small, in which we have engaged, has had at bottom a colonial interest, that is to say, either of a colony or else of a great dependency like India." The impoverishment of India is a classic example of *plunder-by-trade* backed by military might. Before being subdued, colonized, and enforced to become *dependent* upon British industry:

> India was relatively advanced economically. Its methods of production and its industrial and commercial organization could definitely be compared with those prevailing in Western Europe. In fact, India had been manufacturing and exporting the finest muslins and luxurious fabrics since the time when most western Europeans were backward primitive peoples.[7]

Hand weaving was tedious and paid little, so at first the British purchased much of their cloth from India. India had no need or desire for British products, so imports had to be paid for with gold. However, Britain did not make the same mistake as Spain; Indian textiles were embargoed and British cloth was produced with the evolving technology of weaving machinery. After India was conquered, its import and export policies were controlled by Britain, which not only banned Indian textiles from British markets but also taxed them to a disadvantage within India so that British cloth dominated the Indian market. India's internal production of cloth was not only excluded from their own internal market so as to be undersold by Britain's inferior cloth, Britain excluded those beautiful and much higher quality fabrics from England while marketing them all over Europe. Controlling India and the seas "entitled" British merchants to buy for a pittance and sell at a high price. Friedrich List points out that the purpose of this control of trade was building Britain's "productive power":

> Was England a fool in so acting? Most assuredly according to the theories of Adam Smith and J.B Say, the Theory of Values. For, according to them, England should have bought what she required where she could buy them cheapest and best; it was an act of folly to manufacture for herself goods at a greater cost than she could buy them elsewhere, and at the same time give away that advantage to the Continent. The case is quite contrary according to our theory, which we term the Theory of the Powers of Production, and which English Ministry ... adopted when enforcing their maxim of *importing produce* and *exporting fabrics*.... The English ministers cared not for the acquisition of low-priced and perishable articles of manufacture, but for that of a more costly but enduring *manufacturing power*.... They have attained their

> objective to a brilliant degree. At this day [1841] England produces seventy million pounds' worth of cotton and silk goods, and supplies all of Europe, the entire world, India itself included, with British Manufactures. Her home production exceeds by fifty or a hundred times the value of her former trade in Indian Manufactured goods. What would it have profited her had she been buying for a century the cheap goods of Indian manufacture? And what have they gained who purchased those goods so cheaply of her? The English have gained power, incalculable power, while the others have gained the reverse of power.[8]

Through the forced sales of British products and the simultaneous embargoing of, or high tariffs on, the cheaper yet higher quality Indian cloths, India's wealth started flowing toward Britain. "It was [only] by destroying [the] Indian textile industry that [the British textile industry of] Lancaster ever came up at all."[9] Other Indian industries were similarly devastated. In the words of historian Lewis Mumford:

> In the name of progress, the limited but balanced economy of the Hindu village, with its local potter, its local spinners and weavers, its local smith, was overthrown for the sake of providing a market for the potteries of the Five Towns and the textiles of Manchester and the superfluous hardware of Birmingham. The result was impoverished villages in India, hideous and destitute towns in England, and a great wastage in tonnage and man-power in plying the oceans between.[10]

One exceptionally rich sector of India was East Bengal (Bangladesh). When the British first arrived,

> [they] found a thriving industry and a prosperous agriculture. It was, in the optimistic words of one Englishman, 'a wonderful land, whose richness and abundance neither war, pestilence, nor oppression could destroy.' But by 1947, when the sun finally set on the British Empire in India, Eastern Bengal had been reduced to an agricultural hinterland. In the words of an English merchant, 'Various and innumerable are the methods of oppressing the poor weavers ... such as by fines, imprisonment, floggings, forcing bonds from them, etc.' By means of every conceivable form of roguery, the company's merchants acquired the weaver's cloth for a fraction of its value.[11]

Later, still under British control and ignoring the fact that the East Bengalis were being impoverished through dispossession of the land which produced their food and cotton, Bengal produced raw materials (indigo and jute) for world commerce, and poppies for the large, externally-imposed, Chinese opium market. As Adam Smith commented, money was lent to farmers "at forty, fifty, and sixty percent" and this, and other profits of trade, would confiscate all wealth except that paid in wages. Of course, Bengali labor was paid almost nothing so Bengal's wealth was rapidly transferred to Britain. Foreign control enforcing dependency upon British industry and siphoning wealth away through unequal trades in everyday commerce devastated the balanced and prosperous Bengali economy and created the extreme poverty of Bangladesh today. "[O]nce it was the center of the finest textile manufactures in the world ... [with] a third of its people ... employed in non-agricultural occupations.... Today 90 percent of its workers are in agriculture or unemployed."[12] The destruction of the once thriving economy of East Bengal (Bangladesh) was so thorough that even the long-staple, finely textured local cotton became extinct.[13]

Anyone who saw the movie *Gandhi* will remember that Indian citizens were even denied the right to collect salt from the ocean and were required by law to buy their salt and other everyday staples from British monopolies. Such enforced dependencies were little more than a tax upon defeated societies under the guise of production and distribution. Much work was being done, but it could have been done just as well or better by those being dispossessed of their land, denied the right to produce for themselves, and overcharged for monopolized products.

Japan, because it had no valuable natural resources, was the only country not culturally, racially, and religiously tied to Europe that escaped domination during this period. Until Taiwan and South Korea (and now China and Southeast Asia) were industrialized, all under the same protectionist barrier to contain fast expanding socialism, Japan was the only non-white society to industrialize and join the club of wealthy nations.[14]

In *The Discovery of India*, Prime Minister Jawaharlal Nehru wrote, "If you trace British influence and control in each region of India, and then compare that with poverty in the region, they correlate. The longer the British have been in a region, the poorer it is."[15] What applies to British colonialism applies to all colonialism and India and China were actually the least damaged of all colonial regions.

Controlling China was a much more Difficult Problem

In 1800, the per-capita standard of living in China exceeded that of Europe.[16] Like India, China did not need or want Britain's products. However, Britain consumed large quantities of Chinese tea and, to avoid the loss of Britain's gold, it was imperative that something else be traded. Though it was done covertly and not acknowledged by the British government, it became official policy for British merchants to peddle opium to China. "Opium [sold to China] was no hole-in-the-corner petty smuggling trade but *probably the largest commerce of the time in any single commodity*."[17] This injustice was challenged by Chinese authorities (the Boxer Rebellion) but their attempt to maintain sovereignty was put down by a combined force of 20,000 British, French, Japanese, German, and United States troops (5,000 were Americans) led by a German general.[18] It was a blatant attempt to carve up China between those *imperial-centers-of-capital*.

With the sales of opium exceeding the purchases of tea, Britain lost neither gold nor currency. Their capital and labor costs involved only an internal circulation of money. No wealth was lost to another society, which is the essence of a successful mercantilist policy. This appears productive only because the wealth gained or protected by Britain was considered; the much greater losses suffered by China, India, and much of the world were conveniently left uncalculated.

While the *imperial-centers-of-capital* were battling each other in WWII, China was laying its base for economic freedom. Although it is little known to Americans, after the war United States troops were guarding key rail lines and ports for the collapsing Chinese government and the OSS, precursor to the CIA, was busy ferrying Chiang Kai-shek's troops back and forth across China to suppress that revolution. However, China did break free in 1949, was marginalized for years by the imperial nations, yet still built a modest industrial capacity, and—by moving under the same protectionist umbrella as Japan, Taiwan, and South Korea—eventually averaged production gains of well over 10% a year.

Notes

1 E.K. Hunt, Howard J. Sherman, *Economics* (New York: Harper and Row, 1990), p. 144.

2 William Appleman Williams, *Contours of American History* (New York: W.W. Norton & Company, 1988), introduction, especially p. 43.

3 Friedrich List, *The National System of Political Economy* (Fairfield, NJ: Augustus M. Kelley, 1977), pp. 33, 41-60, 72, 323, 342, 357, 369, 391.

4 Gordon C. Bond, *The Grand Expedition* (Athens: University of Georgia Press, 1979), pp. 1-2, 8.

5 List, *National System*, Chapters 6 and 25, pp. 39, 72-73, 85-87, 323, 343-45, 357, 421-22.

6 Paul Kennedy, *Rise and Fall of Great Powers* (New York: Random House, 1987), pp. 151-52, quoted from R. Hyam, *Britain's Imperial Century 1815-1914* (London: B.T. Batsford, 1976), p. 47. Economist John Stuart Mill also believed the colonies were Britain's fields (Frances Moore Lappé, Joseph Collins, *Food First: Beyond the Myth of Scarcity,* rev. (New York: Ballantine, 1979), pp. 63 – 64, reproduced and quoted from Douglas H. Boucher, *The Paradox of Plenty; Hunger in a Bountiful World* (Food First, 1999). See also these subchapters in Chapter 13: "Conceptually Reversing the Process" and "One Huge Plantation System Providing Food and Resources to the Imperial Center."

7 Hunt and Sherman, *Economics*, p. 142.

8 List, *National System,* pp. 43-44.

9 Dan Nadudere, *The Political Economy of Imperialism* (London: Zed Books, 1977), p. 35, 68, especially 86. See also Betsy Hartman and James Boyce, *Needless Hunger: Voices from a Bangladesh Village* (San Francisco: Institute for Food and Development Policy, 1982).

10 Lewis Mumford, *Technics and Civilization* (New York: Harcourt Brace Jovanovich, 1963), pp. 184-85.

11 Hartman and Boyce, *Needless Hunger*, pp. 10, 12.

12 Arjun Makhijani, *From Global Capitalism to Economic Justice* (New York: Apex Press, 1992), p. 79.

13 Adam Smith, *Wealth of Nations*, Modern Library edition (New York: Random House, 1937, 1965), pp. 94, 97; Hartmann and Boyce, *Needless Hunger*, describes this devastation.

14 Hunt and Sherman, *Economics*, 1990, pp. 142-47, 624.

15 Noam Chomsky, *The Prosperous Few and the Restless Many* (Berkeley: Odonian Press, 1993), p. 56.

16 Anthony Sampson, *The Midas Touch* (New York: Truman Talley Books/Plume, 1991), p. 108.

17 Samuel Flagg Bemis, *A Diplomatic History of the United States* (New York: Henry Holt and Company, 1936), pp. 1027-1142; Michael Greenberg, *British Trade and the Opening of China 1800-1842* (New York: Monthly Review Press), p. 104; Eric R. Wolf, *Europe and the People Without History* (Berkeley: University of California Press, 1982), pp. 255-58. (emphasis added)

18 Jack Beeching, *The Chinese Opium Wars* (New York: Harcourt Brace Jovanovich, 1975). See also Michael Bentley, *Politics Without Democracy* (London: Fontana Paperbacks, 1984), p. 154.

5. World Wars: Battles over Who Decides the Rules of Unequal Trade

United States President Woodrow Wilson is known as the most peaceful president America has ever had. But he knew control of resources and trade was the goal of all powerful nations:

> Since trade ignores national boundaries and the manufacturer insists on having the world as a market, the flag of his nation must follow him, and the doors of the nations which are closed against him must be battered down. Concessions obtained by financiers must be safeguarded by ministers of state, even if the sovereignty of unwilling nations be outraged in the process. Colonies must be obtained or planted, in order that no useful corner of the world may be overlooked or left unused.[1]

When two or more powerful nations deny each other equal trading rights, war develops. Spain, Holland, Portugal, and France had been overwhelmed by British sea power and cunning control of markets. Otto von Bismarck, unifier of the German nation, deduced that "free trade is the weapon of the dominant economy anxious to prevent others from following in its path."[2] Studying the development philosophy of Friedrich List, he consolidated the German nation in the late 1800s and industrialized: "factories, machinery, and techniques were bought wholesale, usually from England."[3]

At first German manufactures were of inferior quality, just as Japan's products were later when it first industrialized. However, it did not take the Germans long to learn. By 1913, Germany had 60,000 university students to Britain's 9,000, and 3,000 engineering students to Britain's 350. German industries were not only out-producing Britain, they were producing superior products.[4]

Earlier, in 1888, philosopher T.H. Huxley outlined the disaster that would befall Britain if it should ever lose its dominance in trade:

> We not only are, but, under penalty of starvation, we are bound to be, a nation of shopkeepers. But other nations also lie under the same necessity of keeping shop, and some of them deal in the same goods as ourselves. Our

> customers naturally seek to get the most and the best in exchange for their produce. If our goods are inferior to those of our competitors, there is no ground, compatible with the sanity of the buyers, which can be alleged, why they should not prefer the latter. And if the result should ever take place on a large and general scale, five or six millions of us would soon have nothing to eat.[5] [26 years later, when Britain was threatened with just such a loss, WWI began.]

Outlining that the concern was Germany's threat to British trade, in 1897 the publication *Saturday Review* wrote: "If Germany were extinguished tomorrow, the day after tomorrow there is not an Englishman in the world who would not be richer. Nations have fought for years over a city or right of succession; must they not fight for two hundred fifty million pounds sterling of yearly commerce?"[6]

Britain's survival depended upon selling overpriced manufactured products and losing those markets would collapse her economy. As Britain's "national interest" was at stake, she had signed pacts with France, Austria-Hungary, Italy, and eventually Russia, all designed to contain Germany. Austria-Hungary changed sides and the clash of interests in the Balkans between the competing *imperial-centers-of-capital* led directly to WWI. WWII was simply a replay of WWI.[7] Before that War, Europe

> was "stifling" within her boundaries, with production everywhere outstripping the European demand for manufactured products. All Europe was therefore "driven by necessity to seek new markets far away," and "what more secure markets" could a nation possess than "countries placed under its influence?."... The rapid growth of German trade and the far-flung extension of German interests first encouraged in Germany a demand for a larger merchant marine, and then for a larger and more effective navy.... Without a strong fleet, Germany would find herself at the mercy of Britain, a "grasping and unscrupulous nation which, in the course of history, had taken opportunity after opportunity to destroy the trade of its commercial rivals."[8]

As Germany tried hard to break Britain's control of world commerce, Britain

> was reinforcing her position by making a hard and fast alliance with Austria-Hungary and Italy.... In 1904, Britain made a sweeping deal with France over Morocco and Egypt; a couple of years later she compromised with Russia over Persia, that loose federation of powers was finally replaced by two hostile power groupings; the balance of power as a system had now come to an end.... About the same time the symptoms of the dissolution of the existing forms of world economy—colonial rivalry and competition for exotic markets—became acute.[9]

These "two hostile power groupings" were the *old imperial-centers-of-capital*, Britain and her allies, and the *emerging imperial-centers-of-capital*, Germany and her allies. Restrictive trade practices were strangling potentially wealthy countries and "everyone knew it would start but no one knew how or when ... until Archduke Ferdinand was shot."[10]

Except for religious conflicts and the petty wars of feudal lords, wars are primarily fought over resources and trade. President Woodrow Wilson recognized that this was the cause of WWI: "Is there any man, is there any woman, let me say any child here that does not know that the seed of war in the modern world is industrial and commercial rivalry?"[11]

> The real war, of which this sudden outburst of death and destruction is only an incident, began long ago. It has been raging for tens of years, but its battles have been so little advertised that they have hardly been noted. It is a clash of traders.... All these great German fleets of ocean liners and merchantmen have sprung into being since 1870. In steel manufacture, in textile work, in mining and trading, in every branch of modern industrial and commercial life, and also in population, German development has been equally amazing. But geographically all fields of development were closed.... Great Britain took South Africa. And pretended to endless surprise and grief that the Germans did not applaud this closing of another market.[12]

Financial warfare is a powerful weapon in trade wars:

> It should be recalled that the practically universal use of sterling in international trade was a principal component of Britain's financial sway, and it was precisely into this strategic sphere that Germany began to penetrate, with the mark evolving as an alternative to the pound. The Deutsche Bank conducted "a stubborn fight for the introduction of acceptance [of the German mark] in overseas trade in place of the hitherto universal sterling bill.... This fight lasted for decades and when the war came, a point had been reached at which the mark acceptance in direct transactions with German firms had partially established itself alongside the pound sterling."..."It seems probable that if war had not come in 1914, London would have had to share with Germany the regulatory power over world trade and economic development which it had exercised so markedly in the nineteenth century."[13]

Serious researchers recognize that a dominant currency has "regulatory power over world trade and development." Almost 50 years after the American dollar replaced the British pound as the world's trading currency, the *Washington Post* noted: "Under the Bretton Woods system, the Federal Reserve acted as the world's central bank. This gave America enormous leverage over economic policies of its principal trading partners."[14] Control of a trading currency is a powerful tool and the primary mechanism through which *imperial-centers-of-capital* maintain unequal currency values and unequal trading values which keep the wealth of the periphery flowing to the imperial center as per the formula outlined in Chapter 1.

The British were afraid of both German economic power and the loss of their central bank operating as the world's central bank. Because their industries and economic infrastructures were primitive and could not compete with Britain's highly developed technology and economic infrastructure, all major countries had protective tariffs on the eve of WWI. Historically markets have been both opened and protected by military force. Opening others markets while protecting their own were primary to the national security of virtually every *imperial-center-of-capital.* After that war, Britain thought that

> placing a ring of new nations around Germany (supported by proper guarantees) would do away with the immediate danger of a German-led economic union.... Once Germany's threat to British economic supremacy had abated the prewar crisis inside British politics would resolve itself.[15]

Germany and World War II

German leaders were still angry over their humiliating defeat in WWI, a war fought over trade, and trade was a large component of this second struggle. "The peace conference of 1919, held in Versailles, marked not the end of the war but rather its continuation by other means."[16] The injustice of controlled markets under the guise of free trade was never rectified. A resentful Germany prepared, at first secretly, then more and more openly, to employ military might to break those trade barriers and eliminate the humiliation and restrictions of Versailles:

> The late 1920s and early 1930s began with a series of worldwide financial crashes that ultimately spiraled downward into the Great Depression. As GNPs fell, the dominant countries each created trading blocks (the Japanese Greater East Asia Co-Prosperity Sphere, the British Empire, the French Union, Germany plus Eastern Europe, America with its Monroe Doctrine) to minimize imports and preserve jobs. If only one country had kept imports out, limiting imports would have helped it avoid the Great Depression, but with everyone restricting trade, the downward pressures were simply magnified. In the aggregate, fewer imports must equal fewer exports. Eventually, those economic blocks evolved into military blocks, and World War II began.[17]

This is not a defense of Germany's racist motives or conduct in WWII. The supporters and goals of fascism are the antithesis of this treatise. Fascism would severely restrict rights for the masses; this treatise would expand them to full rights. However, the injustice to Germany in denying her equality in world trade was extreme and injustice breeds extremism. As we have shown, World Wars I and II were caused by the attempt to economically strangle (contain) Germany.[18]

William Appleman Williams, in *The Tragedy of American Diplomacy*, identified control of markets as the cause of both World Wars I and II. He notes that free trade was then called the "Open Door Policy" and "It was conceived and designed to win the victories without the wars.... It does not prove that any nation that resisted (or resists) those objectives was (or is) evil, and therefore to blame for [the] following conflicts or violence."[19]

Both Presidents McKinley and Wilson "unequivocally pointed to Germany as the most dangerous rival of the United States in that economic struggle" and President Franklin Roosevelt and his advisors "explicitly noted as early as 1935 ... that Germany, Italy and Japan were defined as dangers to the well-being of the United States."[20]In fact, on April 10, 1935 (four years before WWII and six years before America entered that war), Roosevelt "wrote a letter to [Britain's] Colonel House telling him he was considering American participation in a joint military and naval blockade to seal off Germany's borders."[21]

Because Germany was bypassing Britain's monopolization of finance capital through barter agreements, that blockade was intended to re-impose neo-mercantilist "free" trade and contain German economic power as well as its Aryan supremacist philosophy. After the war, Secretary of State Cordell Hull reaffirmed that trade was the primary cause of WWII:

> Yes, war did come, despite the trade agreements. But it is a fact that war did not break out between the United States and any country with which we had been able to negotiate a trade agreement. It is also a fact that, with very few exceptions, the countries with which we signed trade agreements joined together in resisting the Axis. The political line-up followed the economic line-up.[22]

Walter Russell Mead concurred that wars are extensions of trade wars. He warned: "The last time the world deprived two major industrial countries, Germany and Japan, of what each considered its rightful 'place in the sun' the result was World War II."[23]

Japan's Greater East Asia Co-Prosperity Sphere and World War II

Under the guns of Admiral Perry's naval task force in 1854, Japan's markets were forced open. They were forced to sign a trade agreement with a tariff limit of 5% while the average tariff on imports into America of almost 30% was immediately raised even higher.[24] Learning the mechanics of becoming wealthy through this experience with neo-mercantilist unequal trade (and on the advice of Herbert Spencer), the Japanese studied Western economic theories carefully and in 1872 formed their trade policies.

Japan copied and improved upon Germany's industrial cartels, and followed the European model of establishing colonial empires to create the pre-WWII Greater East Asia Co-Prosperity Sphere. Both Germany and Japan were following Friedrich List's philosophy of consolidating nations and developing industrial power.

The origin of many of today's Japanese corporations came from the post-Meji Japanese government building the most up-to-date factories and selling them to industrialists for 15-to-30% of building costs.[25] Take specific note on how Germany and Japan's independence, based on military might, gave them the power to create money and thus combine natural resources and labor to produce industrial capital. They could not have built those basic industries quickly, if at all, while remaining dependent upon the British pound as their trading currency. A nation without natural resources need only create the money, build the industry, barter production from that industry for more resources, and pay for it all with the goods produced. Japan provides the model. So long as a country has access to technology to produce quality products and access to markets to sell those products, those industries and products back the money created to produce those industries.

After WWII, under United States protection as a buffer against fast-expanding socialism, Japan reestablished her centrally planned cartels (Germany reestablished theirs at the same time) to maintain low import prices for raw materials, high prices for Japanese citizens, and lower export prices of high-quality consumer goods to penetrate world markets.

Japan's industrialization was a strengthened and fine-tuned copy of Germany's cartel industrialization that was such a threat to England: "America is no longer such a rich country. And Japan is no longer poor. Much of America's wealth has been transferred to the Japanese through the medium of exports and imports. Their exports and our imports."[26]

Japan's pre-WWII conquests cut powerful European traders off from what was once their private domain. This was the common bond between Germany and Japan in WWII and virtually any respectable history of the origin of the war in the Pacific outlines the embargoes against Japan and the trade negotiations carried out right up to the bombing of Pearl Harbor. The total embargo of oil against Japan just before war broke out in 1941 would have squeezed its economy just as effectively as a Middle East embargo would squeeze Western economies today.

America Protects the Imperial Centers

Check a globe and note the enormous expanse of the world where most of the world's natural resources are located, which is undeveloped and impoverished, and which consumes only 14% of the world's resources. Then note the small area of the world which has few resources, which is developed, wealthy and powerful and which consumes 86% of the world's resources.[27] The resources which produce the wealth and power of the imperial centers are primarily in, and thus properly owned by, the impoverished undeveloped world. The secret that can never be acknowledged is that—if the impoverished world had access to finance capital, technology, and markets—it is they who would be wealthy.

As impoverished nations started breaking free from the chains of neo-mercantilist imperialism after WWII and exercising their rights as free people, the words spoken by Western security councils demonstrated they clearly realized their dilemma: "China is moving towards an economy and a type of trade in which there is no place for the foreign manufacturer, the foreign banker, or the foreign trader."[28] "We cannot expect domestic prosperity under our system without a constantly expanding trade with other nations. The capitalist system is essentially an international system, if it cannot function internationally, it will break down completely."[29]

The threat of the governments of half of Europe being no longer allied with the West and the loss of China after that war led to Germany and Japan, as well as Taiwan and South Korea—right on the border of China—being included as allies. The strategy of allowing those *once-threatening imperial-centers-of-capital* access to finance capital, technology, resources, and markets rapidly rebuilt Germany and Japan and much of Southeast Asia.

The Friedrich List protection provided post-WWII Japan, Taiwan, and South Korea (which was *democratic-cooperative-capitalism*) would be a great model to develop the entire world. However, the rest of the colonial world—which was forming their own nonaligned bloc to control its destiny—was not only denied all those protections, they were covertly destabilized and the rules of Adam Smith free trade, as interpreted by neo-mercantilists, were applied. True free trade was nonexistent, all the free trade rhetoric notwithstanding.

America allied with Britain to defeat Germany in WWI, allied with both Britain and the Soviet Union to defeat Germany again, and defeated Japan almost alone, in WWII. The United States then allied with the former *hostile imperial-centers-of-capital* to defeat the *rising center of capital* to the East, the Soviet Union, and suppress the many breaks for economic freedom of the colonial nations. European nations were prostrate after bankrupting each other battling over the world's wealth and America picked up the baton as protector of the *now-allied imperial-centers-of-capital.*

That the Cold War was primarily to maintain control of the world's resources, not to defend against attack, is proven by the fact that even after the collapse of the Soviet Union, the West's supposed imminent military threat, the U.S. military budget alone is becoming equal to that of the rest of the world combined. America and its allies together have at least 20-times the firepower of any possible combination of nations allegedly hostile to their interests.

Western imperialists may need that firepower. Much of Southeast Asia is highly industrialized and, in 2002, China alone graduated over 400,000 Ph.D.s in the hard sciences. We must remember it was Germany graduating 3,000 engineers to Britain's 350 that made the German economy so much more efficient and it was Germany's takeover of British markets with the production of those engineers that led to World Wars I and II. Only a philosophy of sharing resources, sharing productive capacity, and sharing in the wealth produced can avoid Fascist military control of world resources which could easily turn into WWIII.

America's and NATO's rapid-reaction forces snuffing out resistance worldwide is only control of resources and control of the *wealth-producing-process* hiding under other excuses.

Notes

[1] Woodrow Wilson, President of the United States, 1919, Quoted by Noam Chomsky, *On Power and Ideology*, (South End Press, 1990), p.14.

[2] Steven Schlosstein, *Trade War* (New York: Congdon & Weed, 1984), p. 9.

[3] Kurt Rudolph Mirow, Harry Maurer, *Webs of Power* (Boston: Houghton Mifflin Co., 1982), p. 16.

[4] D.J. Goodspeed, *The German Wars* (New York: Bonanza Books, 1985), p. 71.

[5] Petr Kropotkin, *Mutual Aid* (Boston: Porter Sargent Publishing Co.), p. 334.

[6] Frederic F. Clairmont, *The Rise and Fall of Economic Liberalism* (Goa, India: The Other India Press, 1996), pp. 195, 197; William Appleman Williams, *The Contours of American* History (New York: W.W. Norton, 1988), his *Empire as a Way of Life* (Oxford: Oxford University Press, 1980), and his *The Tragedy of American Diplomacy* (New York: W.W. Norton, 1972); Eli F. Heckscher, *Mercantilism* (New York: Macmillan Company, 1955); Fritz Fisher, *Germany's Aims in the First World War* (New York: W.W. Norton, 1967), pp. 38-49; Dwight E. Lee, *Europe's Crucial Years* (Hanover, NH: Clark University Press, 1974).

[7] Williams, *Contours of American History*, pp. 54, 66, 122-23, 128-29, 144-45, 168-70, 221-22, 272, 319, 338-40, 363, 349, 368-69, 383, 411, 417-23, 429, 434-37, 452, 455-58, 461-64; Williams, *Empire as a Way of Life*; Williams, *Tragedy of American Diplomacy*; Heckscher, *Mercantilism*, especially vol. 2, pp. 70-71.

[8] Nazli Choucri, Robert C. North, *Nations in Conflict* (San Francisco: W. H. Freeman and Company, 1974), in part quoting other authors, pp. 58-59, 106-07. See also Samuel Williamson, Jr., *The Politics of Grand Strategy* (London: Ashfield Press, 1969).

[9] Karl Polanyi, *The Great Transformation* (Boston: Beacon Press, 1957), p. 19.

[10] Lawrence Malkin, *The National Debt* (New York: Henry Holt and Co., 1988), p. 11; Williams, *Contours of American History*; Heckscher, Mercantilism; Lloyd C. Gardner, *Safe for Democracy* (New York: Oxford University Press, 1984).

[11] Terry Allen, "In GATT They Trust," *Covert Action Information Bulletin*, (Spring 1992), p. 63; George Seldes, *Never Tire of Protesting* (New York: Lyle Stuart, Inc., 1968), p. 45; Gardner, *Safe For Democracy*, Chapters 1-2. See also Williams, *Contours of American History*, p. 412; Heckscher, Mercantilism, vol. 2.

[12] John Reed, *The Education of John Reed* (New York: International Publishers, 1955), pp. 74-75.

[13] Harry Magdoff, Paul M. Sweezy, *Stagnation and the Financial Explosion* (New York: Monthly Review Press, 1987) p. 167. Quotes are from H. Parker Willis and B. H. Beckhart's *Foreign Banking Systems* and from J. B. Condliffe's *The Commerce of Nations.*

[14] Bookworld, *Washington Post* (April 14, 1994), p. 14 (From McGehee's Database).

[15] Gardner, *Safe for Democracy*, p. 98.

[16] Goodspeed, *German Wars*, pp. 267-68.

[17] Lester Thurow, *Head to Head: The Coming Economic Battle Among Japan, Europe, and America* (New York: William Morrow and Company, 1992), pp. 55-56.

[18] James and Suzanne Pool, *Who Financed Hitler* (New York: Dial Press, 1978), p. 41.

[19] Williams, *Tragedy of American Diplomacy*, pp. 128-29.

[20] Ibid, pp. 73, 128-29, 172-73; see also pp. 72-3, 134-5, 142; Williams, *Contours of American History*, pp. 412, 451-57, 462-64.

[21] Richard Barnet, *The Rockets' Red Glare: War, Politics and the American Presidency* (New York: Simon and Schuster, 1990), p. 194.

[22] Williams, *Tragedy of American Diplomacy*, pp. 163-64, emphasis added.

[23] Walter Russell Mead, "American Economic Policy in the Antemillenial Era," *World Policy Journal* (Summer 1989), p. 422.

[24] James Fallows, "How the World Works," *The Atlantic Monthly*. December 1993, p. 82.

[25] Clairmont, *Rise and Fall of Economic Liberalism*, pp. 169, 268.

[26] Schlosstein, *Trade War*, pp. 9, 13, 55, 99. Fallows, *World Works*, pp. 73, 82. See also J.M. Roberts, *The Triumph of the West* (London: British Broadcasting Company, 1985), p. 33.

[27] *United Nations Human Development Report, 1998.*

[28] Noam Chomsky, "Enduring Truths: Changing Markets," *CovertAction Quarterly* (Spring 1996), p. 49.

[29] Eric Wolf, *Europe and the People Without History* (Berkeley: University of California Press, 1982), p. 9.

6. Suppressing Freedom of Thought in a Democracy

"The great masses of the people in the very bottom of their hearts tend to be corrupted rather than purposely or consciously evil ... therefore ... they more easily fall a victim to a big lie than to a little one, since they themselves lie in little things, but would be ashamed of lies that were too big.

—Adolph Hitler from Mein Kampf

The true dimension of covert violence and intrigue that has gone into controlling thoughts in "free" societies is so insidious that many may question the events we are describing ever took place. Thus this chapter provides a brief outline of how the minds of free people were controlled to make them unaware of, ignore, or accept, covert activities and what can only be described as wholesale terrorism against primarily peaceful nations.

The CIA's *Mighty Wurlitzer* Inoculated the World against Philosophies of Full and Equal Rights

Through the expansion of empires in the 19th-Century, the world had become the "countryside" from which to obtain resources for the *European-centers-of-capital.* The old imperial nations broke themselves battling over the world's wealth—World Wars I and II. America was the only *intact center-of-capital.* The frightened leaders of the old imperial nations handed the baton to the United States to keep the entire world from gaining their *economic freedom* and America has done that job well.

To maintain control of the economies of periphery nations it was essential that the influence of the once rapidly developing former Soviet Union be contained. Their successful development would be a beacon for historians, social scientists, and intellectuals worldwide. Those economic and political philosophies would be followed and controlling the rest of the world would be impossible:

> Even if a small country like Cuba, gained their freedom and their living standards rose, the rest of the world would demand their freedom. Hence the

> otherwise incomprehensible destruction by the world's most powerful nations of small weak nations such as Korea, Vietnam, Chile, Nicaragua, Angola, Mozambique, and the Congo who came close to gaining their freedom. The drumbeat of the West being under imminent threat of attack by these nations was a *strategy-of-tension* so that the citizens of these powerful nations would support the extremely violent and terrorizing suppression of those countries break for freedom.[1]

As the Cold War was being won, Peter Coleman, author of *Liberal Conspiracy*, gained complete and unimpeded access to the archives of the Congress for Cultural Freedom, an American and European writers' support group that had been covertly established by the Central Intelligence Agency (CIA). The path to easy publication of books and articles throughout the "free" world was through this worldwide, CIA-orchestrated and funded *strategy-of-tension* creating the belief within Western populations that they were about to lose their freedom to totalitarian dictators:

> Five years after their victory in 1945, the Western democracies were about to lose the battle for Europe, but this time to Stalinist totalitarianism instead of Nazis. To combat this prospect, an intellectual guerrilla group was formed: over one hundred European and American writers and intellectuals met in Berlin to establish the Congress for Cultural Freedom to resist the Kremlin's sustained assault on Western and liberal values. During the 1950s the Congress spread throughout the world, creating a network of affiliated national committees, a worldwide community of liberal intellectuals fiercely committed to democratic governance, but supported by grants which, unknown to *most* of them, originated in the Central Intelligence Agency. Through the Congress's influential publications, conferences, and international protests, it kept the issues of Soviet totalitarianism and liberal anti-Communism alive in a largely hostile environment.... It was finally dissolved in 1967 amid the revelations of its funding by the CIA.[2]

Frances Stoner Saunders, in T*he Cultural Cold War: The CIA and the World of Arts and Letters*, discusses this further:

> Whether they liked it or not, whether they knew it or not, there were few writers, poets, artists, historians, scientists or critics in post-war Europe whose names were not in some way linked to this covert enterprise.... Defining the Cold War as a 'battle for men's minds' it stockpiled a vast arsenal of cultural weapons: journals, books, conferences, seminars, art exhibitions, concerts, awards.... Endorsed and subsidized by powerful institutions, this non-Communist group became as much a cartel in the intellectual life of the West as Communism had been a few years earlier (and [since it was the intellectual left that was being targeted for control through the establishment of a Non-Communist left] it included many of the same people).... It spied on tens of thousands of Americans, harassed democratically elected governments abroad, plotted assassinations, denied these activities to Congress, and, in the process, elevated the art of lying to new heights.[3]

According to Frances Stoner Saunders and others cited, covert coordination of the writings of Western authors—such as George Orwell (including the CIA producing movies of his books), Hannah Arendt, Irving Kristol (the CIA buying 50,000 of his books for free distribution worldwide), Isaiah Berlin, Sidney Hook, Arthur Koestler, Henry Luce, Bertrand Russell, Arthur Schlesinger Jr., Robert Conquest and Peter Coleman (who wrote the above cited exposure) and the simultaneous sabotage of media they could not control (such as *Ramparts Magazine*, *the Nation* and *the New Statesman* of which only a few were able to avoid bankruptcy from loss of their readers)—was only one of the many "black ops" and covert actions, occasionally breaking out into overt actions, which became the hidden history of the Cold War.

That hidden history was first exposed by the Church and Pike Congressional Committees in 1975 and 1976 and by many researchers and reporters since. To carry out its *strategies-of-tension*, the CIA had its own wire service and publishing companies. It set up and supported magazines, newspapers, and radio stations with solidly biased and beholden editorial staffs. It established the largest news conglomerate in West Germany and major media in many countries (including Radio Free Europe, Radio Liberty, and Voice of America with roughly 100 transmitters each, and many lesser-known regional radio stations beamed to Asia, the Middle East, Latin America, and Africa). Attorney William Schapp says the CIA

> alone—not to mention its counterparts in the rest of the American intelligence community—owned or controlled some 2,500 media entities all over the world. In addition, it has people ranging from stringers to highly visible journalists and editors in virtually every major media organization.[4] [To that we must add those controlled by the intelligence services of other nations.]

Canned Cold War editorials were prepared and sent to large and small newspapers all over the world. These editorials were available for any editor to restructure as his or her own creation. Large independent think-tanks were established, funded, and staffed with ideological supporters, as were think-tanks within universities.

Using negative buzzword labels to describe others such as *communist dictatorship, subversives, and extremists* and using only positive words such as *freedom, justice, rights, and majority rule* when talking of ourselves was the foundation of this, and all other, *social-control-paradigms*. This is designed to create fear (a *strategy-of-tension*) among the populations of the wealthy nations so they would support a policy of worldwide suppression and oppression under the cover of protecting freedoms and rights.

Foundations established and funded by the CIA were only some of the many financial conduits that provided the funds for this immense operation. Money was passed covertly through more than 170 major, seemingly independent, foundations—as well as the Marshall Plan and the American Federation of Labor. The CIA's covert propaganda budget throughout the Cold War exceeded that of UPI, AP, and Reuters even as those news services were the unwitting primary carriers of its carefully crafted views of the world. Control of the thoughts of the world through control of media content was the CIA's biggest covert action expenditure. That the CIA offered reporters news scoops in exchange for publication of fraudulent articles tells us some of the leading columnists in the world were planting these deceptions.

Reporters with a pipeline to sensational stories rise quickly to the top. According to Frances Saunders, well-known Washington columnists such as Joe and Stewart Alsop and Walter Lippman were dinner and social friends with the *managers-of-state* and the CIA leaders (such as William Colby, Frank Wisner, and other managers of the CIA) who were creating this propaganda and were in on the ground floor of cold war planning. Those columnists knew that the *Grand Strategy* was to misinform the nation that it was under dire threat of military assault even as they knew this was pure fabrication. Those columnists knowingly cooperated and never breathed a word of the propaganda (*strategy-of-tension*) scheme. The news media were scandalized when the Pike Committee exposed that over 400 journalists were in the direct employ of the CIA (at $200 a month they were cheaper than prostitutes). Of course, "A central feature of this program was to advance the claim that it [propaganda] did not exist."[5]

Here then is how the propagandizing of the so-called free world was accomplished: CIA leaders moved in the same social circles as—and were personal friends of—leading columnists, newspaper editors, and media owners. With the base of fraudulent books and articles in place for researchers as addressed above the CIA would leak dramatic fictitious stories (missile gaps, Soviet aggression, threats from rogue terrorist nations). It was crucial for the masses to believe such stories because then they would give their support for any suppression of the colonial world's breaks for freedom.

When media leaders published these fraudulent stories they were passed over all the wire services and every media in the nation would publish them, usually as front page news and lead articles. Follow up interviews were channeled to prepared spokespersons and the threats were confirmed. Alternative news may challenge that view eventually but initially no one stands up. In one day, not just the United States but much of the world faithfully believed what, in final analysis, was carefully crafted propaganda. In this way *strategies-of-tension* are still created so the masses will fully support whatever military campaign or covert activity is on the agenda of the State Department/National Security Council/President.

Below the elite group of *misinformers* were accredited reporters who remained accredited only by parroting what was fed them. No one—except those ideologically safe media (personal and social friends of CIA managers and top government officials)—knew this was created propaganda and accredited reporters were straitjacketed. To challenge those planted stories which the whole nation believed fully would be career and social suicide. Thus there were no reporters to seriously challenge such silly notions as El Salvador, Nicaragua, Guatemala, Chile, Cuba, Yugoslavia, and other tiny countries being serious military threats to America.

With the "free" media saturated with those articles carefully crafted to control the masses view of the world, propaganda became, and is still being written as, history. This can be seen in the daily news being nearly identical in today's newspapers and newscasts while only a small portion of the world, national and local news is reported. Generally speaking, these media do not have reporters checking if those are facts, they only have reporters rushing to be the first to report what they are told.

Once a primary *social-control-paradigm* is carried in every newspaper and newscast in the nation as fact and every applicable organ of government is backing it, no reporter or editor would dare challenge that report. This was seen with full force when Iraq was demonized in 2002-03 in preparation for the April 2003 invasion with the goal of installing a puppet government. The majority of Americans firmly believed they were under the dire threats the media reports proclaimed. Any newspaper or TV news that dared take an opposing view would have lost its readers en masse, would lose their lucrative corporate advertising and, though this will vehemently be denied, those editors would have lost their jobs.

The powerful were, and are, writing history to control the thoughts of the general public well into the future (the intention is forever). Unless the process is fully exposed, sincere researchers will forever be citing these fabricated published accounts as they write history. In fact, the British and all other empires have been practicing just such black-ops to protect their empires for centuries, still are, and the OSS and CIA were taught by Britain's MI6. The intelligence services of all nations of what is now one allied empire cooperated in misinforming their citizens to gain their backing supposedly to suppress tyrants but in reality to maintain control of the world. This orchestrated propaganda machine was eventually described by agents of the CIA itself as its *Mighty Wurlitzer*.[6]

The route to becoming well-published and well-known was therefore through parroting what came out of the *Mighty Wurlitzer*. Certainly most writers and reporters had no direct contact with the Congress for Cultural Freedom. But Cold War hysteria created by the intelligence services and government press releases left them no option but to parrot the same line. Thus, almost every political or economic writer and columnist was unwittingly creating the literature/historical base to suppress the world's break for freedom, and protect the current power-structure's control of world resources and markets.

Gross fabrications and crafted propaganda are now not only a major part of Western literature and history—*they are Western literature and history.* It is to the credit of the conscientious academics that did stand up and attempt to tell the American people the truth. But they were quickly silenced by McCarthyism, the House Un-American Activities Committee, and the massive weight of the *social-control paradigms* being imposed.

The destruction of the careers of 300-plus blacklisted Hollywood stars and writers—as was pointed out during the March 21, 1999, Academy Awards when the recipient of an Oscar was acknowledged by all major media as having testified against his friends to the House Un-American Activities Committee—provides just a hint of the thousands of professors and intellectuals whose careers were destroyed or badly damaged. As these conscientious voices were silenced, the careers of academics, reporters, and writers parroting the CIA's *Mighty Wurlitzer* soared. Little did they know that, just like the hard right (Aryan Nations, Posse Commitatus, John Birch Society, et al.) absurdities, which all respectable academics know better than to source, imperial nations were creating their own reality, reporters and academics were unwittingly recording this misinformation as reality, and everyone was referencing each other as authoritative sources.

Ralph McGehee was a career CIA agent who spent the last few years of his career studying CIA archives. He concluded:

> The CIA is not now nor has it ever been a central intelligence agency. It is the covert action arm of the President's foreign policy advisers. In that capacity it overthrows or supports foreign governments while reporting "intelligence" justifying those activities. It shapes its intelligence ... to support presidential policy. Disinformation is a large part of its covert action responsibility, and the American people [and legislators] are the primary target of its lies.[7]

To target the American people, American intelligence services must simultaneously target those the masses look up to for designing and interpreting our world—Congress, academia, and the media. Reformed CIA agent McGehee claimed that "He has never once seen a CIA official tell the truth to Congress. Instead came a steady stream of lies."[8] Even the information going to those with security clearances is controlled. This explains why academics and other intellectuals are so misled and, in turn, mislead the masses. The *Mighty Wurlitzer* was established to write a history that protected powerbrokers as they imposed enormous violence upon the world to protect their wealth and power. Those outright lies and distorted stories are recorded as real history and there is little else in the media of record. Perhaps this is true of all empires but—if that pattern of social control through *strategies-of-tension*, covert actions, military power, and then writing history by distorting the record is ever to be broken—we must recognize and analyze this process.

Controlling Nations on the Periphery of Empire

After WWII, colonial nations were declaring their full independence. Many were electing democratic governments and hoping to emulate the United States' economic successes and freedoms. The loss of the resources in their former colonies meant impoverishment for the war-shattered *historic imperial-centers-of-capital.* For the American led coalition of empires to regain control it was crucial that the educational institutions and the media of emerging countries not be permitted unbiased observation and critiques of the maneuvers of the superpowers. Newly-free democracies therefore had to be covertly overthrown and puppet governments put in place (Indonesia, Iran, Chile, Guatemala, Nicaragua, et al.). Yugoslavia too had to be militarily suppressed and a submissive government installed. .

Even though many of the colonial oppressed fought hard and suffered tens of thousands, hundreds of thousands, and a few millions of casualties; most were unable to break free. Massive military and financial support was put behind puppet dictators to prevent loss of those countries by the vote. The citizens of the imperial centers accepted these interferences into other countries because the information reaching them through the CIA's *Mighty Wurlitzer* essentially reversed reality: dictators were described with the buzzword expression "*authoritarian governments*" while fledgling democracies, defending themselves against overthrow by CIA covert destabilizations, were portrayed as "dictatorships."

Freedom and democracy are taught, preached, and believed in throughout the world. So suppression of any break for freedom could only be accomplished under a cover of "free" elections. Progressive leaders could easily explain true freedom to their followers. To silence them and subvert elections required funding the campaigns of dictators and establishing reactionary newspapers.

But not even these black-ops could fool the people into voting against their own best interests. No matter how idealistic these 2nd-and-3rd tier planners were it was obvious to them that those standing up and preaching freedom for their countries had to be eliminated. Talking to ex-CIA agent Ralph McGehee I said, "America established and orchestrated those death squads." His instant response, "Of course we did." As I write this, December 3, 2001—President Vicente Fox of Mexico has admitted Mexico kidnapped, tortured, and murdered, hundreds of "leftists" during the 1960s and 1970s. Leftists, of course, is a buzzword for any progressives outside the control of the established political powers.

Because they were so thoroughly indoctrinated into the enemy-belief-system, idealistic people—no different than you and I but not having looked deeper—established and orchestrated death squads which assassinated thousands of teachers, professors, labor leaders, cooperative leaders, and church leaders, the budding Washingtons, Jeffersons,

Madisons, Lenins, Gandhis, and Martin Luther Kings of those countries. Then, to protect this exceptionally violent suppression of freedom and democracy by *imperial-centers-of-capital*, the *Mighty Wurlitzers* of those imperial nations created the image to the world that these primarily nonviolent, patriotic, and courageous people were terrorists and a threat to the world.

Insurgents battling for freedom today, who would be praised as heroes if they had been fighting for America's revolution in 1776, or any other major nation's revolution, were dealt with by U.S.-supported military forces. Potential civilian leaders, whose only threat was that they would win at the ballot box, were dealt with by CIA-orchestrated death squads. One marvels at the courage of these men and women who keep standing up for freedom and rights in their country and for their people when they knew their name would go on a death squad list. How can one help but notice that those heroes on the periphery of trading empires are fighting for freedom just as America fought for its freedom in 1776.

With U.S. military forces in over 100 countries around the world, with a military budget reaching the level of the entire rest of the world, and with the largest of those military powers tentatively allied with America, it is impossible for America to deny it is an empire or that, with their military and trading allies, they form an allied empire. Where America was originally one of the smaller colonial empires, today—along with their *allied centers-of-capital*—they are, although somewhat fragile due to internal contradictions and the potential of an economic collapse, the largest and most powerful empire in history.

Of course, "trading empires" is a commonly used term but trading empires expanded and protected by military might are true empires in the deepest and most original meaning of the word. Today's empires are only hiding under the cover of new names (free trade) and new slogans (peace, freedom, justice, rights, and majority rule).

The Cold War required a Master Plan

The Maoist-led revolution in China in 1949 triggered an intense study by the U.S. State Department that culminated in National Security Council Directive 68 (NSC-68) being presented to President Truman on April 16, 1950. Although it was not signed until September 30, 1950 (as NSC-68/2), that document's master plan for the containment of those breaks for economic freedom (actually only an affirmation and expansion of the top secret policies of 1947: NSC-4, NSC-4A, NSC-10/2, and others) officially became America's secret policy of covert and overt financial, economic, political, and military, warfare.[9]

Although the world was theoretically at peace, this directive called for increasing the U.S. arms budget by 350% ($13.5-billion to $46.5-billion). This was just under the $300-billion annual budget (year-1990 dollars) with which the United States fought the Cold War. U.S. economic and military power was being mustered to support the collapsed power-structure of the former colonial empires and suppress those emerging nations' breaks for economic freedom.[10]

While admitting there was no military threat to the West, Dean Acheson's memoir, *Present at the Creation*, unwittingly exposes NSC-68 as the master plan for the Cold War. It was a *Grand Strategy* for increasing the military budget of the United States by 350% to wage a worldwide covert war (or overt when necessary—Korea; Vietnam; the two Gulf Wars; the containment of Cuba, Iran, Iraq, Libya; and the destabilization and fragmentation of Yugoslavia) to suppress the rising tide of social and economic revolutions which were intent on breaking the dependency imposed upon them and turning their resources to the care of their own people.

There are just and necessary covert operations such as those by the Office of Strategic Services (OSS) during WWII. However OSS officers, the primary designers of post-WWII covert actions, and other Western intelligence services had been carrying out major covert operations to suppress the freedom of colonial nations well before the CIA was officially established. Very large military efforts to reinstall or maintain the old ruling elite were undertaken in Greece and China before WWII ended. Tens of thousands of valiant patriots who had held two-thirds of Greece out of Hitler's control were slaughtered. At the same time, with U.S. support, Vietnam was being reclaimed by the French, who killed 20,000 in Haiphong harbor alone and another million Indochinese before America took over the suppression of that break for economic freedom to slaughter another 3-million in the 1960s and 1970s. Britain retained her claim to Malaysia by slaughtering thousands. With American and British support, the Dutch slaughtered 150,000 Indonesians in an unsuccessful attempt to reclaim those resource-rich islands (using Dutch SS battalions which had been fighting for Hitler just weeks earlier). In one bombardment alone, over 90,000 were killed in the suppression of Madagascar's bid for freedom. There were many more, even if smaller, suppressions of the worldwide break for economic freedom.

OSS Cold Warriors were the primary staffers of the CIA when it was first established in 1947.[11] The experiences of these Cold Warriors in suppressing breaks for economic freedom (called insurgencies) between 1945 and 1950 were codified into NSC-68. All previous Security Council directives were on a learning curve which built up to that April 1950 master plan. All later NSC directives were supplemental to it. Most "insurgency" suppressions succeeded in maintaining the dependent status of the crucial "countryside" with its precious natural resources. But China, with one-fifth of the world's people, was a big loss that reverberated in the boardrooms of major corporations, and protective government policies were called for.

Managers-of-state knew well that if these revolutions were successful the imperial center would lose those cheap resources and profitable markets.

To maintain control, it was necessary to suppress and/or contain both the rising socialist centers of capital to the East and the emerging countries that might take the rhetoric of democracy and freedom seriously and either form an independent trading bloc of nonaligned nations or tie their economies to other *emerging-centers-of-capital.* But with the world at peace the planners admitted there was no way to get even $1-billion a year out of either Congress or the American people, and NSC-68 called for an additional $33-billion per year ($300-billion in year-2000 dollars).[12]

Note the simultaneous occurrences of these major events: (1) The Korean War, proving communists were bent on world conquest. (2) The Congress for Cultural Freedom, along with other black ops of the CIA and other intelligence agencies, controlling the information flow to the world. (3) And McCarthyism silencing those with the credentials and authority to tell the people anything different.

These mutually supporting events made their debut in the first half of 1950 and within two months of the finalization of NSC-68, the master plan for the Cold War.[13] None of this was accidental or incidental. It was all part of the *Grand Strategies* of *managers-of-state.*

While McCarthyism—painting any progressive person or philosophy as communist—was in full swing, it was political, social, and career suicide to be objective and intellectually balanced. During those 40-years of suppression of dissenting opinion, the CIA paid compliant professors to write 25-to-30 fraudulent books a year. Right-wing think-tanks were set up to produce thousands of books based on those original planted volumes. Tens of thousands of CIA articles based on, and in turn supporting, those fraudulent books were planted in the media around the world (700 CIA articles were planted worldwide during the overthrow and assassination of Allende in Chile). Reporters were provided news scoops in exchange for publication of fraudulent articles. Some of the leading columnists in the world, therefore, were planting this nonsense.

For over two generations social scientists have used, and are still using, those fraudulent books and articles as the foundation of their research. Such books have been cited by official textbooks for 50 years and will be in the future. The intelligence agencies, corporate think-tanks, and state departments of all powerful nations were busy writing the same distorted history. Intellectual figures and skillful writers throughout the Western world supported and coordinated this massive falsification of history. As the quote above (page 63, also 73-75) on the Congress for Cultural Freedom demonstrates, only academics and intellectuals on the fringe knew the difference and even they could only be very unsure of what was real and what was not. When it was learned that the CIA had supported the printing of these thousands of books, sincere academics sued for the titles to be revealed. But the Supreme Court ruled that this would expose CIA methods and endanger the national security.[14]

The imperial nations of Europe also had to worry about the loss of their heartland by the vote. Post-WWII France and Italy were especially vulnerable to ballot box revolutions. Massive CIA funds were only barely able to avert that loss. It required more than money. The partisans were the only effective political force left in Italy and many were communist. Allied troops released Mafia leaders from Mussolini's prisons, armed them, and placed them in charge of the cities as they reclaimed the Italian peninsula.[15]

Control of the Italian elections was still in question and, besides other methods of funding conservative Italian politicians, the CIA was deeply involved in the super-secret P2 lodge, the primary group trying to prevent that election disaster for the Western world's *managers-of-state*. The only way to obtain a seat of power in the Italian government was through that secret lodge. The risk of an overthrow by the vote was still high. For further belief system protection, the Bologna railway bombing which killed 84 people and injured 150, and other fatal bombings in Italy were *strategies-of-tension* planned and carried out by the CIA-controlled Italian intelligence services and, right by the covert action training manuals that have since surfaced, blamed on the "left." The explosives from that bombing and others were traced to some of the 139 buried weapons and explosives caches for the CIA's "Operation Gladio," under which those bombings were carried out. In Italy alone, the right wing terrorist bombings blamed on the left numbered in the hundreds, killing several hundred and injuring many more.[16]

Operation Gladio was the Italian segment of the CIA's "Operation Statewatch" operating, with the support of other intelligence services, throughout Western Europe. Operation Statewatch was, of course, worldwide and the same dirty tricks were used by the CIA to discredit socialist elements in Japan.[17] Though the cover story when exposed in September 1990 was that these were "stay behind forces" in case the Soviet Union overran those countries, they were really there to control elections through a *strategy-of-tension* and, if that failed, to take back by force (through assassinations, black ops, and military coups) any government lost by the vote. Their permanent in-place numbers ranged from 400 operatives in Belgium to 2,000 in Italy. The super-secret covert operation's bombings and blaming of the left in other European countries within the Western alliance were done more sensibly, where and when no one would be hurt. The purpose of *strategies-of-tension* worldwide, creating terrorist acts and blaming the left, was, of course, to distort what the so-called left (primarily labor leaders) stood for to deny them any wins in the elections.

In 1997-98, there were exposures of South Africa's secret service using and planting Soviet weapons in its own *strategy-of-tension* to blame the massacres of blacks on the African National Congress. Such framing of opponents is an old political trick and planting counterfeit letters, documents, and weapons (black ops) is standard operating procedure for intelligence services. The CIA's *Mighty Wurlitzer* had this all down to a science. Those bombings and other violence blamed on the left within Europe and throughout the world were to provide a base for those planted articles.

In fact, both actual and staged covert violence is used worldwide by *imperial-centers-of-capital* to control elections both on the periphery and within their centers of empire. In dozens of CIA-staged attacks by supposed Communist Huks in the Philippines, the hamlets were rescued by General Magsasay. As planned, the general was popularized as a hero and became America's elected Philippine puppet.[18] *Strategies-of-tension* are standard operating procedures of most, if not all, power-structures. The famed march of the Black Shirts in Italy that supposedly put Mussolini in power was staged three days after Italy's powerbrokers handed to him the reins of power. That showing of unrest was to consolidate that power. Germany's famous Reichstag fire was several months *after* Hitler had been given power in a secret January meeting of German powerbrokers. Again the purpose was to consolidate that power by gaining followers through creating the belief of an imminent threat to social tranquility and security. In Chapter 7 we will be addressing how the Korean War was just such a *strategy-of-tension* staged to provide the loyalty base to support the expense and worldwide violence of the Cold War.

Impositions of Beliefs through Corporate-Funded Think-Tanks

We would do well to study the *CovertAction Quarterly*, put out by disaffected CIA agents (Fall 2002 issue especially). They recognized that corporate America was imposing *social-control-paradigms* upon the world under the cloak of false scholarship, the same way America's beliefs of lurking enemies during the Cold War had been manufactured and also the way Britain imposed the Adam Smith free trade beliefs 200 years ago. This is of such importance we obtained permission to quote Sally Covington at length. Note how her description of corporate control of information (creation of public opinion, a *social-control paradigm*) is a close parallel to the post-WWII imposition by intelligence services of these same beliefs:

> Spearheading the assault has been a core group of 12 conservative foundations: the Lynde and Harry Bradley Foundation, the Carthage Foundation, the Charles G. Koch, David H. Koch and Claude R. Lambe charitable foundations, the Phillip M. McKenna Foundation, The JM Foundation, The John M. Olin Foundation, the Henry Salvatori Foundation, the Sarah Scaife Foundation, and the Smith Richardson Foundation.... From 1992-94, they awarded $300-million in grants, and targeted $210-million to support a wide array of projects and institutions.... The 12 have mounted an

> impressively coherent and concerted effort to shape public policy by undermining—and ultimately redirecting—what they regard as the institutional strongholds of modern American liberalism: academia, Congress, the judiciary, executive branch agencies, major media, religious institutions, and philanthropy itself. They channeled some $80-million to right-wing policy institutions actively promoting an anti-government unregulated market agenda. Another $80-million supported conservative scholars and academic programs, with $27-million targeted to recruit and train the next generation of right-wing leaders in conservative legal principles, free-market economics, political journalism and policy analysis. And $41.5-million was invested to build a conservative media apparatus, support pro-market legal organizations, fund state-level think tanks and advocacy organizations, and mobilize new philanthropic resources for conservative policy change ... Conservative foundations also provided $2,734,263 to four right-of-center magazines between 1990 and 1993, including *The National Interest, The Public Interest, The New Criterion,* and *The American Spectator.*[19]

With millions of dollars in funding at their fingertips, conservative institutions have taken

> the political offensive on key social, economic, and regulatory policy issues.... These institutions have effectively repositioned the boundaries of national policy discussion, redefining key concepts, molding public opinion, and pushing for a variety of specific policy reforms.... These groups flood the media with hundreds of opinion editorials. Their top staff appears as political pundits and policy experts on dozens of television and radio shows across the country. And their lobbyists work the legislative arenas, distributing policy proposals, briefing papers, and position statements.... The American Enterprise Institute has ghost writers for scholars to produce op-ed articles that are sent to the one hundred and one cooperating newspapers—three pieces every two weeks.... The Hoover Institution's public affairs office ... links to 900 media centers across the U.S. and abroad. The Reason Foundation ... had 359 television and radio appearances in 1995 and more than 1,500 citations in national newspapers and magazines. The Manhatten Institute has held more than 600 forums or briefings for journalists and policy makers on multiple public policy issues and concerns, from tort reform to federal welfare policy.... The Free Congress Foundation, in addition to its National Empowerment Television, is publishing *NetNewsNow*, a broadcast fax letter sent around the country to more than 400 radio producers and news editors.[20]

As Karen Rothmyer wrote 19 years ago:

> 'Layer upon layer of seminars, studies, conferences, and interviews do much to push along, if not create, the issues, which then become the national agenda of debate.... By multiplying the authorities to whom the media are prepared to give friendly hearing, [conservative donors] have helped to create an illusion of diversity where none exists. The result could be an increasing number of one-sided debates in which the challengers are far outnumbered, if indeed they are heard at all.'... [The Heartland Institute] introduced *Policy Fax* ... a revolutionary public policy fax-on-demand research service that enables

> you to receive, by fax, the full text of thousands of documents from more than one hundred of the nation's leading think tanks, publications, and trade associations. *Policy Fax* is easy to use and it's free for elected officials and journalists.... The American Legislative Exchange Council and the newer State Policy Network provide technical assistance, develop model legislation, and report about communications activities and conferences. ALEC, well funded by private foundations and corporate contributors, is a powerful and growing membership organization, with almost 26,000 state legislators—more than one-third of the nation's total. The organization, which has a staff of 30, responds to 700 information requests each month, and has developed more than 150 pieces of model legislation ranging from education to tax policy. It maintains legislative task forces on every important state policy issue, including education, health care, tax and fiscal policy, and criminal justice.[21] [a]

During early histories of all developing democracies powerbrokers bought up or established the major information systems, at that time primarily newspapers. That control moved from one center of power to others as media were sold or taken over but they are never released to seriously inform the masses; the occasional, or even many, exposés notwithstanding. The foundation beliefs that maintain unequal internal and external trades are not only unchallenged, they are heavily promoted.

In late February 2002, the attempted establishment within the Pentagon of an Office of Strategic Influence (office of disinformation) to plant fraudulent and distorted news in the world press to control Muslim opinion worldwide was exposed. The media took the tack that this was something new. But it was not new. Every intelligence service (the U.S. has at least 14 of them, most other nations have several) and state department of major countries practice disinformation and corporations and politicians practice it to control who will be elected and what laws will be written.

The corporate-owned media is there to push *social-control corporate philosophies* and scholars have easy access to the massive literature put out by corporate-funded think-tanks. Everyone everywhere feels he or she is thinking independently but when analyzed most information and foundation beliefs come from those disinformation centers or less than straightforward government sources. With little other information available, researchers stay safely inside *permitted-parameters-of-debate*. For those who dare to write or speak truly independently, the market is extremely limited. These heavily-funded schools of thought become the functioning beliefs of

---

[a] In "A Hostile Takeover" (*The American Prospect*, Spring 2003, pp. A16-A18) Martin Garbus explains how The Federalist Society for Law and Public Policy was highly successful in its purpose: packing the federal courts. We were able to condense how the beliefs of legislators, academia, and the media were controlled to protect wealth and power. The serious researcher can study Garbus's article for how the courts are similarly controlled.

These quotes address the fine-tuned control of democracies learned over the centuries. For a view of the ad hoc feeding frenzy, control of elections, and ongoing frauds of corporations read Greg Palast, *The Best Democracy Money can buy: The Truth about Corporate Cons, Globalization, and High-Finance* (London: Penguin Books, 2003).

society (its belief system or social paradigm) and all other views are crowded to the margins.

The massive effort to suppress Henry George's philosophies which spread rapidly when first introduced indicates that the *managers-of-state* knew well that this sensible economic philosophy was available.[22] This philosophy gives equality and rights to all which meant that unearned wealth had to be given up. The powerbrokers were not about to do that. For example: In the 1917 crisis that brought on the Bolshevik Revolution in Russia, in an attempt to avoid total overthrow, the Russian *managers-of-state* (Kerensky in this case) offered to adopt the philosophies of America's Henry George. So they too knew this philosophy for full and equal rights was available and only reached for it in a last-ditch effort to avoid being overthrown. The Bolsheviks following the philosophy of Karl Marx were in no mood for compromise. They overthrew the provisional government and took over. Now *managers-of-state* of the *imperial-centers-of-capital* had a new threatening social philosophy to deal with.

The Residual Effects of McCarthyism

After WWII the *old imperial-centers-of-capital* had shattered each other's power, and the former colonial world was revolting. The only wealth left to suppress those breaks for freedom was in America.

At the end of that war the United States had two *Grand Strategy* choices: join the newly emerging nations in their break for freedom or join the *old imperial-centers-of-capital* and suppress those insurgencies. The behind-the-scenes cultural and financial ties to Western Christian, white Europe were too great. America chose alignment with the old imperial nations and the historical record shows that this choice was chiseled in stone decades before.

For 130 years British intelligence services, the British diplomatic service, and British industry had financed university systems and think-tanks to teach neo-mercantilist free trade. U.S. intelligence services, State Department, and multinational corporations now took over that role as the British Empire crumbled. Most universities and opinion makers in Europe and America then preached those *social-control-paradigms* (most unwittingly) for the next 56 years (1947 to the present) and still do.

Within the *old imperial-centers-of-capital* it was not possible to remain in a position of influence in either government or academia if one promoted anything other than the *social-control-paradigms* protecting that society. The crisis of the Great Depression created openings for other social philosophies to be looked at but WWII and the Cold War permitted the re-imposing of the protective beliefs. While McCarthyism was in full swing—painting any progressive philosophy as Communist—it was political, social, and career suicide to be objective and intellectually balanced.

European professors had for centuries been the carriers of the *social-control paradigms* of imperialism and there was little else taught. There were however conscientious professors in the American universities who knew the history of Americans gaining their economic freedom, who knew that most other colonial nations were still under the control of *imperial-centers-of-capital*, and who recognized the potential of those former colonies joining the brotherhood of free nations. These idealistic and conscientious professors were recognized authorities whose views would be freely expressed through their classes and eventually the media. To take over the imperial mantle and suppress the post-WWII breaks for freedom it was necessary for the America to strip these potential carriers of truth and reality out of the universities.

McCarthyism was no aberration of one individual as recorded in history. Senator Joseph McCarthy was the chosen point man for the House Un-American Activities Committee (whose members themselves were point men for the wealthy and powerful and the first echelon *managers-of-state*) to strip those professors out of the universities and their thoughts out of the media. Hundreds of professors and thousands of others lost their jobs as lower-level *managers-of-state*, congresspersons without security clearances, the universities, the media, and lay intellectuals were conditioned to keep their heads down, their mouths shut, and their typewriters silent.[23]

The major universities' rehabilitation of the reputation of these persecuted souls when the Cold War was won (most were dead by then) proves even the powerbrokers of universities—the very people sworn to provide an honest education to the nation and the world—knew that students and everyone else were being fed a controlled and fraudulent picture of the world. Professors took leaves of absence to organize the CIA and then returned to their ivory towers.[24]

By not telling their students that they had established a massive propaganda organization that was to put all others to shame, which would have been an honest education, they, and all who knew but remained silent, became propagandists just as surely as those within the massive intelligence system they had set up.

The 1975-76 Church Committee and Pike Committee hearings exposed many of these black ops: The thousands of fraudulent books financed by intelligence services (all imperial centers were doing it). The tens of thousands of articles planted all over the world (intelligence agencies of all imperial centers were also doing this, including the CIA making movies as well as newsreels that the 50s and 60s generation watched with almost every movie). The massive literature put out by the subsidized think-tanks and subsidized academics. And the thousands of books written by sincere academics but sourcing that fraudulent literature being passed off as honest scholarly work. On top of this were the massive fiction (novels and movies) written to take advantage of the created hysteria.

This was the rhetorical thunder of the Cold War. After 30-to-40 years of this hysteria during which honest and sober works were dismissed as the works of radicals, misguided souls and conspiracy theorists only a few on the fringes of academia understood how deeply they were involved in suppressing truth through parroting these carefully created beliefs that democracy and freedom was under threat. The truth can be found only through intense research and dedication and few have the time, money, or motivation to do it. Thus, although the claim is made that it is long dead, the legacy of McCarthyism and the orthodoxy it created still rules the halls of academia, the media, and the masses.

The News Media Trapped Themselves

Citizens educated under those far from free thought conditions eventually moved into positions of power and, within the limitations of their power and misinterpretation of free trade, were likely sincere in their efforts to develop the world and eliminate poverty. But those who would question free trade as practiced by neo-mercantilists were silenced; at first by McCarthyism's threat to their career and later by peer pressure and lack of financial or identity rewards. As opposed to the certainty of being cast into oblivion if one tried to stand up against the propaganda, the majority staked their careers on promoting the cosmopolitan philosophy and the high financial and career (identity) rewards that choice offered.

Thus the Brer-Rabbit, don't throw me in the brier patch[a], neo-mercantilist, Adam Smith free trade scam became firmly entrenched. To the extent we believe our own *social-control-paradigms* and force these policies on the world, we will seriously retard world development, continually ratchet down the wages of labor in the developed world, could collapse the world economy into a depression, and could again lay the foundations for war.[b]

While enjoying the followers and income they gained by publishing the *social-control-paradigms* and Cold War hype created by the power-structure, the media trapped themselves. Once a nation was fully propagandized, they were now controlled by their readers and advertisers. With the masses believing enemies were planning to attack them at any moment and intelligence services spending hundreds of millions of dollars continually reinforcing that belief, any media that would dare present a rationalization outside the Cold War belief system that the West was under serious threat would lose both their readers and advertisers in droves.

---

[a] Referring to the children's classic when the captured Brer Rabbit begged not to be thrown into the briar patch. His captor promptly threw him in the briar patch and he escaped.

[b] It does not have to either. If the financial monopolists and military are strong enough, it could freeze the world into the current mold of extremely rich and extremely poor with the resources and labors of the impoverished supporting the lifestyle of the rich and a powerful military maintaining security for that system of theft of the wealth of the weak.

The market then worked its magic. With the world programmed that there were enemies lurking behind every bush, the occasional scholarly and honest critique could not be sold while paranoid and hysterical writings, and the total frauds we have been addressing, sold by the hundreds of millions.

Destabilizing Internal Political Groups

Just as imperial powers did not dare let any nation develop their own social philosophies and become a beacon for other oppressed nations, they did not dare let the voices of the oppressed within the imperial centers nor the voices of those on the periphery aware of suppressions be heard. Preventing awakened political voices from reaching others with their message required destabilizing internal political groups in all allied countries. In the United States, this was the purpose first of the House Un-American Activities Committee and McCarthyism and then of the FBI's Operation COINTELPRO (a replay of the post-WWI shattering of the forming solid labor front: the destruction of the Wobblies [International Workers of the World, IWW]). CHAOS, Cable Splicer, and Garden Plot were American internal destabilizations by military intelligence services carried out in cooperation with the FBI. These synchronized efforts of political police became urgent when over 500 periodicals critical of the Vietnam War, with a peak circulation of 7-million, sprang up.[25]

Through *agent provocateurs, counterfeited letters, planted narcotics, false arrests, poison-pen letters, malicious articles planted in the press, blacklisting from jobs, harassment, electronic surveillance, burglary, mail tampering*, and *other internal strategies of terrorist tension*, hundreds of budding political groupings were destabilized. In March 1998, the Socialist Workers Party (SWP) and Young Socialist Alliance (YSA) won a 15-year legal battle against the FBI for decades of spying, harassment, and disruptions as just described. During that trial, these two groups—out of hundreds spied upon and/or destabilized—proved that the FBI had conducted 20,000 days of wiretaps and 12,000 days of listening "bugs" between 1943 and 1963 as well as 208 burglaries of offices and homes of their members and had photographed or stolen 9,864 private documents.[26] These are only two groups out of hundreds that were compromised and only events that have been proven. (The 2002 Patriot Act legalizes all this.)

The American government was ordered to pay Fred Hampton's family $3-million when it was proven in court that his December 4, 1969 death in Chicago was a political assassination of the above-described black-ops. After 27 years in a California prison, Geronimo Pratt was ordered released and he collected $4.5-million when, though other excuses were used by the courts, he proved that his arraignment and conviction for murder was a conspiracy between the FBI and the Los Angeles District Attorney's Office.

The FBI had him under surveillance, knew he was 400 miles away at the time of the murder, and the prosecutor knew that his witnesses were government informers with no credibility. Proving these conspiracies required some of the longest court cases in American history. As few such targeted people had either resources or determined people behind them, many more innocent people had their lives destroyed by what can only properly be called America's political police. Totally innocent political prisoners have died in prison and others are still there.[27]

If the largest and most politically motivated of these hundreds of groups had been allowed to form and grow, some of their leaders would eventually have been elected to local, state, and national governments. From that position, they would have had platforms to speak to the masses.

Social philosophies not in their best interest, as had been accepted in the past when there were no other choices, are much harder to impose upon a population under conditions of true freedom. The independent views on national and international events that would have been carried by the media when addressed by those new leaders, as opposed to the desired view of *managers-of-state* as they suppressed both internal dissent and the world's break for freedom, were the real threat. For exercising their democratic rights, these innocent people were systematically monitored, systematically destabilized, some were sent to prison, and their voices were never heard except by a few on the margins. Silencing those who stood up on the periphery of empire was a much harder job than silencing dissenting voices within the imperial center but—at least until the financial meltdowns on the periphery—this too was, to a large extent, accomplished.

No profound thoughts which ran counter to the mainstream were permitted on either side of the opposing Cold War blocs, rhetoric about a free, open, and unbiased educational system in the "democratic" West notwithstanding. Classics of alternative thought were taught in the universities, but they were taught negatively and the massive propaganda of the CIA's *Mighty Wurlitzer*, the weeding out of professors with independent thought through loyalty oaths and the threat of—or actual—job loss, and the pressure of propagandized peers assured these philosophies would only be taught as being dictatorial, violent, and/or impractical. The violence of the Cold War was to suppress the implementation of any competing philosophies so that no such example could exist to gain the allegiance of intellectuals, opinion makers, and voters.

Because the masses now have voting rights their perception of the world had to be controlled. These gross fabrications and crafted propaganda provided a firm foundation for the *social-control-paradigms* of the Cold War and are now not only a major part of Western literature and history; *they are Western literature and history*. After the Cold War was won, major universities officially restored the good name of those who were forced out of academia and had their careers destroyed. This proved that the innocence of these accused and shattered people was well understood all along by the information gatekeepers.

Understanding the suppressions and oppressions of the Cold War is essential to understanding this book's primary theses: inequalities in world trade impoverish naturally wealthy regions, and imperial-center social philosophies are imposed to protect that system of laying claim to impoverished nations' wealth. History repeats itself because wealth and power are based on inequalities of both external and internal trade; the rules of which have been fine-tuned for centuries. For the powerful to permit the establishment of equality in trades would be to allow the loss of their massive accumulations of unearned wealth and power. Thus, the suppressions and oppressions of the Cold War are not an aberration. Whenever the threat to wealth and power is high, such violence against idealistic people and societies gaining their freedom is the norm.

With all political, economic, financial, and military options blocked, the defeated, dependent, and impoverished world has no options outside of what the imperial centers have to offer. All plans of the developing world fail (the specific purpose of the covert actions of the Cold War), realization takes hold that the only opportunities are those offered by the powerful, the imposed (re-imposed) social philosophy takes hold, and the old order is restored. This is an exact description of the Cold War and the *re-imposition* of Adam Smith free trade philosophies and neo-liberal economics upon the world that we will be addressing in depth.

We have heard we have freedom, rights, and free press all our lives. To accept that America had, and has, a propaganda system far more extensive than most empires in history is hard to accept. After reading this book we suggest reading Mark Lane's *Plausible Denial: Was the CIA Involved in the Assassination of JFK;* L. Fletcher Prouty's *JFK: The CIA, Vietnam and the Plot to Kill Kennedy*; and Philip Willan's *Puppet Masters: The Political Use of Terrorism in Italy*. In Prouty's authoritative books (he was 1-of-3 who wrote the how-to book on U.S. covert actions) one will learn how staged violence (a *strategy-of-tension*) is used worldwide to control the beliefs of voters so as to control elections both on the periphery of empire and within the imperial centers. When a *strategy-of-tension* fails and a power-structure is faced with loss of power, actual violence is used—including assassinations of leaders of nations, covert destabilizations, and wars.

Public knowledge of each violent event is controlled through carefully crafted press releases before, during, and following those implementations of *policies-of-state*. This is done so effectively that the FBI knew the identities of President Kennedy's assassins but—because the plotters reached high into government circles and the entire government would come crashing down—they did not dare move on this information.[a] Members of the

[a] Even though in charge of governments or departments of governments, these are just mortal men. Not even President Franklin D Roosevelt dared do anything when General Smedley Butler exposed that an organization composed of some of the wealthiest people in the United States had approached him to lead an overthrow of the American government

House Select Committee on Assassinations sat on this same information in 1978 when they learned those same names from the same sources; and America's vaunted institutions—the Justice Department, the media, the universities, and its political leaders—all failed to inform the public even when everything the FBI and the House Select Committee knew was proven in a court of law when one of the assassins sued the *Spotlight* for publishing his name as one of those professional killers.

The assassins were named in the courtroom of Judge James W. Kehoe (verdict February 5, 1985), United States District Court, Miami, Florida, case number 80-1121-civ-JWK, E Howard Hunt [of Watergate fame], plaintiff, versus Liberty Lobby, defendant. It was actually CIA agent E Howard Hunt's lawyers who irretrievably damaged their own client by asking specifically who these assassins were and what the witness knew of their activities and whereabouts as they organized and carried out the assassination. Claudia Furiati came up with the same names as the assassins when she was allowed access to Cuban intelligence files to write her book, *ZR Rifle: the Plot to Kill Kennedy and Castro*.

Part of the CIA's plans to overthrow the Cuban government included control of information reaching the people as that overthrow unfolded and all was in place for history to be written that this externally coached and financed invasion was an internal Cuban revolution. When the Cuban overthrow collapsed at the Bay of Pigs and President Kennedy refused to rescue that covert operation with American air power the Cubans of Miami and their CIA handlers were furious. To them President Kennedy was a traitor to what they viewed was a fight for the survival of the world as they knew it. Being hardened to orchestrating death squad activity worldwide these angry agents, under orders from higher up, assassinated President Kennedy just as they had orchestrated the assassination of thousands of others worldwide so the imperial nations would not lose control of the

---

and set up a fascist government as was being done all over Europe at the time. There were a lot more skeletons in the U.S. government's closet than President Kennedy's assassination. If that assassination had been truly investigated, many powerful people would have been destroyed. Those powerful people knew where the skeletons of any who dared attack them were, it is unlikely these people would go down without taking their attackers with them, and America's Fascist covert violence all over the world and control of the media worldwide would have come to the surface. Both the CIA and the FBI knew about each others' illegal activities addressed above. Not only was there an unwritten agreement that neither would expose the other, each must cooperate to suppress any evidence of the other's illegal activities. That suppression of evidence and placing blame elsewhere was the order of the day for all—the FBI, the CIA, the Warren Commission, the House Select Committee on Assassinations, and the entire U.S. government. Against such a phalanx of power, the media dutifully fell in line. Though the American people had accepted without question many false realities imposed upon them, the majority believed the assassination was a conspiracy. But the propaganda apparatus had accomplished its purpose, through the mechanisms of collective denial, citizens looked everywhere for those conspirators except where they were, right in the top leadership of the American government, the U.S. military, and the CIA.

periphery of empire. The same propaganda machinery that was in place to control the world's belief of how the planned overthrow of the Cuban government was an internal event was now turned to controlling the world's belief in who assassinated President Kennedy.

When the above trial concluded, the jury foreman, Leslie Armstrong, "simply, eloquently, and painstakingly" explained to waiting print, radio, and television reporters that "the evidence was clear ... the CIA had killed President Kennedy, Hunt had been a part of it, and the evidence, so painstakingly presented, should now be examined by the relevant institutions of the United States Government so that those responsible for the assassination might be brought to justice."[28]

Lane points out that a Miami television station that evening reported only that Hunt had lost a libel case and had ignored her eloquent description of the historic importance of this case. The Jury foreman challenged that station on their reporting. It was then accurately reported by that one station but was ignored by all other media, local and national. In contrast, Hunt's winning of the first trial where none of this explosive testimony was given and which was of no historic importance was widely reported.

William F. Pepper's *An Act of State: The Execution of Martin Luther King* was released just before this manuscript went to press. Here too we learn that, in a suit brought by the King family against one of the assassins and others unnamed, it had been proven in Judge Swearingen's courtroom in Memphis, Tennessee, between November 15, 1999 and March 2000, that Martin Luther King had been assassinated by elements of the Memphis police and the Tennessee State Police with the operation overseen by Army Intelligence.[29]

King's murder was part of the well-known Operation COINTELPRO which was established specifically to destabilize rising political groups. We encourage the reader to read the story of the 70-plus witnesses bringing this political assassination to light.

After Mark Lane's exposure of the CIA being behind the shooting of President Kennedy I dismissed the other cited theorists. I should not have. The dynamite testimony of President Johnson's mistress (never used so as to avoid the taint of conspiracy theorists) makes it clear most were on the right trail tracing the many threads of power directly involved in that assassination. Some of those same respected powerbrokers were behind both assassinations. Those movers and shakers were meeting to plan King's demise less then a month after President Kennedy was shot.[30] The media was just as silent on this exposure of the violent elimination of African-American leaders as they were about the assassination of John F. Kennedy.

The assassinations of up and coming leaders in periphery countries by death squads is standard practice. We now know that, when the threat is high, this is also practiced within the imperial centers. Units within the intelligence communities are specially trained for these jobs, the relevant government structures stand ready to cover it up (plausible denial, the title of Lane's book, but better explained in Pepper's), and the media, local and regional police, and the judicial system are, as you and I would be, too cowed to expose what they know.

Bobby Kennedy was loved by Americans as much as his brother. If he was elected president (and he had just won the California primary the eve he was assassinated) he would have had the will, the knowledge, and the power to expose the true assassins of his brother. That could not be permitted.[31]

How and why the true assassins got away with this can be summed up in two sentences: In Chapter 16 we address that anyone in power who exposed that Japan was running a pure mercantilist economy (and their company) would be totally ostracized and destroyed. In the same way if anyone in the media or academia were ever a threat to exposing the power structure they would immediately face the full force of the system and be ostracized to the margins of society or (as we see by the Kennedy and King assassinations) worse.

By studying the above books and this book, one will begin to understand how *social-control-paradigms* are imposed upon an acclaimed "free press" and academia who then, largely unwittingly, impose it upon a population whose government, educational institutions, and press claim to be honest recorders of history.[a]

---

[a] For clear illumination as to who killed President Kennedy, first read the solidly authoritative Mark Lane, *Plausible Denial: Was the CIA Involved in the Assassination of JFK?* (New York: Thunder Mouth Press, 1991); William F. Pepper, *An Act of State: The Execution of Martin Luther King* (New York: Verso, 2003), p. 127 and Claudia Furiati, *ZR Rifle: The Plot to Kill Kennedy and Castro* (Melbourne: Ocean Press, 1994). For further information read Mathew Smith, *Say Goodbye to America: The Sensational and untold Story of the Assassination of John F. Kennedy* (London: Mainstream Publishing, 2001); L. Fletcher Prouty, *JFK: The CIA, Vietnam, And the Plot to Kill Kennedy* (New York: Carol Publishing, 1992); For a view of how the CIA used terrorism and assassinations all over the world, including Europe, to protect the old imperial-centers-of-capital, read Philip Willan's *Puppet Masters: The Political Use of Terrorism in Italy*. After reading those four books, one can spot the solid evidence in the following books: Jim Garrison, *On the Trail of the Assassins* (New York: Sheridan Square Press, 1988); Walt Brown, *Treachery in Dallas* (New York: Carroll & Graf, 1995); Harrison Edward Livingston, *Killing the Truth: Deceit and Deception in the JFK Case* (New York: Carroll & Graf, 1993); Jim Marrs, *Crossfire: The Plot that Killed Kennedy* (New York: Carroll & Graf, 1989); Anthony Summers, *Conspiracy* (New York: Paragon House, 1989). Those books and a documentary, "The Men Who Killed Kennedy," made in Britain for release on the twenty-fifth anniversary of Kennedy's assassination (but self-censored by the American media) was not shown in the U.S. until 11-years later, leave little doubt it was a political assassination (New Video Group, 250 Park Ave. S., NY, NY 10010, 212-532-3392, catalog number AAE-21201 through 21206, or A&E Home Video, Box Hv1, 233 E. 45th St, NY, NY 10017). See also Oliver Stone's outstanding move JFK, Prouty is the man X in that movie which would have been better yet, actually complete and unchallengeable, with the information of Mark Lane and Claudia Furiati. For Bobby Kennedy's assassination read James DiEugenio and Lisa Pease,

We understand why it is so hard to believe that a free media does not inform the public. But that they do not is reality. In *The Best Democracy that Money can Buy* (2003), Greg Palast provides many examples with solid evidence of massive corruption that would have ended the careers of powerful politicians and even brought down governments if exposed but were glossed over and ignored. Through his efforts these stories get on British television but do not get on America's. Any American who wants to stay fully informed should study his website, www.gregpalast.com.

Writing History to Protect Wealth and Power

History is written by the powerful to protect their wealth and power. Those carefully crafted press releases and carefully crafted recordings of events is the writing of history. Because all people are trained to be just (a society could survive no other way), destabilizing other societies to lay claim to, or retain claim to, their wealth requires the imperial center to create the belief that targeted and oppressed people are enemies and/or incompetents.

To justify colonizing the world, confiscating much of the world's wealth, enslaving entire populations to produce that wealth, and actually wiping entire civilizations off the face of the earth in the process, it was necessary to expound the belief that natives of those besieged societies were not really people (they had no soul). When it was no longer possible to ignore the fact that they were people, it was necessary to expound the belief that indigenous people were incompetent, that they could not run their own affairs (a belief only now being slowly set aside), and that technologically advanced and "civilized" societies were helping them (a primary aspect of today's beliefs that we are documenting is also untrue).

When the blatant injustices of mercantilist imperialism became too embarrassing, the belief that mercantilism had been abandoned and true free trade was in place was expounded. In reality the same wealth confiscation went on, deeply buried within complex systems of subtle monopolies and unequal trade hiding under the cover of free trade. Many explanations have been given for wars between the imperial nations when there was really only one common thread: "Who will control resources and trade and the wealth produced through inequalities in trade?" This is proven by the inequalities of trade siphoning the world's wealth to *imperial-centers-of-capital* today just as when *plunder-by-trade* was learned centuries ago. The battles over the world's wealth have only kept hiding behind different protective philosophies each time the secrets of laying claim to the wealth of others' have been exposed.

Thus it is that students of statecraft and foreign policy are openly taught that what the people believe is happening is only a control

---

The Assassinations: Probe Magazine on JFK, MLK, RFK, and Malcolm X (Los Angeles: Feral House, 2003), run a computer search.

mechanism created through a public education campaign (a polite way of saying propaganda), and those planning the *Grand Strategies of state* are "defensive realists" or "offensive realists" dealing with the "realities" of the "real" world. Trained to be "realists," students of statecraft are taught to care for their nation's "national interest." Students with the right connections, along with many more who moved up through the corporate, political, and military world, move into the inner sanctums of government, take a pledge of secrecy, and become the *managers-of-state* we have been discussing throughout this treatise. None of these upper echelon managers are trained to care for the interests of the impoverished world, while those who rose through the corporate, political, and military ranks are deeply ingrained with the need to care for the corporate world and the imperial center. For *managers-of-state* to care for those on the periphery of empire when the confiscation of the natural wealth and labors of that periphery are creating the wealth and power of the imperial center is an oxymoron.

While powerful nations are controlling other people's resources or denying the use of those resources to competing centers of capital, it is necessary to create the belief that people targeted for covert or overt attack, economically or militarily, are a serious threat to "national security." Of course, the ones under threat are the already impoverished whose natural wealth and labor production are being siphoned to the *powerful developed imperial-centers-of-capital.* The belief that imperial nations are under military and terrorist threat and these "good" nations are supporting "good" people on the periphery of empire is accomplished through loudly proclaiming this through the still operational *Mighty Wurlitzer.* Those imposed beliefs establish the parameters of national and international debate and the real problem, monopolies and unequal trade, is not a *politically correct* or *economically correct* subject of discussion.

The low-key approach is used only when there is no serious threat. "No serious threat" means the subject of injustices of imperial centers and unequal trades is far outside the *permitted-parameters-of-debate*. However, when the threat of loss of power and wealth is high, meaning imperial injustices and unequal trades are being placed on the table for discussion on the periphery of empire, Western cultures engage in massive propaganda and covert destabilizations (both internally and externally), which is exactly what we are taught is done in dictatorships.

After the threat of a break for freedom is past, only an occasional violent covert operation is necessary. Populations have been so thoroughly indoctrinated by the propaganda of the Cold War—and there is so little else recorded in articles, books, or history—that the imposed beliefs are firmly in place in the social mind. As both the survival and wealth of most citizens of the imperial centers are based on the system as structured, most are firmly within the aura of a society's protective beliefs. Extending those beliefs to the periphery and maintaining it is what these covert and overt destabilizations are all about.

The line between the controllers and the controlled lies above the university system and the media and below the National Security Council, the State Department, the intelligence services, the few in Congress with security clearances, and other inner-sanctum *managers-of-state.* Whereas the elite and *managers-of-state* know well the *social-control-paradigms* of the masses exist, after all, they created them, the masses—and this includes most within the university system, the media, and elected officials outside the inner sanctums of government—are unaware they are being controlled through *strategies-of-tension* so their governments can do throughout the world just what they are warning others wish to do to them; subvert their governments and steal their wealth.

It would be a difficult task for a professor or journalist to step back and realize that his or her entire education and life's work was little more than spreading *social-control beliefs* that had been imposed upon society for generations.[a] Nor could many accept that these fundamental beliefs with little relevance to reality had been kept in place by extreme violence. Those professors and journalists would instinctively and instantly realize that all the rewards (money, career advancement, acceptance of one's work for publication, acceptance by one's peers, and appointments to government posts) were stacked totally in favor of parroting the *social-control-paradigms.*

After observing those who did stand up being totally ostracized by their peers and denied any of the above described rewards for their achievements, only an insignificant few will stand up. However, after the crumbling of the tiger economies and other nations on the periphery, this is changing. Those who question those unjust and unequal policies and provide different answers are starting to find an audience. That and the collapsing economies on the periphery of empire discrediting the beliefs imposed upon them accounts for President George Bush's national security team's pre-9/11/2001 study concluding that what was needed to retain dominance and control of the world's resources was "some catastrophic and catalyzing event—like a new Pearl Harbor.[b]"

While ignoring all other interpretations of world events as propaganda, crucial Western news comes directly from the CIA's *Mighty Wurlitzer* and

---

[a] Actually it is a residue of Feudalism as is the legal structure which it is protecting. This will become visible as we address the enormous economic efficiency gains when the feudal legal residue that create and protect monopolies is stripped out of our laws.

[b] Keywords: New Statesman, London, December 12, 2002, John Pilger, www.newstatesman .co.uk, http://pilger.carlton.com/print/124759. Legislation has been passed since that attack (the Patriot Act, a recreation of Hitler's Enabling Act) which legalizes all the internal surveillance and covert destabilizations just described. This act was the legal structure of fascism.

other intelligence services' presentation of reality. Intelligence agencies' wordsmiths restructure every world event to the desired spin. It is this reality that ambassadors and other government agencies hand to reporters. Lower-level officials have to parrot the same words they hear from higher officials. With the many years required to reach such a position of authority, every government official has been through this many times and knows what he or she is expected to say. To deviate from the proper script, no matter how much reality demands it, would incur immediate dismissal.

Any accredited reporter seriously challenging these creations at a presidential news conference or any other high-level news briefing would quickly lose accreditation to attend such briefings. To seriously address these creations as the propaganda they are would immediately place one outside the loop, cost most their jobs, and be instant social and political suicide. That peer pressure is at the heart of a primary structure of beliefs, so little else is heard or read. Thus, children can quickly understand what adults find incomprehensible. Children are honest and have nothing to lose while adults have everything to lose and following the crowd can quickly quiet their conscience. No one challenges them there but they would face big challenges if they tried to peel aside any major portion of the *social-control-paradigms* and expose the truth.

The Untold Secrets of "National Security" and the "National Interest"

Three tenets of capitalism are: pay the lowest possible price, charge all the market will bear, and give nothing to anybody. That is great philosophy for powerbrokers with a subtle monopoly on capital, technology, markets, and military might. It takes no deep thought to realize that these tenets of classical economic philosophy were implanted by an earlier power-structure to maximize its claims to the wealth of others (that feudal residue in our philosophy, laws, and customs). Landed aristocracy and financial aristocracy, through control of all positions of power in the Church and universities, had full control of what was taught. The *social-control paradigms* taught (and still with us) were philosophical tenets chosen for the protection of that society and/or its power-structure, not philosophical tenets chosen by free thought to maximize the well-being of all within that society—let alone the welfare of the rest of the world's citizens whose natural wealth and labors were confiscated to create the wealth of the *imperial-centers-of-capital.*

It is the trumpeting of *peace, freedom, justice, rights, and majority rule* that requires that those *Grand Strategies* for controlling other people and their resources be kept secret. (It is also a key part of keeping it secret.) What is practiced is the total antithesis of what is preached.

Professors and Intellectuals are Conscientious and Sincere

Professors are conscientious and sincerely want to teach true history, honest economics, and honest political science. However, when a society is under extreme threat such as the *managers-of-state* of the *imperial-centers-of-capital* were all through the Cold War, honest expressions of threatening thoughts are not permitted in the mainstream of these soft sciences. Honest analysis can be found at the margins but those are effectively "voices in the wilderness." Professors and intellectuals who could, and did, challenge the Cold War beliefs being imposed upon the world as a cover for those suppressions of economic freedom were stripped out of the universities and the media or were silenced.[32] Instinctively understanding this process, and with the exception of a few forced to the margins, professors and the media who are aware, with a few exceptions, keep their head down.

French economic students understood that economic theory as taught had no relation to reality and in the fall of 2000 they protested and academic administrators agreed to address what heretofore had been "controversial" subjects. Twenty-seven Ph.D. economic students at the University of Cambridge, UK, signed a similar, but milder, letter of protest in 2001.

Now that the Cold War is over, opposing thought is surfacing. However those thoughts are only a whisper against the thunder of *social-control-paradigms* that have been carefully cultivated by the *managers-of-state* of powerful nations for 50 years. Biased and compliant historians of the winners of the hot wars—wars over who will set the rules of unequal trade and thus who will be wealthy and powerful—wrote this history without an understanding of the real causes of those wars. President George W. Bush's Patriot Act, copied from Hitler's Enabling Act (the legal foundation for Fascism) threatens to again silence academia and the press.

Providing a Beacon for Intellectuals throughout the World

Though one would never know it listening to the operational philosophic rhetoric, the efficiencies of centralized planning were crucial to the West's post-WWII success. The Cold War military buildup, the economic rebuilding of the *old shattered imperial-centers-of-capital* (Japan and Western Europe), and the rise of *new allied centers-of-capital* (Taiwan and South Korea) to prevent expansion of socialism were all a part of the centralized plans of corporate capitalism.

The question of whether socialism and central planning will work or will not work has been thoroughly established. The only two functioning economies during the Great Depression were Germany's and the Soviet

Union's, both were centrally planned (Germany's only because it had to usurp the rhetoric of National Socialism or be forced by its politically aware labor movement to accept Soviet socialism), and both were building industrial capital faster than had ever been built before.

Because it is viable and thus threatening, socialism has always faced the full military might of capitalism's propaganda. If it were not viable, there would be no need to demonize it. Destabilizations have prevented socialist centers of capital from becoming established, and its efficiencies have been utilized only by dictators attacking socialism (Hitler attacking the Soviet Union in WWII) and utilized by socialism when defending against not only those attacks but against the ring of steel put around them by the entire *allied developed centers-of-capital* after that war.

While the well-funded think-tanks were pouring out the rhetoric against central planning, covert—and occasionally overt—destabilizations (and the enormous military expenditures of emerging nations defending against the threat of military overthrow) were preventing the Soviet Union, Cuba, all Africa and Latin America, and many other nations from putting their economies together. (The hoped-for co-opting of China as she develops is still ongoing.) The reason for these destabilizations is obvious: an efficient social system providing a better standard of living for its people becomes a beacon drawing the loyalty of intellectuals and the impoverished worldwide.

The rapid restructuring of the German economy, which successfully cared for its citizens during the depths of the Great Depression even as they were being denied equality in world trade, caught the attention of the world. During the crisis of that depression, German "Bunds" were forming in every corner of the globe. Both the rapidly developing Soviet form of socialism and Germany's rapidly developing Fascist (corporate) socialism were drawing intellectual followers away from neo-liberal capitalism that was collapsing under the weight of the Great Depression.

Maintaining both power and wealth of established imperial powers required that both socialism and Fascist National Socialism be contained and both were contained by military force: WWII contained Germany and the Cold War (on top of the severe Soviet losses in WWII) both contained the Soviet Union and suppressed others' break for freedom worldwide.

Even though most of those attempting to gain their freedom looked to the United States as their political and economic model, they had the universal danger of popular leaders who were not puppets and who would turn those resources to sustaining their own people. Empires whose economies depended upon the resources of those countries for raw material for their industries would be faced with a disaster of the first order if their countryside gained its economic freedom. Those breaks for freedom had to be suppressed.

Who are the Powerful?

So who are the powerful? It could, unwittingly, be you or me. We all have some power. Only it is, through imposition of beliefs, turned to the protection of what we would never tolerate if we ever knew: the suppression of other peoples' freedom and confiscation of their wealth. After all, most of us unwittingly provided full support as corporate imperialism suppressed breaks for freedom worldwide.

The CIA could not have suppressed those worldwide breaks for freedom without the support of American citizens. The fact that most did not know their government was avoiding democratic choice worldwide through an offensive military policy only outlines the imposed beliefs which protect this system of claiming the wealth of others through inequalities of trade. Fully believing they live in a true democracy with a free press and educational institutions of free thought, most Americans find incomprehensible any suggestion that a belief has been imposed upon them.

Only a small number of the wealthy or moderately wealthy pay any attention to imposing beliefs on the masses but they do provide generous financial support to those who do. The wealthy recognize that it is this belief that is the source of, and the protection of, their wealth. It is likewise with the middle class. They recognize their living is tied to the current arteries of commerce and thus easily believe their security is under threat. They are totally unaware that much of this wealth comes from their society imposing inequalities of trade on weaker societies and perpetuating others' impoverishment. Thus, a propagandized population provides the power base for *managers-of-state* to inflict such violence upon defenseless people, at times even upon their own people.

As in all indoctrinated societies, we each parrot what propaganda wordsmiths have carefully crafted for us. Thus, again as in all such societies, we keep persuading each other with these distortions of reality. As the need to belong to a group is paramount and beliefs define a political group, peer pressure keeps a society locked within those beliefs.

Who are the Violent and Powerful?

A study of CIA powerbrokers and others deeply involved in leadership positions pushing the Cold War will expose that they are powerful corporate lawyers, have developed close ties to the powerful while being educated in elite educational institutions, have other close ties to wealth, or are themselves extremely wealthy. Thus when Guatemala's elected government was overthrown and a dictator imposed to protect United Fruit, "the head of the CIA, General Walter Bedell Smith, joined the board of the United Fruit Company, while United Fruit's president, Allen Dulles, became CIA director."[33] Kermit Roosevelt, former Vice President of Gulf Oil, oversaw the destabilization of Iran (Operation Ajax).

John F. and Allen Dulles, both long-term powerbrokers in the State Department and CIA, came from entrenched wealth and were also corporate lawyers for others of the world's wealthy. Probably no one else except William Casey, another CIA director and leading corporate lawyer, was in on the planning for the covert actions of the Cold War throughout the CIA's first 45 years more than they were.

The violent and powerful who carry out corporate policies, such as described in Chapters 7 and 8, are good citizens, good neighbors, good husbands, and good parents who kiss their children when they put them to bed. But their loyalty is to their wealth or the wealthy who put them in power. They do not expand their view of rights to include all people.

To justify their oppression, it was once convenient to tell one another that colonial natives had no souls, and thus were not people. To redefine rights in the broadest sense and act accordingly (full rights and equality for all people), would not only shatter everything the world's wealthy believed and everything the powerbrokers have done in our name—it would mean a total repudiation of the philosophy the imperial nations were functioning under.

Damage Control

If one has any doubts as to how thorough propaganda and thought control are consider the 730 American airmen shot down or crashed as they were flying sabotage and assassination teams into Byelorussia and the Ukraine and photographing territory in the heart of the Soviet Union as addressed in Chapter 7.[34]

Much effort went into "damage control" to tone down that explosive story. In later documentaries and feature articles the admission of over 730 airmen lost over the Soviet Union was downgraded to 130, but, knowing they had been deceived once, each documentary noted the story might be much bigger. A few years after the exposure of the air assaults on the Soviet Union, a military spokesman in a news interview said that, "Americans would be surprised if they knew how many airmen had been lost over the Soviet Union and China." A documentary on the subject of the downed pilots showed their routes over the Baltic Sea and claimed that all planes veered off before going over Soviet territory. That falsification of history—telling a part of the story as the full story and ignoring the major story of over 10-thousand flights into the heart of the Soviet Union—required both a careful selection of facts by the Pentagon and a cooperative producer. Even as Western citizens were being brought to near hysteria that they were under dire threat of attack, there were no planes from either Eastern Europe or the Soviet Union flying towards the West with teams trained for sabotage and assassination, or any other kind of destabilization. No politician of substantial stature seriously believed the Soviets were going to attack anyone and our next chapter will document that many countries were under attack from the West.

Damage control was exercised again when *CNN* and *Time* magazine spent two years documenting over 20 instances of the use of nerve gas by Americans in Vietnam (at times against defecting U.S. Soldiers). The story (Operation Tailwind)—aired and printed in July 1998—was withdrawn, senior editors who stood by their story were fired, others demoted or chastised, and the story was successfully suppressed. That surfacing of true history was quickly erased from history. When such revelations get into the mainstream media they cannot be permitted to stand.

Whenever the powerful are challenged, the longstanding tradition of the owners of newspapers backing their editors and editors backing their reporters (at least we have always been told it is so) is blown out the window. Witness reporter Ray Bonner's banishment to obscurity by the *New York Times* for exposing the El Mozote massacre by U.S.-trained soldiers in El Salvador; Robert Parry's departure from *Newsweek* after "path-breaking work on the Iran-Contra scandal"; *The San Jose Mercury News* retraction of its exposure of CIA involvement in drug trafficking and subsequent resignation of its star reporter, Gary Webb; and James Fallows' disappearance from *U.S. News & World Report* for trying to insert a little reality into that publication. This author was especially appreciative of James Fallows' writings and wondered how his broad and sensible view of the world could ever be tolerated at *U.S. News*. It wasn't.

And if all we have documented to this point is not enough to prove that the West was never under threat of a military attack, that the *managers-of-state* knew this well, and that there was no need for intelligence agencies to alert the West about any such attack, consider this: Immediately after WWII, U.S. intelligence co-opted Switzerland's Crypto-Ag (and other encryption companies) to obtain the codes to the most secure encryption machines sold to nations all over the world. With these codes, U.S. intelligence officials read the most secret messages of most nations, friend and foe, as easily as they might read the morning newspaper.[a] The National Security Agency's ECHELON listens in on almost every conversation in the world. Its computers are keyed to detect key words and phrases and

---

[a] Wayne Madsen, "Crypto Ag: The NSA's Trojan Whore?" *CovertAction Quarterly* (Winter 1998), pp. 36-42; William Blum, Rogue State: A Guide to the World's Only Super Power (Monroe, ME: Common Courage Press, 2000), Chapter 21. The CIA uses many methods for plausible denial. For example: Inter-Arms was established by ex-career CIA agent Samuel Cummings was supposedly separated from the CIA to establish the world's largest small arms dealership, Inter-Arms Incorporated, a plausibly deniable conduit for weapons shipments anywhere in the world. With an established arms conduit for covert actions, and a record of serial numbers of other sales so intelligence agencies could keep track of who was using those arms, one would be in deep denial if they thought Cummings was really independent of the CIA.

divert all communications with those words to be looked at. Important communication sources and destinations have all communications checked. American intelligence services and *managers-of-state* not only knew well there was no planned attack, they knew how weak and defenseless against the full power of the west these besieged people really were. [a]

Assassinations and covert actions were the least of what interested the West as they read other nations' mail; they were responsible for most of them anyway. The economic plans of those nations were their primary interest. Playing the high-stakes diplomatic poker game of international trade with a mirror behind everyone else's back gave the United States an insurmountable advantage in trade negotiations. They knew the most intimate secrets of nonaligned nations attempting to ally together to develop their industries and internal economies.

Few of those nations had any intention of allying their economies with the Soviet Union. Although a nation embargoed by the West would be forced to trade with the Soviet Union, their goal was freedom to control their resources and economies and trade with any nation they chose. (By 1998, 70 countries—66% of the people on earth—were under some form of American embargo or sanction.[35] Control of trade hides behind a rhetorical cover of human rights abuses. If a nation is recalcitrant, those human rights abuses provide the legitimacy for sanctions, destabilizations, and wars.)

Though hundreds of billions of dollars were spent to destabilize emerging nations, funds can no longer be found to rebuild these shattered nations (it took over 50 years, trillions of dollars, and many millions killed to destabilize the Soviet Union). Without development funds and without access to technology and markets, the weak are again relegated to providing cheap commodities and labor to *imperial-centers-of-capital.* However, if the threat of loss of the countryside to the imperial centers returns, massive funds will again be available for development of those countries crucial for allies and even more massive funds for destabilization of all others.

Knowledge of how propaganda works in the world's so-called "free" press is sobering. The post 9-11 Patriot Act is a recreation of Germany's post Reichstag fire Enabling Act under which Hitler established Fascism and took all rights away from, and jailed and executed, targeted people. Entire ethnic groups are targeted in both cases, databases of potential

---

[a] The lead article in CovertAction Quarterly, Fall 2002, is titled "Imperial Wizard: Soros is not just doling out cash—he's fleecing entire countries," by Heather Cottin. This is a must-read for serious researchers on how propaganda works. While being portrayed, and portraying himself as a great philanthropist, George Soros is obviously working closely with the IMF, the World Bank, the National Endowment for Democracy, and many other offshoots of American intelligence to subvert the economies of entire nations. He then picks up prime assets for pennies on the dollar. There has to be many others in on that blatant fleecing of the weak impoverished world.

enemies are created, those enemies are watched by a newly reorganized or newly created internal intelligence service, neighbors are asked to report on neighbors, people have disappeared with—as of this writing—no rights to lawyers, torture of suspects is openly discussed even as it is obviously practiced but not admitted. We must remember that the overwhelming masses of the German people were not targeted, were instead told that it was they under threat, and it was not until Fascism was defeated that the excesses and abuses of other people—very similar to the abuses of other societies and other cultures we are addressing—were exposed.

Notes

[1] J.W. Smith, WHY?: The Deeper History Behind The September 2001 Terrorist Attack On America (ied.info/cc.html: The Institute for Economic Democracy, 2003.), Chapter 3.

[2] Peter Coleman, *Liberal Conspiracy* (London: Collier Macmillan Publishers), dustjacket; Frances Stoner Saunders, *The Cultural Cold War: The CIA and the World of Arts and Letters* (New York: The Free Press, 1999).

[3] Saunders, *The Cultural Cold War*, pp. 1-3, 197.

[4] William F. Pepper, *An Act of State: The Execution of Martin Luther King* (New York: Verso, 2003), p. 135.

[5] Saunders, *The Cultural Cold War*, pp. 1-3, 37, 60-63, 68, 71, 91, 101-39, 142, 150-51, 166, 201, 206, 245, 294-99, 353-58, 382, 403-403, 409-411, 420, more author's names were listed on the dustjacket; Angus MacKenzie, *Secrets: The CIA's War at Home* (Berkeley: University of California Press, 1997), pp. 2, 29, 40, 61-72, 185; See also, Coleman, *Liberal Conspiracy*.

[6] Run a Google Internet search using keywords, names, and countries on these pages. The history of America's state terrorism worldwide is deeply hidden and most records have been destroyed. (Witness Bamford's exposure on how General Lemnitzer destroyed the records on the Pentagon's plans for staging an attack on America, which included American deaths, to create an excuse to over throw Fidel Castro of Cuba.) The following books provide a good view of that history: Austin Murphy, *The Triumph of Evil: The Reality of the USA's Cold War Victory* (Italy: European Press Academic Publishing, 2000); James Bamford, *Body of Secrets: Anatomy of the Ultra-Secret National Security Agency* (New York: Doubleday, 2001), especially pp. 70-75; John Quigley, *The Ruses for War: American Interventionism Since World War II* (Buffalo: Prometheus Books, 1992); L. Fletcher Prouty, *The Secret Team* (Englewood Cliffs, NJ: Prentice-Hall, 1973); Ralph McGehee, CIABASE (12-megabyte database on this history), http://come.to/CIABASE/, Box 5022, Herndon, VA 22070 (Caution: Run an Internet search for Ralph McGehee. The CIA is harassing him and may be sabotaging his database.); Peter Coleman, *Liberal Conspiracy*; Michael T. Klare, *Resource Wars: The New Landscape of Global Conflict* (New York: Henry Holt and Company, 2001); Michel Chossudovsky, *The Globalization of Poverty: Impacts of IMF and World Bank Reforms* (London: Zed Books, 1997); William Blum, *Rogue State: A Guide to the World's Only Super Power* (Monroe, ME: Common Courage Press, 2000), *Killing Hope: U.S. Military Interventions Since World War II* (Monroe, ME: Common Courage Press, 1995), and *The CIA: A Forgotten History* (London: Zed Press, 1986), pp. 127-28, 131, 185; Chalmers Johnson, *Blowback: The Cost and Consequences of American Empire* (New York: Henry Holt & Company, 2000), p. 117; John Prados, *The Presidents' Secret Wars* (New York: William Morrow, 1986) and *The President' Secret Wars: CIA and Pentagon Covert Operations From World War II Through the Persian Gulf War* Warwick: Elephant Paperbacks, 1996); John Stockwell, *The Praetorian Guard* (Boston: South End Press, 1991), pp. 100-101; Ted Gup, *The Book of Honor: Covert Lives and Classified Deaths at the CIA* (New York: Doubleday, 2,000); Dan Jacobs, *The Brutality of Nations* (New York: Alfred A. Knopf, 1987); P.V. Parakal, *Secret Wars of the CIA* (New Delhi: Sterling Publishers, 1984); K. Nair, *Devil and His Dart: How the CIA is Plotting in the Third World* (New Delhi: Sterling, 1986); I.F. Stone, *The Hidden History of the Korean War* (Boston: Little Brown and Company, 1952); Victor Marchetti and John D. Marks, *The CIA and the Cult of Intelligence* (New York: Dell, 1980), Chapter 6, especially pp. 152-56, also pp. 53-54, 62-63, 541-42; Ralph W. McGehee, *Deadly Deceits* (New York: Sheridan Square Press, 1983), especially pp. 30, 58, 62, 189; Philip Agee and Louis Wolf, *Dirty Work* (London: Zed Press, 1978), especially p. 262; Loch .K. Johnson, *America's Secret Power* (New York: Oxford University Press, 1989); David Wise, Thomas B. Ross, *The Espionage Establishment* (New York: Bantam Books, 1978), pp. 256, 257; H.B. Westerfield, *Inside CIA's Private World: Declassified Articles from the Agency's Internal Journal 1955-1992* (New Haven, CT. Yale University Press, 1995); Frank J. Donner, *The Age of Surveillance: The Aims and Methods of America's Political Intelligence System* (New York: Random House, 1981); John Prados, *Keepers of the Keys: A History of the National Security Council from Truman to Bush* (New York: William Morrow, 1991); C.D. Ameringer, *U.S. Foreign Intelligence* (Lexington, MA: Lexington Books, 1990); J. Adams, *Secret*

Armies (New York: Atlantic Monthly Press, 1987); T. Powers, *The Man Who Kept the Secrets* (New York: Alfred A. Knopf, 1979); Christopher Simpson, *Blowback* (New York: Weidenfeld & Nicolson, 1988); Ernest Volkman, Blaine Baggett, *Secret Intelligence* (New York: Doubleday, 1989); John Ranelagh, *The Agency: The Rise and Decline of the CIA* (New York: Simon & Schuster, 1987); Darrell Garwood, *Under Cover: Thirty-Five Years of CIA Deception* (New York: Grove Press Inc., 1985); Philip Agee, *Inside the Company: CIA Diary* (New York: Bantam Books, 1975); B. Hersh, *The Old Boys: The American Elite and the Origins of the CIA* (New York: Charles Scribner's Sons, 1992); H. Rositzke, *The CIA's Secret Operations* (New York: Thomas Y. Crowell Company, 1977); E. Thomas, *The Very Best Men Four Who Dared: The Early Years of the CIA* (New York: Simon & Schuster, 1995); D.S. Blaufarb, *The Counterinsurgency Era: U.S. Doctrine and Performance 1950 to Present* (New York: The Free Press, 1977); Michael T. Klare and P. Kornbluh, *Low Intensity Warfare* (New York: Pantheon Books, 1988); Alexander Cockburn and Jeffrey St. Clair, *Whiteout: The CIA, Drugs and the Press* (New York: Verso, 1998); S.E. Ambrose, *Ike's Spies* (Garden City, New York: Doubleday & Company, 1981); Susanne Jonas, *The Battle for Guatemala: Rebels, Death Squads, and U.S. Power* (San Francisco: Westview Press, 1991); C. Andrew, *For the President's Eyes Only: Secret Intelligence and the American Presidency from Washington to Bush* (New York: HarperCollins Publishers 1995); H. Frazier, ed., *Uncloaking the CIA* (New York: The Free Press, 1978); *Covert Action Information Bulletin*, all issues; *Counterspy*, all issues. See also, Wendell Minnick, *Spies and Provocateurs: A Worldwide Encyclopedia of Persons Conducting Espionage and Covert Action, 1946-1991* (Jefferson, North Carolina: McFarland & Company,1992); John Loftus, *The Belarus Secret* (New York: Alfred A. Knopf, 1982); Robin W. Winks, *Cloak & Gown: Scholars in the Secret War, 1939-1961* (New York: Quill, 1987); D.F. Fleming, *The Cold War and Its Origins* (New York: Doubleday & Company, 1961); Nora Sayre, *Running Time: Films of the Cold War* (New York: Dial Press, 1980); Milton Mayer, *They Thought They Were Free* (Chicago: University of Chicago Press, 1955).

To understand financial and economic warfare, read Peter Gowan, *The Global Gamble: Washington's Faustian Bid for World Dominance* (New York: verso, 1999); John Gray, False *Dawn* (New York: The Free Press, 1998); Robert A. Pastor, Ed., *A Century's Journey: How the Great Powers Shape the World* (New York: Basic Books, 1999); Anders Stephanson, *Kennan and the Art of Foreign Policy* (Cambridge: Harvard University Press, 1989); David Mayers, *George Kennan and the Dilemmas of US Foreign Policy* (New York: Oxford University Press, 1988); John R. Commons, *Legal Foundations of Capitalism* (New Brunswick/London: Transaction Publishers, 1995); John R. Commons, *Institutional Economics* (New Brunswick/London: Transaction Publishers, 1995); Carey B. Joynt and Percy E. Corbett, *Theory and Reality in World Politics* (Pittsburgh: University of Pittsburgh Press, 1978); Richard L. Rubenstein, *The Age of Triage* (Boston: Beacon Press, 1983); Peter Rodman, *More Precious than Peace* (New York: Charles Scribner & Sons, 1994); Angelo Codevilla, *Informing Statecraft* (New York: The Free Press, 1992); Arie E. David, *The Strategy of Treaty Termination* (New Haven: Yale University Press, 1975); Francis Neilson, *How Diplomats Make War* (San Francisco: Cobden Press); Jerry Fresia, *Toward an American Revolution: Exposing the Constitution and Other Illusions* (Boston, South End Press), 1988.

For how the purpose of Western intelligence services are to control the beliefs of its citizens, and how much of the violence are covert operations to maintain this control, read L. Fletcher Prouty, *JFK: The CIA, Vietnam, And the Plot to Kill Kennedy* (New York: Carol Publishing, 1992) and Philip. Willan, *Puppetmasters: The Political Use of Terrorism in Italy* (London: Constable, 1991), provides a short description of how strategies-of-tension are used worldwide to control beliefs and thus control elections. Alex Carey's *Taking the Risk out of Democracy; Corporate Propaganda versus Freedom and Liberty* (Chicago: University of Illinois Press, 1995) is an in-depth analysis of corporate propaganda pushed through the government, media, and academia throughout the 20th century.

For more scholarly studies on the media read: Richard O Curry, *An Uncertain Future: Thought Control and Repression During the Reagan-Bush Era* (Los Angeles: First Amendment Foundation,

1992); John Downing, Radical Media.(Boston: South End Press, 1984); Edward S. Herman and Noam Chomsky, *Manufacturing Consent: The Political Economy of the Mass Media* (New York: Pantheon, 1988); Brooks Jackson, *Honest Graft: Big Money and the American Political Process* (New York: Alfred A Knopf, 1988); Naomi Klein, *No Logo* (New York: Random House, 1999); Martin A. Lee and Norman Solomon, *Unreliable Sources: A Guide to Detecting Bias in the news* (New York: Carol Publishing, 1990);. Walter Lippman, *Public Opinion* (New York: Simon & Schuster, 1949); David W. Moore, *The Super Pollsters: How they Measure and Manipulate Public Opinion in America* (New York: Four Walls Eight Windows, 1992); Michael Parenti, *Inventing Reality: The Politics of the Mass Media* (New York: St Martins's Press, 1986); John Stauber and Sheldon Ramption, *Toxic Sludge is Good for You: Lies, Damn Lies and the Public Relations Industry* (Monroe, ME: Common Courage Press, 1995).

7 Ralph McGehee, *Deadly Deceit.* (New York: Sheridan Square Press, 1983), p. 192.

8 McGehee, http://come.to/CIABASE/, check Wade Frazier's review of McGehee's Deadly Deceits. (Caution: McGehee is being harassed by the CIA and his website may be disabled.)

9 Dean Acheson, *Present at the Creation* (New York: W.W. Norton & Company, 1987), pp. 373-379; the complete NSC-68 document can be found in Thomas H. Etzold and John Lewis Gaddis, *Containment: Documents on American Policy and Strategy, 1945-50*, (New York: Columbia University Press, 1978), Chapter 7. See endnote 6.

10 Acheson, *Present at the Creation* p. 377; Etzold and Gaddis, *Containment*, Chapter 7.

11 See endnote 6. Run a Google Internet search using keywords, names, and countries on these pages

12 Acheson, *Present at the Creation,* p. 377. See also Stone, *Hidden History,* and Etzold and Gaddis, *Containment.*

13 Stone, Hidden History; Coleman, Liberal Conspiracy; Saunders, The Cultural Cold War; Schrecker, No Ivory Tower; Etzold and Gaddis, Containment, Chapter 7.

14 See endnote 6 (Coleman's *Liberal Conspiracy*, especially Appendix D, lists almost 200 of these thought control books); Saunders, *The Cultural Cold War*, pp. 60, 63, 111, 140, 294-96, 105-106; see Chapters 6, 7, and 9 of this work.

15 See endnote 6. Run a Google Internet search using keywords, names, and countries on these pages

16 William Blum, *Rogue State:*, Chapter 4; Willan, *Puppetmasters* , Chapters 1-3, pp. 146-159; Thomas, Very Best Men, pp. 65-66; David A. Yallop, *In God's Name* (New York: Bantam Books, 1984); Saunders, *The Cultural Cold War*, p. 143; See endnote 6. Gladio and Operation Statewatch was not uncovered until November 1990, too late for most books listed here, so one must go to McGehee's CIABASE for articles and later sources. See also Prouty, *JFK,* Chapter 3 and Blum, *Rogue State*, chapters 4 and 16.

17 Chalmers Johnson, *Blowback: The Cost and Consequences of American Empire* (New York: Henry Holt & Company, 2000), p. 117.

18 See endnote 6, especially Prouty, *JFK*, Chapter 3 and Blum, *Rogue State*, Chapter 4.

19 Sally Covington, "Right Thinking, Big Grants, and Long Term Strategy: How Conservative Philanthropies and Think Tanks Transform U.S. Policy," *CovertAction Quarterly* (Winter 1998), pp. 6-16; see also Frances Stoner Saunders, *The Cultural Cold War: The CIA and the World of Arts and Letters* (New York: The Free Press, 1999), pp. 116, 135, 138-39, 142, 353-58, 409.

20 Ibid. Run a Google Internet search using keywords, names, and countries on these pages

21 Ibid. Run a Google Internet search using keywords, names, and countries on these pages

22 Mason Gaffney, Fred Harrison, *The Corruption of Economics* (London: Shepheard-Walwyn, 1994).

23 Ellen Schrecker, *No ivory tower: McCarthyism and the Universities* (New York: Oxford University Press, 1986).

24 Robin W. Winks, Cloak and Gown; Saunders, The Cultural Cold War.

25 Ibid; MacKenzie, *Secrets,* pp. 2, 4-6, 27, 29-41; Michael Parenti, *History as Mystery* (San Francisco: City Lights Books, 2000), pp. 178, 183-89; Holly Sklar, *Washington's War on*

Nicaragua (Boston: South End Press, 1988), p. 359; Rositzke, *CIA's Secret Operations*, pp. 218-20; Powers, *Man Who Kept the Secrets*, pp. 246-70, 364.

26 Angus MacKenzie and David Weir, *Secrets: The CIA's War at Home* (University of California Press, 1997); M. Wesley Swearingen, *FBI Secrets: An Agent's Exposé* (Boston: South End Press, 1995); Ward Churchhill, *Cointelpro Papers: Documents from the FBI's Secret Wars Against Domestic Dissent* (South End Press, 1990); Margaret Jayko, *FBI on Trial: The Victory in the Socialist Workers Party Suit against Government Spying* (New York: Pathfinder Press, 1989); Nelson Blackstock, *Cointelpro: The FBI's Secret War on Political Freedom* (New York: Anchor Foundation, 1988); Margaret Jayko, *FBI on Trial: The Victory of the Socialist Workers Party Suit Against Government Spying* (New York: Pathfinder Press, 1989): Nelson Blackstock, *Cointelpro: The FBI's Secret War on Political Freedom* (New York: Anchor Foundation, 1988); Ward Churchhill, *Agents of Repression : The FBI's Secret Wars Against the Black Panther Party and the American Indian Movement* (Boston South End Press, 1989); Martin Luther King Jr, Philip S. Foner, editor, *The Black Panthers Speak* (New York: Da Capo Press, 1995); Hugh Pearson, *The Shadow of the Panther: Huey Newton and the Price of Black Power in America* (Readings, MA: Perseus Press, 1995); also see endnote 6. Run a Google Internet search.

27 Blum, *Rogue State,* pp. 258-59. The full story of Post World War II suppression of dissent in America has not been written yet: Stephen M. Kohn, *American Political Prisoners: Prosecution under the Espionage and Sedition Acts* (Westport: Praeger Publishers, 1994), covers that history before and after WWI.

28 Lane, *Plausible Denial,* pp. 239-323, especially 320-22.

29 William F. Pepper, *An Act of State: The Execution of Martin Luther King* (New York: Verso, 2003), pp. 11, 15, 65, 76, 107.

30 Ibid, p. 127.

31 Run a Google Internet search.

32 Ellen Schrecker, *No Ivory Tower* (New York: Oxford University Press, 1986).

33 Frederic F. Clairmont, *The Rise and Fall of Economic Liberalism* (Goa India: The Other India Press, 1996), pp. 7, 18, taken from Gerald Colby, *DuPont: Behind the Nylon Curtain* (Englewood Cliffs, N.J.: Prentice-Hall), 1974.

34 Michael Ross, "Yeltsin: POWs 'Summarily Executed'," *The Spokesman Review* (November 12, 1992): pp. B1, A10; Ernest Volkman, Blaine Baggett, *Secret Intelligence* (New York: Doubleday, 1989), p. 187; John Loftus, *The Belarus Secret* (New York: Alfred A. Knopf, 1982), Chapters 5-8, pp. 109-10; William Blum, *The CIA*, Chapters 6, 7, 8, 15, 17, especially p. 124; See endnote 6.

35 Thomas Omestat, "Addicted to Sanctions," *U.S. News & World Report,* June 15, 1998, pp. 30-31.

7. The World Breaking Free frightened the Security Councils of every Western Nation

The security councils of the historical colonial empires were horrified to observe that not only were populations on the periphery of empire who provided their cheap resources taking the rhetoric of democracy seriously and breaking free, but that the empires were losing traditional allies. After WWII, a Soviet system of government was installed in all but Hungary and Czechoslovakia when Hitler's armies were driven from Eastern Europe. The security councils of all major Western nations were traumatized as:

(1) Hungary and Czechoslovakia, with diplomatic pressure from the Soviet Union but still of their own choice, quickly slipped into the Soviet orbit and labor now governed half of Europe.[a]

(2) In Greece, only an alliance with Hitler's puppets, massive repression, and massacres of the partisans who had kept two-thirds of the country out of Hitler's control throughout WWII kept the Greek nation in the Western orbit (the first battle of the Cold War started before WWII ended and was fought strictly against our former allies; the awakened workers of Greece).[1]

3) Through nonviolent protest, Gandhi freed India from Britain.

(4) In spite of large expenditures of money and arms, military advisors, and the United States transporting Chiang Kai-shek's troops back and forth across China, one-fifth of the world's population was lost to the West: China was suddenly free to chart her own destiny.

(5) World opinion forced the dictation of the U.S. presidential "white paper" that would return Taiwan (Formosa) to China.[2]

(6) South Korea was having massive riots (over 100,000 killed[a]), the collaborationists of the United States installed dictator Syngman Rhee (who

---

[a] Certainly there was repression within Hungary and Czechoslovakia as the Soviet Union suppressed the political elements who wished to ally with their cultural and religious cousins in the West. But, as will be demonstrated in the next chapter, the repression exercised to maintain the Eastern European bloc pales alongside the massive repression required worldwide to suppress the many attempted breaks for freedom from Western capital.

had spent 20 years in exile in Hawaii) were overwhelmingly voted out of parliament, "several crack South Korean military units [had] defected to leftist forces," and South and North Korea were rejoining as one nation outside the control of imperial capital.[3]

(7) Japan, Germany, and Italy—being far from friends with their recent conquerors—made it uncertain that the facade of democratic control of those populations would hold, and France was equally insecure.[4]

(8) Workers in all nations of Europe were developing a political consciousness and not only were the Western economies not picking up as planned, they were moribund. The beacon of capitalism—the receptacle of power for the descendants of the old First and Second Estates and philosophical foundation for their *social-control-paradigms*—was not shining brightly enough to claim the loyalties of the world's intellectuals or that of the stirring masses. The Marshall Plan to rebuild Europe and retain its loyalty went forward at full speed and only by expenditure of tens of millions of dollars in the Italian and French elections (a practice that lasted two decades in France and four decades in Italy) were those two countries kept within the system of *allied imperial-centers-of-capital.*

(9) Virtually the entire colonial world was breaking free, their resources would be turned to the care of their own people, and those resources could no longer be siphoned to the *old imperial-centers-of-capital* for a fraction of their value.

(10) China and Eastern Europe were now allied with the Soviet Union. If India and the rest of the world's former colonies continued to take the rhetoric of democracy seriously and form the nonaligned bloc as they were planning, over 80% of the world's population would be independent or on the other side of the ideological battle. And, if Japan, Germany, Italy, and France could not be held (it was far from sure they could be), that would leave only the United States, Britain, Canada, and Australia, about 10% of the world's population, still under the old operational philosophies, and even there the ideological hold would be tenuous at best. After all, if there were no countryside under the firm control of an imperial center, the entire neo-liberal/neo-mercantilist philosophical system will have disappeared.

What Western nations were observing, of course, was the same potential loss of resources and markets, their "countryside," as the cities of Europe had experienced centuries earlier. "National security" and "security interests," which citizens were coached (propagandized) to believe meant fear of a military attack, really meant maintaining access to the weak, impoverished world's valuable resources. The "domestic prosperity" worried about was only their own and the "constantly expanding trade"

---

[a] One has to research deep to find the true level of South Korean massacres of civilians. These slaughters of dissidents to maintain control of South Korea and prevent its rejoining the North were still going on as late as 1980 (Lee Jai-eui, *Kwangju Diary: Beyond Death, Beyond the Darkness of Age*. (Los Angeles: University of California, 1999).

were unequal trades maintaining the prosperity of the developed world and the impoverishment of the undeveloped world as the *imperial-centers-of-capital* siphoned the natural wealth of their "countryside" to themselves.

A Crisis of Overproduction had to be averted

With industrial capacity having increased 50% during WWII, U.S. industry was calculated to be twice what was necessary for America's needs and almost enough to produce for the entire world at its pre-war level of consumption.[5] One of the primary tenets of a capitalist market economy is that surplus production at much smaller levels than that spells an economic depression.

The eighth conclusion of NSC-68, the master plan for the Cold War, states: "There are grounds for predicting that the United States and other free nations will within a period of a few years at most experience a decline in economic activity of serious proportions unless more positive government programs are developed than are now available." In a democracy, the legitimacy of both ideology and leaders are judged at the ballot box by how well its citizens are cared for. Every leader in the developed world still remembered how near the world was to a ballot box revolution during the Great Depression; a market for that excess productive capacity was crucial. In short, the waste of building arms and covert and overt wars was both to protect the existing trade structure and to be a Keynesian infusion of money into the economy to prevent a replay of the Great Depression and the threat of a voter's revolution.

But the post-WWII stirring of the masses worldwide was a more immediate concern. Noting the threat to their commerce and wealth as the entire world was taking the rhetoric of freedom and democracy seriously, corporations, through control of policy of the one remaining wealthy nation (America) and the devastated nations of Europe and Japan, made the same decision as the free cities of Europe centuries earlier. Threatened with loss of their cheap, but valuable, resources and profitable markets, they had to reclaim control of their countryside:

> Fostering a world environment in which the American system can flourish ... embraces two subsidiary policies. One is a policy which we would probably pursue even if there was no Soviet threat. It is a policy of attempting to create a healthy international community. The other is a policy of "containing" the Soviet system. These two policies are closely interrelated and interact with one another.[6]

Of course, the "healthy international community" Secretary of State Dean Acheson, one of the primary architects of the Cold War, had in mind as he was justifying NSC-68 was only from the perspective of those who watch the wealth of others roll into their vaults. A healthy community as enforced by the Free cities of Europe 800 years ago meant wealth to them and poverty for the defeated neighboring cities. A healthy international community, from the perspective of corporate imperialism, means wealth for the developed corporate world and poverty for the formerly colonized, still defeated, and re-colonized undeveloped world.

Control had to be reestablished. Although done in the name of *peace, freedom, justice, rights*, and *majority rule* (*social-control-paradigms*, especially when girding for war), the fundamental goal of the forming IMF/World Bank/GATT/NAFTA/WTO/MAI/GATS/FTAA/ military colossus and the covert actions authorized by NSC-68, and many lesser Security Council directives both before and after that master plan, was the reclamation and maintenance of control over valuable resources and profitable markets and the very negation of the principles so loudly touted as their rationale. The real fear was people taking democracy seriously, deciding their own destiny, and corporations losing access to those cheap resources and valuable markets.

National Security Council Directive 68

A study of NSC-68 will conclude that, besides being a master plan for the Cold War, this directive was also a propaganda instrument to stampede government officials into accepting that military posture. That analysis and the crisis facing the developed Western world are confirmed. Secretary of State Dean Acheson, one of the primary architects of NSC-68, sums it up for us:

> Western Europe ... shattered by its civil war, was disintegrating politically, economically, socially, and psychologically. Every effort to bestir itself was paralyzed by two devastating winters and the overshadowing fear of the Soviet Union no longer contained by the stoppers on the east, west, and south—Japan, Germany, and British India.... It was in this period [the first 3 years after the beginning of the Cold War] that we awakened fully to the facts of the surrounding world and to the scope and kind of action required by the interests of the United States; the second period, that of President Truman's second administration, became the time for full action upon those conclusions and for meeting the whole gamut of reactions—favorable, hostile, and merely recalcitrant foreign and domestic—that they produced. In the first period, the main lines of policy were set and begun; in the second, they were put into full effect amid the smoke and confusion of battle.... *The purpose of NSC-68 [the master plan for the Cold War] was to so bludgeon the mass mind of "top government" that not only could the president make a decision but that the decision could be carried* out.[7]

Although President Truman may have been fully aware, the fact that the finalized NSC-68 was presented to him on April 16, 1950, but that it was not signed until September 30, 1950 (as NSC-68/2) three months after the start of the Korean War, demonstrates the likelihood that the American president was one of the "top government officials" the designers of the

Cold War were stampeding into a war posture through the *strategy-of-tension* of the communists as the aggressor of the Korean war and this foretelling more communist aggressions worldwide.

The Korean War, a *Strategy-of-Tension*

Any power-structure, "democratic" or dictatorship, facing the loss of control on the periphery of empire, will find or create an excuse for war. Because all the records were not destroyed as ordered, it is now known the American Joint Chiefs of Staff had just such a *strategy-of-tension* planned to create support for a war with Cuba. They urged President Kennedy to justify their planned war by staged covert terrorist acts, some of which would have caused the deaths of innocent Americans[a]:

> In the name of anticommunism, they proposed launching a secret and bloody war of terrorism against their own country in order to trick the American public into supporting an ill-conceived war they intended to launch against Cuba. Codenamed Operation Northwoods, the plans which had the approval of the Chairman and every member of the Joint Chiefs of Staff, called for innocent Americans to be shot on American streets; for boats carrying refugees from Cuba to be sunk in the high seas; for a wave of violent terrorism to be launched in Washington D.C., Miami, and elsewhere. People would be blamed for bombings they did not commit; planes would be hijacked. Using phony evidence, all of it would be blamed on Castro, thus giving Lemnitzer and his cabal the excuse, as well as the public and international backing, they needed to launch their war.[8]

The political instrument to put NSC-68 into effect was the Korean War that started 72 days after that directive was finalized and presented to President Truman. When I.F. Stone wrote *The Hidden History of the Korean War* in 1952, NSC-68 was still classified. However, in that book, Stone demonstrated the Korean War was a *strategy-of-tension* imposing the policies of America's *managers-of-state* upon the world and the most important political event since WWII.

No empire (or nation) instigates a war on the periphery that is already politically won but they do instigate actual wars when loss of control is imminent. But this planned war was not only to save an outpost on the periphery of empire; this was a war to save the empire. There was nothing

---

[a] Historians should look close the anthrax scare after 9/11/2001. Those anthrax spores were proven to be biologically identical to that produced at the U.S. germ warfare facility at the Dugway Proving Grounds in Utah. John Pilger stated in the *New Statesman,* December 16, 2002, that America's leading powerbrokers spoke of "needing "some catastrophic and catalyzing event—like an new Pearl Harbor"—so as to gain the loyalty of the American people for their violent foreign policy. The source of that anthrax is not in dispute. The probability is very high that propagandists took advantage of the September 11th terrorist attack to further their *strategies-of-tension* to maintain that loyalty. Run Google Internet searches using the many keywords on this page.

to lose in Korea; without a war it was going to be lost anyway and there was an entire world to gain through a *strategy-of-tension* mobilizing the citizens of the imperial centers for a war to suppress the renewed breaks for economic freedom of the emerging world. Though the plans were made in State an analysis of our sources will conclude the excuse for the Korean War was obviously staged by General Douglas MacArthur, South Korean President Syngman Rhee, and Chiang Kai-shek of Formosa under the political cover of the American hard right (called the China Lobby), McCarthyism, and the CIA's *Mighty Wurlitzer*."

Highlights from Stone's book outline a war created by those threatened with the loss of their power and wealth. Massive riots were breaking out all over South Korea with the goal of North and South Korea reuniting, over 100,000 were killed. Crack military units were defecting to the so-called left and the CIA and South Korean government were unable to control the elections. Syngman Rhee's puppet government was voted out wholesale and the next to go would be Syngman Rhee.

North and South Korea were going to rejoin outside Western control, South Korean troops pulled back from the 38th parallel the day before the war started, South Korean government press releases were saying a North Korean attack was imminent, the UN inspected the 38th parallel—just hours before the war started—concluding there was no imminent attack, and intelligence briefings stated that North Korea was not prepared for war. Yet ships were in place to evacuate American families. Everything was set to fabricate an excuse for a war, a *strategy-of-tension*, to gain followers for the immense military budget and casualties it would take to suppress the world's break for freedom.

But the clincher that the invasion of South Korea was a much more elaborately staged war than Hitler's staged invasion of Poland was North Korea's announcement that South Korea had invaded North Korea in three places and had been hurled back. Author John Gunther, General Douglas MacArthur's personal biographer, just happened to be in the General's personal railroad car when a high-level occupation official returned from being called to a phone, saying, "A big story has just broken. The South Koreans have attacked North Korea."[9]

That verification which accidentally slipped into history and Stone's cold political analysis verifies the North Korean claim that South Korea, under American guidance and promise of protection by America's full military might, started that war. (A third verification was the few days it took to dislodge South Korea from Heiju, several miles above the 38th parallel.) I.F. Stone describes how many of the massive battles with hordes of Koreans and Chinese attacking were nothing more than military press releases (*social-control-paradigms* manufactured by intelligence service wordsmiths and passed out through military and government channels).[a] Stone would quote the headlines built from those press releases and then print the communiqués from ground commanders who were essentially searching for enemies they could not find.

Certainly 4-million were killed but they were primarily killed by an unopposed air force that napalmed North Korea to the ground, an unopposed navy that shelled North Korean coastal cities to rubble, and massive artillery that extracted a horrendous price in lives when a real attack was faced. This accounts for only 35,000 Americans being among the 4-million who died. Half those numbers were women and children who died in this carnage when defenseless and totally undefended North Korean cities and villages were napalmed and bombarded to the ground.

Neither China nor the Soviet Union provided any great support to North Korea until that tiny impoverished nation was essentially destroyed. Couple that war by press release with the documented efforts of the North Koreans, Chinese, and Soviets to bring that war to an end—every such effort unreported in Western media and thwarted by either a massive air attack or ground offensive—clearly mark it as a political event.

John Quigley wrote *The Ruses for War: American Interventionism since World War II* in 1992 and he came up with the same conclusions: The Korean war was started under NSC-68 and by the West as a *strategy-of-tension* so citizens and governments would support the militarization of the West for control of the world's resources. Besides unearthing evidence we missed that America instituted that war, Quigley agrees that the West was at all times militarily superior to the North Koreans, that the North Koreans were not ready for war, and Western armies were many times looking for forces that simply were not there.[10]

Thanks to the hysteria of the Korean War, which legitimized the West's primary *social-control-paradigm* (that the West was under imminent threat of attack), South Korea and Taiwan were kept within the sphere of Western influence; so called "leftist" dissidents in Germany, Italy, France, and Japan were totally suppressed (by a *strategy-of-tension* identical to American McCarthyism); the military budget did increase 350% as planned in NSC-68; the Cold War was on full force; and—after an intense 40-year battle—that struggle to regain control worldwide to protect those cheap resources, those markets, and the very right to govern the imperial centers, was won.

That 4-million people were killed (half women and children), millions more wounded, that the entire Korean peninsula was scorched earth, that another 10-million would be violently killed as other breaks for economic freedom were suppressed all over the world, that tens of millions more

---

[a] When China joined the war and pushed the Americans back to the 38th parallel the West did face a capable enemy. But the 35,000 Americans killed while 4-million North Koreans and Chinese were killed fully supports I.F., Stone's analysis.

would be wounded, that hundreds of millions would die from starvation and disease as the economies of impoverished countries struggling for freedom were shattered, that billions would remain impoverished as their governments were covertly overthrown or that trillions of dollars of the world's resources would be wasted, could not deflect the *managers-of-state* from their decisions. They, like *imperial-centers-of-capital* for centuries, felt they had no other choices. To lose those natural resources, that cheap labor, and those markets was to lose their power and their wealth. As we will be addressing below, other choices are not only available today; they are imperative.

The security councils of all the Western European nations had long since realized that they could not rebuild their WWII devastated societies if they lost control of the resources of the world, nor could they rebuild if their industry, money, and labor were expended on arms. British Prime Minister Winston Churchill made it clear that, even though Britain was damaged less than 10% as much as Eastern Europe and Western Europe was damaged possibly only 20% as much, "If rearmament is not spread out over a longer time the nations of Western Europe will be rushing to bankruptcy and starvation."[11]

The *Grand Strategy* paid off. Except for China and all Southeast Asia slipping in under the umbrella of protection provided to Japan, Taiwan, and South Korea, the natural-resource-wealthy developing world remained poor. This left those resources available for the use of the imperial centers and the resource-depleted developed world rebuilt its wealth to a level far higher than before.

Fabricating Incidents to Start Wars

Fabricating incidents to start wars empires feel they can win—such as Hitler's *strategy-of-tension* through faking an attack by Poland on a German radio station and America's *strategy-of-tension* through creating the Gulf of Tonkin incident in order for President Johnson to get congressional backing to widen the war in Vietnam to justify a heavier assault on North Vietnam—is standard practice. This is the careful writing of history by the powerful. United States documents on the destabilization of Cuba, declassified in 1998, titled "Pretexts to Justify U.S. Military Intervention in Cuba" demonstrate how it is done. Plans for those in-depth deceptions were:

> Fake an attack on the U.S. naval base in Guantanamo, Cuba, with friendly Cubans masquerading as attackers.... Arrange for an unmanned vessel to be blown up near a major Cuban city.... Stage a 'Communist Cuban terror campaign' in the Miami area.... Plant arms in a Caribbean country and send jets painted to look like Cuban Migs, creating the appearance of a 'Cuban based, Castro supported' subversion.... Blow up an unmanned U.S. plane that would surreptitiously replace a charter flight of civilians (and much more).[12]

L. Fletcher Prouty was one of three officers who wrote the how-to book on covert operations for the CIA. In his *JFK: The CIA, Vietnam, And the Plot to Assassinate John F. Kennedy*, we learn that *strategies-of-tension*s (terrorist bombings, attacks by our own covert forces dressed as the enemy, counterfeit papers, and the drumbeat of the CIA's *Mighty Wurlitzer*) were used throughout the world to control elections and to gain acceptance for the military suppressions of the many breaks for freedom. In fact, American intelligence service manuals on terrorism teach that, whenever they carried out one of their many acts of state terrorism, to always leave evidence that the opposition was responsible.[13]

Peace in Korea could not be permitted

Attacks on defenseless civilians In North Korea were specifically to create anger and prevent negotiation. For a government to sign a peace treaty under such conditions is essentially unconditional surrender. For two years of negotiations at Panmunjom, every time it appeared a peace settlement was near there would be a massive air raid, a ground offensive, a naval bombardment, or all three.

When it appeared the Chinese were willing for a cessation of hostilities at the 38th parallel where it all began, three defenseless North Korean port cities were subjected to 41 straight days and nights bombardment by the navies of three nations and America's Air Force.

That most intense naval and air bombardment of any city in history, against totally defenseless women and children, went totally unreported in the Western press.[14] Instead of dictatorial powers planning to overwhelm the West militarily, those we were told were a dreaded dictatorial enemy were making every effort to return to peace and were being bombed and shelled to prevent a peace settlement.

The Korean War could not be permitted to end until the West's war machine was fully rebuilt, until treaties were signed with Japan and Germany that fully committed them to the West and until the entire Western world was raised to a high level of tension believing that it was at high risk of being attacked. The Korean War was necessary to gain full support from governments and the masses so that other overt and covert wars to suppress the world's break for economic freedom could be successfully fought.

To understand that the deciding factor in imposition of beliefs to control people is military power, read this book on how inequalities of trade are militarily imposed, then read NSC-68 while noting Acheson's statement quoted above that its purpose was to "*bludgeon the mass mind of "top government" that not only could the President make a decision but that the decision could be carried out*," and then read I.F. Stone's *The Hidden History of the Korean War*.

We are not exaggerating. These wars, in which we were told we were in such imminent danger of being attacked, were only to maintain control of the developed world's countryside with their immense natural resources and markets so crucial to those corporate industries. Voters would quickly change leaders if they knew that the *Grand Strategy* was to maintain control of the countryside through violence. Thus it was necessary to maintain control of the beliefs of the masses through a *strategy-of-tension* designed by the secretly functioning national security state.

The decisions had been made. America's *managers-of-state* were accepting the reality that only they had the economic and military power to re-impose control upon the world, and, though most of the planning (such as NSC-4, NSC-4A, NSC-10/2 and NSC-68) had yet to be done, most of world history since Churchill's famous 1946 Iron Curtain speech has been efforts to re-impose that control and the efforts of others to resist that imposition of control. We know this struggle as the Cold War and it was fought just as fiercely around the world as it was against the Soviet Union.

The First Efforts to Contain the Soviet Union

To understand how even powerful, threatening rising centers of capital can be destroyed we will encapsulate the short 73 year history of the former Soviet Union. The Soviet reorganization to unwieldy community ownership, equally inefficient direct distribution, yet very sensible community mutual support principles, had barely begun when 14 countries sent in 180,000 troops and armed 300,000 dissidents within Russia to overthrow that revolution.[15] Reclaiming this breakaway nation for capitalism's *managers-of-state* almost succeeded; nearly two-thirds of the Soviet Union came under interventionist and counterrevolutionary control before the Soviets defeated the allied invaders.

The effort was more successful than the history books acknowledge—Finland, Latvia, Lithuania, Estonia (these four countries having been a part of the Old Russian Empire for over 100 years) and the Eastern half of Poland, and Bessarabia were carved from the forming Soviet nation by that intervention.[16] Except for Leningrad, this barred the Soviet Union from Atlantic ports and restricted its access to world trade. Note the similarity of the carving off of these historic sectors of Russia 1917 to 1921 to the later carving up of the Soviet Union after 1990, the carving up of Yugoslavia still on-going as this book goes to press, and the continued moving East of the line between Eastern Orthodox Christianity and Western Christianity. The shattering of empires has a long and repetitive history.

Where only a few thousand died in the Bolshevik revolution possibly 15-million Soviets died of disease and starvation in the interventionist battles between 1918 and the withdrawal of the last foreign forces in 1922.[17] We hear of the millions who then died from famine in the decade of the

1930s in the wake of social disruptions caused by putting farms under collective or state ownership. But we are now alert to how intelligence services, furthering the policies of *managers-of-state*, expand or even create these images of *threatening-centers-of-capital* as terrorist states. The truth is that the citizens of the former Soviet Union were fiercely loyal to, and worked hard for, their revolution and one should be very skeptical of those figures. The real threat was the potential for success of this new economic system.

Russian pre-WWI industrial capacity, 3% that of America, was not replaced until 1928. But, once the people were educated and the political and industrial bases were laid, the successes came quickly. In the next 12 years the Soviets soared well past France, Japan, and Italy, matched Britain, and their industrial capacity was now 25% that of the United States.[18]

The Soviet Union's rapid development was matched by that of Germany. The plans of the *managers-of-state* are too well hidden to fully document but the similarities between the wars against these *emerging centers-of-capital* and previous such threats to *imperial centers* are high. Germany's second in command, Rudolf Hess, supposedly fled to England 43 days before Germany's attack on the Soviet Union.[a] His lifetime incarceration at Spandau prison, where he was denied the right to speak on any except the most mundane subjects, allows only a glimpse of the hopes of fascists in Germany and Britain for an alliance against the Soviet Union and a reallocation of the world's industries, resources, and markets among Western powers. The nations already overrun by Hitler were of Aryan descent and many countries of Europe had accepted Fascist governments during the recent Great Depression. So a restructured European Fascist alliance would have been easily organized if Britain had agreed.

Except that German sympathizers were automatically kept out of the British government both before and during the war, a defecting Hess would have been welcomed by fascist elements in Britain. There are no other logical reasons for his flight except to form an alliance against the rapidly developing Soviets. Hitler and Hess were taking a gamble on Britain accepting a realignment of power to avoid a long war and they lost.

There were elements in Britain amenable to such alliance plans but Germany's fascist violence, Britain's treaty commitments with countries invaded by Germany, the impossibility of restructuring the *social-control paradigms* of the masses of Britain in that short a time, and the almost certain eclipse of British economic, financial, and military power as Germany drew on a defeated Soviet Union's vast resources and sold the

---

[a] James Douglas-Hamilton, *Motive For a Mission: The Story Behind Rudolf Hess's Flight to Britain*, (New York: Paragon House, 1979). As it does not even mention the "Clivedon Set" of Britain who were supporters of Fascism, this book's analysis is far too soft. There is a serious school of thought on the pre-World War II worldwide alliance of fascists but that history is too well hidden and unsure for us to address

products manufactured from those resources on Britain's historic markets precluded any such alliance.

While the Germans felt for a political settlement in the West, their June 22, 1941 offensive against the Soviet Union, Operation Barbarossa, took the invading troops to the outskirts of Stalingrad and within sight of Moscow. In desperation, the Soviets moved their industrial machinery ahead of the invading army and rebuilt beyond the Ural Mountains. Industrial technology is not only the key to a wealthy economy, it is the key to modern warfare and the Soviets, who only 13 years earlier were a minor industrial power, produced far more weapons than Germany for the remainder of the war. By the beginning of 1945, "on the Byelorussian and Ukrainian fronts alone, Soviet superiority was both absolute and awesome, fivefold in manpower, fivefold in armor, over sevenfold in artillery and 17-times the German strength in the air."[19]

Essentially unrecorded in Western history is what the West owes the Soviets in that war. The estimation that 85% of Germany's firepower was expended against the Soviet Union alerts the serious researcher. Simple history and battlefield statistics tell the story well: Once the Germans were stopped, the massive 17-month battle for Stalingrad (liberated on February 2, 1943) ended with the death or capture of 1.5-million Germans, the death of 800,000 Soviets and wounding of hundreds of thousands more. That victory was followed by the greatest tank and artillery battle in history at Kursk and the immense battles at Kharkov and Orel; all of which the Soviets decisively won. The Soviet Union had been holding off the Germans for three years and had cleared the Germans from half the occupied area six months before the Allies landed at Normandy on June 6, 1944.

As the Allies fought inland the last year of the war, over two German soldiers out of every three were still on the Soviet front. In a replay of their 1944 offensive to take the pressure off the West's Normandy beachhead, the Soviets launched an all-out attack on January 11, 1945, to take the pressure off the West's Battle of the Bulge. The German counterattack collapsed five days later as they rushed troops to the Eastern front to stem that Soviet offensive. By the end of March, 6 weeks before the German surrender, there were seven German soldiers on the Eastern front for every one in the West and the Soviets would still reach Berlin first.[20]

World War II's Huge Costs for the Soviet Union

But a huge price was paid for that victory. The Soviets destroyed industries, railroads, and bridges as they were pushed east and the Germans destroyed what basic infrastructure the Soviets missed (oil wells, coal mines, dams, et al.) as they were forced back West. The Germans burned the cities and villages to the ground and hauled 7-million horses, 17-million cattle, 20-

million hogs, 27-million sheep and goats and 110-million poultry away to feed Germany.[21]

That the Soviet Union was scorched earth, there can be no doubt. The destruction was there for all to see and 25-million Soviets were eating sunflower seeds and living in holes in the ground. By comparison, the United States had only 12.3-million men and women under arms, lost 405,399, its homeland was untouched, and its industrial capacity had increased 50%.[22]

The creation of beliefs to control people are never-ending. The first figure for total Soviet citizens killed of 20.6-million was quickly upgraded to 27-million. But Stalin's response to Churchill's 1946 Iron Curtain speech in Fulton, Missouri, states the true losses at 7-million.

World War II was over and the Soviet Union was again reduced to less than 20% of the industrial capacity of the U.S. More important, social infrastructure is much more expensive to build than industrial capacity, and the Soviets had to remove all the rubble first.

In 1947, U.S. Secretary of State General George C. Marshall made a trip across Western Europe and Eastern Europe all the way to Moscow. Western Europe, damaged possibly 20% as much as Eastern Europe and Russia, was prostrate under capitalism's laissez-faire principles while the shattered Eastern Europeans and even more badly damaged Soviets with their community support structures were rapidly rebuilding. Marshall rushed back to Washington to report that obviously capitalism's security interests were at stake. His comments mirrored the concerns of all *managers-of-state*:

> "All the way back to Washington," [fellow diplomat] Bohlen wrote, "Marshall talked of the importance of finding some initiative to prevent the complete breakdown of Western Europe."... [In a speech to the nation, Marshall gave a bleak report.] We cannot ignore the factor of time. The recovery of Europe has been far slower than had been anticipated. Disintegrating forces are becoming evident. The patient is sinking while the doctors deliberate. So I believe that action cannot [a]wait compromise through exhaustion. New issues arise daily. Whatever action is possible to meet these pressing problems must be taken without delay.[23]

Those *managers-of-state* placed the Marshall Plan into effect in 1948 and, under those Friedrich List protection principles, Europe was rebuilt in about five years. The race for industrial and technological supremacy that had triggered the recent world war and many other wars was on again. The containment of the Soviet Union and the simultaneous suppression of the world's break for economic freedom was going to require an enormous amount of expensive arms and, as addressed above, the Korean War and the CIA's *Mighty Wurlitzer* provided the *social-control paradigm*—the belief the West was under imminent threat of attack from the East, a *strategy-of-*

tension—under which the increasingly tense citizens of the West would support the expensive arms race and violence that would be required.

There is nothing in capitalism's philosophy to give anything to anyone. Each person and each country are to succeed on their own in competition with all others and the fittest accumulate the wealth. The West has long been boasting that their welfare capitalism is superior to the Soviet Union's communism. Not only was that not true, they fail to mention that welfare capitalism only exists because the West needed a philosophy to counter the obvious superiority of a cooperative/sharing philosophy over that of raw capitalism's winner take all.

Thus the unwritten contract between labor and capital that organized labor would be well paid to fight capitalism's battle. Without the threat from the East, labor in the West would not have been given the high wages which provided the quality life they came to believe was normal and their right. As demonstrated by the steady loss in wages of American labor 1973 to 1998, as soon as capital was sure they would win this battle, they immediately started lowering labor's share of the wealth produced. All labor throughout Europe are watching their earnings decline and structural adjustments throughout the world are forcing the same race-to-the-bottom logic of lowering the pay of labor that competition requires.

Fictional Missile Gaps were *Strategies-of-Tension*

Professor George Kistiakowsky's impeccable credentials include a position as head of the explosives division, for the Manhattan Project that built the atomic bomb, professor of chemistry at Harvard University, and later science advisor to Presidents Eisenhower, Kennedy and Johnson. Professor Kistiakowsky had a rude awakening as he observed the workings of the "defense" planners from the inside.

> I attended all the National Security Council meetings, by order of the President. I began to realize that policy was being formed in a way which really was quite questionable. It was being formed by people who didn't really know the facts and didn't have time to learn them because of bureaucratic preoccupation.... But it took time for all this to sink in. And then I began to see all of the lies, such as the so-called missile gap. I knew there was no missile gap, because our U-2 reconnaissance flights over the Soviet Union could not find any missile deployment. This was 1958—after the U-2s began flying. We put a lot of effort into detecting possible deployment sites. And we could find only one, north of Moscow. This was really a test site. It wasn't really an operational site. Those first ICBMs were so huge that you couldn't hide them.[24]

With full knowledge that the Soviets had no missiles pointed at anyone, the *managers-of-state* requested that the CIA crank up their *Mighty Wurlitzer* and propagandize American citizens that the Soviets had them targeted with 50 intercontinental ballistic missiles (ICBMs).

The truth of the arms race was that the West led the Soviets by 5-to-10 years in the development of every super weapon and that the devastated Soviets, who desperately both wanted and needed peace, were encircled with immense firepower by many of the very nations that had invaded them in 1918 in an attempt to overthrow their government and who still loudly proclaimed they were evil and should be destroyed.

The Soviet Union had paid a huge price and was owed an enormous debt for saving the world from fascism. The *imperial-centers-of-capital* repaid that debt by encircling the Soviets with steel, embargoing them from technology and trade, and vilifying them throughout the world through the CIA's *Mighty Wurlitzer* and those of other Western intelligence services. The basic principles of world trade had not changed. Any rising center of capital may take over scarce resources and markets—that is the base of wealth and power of *established imperial-centers-of-capital.* The proof is that the West's military actually expanded since the Soviet Union collapsed.

Twelve years after that collapse, America alone was spending more for arms than the entire rest of the world and the most powerful of those nations are allied with America as *one imperial-center-of-capital.* The combined military power of the now *allied centers-of-capital* is truly immense and this 12th year after the Cold War ended (2003) military expenditures are set to rise by over 50% as, under the flag of the War on Terrorism, the struggle for control of crucial resources and markets continues.

The Massive Resources of the Soviet Union and the More Massive and Cheaper Resources of the West

Soviet successes under extremely harsh conditions were what was worrying Western *managers-of-state.* Covering one-sixth of the world's land surface, the Soviet Union had massive natural resources. However, its citizens lived primarily in Europe while its major natural resources were in Asia 3,000 miles away, and much of that under frozen tundra. To mine and process those resources, entire cities had to be built in a cold and hostile climate. Shipping those raw materials to Soviet industries in their West and supplies from those industries to those new cities in their Eastern tundra required construction of expensive roads and railroads. Transportation is a major part of production costs, the Soviets estimated their costs of production at 1.8-times those in America, and Americans and other Western nations obtain much of their resource needs from their even cheaper periphery of empire.

We discussed Britain's rich coal and iron ore deposits being only 15 miles apart and her cheap water transportation to anywhere in the world. Those largely unspoken-of advantages allowed Britain to produce more cheaply, sell more cheaply, and thus accumulate more capital and industrialize more quickly, than other nations. The West had the same advantage over the Soviet Union and that advantage continues to this day. Not only were the natural resources of America closer to population centers and cheaper to mine and process, their roads, railroads, and factories were already in place.

And the West has advantages far beyond that. Paying equally-productive developing world labor 20% of the wages of developed world labor denies buying power to the periphery of empire. This leaves the only market for resources and products in the developed world which effectively gives the West title to the richest resources all over the world.

Not only was the harvesting of Soviet resources, and thus the production of Soviet wealth, far more labor-intensive than in the West, the Soviets provided those resources and industrial technology to the periphery of their sphere of influence (Eastern Europe, China, Cuba, et al.) at far below world prices. Thus the Soviets denied themselves a large share of the wealth produced by their own labors. With adequate resources within their borders, the Soviets were taxing their center to build their periphery, exactly the opposite of Western empires.

Errors in Soviet Planning

Thirty percent of Soviet industrial capacity and an even greater share of Soviet infrastructure and social wealth were destroyed in WWII. As soon as Germany was defeated, the Soviets started rebuilding. By the 1980s Soviet industrial production was approaching that of the United States and pulled ahead in steel, oil, coal, and a few other industries. In only 70 years the Soviets had moved from the bottom among industrial nations to number two and they had accomplished this while fighting off the 4-year effort of 14 nations to overthrow her, under the massive losses of WWII, and while being forced to arm to offset the ring of steel being placed around her by the West. One can only wonder at the amenities of life the Soviet Union could have provided its citizens if it had been left in peace.

But a serious error was being made in Soviet planning. Some 77% of manufactured products were produced by only 1-or-2 huge factories for each consumer product.[25] If technologies were equal, these huge factories could initially produce consumer products more cheaply than many competing companies, each with separate production, publicity, and distribution networks.

But they could not keep up with ongoing technological developments. Retooling factories is expensive. When there is no competition, managers will not retool a huge factory, while market capitalism—with its virtually hundreds of initial producers—will typically shake out to three competing producers of roughly equal economic strength, each with several factories. The others disappear from the scene. But those three or more remaining competing producers innovate, develop, retool, produce, distribute, train repair people, and receive feedback from all elements of society for further innovation and retooling, and the cycle keeps repeating itself. Thus, in a competitive society, factories become ever more efficient.

Soviet industry did not have that technological innovation and retooling cycle. Without feedback from society, innovating, retooling—and thus producing and distributing better products—the Soviet civilian economy became moribund.

Containing the Soviet Union through forcing it to Waste its Industrial Production

There were far greater costs to the Soviet Union than their errors. The rubble of WWII had to be cleared away and homes, stores, and their complete economic infrastructure had to be rebuilt to the level of a modern nation. The Soviets had made the decision to sacrifice the present to build for the future.

But the arms race short-circuited those plans. We must remember British Prime Minister Churchill's warning that Britain and Western Europe could not rearm quickly without facing poverty and starvation. Britain and Western Europe were damaged possibly only 20% as bad as the Soviet Union and Eastern Europe. The result of offsetting the ring of steel being placed around the Soviet Union while simultaneously cleaning up the rubble, building homes (25-million were homeless), repairing the damaged infrastructure and then building new dams, highways, railroads, and industry was an economic nightmare.

"The estimate of a Soviet economist [is] that 51.4% of total Soviet industrial investment between 1950 and 1985 went into military production." A large share of the rest—roughly 43%—was going into building and rebuilding basic infrastructure (roads, railroads, steel mills, et al.) and providing industry and resources to the embattled periphery (China, Eastern Europe, Cuba, et al.), and a minuscule 5% was left for producing consumer durables.[26]

Any serious study of economic growth rates will conclude that the Soviet socialist system accumulated capital and industrialized far faster than any capitalist country except those essentially given capital and technology after WWII so as to contain fast expanding socialism. Before they collapsed in 1990, the Soviets were able to raise their technology to about 1982-83 U.S. levels.[27] But their expenditure of labor and resources toward rebuilding from the rubble of WWII, their building of expensive infrastructure, the necessity of turning their industry to producing arms to offset the West's determination to destroy them, and their transfer of a share of their production to the periphery, as well as errors in Soviet planning, denied them the opportunity to apply that technology to consumer production. The mining of resources and land transportation in the arctic tundra thousands of miles away from their population centers were simply too expensive to overcome those hurdles.

Though it ended up a close race militarily and technologically as the Soviets fought for survival, the enormously expensive arms race imposed by the very wealthy and undamaged United States precluded the development of a Soviet consumer economy and eventually bankrupted the severely damaged and impoverished Soviet Union just as the *managers-of-state* in the West planned.

Wasting the resources of the entire world building arms has been very profitable for corporate imperialists in a system that, as acknowledged by America's President Eisenhower, in the final analysis is paid for by the world's poor. Where building arms is highly profitable for capitalists, both in the actual production and in those arms being used to maintain control of others' resources, processing their own resources into arms is always an enormous loss to a socialist economy attempting to live on its own resources. Through the multiplier factor, fully 30% of American jobs were attributable to arms expenditures. Thus the waste of the arms race was a wealth distribution mechanism for the West even as it greatly reduced real wealth throughout the world.

Destabilizing Eastern Europe and the Soviet Union

Peter Gowan, senior lecturer in European politics at the University of North London, describes the neo-mercantilist policy towards the East which eventually shattered the Soviet Bloc:

> [I]n the closing decades of the Cold War, the Atlantic Alliance had combined a formidable economic blockade against Eastern Europe.... The West possessed two principal means of control. Through the IMF, it exerted political control over international finance and currency matters. Furthermore, it could restrict commercial access to Western markets through bilateral export policy, through the Coordinating Committee for Multilateral Export Controls (Cocom) on high technology, and through import duties—largely imposed by the European Community (EC)—on ECE goods.... It is scarcely an exaggeration, therefore, to say that following the upheaval of 1989 the West had the capacity to shape events in ECE to an extent comparable to that enjoyed by the Soviet government in the region after 1945. In field after field the ability of governments to deliver to their people depended on the intervening decisions of the G7 [the seven leading Western countries]. Employing this power, Western policy makers could shape the destiny of the region according to a very particular, and very political, agenda. The Western powers did not respond to the challenge of 1989 in a piecemeal fashion. Although the form and speed of the collapse took most policy makers by surprise, the G7 had, by the summer of 1989, established new machinery for handling the political transformation of Poland and Hungary and had worked out both the goals and the means of policy. Even before the region's first noncommunist government ... took power in Poland in September 1989, the

> G7 framework was in place.... Coercive diplomacy, not persuasion, became the tool by which the West established market economies in the East.[28]

Peter Gowan explains further how coercion was practiced by outside powers:

> The EC, the G7, and the IMF treated each country separately according to its domestic program, setting off a race among the governments of the region to achieve the closest relations with, and best terms from, the West.... The economic "liberalization" measures urged upon the new governments of ECE by Western agencies were bound to push these economies into serious recession, a situation only made worse by the disruption of regional economic links and the collapse of the Soviet Union. The result has been less a move to the market than a large-scale market destruction.... G7 experts were well aware that the drive for social system change would thoroughly destabilize ECE economies.[29]

The East was destabilized; those countries did not just collapse. The above destabilizations were the policy decisions of America's 1982 National Security Council Directive 54 (NSD-54) to destabilize all East European countries, except Yugoslavia, which throughout the Cold War was provided financial aid and some access to markets so as to wean it away from the Soviet Union. Yugoslavia prospered. They had a respectable standard of living, education and medical care were free, and each citizen was guaranteed a job and 30 days vacation with pay. This multi-ethnic melting pot was provided cheap transportation, cheap housing and inexpensive utilities. Such a wealthy socialist society could not be permitted.

Now it was Yugoslavia's Turn to be Destabilized

The opening guns of financial warfare for the destabilization of the relatively prosperous Yugoslavia were the IMF's 1980-84 demands for currency devaluation and an increase in the Yugoslavian Central Bank's discount rate. That currency devaluation immediately increased the debt; the interest rate hike slowed the Yugoslav economy. The drop in living standards created by those structural adjustments led to economic and political turmoil.

Then the 1984 U.S. National Security Council Directive 133 (NSD-133) titled "United States Policy towards Yugoslavia" and labeled "SECRET SENSITIVE," contained the marching orders for the final fragmentation of that nation: Further IMF-imposed structural adjustments denied the Yugoslav government the right to credit (money creation) from its own central bank, thus losing them the ability to fund crucial economic and social programs (industry and health care). Those structural adjustment policies included imposing a freeze on all transfer payments from the central governments to the outlying provinces.

The results were planned and predictable: A growth rate of 7.1% from 1966 to 1979 "plummeted to 2.8% in the 1980-87 period, plunging to zero in 1987-88 and to a minus 10.6% in 1990." Another currency devaluation (30%) accelerated the 140% inflation to 937% in 1992 and 1,134% in 1993, with GDP dropping 50% in four years. Imported commodities flooded in to further disrupt domestic production and drain Yugoslavia's hard currency reserves. It was calculated that, under those policies, 1.9-million workers—out of a total workforce of 2.7-million—were headed for unemployment.[30]

Simultaneous with the denial of Yugoslavia's right to fund her outlying regions were offers to those provinces for funds and trade if they declared their independence. German foreign minister Hans Dietrich Genscher was in almost daily contact with his Croatian counterpart, promoting independence. The 1990-91 U.S. "Foreign Operations Appropriations Bill" (an annual event funding destabilizations) demanded separate elections in each of the six Yugoslav provinces with State Department approval of their conduct and outcome and, again, all aid to go to independent republics and none to the central government. A total embargo imposed in 1991 was still in effect in June 1999 during the final breakup of Yugoslavia. Independence meant funding and trade for the provinces while continued federation with Yugoslavia meant continued embargoes and no funds.

A country that had been peaceful and relatively prosperous since WWII, with 30% of the marriages interethnic, erupted into civil war and, with continued overt and covert support from Germany and America, Macedonia, Slovenia, and Croatia were torn away from the Yugoslav federation. The Serbian populations of the seceding provinces, who had forgiven the Western Christians for the slaughter of one-third of the Serbian men during Hitler's holocaust and formed the multiethnic nation of Yugoslavia after WWII, were again facing second-class citizenship.

Now it was Bosnia-Herzegovina's Turn.

Western Christians allied with Muslims to give the Bosnia-Herzegovina secession the necessary majority voice. The November 1995 Dayton Accords, established under the threat of NATO intervention to suppress the ensuing struggle over who should govern, established a virtual colonial government which allowed the U.S. and the European Union to appoint a High Representative (HR) with full executive powers in civilian matters. A constitution for the Bosnian Federation was written at those peace talks by the U.S. State Department stipulating that the HR could overrule the government. That façade of democracy (the Parliamentary Assembly) simply rubber-stamped the decisions of the HR and his expatriate advisors. Those dictates (called "Accords") actually stipulated that, "the first governor of the Central Bank of Bosnia and Herzegovina is to be appointed by the IMF and 'shall not be a citizen of Bosnia and Herzegovina or a neighboring state.' " The elected president of the Serbian segment of Bosnia—who objected to forcibly selling off banks, water, energy, telecommunications, transportation, and metal industries, at firesale prices—was forcibly removed by NATO.[31] Of course, these dictates were all carried out under the flag of "democracy."

Then it was Kosovo's Turn

As Bosnia-Herzegovina was being digested by the NATO alliance, the foundation for the breaking away of Kosovo was being laid. Due to fear of secession, the autonomous status of Kosovo had been revoked by Yugoslavia as ethnic Albanians increased from 40% at the end of WWII to 80%. That political stalemate became violent when German and American intelligence armed the Kosovo Liberation Army (KLA). Before that arming and training of the KLA into a force of 30,000 by outside powers, the Kosovar rebellion had been a peaceful one similar to Gandhi's peaceful rebellion in India 50 years earlier. Armed by German intelligence for years, the KLA surfaced in 1997 and started assassinating Serbian police officers and ethnic Albanian collaborators. Yugoslavia sent in the army to suppress that externally armed insurrection. In February 1998, and a sure sign that America's CIA, Germany's BND, and the Military Professional Resources (MPRI, retired U.S. generals under Pentagon contract) were still orchestrating this destabilization, the Croatian General, Agim Ceku—who had been in command of artillery in the ethnic cleansing of Serbs from the Krajina region of Croatia—took over command of the KLA.[32]

In a replay of the Dayton Accords, an assembly was convened in Rambouillet, France, to essentially dictate the carving off of Kosovo. The prepared accords allowed for 50,000 NATO troops overseeing that autonomous republic: NATO was to be granted the use of airports, roads, rail, and ports free of any charges, NATO troops were not only not to be subject to Yugoslav law they were to have supremacy over Yugoslav police and authorities, they were to be given the right to inspect any part of not just Kosovo but Serbia itself, and the Kosovo economy was to be structurally adjusted as per the Bosnian-Herzegovenan economy described above. NATO gave Yugoslavia only two choices: sign the accords (dictates) or be bombed. Virtually every serious diplomat of good conscience agreed that these were articles of surrender that no sovereign nation could sign. In short, those accords were little more than a disguised declaration of war. The world, of course, heard only the prepared press releases of an intransigent Yugoslavia as, with the support of the majority of their citizens who patriotically believed what they were told about Serbian atrocities, NATO proceeded to bomb the regional Orthodox Christians back to the 19th-Century.[33]

The destabilization of Yugoslavia is a classic on how propaganda works in what are called "democracies" with "freedom of the press." Before the bombing, Yugoslavia had opposition radio stations, dissident publications, had several major political parties and each party had its own newspapers, radio stations, and TV stations. Milosevic had been elected three times, twice as president of Serbia and later as president of Yugoslavia. The Yugoslav president had a cabinet to discuss and decide policy and an elected coalition parliament which included four major political parties, more than any other country in Europe and they ranged fully from the left political spectrum to the right, that approved all decisions, and this governing process had even been shown occasionally on Western TV.

During the Western orchestrated coup that overthrew Milosevic, armed units seized all major TV, Radio, and newspaper outlets. When the dust settled, there remained essentially only one media. Just as in the West, all papers published the same stories and all were written the same. Just as Americans can see the same news with the same slant on all TV channels, Serbs now found the same news with the same slant on all their TV channels. A nation which once had a wide choice of views suddenly had only one view, that of the West.

On news beamed into Yugoslavia and to the citizens of the West, Milosevic was labeled a dictator in almost every news report, while Croatian descendants of Hitler's Ustase[a]—who ethnically cleansed Jews, Gypsies, and Serbs during WWII (the Three-Thirds Doctrine: one-third of the Serbs to be deported, one-third forced to become Catholics, and one-third to be annihilated), who had just imposed a one-party press, and who had just ethnically cleansed several hundred thousand Serbs from Croatia and Bosnia—were simultaneously labeled democratic. While Western puppets purge their territory of ethnic minorities even as the West is accusing Serbia of these atrocities, that besieged nation is the home to 26 ethnic groups, 1-million are refugees ethnically cleansed from former provinces of Yugoslavia, including 350,000 Serbs and others who fled Kosovo after NATO's takeover of that province.[34]

There will be an occasional mild analysis of this propaganda process after the fact but, as every social system protects itself and its own, even those cautious reflections will not become part of assigned, well-read history. Thus it will remain largely unknown to most that the Kosovo rebellion was a civil war covertly organized and supported by the same governments militarily imposing the Rambouillet Accords. Some reality was expressed in a German documentary:

> "On Feb. 8, the major German television network ARD broadcast a special on the war entitled "It Began with a Lie." This showed that the charges of

---

[a] The Romanian death squads under Hitler's occupation were called The Iron Guard. In Latvia they were called Vanagas.

> mass murder, genocide and organized "ethnic cleansing" made against Belgrade were inventions of the U.S., German and other governments.[35]

The Serbs knew the KLA had been armed and coached by U.S. and German intelligence to carve Kosovo off from Yugoslavia. They refused to sign the capitulation Rambouillet Accords, and—when the bombing began with the purpose of forcing Yugoslavians to sign away their sovereignty—was accused to have reacted by expelling the Albanian Kosovo population.[a]

The excuse for bombing Yugoslavia was the ethnic cleansing and genocide of Kosovar Albanians from Kosovo. The "free" press should be called to account for not alerting the public to this fiction and that it was NATO members acting and Yugoslavia reacting just as any student of foreign policy would expect. Yugoslavia was not threatening anyone outside its borders, the Kosovar Albanians were not threatened with violence before the external orchestration of the KLA for a civil war (over 1,100 attacks on Serb police and Kosovar Albanian collaborationists, many fatal), and the holocaust within their borders was a reaction to this destabilization and forthcoming loss of a province Serbians consider the cradle of their civilization. Houses were destroyed as the KLA were rooted out from where they were firing on Serb soldiers but no ethnic cleansing occurred until after NATO took over Kosovo and then it was an ethnic cleansing of Serbs.

That will make no difference. Knowing the bombing was Western pressure that Serbs accept the loss of the heart of their culture, some of the atrocities required to demonize the Serbs occurred and these will be kept in the world news through war crimes trials even as the far greater violence against the Serbs (the total shattering of their country with the deaths of tens of thousands) disappears from all except the most deeply researched history.

Researchers should note that original propaganda figures of over 100 massacres with 100,000 to 500,000 Albanian men missing and thought to be slaughtered were reduced to a still sensationalized 10,000 expected to be found in mass graves when NATO first entered Kosovo. Inspection of the alleged 30 mass gravesites by an FBI team turned up 200 bodies and dropped the Kosovar externally orchestrated civil war body count to 2,108 killed by all participants—the Serbs, the KLA, *local grudge settlements*, and

---

[a] The KLA engineered the ethnic Albanian exodus from Kosovo under the coaching of Western Intelligence services who were carefully writing history to justify the destruction of Yugoslavia. Only an alert researcher on the ground in Kosovo can research the truth. Jared Israel, "Why Albanians Fled During the NATO Bombing: The Truth About What Happened," Interview with Cedda Pralinchevich, http://emperors-clothes.com/interviews/keys.htm, will provide insights. Cedda Pralinchevich is very persuasive that Albanians were fleeing upon orders of their leaders and in their culture and not obeying was not an option. History will prove the claims of NATO of preserving Kosovo as a Serbian province was only a cover story for it being carved from that nation.

NATO bombs. Emilio Perez Pujol, the head of the Spanish Forensic team conducting the investigation, said not one mass grave was found.[36]

No mass graves in Kosovo and this rather low body count when an entire nation was being militarily fragmented by covertly funded and orchestrated opposition forces and under direct attack by those same foreign military forces as well as the 1-million refugees within Serbia from the destabilization and fragmentation of Yugoslavia testifies to a successful NATO propaganda blitz (that *Mighty Wurlitzer* again) that was never addressed in depth by the media of record. When to the above disinformation we add the Pentagon wordsmiths' claim of the destruction of one-third of the Serbian military (122 tanks, 454 artillery pieces, and 222 armored personnel carriers) and the postwar investigation by General Wesley Clark, the commander of that war, that only 14 tanks, 20 artillery pieces, and 18 armored personnel carriers" were destroyed, the outline of a planned propaganda campaign becomes clear.[37]

Quite simply, the American/NATO assault on Serbia/Kosovo destroyed about 50 of Serbia's major weapons of war and very few soldiers while killing more civilians than Serbia and creating massive destruction of the obvious real target, Serbia's economic infrastructure. Under the ultimate oxymoron of a "humanitarian war," which depicted the West as saviors as they bombed 15 essentially defenseless cities around the clock for 78 days, the successfully destroyed real targets of precision bombing were: heating plants for entire cities, 344 schools, 33 clinics and hospitals, power plants, food processing plants, pharmaceutical plants, bus and train depots, electrical grids, bridges, factories, power stations, trains, airports, water supply systems, warehouses, oil refineries, fuel storage, chemical factories, museums, and TV and radio stations. Among the commercial buildings destroyed were twin tower skyscrapers eerily reminiscent of the World Trade Center destroyed in the 9/11/2001 terrorist attack on America.

After the destruction of Yugoslavia was carried out under the false flag of oppression and genocide in Kosovo, 350,000 Serbs, Gypsies, Slavic Muslims, Croations, Jews, Turks and anti-fascist Ethnic Albanians were driven out of Kosovo. After defeating the defending Serbian army, the Kosovo occupation army claims not to have been able to prevent this ethnic cleansing by the very forces they were financing, arming, and coaching.

Powerbrokers within NATO are concerned with Yugoslavia only as a small battle within one or more of a centuries-long struggle:

(1) The splitting of the Roman Empire into Eastern Orthodox Christianity and Western Christianity starting in the 4th-Century. This created the Christian East and Christian West that are fighting over territory on the boundaries between those religions yet today, and it is obvious that, without the support of NATO nations, Yugoslavia's Western Christians

would not have had the political strength to shatter that once peaceful federation.

(2) The 1,300-year struggle between both Eastern and Western Christians and Muslims, a battle between the Muslim East and the same Christian West. The current alliance of the West with Balkan Muslims is only a temporary strategic decision of *managers-of-state*.

(3) The 70-year battle between communism and capitalism, the Cold War. Most, but not all, communists were Eastern Orthodox and most, but not all, capitalists were Western Christian. This is the historic in-step march of religion and governments as empires expand and contract.

(4) And then, the centuries of battles over who will control world trade and thus who will claim title to wealth. This battle over the world's wealth is between the fragmented periphery of empire and the same allied, coordinated, and powerful West.

That last struggle, *managers-of-state* utilizing religious and political loyalties to control the *wealth-producing-process*, is the one that counts. At any one moment, what is motivating any one person's vision of these historic events depends upon that person's position and loyalties within those four struggles. For those deeply committed to religion, or moderately religious and not interested in politics, which covers most of the masses, religious loyalties will determine their opinions. Those committed politically will be on one side or the other of the battle between capitalism and any form of cooperative society. If one is a corporate strategist, a *Manager-of-State*, or aware that one's livelihood is deeply affected—either positively or negatively—by the inequalities of trade, then some subdivision of the battle over world trade will be primary in their considerations.

Clinton's Energy Secretary Bill Richardson spelled out America's Balkan policy a few months prior to the 1999 bombing of Yugoslavia:

> This is about America's energy security.... It's also about preventing strategic inroads by those who don't share our values. We're trying to move these newly independent countries toward the west.... We would like to see them reliant on western commercial and political interests rather than going another way. We've made a substantial political investment in the Caspian, and it's very important to us that both the pipeline map and the politics come out right.[38]

The *policies-of-state* here are obvious, isolating Russia politically, reducing its control over the oil and gas deposits in the Caspian basin, and piping those hydrocarbons to Europe. Germany reached an agreement with Croatia (announced in the UN) for a pipeline through its territory and—even as the bombs were falling on Yugoslavia—officials of Georgia, Ukraine, Uzbekistan, Azerbaijan, and Moldova were in Washington, DC, signing a regional alliance (GUUAM) that included discussions of oil pipeline export routes to the West. There was also high interest in the rich minerals of Kosovo (the Trepca mining/manufacturing complex, which was too valuable to bomb and now arbitrarily turned over to Albanian Kosovars), the suspected oil and gas deposits within the Dinarides Thrust, and other mineral wealth of Yugoslavia (coal, bauxite) planned for diversion to the west, which will deprive Eastern Orthodox Christians of that wealth, will weaken that tiny enclave of socialism while simultaneously increasing the wealth of Western Europe.[39]

The foundation of all property rights is military power. While the Trepca mines rich in gold, lead, zinc, cadmium, silver, and coal were considered the most valuable piece of real estate in the Balkans (Soros tried to own them), note that the world's great oil bearing sands go from the Middle East, through the Caspian Basin, and end at Romania. The straightest route to Europe for that oil is through Yugoslavia.

Though the human cost is greater today, the destruction of the economic infrastructure of Yugoslavia and demonstration in Iraq of the ability to decapitate any leadership and destroy an entire army from a safe distance is a replay of the raiding parties of the cities in the Middle Ages controlling the countryside to maintain its dependency upon the city.

That empires manufacture excuses to gain the support of the people to destroy a potential rival is documented history.[40] One need only analyze how far worse human slaughters failed to affect strategic decisions to convince one that the death of 2,108 Kosovars (both Albanian and Serb Kosovars and killed by the Serb military, the Kosovo Liberation Army, and by Western bombs) in Kosovo's NATO designed and supported civil war was not the reason for NATO's bombing of Yugoslavia. (Note how that statement answers its own question.) Over 1-million children and weaker old people have died in Iraq due to American-led sanctions and a few hundred thousand in the two American-led Gulf Wars.[41] One-third of the East Timorese (200,000) have died in the Indonesian suppression of their independence (utilizing American-supplied weapons). Estimated number killed in five years of ethnic cleansing in Rwanda, 500.000. Fifty thousand have perished in the 20-year conflict between Ethiopia and Eritrea (a province of Ethiopia, the independence of which was covertly supported by America during the Cold War). Two million have perished in the 16-year struggle in neighboring Sudan. The estimated number killed in Russia's ongoing Chechnya suppression, 80,000. And thousands were killed when Croatia —with the backing of the United States and Germany—"ethnically-cleansed" her territory of over 500,000 Serbs when breaking from Yugoslavia.[42]

Note how, after the fragmentation of Yugoslavia, the Eastern Orthodox Serbs are surrounded by the Western Christian nations of Romania, Bulgaria, Hungary, Slovenia and Croatia, all of which are being brought within NATO. One must remember that the West had Yugoslavia embargoed throughout the decade of the 1990s as she was being destabilized and the Serbs simply refused to collapse. Until its destabilization, and despite the embargo, Yugoslavia was quite prosperous relative to the surrounding nations before the total shattering of her industry by NATO bombs and her subsequent loss of access to resources.

Just as Cuba is still under economic and financial assault to prevent the world from observing the higher standard of living obtained by her citizens when free of domination by Western capital, Eastern Europe could not be totally restructured along Western political and economic lines so long as Yugoslavia remained intact with her citizens well cared for and her industry underselling Western products throughout Eastern Europe. Nor could NATO permit an opposing ideology with an intact military west of the planned new line of defense, Romania, Bulgaria, and Greece. It is for this reason that the Serbian economic infrastructure was pulverized by NATO bombs and missiles. Once the richest, Serbia is now expected to become one of the poorest nations in Eastern Europe, her citizens cannot be properly cared for, she cannot arise as an example for other dependent countries for generations, and she cannot afford to maintain a powerful military.

If Western capital dominates the economies and controls the governments of the fragmented former Yugoslavia, if oil pipelines from the Caspian oil basin (according to the U.S. Energy Information Association, possibly nine-times more oil reserves than in the U.S.) and the Middle East are built across Turkey and the former Yugoslavia to reach Europe, if Montenegro also breaks away, if the natural resources of the Balkans comfort Western consumers, and if that once relatively prosperous region becomes a market for Western industries, we will be observing the success of the *Grand Strategy* of the breakup and impoverishment of Yugoslavia by international capital.

As products and services produced under the management of labor and direct financing of industry by the central bank could be sold or contracted much cheaper than Western products (there was not the massive unearned monopoly profits as in a subtly-monopolized capitalist economy, see below), without the fragmentation and embargo of Yugoslavia it is the Yugoslavs who would have dominated those markets. It is they who would have become wealthy, and, the most dangerous of all, the rest of Eastern Europe had a similar industry/labor history, they and the entire world would have observed the Yugoslav success under their alternative form of government and labor/management relations, and many would establish a similar socialist market economy.

Thus, in final analysis, the *managers-of-state* in the West understood well that protection of the markets of Eastern Europe for Western industry and emerging subtle monopoly Eastern European industry, and the very survival of Western neo-liberal economic philosophy required the destabilization of Yugoslavia, severe crippling of their industrial infrastructure, and that of any other nations that dared maintain their independence—Cuba for example.

A full accounting of the profits from those Eastern markets as well as the multiplier factor as the money from locally employed labor circulates within the economies of Western nations will show that, to the winners, the breakup of Yugoslavia was one of the most profitable combinations of economic, financial, covert, and overt warfare in history. It is nothing less than Germany's 100-year dream of gaining control of Eastern and Central Europe to obtain their resources and markets for the 1000-year Reich. The only difference is that the Western imperial nations had given up on battling between themselves over the world's resources, have allied together to maintain control of the wealth-producing process, and their East European Cousins are joining that alliance.

In September, 2000—the very month the hardcover edition of this book came out with the above revelations—that American money was covertly financing elections in both Serbia and Montenegro became common knowledge and the U.S. Congress openly authorized $10-million to Serbs and Montenegrins economically and politically breaking ranks with their government and thus were prime prospects as puppets to run that part of the world. This standard covert policy of the Cold War was secret and thus unknown to citizens of the Western imperial nations. But, where previously it was all covert, ever since the collapse of the Soviet Union, and with the exception of China and a few others, the U.S. has been both covertly and overtly financing elections of emerging nations throughout the world.

The final destabilization of Yugoslavia provides a textbook example of what has been standard covert practice destabilizing functional democratic governments worldwide throughout the Cold War that were not accepting control from the imperial center:

(1) A ring of radio stations were established around Serbia beaming in propaganda;

(2) suitcases full of American and German cash supporting opposing newspapers, news agencies, broadcasters, political parties, think-tanks, student groups, "human rights" organizations, and trade unions were passed out;

(3) opposition forces were given access to satellite communications while Yugoslav loyalists were denied access;[a]

---

[a] Los Angeles Times, September 26, 2000; *New York Times*, September 20, 2000; Senator Joseph Biden's Senate Hearings on Serbia, July 29, 1999; Serbian Democratization Act, HR1064, September 5, 2000; sourced on various webpages at http://emperors-clothes.com. We have barely opened the door on the all-out financial, economic, covert, and overt warfare destabilization of Yugoslavia. The definitive books have not yet been written on this hidden history. We suggest early readers to study the website http://emperors-clothes.com and later readers watch for books and articles by Michel Chossudovsky, Jared Israel, Peter Gowan, Greg Palast, Michael Parenti, Noam Chomsky, and authors in Eastern Europe, Yugoslavia and Russia.

(4) and in the final push mobs were armed, coached, and financed to take over the media. The Serbs no longer controlled any major media within their own country.

All who follow how overthrows of governments were accomplished all over the world by the imperial nations during the Cold War knew that the leaders of the mob which burned the Yugoslav parliament and other centers of power of the Milosevic government were coached, financed, and even armed by German and American intelligence.[a]

In any of the nations allied against Yugoslavia, any opposition political group would be arrested if they were funded by outside powers trying to overthrow the government. Yet, even as they were being labeled as dictators, the Yugoslav government was not even arresting those that were openly funded by the very outside powers overthrowing them even though how this money was pouring in and funding the opposition was discussed over the Yugoslav national news.

Even as Western media parroted Western intelligence service wordsmiths as Yugoslavia being a "dictatorship," Canadian observers reported the election as open as any election in Canada, with no police visible, and opposition literature widely distributed. When a nation is targeted for destabilization, or there is need to suppress a tendency for independence in countries already under control, the National Endowment for Democracy (NED), George Soros' *destabilization foundations* (such as the Open Society Institute), and others fund opposition groups (such as the: Center for International Private Enterprise, Humanitarian Law Center, Center for Democracy Foundation, Belgrade Center for Human Rights, European Movement of Serbia, G-17 economists, Center for Anti-War Action and Media, think-tanks, student groups, and many others), all claiming to be private groups but they and many more are actually funded by the American Congress through the NED, provides the crucial service of funding puppet media and politicians.[b] This covert funding of opposition

---

[a] Six months after this was written, Milosevic's trial started and this was his first defense. His continued defense outlined the entire process of the West's destabilization of Yugoslavia far more thorough than we have outlined it here. A lady spectator who came for the purpose of seeing Milosevic convicted said, "We have been deceived." As that deception will not leak out through the media or into the history books for the reasons outlined in Chapter 6, sincere researchers will have to study Milosevic's defense to write honest history.

[b] Heather Cottin, "Imperial Wizard: Soros is not just doling out cash—he's fleecing entire countries" *CovertAction Quarterly* (Fall 2002, pp. 1-6). In "Regime Change: A Look at Washington's Methods and Degrees of Success in Dislodging Foreign Leaders," *The Christian Science Monitor*, January 27, 2003, Peter Ford outlines the 50 years of America destabilizing other governments we are addressing, including the demonization of progressive leaders like Milosevic and how George Soros' *destabilization foundations* work. When knowledge of American covert funding of other nations' elections surfaced, the U.S. Congress established the National Endowment for Democracy (NED) in 1983 to fund openly a part of what the CIA had been funding covertly (*Washington Post*, September 21 and 22, 1991 and William

forces through NED and other means is standard practice worldwide. In short, Western powers were practicing total control of governments and media and military suppression of dissent, the very accusations of dictatorship they level at every country not safely under their imperial umbrella.

Before they had even taken office, Serbian opposition leaders met in Bulgaria with the IMF, the World Bank, and the leaders of NATO countries to finalize the fine points on the takeover of Yugoslavia.[43] This included structural adjustment abandonment of protection of citizens imposed upon most nations on the periphery of empire and will almost certainly include the takeover of their economy by the German mark and eventually the Euro. Once the various former Yugoslav provinces use the German mark or the Euro as their currency (as all but Serbia now do including Kosovo and Montenegro), Serbians can no longer create their own money and their funding of essential industries and services will be severely curbed.

Where the Western-imposed new leaders of Croatia, Slovenia, and other regions were direct descendents of Hitler's Ustase death squads with every intention of making second class citizens of their Eastern Orthodox neighbors, the new leaders being installed in Serbia have no illusions as to the hard future the West will be imposing upon them. After all, poverty is many times higher in the collapsed East and the former Soviet Union than it was under Communism. Even the Ukraine, the breadbasket and industrial heartland of the East—which dutifully followed all the prescriptions of the IMF, the World Bank, and NATO—is prostrate and essentially begging the West for food. Of course, these leaders are aware that Western promoted structural adjustment prescriptions created that poverty but they are equally aware that they have been left with no other choices.

President Milosevic is being tried in The Hague as a war criminal. The winners write history and—as the allied nations named the judges and prosecutors and financed it all—the current International War Crimes Tribunal at the Hague was designed, established, and funded specifically to write history with the former leaders of Yugoslavia as the war criminals. The judges and prosecutors were handpicked by NATO, primarily the U.S., and their focus was preordained. The same powers which directly orchestrated the destabilization and destruction of the peaceful and relatively prosperous Yugoslavia are prosecuting their targets as war criminals.[44]

The *managers-of-state* of the now allied *imperial-centers-of-capital* know well their power, use it ruthlessly, and leave weak countries no alternative. Once the powerful Soviet Union was destabilized, virtually every country in the

---

Blum, *Rogue State: A Guide to the World's Only Super Power* (Monroe, ME: Common Courage Press, 2000), Chapter 19.

world was at the mercy of the well organized, and allied, *imperial-centers-of-capital.*

The guarantees of all Yugoslav workers for jobs, free health care and education, pensions, paid maternity leave and vacations, low-cost recreation, and cheap food and rent was replaced in the breakaway provinces with 20% unemployment and a lowered average standard of living. Analyzing the sharply lowered living standards of the dozen Eastern European countries religiously and culturally tied to the West and slated to be allies, provides a clue to the bleak future of countries not religiously and culturally tied to the West and not viewed as natural allies.[a] The very word "slave" is derived from what are now the Eastern Orthodox Slavic people of Eastern Europe (check a major dictionary).

The fate of the highly efficient VSZ steel complex in Slovakia provides another glimpse. With the breakup of Czechoslovakia, the collapse of all Eastern European countries, and the imposition of IMF/World Bank structural adjustments, the local markets for VSZ steel disappeared (markets in the West were protected from VSZ's low priced, high quality, steel), the once-booming steel complex ran out of money, and under IMF/World Bank rules they could not be financed by the Slovakian central bank. This prostrate industrial jewel was picked up by America's U.S. Steel for the bargain basement price of $450-million and now provides 25% of their steel making capacity. Slovak steel workers are paid roughly $2 an hour against U.S. Steel workers pay in America of $35 to $45 an hour.[45] High quality Slovakian steel will be sold on the world steel market, those mills will operate at full capacity, any overcapacity will be alleviated through lowered production in America, West Europe, and Japan and the huge profits generated in the Slovakian mills will disappear into the accounting books of U.S. Steel. The labor of both Slovakia and America will take a loss and all gains will go to the owners of U.S. Steel. This same scenario will play out in other industries.

Like the underpaid developing world, Eastern Europe will gain only a little because their pay is too low to provide adequate buying power, labor in the developed world will eventually lose buying power as their jobs are taken by underpaid Eastern European workers, Japanese and other steel producers will have to lower steel and labor prices or lose market share. This will be the well-understood cyclical crisis of over production of capitalism compounded by the abandonment of economies once seen as crucial to protect against fast expanding socialism and further compounded

---

[a] Russia fears the Muslims on her Eastern borders. After all, it is they who pushed Eastern Orthodox Christianity out of their birthplace around Constantinople and it is they, far more so than Western Christianity, which has been their primary enemy. We must leave open the possibility that Russia and other Eastern Orthodox countries may join the alliance of industrialized nations against the impoverished world. President Vladimir Putin is showing signs that he is amenable to such an alliance.

by the melding of high-paid capitalist economies with low-paid former socialist economies.

Economic statistics showing a steadily advancing world economy can only be through ignoring the shrinking of 40% of the world economy.[46] The standard of living of all Eastern Europe is lower than 15 years ago. The collapse of currencies, buying power, and industries in Mexico, Southeast Asia, parts of Latin America, and the former Soviet Union meant their citizens were impoverished as their resources and production of their labor were purchased by the imperial centers well below the previous norm. Low-priced oil contributes to maintaining healthy economies for the imperial centers. Thus a lowering of resources prices from the periphery of empire will, so long as the markets of the imperial center can be protected, be a boon to those economies even though the periphery may be devastated.

Protecting the markets of the imperial centers may be relatively easy in the short run as the periphery collapses but will be tough in the long run. Underpaid labor on the periphery will not be able to buy their own production while the products produced with that underpaid labor and lower-valued capital will be able to offer consumer products to the imperial center at a price lower than producers in the wealthy world. This will be tempered by capital of the imperial center purchasing much of the industrial capital of the periphery at bargain prices but, as outlined with the Slovakian VSZ steel mill above, this melding of cheap-cost industries with high-cost industries only means it takes a little longer for the cycle of lost buying power and collapsing values to work its way through the economy. And even that extended time span will collapse if stock market values in the imperial centers collapse and destroy buying power and consumer confidence.

Making a deal with the Corrupt of Russia

The majority of the Russian people wanted change, but only slowly and carefully. They were not so foolish as to throw away their livelihood and the natural wealth of their nation. But Russian powerbrokers were given the opportunity to immediately own the vast natural wealth of that nation. Fifty percent of Russia's GDP came under the control of what became known as the "Russian Mafia." These thieves sent the money out of Russia as fast as it came into their hands. Thousands of mansions were purchased with this money in Spain, France, Cyprus, Austria, and many other countries and purchasers of each of these homes had many times that value stashed in overseas bank accounts. Thus, by the estimates of Fidel Castro, 200-billion to $500-billion fled Russia in the decade of the 1990s.[47]

When the Soviet borders crumbled, subversive funds flowed in (much of them from the National Endowment for Democracy, NED and George Soros, and other, *destabilization foundations*), political allies were organized, those heavily-funded politicians won enough control to pass the necessary laws, corrupt oligarchs gained title to valuable properties by various subterfuges, predatory capital came across the border to buy up resources at a fraction of its value, and massive consumer products produced in the West were sold to Soviet citizens to soak up and return to the Western *imperial-centers-of-capital* even the small amount of money that was created within that defeated nation.

Western *managers-of-state* made the same alliance with powerbrokers of the defeated former Soviet Union as they have with corrupt leaders throughout the former colonial world. The wealth and power of those corrupt leaders are protected so long as the West has access to their nation's resources at a fraction of its value and so long as there is access to their markets for the wealthy world's manufactured goods. Economic shock therapy in the former Soviet Union was an attempt to compress the 70-years of America's age of the robber barons into 10 years.[48]

Unless Russia allies with the West for protection against the Muslims to her East, it is unlikely those aspirations of the West will hold as they are applied to Russia, Belarus, and Ukraine. To build a wealthy economy those countries will eventually have to limit access to both their resource and consumer markets. When that happens, Western money will be withdrawn and those countries will have to rebuild without access to finance capital, technology, or markets. But the corrupt elite of some of the remaining 12 provinces of the shattered former Soviet Union will accept being paid off and a part of their resources, primarily oil and timber, will continue to flow to the West. The East will be weaker and the West will be stronger and this, of course, is what the battles are all about. [a] The math is quite simple: as per Chapter 1, Western traders and the corrupt of those provinces share the difference between the market price in the West and the pennies per hour paid labor in those collapsed provinces to harvest, mine, and ship those resources.

On an evening news show, Harvard economist Jeffrey Sachs, who was in charge of the U.S. economic team coaching the Soviets in their shock therapy economic collapse said, "the problem with the former Soviets is they do not yet have enough free enterprise." Having just cut economic arteries in the former Soviets with abandon, this same economist, in a later statement, had deep concerns over the "fragility of the world economic system" and expressed fears about U.S. efforts to penetrate the Japanese market which he describes as "reckless."

Simultaneously advocating opposite policies for the collapsed East as under which the booming West operates their economies indicates the

---

[a] If the struggle between Christians and Muslims becomes more intense, there is the possibility that Russia itself will be included in the trading alliance. How much of the wealth-producing process is shared with Eastern Orthodox Christians depends upon how badly they are needed as allies and how willing they are to accept being less than an equal partner.

economic health of the Soviets was of no concern. Sachs was in charge of the Harvard Institute for International Development that oversaw Russia's destabilization. We do not know if there is a connection between the CIA hiring economists during the middle and late 1980s and the Soviet collapse and we do not know if that institute was one established by the CIA as addressed above. But consider these points:

(1) The wholesale shutdown of Soviet industry was done following the advice of that institute.

(2) These same economists would surely not offer the same advice to an allied nation, as the comment on opening Japan's markets demonstrates.

(3) Any student of mercantilism would have recognized these suggestions would destroy Russia's industry and commerce and create a dependency.

(4) Any economist could analyze that there was virtually nothing anywhere to replace the industry that was being defunded and shut down except imports from the West.

(5) And we know that imposing beliefs to protect an imperial nation's "national interest" (the way Adam Smith free trade was imposed upon the world) is an oft-used tactic of *managers-of-state* of already developed nations.

So, how else can the guided collapse of the Soviet Union be interpreted? Any nation which tried such a thoughtless plan would revert to developing world status with its wealth essentially confiscated by intact *imperial-centers-of-capital.* As would be expected, the Soviet collapse rapidly worsened as industries were shut down. The Russians figured that out after it was too late and those advisors were expelled from Russia.[49]

When the Soviets collapsed in 1990 imports rose to an unsustainable officially-acknowledged 39% of Russian consumer products as imported in 1996 and climbed to an official 50% (and an estimated 60%) by 1998 with no compensating manufactured exports.

Documentaries showing both impoverished Russian soldiers begging for food and other soldiers unloading cases of food with American labels on them unwittingly expose the cause of Russia's current impoverishment. The second most powerful country in the world, totally self sufficient—except for bananas, coffee and coconuts—is quickly impoverished through massive consumer imports. A country's economic multiplier is its economic health and Russia's economic multiplier collapsed when its operating currency was spent on importing 50% of its consumer needs. There simply was too little money left in Russia to run their economy.

Meanwhile, 30% of America's consumer products are imported against large compensating manufactured exports, and still many economists, including the "Harvard boys" mentioned above, are concerned. Couple that impoverishing 50-to-60% consumer product import statistic with the fact that Russia has a $35-billion per year trade surplus while its industrial production has fallen 80% and capital investment nearly 90%, this touted

Russian success is really an enormous success for the West's *Grand Strategy* of destabilization of its feared enemy. These statistics tell us that Russia's massive natural resources are being turned to the West to produce consumer needs for Western citizens and a small share of those manufactured products are returned to Russia to pay for those resources.[50] Massive natural resources exported to pay for a small amount of manufactured wealth—this is an exact replay of centuries ago when raiders from the cities of Europe controlled the resources of the countryside, when the science of laying claim to others' wealth through inequalities of trade began (Chapter 2).

The immense sums then loaned to Russia and the former provinces of the former Soviet Union can be repaid only through massive sales of resources and fire-sale prices dictate many years of a depressed economy for those beleaguered souls.

Before their collapse, 1-Ruble equaled $1 in value and would buy more than $1 would within the Soviet Union. At that time, 1-ruble would buy breakfast, lunch, and dinner with change left over. After the collapse, it required 6,000 rubles to buy $1. The Russians traded those old rubles for new ones at the rate of 1,000-to-1 which brought the exchange rate down to six of the new rubles for $1. Then the value of that new ruble fell by two-thirds. Most Russian savings were wiped out in the first currency collapse and the second collapse took two-thirds of what was left.[51] One of the old rubles now would not buy a cup of tea.

A healthy economy requires faith in a nation's currency. Without trust in a nation's banks, the money will flee which is exactly what it did in Russia. Worse yet, once a population has lost their money they thought safely stored in the bank, trust in a nation's banking system cannot be restored for at least 1-to-2 generations. Loss in faith in banks means efficient capitalism cannot be established in Russia for a very long time. This is the outline of a very successful periphery destabilization policy for *imperial-centers-of-capital.*

This has all the marks of a planned destabilization. Jeffrey Sachs knew that Russian citizens had massive savings in the bank. In any other society this would be considered a big plus. But Sachs referred to it as that "pesky overhang." Those private funds would have been a natural to purchase shares in Russian Industry. But the goal was to transfer that social wealth to Russian oligarchs; the rights and well-being of the masses were to be ignored. To eliminate that "pesky overhang" it was necessary to collapse Soviet industries and flood the markets with imported products. That, and the resulting inflation addressed above, stripped Russian citizens of their "pesky" savings.[52]

The First Destabilization of Afghanistan was aimed at the Soviet Union

The CIA's largest covert operation was 1985 National Security Council Directive 166 ordering the destabilization of Afghanistan. However, that directive was only a massive expansion of what the CIA had already been doing since 1980 under a finding signed by President Carter on July 3, 1979, five months before the Soviet forces were invited into Afghanistan to suppress that destabilization. The CIA, working behind the scenes through Pakistani intelligence, provided massive arms (eventually reaching 65,000 tons a year) and training to Afghanistan's Mujahideen and 40,000 Muslim zealots recruited from over 40 countries. All support seemed to be coming from Pakistan and most Muslims would have been unaware that their terrorist operation against Afghanistan and the Soviet Union was a CIA designed, funded, and coordinated operation.

Afghanistan was not the primary target. The goal was to destabilize the six Eastern Muslim provinces of the Soviet Union both by smuggling in subversive propaganda (fraudulent books on Soviet atrocities against Muslim people) and sabotage teams (focused on assassinating Soviet officers and destroying factories and supply depots). The Mujahideen rebels were based safely in Pakistan from which as many as 11 teams at a time would infiltrate across the borders to attack airports, railroads, fuel depots, electricity pylons, bridges and roads.

Satellite reconnaissance guided the Afghan resistance to Soviet targets and they were equipped with hand held stinger missiles to shoot down Soviet helicopter gunships and other aircraft. A stinger missile electronic simulator was brought to Pakistan to train the Mujahideen. Soviet battle plans were intercepted by spy satellites and this information relayed to the resistance which were supplied with secure communications technology. Massive amounts of propaganda books were distributed to the population.

It worked. The progressive government of Afghanistan, and the Soviet forces supporting them at the request of the freely elected government, were defeated and Muslim "freedom fighters" went on to destabilize those Eastern Soviet provinces. Today's civil war in Russia's Muslim Chechnya and Georgia is a residual of that CIA master plan. Those destabilizations were directly coached and financed by Western intelligence services.[a]

---

[a] Energized by the CIA designed Jihad to push Soviet influence out of Afghanistan and the Soviet Union's Eastern provinces, the "freedom fighters" restructured their newly gained knowledge into a Jihad to free all Muslim nations from Western domination. The bombs that fell on Afghanistan in October 2001 were blowing apart the terrorist training camps built by the CIA in the 1980s to train terrorists to destabilize the Soviet Union. These students of terrorism have turned their deadly skills towards destabilizing the nation who trained them and America is now searching out and killing the very terrorists they trained. Control of discourse and self-censorship by the media is so thorough that, even as their

In 1998, after the successful destabilization of Afghanistan, Zbigniew Brzezinski, President Carter's National Security Advisor at the time, admitted that covert U.S. intervention began long before the USSR sent in troops. ""That secret operation [National Security Council Directive 166] was an excellent idea," he explained. "The effect was to draw the Russians into the Afghan trap."[53]

Take note of what was "an excellent idea": It was the peaceful, rapid successes of Afghanistan that were a problem for imperial America. To subvert those successes, a country rapidly developing and moving towards modernization was politically and economically shattered, 2-million Afghanistani (out of a population of 15-million) were killed, millions more became refugees. One of the many forces financed and armed by the CIA to suppress the progress of that impoverished nation were the Taliban.

Activist Muslims worldwide, some of America's most implacable enemies trained in Afghanistan by the CIA, used their CIA terrorist training to blow up American embassies worldwide. They then reached right into the heart of America to hijack planes and fly them into New York's World Trade Center and the Pentagon—killing 260 passengers and almost 3,000 on the ground for one of the greatest terrorist acts against the West.[a] However, that act pales alongside the acts of wholesale terror required to suppress the periphery of empire's break for freedom.

The destabilization of Afghanistan was only one of many covert actions undertaken with the primary goal of destabilizing the Soviet Union. If outside powers would stay out of them, the political conflicts of most countries would be settled peacefully and quickly. But when powerful outside powers offer to finance and arm radical groups to take over and govern, there are leaders in every society willing to take that offer. These impoverished people are given massive funds to fight proxy battles. Even the inexperienced can quickly make a value judgment that they are currently in poverty with little opportunity for a quality life and that, through the patronage of the world's greatest power, they may end up as their nation's leaders and become personally rich and powerful under the largesse of the wealthy world. What would happen in America or Europe if outside forces

---

nation gears up for war against terrorism, the immorality, the injustice, and the lawlessness of the West's training of terrorists to destabilize fundamentally peaceful nations is not even discussed. It is crucial that this state terrorism not be recorded in history. This accounts for terrorists being tried in military tribunals rather than civilian courts. A civilian court would record terrorist testimony that they were trained and financed by America while any such testimony will be suppressed in a military tribunal.

[a] See the endnote to the above paragraph. CIA Director William Casey suggested to the Muslim terrorists they were training that after overthrowing the Afghanistan government that the U.S. would support their terrorizing/destabilizing the Muslim provinces of the Soviet Union. Though virtually every CIA covert action must be plausibly denied, a Google search using various keywords on these pages will come up with the documentation.

supported political grouping, with immense funds and arms to sabotage and destabilize those countries?

The website www.emperors-clothes.com has chosen the destabilization of Yugoslavia and Afghanistan as the focus of their research and they cite solid sources describing the same Muslim terrorists America trained in Afghanistan were later destabilizing Kosovo and Macedonia under the funding and guidance of American and German intelligence services. Later these same intelligence services (MPRI and other supposed private armies under the supervision of the Pentagon's Special Operations Command, SOCOM.[a]) were organizing the Ethnic Albanian insurgency in Macedonia, utilizing some of these same Western trained Muslim extremists. The escort to safety of surrounded and trapped Ethnic Albanian insurgents by American troops provides strong support for these reports. For those sources in the media of record the reader will have to do a Google search, especially that website, and check future books by the authors cited.[54]

The Soviets withdrew from Afghanistan in 1989, the government was soon overthrown, and those progressive leaders attempting to build a modern Afghanistan were promptly hanged. All this was made palatable to the world by intelligence agency wordsmiths (that *Mighty Wurlitzer* again) use of terrorist adjectives (butchers) to describe the progressive leaders they had overthrown and assassinated.

The CIA and all *managers-of-state* knew better. CIA study-books available in most libraries described this government as freeing women and peasants, establishing clinics and schools with massive literacy programs, returning the land to those who farmed it, canceling the mortgage debts of small farmers, and canceling usurious debts. Sale of brides was prohibited and women were able to choose their own husbands. In fact, Afghanistan was then one of the leading nations in the world for providing women's rights. More women were in universities than men.

Because *one imperial-center-of-capital* had targeted another powerful *emerging-center-of-capital*, Afghanistan went from one of the fastest developing nations in the world with full rights extended to all citizens to one of the most repressive in the world where a woman did not dare show her uncovered face in public, could not go to school, and could not hold a job.

---

[a] Linda Robinson, America's Secret Armies, *U.S. News & World Report* (Nov. 4, 2002), pp. 38-43. In *Dollars for Terror* (New York: Algora Publishing, 2000), Chapter 10, Richard Labeviere explains that Special Operations Command (SOCOM) overseas MPRI and other private military groups and interfaces between those groups and the Pentagon. Occasionally a news broadcast or talk show will address lightly the covert activities of the CIA. On one of those occasions, the TV camera turned to a younger Congressman who evidently had been in on covert activity briefings. He said, "We think of the CIA as carrying out these covert operations but the really big covert operations are carried out by the military." Of course it is in support of the CIA that special operations forces of the military are called upon. These are the military covert operations that have gone under the deeper cover of MPRI and other supposedly private armies.

Take note of how the label "butchers" were placed upon what was one of the most progressive governments in the Muslim world. Research very deep before accepting one of the labels placed on people and nations by any nation's *Mighty Wurlitzer.* The feudal structure of much of the Muslim world today is specifically because *Western imperial-centers-of-capital* reestablished that feudal structure when they collapsed the Ottoman Empire and overthrew or contained every democratic government that emerged.

As Afghanistan is of strategic importance for the allied *imperial-centers-of-capital* to control the oil and other resources in the former Eastern Soviet republics, we were told that immense funds would be spent to rebuild that shattered nation and incorporate it into world trade and the *wealth-producing-process.* True to form, this is not happening. Money for destabilization is plentiful while money for rebuilding is scarce to unavailable. As there are no economic threats out there, this is not to be a replay of the industrialization of Japan and the Asian tigers to stop fast expanding socialism 50 years ago.

Exactly what the deepest secrets of the current War on Terrorism are we cannot be sure. But this we do know: Terrorists had already attacked American embassies and infrastructure overseas and that they were going to attack targets within mainland America was a known. After all, such terrorist efforts generate a lot of phone traffic and ECHELON, America's electronic intelligence gathering service, intercepts and analyzes (through keywords picked out by powerful computers) virtually every message in the world that is sent through space and much of what is sent by ground. Clearly dangerous messages lead to detailed analysis of all traffic to and from those phone numbers. Over time, almost all terrorist cells and a rough outline of their plans become known.

The current prime target of the War on Terrorism, Osama Bin Laden, worked with the CIA and Pakistani Intelligence in establishing terrorist training camps in Afghanistan and training terrorists. So long as he and Al-Qaeda members were terrorizing capitalism's competitors, they were classed as "freedom fighters." As soon as they turned their training to blowing up American political and economic emblems, they became terrorists. Terrorists, of course, are what they were all along. Western media simply ignored the destruction of political and economic infrastructure of ideological competitors.

We do know that every empire creates enemies to justify expansionist and suppressionist policies. We know that excuses for war are created so as to gain the political backing of a nation's citizens and these excuses include permitting attacks on, and deaths of, citizens. History is rife with examples but America has its destruction of the battleship Maine in Havana which rallied citizens for the Spanish American War and Pearl Harbor which rallied them for WWII.

So much terrorism of others by the imperial centers has been neglected by the media and there has been so much distortion of reality by the greatest propaganda system in history that figuring out what is real is very slippery. We do know Osama Bin Laden praised the terrorist attacks on America. But so did Western leaders praise their terrorist attacks on the empire's competitors. We do know that Al-Qaeda is dedicated to the destruction of America. But America trained them to terrorize and destabilize both Afghanistan and the Soviet Union and millions were killed in the process as opposed to the few thousand killed so far as these terrorists turned on their trainers and benefactors.

More that we know is that the West feels they must control the vast oil fields around the Caspian Sea, Afghanistan is one of the keys to that control, and that control is now in place. Besides planned oil pipelines being now more secure, virtually all the former Eastern provinces of the Soviet Union have joined NATO's Orwellian-named Partnership for Peace (PfP) military bloc. Those former Soviet provinces will receive arms from, and be doing training maneuvers with, NATO troops.

Major wars have been fought over far fewer resources. Sincere researchers should look close at the War on Terrorism being a cover for control of those largely untouched resources. But they will have to look deep, this will not be the analysis recorded in history. Instead of the destabilization of the Soviet Union and Afghanistan, history will record only a collapse of the Soviet Union and a War on Terrorism. For example: Running a Google Internet search using the keywords "Defense Planning Guide, Cheney, Wolfowitz, 1992" will alert one that the overthrow of Saddam Hussein was planned 11 years earlier.

We discuss what is a known only to point out that there is much more to the story of the terrorist attack on America than Osama Bin Laden and Al-Qaeda. These terrorists must be neutralized but so must the massive violence, suppressions and oppressions of the West we discuss be abandoned.

The one aspect of this history that stands out is how these American trained terrorists were freedom fighters when terrorizing and destabilizing America's competitors and terrorists when they turned on America.

The Decision to restructure to a Market Economy was made by Soviet Intellectuals

Soviet intellectuals studied both their economy and that of the West closely and made a conscious decision for change. Once the decision to change to a market economy was made, these same intellectuals had little to say about the actual restructuring:

> When I [Fred Weir] came here seven years ago at the outset of *perestroika*, there was very little belief in socialism among the generation dubbed the golden children. These sons and daughters of the Communist party elite had received excellent educations, had the best that the society could give them,

> and only aspired to live like their Western counterparts. Many had high positions in the Communist Party, but were absolutely exuberant Westernizes, pro-capitalists, and from very early in the perestroika period, this was their agenda.... People who thought they were going to be the governing strata in a new society are [now] losing their jobs, being impoverished and becoming bitter. The intellectuals, for instance—whose themes during the Cold War were intellectual freedom, human rights, and so on—had a very idealized view of Western capitalism. They have been among the groups to suffer the most from the early stages of marketization as their huge network of institutes and universities are defunded.[55]

Those golden children of the communist elite are undoubtedly quite silent as they gaze at their once proud country lying prostrate at the feet of imperial capital. The population of Russia is falling at the astounding rate of 800,000 a year, birth rates have plummeted to the lowest in the world, and only 1-in-4 children are born healthy. There are dramatic increases in the number of children born with physical and mental impairment, disease is rampant, and the average lifespan of Russian men has fallen from 65 years to 58, below that of Ghana.[56]

Sale of the Century by Chrystia Freeland is a highly recommended masterly study on the collapse of Russia after the breakup of the Soviet Union.[57] However, as a correspondent for the *Financial Times* when doing her research, the author focuses only on finance and politics and ignores other crucial factors. Ignored were: basic economics, Russia's highly motivated labor ready to make the transition to capitalism as addressed above by Fred Weir, the National Endowment for Democracy's funding and management of Yeltsin's election, the American election specialists orchestrating of that election,[a] the Harvard Institute for International Development's advising Russia's "young reformers" throughout that collapse, and how the massive imports of consumer products both collapsed the economic multiplier and sucked the wealth out of Russia.

Without the economic multiplier as money from wages circulates, a country essentially has no economy. Yet, while intending to document the full history of the attempt to restructure the Russian economy, the author fails to notice that the "young reformers" paid no attention to primary production in Russia. These neophytes were so immersed in classical Western philosophy that they thought all there was to establishing capitalism was to create rich capitalists by giving title of valuable resource industries and banks to a few "oligarchs," who, without a doubt, pulled off one of the greatest thefts of social wealth in history.

In the West, preventing the rise to political power of labor is a primary consideration. Thus the highly motivated "golden children" (the latest

---

[a] This was very successful. Through covert black ops and political pressure, even Michael Gorbachev was denied access to local reporters, media, or even an audience to speak to, wherever they went. Freeland, *Sale of the Century*, Chapter 9.

generation of leaders) who were ready to restructure Russia's economy were never given the opportunity. Instead, the neophyte agents of capitalism (the "Young Reformers") were intent on the obviously impossible job of telescoping the 50 years of the age of American robber barons into less than 10 years. The "golden children" running Russia's economy wanted to restructure to capitalism and would have understood how to do so. But labor in charge of any part of an economy is anathema to theorists of Western philosophy. So the only people offered a serious opportunity to buy Russia's productive industries for a fraction of its true value were the new "oligarchs" with no experience in running any part of the Russian economy. Without any background on running industries or much of anything else, these oligarchs were expected to become the leading capitalists of Russia.

No country has ever developed under the principles imposed upon post Soviet Russia. In fact, economic protections for the developed world are all in place and functioning and no wealthy nation would consider subjecting their economies to such harsh economic medicine as was imposed on Russia. To double, triple, and quadruple prices while shutting down industry right and left and destroying consumer savings would be taught as a recipe for disaster in any economics class.

The easiest way to understand the failure of the restructuring of the Russian economy is by outlining a sensible restructuring plan:

(1) The massive savings of Soviet citizens should have been protected;

(2) Industry and media shares should have been distributed to those workers;[a]

(3) modern consumer product industries should have been built, the bonds to be repaid from profits (the workers being owners will help insure those profits);

(4) until those industries were established and the economy competitive, import restrictions should have stayed in force;

(5) as fast as those modern industries came on stream, Russia's obsolete huge factories would have reduced production and shut down in stages;

(6) an inescapable landrent tax, as per Chapter 24, should have been placed into law, including royalties on natural resources such as oil, minerals, timber, and communications spectrums;

(7) citizens should have received title to their homes through paying the first year's landrent taxes in advance;

(8) farmers should have been given title to their land through landrent bids, again as per Chapter 24;

(9) locally owned banks should have been put in place to fund consumers, farmers, and producers;

---

[a] This was done through vouchers but, as Chrystia Freeland documents, there were many schemes for the oligarchs to buy up those vouchers, not the least was they had to be sold for survival.

(10) and, with those massive consumer savings and financing available, retailers would spring up automatically and this would be the ideal moment to establish an efficient distribution system as per Chapters 27 and 28.

There are many other factors to consider but the above would have been the foundation of a workable restructure plan. Subtle monopolization of technology is the biggest barrier. Virtually any successful restructure plan must provide access to technology, resources and markets and Russia's massive resources could have been bartered for that technology. Also, patent licensing could have been imposed by law. This is accepted as legal in international law, was being tested in court with AIDS drugs in South Africa, and the major drug companies capitulated rather than go to trial.

The reason these suggestions were not followed is obvious, labor would have ended up with enormous wealth and political power. If they had been given the chance, those egalitarian trained and idealistic "golden children" could have established *democratic-cooperative-capitalism* as opposed to today's dependency on the periphery of *imperial-centers-of-capital.* If that had happened, the secret that no power-structure in the imperial centers had yet given their citizens full rights would have been exposed.

Could the Soviet Union have avoided the Cold War?

From the Soviet side it certainly looked as if war was coming. From 1945, and up to at least 1956 when the U-2 spy flights started, thousands of U.S. "ferret" spy flights photographed Soviet territory and raced back before they could be identified and attacked. In 1946 and 1947 alone (note this was before the Cold War officially started), 30 such planes were shot down, at least 20 U.S. airmen were captured alive, never acknowledged by their government, they finished out their lives in Soviet prisons, and their families were told they died in various accidents. As acknowledged by the highly respected *U.S. News and World Report*, between 1950 and 1970 (after the Cold War officially started but those overflights had been going on since the end of WWII) there were over 10,000 and possibly over 20,000 such overflights deep into Soviet and Chinese territory by military aircraft.

There was a lot more going on than just the acknowledged photographing of Soviet territory. Sabotage and assassination teams were being dropped in to hide among their relatives and ethnic brothers. Almost universally these acts of war failed, with large losses among the agents and their relatives who were to hide them.[58]

In June 1992, when Russian President Boris Yeltsin met with President Bush and said, "We may have American prisoners yet," quite a stir was created. News anchor Tom Brocaw reported this disturbing news and the congressional uproar over these possible prisoners. The next night Brocaw said, "These were American airmen shot down during the Cold War. This is the first time Americans have been apprised of this." Then for weeks, except for an occasional highly sanitized statement, all went silent on that explosive subject. A few months later, the headlines read, "Yeltsin: POWs 'Summarily Executed.'" But the last line of that front-page article depicting these execution horrors told the real story. "The largest group of Americans imprisoned in the Soviet Union included more than 730 pilots and other airmen who either made forced landings on Soviet territory or were shot down on Cold War spy and sabotage flights."[59]

The intelligence agencies of Britain, France, and Germany were running similar, but smaller, covert operations against the Soviet Union and other nations of the Eastern bloc. This was a massive assault on Soviet sovereignty, actually outright acts of war, by essentially the same powers that had invaded Russia 25 years earlier and also the same powers that owed an enormous debt to the Soviets for saving them from fascism in WWII.

The fact that there were no Soviet spy planes carrying assassination and sabotage teams, overflying Western territory during this period is something scholars should note. Nor should the internment of U.S. pilots in the Soviet Union have been news to U.S. newscasters. With the Soviets complaining to Washington, DC, to the United Nations, and holding many trials, for the American people not to be informed of these assaults on Soviet territory can be due only to cooperation by the major media of record in misinforming of America. These illegal flights remaining a secret only to Western citizens testifies to how *social-control-paradigms* require suppression of information about acts of war by *managers-of-state* simultaneously with depictions of imminent attack from the targeted society. That is, of course, the creation of enemies to protect a power-structure.

As in any society after any revolution, there were those within the Soviet Union who were sympathetic to, and subject to manipulation by, their religious and cultural cousins in the West. Thus, when Germany invaded the Soviet Union, whole communities of ethnic Germans and other communities that still had religious ties and loyalties to the West joined the invading army.

When that war was over, entire communities were resettled in Siberia where they could not link up with outside powers still threatening to overthrow the Soviet government. Millions of innocent people (even many dedicated and loyal communists) were rounded up for resettlement and many were executed. But many executed had been harboring trained saboteurs who had been parachuted into the Eastern European countries all the way to Byelorussia.[a] Struggles for power became mixed with the

---

[a] Besides those with ethnic ties to the West who betrayed their new country by joining forces with the Nazi invaders (such as Vlasov's army and Byelorussian, Ukrainian, Croatian, and Polish volunteers for the mobile death squads; 20,000 were volunteers; the rest were conscripts who were granted amnesty). John Prados, *The Presidents' Secret Wars* (New York: William Morrow, 1986), Chapters 2 and 3; Loftus, *Belarus Secret*, Chapters 1-3, pp. 51-53, 49, 102-03, especially p. 43; Ranelagh, Agency, p. 156.

legitimate battle to defend the revolution, and many were swallowed up in that holocaust. (America facing a much weaker terrorist threat is reacting even more violently but primarily outside its borders.)

But note! It was protecting their country from being overthrown by external powers manipulating internal ethnic groups that created these suppressions. Where America faced no such threat after its revolution, the cooperative efforts of many nations to overthrow the Soviets had been ongoing for 70 years. These included direct intervention in their revolution, the WWII effort to exterminate them, years of covert actions such as training and flying in assassins and saboteurs, being embargoed from world trade, and their post-WWII military encirclement.

Ignoring the background behind the forced migrations to Siberia, and in its constant search for drama, the Western press openly pushed the governing *social-control-paradigm*, giving the death toll as 60-million. But then it became 40-million, then 20-million, then 10-million, and the figures are still coming down towards the true number killed under "Stalinism"—certainly under 100,000 and most likely fewer than 50,000.[60]

These are the same principles that peddlers of crisis have been using for thousands of years. The greater the lie, the more surely it will be believed by their followers. Even if it is done only verbally and the accuser is in no personal physical danger, the surest way to be recognized as a leader is to lead an attack against an enemy.

There has been so much fabrication that it is impossible to know what is true. We are satisfied that, of the citizens of those Soviet communities who welcomed the German armies and were the contacts for the saboteurs the West was infiltrating into those countries, and thus were a threat to the security of this new nation, many were relocated to Siberia. This was a full-fledged war, the Soviets knew it, and many innocent people died from the 70-years of intense destabilization efforts and outright wars.

The names of the now declassified plans for war against the Soviet Union (Bushwhacker, Broiler, Sizzle, Shakedown, Dropshot, Trojan, Pincher, and Frolic) graphically portray their offensive purpose. Some of those plans included the actual occupation of the Soviet Union. [61] Papers in President Johnson's library testify to a planned nuclear strike to destroy the rising economic and philosophical threat. Make no mistake about it, the intention was to both destroy the Soviet Union and suppress any other breaks for freedom and both goals were reached. Those destabilizations cost trillions of dollars, 12-million to 15-million lives, and hundreds of millions of deaths from disease and hunger as those nations' economies were destroyed.

Analysts are right when they say the West would not have attacked the Soviet Union. But that is only because the Soviets developed the atomic bomb too quick. One hydrogen bomb getting through to America would be one too many.

Study the history of suppressions worldwide we are addressing, study why tiny impoverished Vietnam faced such an assault, study why Cuba is under such an assault even though their revolutionary government provided Cubans with health care and education equal to America and eliminated hunger, and study why every offer of the Soviets for mutual disarmament was ignored.

A key part of Western propaganda was the lack of rights in the Soviet Union and secret police everywhere. Not only was this fundamentally not true, America and most of Western Europe could give more freedom and rights to their citizens because they were not subject to bombings, assassinations, and threats of invasion; the CIA's *Mighty Wurlitzer* saying otherwise notwithstanding.

Propaganda was the Essence of the Cold War

Former attaché to the Soviet Embassy George Kennan, undoubtedly the U.S. citizen most knowledgeable about the Soviet Union (one of the prime promoters of the Cold War, and one who eventually had a change of heart about the morality of that deception), is quoted as saying that those executed in the Soviet Union were in the tens of thousands, meaning the total is under 100,000 as addressed above.[62] Tens of thousands is still a large number to be sure, but, even though many—even possibly most—were innocent, a large number were attempting to overthrow that new government, and that is a capital offense in any country. (For a balanced perspective, compare the under 100,000 killed within the former Soviet Union as they searched for those being supported by the West to overthrow the government with the 12-million to 15-million killed on the periphery of empire by the West as documented in the next chapter.)

Many innocent people within the Soviet Union were swallowed up in this mass hysteria. The Soviets opened their records and restored the good names of these people. Historians are tracing what happened to each individual so their families can know their fates. Perhaps the world may someday know the true numbers of those unjustly persecuted souls.

We caution the reader on the statistics that will be published. The slaughters of defeated centers of capital and others threatening to break free will be exaggerated, while the suppressions and oppressions by the dominant centers of capital will be camouflaged as defensive actions and their slaughter of innocents will be recorded in history as a response to others' aggressions.

When Hitler was planning WWII, Reinhard Heydrich, deputy chief of Hitler's SS, operated a covert operation that counterfeited letters from top Soviet military officers to falsely indicate a counterrevolution by these officers.[63] Possibly 35,000 highly loyal officers were executed. We say possibly because again we must remember how intelligence services create and exaggerate facts to demonize an enemy; these exaggerated figures then tend to become recorded history.

After WWII, copying Heydrich's successful destabilization efforts, Western secret services counterfeited papers and letters that caused massive arrests of innocent people in Eastern Europe and the Soviet Union. Citizens of the West heard all about the repressions but nothing about the causes or that, when the Soviets caught on to the scam, they released those imprisoned and even paid compensation to an innocent American couple who were caught up in that intrigue and imprisoned for several years.[64]

Even as the Russian revolution succeeded, the British were attempting to destroy Lenin's reputation to the world. By the same methods that placed Napoleon in history books as a megalomaniac, the leaders of the Bolshevik Revolution will be in future history books as mass terrorists.[65] That creation of history will be accomplished through financing already highly biased historians to research executions and point out the total innocence of those executed, and will simultaneously totally ignore the counterfeit papers fingering innocent people, the destabilization/ assassination teams inserted, the many who were guilty, or the massive amounts of money spent placing a ring of steel around the Soviet Union.

The alert can watch this writing of history unfold. Alternative views typically find little financing and, due to the already programmed masses, no audience. Once imposed, a society's belief in an enemy continues to control a population even after the defeat of that enemy. Major publishers publish only books they think can make a profit, the loyal and patriotic masses read only books which support the *social-control-paradigms* that have been imposed upon them, and thus books based on this fraudulent history are best sellers while there is little audience for a book that documents honest history.

Conceptually Reversing the Process

Remembering how close the Soviets came to winning the arms race and thus winning the Cold War, does anyone doubt what would have happened if the Soviet Union was untouched and America was the one that had been invaded, the nation which lost 30% of its prime labor, and the nation in which everything above the Mason-Dixon line and east of the Mississippi River had been blown up or burned to the ground? The conclusions are obvious. The expensive arms race imposed upon it broke the Soviet Union. Their cooperative ways explain why the Soviets developed so fast under such adverse conditions and our research demonstrates that development could even be much faster yet under *democratic-cooperative-capitalism*.

If the Soviets had been incompetent, as we hear so often, they would have been no threat and there would have been no Cold War. They would have simply been quietly overwhelmed by capitalism. It was their competency that was the problem. To have advanced as far as they did under such adverse conditions before finally collapsing under the weight of assault by the Western world testifies to a fiercely loyal population working hard for their country. They were not a terrorized and sullen population.

Keeping the World in Chains

Forces in the former Soviet Union to take back their country are rapidly rebuilding. This means the property titles of those who bought Russia's wealth for pennies on the dollar are at risk. But for a quick lesson on what Marx meant by "monopoly capital," and what "debt traps" mean, look at what those shattered economies face. If they repudiate or default on any external debts, any assets outside their borders can be, and will be, attached. This means businesses, property titles, bank accounts, goods-in-transit, ships, or planes. Those beleaguered societies would be in one of the tightest containment traps that any *imperial-center-of-capital* ever devised. Every ship or plane that left their ports would be subject to seizure to repay those debts. Without unimpeded access to the world, no economy of any country can function efficiently. The trap structured in law designed to keep the world in chains becomes fully visible.

Notes

[1] Lawrence Wittner, *American Intervention in Greece* (New York: Columbia University Press, 1982), especially pp. 162, 283; Kati Marton, *The Polk Conspiracy: Murder and Cover-up in the case of Correspondent George Polk*, (New York: Farrar, Straus, and Giroux, 1990); C.M. Woodhouse, *The Rise and Fall of the Greek Colonels*, (New York: Franklin Watts, 1985); Stephan Rosskamm Shalom, *Imperial Alibis* (Boston: South End Press, 1993) pp. 26, 26; William Blum, *CIA: A Forgotten History* (London: Zed Books, 1986), pp. 31-36; David Leigh, *The Wilson Plot* (New York; Pantheon, 1988), pp. 17-18; William Manchester, *The Glory and the Dream* (New York: Bantam Books, 1990), pp. 433-43; Michael McClintock, *Instruments of Statecraft* (New York: Pantheon, 1992), pp. 11-17. See Chapter 6, endnote 6.

[2] Eric Wolf, *Europe and the People Without History* (Berkeley: University of California Press, 1982), pp. 99-100.

[3] Ibid, pp. 99-100; I.F. Stone, *The Hidden History of the Korean War* (Boston: Little Brown and Company, 1952); Chalmers Johnson, *Blowback: The Costs and Consequences of the American Empire* (New York: Henry Holt & Company, 2000), Chapter 4.

[4] Ibid, Chapter 3, pp. 43, 61, 97, 108, 110, 119; Gabriel Kolko, *The Politics of War* (New York: Pantheon, 1990), Chapters 3 and 4.

[5] Sidney Lens, *Permanent War* (New York: Schocken Books, 1987), pp. 20-21;William Appleman Williams, *The Tragedy of American Diplomacy*, (New York: W.W. Norton, 1988), pp. 208, 235.

[6] Arjun Makhijani, *From Global Capitalism to Economic Justice* (New York: Apex Press, 1992), pp. 25-26, quoting a memorandum on NSC-68.

[7] Dean Acheson, *Present at the Creation* (New York: W.W. Norton, 1987), pp. 374, 726; see also p. 377; emphasis added.

[8] James Bamford, *Body of Secrets: Anatomy of the Ultra-Secret National Security Agency* (New York: Doubleday, 2001), pp. 70-91, especially p. 82; Linda Robinson, "What didn't we do to get rid of Castro," *U.S. News & World Report,* October 26, 98, p. 41; Castro, *Capitalism in Crisis,* p. 215-17; John Quigley, *The Ruses for War: American Intervention Since World War II* (Buffalo: Prometheus Books, 1992).

[9] Stone, *Hidden History,* pp. 1-3

[10] Quigley, *Ruses for War*, Chapter 3.

11 John Ranelagh, *The Agency: The Rise and Decline of the CIA* (New York: Simon & Schuster, 1987), p. 257.

12 Linda Robinson, "What didn't we do to get rid of Castro," *U.S. News & World Report*, October 26, 98, p. 41; Fidel Castro, *Capitalism in Crisis: Globalization and World Politics Today* (New York: Ocean Press, 2000), p. 215-17. See also, John Quigley, *The Ruses for War: American Intervention Since World War II* (Buffalo: Prometheus Books, 1992).

13 L. Fletcher Prouty, *JFK: The CIA, Vietnam, And the Plot to Kill Kennedy* (New York: Birch Lane Press, 1992), Chapter 3; James Bamford, *Body of Secrets: Anatomy of the Ultra-Secret National Security Agency* (New York: Doubleday, 2001), especially pp. 70-75;

14 Stone, *Hidden History*, pp. 263-64.

15 Lloyd C. Gardner, *Safe for Democracy* (New York: Oxford University Press, 1984), pp. 197-8; Philip Knightley, *The First Casualty* (New York: Harcourt Brace Jovanovich, Publishers, 1975), Chapter 7; Mikhail Gorbachev, *Perestroika* (New York: Harper and Row, 1987), p. 33, note 2; Edmond Taylor, *The Fall of the Dynasties* (New York: Dorset Press, 1989), p. 359; Ernest Volkman, Blaine Baggett, *Secret Intelligence* (New York: Doubleday, 1989), Chapter 1.

16 Walter Isaacson, Evan Thomas, *The Wise Men* (New York: Simon and Schuster, 1986), p. 150; Michael Kettle, *The Allies and the Russian Collapse* (Minneapolis, University of Minnesota Press, 1981), p.15; Taylor, *Fall of the Dynasties*, p. 381.

17 Philip Knightley, First Casualty, p. 138; D. F. Fleming, *The Cold War and its Origins* (New York: Doubleday, 1961, 2 vols.), pp. 26, 1038

18 Paul Kennedy, *The Rise and Fall of the Great Powers*, (New York: Random House, 1987), pp. 321, 323.

19 Vilnis Sipols, *The Road to Great Victory* (Moscow: Progress Publishers, 1985), pp. 109, 132, 179-80; Kennedy, Rise and Fall, especially pp. 321, 323, 352, in part quoting J. Erickson, *The Road to Berlin* (London: 1983), p. 447.

20 Jeffrey Jukes, *Stalingrad at the Turning Point* (New York: Ballantine Books, 1968), p. 154; *National Geographic TV* (August 23, 1987); Fleming, *Cold War and its Origins*, p. 157; Kolko, *Politics of War*, pp. 19, 351, 372.

21 Kennedy, *Rise and Fall*, pp. 357-58; David Mayers, George Kennan (New York: Oxford University Press, 1988), pp. 190-91; Oleg Rzheshevsky, *World War II: Myths and the Realities* (Moscow, USSR: Progress Publishers, 1984), p. 175.

22 Lens, *Permanent War*, pp. 20-21; Williams, *Tragedy of American Diplomacy*, pp. 208, 235.

23 Don Cook, *Forging the Alliance*, (London: Seeker and Warburg, 1989), pp. 78-9.

24 E.P. Thompson and Dan Smith, *Protest and Survive*, (New York: Monthly Review Press, 1981), p. 123.

25 Lester Thurow, *The Future of Capitalism: How Today's Economic Forces Shape Tomorrow's World* (England: Penguin Books, 1996), p. 56; Lester Thurow, *Head to Head: The Coming Economic Battle Among Japan, Europe, and America* (New York: William Morrow and Company, 1992), pp. 92, 95; David Kotz, "Russia in Shock: How Capitalist 'Shock Therapy' is Destroying Russia's Economy," *Dollars and Sense*, June 1993, p. 9.

26 Patrick Flaherty, *"Behind Shatalinomics: Politics of Privatization,"* Guardian. Oct. 10, 1990, p. 11.

27 Rich Thomas, "From Russia, with Chips," *Newsweek*, August 6, 1990.

28 Peter Gowan, "Old Medicine in New Bottles," *World Policy Journal* (Winter 1991-92), pp. 3-5.

29 Gowan, "Old Medicine in New Bottles," pp. 6-8, 13.

30 *Ramsey Clark,* Hidden Agenda: U.S./NATO Takeover of Yugoslavia *(New York: International action Center, 2002); Michel Collon,* Liars Poker: The Great Powers, Yugoslavia and the Wars of the future *(New York:: International action Center, 2002); Michel Chossudovsky,* The Globalization of Poverty: Impacts of IMF and World Bank Reforms *(London: Zed Books, 1997), Chapter 13; Michel Chossudovsky, "Dismantling Yugoslavia, Colonizing Bosnia,"* CovertAction Quarterly *(Spring, 1996), pp. 31-37; Michael Parenti,* To Kill a Nation: The Attack on Yugoslavia *(New York: Verso, 2000), p. 26; William Tabb,* The Amoral Elephant: Globalization and the Struggle for Social Justice in the Twenty-First Century *(New York: Monthly Review Press, 2001), Chapter 6, espec. pp. 149, 153-54; Sean Gervasi, "Germany, U.S., and the Yugoslavian Crisis,"* CovertAction

Quarterly *(Winter 1992-93), pp. 41-45, 64-66; David Lorge Parnas, "Con: Dayton's a Step Back—Way Back,"* Peace *(March/April 1996), pp. 17-22; McClintock,* Instruments of Statecraft, *pp. 71-82; Catherine Samaray,* Yugoslavia Dismembered *(New York: Monthly Review Press, 1995; Charles Lane, Theodore Stranger, Tom Post, "The Ghosts of Serbia,"* Newsweek. *April 19, 1993, pp. 30-31; Dusko Doder, Yugoslavia: "New War, Old Hatreds,"* Foreign Policy *(Summer 1993), pp. 4, 9-11, 18-19; Thomas Kielinger, Max Otte, "Germany: The Presumed Power,"* Foreign Policy *(Summer 1993), p. 55. This was essentially acknowledged by former Acting Secretary of State Lawrence Eagleburger on the* McNeil/Lehrer Report *(May 6, 1993), and many other talk shows and news programs, pointing out that there were those who pushed for the collapse of Yugoslavia, specifically pointing to Germany. On that same show, Michael Elliot of the respected British publication,* The Economist, *agreed.*

[31] Ibid

[32] Ibid and Parenti, *To Kill a Nation,* Chapter 10, p. 105. check *Jane's Defense Weekly*, especially the May 10, 1999 issue; Linda Robinson, "America's Secret Armies," *U.S. News & World Report* (November 4, 2002), pp. 38-43.

[33] Ibid; Be sure and check later articles and books by those same authors; Parenti, *To Kill a Nation,* Chapter 11.

[34] Parenti, *To Kill a Nation*, Chapter 15, p. 12, 28-29; Fidel Castro, *Capitalism in Crisis: Globalization and World Politics Today* (New York: Ocean Press, 2000), p. 209.

[35] "Big Lie Exposed," *Workers World,* April 12, 2001.

[36] Parenti, *To Kill a Nation,* Chapter 14.

[37] See endnote 32. For reduced Serbian losses: Parenti, *To Kill a Nation,* Chapter 16; Richard J. Newman, "A Kosovo Numbers Game," *U.S. News & World Report,* July 12, 1999, p. 36.

[38] George Monbiot, A Discreet Deal in the Pipeline, *The Guardian*, 15 February 2001.

[39] See endnote 32; Parenti, *To Kill a Nation,* Chapter 16. Run a Google Internet search.

[40] Castro, Capitalism in Crisis, pp. 215-17; James Bamford, Body of Secrets: Anatomy of the Ultra Secret National Security Agency (New York: Doubleday, 2001), pp. 70-75.

[41] Anthony Arnove, Iraq Under Seige: The Deadly Impact of Sanctions and War (Cambridge: South End Press, 2002).

[42] Parenti, *To Kill a Nation,* pp. 12, 28-29, Chapter 15.

[43] United Press International, September 27, 2000.

[44] Parenti, *To Kill a Nation,* Chapter 12.

[45] Deirdre Griswold, "Marxism, Reformism and Anarchism: Lessons from a Steel Mill in Slovakia" *Workers World* (December 14, 2000).

[46] Mark Weisbrot, "The Mirage of Progress." *The American Prospect* (Winter 2002), pp. A10-A123.

[47] Castro, *Capitalism in Crisis*, pp. 42, 104.

[48] John Gray, *False Dawn* (New York: The Free Press, 1998), Chapter 6; Alexander Buzgalin and Andrei Kolganov, *Bloody October in Moscow: Political Repression in the Name of Reform* (New York: Monthly Review Press, 1994); Boris Kagarlitsky, *Square Wheels: How Russian Democracy Got Derailed*, (New York: Monthly Review Press, 1994). The tables of contents of most good magazines, both mainstream and alternative news, will have many good articles on the legal theft of the wealth of the Soviet Union through privatization.

[49] Janine R. Wedel, "The Harvard Boys Do Russia," *The Nation.* June 1, 1998, pp. 11-16.

[50] Thurow, *The Future of Capitalism*, pp. 43-45; Castro, *Capitalism in Crisis*, pp. 99-104; "Proud Russia on Its Knees," *U.S. News & World Report*, February 8, 1999, pp. 30-36; David R. Francis, "Debt -riddled Russia to Ask for Forgiveness," *The Christian Science Monitor*, April 5, 1999, p. 17; Katrina vanden Heuvel, editorial, *The Nation*, August 10-17, 1998, pp. 4-6. See also Julie Corwin, Douglas Stranglin, Suzanne Possehl, Jeff Trimble, "The Looting of Russia," *U.S. News & World Report*, March 7, 1994; John Feffer, "The Browning of Russia," *CovertAction Quarterly* (Spring 1996).

[51] Castro, Capitalism in Crisis, pp. 99-104.

[52] Ann Williamson, "An Inconvenient History," *http://www.geocities.com/Athens/7842/* wcessay04.htm

[53] Greg Guma, "Cracks in the Covert Iceberg" *Toward Freedom* (May 1998), p. 2; Yousai Mohammad and M. Adkin, *The Beartrap: Afghanistan's Untold Story* (London, England: Leo Cooper, 1992); Blum, *Rogue State*, Chapter 2; K. Lohbeck, Holy War, *Unholy Victory: Eyewitness to the CIA's Secret War in Afghanistan* (Washington DC: Regnery Gateway, 1993); J. Peterzell, *Reagan's Secret Wars, CNSS Report 108* (Washington, DC: Center for National Security Studies, 1984); T. Weiner, *Blank Check: The Pentagon's Black Budget* (New York: Warners Books, 1990); E.T. Chester, *Covert Network: Progressives, the International Rescue Committee, and the CIA* (New York: M.E. Sharpe, 1995); D. Cordovez, and S.S. Harrison, *Out of Afghanistan: The Inside Story of the Soviet Withdrawal* (New York: Oxford University Press, 1995); S.

Emerson, *Secret Warriors* (New York: G.P. Putnam, 1988); Westerfield, Inside *CIA's Private World*; L.K. Johnson, *America's Secret Power*, R. Kessler, *Inside the CIA: Revealing the Secrets of the World's Most Powerful Spy Agency* (New York: Pocket Books, 1992); Duane A. Clarridge, *A Spy for all Seasons: My Life in the CIA* (New York: Scribner, 1997) ; see Chapter 6, endnote 6.

54 Linda Robinson, "America's Secret Armies," *U.S. News & World Report* (November 4, 2002), pp. 38-43; Greg Guma, "Cracks in the Covert Iceberg" *Toward Freedom* (May 1998), p. 2; Ahmed Rashid, *Taliban: Militant Islam, Oil and Fundamentalism in Central Asia* (New York: Yale University Press, 2001); Michael Griffin, *Reaping the Whirlwind: The Taliban Movement in Afghanistan* (Sterling, VA: Pluto Press, 2001); John Cooley, *Afghanistan, America, and International Terrorism* (Sterling, VA: Pluto Press, 2000); Yousai Mohammad and M. Adkin, *The Beartrap*; William Blum, *Rogue State: A Guide to the World's Only Super Power* (Monroe, ME: Common Courage Press, 2000), Chapter 2; K. Lohbeck, *Holy War, Unholy Victory: Eyewitness to the CIA's Secret War in Afghanistan* (Washington DC: Regnery Gateway, 1993); J. Peterzell, *Reagan's Secret Wars*, CNSS Report 108 (Washington, DC: Center for National Security Studies, 1984); T. Weiner, *Blank Check: The Pentagon's Black Budget* (New York: Warners Books, 1990); E.T. Chester, *Covert Network: Progressives, the International Rescue Committee, and the CIA* (New York: M.E. Sharpe, 1995); D. Cordovez, and S.S. Harrison, *Out of Afghanistan: The Inside Story of the Soviet Withdrawal* (New York: Oxford University Press, 1995); Yonah Alexander and Michael S. Swetnam. *Osama Bin Laden's al-Queda: Profile of a Terrorist Network* (Ardsley NY: Transnational Publishers, 2001); Peter L. Bergen, *Holy War Inc.: Inside the Secret World of Osama Bin Laden* (New York: Simon & Schuster, 2001); John K. Cooley, *Unholy Wars: Afghanistan, America, and International Terrorism*, 2nd edition (London: Pluto Press, 2000); M.J. Gohari, *The Taliban: Ascent to Power* (New York: Oxford University Press, 2000); Larry P. Goodson, Afghanistan's *Endless War: State failure, Regional Politics, and the Rise of the Taliban* (Seattle: University of Washington Press, 2001; Robin Wright, *Sacred Rage: The Wrath of Militant Islam* (New York: Simon & Schuster, 1985; S. Emerson, *Secret Warriors* (New York: G.P. Putnam, 1988); Westerfield, *Inside CIA's Private World*; L.K. Johnson, *America's Secret Power*, R. Kessler, Inside the *CIA: Revealing the Secrets of the World's Most Powerful Spy Agency* (New York: Pocket Books, 1992); Duane A. Clarridge, *A Spy for all Seasons: My Life in the CIA* (New York: Scribner, 1997).

55 Fred Weir, "Interview: Fred Weir in Russia," *CovertAction Quarterly* (Summer 1993), pp. 54-55.

56 Castro, *Capitalism in Crisis*, pp. 42, 99-104; *60 minutes*, May 19th, 1996.

57 Chrystia Freeland, *Sale of the Century: Russia's Wild Ride From Communism to Capitalism* (New York: Crown Publishers, 2000. See also, Stephen Cohen, *Failed Crusade: America and the Tragedy of Post-Communist Russia.* (New York: W.W. Norton, 2000).

58 Michael Ross, "Yeltsin: POWs 'Summarily Executed'," *The Spokesman Review* (November 12, 1992), pp. B1, A10; Volkman and Baggett, *Secret Intelligence*, p. 187; *John Loftus, Belarus Secret* (New York: Alfred A. Knopf, 1982), especially Chapters 5-8, pp. 109-10; Blum, *A Forgotten History*, Chapters 6, 7, 8, 15, 17, especially p. 124; *U.S. News & World Report*, March 15, 1993, pp. 30-56; see Chapter 6, endnote 6.

59 Ross, "POWs "Summarily Executed,"" pp.B1, A10. Later TV documentaries on this episode claimed 130 airmen lost, the above referenced U.S. News article claimed 252, but all pointed out that the losses may have been much higher.

60 Blum, *The CIA: A Forgotten History*, pp. 127-28, 131, 185; Victor Marchetti and John D. Marks, *The CIA and the Cult of Intelligence* (New York: Dell Publishing Co., 1980), Chapter 6, especially pp. 152-56; Philip Agee, *Inside the Company* (New York: Bantam Books, 1975), especially pp. 53-54, 62-63, 541-42; John Stockwell, *The Praetorian Guard* (Boston: South End Press, 1991), pp. 100-1; Ralph W. McGehee, *Deadly Deceits* (New York: Sheridan Square Press, 1983), especially pp. 30, 58, 62, 189; Philip Agee, Louis Wolf, *Dirty Work* (London: Zed Press, 1978), especially p. 262; David Wise, Thomas B. Ross, *The Espionage Establishment* (New York: Bantam Books, 1978), pp. 256, 257; Ellen Schrecker, *No ivory tower: McCarthyism and the Universities* (New York: Oxford University Press, 1986); Frank J. Donner, *The Age of Surveillance: The Aims and Methods of America's Political Intelligence System* (New York: Random House, 1981). See also Introduction, note three.

61 Michio Kaku and Daniel Axelrod, *To Win A Nuclear War*, (Boston: South End Press, 1987), especially p. x

62 Alexander Cockburn, "Beat the Devil," *The Nation*, March 6, 1989, p. 294; David Corn and Jefferson Morley, "Beltway Bandits," *The Nation*, April 9, 1988, p. 488. An interesting appraisal of Stalinist terror is made by Soviet dissident Roy Medvedev, "Parallels Inappropriate," *New Times* (July 1989), pp. 46-47. See also Volkman and Baggett, *Secret Intelligence*, p. 187; Loftus, *Belarus Secret*, especially Chapters 5-8, pp. 109-10; Blum, The CIA: *A Forgotten History*, Chapters 6, 7, 8, 15, 17.

63 Donald Cameron Watt, *How War Came: The Immediate Origins of the Second World War* (New York: Pantheon Books, 1989), p. 45.

64 Blum, A Forgotten History, Chapter 7.

65 Volkman and Baggett, Secret Intelligence, p. 9, and see Chapter 6, endnote 6.

8. Suppressing the World's break for Economic Freedom

The public has been, through *strategies-of-tension*, them that that they were battling communism all over the world but, of the governments overthrown, only Afghanistan and Chile were originally communist. During the seven years William Casey was CIA director (1981 to 1987), 50 major CIA covert operations were initiated throughout the world and thousands of minor ones.[1] Those major destabilizations caused massive deaths and destruction while the minor operations controlled the media on both the periphery and in the imperial center and destabilized small democratic groups before they could gain a following. As Casey was director for only seven of the CIA's 55 years, one starts to get a sense of the massive covert destabilizations it took to suppress these breaks for freedom.

America as an Empire predates the Cold War

That America won the Spanish-American War in 1898 is recognized by all but even some encyclopedias do not inform the reader that "Spain ceded Cuba, Puerto Rico, Guam, and the Philippines" to the United States for $20-million. Similarly, but not totally, ignored, is that the Philippine patriots' struggle for freedom from America was violently suppressed from 1899 through 1903 in a manner very similar in tactics and level of violence of the Vietnam War. In that break for freedom, an estimated 600,000 Filipinos died from combat and starvation.

Control through a puppet government was substituted for outright colonial control as authorized by the ceding of these lands by Spain. As the rest of the colonial world was breaking free after WWII, the Filipinos again fought for their freedom. Tens of thousands of Filipinos were killed, primarily by private death squads (orchestrated by the CIA's General Edward G. Landsdale), as the elite fought to retain control of the government and the land, and that suppression of true independence through covert American support is still ongoing.[2]

History as General Smedley Butler knew it while he was helping create it does not get into high school, or even university, history books:

> I spent thirty-three years and four months in active service as a member of our country's most agile military force—the US Marine Corps.... And during that period I spent most of my time being a high-class muscle man for big business, for Wall Street and for the bankers. In short, I was a racketeer for capitalism.
>
> Thus I helped make Mexico and especially Tampico safe for American oil interests in 1914. I helped make Haiti and Cuba a decent place for the National City Bank boys to collect revenues in. I helped purify Nicaragua for the international banking house of Brown Brothers in 1909-12. I brought light to the Dominican Republic for American sugar interests in 1916. I helped make Honduras 'right' for American fruit companies in 1913. In China in 1927 I helped see to it that Standard Oil went its way unmolested.[3]

The highly competent historians Gerald Colby and Charlotte Dennett researched the "conquest of the Amazon" and wrote *Thy Will Be Done: The Conquest of the Amazon: Nelson Rockefeller and Evangelism in the Age of Oil.* Their research soon showed that corporate powers, working in part through missionary groups first to gain control of indigenous societies and then to gain control of their land, had been behind these destabilizations and genocides throughout the 20th-Century. Since WWII the CIA had been deeply involved in the same process for the same purpose. Equally of interest is that key cloak and dagger figures involved in guiding the destiny of the natives to their impoverishment and destruction were assigned positions of power in the American government developing Latin America policy.[4]

As we outline examples of a few of the major destabilizations of post-WWII democratic governments that were breaking out from under the control of the imperial centers, remember that these destabilizations were done by good people just like you and I who believed fully in what they were doing. Quality people throughout the world were firmly locked within a *social-control paradigm* carried by a political, academic, and media system from which many conscientious scholars had been either purged or silenced. Those carrying out the orders of *managers-of-state* had never heard anything other than that they were battling the world's worst elements that were attempting to take away our democratic freedoms.

Iran Breaks Free

When Iranians gained their freedom after WWII under the leadership of Dr. Mohammad Mossadeq, they were America's friend and wished to emulate both its democratic government and its economic success. Operation Ajax (with Kermit Roosevelt, future Vice President of Gulf Oil, in charge of reinstalling the Shah and training SAVAK, the Iranian Secret Service) was the CIA's covert operation to stem that burst of democracy.

Under the reinstalled Shah, Gulf Oil, Standard Oil of New Jersey, Texaco, and Socony-Mobil gained a 40% share of Iranian oil rights (Britain, the original planner of this regime change, claimed the remaining rights). Thousands of Iranians were tortured by SAVAK and a few thousand were killed.[5]

The Iranians were as angry as any American or European would be if a foreign power overthrew their government. But government press releases (most news can be traced to press releases of governments or corporate-funded think-tanks) and planted articles (traceable to the CIA's *Mighty Wurlitzer*) building the image of a great enemy denied all knowledge of this suppression of democracy to the masses in Western nations. That enemy is, of course, then not hard to prove. The overthrow of its government to control its oil and its destiny made Iran that enemy.

On November 4, 1979, activist Muslims overthrew America's puppet dictator, overran the American Embassy, and held 52 Americans hostage for 444 days.[6] This was the greatest peacetime tweak of America's nose in its history.

Considering the imperial nations were actively fomenting intrigues, overthrowing budding democracies with immense loss of life, and installing and supporting puppet dictators all over the world to control resources and markets, to think that America would peacefully take that nose tweaking as well as the loss of control of Iranian oil would be an exercise in extreme denial.

To our knowledge the true history has not been uncovered yet, and may never be, but by accident we do have a hint. The Iran-Iraq War started four months before those hostages were released. Through the CIA's *Mighty Wurlitzer*, the American people were being told the Soviet Union was backing Iraq. The truth came out when the Iraqis gassed their own Kurdish population. (A CIA study concluded it was really Iran. Run a Google search.) A U.S. senator angrily fumed on national news, "We have $800-million of arms in the pipeline to Iraq and we should cancel it all."

With the surfacing of that piece of hidden history, simple common sense tells us that any imperial nation would pursue every option to damage a nation that was holding their citizens hostage and Iraq was likely coached into that invasion with the promise of backing for their claim of title to the oil fields right across its borders. With the strongest nation in the world behind it and Iran in turmoil, Iraq would have felt assured of success.

Containing Iraq

Before the early 20th-Century subdivision of the Middle East, Kuwait was a province of Iraq. Badly bruised from the Iran/Iraq war, upset about Kuwait's horizontal, cross-border, drilling stealing oil from Iraq, and feeling America was now their friend after their immense support, Iraq moved to bring her lost province back into the fold.[a] This led to the 1991 Gulf War which cost Iraq 200,000 killed, destruction of her industry and infrastructure, a 12-year embargo in which another million Iraqis died for lack of food and medicine, and the destruction of a 2nd Gulf War.

The price of oil rising to over $30 a barrel threatens the economies of the *imperial-centers-of-capital.* Powerbrokers feel that oil priced under $20 a barrel will give the world economy a boost.[7] There are deeper reasons. According to Neil Mackay of The Sunday Herald in Scotland, a meeting of President George W. Bush's advisors was held within days after his election in 2000 in which the decision to depose Saddam Hussein was made. U.S. Intelligence would have known that Iraq, Venezuela and Iran were considering switching to euros as their reserve currency which could crash the American economy.[8]

As soon as the war was over the Economic and Social Commission for Western Asia (ESCWA,) met and concluded that the first Gulf War cost them $600 billion and anticipated this 2nd Gulf war will cost them $1 trillion. All the destabilizations and overthrows of governments we are addressing were because of potentials for success if those countries gained or retained their freedom. There is no reason to doubt that the same reason applies to this war (search for ESCWA, $600 million, 1,000 billion).

As of this goes to press the war is on to install a "democratic" government in Iraq. But we must remember that democratic in this context means a government subservient to the West. Puppet governments are as old as history but a "democratic" Muslim government suppressing Muslim interests and supporting Western interests is a contradiction in terms. (For by far the best analysis on American foreign policy as it relates to Yugoslavia and Iraq read Michel *Chossudovsky, War and Globalization: The Truth behind September 11.*)

Economic Freedom for Indonesia was a Big Threat

Indonesia, rich in oil and other resources, was gaining its economic freedom and taking control of its destiny. Besides having massive resources coveted by the imperial nations, Indonesia was establishing an honest democracy. Twenty-five percent of the nation's citizens were following the Communist Party so they were to be entitled to 25% representation in the government. This could not be permitted. On the second try, the CIA overthrew Sukarno and installed Suharto. The managers of the American state were still not secure enough: their newly installed puppet was not actively suppressing that 25% of the voters who were such a threat. If they were left intact, Indonesians may have successfully taken control of their destiny.

---

[a] Most destabilizations were of progressive governments. Saddam Hussein's wars against his neighbors and suppressions internally mark him as a leader easy to justify being deposed.

How Indonesians were coached into slaughtering their own innocent civilians provides a textbook example of how *strategies-of-tensions* work. Arms were beached on the islands, papers were counterfeited to make it appear a revolution was imminent, and a list of over 4,000 political leaders and activists targeted for assassination was passed to the Indonesian military. The tension of Indonesian leaders rose rapidly and, by the lowest estimate, 500,000 Indonesians were slaughtered; by the highest, 1,000,000; and by the CIA's own estimate 800,000. As they tried to change their image in the riots in the year 2000 against the holdovers of Suharto's regime, Indonesia's Special Forces Command, Kopassus the military forces responsible, did not even deny these atrocities.[9]

These innocents were not slaughtered because they were going to overthrow anybody, as the citizens of the Western world were told. They were overthrown because with their enormous resources a truly democratic Indonesian government had a high potential for both political and economic success and that success would catch the attention of other nations who would then insist on their freedom. That suppression of freedom was handled by such fine control of the news that it was almost unknown to the citizens in the Western world and what little was in the news seldom mentioned the immense slaughter and America's connection was totally ignored.

Nigeria tried but did not break Free

In Nigeria, 1966 to 1971, it was oil again and possibly 2-million Biafrans, mostly children, starved as, during that nation's destabilization, relief was prevented from reaching the starving Ibo people. Dan Jacobs, a United Nations relief worker trying to help avert that tragedy, who later researched its causes, was aghast to discover that *British managers-of-state*, with the passive support of *American managers-of-state*, were behind that disaster: "I went to a National Security Council staff man and said: 'The British did this.' 'Oh, of course,' he responded. 'The British orchestrated the whole thing.'" Newsreels were constantly showing footage of starving Nigerians but not a hint did one see that—to prevent a nation with huge natural resources and oil from gaining control of its own destiny—this civil war was externally orchestrated by Britain with the passive diplomatic support of the United States.[10]

Vietnam Gained Political but not Economic Freedom

During WWII, while working directly with American agents to rescue downed U.S. pilots, Ho Chi Minh sent six letters to the U.S. government asking for support and stating that the Vietnamese wished to pattern their constitution after America's. Only after America *refused* to recognize and support their freedom, and instead supported the French suppression of their freedom, were the Vietnamese forced to turn to China and the Soviet Union.[11] It is said that America lost in Vietnam but 3-million people were slaughtered (4-million if one included the previous 15 years of French suppression), millions of acres of forest poisoned with herbicides were destroyed and, after winning its freedom, Vietnam was further decimated by embargoes.[12] We want to remember the revolution only gained America its political independence and it required the war of 1812 to gain its economic independence. Vietnam gained only its political independence, not its economic independence. Vietnamese resources are now available to *imperial-centers-of-capital*. This makes that war a success. After all, control of resources to feed the industries of imperial centers is what these wars are all about.

During the Vietnamese struggle, a treaty was signed in Paris in 1973 for the future of that nation to be decided by free elections. The South Vietnamese puppet government and their American backers knew well that over 80% of the votes would be for rejoining with North Vietnam. So the treaty was ignored and that tiny country and its theoretically neutral neighbors, Laos and Cambodia, were pummeled with more firepower than was expended in WWII (15.5-million tons). The 6.3-million tons of bombs dropped were 50% more than dropped in WWII and created over 5,000 square miles of craters. At the officially acknowledged cost of $800-billion (1990 dollars) to conduct that war and another $800-billion for the cost and damage incurred by the Vietnamese, for a total of $1.6-trillion, America could have given every man, woman, and child in Vietnam (62-million people) $13,000 or about $90,000 per family.[13]

Guatemala Broke Free Briefly

In 1951, the Communist Party was one of the smallest of four parties which supported the election of Jacobo Arbenz as president of Guatemala. Knowing that foreign-owned land titles had been obtained under far from free market conditions, President Arbenz started the legal process of reclaiming several hundred thousand acres of idle land from America's United Fruit Company. For the first block of 178,000 acres, United Fruit was offered a 24-year bond valued at $525,000, its valuation on United Fruit's tax records.

But United Fruit had close connections to the old-boy network of the National Security Council and in the CIA: The brothers John Foster Dulles (appointed Secretary of State one year before the overthrow of Arbenz), Allen Dulles (appointed director of the CIA the year of that overthrow), General Walter Bedell Smith (director of the CIA when Arbenz was elected), and John J. McCloy (World Bank president who refused loans to Guatemala during its destabilizations). In a replay of a future Vice President of Gulf Oil, Kermit Roosevelt, overseeing the overthrow of Iran, all four of these powerful men in American intelligence and the World Bank either had a longstanding connection to United Fruit before Arbenz's overthrow, or became directors of that company shortly afterwards.[14]

An earlier coup attempt with the CIA backing the remnant colonial elite with money and arms failed, so the CIA prepared more thoroughly for Arbenz's overthrow in 1954. A propaganda campaign was launched throughout Latin America claiming that Arbenz was a Communist. Russian-made arms were parachuted into Guatemala to be found and support the claim of a Communist takeover. The CIA and the United States Information Service (USIA, an integral part of the *Mighty Wurlitzer*) cooperated in a media blitz. The USIA created over 200 propaganda articles on Guatemala and provided them to Latin American newspapers for anonymous use. Over 100,000 pamphlets titled "Chronology of Communism in Guatemala" and 27,000 copies of anticommunist cartoons and posters were distributed. The USIA produced three propaganda movies on Guatemala. Seven weeks before the successful coup the CIA launched a clandestine radio misinformation campaign.[15]

When all was ready, powerful transmitters broadcasting messages of confusion overrode Guatemala's national radio while fighter aircraft bombed oil and ammunition dumps, strafed Guatemala City, and dropped smoke bombs to make it appear the attack was even larger. Although the CIA army of expatriate Guatemalans never numbered over 400 and were staying close to the Honduran border so they could escape if the Guatemalan army was activated, the bluff worked. Arbenz was overthrown.[16]

Undestroyed documents eventually forced out of the CIA under the Freedom of Information Act showed that 58 of Guatemala's freely elected officials were targeted for assassination. A comparable number of elected officials and intellectuals targeted for death so as to control the American government would be 2,300. Only the CIA knows how many of those original 58 leaders were assassinated, but with 200,000 killed and unaccounted for during the 35 years Guatemalans attempted to wrest back their government, and with Guatemala's U.S.-supported military and CIA-orchestrated death squads being responsible for a documented 93% of the slaughters, it is highly likely that most were.[17]

Chile Broke Free Very Briefly

Thinking there were no serious problems in Chile and spending only a modest amount of money to influence its 1972 election, Cold War *managers-of-state* went into shock when Salvadore Allende was freely elected president on a platform of control of Chilean resources for Chileans.

The CIA immediately financed 10 economists, primarily from the Chicago School of Economics, to put together an alternative economic program for Chile to assure stability once that errant nation was brought back within the fold. To assure its return, the *managers-of-state* embargoed Chile and the CIA and America's military, primarily the Navy, coordinated plans for Allende's overthrow. This included picking Chilean military personnel for training at the School of the Americas (then in Panama, later in Fort Benning, Georgia, then renamed to the Center for Inter-American Security Cooperation, but properly nicknamed The School of Assassins or School of Coups). Among those hand-picked recruits would be dependable supporters for a coup when the time was ripe. Guns used to assassinate President Allende were proven to have been given to the assassins by the CIA which then must abide by the rules of plausible denial and disclaim any responsibility.[18] Among those killed the first year of Pinochet's regime were citizens of the United States, Spain, and a few other countries. The Chilean government's official figure of 3,197 killed by its security forces in the suppression is almost certainly many times too low.[19]

Pinochet was under house arrest in Britain for over a year in response to a petition to be extradited to Spain to stand trial for killing 300 Spanish citizens.[a] Although he escaped that attempt to put him on trial, eight Chilean generals and 80 military and intelligence officials have been indicted and virtually everyone agrees that even though Pinochet has been declared mentally incompetent to stand trial, he will be recorded in history as being in charge of the torture and slaughter of over 3,000 innocent Chileans.[20] Argentineans have similarly been able to correct the history of the suppression of democratic voice in their country but most such suppressions get falsely recorded as civil wars and uprisings.

Chile since the overthrow of Allende is trumpeted as a great success story of Adam Smith free trade. But when all wealth is accounted for, it is a testimonial to Chilean resources and wealth going to the *imperial-centers-of-capital* and their wealthy puppets now running Chile. In statistics, where you

---

[a] A part of those assassinations were carried out under Operation Condor, a joint operation set up by Chilean, Argentinean, Brazilian, Uruguayan, Paraguayan, Ecuadorian and Bolivian intelligence (see *The Nation* August 9, 1999 and the New York Times March 6, 2001) to assassinate expatriates whom they considered a danger to the security of their then Fascist governments and who had fled their home country, including some in Spain, Italy, the United States, and other countries,. The problem, of course, was that these people knew too much about the Fascist suppressions in these countries. The assassination in Washington DC of former Chilean official Orlando Letelier was carried out under Operation Condor. American Ronni Moffit was riding in the car alongside Letelier and killed in that blast. A Google search using keywords on these pages will come up with tons of citations.

As this is written 86 nuns, priests, veterans, students, grandmothers, and grandfathers are being sentenced for protesting at the gates of the terrorist training center (school of the Americas addressed above) operating in America. This is an annual event essentially unreported in the American media. As the imperial centers write history through placing defeated leaders on trial as mass murderers, the defendants were denied the right to use an international law defense but these courageous people would not be silenced and spoke forcefully on the atrocities committed worldwide by graduates of this terrorist training center.

start and where you quit is everything. After Allende's overthrow, national output dropped 15%, the unemployment rate rose to 20%, wage reductions averaged 15%, and that low level provides the base for most statistics.

But a proper statistical base would start from Chile's production level under Allende. Chile's GDP 16 years after Allende (1986) had only regained that 1970 level, real wages were still below that year's level, per-capita consumption was 15% lower (some calculate 23% lower). In the next five years (1985 to 1990) the income of the top 10% of Chileans rose 90% while the share of Chile's wealth for Chile's poorest 25% fell from 11% to 7%.[21]

The percentage share of national income going to labor dropped from 47.7% in 1970 to 19% 20 years later. Likewise, Argentina's labor share dropped from 40.9% to 24.9%, Ecuador's from 34.4% to 15.8%, Mexico's from 37.5% to 27.3%, and Peru's from 40% to 16.8%.[22] The real story of Chile and other emerging nations is that the earnings of laborers have declined significantly, their rights have declined precipitously, the earnings of the already wealthy have climbed astronomically, and the natural wealth of Chile and the rest of Latin America is being rapidly mined, harvested, and shipped to the *imperial-centers-of-capital*, a classic example of a successful neo-mercantilist policy.

El Salvador did not gain even its Political Freedom

With the exception that a free election was never permitted, the 1980 through 1992 suppression of El Salvador's break for freedom paralleled that of Guatemala as described above. When tortured bodies with their thumbs wired behind their backs show up outside the El Salvadoran capital almost daily and since there was no serious effort by the officials to get to the bottom of those tortures, one can safely assume these are government assassinations of the political opposition.

This was the conclusion of the United Nations El Salvador Truth Commission. Its 1993 report placed responsibility for 85% of the 70,000-plus deaths on security forces trained, armed, and advised by the American military and another 10% upon the El Salvadoran elite's private death squads which, of course, could only function with the silent approval of the both the El Salvadoran and American governments. The suppression was successful and El Salvador remains as a provider of cheap resources and labor. [23] It is now "the 8th-largest exporter worldwide of apparel to the United States. This year it will send the U.S. 268-million garments." A Google search for Truth Commissions will be an education.

Nicaragua never attained Economic Freedom

Nicaragua gained its freedom July 19, 1979, when the Sandinista liberation forces overthrew President Somoza. Under the guidelines of NSC-68, American *managers-of-state* immediately made plans to reverse that revolution. The CIA armed, trained, and oversaw the sabotage and assassinations within Nicaragua by Nicaraguan defectors called Contras. While tens of thousands of people were killed under the oppressive—U.S. sponsored—Somoza dictatorship, only a few thousand died in as Nicaragua fought for its freedom, all at the hands of the Contras. The Nicaraguan government was protecting its citizens as opposed to being the primary source of murderous assault upon its own people as in Chile, Guatemala, El Salvador and in Nicaragua under Somoza. The immediate improvement in education, health, and living standards under the Sandinistas was reversed by the destabilization process.

The beleaguered Sandinistas eventually agreed to a free election, massive U.S. funds illegally financed the opposition, the people knew the war of attrition would continue if Ortega and the Sandinistas still governed, and the American-backed Violeta Chammoro became president of Nicaragua in February 1990.[24] Though the Chammoro government was not the thief and oppressor the old guard Somoza government had been, that suffering nation has not yet (2003) attained the standard of living of the early years of their revolution, their resources again feed the industries and populations of the *imperial-centers-of-capital*, 1-in-9 Nicaraguan children face serious malnutrition (BBC news used the word starving), and Nicaragua is again a country going nowhere.

Southern Africa's Frontline States

As the Vietnam War wound down in 1976, the CIA, under the instructions of Secretary of State Henry Kissinger, was getting deeper into Angola and other regions of the world. John Stockwell, former CIA officer in Langley, Virginia, overseeing the destabilization of Angola, emphatically points out that America was supporting the National Union for Total Independence of Angola (UNITA) while the vast majority of Angolans supported the Popular Movement for the Liberation of Angola (MPLA). Moreover, it was well recognized that the MPLA was "best-qualified to run Angola; nor was it hostile to the United States," while the leader of UNITA, Jonas Savimbi, had taken training in the Soviet Union and was distinctly more ideologically tuned to the Soviet Union than MPLA. Obviously the political and economic shattering of Angola was the purpose of supporting Savimbi, not the establishment of a functional friendly government.[25]

Facing the greatest threat from black Africans gaining their freedom, South Africa's white minority government orchestrated Renamo's terror campaign in Mozambique and, in conjunction with the remnant colonial power-structures, ran similar covert destabilization campaigns in Zambia, Namibia, Zimbabwe, and Botswana.[26]

The CIA, with support from Belgium, destabilized the Congo and assassinated the charismatic and popular Patrice Lumumba (run a Google search) before he could be legitimized as their leader through elections.

Control still could not be assured, so Zaire was created to remove those rich copper deposits from the uncontrollable Congolese and Joseph Mobutu was installed as the Belgian/American puppet. That it was business interests that were being protected in the Congo is just as obvious as in General Smedley Butler's overseas incursions by U.S. marines addressed above.[27]

As they were breaking free after WWII, many countries of Africa were looking forward to cooperating, building their infrastructure, educating their citizens, building modern industry, and joining the world of developed nations. The suppressions to prevent those breaks for freedom on the southern cone of Africa cost between 1.5-million and 2-million innocent lives and left those nations shattered, deeply in debt, and torn apart by factions fighting for political supremacy yet today.

The Libyan Threat

After Libya declared its freedom, Britain tried several times to covertly overthrow Libya's leader who responded by supporting violent anti-Western political movements. After direct bomber attacks, which killed President Muammar Khadaffi's adopted daughter, such support was abandoned. Though Libya's human losses have been small, there have been some killed and, through embargoes, their economy has been successfully contained.

Libyan, Iranian, and Iraqi economic freedom meant they, along with other newly developing oil-rich nations which would follow their lead, would build their own refineries and take over a significant share of the world's oil industry. With their cheap oil and massive reserves (pennies per barrel as both raw material and fuel for their refineries and factories against $17 to $30 a barrel for others to import), they would also control all the thousands of derivative products of oil (medicines, plastics, synthetic fibers, et al.) as well as other fuel-intensive production processes.

What really threatens the imperial center is the potential of success of Libya's and other resource-wealthy nations' development plans and the loss not only of control of that oil and other resources but of the current monopolization of other industries through those nations' use of the immense profits to take over industries and markets.

Cuba: almost Free and may yet Succeed

In 1959 the American-backed Cuban dictator, General Batista, fled as Fidel Castro's forces freed Cuba. The new Cuban government was not Communist and attempted to maintain friendly relations with America. But the redistribution of the *wealth-producing-processes* in Cuba from foreign ownership to Cuban ownership and their regaining control of their destiny was the very thing that threatened American *managers-of-state* the most.

Embargoes were put into effect to force a rescinding of those policies. Cuba promptly turned to the Soviet Union for technological and economic support and embraced the Communist ideology. The Cuban economy developed rapidly. Cuban students now lead the world in education, their health care equals America's, and infant mortality is lower.[a] No Cubans were hungry, housing was being rapidly built, and a sign outside Havana read: "Millions of children in the world sleep in the street and not one is Cuban."

All this was accomplished even as Cuba was totally embargoed by the West. No ship trading with America dared dock in a Cuban port; if they did they could not dock in the United States. No corporation dared trade with Cuba; to do so would result in fines or withdrawal of trading rights in the United States. Such rapid development of a nation breaking free was the great fear of *managers-of-state*. Saboteurs—trained, armed, financed, and managed by the CIA—counterfeited Cuban money and ration books, burned cane fields and infected them with fungus, infected tobacco fields with mildew, and infected potato fields with the potato-ravaging insect Thrips palmi. African swine fever, never before seen in the Western hemisphere, ravaged Cuba twice and 500,000 pigs had to be destroyed. Over 300,000 Cubans were infected with dengue fever, 158 died of which 101 were children under 15 years old. Enough operatives have acknowledged their part in this biological warfare that serious researchers accept the accuracy of these allegations. Newly released CIA documents alerted researchers that crop warfare was practiced against a number of impoverished countries.[28]

This author watched a news broadcast where one operative boasted of over 50 forays into Cuba creating such havoc, including blowing up a Cuban railroad trestle and "watching the train go into the ravine just like in the movies." The reader should note that, until the 9/11/2001, terrorist attack on America, no one was blowing up American or European trains and refineries, no one was burning American or European grain fields, no one was poisoning the West's dairy cattle (7,000 East German dairy cattle were poisoned by the CIA) and no one was practicing germ and crop warfare against the West. In short, the truth is exactly apposite of what the CIA's *Mighty Wurlitzer* has propagandized the world to believe. No countries were attempting to overthrow Western nations. It is the rest of the world which was under assault by the West for the purpose of controlling their governments, their resources, and the *wealth-producing-process*.

After the 9/11 terrorist attack Americans are very justly waging a war on terror. Yet five Cuban agents infiltrating the Cuban-American community so Cuba could be forewarned of U.S. coached terrorist attacks

---

[a] It is this success that terrifies imperial nations not their failures. The fear is that such successes will expose that Western Democracies are not full democracies, that they do not provide their citizens full rights, and that they are not the most efficient economies.

against them were sentenced to 15-years-to-life as spies. A serious analysis would conclude that charging those Cuban heroes with spying is an admission that America was behind the same covert attacks against Cuba as they fear others are now waging against Americans. The imperial center is retaining the right to interfere covertly, overtly, and violently with any nation on the periphery and simultaneously denying these besieged people even the right of self-defense.

Note how successful these *strategies-of-tension* are for controlling the mindset of a population. American people remained blissfully unaware that Cubans had attained a level of education and health care equal to America and had eliminated hunger while the rest of Latin America remained in poverty. Talk to any American on the street, most will know nothing of Cuba's successes and, even though it is Cuba being terrorized by America and Cuba is not terrorizing anyone, they believe Cuba is a terrorist state in poverty.

Many times this author would test his peers by bringing up the subject of Cuba. Their immediate angry response casting Castro as a dictator and killer testify to the effectiveness of the American propaganda machine. Rather than being an autocratic dictator, any leaders that led a country to freedom and made such great progress in eliminating poverty and hunger would gain the very loyalty and respect the Cuban people give their government. Far fewer people died in the Cuban revolution than most and those who were killed were Cubans cooperating with the American government in the attempted suppression of Cuban freedom.

That Cuba was ever a military threat is totally silly. No serious diplomat of state thought the Soviets, China, or anyone else was going to invade anyone in the powerful Western bloc. It was Cuba's rapid, exemplary successes in bettering the living standards of her people, which, if allowed to succeed, would have made it impossible to control the governments and resources of other impoverished nations that was the threat.

When the Soviet Union collapsed, one of the conditions for financial help was that it withdraw its support of Cuba. This effectively isolated their economy. Building cranes went silent for lack of building materials, machinery was idled for lack of spare parts, and the once prosperous Cuban economy rapidly regressed. As this book goes to press, the Cubans have found a few countries to trade with and have turned their economy back up. But it appears that they will stay embargoed until they abandon control of their destiny and accept control by the imperial center.

On a positive note, Cuban doctors have gone to the poorest regions of the world's poorest countries to provide medical care. Cuba is now providing free medical scholarships to students from poor nations and has provided 50 free scholarships to poor American students with the understanding that they will practice in the poorer parts of the U.S. which have a shortage of good doctors.[29] So much for Cuban terrorists.

Orchestration of Death Squads and Writing History

Those who control history control the future. It is understandable that the United States is using its immense power to prevent the establishment of an International Criminal Court with authority to judge the planners and perpetrators of these atrocities. If such a court were ever established and given the investigative authority and funds, true history might be recorded. The powerful, currently protected because their acts are unrecorded in history and thus unknown, would be immediately weakened as their illegal acts were put on record, and the power of the suppressed masses would be simultaneously strengthened.

When U.S.-trained covert operatives are caught in criminal acts that are extensions of these operations, typically they are not charged in U.S. courts. To do so would require opening those CIA records so—since every operation is the total antithesis of law, justice, honesty, and right—these charges are dismissed or never brought in the first place. We are watching this scene play out with four long-term CIA agents set for trial in Puerto Rico for plotting to kill Fidel Castro of Cuba. They are threatening to expose the fact that their assassination project was only an extension of the spreading of exotic livestock diseases and exotic human diseases in Cuba, burning Cuban cane fields, blowing an airliner with a champion Cuban fencing team (and other innocent people) out of the sky, and many other covert operations they were trained to do by the CIA, including the now well-known 30-year CIA effort to assassinate Castro.

An attempt was made to assassinate Chou En Lai of China, second in power only to Mao Ze-dong. The plane was successfully sabotaged when it landed to refuel outside of China and all aboard were killed. However, Chou En Lai had taken another plane. This was a precursor to sabotaging the plane with the Cuban champion fencing team, and these were far from the only such Western state-sponsored assassinations of fundamentally nonviolent and peaceful leaders and potential leaders. [30] Those death squads were killing teachers, professors, labor leaders, cooperative leaders, and church leaders. Those killed were not the terrorists and killers that we are told. They were the budding Washingtons, Jeffersons, Madisons, Gandhis, and Martin Luther Kings of those countries.

It is possible that U.S.-sponsored state terrorism was greater than all other world terrorism combined, state and private, and it is a certainty that all Western nations together supported and guided several times more terrorism than the entire rest of the world.[a] And remember, much, if not

---

[a] Feisal Mansoor of Sri Lanka informed us that "idealistic youths were being murdered by the SL state in 1987-1992, the elite did not move until one of their own (Richard De Zoysa, journalist and doyen of Colombo society) was taken away from his home at night and found the next morning shot through the head on a beach South of Colombo." Like the

most, private world terrorism is in reaction to these assaults (overt, covert, financial, and economic) that subvert the governments and economies of defenseless societies.

Imperial nations fear a true International Criminal Court[31] but they have no fear of the current International War Crimes Tribunal indicting and trying war criminals. Since the U.S. and NATO established and financed this court and provided the researchers and judges, there is no danger of it seriously looking into terrorist acts of their own such as we are addressing.

On May 10th, 2000 at a speech in Berkeley, California, Secretary of State Madeleine Albright (one of the primary designers of trying Yugoslavs for war crimes) admitted what all diplomats knew: the U.S. "raised the bar" high enough during the Rambouillet negotiations so that "Milosevic could not jump over it" because "Yugoslavia needed a little bombing." The U.S. dictated at Rambouillet that Yugoslavia accepts the total occupation of Yugoslavia by NATO or be bombed. As all diplomats agree that no nation could sign such an agreement, Rambouillet was a declaration of war, not a negotiation, and this means that all who planned that war and the massive destruction of Yugoslavia's civilian infrastructure are war criminals.

Though a few officers of the puppet forces in the Yugoslav destabilization will necessarily have to be sacrificed, the focus will be on indicting and convicting Serbian leaders and military officers while the primary planners and enforcers of this externally planned destabilization of Yugoslavia will be untouched. This court will feign balance by investigating the Rwandan slaughter of 500,000 but the terrorist acts of *imperial-centers-of-capital* will not go on this court's calendar. Quite simply, those court records are the writing of history and these courts are designed to write history through destroying the reputation of targeted societies and leaving the imperial nations unblemished.[a]

Future Leaders of Nations Picked and Trained

The CIA picks candidates in the developing world for an all-expense-paid education at Milton Friedman's Chicago School of [neo-liberal] Economics and other conservative institutions and these students go back to teach and run governments. To regain control of Chile, the CIA handpicked several

---

Inquisitions of the Middle Ages, the tortures and deaths abated when it reached into the ruling classes. Obviously orchestrated death squads were operating in many countries we have not addressed.

[a] As these subjects are not touched by Western media, we must depend upon www.emperors-clothes.com, and Google searches on the Internet using keywords off these pages, for this information so crucial to deciphering the true *policies-of-state*. Our statement barely scrapes the surface of evidence of Western war crimes and we encourage the reader to look at the in depth analysis on that website. William Blum, *Rogue State: A Guide to the World's Only Super Power* (Monroe, ME: Common Courage Press, 2000), especially pp. 73-77, addresses the subject well. Also, Christopher Hitchens, *The Trial of Henry Kissinger* (New York: Verso, 2001).

hundred Chilean students for training at the Chicago School. These graduates returned to Chile, and are—along with the graduates of the School of the Americas (School of Coups/School of Assassins) addressed above—professors and political leaders in Chile today.

So it goes with military officers and students from all over the world. Money is always available for the "right students" to take the "right classes" under the "right professors" in America, others must fend for themselves [32] This is a continuation of William Pitt's imposition of Adam Smith free trade philosophy (as interpreted by neo-mercantilists) upon the defeated world to maintain its dependency. History is then written through the lens of that imposed belief.

Writing History through Erasing the Records

Strategies-of-Tension would fail if exposed. CIA agents are trained on how to write the historical record to protect themselves and purging the records of damaging information is standard practice. In the Iran Contra hearings, Americans watched on their nightly news as Colonel Oliver North testified that he had shredded all records of that covert operation. When Congress was questioning the covert actions in Angola, John Stockwell, in charge of that destabilization, explained that the CIA director, George Bush, sent a young lawyer to his office to purge his files of any such records. Bush then testified to Congress, "that no files in the Agency corroborated any of the Congressional allegations." The CIA and other intelligence agencies are going even further. They are finishing their writing of this history by destroying their covert action records, which, of course, then leaves only these tens of thousands of fraudulent articles and books, and no record of their dishonest creation or the orchestration of those destabilizations by *powerful imperial-centers-of-capital*.[33]

Argentina has also destroyed their records on assassinating 30,000 essentially peaceful people (among them nuns and teenagers, about 500 of them pregnant women who, after giving birth, went straight to the plane which dropped these drugged people into the Atlantic Ocean[34]), and it is a safe bet that other allied imperial nations and puppet governments have destroyed their incriminating records.

Due to the perseverance of mothers, the violence that Argentina imposed on its own people is being recorded even if it is 30 years late. But the ironclad rule of all imperial nations is "plausible denial." These government-sponsored terrorist acts against other people, or their own people, are not to be traceable to those governments and thus unrecorded in history.

Only what is acknowledged or proven can be recorded in history. When someone does bring this government-imposed violence to light, the very people planning or carrying out this violence testify in front of Congress that it is not happening, the government denies to the people and the world that it is involved, and most of those records of covert terrorism are erased before the 30 to 100 years the secrets legally run out. So even if recorders of history (the media) are somehow informed that their government is responsible for extreme violence against innocent people, it does not get recorded in the papers and magazines of record and thus does not get recorded in history. We owe defecting CIA agents and good researchers an enormous debt for bringing enough to light before those records were destroyed so the story can be told.

South Africa's policy of amnesty for all who fully tell the story of their involvement in that country's state terrorism has exposed these practices. But the South African government's poisonings, tortures, and assassinations pale into insignificance alongside those carried out under Western destabilization policies.

We must remember the title of George Seldes's book, *Even the Gods Can't Change History*, and his many examples of totally falsified events recorded as fact that simply cannot get changed in the history books. Quite simply, the winners of wars write history, claims of a free press and free thought notwithstanding. Those old history books become the source for new history books and the same falsifications of history are repeated.

When listening to someone on a podium mouthing the politically correct statements of dictators and killers in Cuba or any other country that has been demonized as wanting to rule the world, you as an individual can break through that propaganda blockade. When recognized to ask questions from the floor, here are some questions that will alert an audience that much in world history and world politics that they took for granted was far from true::

(1) "How come our media and our political leaders did not inform us that Cuba—once as impoverished as other Latin American nations—attained the education and health care level of America?

(2) How come Cuba eliminated hunger while the rest of Latin America did not?

(3) How come tens of millions of children in the world sleep in the street and not one is Cuban?

(4) How did they do this even as they were under almost total embargo by the West and American covert assaults burned their cane fields, spread exotic diseases to their livestock and within the human population killing over 150 Cuban children and forcing the slaughter of thousands of livestock, blew up railroad trestles dumping trains into the ravine, and blew a Cuban airliner out of the sky with Cuba's champion fencing team aboard?

(5) Why were we not informed of the 730 American airmen who were shot down over the Soviet Union who were either killed in the crash or finished out their lives in Soviet prisons while their family were told any of dozens of cover stories of how they died?

(6) It is undemocratic and illegal in America and any other country for another country to be involved in their elections. How come America heavily financed and guided elections in almost every country of the world including those in Western Europe?

(7) By what right did America orchestrate the assassination by death squads of thousands of budding Washingtons, Jeffersons, Martin Luther Kings, and Gandhis when they were losing control of elections in El Salvador, Guatemala, Nicaragua, and dozens of other tiny countries?

(8) By what right did America destabilize governments that, in spite of the above named covert U.S. efforts, were democratically elected (Chile, Guatemala, Iran, Indonesia, and Nicaragua is an incomplete list)?

(9) What does dictating policy to the world do to our language when those assaulted countries with multiple political parties and some, such as the former Soviet Union whose citizens' representatives had direct instructions from the voters on how to vote on issues (similar to American ballot initiatives), are labeled dictatorships while the countries which did all I have just described, and which have effectively kept true democratic choice out of their political systems, label themselves as democracies?

The Battle for Trade Supremacy Continues

As a participant who helped write the training manuals and briefed presidents and pentagon chiefs on these covert operations, Colonel Prouty points out:

> One of the least-known divisions of the CIA is that headed by the Deputy Director of Economics. This division moves into a country to work with a new regime and to begin the task of selecting and setting up new franchise holders for as many goods as possible to assure that they are imported from American companies and that those from other sources, formerly the Soviet sphere in particular, are excluded.... The CIA screens and selects these new "millionaires' and arranges for them to meet with various companies they will front for under the new regime. It might be said that this cleansing of the economic system is the real reason for most of the coups d'état and that political ideology has very little to do with it.... Some of the more daring, in an attempt to escape the severe financial and profit-making controls placed upon them and their government by U.S. manufacturers and by the canopy of international banks that is spread over all imports and exports to their country, attempt to make deals with other countries. They believe they may be able to buy essential goods cheaper that way and to sell their labor and resources at better rates.... As such actions increase, the national leadership will be increasingly attacked by the United States on the grounds that it is turning toward communism and becoming a base for the infiltration of the communist ideology and military system into the hemisphere.[35]

Various countries have proven that America's worldwide listening posts utilizing ECHELON software operated by the National Security Agency, have stolen proprietary corporate and government information and passed that information on to American corporations and trade negotiators. American corporations were then able to patent what was invented by others and American trade negotiators knowledge of other governments' bottom lines gave them an unassailable advantage in negotiations.[36]

There we have it. All intelligence agencies have been, and are still in, the business of destabilizing undeveloped countries so as to maintain their dependency. It is the dependency of weak nations that maintains the flow of the world's natural wealth to powerful nations' industries at a low price and provides markets for those industrial products at a relatively high price. The military forces of today's powerful nations are for the same purpose as those raiding parties from the city states 800 years ago as addressed in Chapter 2 control of the *wealth-producing-process..*

---

[1] *Covert Action Information Bulletin* (Summer 1987): p. 28; see Chapter 6, endnote 6.

[2] Bernard Grun, *Timetables of American History* (New York: Simon and Schuster, 1979); L. Fletcher Prouty, *JFK: The CIA, Vietnam, and the Plot to Assassinate John F. Kennedy* (New York: Birch Lane Press, 1992), pp. 33-36; W. Bello, *U.S. Sponsored Low Intensity Conflict in the Philippines* (San Francisco: Institute for Food & Development Policy December, 1987); S. Karnow, *In Our Image: America's Empire in the Philippines* (New York: Random House, 1989); Fred Poole, and Max Vanzi, *Revolution in the Philippines: The United States in A Hall of Cracked Mirrors* (New York: McGraw-Hill, 1984); Daniel B. Schirmer and Stephen Rosskamm Shalom, *The Philippines Reader: A History of Colonialism, Dictatorship, and Resistan*ce (Boston: South End Press, 1987); William Blum, *The CIA: A Forgotten History* (London: Zed Books, 1986); C.B. Currey, Edward Lansdale: *The Unquiet American* (Boston: Houghton Mifflin Company, 1988); R. Constantino and L.R. Constantino, The Philippines: The Continuing Past (Quezon City, Philippines: The Foundation for Nationalist Studies, 1978); G. Porter, "The politics of counterinsurgency in the Philippines: Military and Political Options," *Philippine Studies Occasional Paper No. 9* (Honolulu, HI: University of Hawaii, Center for Philippine Studies, 1987); R. Bonner, *Waltzing with a Dictator* (New York: Times Books 1987); J. Prados, *The Presidents' Secret Wars* (New York: William Morrow, 1986) and *The President's Secret Wars*, rev. Warwick: Elephant Paperbacks, 1996; K. Nair, *Devil and His Dart: How the CIA is Plotting in the Third World* (New Delhi: Sterling Publishers, 1986); *Bulletin of Concerned Asian Scholar*s, Boulder, CO, many issues; E. G. Lansdale, *In the Midst of Wars* (New York: Harper & Row, 1972); D.S. Blaufarb, *The Counterinsurgency Era: U.S. Doctrine and Performance 1950 to Present* (New York: The Free Press, 1977); E. Thomas, *The Very Best Men, Four Who Dared: The Early Years of the CIA* (New York: Simon & Schuster, 1995); J. Ranelagh, *The Agency* (New York: Simon & Schuster, 1986); Michael T. Klare and P. Kornbluh, *Low Intensity Warfare* (NY: Pantheon Books, 1988); see Chapter 6, endnote 6.

[3] Frederic F. Clairmont, *Rise and Fall of Economic Liberalism* (Goa, India: The Other India Press, 1996), p. 223.

[4] Gerald Colby, Charlotte Dennett, *Thy Will Be Done: The Conquest of the Amazon: Nelson Rockefeller and Evangelism in the Age of Oil* (New York: Harper Collins, 1995). Conversation with the authors shortly after their book was published.

[5] Amir Taheri, *Nest of Spies: America's Journey to Disaster in Iran* (New York: Pantheon Books, 1988); Said K. Aburish, *A Brutal Friendship: The West and the Arab Elite* (New York: St. Martin's Press, 1998); *Richard Labeviere, Dollars for Terror: The United States and Iran* (New York: Algora Publishing, 2000), p. 44; Burton Hersh, *The Old Boys: The American Elite and the Origins of the CIA* (New York: Charles Scribner's Sons, 1992), 330-34; Kermit Roosevelt, *Countercoup: The Struggle for the Control of Iran* (New York: McGraw-Hill 1979): C. Andrew, *For the President's Eyes Only: Secret Intelligence and the American Presidency from Washington to Bush* (New York: HarperCollins Publishers, 1995), pp. 203-05; see Chapter 6, endnote 6.

6 Taheri, *Nest of Spies*, pp. 122-126.

7 Neil Mackay, "Bush Planned Iraq 'Regime Change' Before Coming President," *The Sunday Herald* (Scotland), September 15, 2002; Dan Morgan and David B Ottaway, "In Iraqi Oil Scenario, Oil is Key Issue: U.S. Drillers Eye Huge Petroleum Pool," *Washington Post*, September 14, 2002; Scott Peterson, "In War, Some Facts Less Factual," *The Christian Science Monitor* September 6, 2002; Bill Powell, "Iraq We Win, Then What, *Fortune* November 5, 2002, pp. 61-72; Milan Rai, *War Plan Iraq* (London: Verso Press, 2002); William Rivers Pitt, Scott Ritter, *War on Iraq* (New York: Context Books, 2002).

8 Mackay, "Bush Planned Iraq 'Regime Change'"; W. Clark, "The Real Reason for the upcoming War with Iraq, http://www.ratical.org/ratville/CAH/RRiraqWar.html

9 Dan Murphy, "Indonesia Confronts Unruly Past" (*The Christian Science Monitor*, November 20, 2000), pp. 1, 10; Blum, *Rogue State*, Chapter 17; Philip Agee, *Inside the Company* (New York: Bantam Books, 1975), p. 9; .Steve Weissman, *The Trojan Horse* (Palo Alto: Ramparts Press, 1975); McT Kahin, *Subversion as Foreign Policy: The Secret Eisenhower and Dulles Debacle in Indonesia* (New York: New Press, 1995); Wendell Minnick, *Spies and Provocateurs: A Worldwide Encyclopedia of Persons Conducting Espionage and Covert Action, 1946-1991* (Jefferson, North Carolina: McFarland, 1992), especially pp. 183-84; S.E. Ambrose, *Ike's Spies* (Garden City, New York: Doubleday, 1981), p. 251; M. Caldwell, Editor, *Ten Years Military Terror Indonesia* (Nottingham: Spokesmen Books, no date); Blum, *The CIA*, especially p. 221; search databases for articles or books by Kathy Kadane, reporter for States News Service; see Chapter 6, endnote 6..

10 Dan Jacobs, *The Brutality of Nations* (New York: Alfred A. Knopf, 1987), especially p. 5.

11 Stockwell, *Praetorian Guard*, p. 78.

12 John Prados, *The Hidden History of the Vietnam War* (Chicago: Elephant Paperbacks, 1995); G.M. Kahin and J.W. Lewis, *United States in Vietnam* (New York: Dell Publishing Company, 1969); M. Gettleman, J. Franklin, M. Young, and B. Franklin, *Vietnam and America: The Most Comprehensive Documented History of the Vietnam War* (New York: Grove Press, 1995); *Pentagon Papers: The Defense Department History of United States Decision Making on Vietnam,* Senator Gravel, ed. (Boston: Beacon Press, 1971); L. Ackland, *Credibility Gap: A Digest of the Pentagon Papers* (Philadelphia, PA: The National Literature Service. 1972); O. DeForest and D. Chanoff, *Slow Burn* (New York: Simon and Schuster, 1990); N. Sheehan, *A Bright Shining Lie* (New York: Random House, 1988); Currey, Edward Lansdale; Prouty, *JFK*; Committee of Concerned Asian Scholars, *The Indochina Story: A Fully Documented Account* (New York: Pantheon Books, 1970); Frank Snepp, *Decent Interval* (New York: Random House, 1977); M. Young, *The Vietnam Wars 1945-1990* (New York: HarperCollins, 1991); Douglas Valentine, *The Phoenix Program* (New York: William Morrow, 1990); D. Kaplan, *Fires of the Dragon: Politics, Murder and the Kuomintang* (NY: Atheneum, 1992); K. Conboy and J. Morrison, *Shadow War: The CIA's Secret War in Laos* (Bolder, CO: Paladin Press, 1995); *Bulletin of Concerned Asian Scholars*; see Chapter 6, endnote 6.

13 The Costs of War," *The Nation*, December 24, 1990: p. 793; Matthew Cooper, "Give Trade a Chance," *U.S. News & World Report*, February 14, 1994, p. 20; C. Robbins, *The Ravens: The Men Who Flew in America's Secret War* (New York: Crown Publishers, 1987), p. 332; Prouty, *JFK*, p. 55; V. Levant, *Quiet Complicity: Canadian Involvement in the Vietnam War* (Toronto, Canada: Between the Lines, 1986), p.46.

14 B. Cook, *The Declassified Eisenhower* (Garden City, NY: Doubleday, 1981), pp. 228-29; see also L. Shoup, W. Minter, *Imperial Brain Trust: The Council on Foreign Relations & United States Foreign Policy* (New York: Monthly Review Press, 1977); Hersh, *Old Boys*; Robin Winks, *Cloak & Gown: Scholars in the Secret War, 1939-1961* (New York: Quill, 1987); see Chapter 6, endnote 6.

15 Stephen Schlesinger and Stephen Kinzer, *Bitter Fruit* (New York: Anchor Press/Doubleday, 1984); Peter Grose, *Gentleman Spy : The Life of Allen Dulles* (Boston: University of Massachusetts Press, 1996).

[16] N. Miller, *Spying for America* (New York: Paragon House, 1989); P. Gleijeses, *Shattered Hope: The Guatemalan Revolution and the United States 1944-1954* (Princeton, NJ: Princeton University Press, 1991); H.J. Hunt, *Undercover: Memoirs of an American Secret Agent* (New York: Berkeley Publishing, 1974).

[17] *United Nations Guatemalan Truth Commission Report* carried on AP wires February 25, 1999; Beatriz Manz *Refugees of A Hidden War: The Aftermath of Counterinsurgency in Guatemala* (New York: State University of New York, 1988); Jean-Marie Simon, *Guatemala: Eternal Spring Eternal Tyranny* (New York: W. W. Norton, 1988); Susanne Jonas, *The Battle for Guatemala: Rebels, Death Squads, and U.S. Power* (San Francisco: Westview Press, 1991); Michael McClintock, *The American Connection: State Terror and Popular Resistance in Guatemala* (London: Zed Books, 1985); B. Cook, *The Declassified Eisenhower*, Thomas, *Very Best Men*; D.A, Phillips, *The Night Watch* (New York: Atheneum 1977); T. McCann, *An American Company: The Tragedy of United Fruit* (New York: Crown Publishers, 1976); Andrew, *For the President's Eyes Only*; Eduardo Galeano, *Guatemala: Occupied Country* (New York: Monthly Review Press, 1969); J. Heidenry, *Theirs Was the Kingdom: Lila and Dewitt Wallace and the Story of the Reader's Digest* (New York: W.W. Norton, 1993), pp. 594-97; *CovertAction Quarterly; Counterspy*; run library database searches for anything written by Allen Nairn; Blum, *The CIA*; Blum, *Rogue State*, Chapters 3-10 and Chapter 17; and his book *Killing Hope: U.S. Military Interventions Since World War II* (Monroe, Me: Common Courage Press, 1995); see Chapter 6, endnote 6.

[18] Lucy Komisar, "Documented Complicity: Newly Released Files set the Record Straight on U.S. Support for Pinochet," *The Progressive*, September, 1999, pp. 24-27; Blum, *Rogue State*, Chapter 17; Samuel Chavkin, *The Murder of Chile* (New York: Everest House, 1982); John Dinges, Saul Landau, *Assassination on Embassy Row* (New York: Pantheon Books, 1980); Blum, *Forgotten History*, pp. 232-43; Blum, *Killing Hope*; R.L. Borosage and J. Marks, ed., *The CIA File* (New York: Grossman Publishers, 1976); *Church Committee Report* (1975-1976); William Colby, *Honorable Men* (New York: Simon & Schuster, 1978), pp. 302-06; M. Copeland, *Beyond Cloak and Dagger* (New York: Pinnacle Books, 1975), Note 221; *Counterspy*, Spring/Summer 1975, pp. 43-47; Louis Wolf, *review of The American Federation of Teachers and the CIA*, by George Schmidt, *CovertAction Quarterly* 2 (October 1978); Fred Landis, "*CIA Media Operations in Chile*, Jamaica, and Nicaragua," *CovertAction Quarterly* 16 (March 1982), pp. 42-43; Fred Landis, "Opus Dei: Secret Order Vies for Power," *CovertAction Quarterly* 18 (Winter 1983), pp. 14-15; Louis Wolf, "Inaccuracy in the Media: Accuracy in Media Rewrites the News and History," *CovertAction Quarterly* 21 (Spring 1984), pp. 31-32; Fred Landis, "Moscow Rules Moss's Mind," *CovertAction Quarterly* 4 (Summer 1985), pp. 37-38; Stella Calloni, "The Horror Archives of Operation Condor," *CovertAction Quarterly* 50 (Fall 1994), pp. 11, 13, 58-59; Darrin Wood, "Mexico Practices What School of America Teaches," *CovertAction Quarterly* 59 (Winter 1996-97), pp. 38-53; Lisa Haugaard, "Textbook Repression: US Training Manuals Declassified," *CovertAction Quarterly* 61 (Summer 1997), pp. 29-38; Michael Ratner, "The Pinochet Principle," *CovertAction Quarterly* 66 (Winter 1999), pp. 46-48; H. Frazier, ed, *Uncloaking the CIA* (New York: The Free Press, 1978), 34-54, 60-63; Darrell Garwood, *Under Cover* (New York: Grove Press, 1985), pp. 104, 127; F.S. Landis, "*Psychological Warfare and Media Operations in Chile 1970-1973*" (Doctoral dissertation, University of Illinois, 1975): pp. 4, 14, 235, 254, 309-312; Victor Marchetti, J.D. Marks, *The CIA and the Cult of Intelligence* (New York: Alfred A. Knopf, 1974), especially p. 17; Nair, *Devil and His Dart*; Prados, *Presidents' Secret Wars*, 1996 ed., p. 319; Ranelagh, *Agency*, pp. 514-520; J. Richelson, *American Espionage and the Soviet Target* (New York: William Morrow, 1987), pp. 232-33; R.R. Sandford, *The Murder of Allende*, trans. A. Conrad (New York: Harper & Row, 1975); F.F. Sergeyev, *Chile: CIA Big Business*, trans. L. Bobrov, (Moscow, USSR: Progress Publishers, 1981), pp. 52-53, 93, 98, 108, 114, 163; Stansfield Turner, *Secrecy and Democracy: The CIA in Transition* (Boston: Houghton Mifflin Company, 1985), pp. 80-81, 113, 191; A. Uribe, *The Black Book of American Intervention in Chile* (Boston, MA: Beacon Press, 1975); Rayack, *Not So Free to Choose: The Political Economy of Milton Friedman and Ronald Reagan*

(Westport, Conn: Praeger, 1986); Hersh, *Old Boys*; Winks, *Cloak & Gown*; Juan José Arévalo, *Anti-Kommunism in Latin America* (New York: Lyle Stewart, 1963); see Chapter 6, endnote 6.

19 P. Gunson, A. Thompson, G. Chamberlain, *The Dictionary of Contemporary Politics of South America* (NY: Routledge, 1989), p. 228; Rayack, *Not so Free to Choose*. See also note 18 above and Chapter 6, endnote 6.

20 Marc Cooper, Chile and the End of Pinochet," *The Nation* (February 26, 2001), pp. 11-18.

21 Greg Palast, *The Best Democracy Money Can* Buy, has a much deeper analysis that is a must read for the serious researcher. Duncan Green, *Silent Revolution* (London: Cassel, 1995), pp. 101, 108; Noam Chomsky, *Deterring Democracy* (New York: Verso, 1992), p. 231; Thomas Skidmore, Peter Smith, "*The Pinochet Regime," Modern Latin America* (New York: Oxford University Press, 1989), pp. 137-38.; Rayack, *Not so Free to Choose*; Silvia Bortzutzky, "The Chicago Boys, Social Security and Welfare in Chile," *The Radical Right and the Welfare State*; Howard Glennerster, James Midgley, editors (Barnes and Noble import, 1991), pp. 88, 91, 96; See also above two notes.

22 Rayack, *Not so Free to Choose*; Bortzutzky, " Chicago Boys," pp. 88, 91, 96; Walden Bello, Dark Victory: *The United States and Global Poverty* (San Francisco: Institute for Food and Development Policy, 1999), pp. 42-45, 58-59. See also above three notes. Statistics on labor's share of income is from James Petras and Henry Veltmeyer, "Latin America at the End of the Millennium," *Monthly review* (July/Aug. 1999), p. 44.

23 *United Nations Commission on the Truth in El Salvador, From Madness to Hope: The 12-Year War in El Salvador* (U.N. Security Council, 1993); Charles Kernaghan, "Sweatshop Blues," *Dollars and Sense* (March/April, 1999); Blum, *Rogue State*, Chapter 17; Michael McClintock, *The American Connection: State Terror and Popular Resistance in El Salvador* (London: Zed Books, 1985); Blum, *The CIA*, pp. 232-43; Blum, *Killing Hope*; Dennis Volman, "Salvador Death Squads, a CIA connection?" *The Christian Science Monitor*, May 8, 1984, p. 1; many issues of the *CovertAction Quarterly* and *Counterspy*; Klare & Kornbluh, *Low Intensity Warfare*; Edward S. Herman, F. Broadhead, *Demonstration Elections: U.S. Staged Elections in the Dominican Republic, Vietnam, and El Salvador* (Boston: South End Press, 1984); Jonathan Kwitny, *Endless Enemies: The Making of an Unfriendly World* (New York: Congdon & Weed, 1984) ; see Chapter 6, endnote 6.

24 Blum, Rogue State, Chapter 17; William I. Robinson, A Faustian Bargain: U.S. Intervention in the Nicaraguan Elections and American Foreign Policy in the Post-Cold War Era (Boulder, CO: Westview Press, 1992); Peter Kornblush, Nicaragua, The Price of Intervention: Reagan's War Against the Sandinistas (Washington, DC: Institute for Policy Studies, 1987); Reed Brody, Contra Terror in Nicaragua: Report of A Fact Finding Mission: September 1984-January 1985 (Boston: South End Press, 1985); The Rise and Fall of the Nicaraguan Revolution (New York: New International, 1994); Garvin, G., Everybody Has His Own Gringo: The CIA and the Contras (New York: Brassey's,1992); Peter Kornbluth and M. Byrne, The Iran-Contra Scandal: The Declassified History (New York: A National Security Archive Documents Reader, The New Press, 1993); Twentieth Century Fund, The Need to Know: The Report of the Twentieth Century Fund Task Force on Covert Action and American Democracy (New York: The Twentieth Century Fund Press, 1992); E. Chamorro, "Packaging the Contras: A Case of CIA Disinformation." Institute for Media Analysis, Inc. Monograph Series Number 2 (New York, Institute for Media Analysis, Inc, 1987); Minnick, Spies and Provocateurs; John Prados, Keepers of the Keys: A History of the National Security Council from Truman to Bush (New York: William Morrow, 1991); Loch .K. Johnson, America's Secret Power (New York: Oxford University Press, 1989); C,D. Ameringer, U.S. Foreign Intelligence (Lexington, MA: Lexington Books, 1990); H.B. Westerfield, ed., Inside CIA's Private World: Declassified Articles from the Agency's Internal Journal 1955-1992 (New Haven, CT. Yale University Press, 1995); J. Adams, Secret Armies (New York: The Atlantic Monthly Press 1987); Tony Avirgan and M. Honey, eds., Lapenca: On Trial in Costa Rica (San Jose, CA: Editorial Porvenir, 1987); J. Marshall, P.D. Scott, and J. Hunter, The Iran-Contra Connection (Boston, MA: South End Press, 1987);

P.V. Parakal, Secret Wars of the CIA (New Delhi: Sterling Publishers, 1984); Christopher Simpson, Blowback (New York: Weidenfeld & Nicolson, 1988); National Endowment for Democracy, Annual Report; see Chapter 6, endnote 6.

[25] Blum, *Rogue State*, Chapters 3-10; John Stockwell, *In Search of Enemies* (New York: W.W. Norton, 1978), especially pp. 43, 63-64, 272; Stockwell, *Praetorian Guard*; Jonathan Kwitny, *The Crimes of Patriots* (New York: W. W. Norton, 1987); Clarridge, *A Spy for all Seasons; H. Rositzke, The CIA's Secret Operations* (New York: Thomas Y. Crowell Company, 1977); S. Gervasi and S. Wong, "The Reagan Doctrine and the Destabilization of Southern Africa" (Unpublished paper from McGehee's CIABASE, April 1990); B. Freemantle, *CIA* (New York: Stein and Day, 1983), p. 68.

[26] Blum, Rogue State, Chapter 17; Gervasi and Wong, *Reagan Doctrine*, pp. 56-57; W. Minter, *Apartheid's Contras: An Inquiry into the Roots of War in Angola and Mozambique* (London, ZED Books, 1994).

[27] Stockwell, *In Search of Enemies*, pp. 10, 105, 137, 169, 172, 236-37; Blum, *Rogue State*, Chapter 17; Sean Kelly, *America's Tyrant: The CIA and Mobutu of Zaire* (Washington DC: American University Press, 1993); D. Gibbs, *The Political Economy of Third World Intervention: Mines, Money and U.S. Policy in the Congo Crisis* (Chicago, IL: University of Chicago Press, 1991); R. L. Borosage, J. Marks, *The CIA File* (New York: Grossman Publishers, 1976); Gervasi and Wong, *Reagan Doctrine*; Prados, *Presidents Secret Wars*; Kwitny, *Endless Enemies*; Blum, *Killing Hope*; see Chapter 6, endnote 6.

[28] Blum, *Rogue State*, Chapters 3-10; Stephen Endicott and Edward Hagerman, *The United States and Biological Warfare: Secrets from the Early Cold War and Korea* (Bloomington, IN: Indiana University Press, 1998); Minnick, *Spies and Provocateurs*, especially p. 262; R. Ridenour, *Back Fire: The CIA's Biggest Burn* (Havana, Cuba: Jose Marti Publishing House, 1991), especially pp. 73, 77-78, 145-49; Prados, *Presidents Secret Wars*, 1996 ed., pp. 333, 337, 349; Prados, *Keepers of the Keys*, especially pp. 142-44, 203-317; J.T. Richelson, *The U.S. Intelligence Community* (Cambridge, MA: Ballinger Publishing Company, 1985), especially p. 231; P.V. Parakal, *Secret Wars of the CIA* (New Delhi: Sterling Publishers, 1984); R. S. Cline, *Secrets, Spies, and Scholars* (Washington, DC: Acropolis Books, 1976), especially p. 195; Garwood, *Under Cover*, especially p. 92; P. Wyden, *Bay of Pigs, the Untold Story* (New York: Simon and Schuster, 1979); D. Martin, *Wilderness of Mirrors* (New York: Harper & Row, 1980), especially pp. 151-53; Ranelagh, Agency, especially pp. 356-60; G. Treverton, *Covert Action, The Limits of Intervention in the Postwar World* (New York, NY: Basic Books, Inc., Publishers, 1987); D. Corn, *Blond Ghost: Ted Shackley and the CIA's Crusades* (New York: Simon & Schuster, 1994); L.F. Prouty, *The Secret Team* (Englewood Cliffs, NJ: Prentice-Hall, 1973); Borosage and Marks, *CIA File*; Hersh, *Old Boys*; Thomas, *Very Best Men*; Jeffreys-Jones, R., *The CIA & American Democracy* (New Haven: Yale University Press), 1989; B. Watson, S. Watson, and G. Hopple, *United States Intelligence: An Encyclopedia* (New York: Garland Publishing, 1990); *Covert Action Information Bulletin*; Counterspy; see Chapter 6, endnote 6.

[29] Castro, *Capitalism in Crisis*, p. 138; Nadia Marsh, M.D., "U.S. Med Students Arrive in Cuba," The *Workers' World*, April 19, 2001.

[30] Blum, *Rogue State*, Chapters 3-10; Prados, *Presidents' Secret Wars*, 1996 ed., pp. 333, 337, 349; Garwood, *Under Cover*, pp. 60-64; *Church Committee Report* (1976), Congressional Record; Blum, *The CIA*, p. 108; check Chapter 6, endnote 6 for other successful and unsuccessful attempts to assassinate leaders and potential leaders of other countries.

[31] Tuva Raanes, "A Divine Country All on Its Own," *World Press Review*, October 2002, p. 17.

[32] Prouty, *JFK*, pp. 244-45.

[33] Stephen Schlesinger, "The CIA Censor's History," *The Nation*, July 14, 1997, pp. 20-22; Stockwell, *Praetorian Guard*, p. 21.

[34] Epstein, Jack, "Argentina's 'Dirty War' Laundry May Get a Public Airing," *The Christian Science Monitor*, December 4, 1997,p. 7; Blum, *Rogue State*, Chapters 3, 5, 14, 17, and 18.

[35] Prouty, *JFK*, pp. 236-37, 341.

[36] Blum, *Rogue State*, Chapter 21.

9. Creating Enemies for the Masses

The Inquisitions of the Middle Ages

The Inquisitions of the Middle Ages were, and the Inquisitions of today still are, to prevent democratic choice. The Roman emperors Constantine and Theodosius I, in the 4th-Century AD, stopped the persecution of the Christian church and, along with Justinian I, essentially made the Catholic Church the state religion. Just as the wealth of today migrates toward tax shelters, over the next 700 years aristocracy migrated towards positions of power in the higher offices of the church—those of bishops, cardinals, and pope. Where the church and its people were once one, the church hierarchy (First Estate) and aristocracy (Second Estate) were now one; there was now a distinct division between the church leaders and the common people. From their new power base running the church, the combined First and Second Estates sold indulgencies and salvations. The common people were terrified of Purgatory and the last bit of wealth could be extracted from those who hoped to be saved and go straight to heaven. Edward Burman, in *The Inquisition*, from which this chronology is taken, explains that with the returning Crusaders in the late 11th and early 12th centuries came various unorthodox Christian beliefs filtering into Europe from Jerusalem.

Some of these beliefs permitted each person to find his or her own way to heaven and (primarily the well-organized and rapidly expanding Cathars and Waldensians) openly frowned on a wealthy, licentious church. Others were drawing away church members by competing claims of miraculous cures. All powerbrokers fear the expansion of the political powers of others while their own power shrinks.

Such was the Church's fear of these competing beliefs. The Albigensian Crusade (1209-1229) was organized by Pope Innocent III to destroy the Cathars of southern France with their threatening doctrines and parallel organization of dioceses headed by bishops. This was only the largest of various efforts to suppress heresies since the middle of the 10th-Century. As with all crusades (the crusade of the Cold War is a good example), this required a massive *social-control-paradigm*; a *strategy-of-tension* portraying the

Cathars as a dangerous enemy, in this case as infidels and heretics, to justify their slaughter and the theft of their wealth.

The burning of heretics at the stake for 200 years coalesced between 1123 and 1206 into the formal Inquisition. In 1206 and 1210 Pope Innocent III founded the Franciscan and Dominican Mendicant Orders to preach against heresy; and in 1215 the Latern Council was held which listed "clause by clause" heretical interpretations of the faith, the removal from office of heretics, confiscation of their property, excommunication, and their referral to the feudal lords for punishment.

With the Cathars fleeing to other sections of Europe to escape certain death from zealous inquisitors and secular lords, between 1227 and 1252 Pope Gregory IX and Pope Innocent IV issued several bulls that further encoded and formalized the form of the Inquisition.

"The Inquisition was ready to start work on a grand scale shortly after the mid-point of the thirteenth Century" and, as the Christian sects went underground, Popes Alexander IX, Urban IV, Clement IV, and Boniface VIII issued bulls to maintain that momentum and root out the last vestiges of threat to their power.

Franciscan and Dominican priests organized to lead heretics back to the fold evolved into a few zealous priests becoming inquisitors and torturers. They condemned hundreds of thousands of heretics to burn at the stake over a period of 700 years, the majority being Cathars, Waldensians, Jews, and Muslims. As those religious competitors disappeared, Freemasons, alleged witches, midwives, and personal enemies were targeted.

"Only the fear of losing power acquired over a period of a thousand years can satisfactorily explain such violent reactions."[1] Because they did not believe in buying one's way out of salvation and would draw people from the state church, the Cathars were headed for extinction. They, the Waldensians, and smaller sects in most of Europe were suppressed by 1270 but Jews and Muslims survived as a political force on an ever-shrinking part of the Iberian Peninsula.

We are taught how Roman pagans tortured Christians. But in reality the alliance between the state and the Church extinguished both paganism and competing Christian sects through extreme violence and "the number of Christians executed by other Christians in a single province during the reign of Charles V [alone] far exceeded that of all the martyrs who perished at the hands of the pagans throughout the Roman Empire in the space of three centuries."[2]

The Spanish Inquisition

With the inquisitorial pattern well established, starting in 1478 the Christian secular powers of Spain proceeded to eradicate Jews and Muslims from their territory. The choice was between leaving Spain, converting to Christianity, or being burnt at the stake. It is only because the power of the Spanish empire was a threat to British and other empires that the world knows so much about the Spanish Inquisition and so little about the French, Italian, and British Inquisitions. Although all were equally violent, the history of each culture suppressed the exposure of their inquisitorial violence and emphasized the violence in their archenemy Spain. This is the "creation of enemies" through a *strategy-of-tension* to protect a power-structure as it has functioned throughout history.

The Inquisitorial Suppression of the Templars

The Knights Templar were industrious and faithful servants of Christianity. Their history began in 1119 when nine knights formed an association to protect pilgrims in the Holy Land. They fought so valiantly that

> gifts in abundance flowed in on the Order, large possessions were bestowed on it in all countries of the west.... By the Bull, *Omne datum optimum*, granted by Pope Alexander III in 1162, the Order of the Templars acquired great importance, and from this time forth, it may be regarded as totally independent, acknowledging no authority but that ... of the supreme pontiff.[3]

The Templars fought many battles for Christianity, and by 1302 they had spread over much of Europe and were enormously wealthy and powerful. Much of the land owned by the Templars had been given to their forebears by the grateful ancestors of local aristocracy (in trade for the slaughter of non-Christian or heretical Christian populations) and by a Church whose successors resented and feared the power of this great order. Local bishops and clergy made many complaints to the pope about the Templars' refusal to recognize local religious authority.

When a French pope was consecrated in 1305, he rewarded King Philip IV of France and other nobles by supporting an intrigue against the respected Templars. The French secret service established a *social-control-paradigm* (a *strategy-of-tension*) to protect the power-structure as they destroyed the Templars and stole their wealth. They spread vicious rumors and

> on the night of the 13th of October, [1307], all the Templars in the French dominions were simultaneously arrested.... They were accused of worshipping an idol covered with an old skin, embalmed, having the appearance of a piece of polished oil-cloth. "In this idol," we are assured, "there were two carbuncles for eyes, bright as the brightness of heaven, and it is certain that all hope of the Templars was placed in it: it was their sovereign god, and they trusted in it with all their heart." They are accused of burning the bodies of the deceased brethren, and making the ashes into a powder, which they administered to the younger brethren in their food and drink, to make them hold fast their faith and idolatry; of cooking and roasting infants, and anointing their idols with the fat; of celebrating hidden rites and mysteries, to

> which the young and tender virgins were introduced, and of a variety of abominations too absurd and horrible to be named.[4]

Like all inquisition charges, the fabrications of this *social-control-paradigm* (system of beliefs) could not be defended against and confessions were obtained by torture. King Philip then sent the findings to other European countries. These preposterous accusations were at first rejected, but by 1314 the Templars were totally discredited and destroyed; over 2,000 of them confessed under torture and were quartered or burned at the stake. In only nine years the Templars, who had been perceived for centuries as elite warriors and builders of the Christian world, and who commanded both large resources and respect, were labeled enemies and cast into oblivion. The First and Second Estates had acted together to reclaim their wealth and power.[5]

Winding Down the Inquisitions of the Middle Ages

As the Inquisition wound down in Europe in the 18th-Century (except in Spain), its dying flame, now picked up by Protestant evangelists, reached America in the form of the Salem witch trials. Small inquisitorial flames in Peru and Columbia died out in the 17th-Century but in Spain and Mexico it was a primary political tool well into the 19th-Century.

Although under a different name (changed twice, in 1908 and 1965), the Inquisition still exists as "The Sacred Congregation for the Doctrine of the Faith," the conservative political arm which suppresses liberal elements within the Church.[6]

The world will never know the true number slaughtered. Some authors claim reliable estimates of between 200,000 and 1-million burned at the stake in the witchcraft craze of the 16th and 17th centuries alone. Others claim 500,000 burned at the stake over a period of 400 years before the witchcraft craze even started.

There was a far greater number killed in the sweeps of military forces organized specifically to slaughter entire communities of Cathars, Waldensians, Jews, and Muslims. And Templar and Hospitaler knights gained much of their land through local Christian feudal lords giving them free rein to slaughter heretical populations and sharing with them the spoils.

So, when one includes those killed other than by burning at the stake—which is by far the greater number—deaths at the hands of inquisitors to increase the power of the already powerful throughout the full 700 year inquisition history is truly massive.

The Inquisitorial Suppression of the Illuminati

In 1776 Professor Adam Weishaupt of the University of Ingolstadt in Bavaria (Germany) established the Bavarian Illuminati ("enlightened ones"), a secret group to expand the rights of the people. Thirteen years later, the French Revolution's promise of more extensive rights created even greater fear in the First and Second Estates.

The Third Estate, bourgeoisie with the support of the common people, now ruled France. The potential for full rights for everybody could have become contagious. The Illuminati supported those increased rights. In a replay of earlier inquisitions, managers of the religious state immediately asserted their control by frightening the population into a witch hunt. A *social-control-paradigm* of an imminent enemy was put into place. The war cry went out that in effect said, "Look out for the Illuminati! Look out for the Illuminati! They want to take over your country! Your church! The world!"[7] Note that no one today will dispute that it was the king, aristocracy, and church (those who created those *strategies-of-tension*) that then controlled the so-called civilized world.

That the Illuminati are active today and a threat to freedom is a fiction kept alive by the far right wing, whose politics are too extreme even for most of those who do hold the reins of power. It was the ruling powers who created these *social-control paradigms* to control the masses to protect their wealth and power. It is ironic to note that when people without sufficient education—or of radical bend— dig up those old writings about the Illuminati (the *social-control-paradigm* at that time), they point to the current organizations of the powerful (such as the Trilateralists) as being the Illuminati attempting to rule the world. Poetic justice!

However, the forward march of history could not be stopped. The intense efforts of the Church and aristocracy to overthrow the French Revolution resulted in Napoleon Bonaparte taking the reins of power in France. Through the conquest of many of the nations which had conspired to overthrow the French Revolution and were conspiring to overthrow this latest upstart, Napoleon spread throughout Europe many of the rights declared for all men by that revolution. Known as the Napoleonic Codes, "they are the basis for the law of over thirty nations today."[8]

The twin threats of loss of trading rights in Europe (Napoleon's Continental System) and the threat of replacing aristocratic privilege with rights for all people led to a "Holy Alliance" (more often called a "Monarchical Alliance" but the church was always a crucial ally) between European monarchies and the church to reclaim their aristocratic rights.

Though Napoleon freed most of Europe, he was ultimately defeated at Waterloo in 1815. Aristocracy and European monarchies immediately convened the Congress of Vienna to abrogate the newly gained rights of the masses. However, "Napoleon's omelet couldn't be unscrambled.... It was a force destined to destroy the dynastic system."[9]

History teaches of Napoleon's desire to be a world dictator, when he was really destroying the power of the First and Second Estates who did rule the world. Because Napoleon was such a threat to the powerful, the secret services and state departments of the European monarchies guided the writing and publication of books depicting Napoleon as a megalomaniac and tyrannical dictator. These concepts saturated the literature of the time and still saturate the literature of today. In a replay of the Illuminati nonsense, once Napoleon was demonized as an enemy of the people, the masses remained, and still are, unaware that Napoleon really stood for reclaiming their rights.

Czarist Secret Police Demonize the Jews

Another example of a *strategy-of-tension* to justify assault on a specific people to destroy their power and steal their wealth was *The Protocols of the Learned Elders of Zion*. The Czarist (Russian) secret police created this alleged Jewish/Zionist master plan for world domination out of thin air in 1903 to condition the population for pogroms (government-sponsored riots) against the created enemy, the Jews.

English and French translations appeared in 1920, but in 1921 a correspondent for the *Times*, Philip Graves, proved they were forgeries. With the cooperation of a Russian refugee who had helped create the deception, it was shown that the forgers "plagiarized paraphrases from a satire on Napoleon."[10] That satire was no doubt a previous creation intended, as explained above, to demonize Napoleon because his egalitarian concepts of justice were a threat to the privileged groups.

Though the fraud of the *Protocols of Zion* is well known, there are many instances of such hoaxes that are recorded in history and accepted as fact. Those tens of thousands of CIA-created fraudulent articles and thousands of fraudulent books put out by compliant professors and reporters addressed above are good examples. As intelligence services of all imperial centers do this, one society will have its created version of history and another society a different history favorable to its desired view of the world. The holocaust of WWII was just the climactic finale of over 1,000 years of hate rhetoric against the Jews, preached from the pulpit, supposedly for killing Jesus. Just as the power of right-wing extremists in U.S. society ebb and flow, the power of church right-wing extremists ebb and flow.

Where it was once common to persecute the Jews openly, the horrors of the holocaust made it no longer acceptable. All who would advocate such a thing are now outside the permitted parameters of political or religious debate. Today most Christians are supportive of the rights of Jewish people. This stems from the positive statements of church leaders, as opposed to the previous violent rhetoric of the right-wing minority creating tensions of an imminent enemy so as to gain followers for their agenda.

Barnet Litvinoff, in his masterly work on the 2,000 years of Jewish persecution, *The Burning Bush*, points out that the persecutors and supporters of the Jews have periodically changed sides.[11] Each of these changes required the targeted population to be programmed either as an enemy or a friend. That change is the necessary paradigm shift to gain a following that telegraphs the intentions of the *managers-of-state.*

The World starts Breaking Free from Imperial Centers

Fear gripped the powerful when Russia broke free in the 1917 Bolshevik Revolution. The Third Estate, the bourgeoisie, with the support of the common people, had revolted and taken the reins of power from the 1st and 2nd Estates. As WWI ground to a halt, Communist revolutionaries were taking over railroads and factories as Germany collapsed. The disillusioned German navy and much of the army were hoisting the red flag. Only an alliance between Social Democrats and the socialist wing of labor gave private armies called "free corps" enough time to wrestle those railroads, factories, and disaffected military from the Communists.[12] That Social Democrat/Socialist alliance was broken when the old powerbrokers reclaimed control through the installation of Hitler and his Fascists.

The *managers-of-state* of the old imperial nations knew how close the Bolshevik Revolution in Russia came to spilling over into Poland, Austria, Germany, and even Italy. They knew that, if those major nations were lost, the rest of Europe was sure to follow. A firewall to prevent that threatening philosophy from sweeping them from power had to be built. The scourge of Bolshevism (Communism) was created as the primary *social-control paradigm.* Copied from the old Illuminati and Zionist scare, the message, increasing the level of tension so the masses could be controlled, was the same, "Communism! Communism! They want to take over your country! Your church! The world!" Under that call to arms between the two world wars, most of the governments of Europe were turned over to Fascists.

In the United States, in 1920, the suppression of American political rights took the form of the Palmer Raids, in which thousands, mostly labor unionists suspected of Soviet sympathies, were arrested in the middle of the night. Hundreds were deported, and hundreds more were sent to prison.[13] Again take note that most of the world was still under the control of the *managers-of-state* of those countries sounding the warning. The country that had broken away from capitalism's control was, by comparison, extremely weak.

What the *managers-of-state* really feared was the failure of the 14-nation attempt to overthrow the Bolshevik Revolution, the governing of that country by the common people, and how close Germany, Italy, and a few other countries had come to being lost to the same revolutionary forces. Lest taking democracy seriously would spread and destroy the power-structure of the imperial nations operating under a limited democracy at best, the masses of these "free" countries had to be inoculated against the ideology of that revolution through creation of the Bolshevik (Communist) "enemy."

But during the crisis of the Great Depression that soon followed, the inoculation was quickly wearing off. The *managers-of-state* of European countries knew that the leaders of labor would govern if honest elections were permitted, so they turned the governments over to Fascists. *Managers-of-state* all over Europe acted to avoid a ballot-box revolution such as occurred in Spain. The Fascist takeovers of the governments of Europe were a sham to suppress the democratic voice of the people:

> Hitler was eventually put in power by the feudalist clique around President Hindenburg, just as Mussolini and Primo de Rivera were ushered into office by their respective sovereigns.... In no case was an actual revolution against constituted authority launched; fascist tactics were those of a sham rebellion arranged with the tacit approval of the authorities who pretended to have been overwhelmed by force.[14]

Note how the Fascists were put in power by back-room political deals, specifically for the protection of power and wealth and to avoid democratic solutions, yet are recorded in history as only Fascism. The preceding quotation was from economic historian Karl Polanyi, who recognized that desperate powerbrokers used the violence of Fascism to suppress democracy.

Hitler was a German intelligence officer throughout Germany's post-WWI crisis and it is highly likely his rise to power was orchestrated by German intelligence specifically to protect a power-structure that was crumbling.[15] That these realities can be found only by in-depth reading, or by chance, is because much of history has been written, and is being written, to protect a power-structure.

The famed march of the Black Shirts that supposedly put Mussolini in power took place three days *after* Italy had been effectively handed over to Fascist control. Germany's famous Reichstag fire was several months *after* Hitler had been given power in a secret January meeting of German powerbrokers.[16] Those acts were *strategies-of-tension* depicting the opposition as terrorists and enemies and thus weakening them politically before the national election that legitimized Hitler's rule.

Only in Spain were free elections permitted and, to the horror of the captains of capitalism, labor won the right to govern. The connection between the powerbrokers, Fascism, and the fear of ballot-box revolutions was evident when troops from Germany and Italy (with unspoken but real support from America, Britain, and France) supported the dictator Franco, and, in a bloody foreshadow of WWII, overthrew that election.[a]

---

[a] The wrongly titled Spanish Civil War is a textbook study how the battle cry of communism has been used to motivate populations to support the overthrow of some of the world's most democratic elections. The competing parties in Spain's election "consisted of two

The real target of the back-room political deal in Germany was labor that was poised to take over the reins of the German government by the vote. When Hitler seized power in 1933, police were ordered to shoot key labor leaders on sight and within a year 100,000 politically aware persons were in prison.[17] Witness the comments of a member of Hitler's cabinet, Colonel Walther von Reichenau. His analysis of the crisis in Germany could be used almost without changing a word to describe labor's position in America since 1980 and in the collapsed economies on the periphery of empire since 1997:

> The trade unions have been smashed, the communists driven into a corner and provisionally neutralized, the Reichstag has surrendered its rights with the Enabling Law. The workers are keeping their heads down and, after the previous slump, their wage packets will be more important to them than any politics.[18]

Although there had previously been much rhetoric against, and individual persecution of, the Jews within Germany, organized attacks against them did not start until November 9, 1938—*Kristallnacht* (The Night of Broken Glass).[19] The onslaught against the Jews by Fascists was undertaken to repay the super-secret Thule Society (surely now rebuilding in Europe and roughly similar to America's Aryan Nations) for their early financial support of Hitler. The Thule Society organized Hitler's German Workers' Party and supported it financially. Their symbol was the swastika, and this became the symbol of German Fascism. It is reasonable to assume that Hitler put these fanatics into positions of power because they were the power behind him.[20]

When the original targets of the Inquisition (Christian Cathars and Waldensians) were eliminated, the inquisitors turned towards searching for witches and satanic cults to justify their existence and maintain their power.[21] Those first accused of practicing the "black arts" and burned at the stake were rather defenseless people. However, as the hysteria continued, the accusatory finger pointed higher and higher and eventually pointed towards those in power. When these powerful became the target, the hysteria died down. After a respite, the witch hunts would start again.

The same pattern was observed when McCarthy's "witch-hunts" started destroying those in power, the powerful turned and destroyed him and the hysteria died down. Whenever the personal risk to leaders is high, they are motivated to defend themselves. This demonstrates that the

---

Republican parties with 126 representatives in the Cortez, ninety-nine socialists, thirty-five Catalan Separatists, and just seventeen Communists" (George Seldes, "The Roman Church and Franco," *The Human Quest*, March-April, 1994, pp. 16-18). George Seldes, *Even the Gods can't Change History* (Secaucus, N.J: Lyle Stuart, Inc., 1976), part II, Chapter 3). Likewise, due to the CIA's Mighty Wurlitzer propaganda tagging them as communist, Americans were unaware that the Communist Party was one of the smallest of 14 political parties in the 1984 Nicaraguan election that legitimized the Sandinista government.

process can be controlled and the public protected if the leaders ever decide they wish to do so.

Notes

[1] Edward Burman, *The Inquisition: Hammer of Heresy* (New York: Dorset Press, 1992), p. 39.

[2] Michael Parenti, *History as Mystery* (San Francisco, City Lights Books, 1999), p. 38.

[3] James Burnes, *The Knights Templar* (London: Paybe and Foss, 1840), pp. 12-14. See also Stephen Howarth's *Knights Templar* (New York: Dorset Press, 1982).

[4] Charles G. Addison, *The Knights Templar* (London: Longman, Brown, Green, and Longman, 1842), pp. 194-203, especially p. 203. See also Burman, *Inquisition*, pp. 95-99.

[5] Burman, Inquisition, pp. 95-99.

[6] Ibid, pp. 213-14.

[7] David Caute, *The Great Fear* (New York: Simon and Schuster, 1978), pp. 18-19; Richard Hofstadter, *The Paranoid Style in American Politics* (Chicago: University of Chicago Press, 1979), pp. 10-11; Arkon Daraul, *A History of Secret Societies* (Secaucus, NJ: Citadel Press, 1961); James and Suzanne Pool, *Who Financed Hitler?* (New York: Dial Press, 1978); Barnet Litvinoff, *The Burning Bush* (New York: E.P. Dutton, 1988); Heiko Oberman, *The Roots of Anti-Semitism* (Philadelphia: Fortress Press, 1984); David H. Bennet, *The Party of Fear* (London: University of North Carolina Press, 1988), pp. 23-26, 205-06.

[8] Daniel J. Boorstin, "History's Hidden Turning Points," *U.S. News & World Report*, April 22, 1991, cover story.

[9] Ibid, p. 61.

[10] David Fromkin, *A Peace to End all Peace* (New York: Avon Books, 1989), pp. 468-69; Michael Kettle, *The Allies and the Russian Collapse* (Minneapolis, University of Minnesota Press, 1981), p. 17. For how the Protocols evolved further to support Fascism in Europe read F.L. Carsten, *The Rise of Fascism* (Berkeley: University of California Press, 1982), pp. 24, 29, 118. 184. The Thule Society's efforts to promote anti-Semitism through Hitler would likely have not had much effect on the world except for Henry Ford, through his Dearborn Independent newspaper, spreading those Protocols to every corner of the world, and imprinting anti-Semitism into the world's mind (Pool and Pool, *Who Financed Hitler*, pp. 3, 23, Chapter 3).

[11] Litvinoff, *Burning Bush.*

[12] Edmond Taylor, *The Fall of the Dynasties: The Collapse of the Old Order, 1905-1922* (New York: Dorset Press, 1989), Chapters 17-19.

[13] Bennet, *Party of Fear,* pp. 191-98, 205-206.

[14] Karl Polanyi, *The Great Transformation* (Boston: Beacon Press, 1957), pp. 237-241; see also F. L. Carsten, *Britain and the Weimar Republic* (New York: Schocken Books, 1984), especially Chapter 8; Carsten, *Rise of Fascism.*

[15] Taylor, Fall of the Dynasties, p. 366.

[16] Carsten, *Rise of Fascism,* pp.150-55.

[17] Carsten, *Weimar Republic,* especially Chapter 8; also Michael N. Dobbowski and Isodor Wallimann, *Radical Perspectives on the Rise of Fascism in Germany* (New York: Monthly Review Press, 1989), especially pp. 194-209.

[18] J. Noakes and G. Pridham, eds., Nazism 1919 - 1945, vol. 2 (New York: Schocken Books, 1988), p. 626.

[19] Ibid

[20] Pool and Pool, *Who Financed Hitler?* pp. 7-8, 19-21.

[21] Burman, *Inquisition*; Henry Charles Lea, *The Inquisition of the Middle Ages* (New York: Citadel Press, 1954), a condensation of his 1887 three-volume monumental work, *A History of the Inquisition of the Middle Ages.*

External Trade

Part II.

Capital Destroying Capital

10. The Enforcers of Unequal Trades

"The heart of the GATT—Bretton Woods system is what is known as MFN—most favored nation."[1] GATT, NAFTA, WTO, MAI, GATS, and FTAA, though supposedly defining equality, bend weak nations to the will of powerful nations. That process determines which nations will industrialize and which nations will remain as providers of resources for *imperial-centers-of-capital.* Those needed as allies and permitted to industrialize will accumulate capital and those reserved to provide natural resources to feed those industrial nations will remain poor and in debt:

> Debt is an efficient tool. It ensures access to other peoples' raw materials and infrastructure on the cheapest possible terms. Dozens of countries must compete for shrinking export markets and can export only a limited range of products because of Northern protectionism and their lack of cash to invest in diversification. Market saturation ensues, reducing exporters' income to a bare minimum while the North enjoys huge savings.... The IMF cannot seem to understand that investing in ... [a] healthy, well-fed, literate population ... is the most intelligent economic choice a country can make.[2]

An IMF managing director claimed, "An international institution such as the fund cannot take upon itself the role of dictating social policy and political objectives to sovereign governments." That this, "politely put, is rubbish" is obvious, given the control exerted by the IMF/World Bank/GATT/NAFTA/WTO/MAI/GATS/FTAA/military colossus:[3]

> Many people learned for the first time at Seattle [first major anti-globalization protest] of the existence of the QUAD, the Quadrilateral Group of Trade Ministers, which was formed in 1981 and acts as an informal committee guiding the global trade regime. Before public meetings of the WTO, members of the Quad—the United States, The European Union, Japan, and Canada [all CEOs of, or closely connected with, global corporations]—meet privately, making key decisions without the participation of other representatives of the world community. Once the QUAD reaches agreement, a larger, select group of twenty to thirty countries are invited to come together in informal meetings. Only after that do the 143 members of the WTO discuss and vote on proposals that are typically, by this point, faits accomplis.

> The poor countries of the world are forced to fall in line by the pressure of the economic and political muscle arrayed against them.[4]

Howard Wachtel explains further:

> When the WTO replaced GATT on January 1, 1995, all of the GATT rules and its 47 years of precedents were folded into the WTO.... The WTO is an organization of some 500 highly paid professionals, mostly lawyers ... [which] make significant decisions about international trade out of the public's view. It has no written bylaws, makes decisions by consensus, and has never taken a vote on any issue. It holds no public hearings, and in fact has never opened its processes to the public. ... Its court-like rulings are not made by U.S.-style due process. Yet WTO today [because it has a dispute settlement mechanism with enforcement powers] rivals the World Bank and International Monetary Fund in global importance.... Three minimalist GATT principles continue to operate through the WTO. The first is the famous most-favored-nation status (MFN): Products traded among GATT members must receive the best terms that exist in any bilateral trading agreement.... [The second:] Goods produced domestically and abroad must receive the same "national treatment"—equal access to markets.... [The third] is "transparency," which requires that any trade protection be obvious and quantifiable—like a tariff.... The WTO has the authority to resolve disputes and to issue penalties and sanctions.[5]

A further attempt to structure inequality into law, the Multilateral Agreement on Investments (MAI), was described by Business Week as, "The Explosive Trade Deal You've Never Heard Of." The then Director General of the WTO called the secretive MAI rules as, a "Constitution for a single global economy."[6] Structural adjustment demanded by the IMF/ World Bank/GATT/NAFTA/WTO/MAI/GATS/FTAA strictly forbid government support of developing world industry. Yet Japan's industry pays possibly only 30% for its industrial capital (the public pays the rest). U.S. states and cities pay ransoms in the form of tax breaks, land donations, below cost services, wage subsidies, and outright cash incentives for industries to be built in their region. High tariffs are placed on imported manufactured products, low or no tariffs on raw materials.

An established infrastructure (roads, airports, harbors) is already in place in the developed world, built and maintained with public funds. Agriculture and industry in the wealthy world receive enormous support in the form of payments for land development, price supports, export supports, payments for leaving land idle, as well as major tax breaks. Germany subsidizes her mining industries to the tune of $85,000 per miner and "more than a third of annual U.S. government spending, an estimated $448-billion, consists of direct and indirect subsidies for corporations and wealthy individuals, indirect violation of free-market principles."[7] Not only are there massive subsidies and protections for *imperial-centers-of-capital*, the United States has some level of embargo against over 70 countries, 66% of the people on earth.[8] As structural adjustment rules deny dependent nations the right to protect their industry and agriculture, all these advantages are denied the developing world.

Society is a machine efficiently producing social needs and the well-developed, highly-subsidized, transportation, education, and research systems of the developed world mean it can produce much more efficiently and cheaply than the undeveloped world. This gives insight into why structural adjustments insisted on by the IMF/World Bank/GATT/NAFTA/WTO/MAI/GATS/FTAA reduce supports in these crucial areas. So long as a belief can be imposed upon emerging nations that is the opposite of how every successful nation developed, they can never be a serious industrial threat to the *imperial-centers-of-capital* and their resources will always be available to the imperial nations for less than full value.

Cuba was able to develop an education and health system equal to America precisely because she escaped the clutches of the IMF/World Bank and the structural adjustments they would have imposed.[9] When former World Bank Chief Economist Joseph Stiglitz was eased out of the World Bank for suggesting they relax those structural adjustment rules he was asked by interviewer Greg Palast of the *London Observer* if any nation avoided the fate of structural adjustments. Stiglitz replied, "Yes! Botswana. Their trick? They told the IMF to go packing."

That 90-minute interview on BBC Television's *Newsnight* went much further and confirmed everything we are outlining about these imposed structural adjustments. A reading of Palast's *The Best Democracy that Money can Buy: The Truth about Corporate Cons, Globalization, and High-Finance Fraudsters* (2003) tells us that the purpose of this unspoken and disguised economic warfare through imposed structural adjustments is specifically to hold down the price of developing world resources and labor and to transfer that wealth, natural and processed, to the imperial centers. Joseph Stiglitz was awarded a Nobel Prize in economics in 2001. We would hope the primary reason was to reward him for his courageous stand.

The Greatest Peacetime Transfer of Wealth in History

The corporate assault on labor started in earnest in 1972 and gained substantially more momentum under Reagan in the early 1980s. Even as "the real per-capita gross domestic product ... climbed by a third," before the 1997-99 increase in labor pay, that policy had reduced wages for 80% of Americans, with the poor losing the most. Simultaneous with that loss, the share of the national income and national wealth held by the wealthy climbed to levels normally seen only before collapse of economic bubbles or revolutions. The income share of America's richest 20% and poorest 20% stood at 30:1 in 1970 and at 78:1 in 1999. "Probably no country has ever had as large a shift in the distribution of earnings without having gone through a revolution or losing a major war."[10]

Gone unnoticed by most in the developed world but felt crucially in the poor countries were the same assaults ongoing against the developing world. The Reagan/Bush team had, through their subtle monopolization of finance capital (financial warfare) imposed a far more severe Reaganism/Thatcherism on the world. During their 12 years at the helm of government, IMF/World Bank loans came with structural adjustment conditions: all who take such loans to devalue their currency, lower their import barriers, remove restrictions on foreign investments, remove subsidies for local industry, lower their social welfare funding, pay lower wages, reduce government in general, and expand production and export of their timber, minerals, and agriculture. The result was almost universally the same: wages went down, hunger increased, health care decreased, education decreased and the price of developing world export commodities went down. The purchasing power of commodities exported by poor nations in the year 2000 were 40% of their purchasing power 30 years earlier and Professor Lester Thurow anticipates their price to collapse another 60%.[11]

Meanwhile, these same *managers-of-state* did precisely the opposite for poorer nations within their trading bloc. They easily agreed that West Germany must put $1.5-trillion into the former East Germany to simultaneously build industry, social infrastructure, and buying power.[12] And when Greece, Portugal, and Spain, relatively poorer than the rest of Europe, wanted to join the Common Market, these leaders implemented a 15-year plan that reads as if it came right out of Friedrich List's protectionist classic. This included "massive transfers of direct aid ... to accelerate development, raise wages, regularize safety and environmental standards, and improve living conditions in the poorer nations."[13] Emerging former colonies receive no such care for developing consumer buying power and protection of tender industries so their economies can become viable.

The inefficiency of capitalism as currently structured is highly visible in the rejoining of West and East Germany. Though it will eventually succeed, that expenditure of $1.5-trillion has, at this point in time, failed. Even as massive amounts of money were being transferred from West to East over half a million East Germans moved to West Germany and yet the official unemployment in the East is still 17.5% while that in the West is 7.5%.

Why this is so is rather straightforward. West German labor and industry can produce all the products necessary for East Germany, no West German industry is going to voluntarily release a part of its market share, and no West German worker is going to voluntarily give up his or her job. Both industry owners and workers are solidly within the current flow of commerce and they are not about to voluntarily give any of that up.

Without a change in capitalism's philosophy similar to the support and protection provided by Germany for East Germans and that provided by the European Union to Spain, Greece, and Portugal, the economies of other East European and Central European countries will never gain equality with Western Europe. Quite simply, Eastern and Central Europeans industrialists do not have the technology, industrial capital, and finance capital to compete with Western industries, their labor is not paid enough for their economies to accumulate that capital, and the capitalists and labor of Western Europe will not willingly share.

The day may come, theoretically, when the wages of all Europe will equalize. But by that theory the wage levels will be that of the lower-paid nations. West Europeans will never tolerate their standard of living dropping anything close to the level of the East and West European industries will do everything possible to prevent the lowering of the value of their industries to a level that would permit product sales to workers receiving East European and Central European wages.

The difficulty in bringing Eastern and Central Europe's white, Western Christian, Western-cultured nations in as equals into an allied European imperial-center-of-capital, even when that is the desired goal of managers-of-state of those imperial centers, emphasize the even greater difficulty nations of people of color on the periphery of empire have of entering the flow of world commerce as equals. One can set all the rhetoric of equality and rights aside. Since Western wealth is built and maintained through the periphery providing cheap resources and labor, equality for peripheral nations with different cultures cannot be in the plans of the managers-of-state of those imperial centers.

Those managers-of-state are not about to abandon a plan that has been so hugely successful for them. In 1970, the poorest 20% of the world's people received 2.2% of the world's income while the richest 20% received 70%. By 1990, the poorest 20% received only 1.4% while the richest 20% received 83.4% and this differential can only have increased sharply as currency values on the periphery of empire collapsed in 1997 and again in 2002.[14] When the universal result is low resource export prices and increased poverty in the developing world, the IMF/World Bank/ GATT/NAFTA/WTO/MAI/ GATS/FTAA/military colossus can hardly claim its intent was to develop those countries:

> Structural Adjustment [demanded by the IMF] is best summed up in four words: earn more, spend less. While such advice might be valid if it were given to only a few countries at once, dozens of debtors are now attempting to earn more by exporting whatever they have at hand; particularly natural resources including minerals, tropical crops, timber, meat and fish. With so many jostling for a share of limited world markets, prices plummet, forcing governments to seek ever-higher levels of exports in a desperate attempt to keep their hard currency revenues stable. The "export-led growth" model on which the fund and the World Bank insist is a purely extractive one involving more the "mining" than the management—much less conservation—of resources.[15]

Susan George's "earn more, spend less" is nothing less than a quick snapshot of futile attempts to break out of debt traps. Their efforts are futile because trades are so unequal that the weak and impoverished just go deeper into debt as their irreplaceable natural resources flow to the *imperial-centers-of-capital* to service their ever-increasing debt with its compounding interest.

The purpose of IMF/World Bank Loans to the Periphery of Empire

"The IMF has repeatedly stated that it is not, and was never intended to be, a *development* institution." Neither was the World Bank: "The fundamental goal of creating markets for industrialized countries' exports was written into [their] charter."[16] That means that debt traps and mercantilist dependency were the goals all along. Most investment in the developing world has been geared toward producing low-priced commodities for corporate industries to fabricate into products for the developed world. Investing in development of resources to produce the same product in various parts of the world ensures a surplus of those commodities at low, or very low, prices. The need to service their debts compels the dependent developing world to produce more and more of the commodities desired by the developed world. Through simultaneous investments in various parts of the world in commodities desired by the developed world, surpluses develop and, as low wages ensure there is little buying power and thus no markets in the developing world, prices are kept low for the *imperial-centers-of-capital*. It is really the old colonial plantation system that once produced for Europe, restructured on a massive scale to produce for the industrialized world.[17] (Please consider the subchapter "The Periphery of Empire is a Huge Plantation System Providing Food and Resources to the Imperial Center" of Chapter 13 as an integral part of this subchapter.)

The IMF/World Bank/GATT/NAFTA/WTO/MAI/GATS/FTAA colossus lays down the rules of unequal trade and the military forces of the imperial nations are there to enforce the rules. The developing world is expected to lower its living standards and export more minerals, lumber, and food, all to pay debts that did little for its economic development. Typically those debts were incurred for investments to extract resources, produce agricultural exports, and build the infrastructure to ship these commodities to the developed world. From the late 19th-Century to shortly before WWII, when empires had absolute control of their colonies, the price of primary commodities dropped 60% relative to manufactured commodities prices and leading economists had their bets on another 60% decline.[18] During the battle between the *imperial-centers-of-capital* over the wealth of the undeveloped world (WWII), the developing world was better paid for their resources and labor and they paid off their debts. But, after that war, imperial capital again gained control of the rules of unequal trade and that pre WWII success of low import prices and, under the flag of free trade, high export prices for the *imperial-centers-of-capital* in the first half of the 20th-Century has been far exceeded in the second half.

America's Foreign Trade Act is littered with discriminatory options, allied imperial nations' trade laws are similarly unequal, and under these discriminatory laws the buying power of developing world commodity exports in the year 2000 dropped to a fraction of that in 1960. The low pay for their resources and labor created the developing world's debt of $2.5-trillion in 2003 and it is that debt which places the final chain of low-wage slavery upon the developing world. Financial warfare (IMF/World Bank), economic warfare (those laws just described), diplomatic warfare (sanctions against any who resist), covert warfare, and overt warfare are each a link in those enslaving chains. The final chains will be the courts. Any who attempt to break out will have their commerce in world trade attached. That will bring the economy of any country to an immediate halt.

Investment in the same primary-export commodities throughout the developing world competes for markets creating surpluses and low export prices. As those export commodity surpluses build there is little investment in local industry for local consumers. As wages are too low to provide buying power, the products and services needed for the local population's everyday use are not produced within that society and thus there is no balance of industry, social capital, local purchasing power, commerce, and markets for a prosperous market economy. The dependent countries end up "producing too much of what [they do not] consume, and consuming too much of what [they do not] produce." This denies these people their natural comparative advantage and creates dependent economies. Then, while the prices of developing world commodities plummet because of excessive investments in export products (as opposed to balanced investments and adequate pay in a regional economy to create buying power), the prices of developed world products soar, the very signature of a successful mercantilist dependency policy.[19]

In only seven years, the price of a tractor for Tanzania, measured by the export value of Tanzanian sisal, doubled. The relative value for rubber exporters dropped 300% between 1960 and 1975. Cotton exporters lost 60% of their buying power in the same time span.[20] In 1996, prices for primary commodities exported by the developing world were the same price as 21 years earlier while prices for their imported manufactured products had soared, forcing the developing world to export more and more while importing less and less. The austerity rules of the IMF/World Bank/GATT/NAFTA/WTO/MAI/GATS/FTAA seldom restricts the purchase of arms, toys for the elite, or consumer purchases from the developed world.

To become prosperous or maintain prosperity, the developed world knows they must educate their citizens, they must provide them with health care, they must build transportation systems so people and goods can be moved, they must support the building of efficient industries to process their natural resources, they must pay their labor well to generate consumer buying power, they must maintain a healthy economic multiplier through a proper balance between manufacture of their own consumer products and their imports and exports, and they must not permit their wealth to be claimed by another center of capital through unequal trades.[a]

However, *managers-of-state* of the *imperial-centers-of-capital* simply do not stand up and acknowledge that what is right for the wealthy nations is even more right for the impoverished world whose resources and labor are exploited for the benefit of those *imperial centers*. Their slogans of peace and rights are not only meaningless; they are actually covers for financial, economic, diplomatic, covert, and overt warfare. After all, these *managers-of-state* have spent centuries perfecting the political, legal, and military mechanisms that maintain the rules of trade in their favor.

These *managers-of-state* are highly intelligent, they have massive resources, they are not working in a vacuum, and they are not reacting to oppression upon the imperial center. They are only reacting to others' efforts to break out from under their oppressions. We have provided only a broad outline of the *Grand Strategies* of corporate imperialists. Author Robin Hahnel explains what happens when the financial warfare plans, the economic warfare plans, and the diplomatic warfare plans succeed and all the ducks are lined up in a row for the corporate imperialists to slaughter:

> Multinational corporations and banks will soon have reacquired the most attractive economic assets the developing world has to offer, at bargain basement prices. They may succeed in doing this in a fraction of the time—the next 3-to-5 years—it took progressive and nationalist developing world movements and governments to [regain] control of their natural resources from colonial powers—50 to 100 years.... All of the gains of the great anti-imperialist movements of the 20th-Century may soon be wiped out by the policies of neo-liberalism [corporate imperialism] and its ensuing global crisis. What may become the greatest asset swindle of all time works like this: International investors lose confidence in a developing world economy, dumping its currency, bonds, and stocks. At the insistence of the IMF, the central bank in the developing country tightens the money supply to boost domestic interest rates to prevent further capital outflow in an unsuccessful attempt to protect the currency. Even healthy domestic companies can no longer obtain or afford loans so they join the ranks of bankrupted domestic businesses available for purchase. As a precondition for receiving the IMF

---

[a] Due to the economic multiplier, a small amount of wealth siphoned from a nation or region can become a big loss. Zambia had 40 small industries producing clothes for Zambians. A flood of used clothes from America undersold those producers, those industries all closed down, the multiplier factor went into reverse, and the number of impoverished Zambians rose rapidly.

> bailout the government abolishes any remaining restrictions on foreign ownership of corporations, banks, and land. With a depreciated currency and a long list of bankrupt local businesses, the economy is ready for the acquisition experts from Western multinational corporations and banks who came to the fire sale with a thick wad of almighty dollars in their pockets.... [In Thailand alone,] 'foreign investors have gone on a $6.5-billion shopping spree this year [1999], snapping up bargain basement steel mills, securities companies, supermarket chains, and other assets.'[21] (Be sure and compare this quote with Heather Cottin's article on George Soros *destabilization foundations*, "George Soros, Imperial Wizard, Master-Builder of the New Bribe Sector, Systematically Bilking the World," CovertAction Quarterly (Fall 2002).

In a final analysis, if control cannot be maintained by financial, economic, and diplomatic means, then the covert forces are called upon. If those combined efforts cannot stem a break for freedom on the periphery of empire, the navy, marines, and army are called out, intelligence agency wordsmiths lay the propaganda base of an enemy, if necessary an aggression pretext is engineered, and another break for freedom is militarily suppressed.

Friedrich List Supports for the Developed World, Adam Smith Structural Adjustments for the Developing World

"The developing world has a simple answer to the question of primitive accumulation [of capital]: the West stole it."[22] The wars struggling over resources and markets, the poverty within the underdeveloped World, and the poverty remaining in the "wealthy" countries all testify to the bankruptcy of this *residual-feudal,* neo-mercantilist, corporate-mercantilist, policy as a route to a truly free and prosperous world.

The IMF/World Bank/GATT/NAFTA/WTO/MAI/GATS/FTAA/ military colossus insists that nations on the periphery of empire reduce their education, reduce their health care, eliminate supports for industry, reduce the wages of an already impoverished labor force, and enforce the developed world's monopoly on industrial technology. The entire process imposes unequal trades upon the periphery of empire.

The funds to purchase industries, when weak nations are forced to privatize publicly-owned businesses, are primarily in the developed world. Thus, the same powerful people who impose these harsh conditions upon the weak are the ones who buy up their resources and industries at a fraction of true value when those harsh conditions trigger a collapse. Not only does privatizing the world's industries and resources under corporate imperialism provide opportunities for the investment of subtly-monopolized capital and control of industries, resources, and markets, but a portion of that monopolized capital (a small portion) owned by the emerging "robber barons" of the dependent nations gives the appearance of equality and makes it difficult to identify and target a nation, or block of nations, as an enemy imposing the harsh conditions of financial warfare.

That the structural adjustments forced upon the developing world are exactly opposite the policies under which every wealthy nation developed tells us the *managers-of-state* of the *imperial-centers-of-capital* know exactly what they are doing. Their *Grand Strategy* is to impose mercantilist unequal trades; that formula high pay divided by the low pay squared as outlined in Chapter 1, to lay claim to the natural wealth and the labors of weak nations.

The Privatization of the Commons of other Societies

If land, energy, water, or other basic needs are monopolized, others must pay a monopoly price. That a railroad, a water company, an electric company, a natural gas company, a TV cable company, a telephone company, or a garbage company can provide cheaper services because of competition is pure fiction. Two railroads, two water lines, two electric lines, two gas lines, two TV cables, two telephone lines, two sewer lines, and two garbage companies serving the same customers would be economic nonsense.

The only possible way competition could enter into basic services to a community is if the community contracted the building of the infrastructure (they then own those structures) and if they then took bids on operating those services. Basic services to a community publicly owned but privately operated would preserve everyone's rights to the modern commons while retaining the benefits of competition. Yet the structural adjustment rules of the IMF/World Bank/ GATT/ NAFTA/ WTO/ MAI/ GATS/ FTAA/ Military Colossus demand that societies on the periphery give up their rights for local control of land, resources, water, and even basic services.

These structural adjustments and the violence outlined in previous chapters suppressing weak nations' breaks for freedom are only extensions of the violent privatizations of the commons during the Middle Ages. The one difference is that it is the commons of other societies which is being privatized and claimed by the wealthy of the imperial centers. Thus the real purpose of the IMF/World Bank/ GATT/NAFTA/WTO/MAI/GATS/ FTAA/military colossus is to monopolize resources and services worldwide for the owners of capital.

But why is capital insisting on privatizing the world's water systems, electric systems, natural gas systems, et al, and doubling, tripling, and even quadrupling the charges?? In spite of the enormous waste of *capital destroying capital*, despite the waste of wars, and despite the waste of monopolies within internal economies (see the first five chapters of this author's *Cooperative Capitalism*) capital accumulations are so enormous there are no other safe and profitable areas to invest it. An analysis of the capital and resources wasted within those three areas of the economy will conclude that the alleviation of poverty in 10 years and sustainable development of the world within 50 years under *democratic-cooperative-capitalism* is an achievable goal.

Notes

[1] Lester Thurow, *The Future of Capitalism: How Today's Economic Forces Shape Tomorrow's World* (England: Penguin Books, 1996), p. 131, 137.

[2] Susan George, *A Fate Worse Than Debt*, (New York: Grove Weidenfeld, 1990), pp. 143, 187, 235.

[3] George, *Fate Worse Than Debt*, Chapter 3, especially pp. 53, 93.

[4]. William K. Tabb, *The Amoral Elephant: Globalization and the Struggle for Social Justice in the Twenty-First Century* (New York: Monthly Review Press, 2001), pp. 9-10.

[5] Howard Wachtel, "Labor's Stake in WTO," *The American Prospect* (March/April 1998), pp. 34-38.

[6] Tabb, The Amoral Elephant, p. 196.

[7] Frances Moore Lappé, *World Hunger: Twelve Myths* (New York: Grove Press: 1998), p. 98; Ousseynu Gueye, "Let African Farmers Compete," *World Press Review* (October 2002), p. 12.

[8] Laura Karmatz, Alisha Labi, Joan Levinstein, Special Report, "States at War," *Time* (November 9, 1998), pp. 40-54; Donald L, Bartlett, James B. Steele, "Fantasy Island and Other Perfectly Legal Ways that Big companies Manage to avoid Billions in Federal Taxes," *Time* (November 16, 1998), pp. 79-93; Donald L Bartlett, James B. Steele, "Paying a Price for Polluters," *Time* (November 23, 1998), pp. 72-82; The Banneker Center's Corporate Welfare Shame Links, http://www.progress.org/banneker/cw.html; Thomas Omestat, "Addicted to Sanctions," *U.S. News & World Report*, June 15, 1998, pp. 30-31.

[9] Speech by Cuban President Fidel Castro at the Group of 77 South Summit Conference, April, 2, 2000.

[10] Richard Douthwaite, "Community Money," *Yes,* Spring 1999, pp. 35-37; "In Fact," *The Nation*, March 25, 1996, p. 7. Read also John Gray, *False Dawn* (New York: The Free Press, 1998), especially Chapter 2, and Peter Gowan, *The Global Gamble: Washington's Faustian Bid for World Dominance* (New York: verso, 1999).

[11] Thurow, *The Future of Capitalism*, p. 67; Frederic F. Clairmont, *The Rise and Fall of Economic Liberalism* (Goa India: The Other India Press, 1996), p. 308. See also: Fidel Castro, *Capitalism in Crisis: Globalization and World Politics Today* (New York: Ocean Press, 2000), p. 57; speech by Cuban President Fidel Castro at the Group of 77 South Summit Conference, April, 2, 2000; Gray, *False Dawn*, pp. 39-54. See also: Duncan Green, *Silent Revolution* (London: Cassel, 1995), pp. 22-57, especially pp. 44, 50, 100-111, 131-36, 200-22; Susan George and Fabrizio Sabelli, *Faith and Credit* (San Francisco: Westview Press, 1994), pp. 18-19, 31-33, 65-72, 126-25, especially 130-34, 161, 216-22; Graham Hancock, *Lords of Poverty* (New York: Atlantic Monthly Press, 1989).

[12] Lester Thurow, *Head to Head: The Coming Economic Battle Between Japan, Europe, and America* (New York: William Morrow, 1992), p. 89.

[13] AFL-CIO Task Force Bulletin on Trade (1992).

[14] Harry Magdoff, "A Note on the Communist Manifesto," *Monthly Review* (May 1998), p. 12.

[15] Susan George, *The Debt Boomerang* (San Francisco: Westview Press, 1992), pp. 2-3.

[16] Arnold J. Chien, "Tanzanian Tales," *Lies of Our Times*, January 1991, p. 9. See also Michael Barratt Brown, *Fair Trade* (London: Zed Books, 1993), p. 108.

[17] subchapters "Conceptually Reversing the Process" and "The Periphery of Empire Functions as a Huge Plantation System" in Chapter 13; also Duncan Green, *Silent Revolution*, especially Chapter 4; Hancock, *Lords of Poverty*; George and Sabelli, *Faith and Credit*; Philip Agee, Louis Wolf, *Dirty Work* (London: Zed Books, 1978), Chapter 11.

[18] Thurow, *The Future of Capitalism*, p. 67; Fidel Castro, *Capitalism in Crisis: Globalization and World Politics Today* (New York: Ocean Press, 2000), p. 57; Clairmont, *The Rise and Fall of Economic Liberalism*, p. 308.

[19] Hancock, *Lords of Poverty*, pp. 47-75, especially p. 65; George, *Fate Worse Than Debt*, especially pp. 62, 78.

[20] Susan George, *How the Other Half Dies* (Montclair, NJ: Allen Osmun, 1977), p. 17. The developing world exports sugar and imports candy, exports iron and imports machinery, exports timber and imports paper, exports oil and imports fuel and petroleum products, et al.

[21] Robin Hahnel, "Capitalist Globalism in Crisis," *Z Magazine,* March 1999, pp. 52-57.

[22] Walter Russell Mead, *Mortal Splendor* (Boston: Houghton Mifflin, 1987), p. 197.

11. Emerging Corporate Mercantilism

With corporate fronts established in 39 tax havens around the world and firm neo-mercantilist control of the national policies of both strong and weak nations (reversible if full and true democracies evolve), corporate industries began moving offshore, essentially becoming stateless, and laying the foundation for corporate mercantilism.

To avoid sharing those quasi-aristocratic privileges with labor, control of the economies of other countries from the bastion of protective laws of another nation is the norm. Different forms of this process have constituted proto-mercantilism, mercantilism, and neo-mercantilism for over 800 years. Today it is taking the form of corporate mercantilists moving their wealth offshore where they can avoid paying their share of taxes, avoid environmental laws, extort subsidies from desperate communities, pay subsistence wages to extract and process rich natural resources, and sell their manufactured products in any market. Mercantilist unequal trade enforced by the military power of the state is the very signature of a colonial empire.

Fifty years after the Bretton Woods agreement established the rules for post-WWII banking, the respected *U.S. News and World Report* commented: "Under the Bretton Woods system, the Federal Reserve acted as the world's central bank. This gave America enormous leverage over economic policies of its principal trading partners:"[1]

> Currencies produced by one group for use by another have been instruments of exploitation and control. For example, whenever Britain, France, or one of the other colonial powers took over a territory during the "scramble for Africa" towards the end of the [18th] Century, one of their first actions was to introduce a tax on every household that had to be paid in a currency that the conquerors had developed for the purpose. The only way the Africans could get the money to pay the tax was to work for their new rulers or supply them with crops. In other words, the tax destroyed local self-reliance, exactly as it was designed to do.... Very little has changed. Over 95 percent of the money supply in an industrialized country is created by banks lending it into existence. These banks are usually owned outside of our areas, with the result

> that we have to supply goods and services to outsiders even to earn the account entries we need to trade among ourselves. Our district's self-reliance has been destroyed just as effectively as it was in Africa, and whatever local economy we've been able to keep going is always at the mercy of events elsewhere, as the current world economic crisis is making too clear.[2]

The rules of modern world trade (the IMF/World Bank/GATT/NAFTA/ WTO/MAI/GATS/FTAA) defined by corporations, and those rules enforced by the financial and military might of powerful nations essentially governed by those same corporations, define today's world trade as corporate imperialism.

Besides the military, which is the final arbiter, the power of the *imperial-centers-of-capital* to lay claim to the wealth of the developing world rests in their subtle monopolization of finance capital. No bank in the world will loan to a country blacklisted by the World Bank. To obtain funding from any bank, developing world governments must adjust their policies (called structural adjustments) to the dictates of the IMF/World Bank/NAFTA/ GATT/WTO/MAI/GATS/FTAA/military colossus. It is specifically under the imposed structural adjustment rules of that colossus that protections for the fast developing nations were withdrawn.

Not only is the developing world locked within the parameters of the decisions of international capital, if any developed world government veers from the prescribed path, enough capital will flee to turn the economy downward, the politicians (not the subtle finance monopolists) will be blamed and—to maintain themselves within the good graces of the voters—the politicians will bend to the wishes of capital, even if it is to the detriment of the nation of their birth or of the world.

The Cold War was only an instrument of interim control as the world was guided towards the acceptance of rule by corporations with the IMF/World Bank/ NAFTA/GATT/WTO/MAI/GATS/FTAA colossus —backed by their financial and economic power and allied nations' military power in which corporations had the dominant voice on foreign policy—enforcing its laws.

We must remember that the pre-WWII power-structure of both Germany and Japan was a corporate-dominated alliance of wealth and government to protect and expand their empires. This alliance and the violence of those empires are the defining attributes of fascism. Transnational corporations have applied the principles of fascism to their attempt at world rule. As they effectively run the major governments of the Western world, the above described banking/trade agreements/military colossus effectively rule the world. Under the umbrella of the Cold War, that colossus established an unseen (except when the military is activated) world government ruled by stateless multinational corporations superseding the laws of the most powerful countries. As it is ruled dictatorially and not democratically (labor and weak nations are essentially voiceless), that is a corporate-ruled empire.

The Legal Structure for Corporate Imperialism

Averell Harriman, Dean Acheson, and George Marshall, three of America's leading post-WWII State Department Cold War planners, "devoted a great deal of time and energy formulating the legal structure for the transition to corporate imperialism. The General Agreement on Tariffs and Trade (GATT), signed by 28 nations in Geneva on October 30, 1947 (later to become the World Trade Organization [WTO] and to be strengthened further by the Multilateral Agreement on Investments, MAI [stalled when the world learned its true purpose but resurfacing under the General Agreement on Trade in Services {GATS}]), was the continued privatization of the commons, the legal cornerstone of this new world order:"[3]

> [A]ny member can challenge, through the WTO, any law of another member country that it believes deprives it of benefits it is expected to receive from the new trade rules. This includes virtually any law that requires import goods to meet local or national health, safety, labor, or environmental standards that exceed WTO accepted international standards.... [Both national and local governments] must bring its laws into line with the lower international standard or be subject to perpetual fines or trade sanctions.... Conservation practices that restrict the export of a country's own resources—such as forestry products, minerals, and fish products—could be ruled unfair trade practices, as could requirements that locally harvested timber and other resources be processed locally to provide local employment.[4]

The equality and transparency in world trade supposedly guaranteed by GATT, NAFTA, The WTO, GATS, or FTAA are fraudulent. While weak nations are forced to open their markets, legal structures, and financial institutions, tariffs between the organized and allied *imperial-centers-of-capital* remain one-quarter that between the developing world and those imperial centers and the buying power of developing world export commodities and labor continue to fall as the imperial nations continue to tighten the screws of financial, economic, diplomatic, covert, and overt warfare. Cuba was able to develop an education and health system equal to America precisely because it escaped the clutches of the IMF/World Bank and the structural adjustments they would have imposed.[5] The purpose of this unspoken and disguised warfare is specifically to hold down the price of developing world resources and labor and transfer that wealth, natural and processed, to the imperial centers.

With the intention of imposing a fait accompli upon an unaware world, negotiations on the Multilateral Agreement on Investment (MAI) is designed to grant transnational investors the unrestricted "right" to buy, sell, and move businesses and other assets wherever they want, whenever they want. It would ban regulatory laws now in effect around the globe and preempt future efforts to hold transnational corporations and investors accountable to the public. The intent of the backers (the United States and the European Union) is to seek assent from the 29 countries that comprise the OECD (Organization for Economic Cooperation and Development) and then push the new accord on the rest of the world.

GATT/NAFTA/WTO guidelines for food purity standards would be those of the heavily corporate-influenced Codex Alimentarius Commission, an obscure agency in Rome that issues advisory food standards often much weaker than those of the United States."[6] Labor leaders are essentially excluded from designing and negotiating GATT/NAFTA/WTO/MAI/GATS/FTAA agreements and their rights are only addressed in the breach.[7] World banking and trade rules are designed for corporations by corporate lawyers to obscure the real meaning, leaving affected parties all over the world to decipher what those agreements really say. For example, it was a requirement of the 1974 Trade Act that labor be included in trade negotiations but the Labor Advisory Committee was given a text of the NAFTA agreement only 24 hours before their comments were due to be filed (September 9, 1992). Those several hundred pages would have required weeks of study by the world's best minds to be fully understood.[8] The current plan under negotiation, known as the Dunkel Plan,

> if approved, would give GATT a "legal personality," known as the Multilateral Trading Organization (MTO) [later organized as the World Trade Organization or WTO], that could strictly enforce global trading laws.... MTO [now WTO] will have the power to pry open markets throughout the world.... The proposed agreement would also extend GATT oversight from "goods" (machinery for instance) to "services" (insurance, banking). In order to protect trade in services, GATT would guarantee intellectual property rights—granting protection for patents and copyrights.... MTO would have the authority to restrict a developing nation's trade in natural resources (goods) if it didn't allow a first world country's financial service company sufficient access to its markets.... GATT panels may some day rule on the trade consequences of municipal recycling laws or state and local minority set-aside programs. In any trade dispute, the nation whose law is challenged must prove its law is not a trade barrier in secret hearings. The new GATT says plainly, "Panel deliberations shall be secret." Under this system, newly elected federal executives could allow the trade or environmental laws of their predecessors to be overturned by mounting a lackluster defense of the laws. And since the defense would occur in secret, without transcripts, interest groups and the public would never know the quality and vigor of the defense. Environmental or health and safety laws (and possibly labor rights and human rights laws) affecting another nation's commerce, no matter how well intended, will be more easily challenged. Again, the executive branch from the challenged nation would defend the law in star-chamber proceedings in Geneva—out of view of media and interest groups back home.[9]

David C. Korten titled his book *When Corporations Rule the World*,[a] pointing out,

> the burden of proof is on the defendant to prove the law in question is not a restriction of trade as defined by the GATT.... Countries that fail to make the recommended change within a prescribed period face financial penalties, trade sanctions, or both.... The WTO is, in effect, a global parliament composed of unelected bureaucrats with the power to amend its own charter without referral to legislative bodies.... [It] will become the highest court and most powerful legislative body, to which the judgments and authority of all other courts and legislatures will be subordinated.[10]

Through the above-described colossus, multinational corporations have gained control of other countries' internal policies, a reestablished colonialism that has colonized both the developed and undeveloped worlds. These laws, essentially created by corporations, can bypass national laws protecting environments and economies throughout the world. Legal challenges are now starting to come in and the rulings—all made behind closed doors and not subject to challenge or appeal—have sided with the corporations. Early examples are the governments prevented from protecting Pacific salmon runs; forced to abandon strengthening pesticide laws; blocked from enacting laws to reduce emissions of lead, zinc, and copper from smelters; blocked from banning dangerous chemicals in fuels; and prevented from setting up a single-payer automobile insurance plan modeled on Canada's national health insurance system, which could have saved consumers 50% in insurance costs.[11] Nations' laws denying the right to market fish catches by trawlers who use netting methods that fail to protect turtles, dolphins and other endangered species and thousands of other environmental protection laws can be overruled by what amounts to a court system established, run, and the decisions made, by corporations.

The legal changes necessary to break the multinational corporations' control of world resources and profitable markets, and their control over labor, are not permitted under corporate-utopian world banking and trade agreement guidelines. Those guidelines, backed by financial and military power (exercised through control of foreign policy of governments), lock the world into the corporate mercantilist system of siphoning the world's wealth to these enormous blocks of international capital that have no loyalty to any country, or anyone, except themselves.

---

[a]Very few corporations will be directly involved in covertly controlling thoughts of others. But there is a hard core that does. Trace the covert and overt foreign policy violence to its source and one will arrive at that hard core. Trace the funding of the think-tanks which pour out the books and articles and the lobbyists which essentially write our laws and one arrives at the door of the same hard core. So David Korten's book title, *When Corporations rule the World*, is quite accurate.

Wealthy citizens domiciled in mother countries and subject to the laws of that country are being replaced by a legal system to siphon the wealth of both the developed and developing world to stateless corporations domiciled in offshore tax havens and subject to no law but their own. For example, suppose country A has wage rates averaging $10 an hour, environmental laws that prevent pollution and increase the cost of production, and equal property and income taxes on corporations. And suppose country B's wage rates are $1 an hour, it has no environmental laws, and low taxes for corporations.

The corporate boardroom response, and the foundation which gives corporate mercantilists more power than nations, would be transfer pricing:

(1) On paper, move their headquarters to, or establish a subsidiary in, a third country tax haven;

(2) build their factory in a low-wage developing country with a low unit cost of production, say $10;

(3) invoice (bill) their production to the offshore tax haven at a price that leaves no profit, that same $10 production cost;

(4) invoice that production from the tax haven to a high-wage country at a price that will show a profit in the paper corporation in the tax haven and none in the real corporation in the high-wage country, let's say $30 per unit;

(5) ship their products directly from the low-wage developing country to the high-wage developed country;

(6) and bank those tax-free profits in the tax haven which is nothing more than a mailing address and a plaque on a door.

No products touch that offshore entity; even the paperwork is done in corporate home offices. There are over 11,000 such corporations registered in the Cayman Islands alone, which has a population of only 10,000. William Walker says, "We are directors of about 500 of them.... We funnel a lot of money out of Central and South America." Corporate mercantilists are doubly insulated from accountability. "Of the thousand American holding companies that control U.S. firms and their subsidiaries throughout the world, *six hundred have their registered offices in Switzerland*."[12] With 39 tax havens worldwide, this is a conservative analysis.[13]

A corporation practicing this "transfer pricing" (and almost all transnationals do, 40 to 50% of world trade is intra-firm trade between corporation transnational subsidiaries) could pocket the greater share of the value of production. The wealth of the low-wage country would continue to be siphoned to the *imperial-centers-of-capital*, and the high-wage country would have its wealth siphoned to the powerful company's bank account in the offshore tax haven. Corporations have formed enclosed and controlled trading systems which create comparative advantage within corporate structures (complex words to say they have created monopolies.)[14] This is neo-mercantilism restructured into corporate mercantilism functioning to perfection, siphoning both the wealth of the imperial center and that of the impoverished periphery.

A friend purchased a power tool for $75 from Harbor Freight that was advertised by another store for $250. Another friend paid $330 for a rotary drill press that he knew should cost $800. Obviously the tools at Harbor Freight were manufactured in China and had only a modest price markup. This bypassed the above-described monopoly process and permitted the final buyer to gain that wealth. Assuming the tools were imported for the same low import price but the traders lowered the retail price only a little, it is they who would have gained that wealth, not the final consumer. But in both instances that wealth would have been gained by the imperial center.[a]

Expand that concept theoretically to all consumer products and America and Europe will be rapidly accumulating wealth. Only a few high priced products and services exported would pay for those enormous imports. This accounts for the great wealth accumulated by the imperial centers during the decade of the 1990s. To my knowledge this simple mechanism for transferring wealth from the underpaid to the well-paid is not addressed in economic literature.

Those corporate owners will abandon any country that restricts what they view as their rights and move that wealth to a country that has few, or no, financial scruples. The reason is greed. "Transnational entities [are] loyal only to themselves. To continue making exaggerated profits, they are quite willing to sell the U.S. economy [or any other economy] down the drain."[15] If capital maintains control of the world's legislative bodies, labor's earnings will continue their rapid decline and capital will pull ever more of the world's wealth to itself.

Here is where the logic of capital, as currently structured and taught, falls apart and exposes this massive accumulation of the world's wealth as only a cover for the same greed that has collapsed societies since time immemorial.[16] As the buying power of the middle class declines, capital will continue to destroy capital battling for that limited or even shrinking market. The world will continue its equalization march towards the lowest common denominator, which is the subsistence wages of the steadily declining labor requirements necessary to operate the steadily declining economic system.

Corporate mercantilists moving to areas with cheap labor, tax breaks, ransom payments, and no environmental protections are transferring to society what are properly industrial production costs and banking those unpaid costs as profits. So long as capital sets it own rules, as current developed and developing world labor remain at a higher level for one and a lower level for the other, the logic of capital grasping for every surplus in

---

[a] Primarily traders will drop prices only enough to gain market share. It seems Harbor freight is the exception.

every niche in the economy will reach into the mass of unemployed humanity for lower-paid labor and the march towards the lowest common denominator will continue.

The flaw is in capitalism's foundation philosophy. Surplus, by Adam Smith's law of wages, is nothing more than wealth produced above subsistence. If labor is to be paid only a subsistence wage, we are following a philosophy of no middle class; there will only be the impoverished masses, the enormously wealthy, and a few well-to-do managing the wealth confiscation (surplus appropriation) system. The massive wealth accumulated by the greedy is only temporary, when economies collapse those values collapse.

Thinking in terms of Units of Production

To understand that today's competitive monopolies are a massive throwing away of wealth, one need only think in terms of "units of production," such as a farm. No one would shut down and abandon a farm (a unit of production) and move to an equally-productive farm (an equal unit of production) on the other side of the world because labor is cheaper. The farm is sold to another farmer, the first farmer moves, and both units of production are kept producing food for their regions and selling their surplus to the world. Idle land alongside of hungry people would be an oxymoron. Yet that is what happens when industries are abandoned and rebuilt across borders or on the other side of the world.

Hunger while a region's most productive land is producing for export to the developed *imperial-centers-of-capital* outlines the obvious: the developed world has firm control over the resources of its countryside, the impoverished developing world. Pick any consumer item—stoves, refrigerators, utensils, tractors, trucks, shoes, cloth, clothes, cars, or steel—virtually any item you think of is desired and typically badly needed by people in many parts of the world. If the previous perfectly good factory producing any one of those consumer items had continued producing instead of shutting down, the productive capacity of those "units of capital" would be double over today's subtly-monopolized system and (through payment of adequate wages so labor could have buying power and the circulation of money within the local economy would produce more buying power, the multiplier factor), those new factories could be producing for the impoverished world.

The concepts that need reevaluation are: measurement of that wasted capital, rights of all people to their share, and the logic of productively increasing the buying power of needy people to expand the market to them rather than shutting down perfectly good factories (productive units), rebuilding those factories in the impoverished world, and then shipping the production back around the world to the same consumers. The system, as structured, is designed to monopolize the tools of production, maintain the flow of resources to developed world industries at a fraction of their value, and maintain the flow of manufactures to the same developed world consumers. This is identical to the monopolization of the tools of production and control of industrial capital, resources, and trade that took place when siphoning the wealth of the countryside to *imperial-centers-of-capital* was designed centuries ago (see Chapter 2).

Although using the comparative advantages of soil and climate to trade bananas, grapes, wool, cotton et al. is fine, shipping manufactured products halfway around the world to another industrial society, when that region has the surplus resources and labor to produce its own, is economic (and ecological) insanity. There is no gain to the world in destroying an already efficiently operating factory and rebuilding an identical one elsewhere because the corporate mercantilists wish to move to areas without labor rights, environmental protection laws, or adequate taxes to build and maintain social infrastructure. Today's policies only look efficient because the primary measurement used is the corporate bottom line, which measures excessive accumulation of wealth produced by, and siphoned from, others.

Notes

1 Bookworld, *Washington Post* (April 14, 1994), p. 14 (From McGehee's Database).

2 Richard Douthwaite, "Community Money," *Yes* (Spring 1999), pp. 35-37.

3 John Ranelagh, *The Agency: The Rise and Decline of the CIA* (New York: Simon and Schuster, 1986), p. 120.

4 David C. Korten, *When Corporations Rule the World* (West Hartford, CT, Kumarian Press and San Francisco, Berrett-Koehler, 1995), pp. 174-75; Susan Strange, *The Retreat of the State: The Diffusion of Power in the Global Economy* (Cambridge, UK: Cambridge Studies in International Relations, number 49, 1998); Chakravarthi Raghavan, *Recolonization: GATT, the Uruguay Round & the Developing World* (London: Zed Books, 1990).

5 Speech by Cuban President Fidel Castro at the Group of 77 South Summit Conference, April, 2, 2000.

6 Korten, *When Corporations Rule*, p. 179; Kathy Collmer, "Guess Who's Coming to Dinner?" *Utne Reader*, July/August, 1992, pp. 18-20.

7 Brian Burgoon, "NAFTA Thoughts," *Dollars and Sense*, September/October 1995, pp. 10-14, 40.

8 Noam Chomsky, *The Prosperous Few and the Restless Many* (Berkeley: Odonian Press, 1993), p. 23.

9 Don Wiener, "Will GATT Negotiators Trade Away the Future?" *In These Times*, February 12-18, 1992, p. 7. See also Raghavan, *Recolonization*.

10 Korten, *When Corporations Rule*, pp. 174-77.

11 Noam Chomsky, Year 501: *The Conquest Continues* (Boston: South End Press, 1993), pp. 57-58; Andrew A. Reding, "Bolstering Democracy in the Americas," *World Policy Journal* (Summer, 1992), p. 410; J.W. Smith, *The World's Wasted Wealth 2* (*www.ied.info*/cc.html: Institute for Economic Democracy, 1994), Chapter 1.

12 Jean Zeagler, *Switzerland Exposed* (New York: Allison & Busby, 1981), p. 35, emphasis in original.

13 Ingo Walter, *The Secret Money Market* (New York: HarperCollins, 1990), p. 187, Chapter 8.

14 Alfred E. Eckes, Jr., *Opening America's Markets: U.S. Foreign Trade Policy Since 1776* (no city named: University of North Carolina Press, 1995), p. xviii; Richard C. Longworth, *Global Squeeze: The Coming Crisis of First-World Nations* (Chicago: Contemporary Books, 1999), pp. 31, 259-60.

15 John Stockwell, *The Praetorian Guard* (Boston: South End Press, 1991), p. 129.

16 William H. Kötke, *The Final Empire: The Collapse of Civilization and the Seed of the* Future (Portland, OR: Arrow Point Press, 1993).

12. Impoverishing Labor and eventually Capital

Wages of non-supervisory labor in the United States declined 19% between 1973 and 1996 even as labor efficiency steadily increased. Just as Britain, 100 years ago, sold industrial technology to Germany, who then used it to take over profitable world markets (leading to the two world wars), U.S. labor has lost both industrial jobs and buying power through American technology and capital employing labor in other countries. The "miracle" of more Americans employed than ever before even as high-paying primary jobs shrank has been accomplished by expansion of lower-paying service jobs and wives going to work to make up the shortfall in pay.

Before the 1996-98 increase in the minimum wage, the buying power of low-paid labor was declining at a rate exceeding 1% per year.[1] Though the buying power of American labor initially rose when the Asian tigers and Russia underwent their 1997-98 financial meltdown, and the buying power of those who owned stocks rose sharply through the price spread between production costs on the periphery and sales prices in the center, the continued cheap imports (if permitted) will eventually result in a quickening pay loss for European and American labor and a shrinkage of business profits.

In 1987, it took only 40% as much labor to produce the same amount of goods as in 1973. During that time span, even as U.S. industrial productivity remained the highest in the world, the earnings of German and other European labor increased. The industrial wages of 14 nations are now greater than the industrial wages in the United States. At $23 an hour as opposed to $14 an hour, Germany's industrial labor is 64% ($17,000 a year) better paid.[2] In 1979, a U.S. worker had to work 23 weeks to earn enough to buy an average-priced car. Having to work 32 weeks a decade later to buy the same quality car indicates labor has lost more buying power than the above-calculated 19%. However, this loss has not translated into political action. "Wall Street economists did not anticipate any great rebellion. *Wages have been falling for nearly two decades*, they noted, and *so far the American people have accepted it with patience and maturity*."[3]

The world's workers should be aware what the *managers-of-state* have in store for them. William Greider explains:

> [O]rthodox economists routinely assume that the American wage decline must continue for at least another generation.... Wall Street economists, *without exception*, predicted further erosion for the next twenty to twenty-five years. Unfortunate but inevitable, they said ... wage patterns are moving toward equilibrium—a "harmonization" of labor costs among nations.[4]

While a bonanza for corporate mercantilists, that "harmonization of labor costs among nations" is, for the simple reason that their wages will continue to drop, a disaster for developed world labor. The story of the Jim Robbins Seat Belt Company illustrates the process. In 1972, it moved from Detroit, Michigan, to Knoxville, Tennessee, and reduced its labor costs from $5.04 an hour to $2.58 an hour. In 1980, the company started moving its operations to Alabama, where wages were about 60% those at Knoxville. Then in 1985 the factory was moved to Mexico, where wages were about 37-cents per hour.[5]

The claims that labor is too small a share of production costs to influence major corporations to rebuild factories in low-wage countries are not valid. If labor costs of a runaway industry are 20% of production costs in the high-wage country, they will be only 5% in a country with one-quarter the wage rate. Add in tax savings, lack of pollution controls, cheap land, and cheap construction labor, and a former 10% profit rate becomes 25-to-40%. It is only in the markets of China and Southeast Asia, who had moved under the protection umbrella the United States placed over Japan, that wages had been consistently rising (until their 1997-98 financial meltdown). William Greider explains:

> On the streets of Juarez [Mexico] ... [t]heir incomes are not rising, not in terms of purchasing power. They have been falling drastically for years.... In 1981, the industry association reported, the labor cost for a *Maquila* worker was $1.12 an hour. By the end of 1989, the real cost had fallen to 56-cents an hour."[6]

Before their approval, radio host Jim Hightower had been alerting America to the realities of the General Agreement on Trades and Tariffs (GATT, now superseded by the WTO/MAI/NAFTA/GATS/FTAA:

> No need to speculate on the impact of NAFTA. We can already see its future. Dozens of big-name U.S. corporations have already moved 500,000 jobs from our country to Mexico.... In 1985, Zenith employed 4,500 Americans making TV sets in Evansville, Indiana, and another 3,000 in Springfield, Missouri. Workers made about $9.60 an hour—hardly a fortune, but enough to raise a

> family. Today, all of Zenith's jobs are gone from Evansville, and only 400 remain in Springfield. No, Zenith hasn't gone out of business—it's gone to Mexico, where it pays Mexican workers only 64 to 84-cents an hour.... Consider this: The average manufacturing wage in Mexico is a buck eighty-five. The average wage U.S. companies pay down there is 63-cents—$29 a week. They're going to buy a Buick from us on that? Our companies aren't creating consumers in Mexico, they're creating serfs.... Academics used by the government to promote NAFTA as a job creator] confessed that instead of a gain of 175,000 jobs for the United States—as they had claimed in their book ... [it] would cause a job loss.... The real purpose behind NAFTA is not to help Mexican workers, but to use their low wages as a machete to whack down ours. "Take a paycut, or we'll take a hike" the companies say. *The Wall Street Journal* even found in a survey that *one-fourth* of the U.S. executives *admit* that this is what they've got in mind.[7]

This power of workers to increase wages peaked and started declining in Western Europe, the United States, and Japan while, until their 1997-98 financial meltdown, it was in the middle stages of increase in Taiwan and South Korea and in the beginning stages in China, Malaysia, and Indonesia. Under free trade rules, and at the expense of developed world workers, wages of developed and developing countries will equalize and integrated economies will eventually balance but, unless the rights of labor and communities are reinstated, it will be at a low level:

> With the growth of worldwide sourcing, telecommunications, and money transfers, there is no pecuniary reason for U.S. firms to pay Americans to do what Mexicans or Koreans will do at a fraction of the cost. This is why "elite" U.S. working-class jobs are being sent abroad and "outsourcing" is the current rage in manufacturing. As a result, American multinationals remain highly competitive and their profits are booming, while the United States itself is becoming less and less competitive. In the 1980s, U.S. capital goods exports have collapsed while imports of both consumer and producer goods have surged, no doubt in part because U.S. firms are now importing these products from foreign lands. In other words, we once exported the capital goods used to manufacture our consumer imports; now we are also importing the capital goods to run what remains of our domestic industry. Even a growing percentage of output in "sunrise" industries like computers and telecommunications is moving offshore. At home, the result is downward pressure on wages and chronic job insecurity for the remaining manufacturing jobholders, who are more docile as a result. Meanwhile, the castoffs from manufacturing and mining plus new labor market participants flock to low-productivity jobs serving coffee, making hamburgers, and running copying machines. Barring protectionism or a decline in U.S. wages to Korean or Mexican levels, this situation will persist and, in fact, will probably get much worse.[8]

We should make no mistake about this: integrating a high-wage developed economy with a low-wage developing economy—without the protection of equalizing managed trade —will be traumatic. The developed society's labor income must take a severe cut and without protection against even lower-paid labor there is no assurance that developing world labor will see an increase. The balance—reached by equalization of labor costs—will not hold. The owners of capital will reach outside the newly balanced economies for even cheaper labor and the downward cycle will continue.

It is the inequalities between, and within, societies that permit evasion of social responsibilities. If all societies—and labor within each society—had achieved equality, the bottom line would still measure capital accumulation but it could only be realized by honest competition:

> Broadly speaking, employers can compete either by offering low wages and ignoring the need for effective environmental and other regulations or by achieving higher productivity and producing higher-quality goods. Without a social and environmental charter, a free-trade agreement will encourage competition of the first kind. If, on the other hand, such a charter is adopted, it will not only protect wider social interests but also encourage firms to seek comparative advantage by concentrating on innovative productivity-enhancing approaches. Equally important, a charter is necessary to ensure that workers share in the benefits of rising productivity, thus creating demand for the goods they produce. Simply put, if workers cannot buy the products they make, manufacturers cannot sell them—a point that Henry Ford stressed more than half a century ago.[9]

For decades, Sweden, Japan, and Germany successfully protected both their labor and capital, and their economies were the envy of the world. But the loss of markets to cheaper producers is forcing those countries to abandon their protection of labor. Their capital is now fleeing and their wages are declining, albeit only slightly. This hollowing out of economies is due to the excessive rights of capital as they escape outside national boundaries (corporate imperialism). The loss of rights of labor as those industries flee is but the other side of the coin of the increased rights of property. A part of the earnings of first world labor has been transferred to the low-wage country and a part to increased corporate profits. In the Industrial Revolution, repressed skilled labor fled to the most productive centers of capital that was protected and firmly rooted within national boundaries. Today it is the reverse: capital is fleeing both national laws and labor.

The trauma to a country's finance structure and to workers within the countries whose economies are declining, and the almost certain restructuring of ideology and replacement of current leaders if that decline continues, are, of course, why countries go to war over trade. But corporate mercantilism provides a new international economic framework. If the economies of all nations are spiraling downward as capital parked outside national borders destroys capital protected within borders and various elements of this externally parked capital continue cannibalizing each other (capital destroying capital), it will be interesting to see who the *managers-of-state* go to war with.

Meltdown on the Periphery of Empire as the Center Holds

The world is watching closely: Will the former economic tigers, Eastern and Central Europe, Russia, and Latin America reenergize? Will the world return to the old balance of a wealthy center and poor, but functioning, periphery (successful financial warfare)? Or has control of technology and control of trade been lost, resulting in ultra-cheap manufactured products pouring into, and collapsing, the center (another great depression and failure of financial warfare)?

The financial collapse of the former Soviet Union, Mexico, Southeast Asia, and South America and the lower living standards of Eastern and Central Europe does not have to spread to the imperial centers. If banking and military monopolies are strong enough, the financial collapse of peripheral nations means lower import prices for the intact *imperial-centers-of-capital.* There was an $11-trillion increase in American stock market values between 1989 and 2000 plus large bond and real estate value increases, over $200-billion was confiscated from the collapsing periphery through currency speculation in 1997-98, and the wealth confiscated as the imperial center buys up high-quality firms on the periphery bankrupted by their nations' currency collapses is many times that.[10] (The $5-trillion loss in the stock market since has been compensated for by higher home prices.)

Over 50% of American households own stock. If stockholders in the imperial centers stay broadly distributed, if speculations continue to lay claim to the wealth of the periphery, if profits increase even further due to higher profits from those lower import costs, if stock prices rise substantially due to money fleeing back to the security of America and Europe being invested in those markets, and if those stockholders spend a substantial share of their increased wealth, the economies of the imperial centers can maintain their vigor.[11] Likewise, if profits fall and stock and land prices fall that created money (borrowing against, or sale of, those increased values) would evaporate and the economy will stagnate or collapse.

Because it is difficult to take rights away once they have been given, strong efforts will be made, and are being made, to protect key South American countries and restart the Southeast Asian economies. However, this is being done under the rules of Adam Smith free trade, not Friedrich List protection under which those tiger economies first gained access to capital, technology, and markets.

Financial capital is safely banked in the currently-intact *imperial-centers-of-capital* and those collapsed economies on the periphery can restart only when finance capital flows back. As those economies restart, many of their industries will have new owners. Subtle finance capital monopolists of the imperial centers will have, during the financial crisis on the periphery, bought title to those industries and resources for a fraction of true value.

Under that scenario of successful financial warfare, economies on the periphery of empire will not have the same vigor as before. Too much money will have been siphoned off by subtle finance monopolists with their increased titles to others' wealth, money to fight a Cold War will no longer be flowing to the periphery, and there is massive excess capacity relative to the world's buying power. However, if the increased wealth flowing to the center of empire trickles down to the masses through both lower prices and buying power generated from stock market profits and higher real estate values, it is possible for the imperial center to retain its vigor.

But a collapse of Western stock market and real estate values would eliminate the trickling down of wealth and reduce purchases. That reduction could multiply through the economy, and the recessions and depressions on the periphery will have come home to the *imperial-centers-of-capital.* A substantial softening of European and American economies would blow back upon the already collapsed economies of Southeast Asia and put heavy pressure on the Chinese economy. If economies fall to that level, only relaxing the monopolization of finance capital and restructuring world trade (meaning equal rights, equal access to technology and capital, equal trade, et al., along the guidelines of Part III) can establish a vigorous world economy.

Bond and Currency Markets lowering Living standards for the Politically Weak

Through the economic multiplier, jobs, profits, and commerce expand wherever industries are established. A nation rich in commerce provides profits and a tax base to repay bondholders who provided the capital to build infrastructure and industries. Those same taxes fund safety nets within the developed world (environmental and labor protections, Social Security, Medicare, private retirement programs, unemployment benefits, and welfare programs of all kinds) built up to protect labor and society as a whole. The developing world has no such protections for their citizens and imposed structural adjustments deny them the right to provide such supports.

Whenever a nation attempts to pass laws to increase the rights of labor, bond and currency traders move out of those bonds and currencies and into bonds and currencies of nations not imposing those costs upon capital.[12] Rather than promote labor rights and social supports on the periphery of empire so as to remain competitive at home, corporations chose to reduce labor rights and social supports to stakeholders within the developed world. To reduce or eliminate government expenditures supporting stakeholders with weakened or non-existent political power, there was first massive rhetoric to cut budget deficits and control national debts. With fears of deficits and national debts firmly in the social mind, corporations, through their heavily-funded think-tanks, then lobbied for drastic reductions in the safety nets within the developed world.

As a group, the same people who make decisions for the bond and currency markets make the decisions of the IMF and World Bank and these two institutions earlier forced the same structural adjustments on the developing world as corporations are now forcing upon labor within the developed world. In short, instead of expanding rights as capital spread across the globe, the rights of all other stakeholders within societies are being lowered as the rights of capital are being raised. As economics correspondent Richard C. Longworth thoroughly illuminates in *Global Squeeze: The Coming Crisis for First World Nations*:

> Nations that insist on these [labor rights and social support] laws, regulations, and standards—the components of a decent industrial civilization—will find their industry gone and their tax dollars, which supports this civilization, dried up.... [Neither corporations nor governments] see the real connection between big government, the welfare state, and the global economy, nor understands that, without the welfare state, the global economy will fail. Nor do they grasp that either the unrestrained global economy or democracy will survive, but not both.[13]

Corporate Welfare

Just as corporations make profits by ignoring worker safety, failure to properly dispose of waste, and failure to pay their full share of taxes, profits are made by direct subsidies. The American government provides this welfare to corporations to the tune of $125-billion a year (1997), much to the wealthiest and most profitable corporations (collectively with $4.5-trillion in profits), while providing under $14.4-billion for welfare for the truly poor, of which a large share is consumed in administration and funds going to people not really in poverty. The equivalent of 4% of the wages of every working American subsidizes the wealthy while the equivalent of less than ½-of-1% of America's wages goes for welfare for the poor and well over half of that goes to some who are not truly needy and to administrative costs.[14]

Federal corporate welfare takes the form of tax credits, tax exemptions, tax deferrals and deductions, a tax rate lower than others pay, price supports, funds to train workers, government-insured transactions of all kinds, government grants for research, government services (such as building logging roads for timber companies), outright subsidies, and lavish corporate lifestyles deducted from taxes.[15]

In attempts to attract industry to their communities, states and cities give corporate welfare in the form of forgiving local taxes; low taxes;

government and municipal bonds floated to build factories and infrastructure; outright grants of land; low-interest loans; free water, sewer, and garbage services due to those tax exemptions; and discounted utility bills. Thus Kentucky taxpayers paid $300-million (equal to the plant's wage bill for 2-to-3 years) for Toyota to build its automobile assembly plant there, Alabama paid Mercedes Benz $253-million for the same purpose, Minneapolis $828-million, Illinois gave Sears $240-million worth of land as an incentive not to move, the Pentagon financed the Martin Marietta/Lockheed merger to the tune of billions of dollars even as the companies were making record profits, and the list goes on and on.[16] "More than a third of annual U.S. government spending, an estimated $448-billion, consists of direct and indirect subsidies for corporations and wealthy individuals, in direct violation of free-market principles."[17]

Cities are bidding against other cities, states are bidding against other states, and nations are bidding against other nations. Cities, states, and nations that bid the lowest taxes, least environmental protection costs, lowest wages, and highest subsidies get the corporate jobs. These ransom payments are competitive bids between societies, not competition by production and distribution efficiency:

> Externalizing environmental and social costs is one way to boost corporate profits. Paying child laborers slave wages in some countries may increase a U.S. firm's bottom line. It is a tragic lure that has its winners and losers determined before it even gets underway. Workers, consumers, and communities in all the countries lose, short-term profits soar, and the corporation "wins."[18]

Looking only at their bottom line, and listening to their own rhetoric, the managers of capital are unaware they are moving society back towards the wealth and rights discrepancies of the early Industrial Revolution. This return to quasi-aristocratic privileges is a recipe for eventual contraction of commerce, and destruction of their own wealth will likely come right behind the collapse of labor's buying power.

Notes

[1] Lester Thurow, *The Future of Capitalism: How Today's Economic Forces Shape Tomorrow's World* (England: Penguin Books, 1996), pp. 2, 6; Lester Thurow, "Falling Wages, Failing Policy," *Dollars and Sense,* September/October 1996, p. 7; Mortimer B. Zuckerman, "Where Have the Good Jobs Gone," *U.S. News & World Report,* July 31, 1995, p. 68; Dean Baker, "Job Drain," *The Nation,* July 12, 1993, p. 68, addresses the 2.7% drop in 1992; Kevin Phillips, *Boiling Point: Democrats, Republicans, and the Decline of Middle Class Prosperity,* (New York: Random House, 1993), p. 24; Lester Thurow, "The Crusade That is Killing Prosperity," *The American Prospect* (March/April 1996), pp. 54-59;. The following sources were published before that year. Lester Thurow, *Head to Head: The Coming Economic Battle Among Japan, Europe, and America* (New York: William Morrow, 1992), p. 53. The 1980 *Economic Report to the President* put the loss from 1973 to 1980 at 8% and that decline has continued even more rapidly; an editorial in *The Nation,* September 19, 1988, p. 187, puts the loss at 16% in weekly income and 11% in hourly earnings. Lester Thurow, "Investing in America's Future," Economic Policy Institute, *C-Span Transcript,* October

21, 1991, p. 9, puts the loss at 12% in hourly pay and 18% in weekly pay; Peter Drucker, *The New Realities* (New York: Harper and Row, 1989), p. 123.

[2] Lester Thurow, *Building Wealth: The New Rules for Individuals, Companies, and Nations in a Knowledge-Based Economy* (New York: HarperCollins, 1999), p. 95; Thurow, *The Future of Capitalism*, pp. 46, 168; Doug Henwood, "Clinton and the Austerity Cops," *The Nation,* November 23, 1992, p. 628. Colin Hines and Tim Lang, Jerry Mander and Edward Goldsmith, eds., *The Case Against the Global Economy and For A Turn Toward the Local* (San Francisco: Sierra Club, 1996), p. 487, cites $24.90 an hour for the Germany, $16.40 for the U.S.

[3] William Greider, *Who Will Tell the People?* (New York: Simon and Schuster, 1992), pp. 395-97, emphasis added; Jerry W. Sanders, "The Prospects for 'Democratic Engagement'," *World Policy Journal* (Summer,1992): 375; Thurow, *Head to Head,* p. 163; Thurow, "The Crusade That is Killing Prosperity."

[4] Greider, *Who Will Tell the People?* p. 396, emphasis added.

[5] Thurow, *The Future of Capitalism,* pp. 2, 227; John Cavanagh, Editor, *Trading Freedom* (San Francisco: The Institute for Food and Development Policy, 1992), pp. 19-23. Read also Jim Hightower, "NAFTA—We Don't Hafta," *Utne Reader,* July/August 1993; Donald L. Barlett, James B. Steele, *America: What Went Wrong?* (Kansas City: Andrews and McMeel, 1992), esp. p. 3.

[6] Greider, Who Will Tell the People?, pp. 381-82.

[7] Jim Hightower, "NAFTA—We Don't Hafta," pp. 95-100.

[8] Michael Moffitt, "Shocks, Deadlocks, and Scorched Earth," *World Policy Journal* (Fall,1987), pp. 359-60.

[9] George E. Brown, Jr., J. William Goold, John Cavanagh, "Making Trade Fair," *World Policy Journal* (Spring,1992) pp. 313.

[10] Chalmers Johnson, Blowback: The Cost and Consequences of American Empire (New York: Henry Holt & Company, 2000), p. 226-27

[11] "The New 'Financial Architecture' Crumbles," *Economic Reform,* March 1999, pp. 10-11; "Marshall Plan for Creditors and Speculators." *Economic Reform,* January 1999, pp. 11, 14.

[12] Peter Gowan, *The Global Gamble: Washington's Faustian Bid for World Dominance* (New York: verso, 1999); John Gray, *False Dawn* (New York: The Free Press, 1998).

[13] Richard C. Longworth, *Global Squeeze: The Coming Crisis of First-World Nations* (Chicago: Contemporary Books, 1999), pp. 56-57, 60.

[14] Laura Karmatz, Alisha Labi, Joan Levinstein, Special Report, "States at War," *Time,* November 9, 1998, pp. 40-54; Donald L, Barlett, James B. Steele, "Fantasy Island and Other Perfectly Legal Ways that Big companies Manage to avoid Billions in Federal Taxes," *Time,* November 16, 1998, pp. 79-93; Donald L Barlett, James B. Steele, "Paying a Price for Polluters," *Time,* November 23, 1998, pp. 72-82; Donald Barlett, James B. Steele, "The Empire of Pigs," *Time,* November 30, 1998, pp. 52-64; "Five Ways Out," *Time,* November 30, 1998), pp. 75-79; http://www.progress.org/banneker/cw.html, *The Banneker Center's Corporate Welfare Shame Links.* For funds not going to the really poor read J.W. Smith, *The World's Wasted Wealth 2* (www.ied.info/cc.html: Institute for Economic Democracy, 1994), Chapter 6.

[15] Ibid

[16] Ibid

[17] Frances Moore Lappé, *World Hunger: Twelve Myths* (New York: Grove Press: 1998), p. 98; Ousseynu Gueye, "Let African Farmers Compete," *World Press Review* (October 2002), p. 12.

[18] Jerry Mander, Edward Goldsmith, *The Case Against the Global Economy* (San Francisco: Sierra Club Books, 1996), p. 106; Joanna Cagan, Neil DeMause, *Field of Schemes* (Monroe Maine: Common Courage Press, 1998); Sadruddin Aga Khan, editor. *Policing the Global Economy: Why, How and for Whom.* Cameron Bay Publishers, 1998.; Susan Strange, *The Retreat of the State: The Diffusion of Power in the Global Economy* (Cambridge, UK: Cambridge Studies in International Relations, number 49, 1998); Joshua Karlinger, *The Corporate Planet: Ecology and Politics in the Age of Globalization* (San Francisco: Sierra Club, 1998); John Elkington, *Cannibals With Forks* (Gabriola Island, B.C., New Society Publishers, 1998); Edward Goldsmith, *The Future of Progress: Reflections on Environment and Development* (Berkeley: International Society for Ecology and Culture, 1995).

13. Unequal Trades in Agriculture

From the perspective of winning trade wars, the United States has an insurmountable advantage in agriculture. However, sales of most U.S. agricultural products are not only unnecessary, they are morally wrong. These exports destroy native agriculture by usurping their local markets. The smaller level of circulating money within the economy (the sabotage of the multiplier factor) due to paying for imported food limits the development of, or even destroys industries in, other sectors of the economy. Overseas markets are developed for U.S. farmers because they must sell, not because others must buy:

> A lot of attention is being paid these days to the developing world as a prime growth market for American farmers.... The United States has become more dependent on the developing world with more than 58 percent of total agricultural exports going to these countries in 1986-87.... Virtually every trade analysis by the USDA stresses the potential sales among developing nations in Latin America, Africa and Asia.... Agriculture Secretary Richard E. Lyng said he most wanted freedom for farmers "to produce what they want to produce" and that to accomplish that would involve solving international trade problems.... [James R. Donald, chairman of the department's World Agricultural Outlook Board, emphasized] "The developing countries likely will continue to increase global grain imports and could be a source of expansion for U.S. agricultural exports."[a]

---

[a] Don Kendall, "U.S. Farmers Look to the developing world," AP, *The Spokesman-Review*, January 5, 1988, p. B5; Diane Johnstone, "GATTastrophe: Free-Trade Ideology Versus Planetary Survival," *In These Times*, December 19-25, 1990, p. 12-13. Brian Tokar, *Redesigning Life? The Worldwide Challenge to Genetic Engineering* (London: Zed Books, 2001) and Vandana Shiva's books, *Biopiracy: The Plunder of Nature and Knowledge* (Boston: South End Press, 1997) and *Stolen Harvest: The HYJACKING of the Global Food* Supply (Boston: South End Press, 2000) addresses how corporations are gaining genetic patent titles to the genes of food plant varieties that societies all over the world have spent thousands of years breeding. Having domesticated 60% of the food plants in use, the American Indians were the greatest horticulturists the world has ever known and both India and China have domesticated far more food plants than Europe. Yet, due to those patent titles, the farmers descended from these early horticulturists (whose intellectual and physical labors for centuries created 99% of

One of the most sacred illusions of America is that its agriculture is above all reproach. Not only is the United States the "breadbasket of the world," but the developing world is somehow incapable of emulating America's productive farming methods. There is one thing Americans are sure about, without their food and generosity, much of the rest of the world would starve.

Yet 40% of the developing world that was once plagued by severe food shortages—China, Guinea-Bissau and—until impoverished by embargoes—Cuba and North Korea produced and distributed the 2,300-to-2,400 calories per day required to sustain an adult. India has finally achieved and maintained self-sufficiency. Angola, Mozambique, and Nicaragua had also achieved self-sufficiency, but their economic infrastructures were sabotaged by anti-government rebels organized, trained, and armed by U.S. intelligence services.[1]

The countries that are newly self-sufficient in food production have far less cultivable land per person than most of the countries still suffering from chronic food shortages. China, for example, has only .13 hectares of arable land per person; the former North Vietnam had .10; and North Korea (self sufficient before the Korean War and the embargo) has .07. Despite having more arable land per person, their neighbors are unable to feed themselves. Pakistan has .40 cultivable hectares per person; Bangladesh has .16; and Indonesia has .15 hectares.[2]

The best-known example of a country that is continually faced with hunger is Bangladesh, where "two-thirds of the population suffers from protein and vitamin deficiencies." Yet the country exists on a fertile plain blessed with plenty of water, and "grows enough in grain alone to provide everyone in the country with at least 2,600 calories a day."[3] It is obvious that nature has provided this country with the ability to feed more than the present population.

The reasons for such anomalies become clearer when one studies Africa and South America, the two continents with the hungriest populations. The United Nations Food and Agriculture Organization estimates that only 60% of the world's arable land is farmed. In Africa and South America, the figure averages 20%, and their grain yields are only one-half that of industrialized countries. Brazil, for example, is burdened with a large hunger problem, but, even without the destruction of more rainforests, it has 2.3 cultivable acres per person. In Brazil, as well as most of South and Central America, one-half the acres being farmed—invariably

---

the use-value in those plants) cannot save seeds from those gene patented crops and are forced to buy from seed companies whose business span the globe. And Terminator seeds, crops which produce food but the seeds will not sprout, totally monopolizing seed stocks, are planned.

the best land—currently grows crops for feeding cattle or for export.[4] The masses are unable to feed themselves because their land is subtly monopolized. Brazil has ranches with up to 250,000 head of cattle (that one owned by the Rockefellers) which monopolizes land capable of feeding hundreds of millions of people.[5] Latin Americans and Africans, despite rampant hunger, consume only a small percentage of their land's agricultural potential while a substantial share is exported.

The remaining hungry nations, mostly in Southeast Asia, have such large populations that the land's capacity to feed the people entails a much smaller margin of safety. Yet, if they controlled their land, these nations could also produce an adequate supply of food. China, probably the best example of rational land reform, now adequately feeds 1.3-billion people. But when the population was one-third what it is today and the land was monopolized, there were massive famines.

Fifteen of the poorest countries in the world raise and export more agricultural products than they keep for their own use.[6] Some of these countries, the exported crops, and the percentage of farmland thus removed from local consumption include: Guadeloupe—sugar, cocoa, and bananas, 66%; Martinique—bananas, coffee, cocoa, and sugar, 70%, and Barbados—sugar cane, 77%. Guatemala plants cotton for export in blocks of 50,000 acres.[7]

These are all familiar developed world consumer items imported from these impoverished countries. In 1973, the United States imported 7% of its beef, much of it from the Dominican Republic and Central America. Costa Rica alone exported 60-million pounds to the United States in 1975, even though its own per-capita beef consumption dropped from 49 pounds per year in 1950, to 33 pounds in 1971. If Costa Ricans had not exported this increased production, their per-capita consumption would have been 3-times as high, or 98 pounds per year.[8]

While the United States imports all this beef, two-thirds of the grain it exports is used to feed livestock and much of the rest is distilled into liquors, both for elite consumption. In addition, it requires 40-cents' worth of imported oil to produce and transport every $1 worth of agricultural exports. "To produce and distribute 'just one can of corn containing 270 calories' consumes 2,790 calories of energy."[9]

During 1992, U.S. food imports are estimated to have been $22-billion and exports $40-billion.[10] Economists teach that there must be balanced trade and, from the perspective of maintaining the status quo, this may be true. However, the status quo reflects the unequal distribution of political and economic power in the world; the "geography of world hunger" is specifically the consequence of entire populations having lost control of their land, and thus their destiny.

The impoverished world does not need America's, or Europe's, surplus food. They only need the right to control their own land, the right to industrial capital, and the right to grow their own food. Given those rights, they will not generally be hungry. However, because only the affluent have money to purchase this production, monopolization of land diverts the production of social wealth to those already well off. "The world can simply produce more than those who have money to pay for it can eat."[11] The results are small well-cared-for elite groups, primarily in the developed world, and hunger for the dispossessed.

Hunger is determined by Who Controls the Land

The often-heard comment that, "There are too many people in the world, and overpopulation is the cause of hunger," is the same myth expounded in 16th-Century England and this *social-control-paradigm* has been revived continuously since. Through repeated parliamentary acts of enclosure, the peasants were pushed off the land so that the gentry could raise more wool for the new and highly productive power looms. They could not have done this and allowed the peasants to retain their historical *entitlement* to a share of production from the land. Massive starvation was the inevitable result of this expropriation.

There were serious discussions in learned circles that decided peasant overpopulation was the cause of poverty. This was the accepted reason because social and intellectual elites were doing the rationalizing and they controlled the educational institutions that studied the problem. Naturally the conclusions (at least those published) absolved the wealthy of any responsibility for the plight of the poor. The absurdity of suggesting that England was then overpopulated is clear when one realizes that "the total population of England in the sixteenth century was less than in any one of several present-day English cities."[12]

The hunger in undeveloped countries today is equally tragic and unnecessary. The European colonizers understood well that ownership of land gives the owners control over what a society produces. Military power is the foundation of all law and the more powerful colonizers redistributed the valuable land titles to themselves, eradicating millennia-old traditions of common use. If shared ownership had ever been reestablished, the "rights" of the new owners would have been reduced. For this reason, much of the land was unused or under-used until the new owners could do so profitably. Profits meant selling primarily to the developed world, the local populations, being far underpaid, had no buying power to purchase from each other (the multiplier factor).

This pattern of land use characterizes most developing world countries today. What causes hunger is external control guiding agricultural production to the wealthy developed world, instead of internal control managing production for indigenous use. These conquered people are kept in a state of relative impoverishment. Permitting them any meaningful share of social wealth would negate the historical reason for conquest, which is ownership of that wealth.

The Market Economy Guides the World's Production to *Imperial-Centers-of-Capital*

Currently the purchasing power of the poor keeps falling further and further behind that of the wealthy and powerful. André Gorz, in his book *Paths to Paradise*, explains why a market economy can only work efficiently when the purchasing power of the poor is increased:

> This is what we have to understand—growing soya for our [and other wealthy nations'] cows is more profitable for the big landowners of Brazil than growing black beans for the Brazilian masses. Because our cows' purchasing power has risen above that of the Brazilian poor, soya itself has got so expensive in Brazil that a third of the population can no longer afford to buy either its beans or oil. This clearly shows that it is not enough to ensure the developing world gets 'a fair price' for its agricultural exports. The relatively high prices that we would guarantee might merely aggravate hunger in the developing world, by inciting the big landowners to evict their shareholders, buy agricultural machines, and produce for export only. Guaranteed high prices have positive effects only if they can be effectively used to raise the purchasing power of the poor.[13]

Thus the market guides the world's production to those with money. The defeated, dispossessed, dependent, and impoverished have no money because their labor is far underpaid, and historically there has been no serious intent to let them have agricultural and industrial capital to produce their own wealth. The world's natural wealth automatically flowed to the money-center countries where these basic commodities were processed into consumer products by high-paid industrial labor to produce both consumer products and buying power which is the essence of a wealthy society.

The industrialized world is the prime beneficiary of this well-established system. Great universities search diligently for "the answer" to the problem of poverty and hunger. They invariably find it in "lack of motivation, inadequate or no education," or some other self-serving, *social-control-paradigm*. They look at everything except the cause; the powerful own the world's social wealth.

The major beneficiaries have much to gain by perpetuating the myths of overpopulation and cultural and racial inferiority. The real causes of poverty must be ignored; how else can this systematic siphoning away of others' wealth through inequality of trades be squared with what people are taught about democracy, rights, freedom, and justice?

If people have rights to their own land and the industrial capital to produce the tools to work it, every country in the world could feed itself. This access would have to be permanent and consistent. Any alienation of land rights, or underselling of regional agricultural production with cheap imports, disrupts food production, retards industrial development, and ensures hunger and poverty.

With capital and undisturbed access to their land, the developing world would have little need for the surplus food of the United States. Consequently, there would be no reason to plant the one-quarter of U.S. crops that are for export.[14] The current U.S. agricultural export multiplier of possibly $100-billion (60% of $50-billion in exports which go to the developing world times a multiplier of 3.5) would then be working its magic in developing countries as they produced, processed, and distributed their own food as well as other consumer products for which the increased buying power would create a market.

Stevia: Sweeter than Sugar

Subsidies, acreage permits, and import restrictions to protect the developed world's beet and cane sugar industries are well-recorded history. But the Indians of South America have known of the leaves of a plant today called Stevia which is 30-times sweeter than sugar and it does not require expensive processing as does sugar beets and sugar cane.

Needing only harvesting, drying, and grinding into powder, the labor costs of raising and processing Stevia are minimal. Requiring one-thirtieth as much to sweeten foods even as it costs roughly 10% as much to raise and process, this natural sweetener would sell for a fraction of the cost of sugar. Scientifically tested for safety and used extensively in Japan, Brazil, and China, Stevia is kept out of American markets by classifying and regulating this beneficial leaf as an herb.[15]

Besides the elimination of substantial amounts of unnecessary labor spent producing sugar, sugar is undoubtedly the primary cause of most developed world health problems. There would be a huge savings to the world's health care industry while simultaneously increasing the quality of life.

Where many monopolies are hard to bypass, the sugar monopoly is not. Using Stevia (or a couple of other similarly sweet plants in Africa) as a sweetener throughout the world would quickly raise the quality of life both by being able to simultaneously enjoy sweet foods and good health.

Beef: "A Protein Factory in Reverse"

In *Diet for A Small Planet*, Frances Moore Lappé teaches that:

(1) The human body can manufacture all the 22 amino acids that are the building blocks of protein, except nine—these are called the essential amino acids;

(2) these nutrients are found in grains, vegetables, and fruits but not all nine amino acids exist in any one non-meat food;

(3) if any essential amino acid is missing or deficient in a person's diet, that sets the limit on the human body's ability to build protein; when consuming vegetables, grains, and fruits that include all nine essential amino acids in adequate amounts, the body builds its own protein; to fulfill the need for human protein, an amino acid is an amino acid whether it is in meat or vegetables;[16]

(4) and chemically there is no difference between an essential amino acid such as lysine, whether the source is meat, vegetables, grains, or fruits.

Ms. Lappé points out that vegetables, grains, and fruits—properly balanced for amino acids—can provide more protein per acre than meat. Each 16 pounds of perfectly edible human food in the form of grain fed to cattle produce only one pound of beef. This is "a protein factory in reverse."[17] Lappé's calculation is conservative; prime-fed cattle have 63% more fat than standard grade, and much of it is trimmed off, cooked away, or left on the plate. Even the fat that is eaten is usually not wanted. Subtracting the unwanted fat demonstrates that it requires more than 16 pounds of grain to produce one pound of meat.

Cattle are ruminants with multiple stomachs that efficiently convert roughage (grass) into muscle. But they are inefficient converters of grain to meat and, in that effort, consume large amounts of this human food. If the grains fed to cattle were consumed directly by the world's hungry, the available protein from those foods would increase by 16-times, 1,600%. But when fed to cattle, the overwhelming share of grain is converted into worthless fat, bone, intestines, and manure. Professor David Pimentel of Cornell University estimates that the grain now fed to livestock worldwide would feed 1-billion people.[18]

While cattle are efficient consumers of roughage, the grain fed to them is subtracting from, not adding to, the already short supply of protein. With a digestive system designed by nature for that purpose, if cattle were fed only roughage, and the high-quality grains they once consumed were consumed by the human population, hunger would be eliminated while reducing the pressure on the environment.

If the developed world returned to the practice of growing cattle on roughage and feeding grain for only a short time before slaughter, the quality of the beef would be higher (measured by leanness, not by marbling) and the quantity available only slightly reduced. At 1991 prices, just eliminating the last 2 weeks of cattle feeding (finishing) would have saved American consumers at least 40-cents per pound.[19]

Counting the grain required to produce the meat they eat, the consumption by the well to do of 8,000-to-10,000 calories per day is a major cause of world hunger.[20] Global production exceeds 3000 calories of food per day for each person, while the daily need is only 2,300-to-2,400 calories, and the potential world calorie production could be raised much more by planting high-protein, high-calorie, crops. On the average, the proper combination of leafy vegetables produces 15-times more protein per acre than grain-fed beef, while peas, beans, and other legumes produce 10-times more, and grain produces only five-times more.[21]

By ignoring the multiplier factor and subsidies highly mechanized farms on large acreages can produce units of food cheaper than even the poorest paid farmers of the developing world. When this cheap food is sold, or given, to the developing world, the local farm economy is destroyed.

If the poor and unemployed of the impoverished world were given access to land, access to industrial tools, and protection from cheap imports, they could plant high-protein, high-calorie, crops and become self-sufficient in food. Consumers would buy their food from local producers, those farmers would spend that money in the community, and the producers of those products and services would spend it on their needs. Purchasing of local production multiplies by however many times that money circulates within an economy.

Although the multiplier factor varies, for simplicity, 350% is a good figure to use. Because the circulation of money energizes production and creates wealth, reclaiming their land and utilizing the unemployed would cost these societies almost nothing, feed them well, and save far more money than they now pay for the so-called "cheap" imported foods.

Conceptually Reversing the Process of Free Food

If American farmers were undersold by subsidized agricultural surpluses from another society or that imported food were given to American consumers, U.S. farmers would go bankrupt, the tractor and machinery companies would go bankrupt, the millions of people depending on these jobs would be without work, production of remaining industries would have to be sold to other societies to pay the import food bill, and America would quickly become impoverished. In a country not yet industrialized, the natural resources must be sold to pay for food and consumer products from the industrialized world and debt traps are put in place to maintain that dependency.[22] This process is currently at work in Mexico. As their food imports rose to 60% of their needs, wages fell drastically, industrial production shrunk substantially, and debts increased dramatically.

Many believe that the developing world "does not understand and will never change." But they do not consider that massive subsidies permitting underselling of regional agricultural production shatters already weak economies. Thus sincere, but misinformed, people go on producing for others what they could produce for themselves if permitted the technology. This process siphons the wealth from the already poor and perpetuates their poverty.

Because they do not have industrial capital to produce manufactured wealth from their natural wealth, undeveloped countries have much bigger problems. To pay for their "cheap" imported food, their natural resources must be sold to pay for that food and other consumer products from the industrialized world and trade rules and debt traps have been put in place to maintain that dependency. Once those monopolies are in place, "free trade" is simply a method to siphon the wealth of the periphery, or even defeated powerful nations (witness what happened to the Soviet Union), to the victorious *imperial-centers-of-capital.*

The Periphery of Empire is a Huge Plantation Providing Food and Resources to the Imperial Center

That the periphery of empire functions as a huge plantation system providing agricultural products and resources to the imperial center can be determined by analyzing who consumes those agricultural products and resources. While Somoza was kept in power in Nicaragua by America, 22 - times more farm land was utilized to produce crops for exports than was used for domestic consumption and 90% of all agricultural credits financed those agricultural exports.[23] Running the same statistical analysis on the agriculture of many countries on the periphery of empire will expose similarly high percentages of their land providing food for the imperial center. The same analysis on natural resources (timber, iron, copper, diamonds, et al.) on the periphery will show an even higher level of consumption by the imperial center and lower level of consumption by the periphery. World hunger exists because:

(1) Colonialism, mercantilism and neo-mercantilism (now transposed into corporate imperialism) dispossessed hundreds of millions of people from their land. The current owners are the new plantation managers producing for the mother countries.

(2) The low-paid undeveloped countries sell to the highly-paid developed countries because there is no local market—the defeated, dispossessed, and underpaid have no money. Thus it is highly unequal pay for equally-productive work that creates *invisible borders* guiding the world's wealth to *imperial-centers-of-capital.*

(3) And—as the periphery producing food and resources for the developing world requires exports from the center to pay for those imports—cheap, subsidized, agriculture exports from the wealthy world is part of the process of stripping the natural wealth from the impoverished world to provide exotic foods, lumber, minerals, and—so long as the developed world financiers and intermediaries still maintain control of the direction of the flow of money—even manufactured products for the imperial center. To eliminate hunger:

(1) There must be equalizing managed trade to protect both the developing world and the developed world, so the dispossessed can reclaim use of their land.

(2) The currently underfed people can then produce the more labor-intensive, high-protein, high-calorie, crops that contain all nine essential amino acids.

(3) And those societies must adapt dietary patterns so that vegetables, grains, and fruits are consumed in the proper amino acid combinations, with small amounts of meat or fish for protein and flavor. With similar dietary adjustments among the wealthy, there would be increased, improved, and adequate food for everyone.

Notes

[1] Frances Moore Lappé, Joseph Collins, *Food First: Beyond the Myth of Scarcity,* (New York: Ballantine Books, 1979) p. 486; Susan George, *Ill Fares the Land* (Washington, DC: Institute for Policy Studies, 1984), pp. 8-9; Susan George, *How the Other Half Dies* (Montclair, NJ: Allen Osmun, 1977), p. 36; David Goodman, "Political Spy Trial in Pretoria." *In These Times,* September 19-25, 1984, "The Buffalo Battalion—South Africa's Black Mercenaries." *Covert Action Bulletin* (July/August 1981): p. 16; "Hunger as a Weapon." *Food First Action Alert* (San Francisco: Institute for Food and Development Policy), undated.

[2] George, How the Other Half Dies, p. 36.

[3] Lappé and Collins, *Food First,* p. 20.

[4] Ibid, pp. 14-19, 48.

[5] Gerald Colby, Charlotte Dennett, *Thy Will Be Done: The Conquest of the Amazon: Nelson Rockefeller and Evangelism in the Age of Oil* (New York: Harper Collins, 1995). Conversation with the authors.

[6] Richard Barnet, *The Lean Years* (New York: Simon and Schuster, 1980), p. 153.

[7] Lappé and Collins, *Food First,* pp. 42, 71.

[8] Ibid, pp. 238-39, 289.

[9] James Wessel, Mort Hartman, *Trading the Future* (San Francisco: Institute for Food and Policy Development, 1983), p. 4; Jeremy Rifkin, *Biosphere Politics* (San Francisco: HarperCollins, 1992), p. 83.

[10] "Ag Export Value Projected to Climb." AP, *Great Falls Tribune,* March 5, 1992, p. 6c.

[11] Lester Thurow, Head to Head: The Coming Economic Battle Among Japan, Europe, and America (New York: William Morrow, 1992), p. 62.

[12] Lappé and Collins, *Food First,* p. 27.

[13] André Gorz, *Paths to Paradise: On the Liberation From Work* (Boston: South End Press, 1985), pp. 94-95.

[14] *Statistical Abstract of the U.S., 1992,* charts 1094, 1112 (1990); "Ag Export Value Projected to Climb": p. 6c.

[15] Linda Bonvie, Bill Bonvie, Donna Gates, "Stevia: The Natural Sweetener that Frightens Nutrasweet, *Earth Island Journal* (Winter 1997-98): pp. 26-27.

[16] Frances Moore Lappé, *Diet for a Small Planet,* (New York: Ballantine Books, 1978), pp. 66-7; Frances Moore Lappé and Anna Lappé, *Hope's Edge: The Next Diet for a Small Planet* (New York: Penguin Putman, 2002). For the full story of how "The Great American Steak Religion" developed, read Jeremy Rifkin's *Beyond Beef* (New York: Dutton, 1992).

[17] Lappé, *Diet For A Small Planet,* pp. 7, 17-18. Agricultural studies show that seven to nine pounds of grain produce one pound of meat. But that is for live weight and Lappé's is for dressed weight.

[18] Jeremy Rifkin, "Beyond Beef." *Utne Reader,* March/April 1992, p. 97. Excerpts from his book, of the same title.

[19] Lappé, *Diet For A Small Planet,* pp. 17-18, roughly adjusted for 1991 beef prices; Low Cholesterol Beef Produced on State Ranches." *The Missoulian,* October 15, 1986, p. 18.

[20] Barnet, *Lean Years,* p. 151; George, *Ill Fares the Land,* p. 48.

[21] Lappé, Diet For A Small Planet, p. 10.

[22] See Bhagirath Lal Das, *WTO: The Doha Agenda: The New Negotiations on World Trade* (London: Zed Books, 2003) and his many other books.

[23] Holly Sklar, *Washington's War on Nicaragua* (Boston: South End Press, 1988), p. 9.

14. Developing World Loans, Capital Flight, Debt Traps, and Unjust Debt

> Under present terms of international lending, a recipient of purchasing power abdicates its authority. The borrower [is] as firmly tied to the apron strings of the lender as he ever was by the chains of colonization.
>
> —CEO and author Alan F. Bartlett, *Machiavellian Economics*

Controlling Puppets of the Imperial Centers

Instead of building basic industry for the impoverished world which could then produce both more industry and consumer products, petrodollars not consumed by externally fomented wars were deposited in American and European banks and then lent to developing world countries for non-productive purposes:

> Banks everywhere, flush with petrodollars, had to struggle to find big customers to whom they could make big loans. Brazil, Mexico, Argentina, Nigeria, and others were wonderful customers, borrowing hundreds of billions worth of these "recycled petrodollars," as they were called.... Just moving that money out the door was an achievement because the sums were so vast. Bankers had to struggle to find clients. Never mind that at least $500-billion of those loans turned sour. Never mind that for a decade the biggest borrowers did not make a single payment. Nor, in all likelihood, will they ever.[1]

The banks ignored their responsibility to make sure their loans were used productively:

> [E]xternal loans were not used to finance large-scale industrial or other projects designed to improve the productivity of the national economy. The military dictatorships used them instead to open up domestic markets to imports in order to allow the middle classes a brief, and therefore all the more passionate, frenzy of consumption.... [Those debts] are still being paid for today with even greater poverty, unemployment and destitution for the majority of the population. Much of the contemporary wealth of such nations,

including Argentina, can be found in numbered Swiss bank accounts rather than between Terra del Fuego and La Plata.[2]

Economic Warfare and Financial Warfare

While bankers were busy converting those hundreds of billions of OPEC dollars into developing world debt, top financial planners were studying how to reduce the financial claims the oil nations had against the industrialized world. Out of those studies came the financial warfare plans of the *imperial-centers-of-capital*, debase their currencies:

> In the early 1970s, the United States and, to varying extents, the other OECD countries, responded to OPEC's increases in oil prices by heavily expanding the money supply. The resulting inflation, together with the administered pricing policies in many basic U.S. industries, sharply increased the prices of U.S. exports and thus the cost of many imports to the developing world. Such an inflationary policy enabled the OECD countries, as a group, to keep their current accounts in balance, despite the large oil prices.... In effect, the United States largely insulated itself from the oil price hikes by passing the burden on to the developing world, whose current accounts deficit mounted. The developing world, in turn tried to ease this burden by borrowing heavily rather than by deflating.[3]

Those petrodollars were transferred to the developing world and then returned to the developed world through export purchases and capital flight; then dollars were printed to lower the value of Arab petrodollar deposits. If the petrodollars lent to the developing world had been used to build industrial capital and agricultural self-sufficiency, inflating the dollar would have effectively reduced their debts along with the intended reduction of developed-world debts to the oil cartel.

But, as this money was spent on consumer goods (that properly should have been, on the average, produced by themselves) and funneled into personal bank accounts in the developed world, the developing world gained only the debt. The gains of the Arab cartel were largely erased as the value of their money was essentially halved and the developed nations retained their subtle monopolization of world capital in the form of a $2.5-trillion debt trap for the developing world (2003) which could only be paid off through sales of valuable resources.

The World's Poor are subsidizing the Rich

Wealth that is skimmed off by the elite of developing countries and deposited in foreign banks is a large factor in the developing world's debt burden. Forty-seven percent of Argentina's and 50% of Mexico's borrowed funds have ended up in other countries via this route. The average loss of borrowed funds for 18 of these impoverished countries was 44%. By 1985, according to economist Howard M. Wachtel, the total exceeded $200-

billion. Susan George calculated that a net of $418-billion in borrowed funds flowed right back north between 1982 and 1990.[4] As of 1998, about half the debts of the southern nations are private deposits sitting in the accounts of Northern banks through deposits in their subsidiaries in tax havens.

The net gain to the developed countries (loss to the underdeveloped) of $418-billion between 1982 and 1990 is more than what was spent to rebuild Europe after WWII. "Capital flight from Mexico between 1979 and 1983 alone [was] $90-billion—an amount greater than the entire Mexican debt at that time."[5]

> The big American banks ... welcomed the money as savings, even though the lending officers in a different department had sent it to those same countries for supposedly productive uses ... 40 percent of Mexico's borrowed money leaked away, 60 percent of Argentina's, and every penny of Venezuela's. Like alchemists, the Latin American elite converted the debt of the public at home into their private assets abroad.... About one dollar out of every three loaned to Latin America by banks between 1979 and 1983 made that round trip.[6]

Corporate mercantilist loans are almost invariably tied to purchases from the creditor nations. Over 80% of America's foreign aid returns immediately through exports tied to that aid.[7] Foreign aid of other nations carries the same self-repatriating provisions. In fact, aid money typically never leaves the donor country; it is credited to other institutions in the donor country to which money is owed. Commenting on such generosity, the Prime Minister of Malaysia pointed out that, "Although Japan furnishes loans; it takes back with its other hand, as if by magic, almost twice the amount it provides."[8]

Central American authorities estimated that by 1986 the wealth drained from Latin America was "more than $70-billion in a single year in the form of money or merchandise for which [Latin America] didn't receive anything in exchange."[9]

If a loan is to be of lasting value to the country to which it is granted, it must be put to *productive*, not unnecessary, consumptive, or wasteful, use. Equally important, if those loan funds were spent in the developing region instead of the loaning country as typically required, that money will be spent several times (the multiplier factor) and create buying power within that region. Producing a healthy economy in the industrial exporting nation through the multiplier factor is the reason most aid is tied to purchase of exports from the donor country. Continuation of that policy provides wealth for the nation exporting manufactured goods and poverty for the nation exporting raw produce and products produced with low-paid labor.

Building the Infrastructure to transfer Natural Wealth to the Imperial Centers

A 1987 *Sixty Minutes* documentary explained how billions of dollars were lent to Brazil to clear rain forest for homesteading. The World Bank's own agricultural experts testified that this plan was not feasible because, once cleared, the thin soil would be unable to sustain agriculture. The bank lent the money anyway and the result was just what the experts predicted and what slash and burn farmers have known for thousands of years.[10] Instead of using the rainforest for the sustainable production of medicines, rubber, timber, and even oxygen, it was clear-cut for about seven years of wasteful grazing at which time the soil nutrients were exhausted.

There were also loans for unsound and disastrous development projects in Kenya, Morocco, the Philippines, Tanzania, Togo, Zaire, Zambia, and other dependent countries, including Poland. The projects produced little or no income and the loans had to be repaid by selling valuable resources and lowering the standard of living of already impoverished populations.[11]

A careful analysis will conclude that the purpose of many loans is to develop infrastructure (mines, roads, railroads, pipelines) to move the resources of the periphery to the *imperial-centers-of-capital.* Much of the timber being cut from Brazil's rainforest ended up in those imperial centers. A minimum infrastructure must be built to move those resources and those resources are then sold to fund a debt that, due to low prices for those exports and the expense of imported food and consumer products, proves unpayable and continues to grow.

Debt Traps: Loaning Excess Accumulations of Capital back to the Producers of that Wealth

Third World development has not had serious consideration. Instead, vastly underpriced developing world natural resource commodities and underpaid labor (essentially dictated by IMF/World Bank/GATT/NAFTA/WTO/MAI/GATS/FTAA structural adjustment policies and unequal currency values) and overpriced developed world manufactures created excessive accumulations of capital in the already wealthy world, which were lent wastefully back to the developing world for purchase of developed world exports (a major share being for arms). This forced the developing world to harvest ever more of their natural resources to pay that debt, which further increased surplus production, which lowered natural resource commodity prices still further, and the process keeps repeating itself. This is the little understood debt trap. Sooner or later the crunch of debt incurred under the massive assault of financial warfare will become unpayable:

> A debtor who repeatedly borrows more than the surplus his labor or business enterprise produces will fall further and further behind in his obligations until, sooner or later, the inexorable pressures of compound interest defeat him ... interest [is] usurious when the borrower's rightful share of profit [is] confiscated by the lender.... The creative power of capital [is] reversed and the compounding interest [becomes] destructive.[12]

Professor Lester Thurow explains:

> The fundamental mathematics is clear. To run a trade deficit, a country must borrow from the rest of the world and accumulate international debt. Each year interest must be paid on this accumulated debt. Unless a country is running a trade surplus, it must borrow the funds necessary to make interest payments. Thus the annual amount that must be borrowed gets larger and larger, even if the trade deficit itself does not expand. As debts grow, interest payments grow. As interest payments grow, debt grows. As time passes the rate of debt accumulation speeds up, even if the basic trade deficit remains constant.[13.]

The size of a financial warfare debt trap can be controlled to claim all the surplus production of a society and the magic of compound interest assures those unjust debts are unsustainable. developing world debt climbed from $100-billion in 1973 to $1.7-trillion in 1999, to $2.5-trillion by 2003. With resource prices having dropped 60% the past 40 years and still dropping, obviously that debt cannot be paid.

Peonage has only changed its Name

Most of these debts are incurred without the recipient country receiving any lasting benefits. In fact, only about $500-billion of that $2.5-trillion debt was borrowed finance capital; the rest was runaway compound interest.[14] The situation is comparable to the loathsome form of slavery known as peonage:

> In classic peonage, workers, though nominally free and legally free, are held in servitude by the terms of their indenture to their masters. Because their wages are set too low to buy the necessities, the master grants credit but restricts the worker to buying overpriced goods from the master's own store. As a result, each month the peon goes deeper and deeper into debt. For as long as the arrangement lasts, the peon cannot pay off the mounting debt and leave, and must keep on working for the master. Nigeria [and most other Third World countries] shares three crucial characteristics with a heroin-addicted debt-trap peon. First, both debts are unsecured consumer debts, made up of subsistence and spending-spree expenses, and with future income as the only collateral. Second, both loans are pure peonage loans, that is loans made not because of the potential of the project the loan is to be used for, but simply in order to secure legal control over the economic and political behavior of the debtor. Third, the only way made available for getting out of both debts is by getting into more debt.[15]

Lending responsibly, a Well-Recognized Tenet of Law

American citizens have won lawsuits against banks that foreclosed on their property for defaulted loans that were less blatantly irresponsible. Developed nations should cancel unjust and unpayable debts and start over; giving serious attention to plans that will eliminate waste, using the savings to capitalize impoverished countries, and developing true equality and balance of industry, agriculture, and trade.

The reason these sensible policies are not followed is that, under current corporate imperialist free trade policies, developing world capitalization would be catastrophic for developed world owners of capital. The development of productive capital with borrowed finance capital would produce profits, pay the debt, eliminate the need to borrow, eliminate dependency, and increase market competition to the detriment of the developed world and gain of the impoverished dependent world.

Canceling Unjustly Incurred Debts

There are compelling reasons for paying attention to this potential for catastrophe as, "every debt crisis in history since Solon of Athens has ended in inflation, bankruptcy or war, and there is no cause to believe we've solved this one, even if it has been postponed."[16]

As much of this imposed debt can never be paid back, most developing world debt is severely discounted. As of June 1990, Argentina's debt traded at a low of 14.75-cents on the $1 while the average price of all developing world debt was 28-cents on the $1.[17] Although it is being traded at a 72% discount, the indebted countries must still pay full price. After the financial collapse on the periphery of empire seven years later, discounts for those debts can only trade at a sharply higher discount.

In the 1800s, the United States defaulted on much of its development debt, as did Latin America and others during the crisis of the Great Depression. American *managers-of-state* knew their nation became wealthy due to avoiding the monopolization of their economy, and their European cousins eventual sharing their industrial capital and markets. America returned that favor by sharing its wealth after WWII to rebuild the ancestral home of their culture.

There was no expectation of that shared wealth being repaid. The rational decision, and one that Professor Lester Thurow and others consider the developed world's only choice, would be to forgive the developing world's unjustly incurred and unpayable debts.[18] The precedent has been set by earlier defaults, by the quickness of decisions to protect trading allies, and an honest accounting would find the developed world owing the developing world for the destruction of their social wealth, the earlier enslavement of their labor, and the long term underpayment for their labor and resources.

Notes

1 Joel Kurtzman, *The Death of Money* (New York: Simon and Schuster, 1993), p. 72.

2 Elmar Altvater, Kurt Hubner, Jochen Lorentzen, Raul Rojas, *The Poverty of Nations* (New Jersey: Zed Books, 1991) pp. 8-9.

3 Arjun Makhijani, *From Global Capitalism to Economic Justice* (New York: Apex Press, 1992), p. 159.

4 Susan George, *The Debt Boomerang* (San Francisco: Westview Press, 1992), p. xiv-xvi; Howard M. Wachtel, "The Global Funny Money Game," *The Nation,* December 26, 1987, p. 786; Fidel Castro, *Nothing Can Stop the Course of History* (New York: Pathfinder Press, 1986), p. 68; Howard M. Wachtel, *The Politics of International Money* (Amsterdam: Trans National Institute, 1987), p. 42; William Greider, *Secrets of the Temple* (New York: Simon and Schuster, 1987), p. 517. See also Susan George, *Fate Worse than Debt,* (New York: Grove Weidenfeld, 1990), especially pp. 16-34, 77-154; Philip Agee, "Tracking Covert Actions into the Future," *Covert Action Information Bulletin* (Fall 1992): p. 6.

5 George, *Fate Worse than Debt,* pp. 20, 236, quoted by Agee, "Tracking Covert Actions," p. 6.

6 Lawrence Malkin, *The National Debt* (New York: Henry Holt, 1988), pp. 106-07; see also David Pauly, Rich Thomas, Judith Evans, "The Dirty Little Debt Secret," *Newsweek,* April 17, 1989.

7 Dan Nadudere, *The Political Economy of Imperialism,* (London: Zed Books, 1977), p. 219; Michael Moffitt, . "Shocks, Deadlocks, and Scorched Earth: Reaganomics and the Decline of U.S. Hegemony," *World Policy Journal* (Fall 1987).

8 Ibid, p. 220.

9 Castro, Nothing Can Stop the Course of History, p. 69.

10 Danaher, *50 Years is Enough,* Chapter 8; CBS, *Sixty Minutes,* April 20, 1987; Bruce Rich, "Conservation Woes at the Bank," *The Nation,* January 23, 1989, pp. 73, 88-91.

11 Susan George, *Fate Worse Than Debt,* pp. 18,19, 30-34, 50-57, 77-168.

12 Greider, *Secrets of the Temple,* pp. 707, 581-82; Susan George, Fabrizio Sabelli, *Faith and Credit* (San Francisco: Westview Press, 1994), pp. 80-84, 215.

13 Lester Thurow, Head to Head: The Coming Economic Battle Among Japan, Europe, and America (New York: William Morrow, 1992), p. 232.

14 Michael Barratt Brown, *Fair Trade* (London: Zed Books, 1993), pp. 43, 113.

15 Chinweizu, "Debt Trap Peonage," *Monthly Review* (November 1985): pp. 21-36.

16 George, Fate Worse Than Debt, p. 196.

17 *CNN News* (June 28, 1990); David Felix, "Latin America's Debt Crisis," *World Policy Journal* (Fall 1990): p. 734.

18 Thurow, *Head to Head,* p. 215. See also, Gowan, *The Global Gamble;* Gray, *False Dawn* (New York: The Free Press, 1998), and Longworth, *Global Squeeze.*

15. The Economic Multiplier, Accumulating Capital through Capitalizing Values of Externally Produced Wealth

Although *social-control-paradigms* have always claimed otherwise, people throughout the world can, on the average, be trained to be equally-productive. All it takes is an education, training, and the opportunity. If adequate capital were equally distributed throughout the world, the reality that picking grapes is just as important to society as building automobiles would quickly become apparent.

The difference in skills hardly qualifies for the difference in pay. There are many grape pickers and other low-paid workers who are just as qualified as many production, construction, and transportation workers. Though not true of all, many high-paid workers learned on the job the same way those low-paid workers learned their skills and the work of a large share of well-paid labor is repetitious, just as simple, yet not as hard or dirty as the work of lower-paid labor.

Look at the difference in capital accumulation through the discrepancy in pay as outlined in Chapter 1: A 10-times pay differential when trading between equally-productive labor nations results in a wealth accumulation advantage of 100-to-1, to be paid twice as much for equally-productive work is to accumulate four-times as much wealth in trades, and being paid 30% greater when trading will still accumulate over twice as much wealth.

But the defeated, dependent, world's loss of wealth is even greater than the above example. Forcing these defeated dependent societies to import a product they do not need, or which they could produce themselves if permitted the requisite technology and capital, is a sale 100% overvalued. Actually, as those societies are also being denied the benefits of the multiple use of this money (the economic multiplier) as it moves through the economy and creates more commerce, this unneeded product is, on balance, several hundred percent overvalued.

For example, if a society spends $100 to manufacture a product within its borders, the money that is used to pay for materials, labor, and other costs moves through the economy as each recipient spends it. Due to this multiplier effect, $100 worth of primary production can add several hundred dollars to the Gross Domestic Product (GDP) of that country.[a] If money is spent in another country, circulation of that money, and thus the wealth generated, is within that exporting country.

If imports and exports are equal in labor input and produced by equally-paid and equally-productive labor, the trades will be equal. But they are not; they are unequal to the extreme. To understand that, we must understand not only multiplication of wealth through the horizontal flow of money (the economic multiplier) but the vertical expansion of wealth in an industrial economy as a society becomes wealthy through increased efficiencies of technology, higher value production, and capitalizing those values.

Friedrich List's Fundamental Thesis

The fundamental thesis of Friedrich List is: "Commerce emanates from manufactures and agriculture, and no nation which has not brought within its own borders both those main branches of production to a high state of development can attain ... any considerable amount of internal and external commerce."[1] Further challenging laissez faire, List points out that governments should support and protect industry and this will utilize unused labor and resources to an ever higher level of production. The new manufacturing industries utilize otherwise wasted agriculture products and natural resources producing valuable products to be marketed in trade for other products, preferably cheap natural resource commodities, to be again processed into finished manufactured goods.

List points out that such importation of natural resources and local manufacturing, as a national policy, would create a wealthy and powerful nation selling only what was surplus above the needs of the population while nations allotted the role of providing those unprocessed natural resources and purchasing back their manufactured products will produce no surplus and will be poor.[2] Adam Smith's analysis is worth quoting a second time:

> A small quantity of manufactured produce purchases a great quantity of rude produce. A trading and manufacturing country, therefore, naturally purchases with a small part of its manufactured produce a great part of the rude produce of other countries; while, on the contrary, a country without trade and manufactures is generally obliged to purchase, at the expense of a great part of its rude produce, a very small part of the manufactured produce of other

---

[a] In this process, the U.S. consumer expenditure multiplier may be about 3.5 but the industrial investment multiplier is just under six. In 1986 there were 108.5-million employed in the United States and 18.4-million of them were employed in basic industry, just under a multiplier of six (*Statistical Abstract of the U.S., 1990,* p. 734, chart 1295).) Increased efficiencies should continually lower employment in basic industries and those savings are available to continually increase the industrial investment multiplier.

> countries. The one exports what can subsist and accommodate but a very few, and imports the subsistence and accommodation of a great number. The other exports the accommodation and subsistence of a great number, and imports that of a very few only. The inhabitants of the one must always enjoy a much greater quantity of subsistence than what their own lands, in the actual state of their cultivation, could afford. The inhabitants of the other must always enjoy a much smaller quantity.... Few countries ... produce much more rude produce than what is sufficient for the subsistence of their own inhabitants. To send abroad any great quantity of it, therefore, would be to send abroad a part of the necessary subsistence of the people. It is otherwise with the exportation of manufactures. The maintenance of the people employed in them is kept at home, and only the surplus part of their work is exported.... The commodities of Europe were almost all new to America, and many of those of America were new to Europe. A new set of exchanges, therefore, began to take place which had never been thought of before, and which should naturally have proved as advantageous to the new, as it certainly did to the old continent. The savage injustice of the Europeans rendered an event, which ought to have been beneficial to all, ruinous and destructive to several [most] of those unfortunate countries.[3]

Friedrich List's thesis restructured as an international policy for all nations to have an equal share (which the highly respected President Franklin D. Roosevelt also suggested and President Kennedy hinted at just before his assassination), would create a peaceful and wealthy world. One hundred dollars paid to a community for what were once wasted resources and labor will create, through the economic multiplier, possibly $350 worth of economic activity within a community and thousands of dollars worth of capitalized values.

Gaining Wealth through the Vertical Building of Industrial Capital and the Horizontal Flow of Money

That $100 worth of formerly exported raw material can be processed ever finer and manufactured into ever more complicated products and services until the costs of the original raw materials are barely detectable in the product or service value (high-value-added products). Money spent building new industry to produce new products or services of continually higher values are continually spent horizontally for products and services that continually increase the economic activity of a newly industrializing nation. The high price received for that high value added product circulates within the economy and multiplies the economy to an ever-higher level.

It requires the proper balance of industry, resources, and agriculture to maintain those increased production values that in turn maintain land, industry, store, office, and home values. The natural resources necessary to maintain the economic balance of industrial nations are primarily in the undeveloped, impoverished, world. Thus the centuries-long effort to control the countryside and maintain the flow of resources to developed world industries at a fraction of its value.

The industrial/agricultural ratio of a nation or region can vary greatly depending on the abundance or lack of natural resources. The scarce resources in the wealthy highly-industrialized Japan and abundant resources in the poor nations cheaply providing Japan's factories with their raw materials dramatically outlines the true cause of wealth in Japan and poverty in those who provide those resources. The poor nations provide the resources and purchase manufactured products. Japan buys the low-value resources and sells high-value manufactured products.

Because the developing world has little industry to utilize their labor and resources to produce high-value consumer products and they are paid a low price for their labor and resources, there is almost no vertical industrialization, little horizontal movement of money, and thus little wealth.

When one adds up both the vertical and horizontal multiplication of wealth in an industrialized country, one has to seriously question the advice given to developing nations by the *imperial-centers-of-capital* that their successful future depends on continued mining and harvesting of raw material and forgoing manufacturing because that is their "comparative advantage."

The small savings on importing any item must be laid against the entire vertical and horizontal gain to the region when manufacturing their own consumer products. Industrial development multiplies consumer buying power and profits from consumer spending further multiplies profits which further multiplies investments, further multiplying profits and consumer spending, and all continually multiplying capitalized values.

Accumulation of Capital through Creation of Scarcity

Wealth can be accumulated by open destruction of a defeated nation's wealth to make a commodity scarce and the world dependent upon the monopolized source.

Adam Smith describes just such a destruction of a peaceful and happy society's wealth and their impoverishment for the accumulation of capital by a few. Spices and silk from the East brought overland comprised the majority of trade between Europe and the East for centuries and efforts to control that trade resulted in many battles, large and small. Muslims shutting off the overland trade routes to the East forced the search for a new route by sea.

Nutmeg and cloves grew wild and plentiful on the Molluca Islands that made them, like air, of high desirability but valueless. Natives made an easy living picking the spicy blossoms and leaves. If all traders had access to those spices, the European market (mostly nobles and wealthy traders, no commoners because they had no money) would become quickly flooded, and the price would collapse.

To create capitalized value for spice traders, it was necessary to monopolize those spice trees and keep spice prices high. So the Dutch burned every spice tree they could not control.[4] The other side of the coin of the immense wealth accumulated by a few Dutch traders through monopolization of the spice trade was the impoverishment and depopulation of the Molluca Islands.

The Molluca Island spice monopoly gives a quick lesson in how value is transferred from defeated nations to the powerful through capitalized value of entitled property. If those islanders had kept title to their islands and spice trees and a free market existed, it is they who, eventually, would have, through furnishing spices to the world, become wealthy. If all traders had access to those spices in those early years, there would have been much more, and cheaper, spices in the world, the islanders would have profited immensely, and they would have quickly learned the mechanics of gaining wealth through trade.

Creation of scarcity through open destruction of commodity production is a well recognized principle of neo-liberal economics. In America during the Great Depression cattle and pigs were slaughtered and buried and paying farmers to not produce is standard practice yet today. Oil, coal, timber, and other natural resources are not openly destroyed to produce scarcity. But wasteful consumption of those resources when plentiful and cheap and their waste for war do produce scarcity. That contradiction of waste of plentiful resources can only be corrected through a democratic, cooperative, coordinated social policy as addressed below.

Residual-Feudal Exclusive Property Titles: A monopoly on what nature produced

Titles can take many forms. Colonial conquest gained title to lands and the wealth it produced. The conquerors were "entitled" to do what they wished with their new property and, of course, they wished to transfer all wealth to themselves. Monopolization of natural wealth and the *wealth-producing-process* through exclusive titles were specifically designed to claim the wealth produced. This subtle monopolization is exposed in Section B through outlining the efficiency increases through *conditional title* to what is a part of nature as opposed to *exclusive title*.

Those parts of nature not built by men or women are land (natural resources only need to be discovered), technology (techniques also only need to be discovered), and money (which is only an already discovered social technique).[a]

Capitalizing Values through Underpaying the Weak on the Periphery of Empire

Due to being underpaid for equally-productive labor, resources on the periphery are harvested, and sold to the imperial centers for far less than full value. With that cheap labor, products are manufactured cheaply but primarily for export; those underpaid workers do not have the buying power to purchase what they produce. Lacking buying power, these nations do not develop industry and wholesale and retail infrastructure for local distribution.

Consumer products could be sold within the low-paid producing region if the value of both the industries and products produced were priced relative to the wages paid to build the industry and produce the products. But high wages in the developed world channel those products to imperial centers. This is graphically demonstrated by current wages paid in the developing world being typically under 2% (never over 5%) a product's sales value in the developed world, even before the 1997-98 currency collapses on the periphery reduced their wages by half.[5]

Theoretically, over time, distribution within the developing world at low prices could develop. But the large buying power in the imperial center and the low buying power on the periphery dictate there will be a limited horizontal flow of money on the periphery and thus a limited development of a balanced regional economy outside the *imperial-centers-of-capital.*

It is impossible for the developing world to capitalize their wealth without owning their own resources, owning and running their own factories, being paid equally for equally-productive labor, and selling on established markets. Nor can they develop social capital without the broad-based local buying power that title to their own productive wealth and equally-paid labor would create.

It is consumer purchasing power (adequate wages, adequate commodity prices, and profits from efficient industry and efficient traders) that determines who ends up with the world's products for a quality life, others have no money. Consumer purchasing power and capitalized values are both derived from title to natural resources, title to industrial capital, title to distribution mechanisms, and adequately paid labor as well as efficient industries. High-capitalized values require mass markets and mass markets develop only from adequately paid labor.

---

[a] Social techniques and discovered secrets of nature are both targets for monopolization: insurance, money, and the communications spectrums are three of many possible examples.

The common thread of a society that is productive and profitable and a high living standard is sharing both work and wealth while using *and sharing* the increased efficiencies of technology. A society with equally-paid labor and properly-paid capital will have more real (consumer) wealth. Properly-paid labor and capital means elimination of monopolies which means capitalized values will be far lower even as use-values are far more broadly distributed and utilized.

Accumulating Capital through Capitalized Values of Internally Produced Wealth

Although the above accumulation of capital from the wealth of other nations through inequalities of external trade is little known, the accumulation of capital through appropriation of wealth produced by internal labor has been written about (and challenged) so many times that we will address it very briefly.

Capitalized values are largely appropriated labor values multiplied between 10 and 20-times (current interest rates determine expected profit rates which determine capitalized value). Simpler, more just, and quicker methods of capital accumulation are outlined in the subchapters "The Creation of Money," "Accumulation of Capital through *Democratic-Cooperative-Capitalism*," and "Investment" in Chapter 27."

Notes

[1] Friedrich List, *The National System of Political Economy* (Fairfield, NJ: Auguatus M. Kelley, 1977), p.260.

[2] List, *National System*, especially p. 260, Chapter XIX, see also Chapters XII, XVII, XX -XXV.

[3] Adam Smith, *Wealth of Nations*, Modern Library edition (New York: Random House, 1965), pp. 413, 426, 642.

[4] Ibid, pp. 600-02.

[5] Jack Epstein, "Dickens Revisited," *The Christian Science Monitor*, August 24, 1995, pp. 1, 8; Amy Kaslow, "The Price of Low-Cost Clothes: U.S. Jobs," *The Christian Science Monitor*, August 20, 1995, p. 4; Christopher Scheer, "Illegals Made Slaves to Fashion," *The Nation*, September 11, 1995, pp. 237-38.

16. Japan's Post-World War II Defensive, Mercantilist, Economic Warfare Plan

Few realize the desperation-bred cunning of Japan's post-WWII economic warfare. Stopping fast-expanding socialism required rebuilding as allies the countries which lost that war. Besides providing technology and finance capital, America dropped its import barriers while simultaneously permitting Japan and Germany to protect their industries and markets in the same manner as that which had built America's industry and wealth.[1]

An American investment banker in Japan for 15 years, R. Taggart Murphy had a catbird's view and wrote *The Weight of the Yen*, describing how, in an obvious effort to both survive and revenge the loss of WWII, Japan's postwar economy was structured under pure mercantilist principles to engender "the greatest transfer of wealth in history" (at that time) from America to Japan.[2] Economist Joe Kurtzman's analysis of Japan's international trade is worth quoting at length. Japan has

> developed long-term strategies for entering existing markets and [has] composed detailed plans spanning 20-to-50 years for gaining a share of existing markets, usually by introducing new and highly refined versions of existing products and then slowly upgrading these products.... Beginning with crude copies of advanced German cameras like the Leica and the Rolliflex, the Japanese honed their skills by continually upgrading their entries into these markets until their level of quality and technology began to equal that of the Germans and then surpass it. In the span of less than twenty years, utilizing this long-range managerial approach, the Japanese were able to gain by far the largest share of the worldwide camera and optical goods market, thereby driving the previously dominant Germans to the sidelines. After the Japanese became the primary power in this huge market, they took aim at some of the other existing markets in which they could use their advanced optical skills. Small copying machines, professional video recording devices, and computerized silicon chip etching equipment are markets that the Japanese went after and now dominate. But this time the firms bested by the Japanese were not German. They were American firms that failed to keep pace with the slow, steady unrelenting Japanese technological and managerial advance.... Planning twenty-four months ahead is considered long term by most U.S.

> companies, whereas the Japanese routinely look five, ten, and twenty years into the future when developing their approach to entering a market.... [O]ur companies tend to lose out to those Japanese and other foreign companies that take the long-term view and that have the backing of their governments.[3]

Under protection of *Western imperial-centers-of-capital*, and even as they "chanted the mantra of free trade and laissez-faire," Japan's Ministry of Finance (MOF) and Ministry of International Trade and Industry (MITI) controlled the government's budget; set monetary policy; collected taxes; supervised banks, brokers, and insurers; and established parameters for credit, asset values, capitalization, and lending. Through cross shareholding, designed specifically to prevent outsider takeover and to further their mercantilist goals, Japanese corporations were owned primarily by each other.[4]

Japan's collapsed land and stock markets (down over 80% and 75% respectively) are not the total failures they are loudly touted to be.[a] The preceding bubble economy was specifically inflated to create finance capital with which to build more industry. Earlier we described how Japan first industrialized in the 19th-Century through selling government-built industry to Japanese industrialists at 15-to-30% of construction costs. After WWII, the same rapid industrialization was accomplished through high product prices being protected from imports by arbitrary health, safety and quality standards which permitted charging Japanese consumers three-times the price for consumer products as that paid by the rest of the world.[5] Those high prices were only a hidden tax that, along with other dictated policies and creative accounting, gave Japanese industry the same free finance capital as it received 100 years earlier.

Government financed industry and protected home markets created a comparative advantage that permitted Japanese industry to sell, for a period of time, at what would be a loss for a free enterprise corporation. Now that Japan has built the world's most modern industry and captured markets around the world, so long as trade surpluses are maintained, losses can be absorbed, up to a point, by those high domestic prices taxing back a part of the economic multiplier gains.

Even as its industry is running at only 65% of capacity and its real estate and stock markets have collapsed, Japan's trade surpluses have been consistently in excess of $50-billion a year with the United States alone. Many East Asian countries trade surplus with America were once offset by an equal trade deficit with Japan and those captured markets are released only when forced.[6] (By 20002 China moved ahead of Japan in trade surpluses.) Through health, safety, and quality standards which are never

---

[a] Land and stock prices are still too high and are still falling. Before that collapse, Japanese businessmen proudly claimed that "a square meter of the Ginza, [a part of Tokyo] was worth more than Seattle (Chalmers Johnson, *Blowback: The Cost and Consequences of American Empire* [New York: Henry Holt & Company, 2000], p. 203).

met, instead of tariffs, Japan will prevent others from selling on its home market, and—with the exception that this accumulated wealth was invested in the world's most modern industry, Western financial instruments, and real estate instead of gold, silver and jewels—that is pure mercantilism.[7]

Even though it has the added features of planned industrial financing and good pay for Japanese labor so the economic multiplier will develop a strong economy, mercantilist scholars will easily recognize Japan's wealth-siphoning formula: Buy resources for industry cheaply, build and maintain the most efficient industry in the world, educate their citizens, pay Japanese labor well, charge Japanese citizens above that for the same exported product, price exports just under the products of other nations, and sell enough on the world markets to pay for it all with a substantial cushion to spare.

Japan's Mercantilist policies would appear to be against free trade rules. But Most Favored Nation agreements only required that a nation treat all signed participants the same and all face the same arbitrary health, quality, and safety standards.[8] This accounts for current attempts to, through the WTO/MAI/GATS and FTAA, to require all nations to treat domestic and foreign corporations equally. However, while these rules will be enforced onto weak nations, they will not be enforced upon Japan. To do so would force Japan to close out its worldwide investments in real estate and bonds. If done quickly this could collapse the world economy just as it almost did in 1987 when Japan liquidated some of those equities.

The American/Japanese Debt/Equity Embrace

Japan invested its accumulated surplus values (once half the industrialized world's savings), above that needed for building industry, in U.S. treasury notes and other financial and real properties in the United States. This has locked both Japan and America into a debt/equity embrace that neither knows how to get out of. Japan has only to drop those treasuries and other properties on the market and the U.S. dollar crashes. It was just such a sale of U.S. Bonds by Japan which lowered financial liquidity for all markets and caused America's 1987 stock market collapse.[9] Since then, Japan's continued purchase and holding of those treasuries has been an unwritten agreement between the two countries to maintain the health of both economies.

The United States has the choice of doing what the entire industrialized world did when OPEC raised the price of oil: just print the money to cancel the debt. America's gain would be Japan's loss but there could be much worldwide distress from such an inflationary binge even if America won that financial warfare battle.

Americans would initially have all those TV sets, computers, recorders, and automobiles for the cost of printing the money. When Japan spent those devalued dollars Americans would have to work only a fraction of the time Japanese labor had previously worked to produce the products and services at inflated values.

While the Soviet Union was viable, Americans and Japanese had to protect each other or Japan could not have rebuilt and America's ability to finance the Cold War would have been severely weakened. Now that the Soviets have collapsed, the only need America has for protecting Japan is to protect the reputation of Adam Smith free trade.

Care for another's Economy is only between Allies

Care for another nation's economy is between *allied imperial-centers-of-capital* only. There is no *sincere* concern over economic collapses in either a resource-providing or a competing country. Such collapses mean lower resource prices and higher profits for the imperial centers and are the primary policies of powerful developed nations even if unrealized by second-tier planners.

Except as an ally against China if it threatens to establish a competing trading empire, *Western imperial-centers-of-capital* no longer need Japan. But letting it collapse would be seen as a failure of Adam Smith free trade and loss of philosophical support for capitalism worldwide. So, unless again needed as an ally to contain China, the forecast is for a far less robust Japan.

Some *grand strategists* are discussing America, Japan, and China allying together to bring East Asia out of its financial and economic crisis. But the United States is not going to be signatory to a trade agreement which would result in China's, Japan's, and Southeast Asia's 1.6-billion people (nor the 1-billion in India) becoming equally powerful. Not only will Asia be the world's superpower long before that equality is reached, there are not enough world resources to support the waste of an American style economy for half that many people. However, there are enough resources for a high quality life for all under efficient *democratic-cooperative-capitalism.*

Japanese Industry is being forced offshore

Japan has reached the limits of taxing the public to finance industry (raising sales taxes in Japan the second quarter of 1997 shrank consumer purchases 2.5%) and the lower costs of production are forcing Japan's industry off shore which reduces its economic multiplier. Because the multiplication of high wages paid labor for export production multiplying throughout the economy is the heart of Japan's economic planning,[10] this has a good chance of destabilizing Japan's shaky house of cards.

A simultaneous threat is Costco and other wholesale/retail outlets moving into Japan. Unless historic roadblocks are maintained, efficient supermarkets such as these will quickly replace Japan's enormously inefficient distribution system, lower those extremely high internal prices through which Japan has historically financed her industry and exports, and idle a massive number of workers. Theoretically Japan could force its citizens to spend money by lowering its value through printing more money to create internal inflation. But such a highly devalued Yen would wreck havoc on the world economy. Only war or outside support (externally supplied Friedrich List protection) can save Japan's bubble from massive collapse and that economy has taken a serious turn for the worse as this book goes to press.

It is far from Free Trade wherever One Looks

All major powers, including the historically allied trading blocs and China, have *social-control-paradigms* to keep their own masses in line and a protective negotiating paradigm when dealing with the rest of the world. *The Weight of the Yen* is a textbook on how *social-control-paradigms* work. The MOF and MITI present protective beliefs to the Japanese people, parrot Adam Smith free trade rhetoric back at the rest of the world, and all the time they are operating under Friedrich List protection principles.

Any Japanese industrialist functioning outside MOF/MITI rules instantly loses access to capital, resources, and markets. Any individual within the ruling structure who would expose to the world that Japan is not following Adam Smith and that they operate on partial mercantilist and primarily Friedrich List protection policies suffers immediate loss of job, power, and friends, and the "internal embargoes" are so effective there is no recovery for either errant industry or official.[11]

The major powers, as a group, promote corporate imperialist "free trade" to the undeveloped world to maintain access to their valuable resources while jockeying for advantage among themselves. It is far from free trade or laissez-faire anywhere one looks. Virtually every *imperial-center-of-capital* has massive subsidies for their industries and agriculture and 70 countries, 66% of the people on earth, are under some form of American embargo or sanction. The world needs others within the other six nations of the G7 countries and the IMF/World Bank/GATT/NAFTA/WTO/MAI/GATS/FTAA, world-governing system to defect and tell the whole story. This is a rare occurrence because the primary *social-control-paradigms* are so pervasive that defectors do not find an audience, they become instantly isolated, each person instinctively knows this, and peer pressure keeps them silent.

Mr. Murphy did not defect: he has an audience because Japan's mercantilist/ protection principles were so successful they were damaging other members of the G7 nations and the Japan/Taiwan/South Korea/Southeast Asia barrier was no longer necessary to contain fast-expanding socialism. Anyone who exposed Japan's mercantilist policies 25 years ago would have had no audience because Japan was crucial to the West's economic warfare defense strategy. The exposure of the same protectionist process today is now welcomed with open arms because Japan is no longer necessary as an ally to protect other imperial centers.

Though he does not use those terms, Mr. Murphy has the best outline of *social-control-paradigms* we have seen.[12] Few books could do more to alert one to what is really going on in this world as opposed to the rhetoric (elite-protective *social-control-paradigms*) we hear.

Notes

[1] Alfred E. Eckes Jr., *Opening America's Market: U.S. Foreign Trade Policy Since 1776* (no city named: University of North Carolina Press, 1995), pp. xvii, xix.

[2] R. Taggart Murphy, *The Weight of the Yen* (New York: W. W. Norton, 1996), pp. 13, 109-10, 181, 184, 222, 278. See also: Richard C. Longworth, *Global Squeeze: The Coming Crisis of First-World Nations* (Chicago: Contemporary Books, 1999), Chapter 5.

[3] Joel Kurtzman, *The Decline and Crash of the American Economy* (New York: W.W. Norton, 1988), pp. 107-108.

[4] Murphy, *Weight of the Yen,* pp. 29-30, 72, 77, 108, 185, 197-200, 206, 212-14, 218, 222, 231, 310; Longworth, *Global Squeeze,* p. 35 and Chapter 5.

[5] Lester Thurow, *The Future of Capitalism:* (England: Penguin Books, 1996), p. 201.

[6] Ibid, pp. 133, 194-208.

[7] Murphy, *Weight of the Yen,,* pp. 43, 48, 75-79, 93-99, 106-07, 126, 133, 184-85, 192-93, 195-202, 206, 212, 214, 218-19, 231, 244, 259-69, 279, 286-310, 303, 308; Longworth, *Global Squeeze*, p. 35 and Chapter 5; Chalmers Johnson, *Blowback: Cost and Consequences of American Empire* (NY: Henry Holt & Company, 2000), p. 203.

[8] Longworth, *Global Squeeze,* pp. 39.

[9] Ibid, pp. 53-54.

[10] See endnote 4.

[11] Ibid; especially Murphy, *Weight of the Yen*, pp. 53-55, 72, 98-99, 118-19, 103, 255, 275, 281 and Longworth, *Global Squeeze,* p. 35 and Chapter 5.

[12] Murphy, *Weight of the Yen*, pp. 118-19, 255, 275, 281.

17. Southeast Asian Development, an Accident of History

The current development of China and Southeast Asia due to being given access to technology and markets is accidental: they were only brought within the alliance of wealthy nations to prevent the further spread of socialism. Without a threat there is no basis in capitalism's free trade philosophy to give anything to anybody (and that is Adam Smith, not just a neo-mercantilist interpretation of him). Instead, the stated tenet is pay the lowest possible price, charge all the market will bear, and give nothing to anybody: a great philosophy for powerbrokers with a monopoly on land (resources), capital, technology, markets, and military might. That monopoly was broken only by the need for allies to contain the Soviet Union and suppress the world's break for economic freedom.

Once China and Southeast Asia are industrialized, considering that Japan was destroyed in WWII, this will be the first major accumulation of capital by cultures not tied ethnically and religiously to Europe. If this accident of history continues to succeed, and only war can prevent it, 50% of the world's population will be provided with adequate industrial capital, up from the traditional 15% and 80% of that 50% will be other than descendants of European race and culture. This would be a historic moment and Social Darwinists will take their minority role in the industrialized world as a very serious security threat.

The post-WWII plan was for German economic power to be submerged in the European common market with its 350-million consumers. The neo-mercantilist threat of this historically *powerful imperial-center-of-capital* was to be eliminated through the removal of all trade barriers between Europe, Japan, and the United States, essentially maintaining *one imperial-center-of-capital.* (Japan structured its economy as a sustainable empire within that larger empire.)

This was a sensible plan for the already developed world but unworkable as a development plan for developing nations. It was unworkable because the historic, and still operational, pattern of siphoning wealth from the weak to the strong dictates that there must be a countryside to furnish cheap commodities to both the developed and *developing imperial-centers-of-capital.*

Will Developing Nations Oppose, or Ally With, the Imperial-Centers?

With the collapse of the *Soviet center of capital*, claims that the one *worldwide imperial-center-of-capital* is now threatening to fragment into *three imperial-centers* are likely misplaced. The record of neo-mercantilist wars over trade (between Britain and Holland, Britain and Spain, and Britain and the Allies against Germany and Japan) has been to avoid subsequent battles between themselves by sharing the monopolization of world trade and allying against other *emerging-centers-of-capital.* For example, the developed world cooperated in the assaults against the emerging *Soviet-center-of-capital.* Due to losing trade battles (wars) in previous centuries, Portugal and Spain were left out of earlier sharing in world trade but are being brought into Europe's latest trade alliance.

Because a large bloc of industrial capital had been donated by the former Soviet Union, China had the basic industries with which to begin industrialization. Initially, corporate imperialists had no choice but to permit Southeast Asia and China to develop under that same protective umbrella spread over Japan, Taiwan, and South Korea. Having accommodated to that reality, *managers-of-state* were unable to make a quick paradigm shift to contain China when the Soviet Union collapsed, nor could they control the capital now broadly diffused throughout the periphery of empire. However, with the Soviet collapse there was now little need for allies. Thus there was little need to protect Japan's, Southeast Asia's, or Russia's accumulations of capital or access to resources and markets.

But a quick paradigm shift to openly withdraw protection from China and Southeast Asia would have exposed the fiction of neo-mercantilist free trade and there was now the problem of widely diffused capital fleeing high-priced labor, which would have made embargoing and containment of China a difficult task. As all nations of Southeast Asia were practicing Friedrich List protection rather than the free trade all were mouthing they could have developed, and may still develop, into an *opposing imperial-center-of-capital* with all the risks of trade wars and hot wars that entails. The 12-year stagnation of Japan and the 1997-98 financial meltdown of Southeast Asia after protection was withdrawn have increased that potential.[1]

> It is evidence of the historically illiteracy of western opinion that it expects that economic convulsions in east Asia on a scale that Western countries have not known since the thirties should occur without shifts in government and regime comparable to those experienced by Europe during those inter-war years. … Far from signifying the universal triumph of the free market, the Asian crisis is a prelude to a time of major dislocation for global capitalism. …

> Asia's economies … are not on a phase of decline that terminates with the embracing of free markets. … If history is our guide [most of Europe went Fascist during that crisis], we can be sure that Asian capitalism will emerge from the current crisis altered unpredictably rather than remade on any western model.[2]

Asian countries have thought about protecting their markets and currencies by forming a regional monetary fund. *Grand Strategy* philosophers are speaking of the yen as the primary currency. But true freedom can be only when each country ties its currency values to the value of a basket of commodities as addressed in Chapter 26. Once a region has a stable currency backed by commodities, the central bank of each nation will have the rights of creating money. If economic collapse can be avoided and labor's race to the bottom (the law of wages) can be reversed, the equalization of labor values will substantially expand rights and increase living standards. But there is no assurance that the race to the bottom can be halted. The world is yet locked within the jaws of that centuries-old policy of the countryside providing cheap resources and markets for *developed imperial-centers-of-capital.* It remains to be seen whether the contradictions of lowering the buying power of labor in the developed world, the collapse of buying power on the periphery of empire due to the abandoning of supports (protections) for Southeast Asian countries, and the massive accumulations of capital cannibalizing each other will again create a worldwide economic crisis.

No matter how sincere *managers-of-state* are, to negotiate honestly for world development is not possible under the current rules of neo-mercantilist free trade. Virtually every nation that developed did so while protecting their industries and internal markets. Trade between the developed world and the latest successfully developing countries was carefully managed and to develop the remaining countries requires even more careful management. That, without massive economic restructuring within the developed world, is an extreme contradiction. Historically some societies had to provide those cheap resources. The one best hope for the world is to share those resources and the wealth produced through *democratic-cooperative-capitalism.*

---

[1] Tabb, *The Amoral Elephant,* 2001, pp. 106, 114; Gowan, *The Global Gamble,* Chapter 6.

[2] John Gray, *False Dawn* (New York: The Free Press, 1998), pp. 220-21.

18. Capital Destroying Capital

Factories moving offshore for low-paid labor develop little regional buying power in the undeveloped world, while the loss of those factories in the developed world reduces that regions buying power. The profits from lower cost production sold on the high-priced markets of the imperial centers go into corporate coffers to be distributed to owners of stock, corporate managers, and stock traders. Those increased profits create higher capitalized values which—so long as there is broad ownership of stocks and an increase in taking in each others wash, cooking each other hamburgers, or giving each other heart transplants (service industries) so as to maintain the circulation of money—becomes new money and offsets the loss of buying power of labor.[a]

As subtly-monopolized capital shuts down factories in the developed world and builds new industrial capacity in low-wage areas to produce products for high-paid workers in the developed world, and assuming the service industries do not expand enough to maintain a distribution balance, the wealth of both the low-wage and high-wage regions is claimed by intermediaries and there is eventually insufficient market to fully absorb production. By expanding productive capacity without expanding equal buying power, capital destroys capital. (It is unrealistic to assume that this will be the first time in history those rising stock and real estate values that have been providing the consumer buying power will not go down and collapse the imperial center's buying power.)

In 1987, "world overcapacity was estimated to be 15-to-20% in automobile production, 20% in steel, 25% in semiconductors, and over 20% in petrochemicals."[1] Japan's industrial capacity has operated at 65.5% for 12 years and today, 2003, the entire industrialized world is producing at two-thirds capacity.[2] With such overcapacity in the developed world, and with the buying power—thus the only consumer market—being in the developed world, large sectors of the developing world cannot capitalize.

---

[a] Forty years ago the United States economy was 30% services and 70% industrial. Today it is 30% industrial and 70% services.

The world's powerless cannot obtain their share of industrial capital and high-paying jobs that create buying power, profits, and capitalized values. Michael Moffit quotes Stanley J. Mihelick, executive vice president for production at Goodyear:

> Until we get real wage levels down much closer to those of Brazil's and Korea's, we cannot pass along productivity gains to wages and still be competitive." With factory wages in Mexico and Korea averaging about $3 an hour, compared with U.S. wages of $14 or so, it looks as if we have a long way to go before U.S. wages will even be in the ball park with the competition. That the decline of U.S. industry is the natural and logical outcome of the evolution of the multinational corporate economy over the past twenty-five years has been a bitter pill to swallow and it will become increasingly distasteful as time goes on. *One consequence will be a nasty decline in the standard of living in the United States....* [W]e have the outlines of a true vicious circle: the world economy is dependent on growth in the U.S. economy but the U.S. domestic economy is [now] skewed more towards consumption than production and investment, and this consumption is in turn sustained by borrowing—at home and abroad.... The deal with surplus countries essentially has been as follows: you can run a big trade surplus with us provided that you put the money back into our capital markets.[3]

The excessive accumulation of capital by stateless corporate imperialists and the denial of capital to the world's powerless are two sides of the same coin. There is too little buying power among the dispossessed to purchase all the production of industrial capital. When there is already a surplus, capital building more industry without developing more consumer buying power will destroy other capital:

> So long as global productive capacity exceeds global demand by such extravagant margins, somebody somewhere in the world has to keep closing factories, old and new.... South Korea will be losing jobs to cheap labor in Thailand and even China may someday lose factories to Bangladesh.[4]

In 1988, China offered to launch satellites at one-quarter the price charged by the United States. Under competition from such low-wage cartel-structured industries, even the huge U.S. industries that once dominated the satellite launching market could not survive. That threat to Western industry was eliminated by negotiation and Americans and Europeans still dominate the satellite launching industry (exposing the fictions of free trade and proving that China can be negotiated with rationally).

Currently one-third of the automobiles and 95% of the home electronics sold in the United States are imported, and 30% of all products purchased by the American people are manufactured overseas. In comparison, before the financial meltdown on the periphery of empire, the relatively small populations of Hong Kong, Singapore, South Korea, and Taiwan "account[ed] for 10% of the world's manufactured exports; the U.S. share [was] twelve percent."[5]

If Korea, China, Malaysia, Thailand and other low-wage countries continue their economic development based on industrial cartels and protected home markets while selling to the developed Western markets under the fiction of free trade, industries in America, Europe, and Japan will be destroyed. The one who "distributes" (not necessarily produces) the cheapest and best product captures the market. Cheaper, however, normally means lower-paid labor, lax rules on pollution, and tax avoidance—not less labor expended or a better factory.

The elimination of more expensive manufacturers through free trade appears beneficial and, whenever an inefficient or shoddy producer is eliminated, it is. But many of the factories are closed not because of their low quality or inefficiency but because there are too many factories producing for the established market. The well-paid workers of the relatively developed countries are the logical losers as their industries move offshore and low-paid workers of industries rebuilt in the developing world will gain only a small part of what the former workers lost. When industrial capital is diverted to an undeveloped country to produce for a developed country, the advantage of the former's cheap labor destroys both the established industry and the consumer buying power of the developed country. William Greider explains:

> The world's existing structure of manufacturing facilities, constantly being expanded on cheap labor and new technologies, can now turn out far more goods than the world's consumers can afford to buy.... The auto industry is an uncomplicated example: Auto factories worldwide have the capacity to produce 45-million cars annually for a market that, in the best years, will buy no more than 35-million cars.... Somebody has to close his auto factory and stop producing.[6]

Failure to Expand Buying Power to keep Factories running is Economic Insanity

New industrial capital destroying both established equally-productive industrial capital and the social capital built around that industry is economic insanity. Where industries and jobs disappear as capital destroys capital, both home and business values drop. Through neo-mercantilist free trade the developed nations are destroying each other's industries, while 70% of the world's population are desperately short of industrial capital. *There is currently no mechanism within the market system to build consumer buying power and implant this new technology where it is badly needed while keeping the already producing factories servicing the already established market.*

Industries can be built quickly but Markets only Slowly

While industries can be built quickly, under neo-mercantilist free trade policies markets can be developed only slowly. Instead of building market economies and developing consumers among the world's impoverished giant producers are busy competing with each other for control of current markets and destroying each other's capital in the process.

This cannibalization of each other's industries battling over the current developed markets is ultimately self-destructive. The destruction of industrial capital and social capital by wars is well-known. What is little known is that these struggles over limited purchasing power destroy perfectly good industrial capital, collapse the value of social capital (homes and businesses), and forgo the production of even more wealth; capital destroys capital.

Expanding Buying Power in Step with Increased Industrial Capacity

While nations scramble to build industries to sell to consumers in the *imperial-centers-of-capital*, structural adjustment rules of subtly-monopolized capital deny periphery nations the right to increase their buying power in step with that increased production. The immediate discounting of a nation's currency on the periphery of empire if it attempted to print money to build industry and generate both buying power and products to purchase within its own economy exposes how control of trading currency monopolizes buying power for *imperial-centers-of-capital*.

Only by creating buying power in step with, and in balance with, productive capacity will there be a market for the production from that easily-built industrial capacity. As the productive combining of land (natural resources), labor, and capital (industrial technology) are the three requirements for a wealthy society, buying power is logically created by printing money to combine these economic factors and, so long as the money created is in balance with the wealth produced, that new wealth will back that newly printed money as it circulates within the economy. Equal pay for equally-productive work will create buying power in periphery nations and capital will no longer destroy capital.

The Monopoly Hold on Technology and Markets Is Weakening

"It took Britain and the United States 58 and 47 years, respectively, to double their per-capita output, but Japan did it in 33 years, Indonesia in 17, South Korea in 11, China in 10,"[7] and, if equal free trade under *democratic-*

cooperative-capitalism were economic policy instead of unequal free trade under corporate imperialism, the world could be industrialized to a sustainable level even more quickly.

What we are witnessing is the continued weakening hold of the subtle monopolization of technology. Eliminate fully the control of markets through subtle monopolies and the world economy would become so efficient that poverty could be eliminated in 10 years and the world capitalized to a sustainable level in 50 years.

Democratic-Cooperative-Capitalism will lower Prices and raise Living Standards

That capital is destroying capital while profits are booming outlines the large overcharges required to pay for the continued cannibalism. The cost of moving factories, the cost of perfectly good factories destroyed, the loss of value of social infrastructure in abandoned communities, and the record profits are all part of the overcharge. So too is military expenditure for protection of this wealth-siphoning system. And those losses could become even greater. With static, or even shrinking, world consumer buying power, even more capital will be destroyed.

We see the dramatic forerunner of this in the long-running economic collapse in Japan, the equally long collapse of the Soviet bloc, the 1997-98 financial meltdowns in Southeast Asia, and the current meltdowns in Latin America. Even with an annual $50-billion trade surplus, the Japanese economy has been stagnant for 12 years. Japan has the highest banked savings in the world, the trade surplus continues, massive funds are inserted into the economy, and, as this book goes to press (early 2003) the economy is still shrinking.

The fiction of the trillions in savings while Japan is in a depression will be exposed if the world crisis deepens. All that money is loaned out somewhere. If the equity values backing those loans drop far enough long enough, bankrupt banks will have to close and the money is gone. Those bad bank loans were estimated at $500-billion in 1997, increased to an estimated $1.9-trillion in 1999, and will increase further if property values continue to go down. However, if the Japanese and world economy turns around and those property values rise, the bad loans decline and those savings become valid again. This hope is why Japan refuses to shut down those bankrupt banks. As of March 2003 those values are still dropping.

Underpaying for the raw material to feed those industries and the labor to operate them was a crucial element of the imbalance that created this worldwide crisis. The developing world, which furnished the raw material to feed East Asian and developed world industries, was not paid enough to purchase a balancing share of production, industries were built in cheap-labor countries to sell to consumers in the well-paid world, and workers in the impoverished world were not paid enough to buy their relative share of production. If a financial/fascist fix cannot be put in place (an imperial center utilizing a powerful military to protect the siphoning of the wealth of a powerless periphery), this threatens to pull down the world economy.

Conversely, restructuring to equal free trade (access to technology and markets and equal pay for equally-productive work) and establishing a just legal structure under *democratic-cooperative-capitalism* would eliminate the cost of moving factories, the loss of destroyed industries, and the loss of value of abandoned communities. Those savings could then go towards industrializing the world to a sustainable level, protecting the environment, and reducing poverty.

This wasted industrial capital could just as well produce industrial tools for sale to the developing world. For that matter, why not return a share of this capital, as compensation, to those whose wealth has been confiscated through centuries of inequalities of trade? With the tools provided by that initial capital, and their own natural resources and labor, the developing world could build their regional economic infrastructure. Under *democratic-cooperative-capitalism* the wealthy world would provide the tools for the impoverished world to build their own social capital (homes, roads, stores, et al.) to a sustainable level in two generations. In trade, the Developing World would share their resources with the developed world.

Notes

1 Jeff Faux, "The Austerity Trap and the Growth Alternative," *World Policy Journal,* (Summer, 1988), p. 375.

2 Lester Thurow, Building Wealth: The New Rules for Individuals, Companies, and Nations in a Knowledge-Based Economy (New York: HarperCollins, 2000).

3 Michael Moffitt, "Shocks, Deadlocks, and Scorched Earth," *World Policy Journal* (Fall, 1987), pp. 560-61, 572-73.

4 William Greider, *Who Will Tell the People?* (New York: Simon and Schuster, 1992), pp. 378-79, 399-400.

5 David C. Korten, *When Corporations Rule the World* (West Hartford, CT, Kumarian Press, 1995), p. 128; Steven Schlosstein, *Trade War* (New York: Congdon & Weed, 1984), Chapter 28; Susan Dentzer, "The Coming Global Boom," *U.S. News & World Report,* July 16, 1990, pp. 22-28; Walter Russell Mead, "The Bush Administration and the New World Order," *World Policy Journal,* (Summer, 1991), p. 393.

6 Greider, Who Will Tell the People, p. 399.

7 Samuel P. Huntington, *The Clash of Civilizations* (New York: Simon and Schuster, 1996), p. 103.

19. A New Hope for the World

In 1988, China opened to outside investors coastal economic zones that encompass a population of 200-million cheap laborers. Leading-edge technology started flowing to China. Initially there were great profits for foreign investors as the latest technology, in tandem with China's cheap labor, took over others' markets.

However, most investment capital in China is internally generated (a fact that is studiously ignored) and, once she is developed and this labor force learns modern skills, the scene will change. Like Japan and South Korea while under Cold War protection, and before their financial meltdown when that protection was withdrawn, China will manage her economy to export a surplus. The price charged for products on world markets will drop to just below that of the competition, an ever-increasing amount of the world's consumer products will be produced by Chinese-owned industry, and an ever-increasing share of production costs will be paid to Chinese labor which will, in turn, accumulate ever more capital in China. With that increased capital, China can produce more for export. If this is allowed to reach its logical conclusion, much of the wealth of the United States, Japan, and other countries will then be siphoned to China. It will become the equivalent of 10 Japans competing on world markets.

China's trade surplus with America continues to climb while net imports from Japan and the Asian tigers continue to fall. If mainland China were to achieve the same per-capita surplus as Taiwan ($567), the United States would have an annual trade deficit of an obviously impossible $750-billion with China alone.[1] If India, Malaysia, South Korea, Pakistan, Bangladesh, and Indonesia were to achieve similar success, the U.S. trade deficit with Asia's NICs (Newly Industrializing Countries) would rise to between an even more ridiculous $1.5-trillion and $2-trillion annually.

Before China agreed to limit increases to 3% per year (free trade is avoided when it becomes dangerous), their textile exports to the United States were climbing 19% a year. Their trade surplus with the United States climbed from $3-billion in 1989 to $33.8-billion in 1995, to $60-billion in 1998, and to $84-billion in 2000.[2]

China has the resources, population, and internal cohesion to, by example if it so chooses, force honest trade upon the world. That same economic strength and cohesion can permit it to weather the economic storm that has arrived as the Cold War fades into history and corporate imperialism permits the "law of wages" to operate with full force and drive down the wages of both the developed and developing worlds.

Four Powerful Economic Weapons available for Developing World use

There are four powerful economic weapons the impoverished developing world can use: (1) They can form alliances and barter their resources to the developed nations in trade for technology, finance capital, and access to markets; (2) create their own trading currencies; (3) manufacture their own consumer products for trade within that alliance; (4) and, until the imperial centers negotiate honestly, collectively refuse to mine the ore, cut the timber, drive the trucks, run the trains, or load the ships for export.

If the 1997-2003 economic collapses on the periphery continues, there will be idle natural resources, idle industry, and idle labor. To employ those idle elements of production, a coalition of trading nations can create their own trading currency.[a] A trading currency is only the representation of wealth produced by combining land (resources), labor, and industrial capital. By combining their resources, the developing nations have all three foundations of wealth. If the Developing World allies to create their own trading currencies through tying their currencies' values to a market basket of commodities as outlined in Chapter 26, the *imperial-centers-of-capital*'s financial warfare weapons will have been rendered harmless.

The developing-world countries can then trade with each other for the natural resources to keep their industries and their economies going and barter resources to the developed world in trade for the latest technology for those industries. Bartering avoids hard money monopolization and the resultant unequal trades between weak and strong nations. The developed world needs Developing World resources just as badly as the Developing World needs technology and finance capital. Except for the superior military power of the *imperial-centers-of-capital*, the undeveloped world has the superior bargaining position. The imperial center's superior military forces maintaining control of the world exposes military might as the final arbiter of law.

Barter was how Germany was breaking the financial blockade put in place to strangle her, and World Wars I and II settled that trade dispute.

---

[a] To understand the enormous power the dollar has at this time over other nations' currencies and America's fear of those nations trading in their own or other currencies read W. Clark, "The Real Reason for the upcoming War with Iraq, http://www.ratical.org/ratville/ CAH/RRiraqWar.html..

The *imperial-centers-of-capital* own most those factories and patents. If barter is again tried, then *residual-feudal exclusive* title to technology—and thus monopoly control of others' resources—will be clearly visible. The efforts to prevent those barters will expose the subtle monopolies even further and hopefully they can finally be bypassed.

If an allied region refused to dig ore, cut timber, run trucks and trains, or load ships, the imperial nations would have no choice except to accept equality in trade.

Developing World Regional Trading Blocs to Attain Equal Negotiating Power

If there is no "countryside" to maintain in dependency, there can be no *imperial-centers-of-capital* enforcing unequal trades. The Soviet Union fought so long and so hard that after WWII America (the only remaining *intact imperial-center-of-capital*) was forced to share its capital with Western Europe, Japan, Taiwan, and South Korea to retain them as loyal allies to contain fast expanding socialism. Before the Soviets collapsed, while they were thus still a threat, China and Southeast Asia moved under that sharing protectionist umbrella and, until the Southeast Asia financial meltdown, were rapidly developing. China, just as every other powerful nation in history, will not accept inequality in world trade without a struggle. A powerful and fast developing China that does not fully incorporate Western beliefs is now the new threat to *historic imperial-centers-of-capital.* So long as China can maintain its independence, industrial technology is now so diffuse that the subtle-monopoly power of capital has eroded.

Up until the economic and financial collapses on the periphery in 1997-2003, *managers-of-state* were losing control of technology (industrial capital). The next few years will tell us whether the financial power of the wealthy world has reinstated control (Mexico's and Southeast Asia's 1997-98 implosion, Latin America's 2002-03 collapse); whether the attempt to reclaim control will collapse the world economy; whether fear of a flight from the old beliefs will result in a central plan to re-capitalize those collapsed emerging economies; or whether a fascist combination of financial, political, and military power will organize and maintain firm control of the world economy through financial, economic, and/or military warfare.

If China can maintain its independence it will be impossible to embargo technology from her and a new *social-control-paradigm* with a powerful China as the new enemy will not work while China is rapidly developing and the rest of the world is stagnating. If China (or any other powerful trading bloc) retains the ideology of rights for all the world's people, if it is sincere in that belief (all nations, especially the *imperial-centers-of-capital*, preach that philosophy but none follow it), if it is strong enough to not be subverted and too strong to be attacked, and if this blend of power and sincere caring for others results in all regions of the world gaining access to technology and markets with equal pay for equally-productive work, the world will then have the opportunity for the 50 years of peace it would take to develop the world to a sustainable level and alleviate world poverty.

China could lead the way toward honest free trade. Once its satellite/fiber optic communication system is in place, China could bombard its citizens with rational guidelines for sustainable world development outlining the quality life that could be had for all if that were society's goal. One child per family would shrink a nation's population by 50% in three generations while doubling the amenities of life for each citizen. A steady increase in technological efficiency during the same time span could double the amenities of life again and all that gain would be without increasing the hours of labor, consumption of resources, or pollution of the environment.

We use China as an example because it has the necessary social cohesion. If China succeeds and the lowering of its population results in a rapid rise in her per-capita living standards, others will take note, adopt the same policies, and their living standards will also rise rapidly.

Such a rapid expansion of rights will be a threat of the first order to the imperial nations. They know well that, once resources on the periphery are turned towards the care of their own impoverished, those resources will not be available for the high lifestyles in the imperial centers. The goal of the *allied-imperial-center-of-capital* is to co-opt the powerful within China so as not to be threatened by such expansions of rights, or to prevent such expansion of rights by containing China's access to technology and finance capital, which in turn will contain China's access to world resources and its economic development. Thus, reducing its population and rapidly increasing its per-capita wealth without expansion of resource use is China's, and the world's, best hope for gaining its economic freedom.

Notes

1 Walter Russell Mead, "The Bush Administration and the New World Order," *World Policy Journal* (Summer,1991), p. 404.

2 Wu Yi, "China-U.S. Trade Balances: An Objective Evaluation," *Beijing Review,* June 10-16, 1996, pp. 10-13; John Yochelson, "China's Boom Creates a U.S. Trade Dilemma," *The Christian Science Monitor,* March 1, 1994, p. 19; "China Maneuvering Around Quotas to Market Textiles to United States," *The Spokesman-Review,* January 10, 1989, p. B6; *CNN Headline News,* June, 28, 1990, Jim Mann, "China's Response to U.S.: Slow, Slow," *Los Angeles Times,* October 28, 1998, p. A5.

External Trade

Part III.

Sharing Technology with the World through *Democratic-Cooperative-Capitalism*

20. The Earth's Capacity to Sustain Developed Economies

> [The minerals in concentrated] deposits in the earth's crust, and the capacity of ecosystems to absorb large quantities of exotic qualities of waste materials and heat, set a limit on the number of person years that can be lived in the "developed" state, as that term is understood today in the United States. How the limited number of person years of "developed" living will be apportioned among nations, among social classes, and over generations will be the dominant economic and political issue for the future. World population has grown at around 2% annually, doubling every seventeen or eighteen years.... [For a sustainable, respectable world standard of living], births should equal deaths at low rather than high levels so that life expectancy is long rather than short. Similarly, new production of artifacts should equal depreciation at low levels so that durability or "longevity" of artifacts is high. New production implies increasing depletion of resources. Depreciation implies the creation of physical waste [and consumption of resources], which when returned to the environment, becomes pollution.[1]

Currently, the most effective way to control population is to raise a society's standard of living, provide access to family planning, and provide security for old age. Successful social and family planning was demonstrated in Kerala, one of India's poorest regions, which has a birth rate half that of other low-income countries.[2]

Kerala's per-capita income is only 60% that of India as a whole. Yet when it comes to meeting the needs of the people, Kerala is strikingly ahead of the rest of India, proof that there can be enough resources for a quality life for everyone. It has enforced progressive land reform, and brought about major social benefits precisely for the most disadvantaged. Infant mortality in Kerala is 27 per thousand compared to 86 per thousand in countries at the same income level. Life expectancy in India is 57 years, in Kerala 68. Elementary and secondary schools operate in practically every village as well as health dispensaries, fair price shops, bus stops, and all-weather roads. This is a far cry from village life in the rest of India.[3]

The developing countries of China, Sri Lanka, Colombia, Chile, Burma, and Cuba have a birthrate comparable to that of wealthy nations rather than the high rate of a subsistence economy.[4] With the biggest population problem, China adopted a one-child policy with a 19% salary cut for those who ignored those guidelines. Although still increasing at the rate of 17-million per year in 1990 (a combination of too many young people and longer life spans), it is hoped that China's population, and other heavily populated regions, will eventually stabilize, then, hopefully, shrink.

Each region should have its capacity to feed, clothe, and house its population while still protecting the world's ecosystem mapped. A country's capacity to sustain a population at a respectable standard of living while protecting resources and environment should be statistically analyzed. To reach those goals, family planning information should be universally available. Since most people currently depend on their children in old age, family planning requires that all elderly be guaranteed adequate food, fiber, and shelter. *A reduction of one child per family will save a society far more than it will cost to maintain that family during retirement.*

If it were demonstrated that a lowering of population would give a sustainable secure lifestyle as opposed to poverty without it, individuals would restrict their birthrate to reach that goal. If a reduction of population can be obtained in heavily populated areas while industrializing, the per-capita living standard will increase dramatically and assure acceptance of that policy. A steady increase in technological efficiency could double the amenities of life again and all without increasing consumption of resources or pollution of the environment. There will be great variation in potential depending on how high a living standard is reached for, what resources are used for housing (wood, soil, or salvage), what new technologies are developed, population increase or decrease, and so on. With those statistics common knowledge, goals can be set and reached.

Primary Concerns of World Industrialization

The hydrocarbons that produce much of the energy that fuels society were produced by hundreds of millions of years of plant life taking carbon dioxide out of the air to create those carbon compounds. The amount of carbon dioxide in the atmosphere has increased 25% and it is estimated the world's temperature has risen one degree during the 20th-Century. There is great concern that the burning of those fuels and the release of carbon dioxide and other gasses back into the atmosphere will create a greenhouse effect and seriously disrupt the world's weather. Scientists' primary concerns about world industrialization are:

(1) Fourteen of the warmest years ever recorded were in the last 20 years. "If the current trend of carbon dioxide, chlorofluorocarbon (CFC), nitrous oxide, and methane emissions continues into the next Century, this could subject the entire globe to an increased temperature rise of four to

nine degrees Fahrenheit or more in less than 60 years.... A global warming of [this magnitude] ... would exceed the entire rise in global temperatures since the end of the last ice age. If the scientific projections are correct, the human species will experience the unfolding of an entire geological epoch in less than one lifetime."[5]

(2) Of the estimated 10-million to 80-million animal and plant species on Earth (only 1.4-million of which have been scientifically identified), a minimum of 140 invertebrate species and one bird, mammal, or plant species are condemned to extinction each day. "Within [one] decade, we may lose nearly 20% of all the remaining species of life on earth." That is a rate thousands of times greater than the natural rate.[6]

(3) Chlorofluorocarbons have been in use for about 50 years. It takes 10 to 15 years for one CFC molecule to work its way through the atmosphere to the ozone layer. Once there, those molecules survive for a century or more and, theoretically, each CFC molecule could destroy 100,000 ozone molecules. This 1974 theory of Professor Sherwood Rowland was given credence when a British research team discovered a huge seasonal thinning of the Antarctic ozone. Scientists calculated a 10% ozone depletion in the northern latitudes over a 10 year period but were astounded when that level was reached in only two years and another ozone hole opened in the north. The increased ultraviolet rays that would reach the Earth, if that thinning continues (which it is doing—the first ozone hole is now three-times the size of the United States), are anticipated to cause cancers, harm to immune systems, destruction of some species of microorganisms, and thus, destruction of entire food chains.[7]

(4) The human "species now consumes over 40% of all the energy produced by photosynthesis on the planet, leaving only 60% for all other creatures. With the human population expected to double early in the 21st-century [if limitations are not imposed], our species will be consuming 80% of the planet's photosynthetic energy, leaving little or nothing for millions of other species, and in the process we will be destroying the stable mix of gases in the atmosphere."[8]

(5) Even if new oil finds equal to four-times the present reserves are discovered (which most experts consider unlikely), it will be only 50 years before the total exhaustion of all oil reserves.[9]

(6) If 18% of the world adopted and attained the U.S. living standard of an automobile-throwaway society, it would consume all the annual resource production of the world, leaving nothing for the other 82%.[10]

(7) The first law of thermodynamics says that, "Energy can be neither created nor destroyed. It can only be transformed." The second law of thermo-dynamics says, "This energy can only be transformed one way, from usable to unusable." This means that, do what we may, it is only a matter of time until the world's resources are consumed. Albert Einstein pointed out that this law "is the only physical theory of universal content

which I am convinced that, within the framework of applicability of its basic concepts, will not be overthrown."[11]

(8) To avoid the greenhouse effect, the world must reduce the burning of fossil fuels, reforest the planet to absorb the increased carbon dioxide, and reduce the release of harmful pollutants into the atmosphere, water, and soils.[12] An ecological (resource depletion) tax should be placed upon those fuels and the money generated used to develop and install ecologically safe technology such as solar energy.[13]

Within the next 20 years, scientists should know if the well-documented trend towards global warming, ozone depletion, and species extinction is continuing and be able to estimate the damage.

Civilizations Collapse when Soil Fertility Collapses

Greece's once rich topsoil has eroded down to rocky subsoils. The currently barren North Africa once had lush forests with plentiful wildlife. The "fertile crescent" of the Middle East, the cradle of Western civilization due to its original high fertility, is now largely barren.

As William H. Kötke details in his study, *The Final Empire*, this pattern has continued historically through the destruction of the vast forests of Europe and then has followed the march of empire with European emigration to its colonies. The United States, for example, has already lost one-third of its best topsoils and the loss is accelerating on all other continents. The most recent figure, quoted in *The Final Empire*, indicates world soil loss is on the order of 25- billion tons annually and growing.[14]

Since their origins in Central Asia and Northern China the cultures of empire that term themselves civilized have collapsed their soils. One-half the area of present China was once covered with a vast temperate-zone forest. This forest was eliminated before recorded history by the expansion of the empires of China. For the thousands of years since, China has suffered some of the worst erosion in the world. The Yellow Sea is named for the surrounding land's eroding yellow loess soils carried into it by the rivers.[15]

The empires of Sumer and Babylon in the watershed of the Tigris-Euphrates River collapsed after irrigated agriculture and overgrazing destroyed their land. Today one-third of the arable land of Iraq cannot be used because it is still saline from irrigation 5,000 years ago. The mouth of the Tigris-Euphrates River has extended itself 185 miles into the Gulf as the fertility of that hapless land washed into the sea. Every empire has run, and still runs, a net deficit of the fertility of the earth in order to sustain the unnatural growth and material consumption of its population.[16] The cultural history of Babylon can be traced through time to the denuded Greece and to Rome, which eroded the ecology of that peninsula. Most of North Africa—which once had great forests, broad grassy plains, lions, tigers, and many other plants and animals—became a desert. Both the Greek and

Roman empires used the then-healthy soils of North Africa as their "breadbasket." Cities that once were ports for shipping products to the old imperial centers are five and 10 miles from water as the fertile soils that once produced those exports settled into the Mediterranean Ocean.[17] Before the rising Muslim societies cut Europe off from the light soils of their African breadbasket, there was one vast forest the width of Europe nourished by those heavy soils. That vast forest built ships, smelted ores, warmed homes, and was burned down so the land could be farmed.

The history of this culture can be traced through the deforested lands and exhausted soils of Europe, across North America, and now through the deforestation of the tropical forests of South America, Africa, and the Pacific islands. During the expansion of the American empire, the great forests that lay between the Allegheny Mountains and the Mississippi River (enough to have produced a set of fine hardwood furniture for every family then on earth) were burned to clear the land for farming. Soil scientists estimate that one-half the topsoil of the Great Plains has been exhausted since agriculture began there barely 150 years ago.[18]

Industrial agriculture has learned to create artificial fertilizer from petroleum feedstock so that it trades off biological energy for a finite amount of hydrocarbons. In many areas the soil is exhausted and without such inputs would grow nothing. Modern industrial agriculturists say this is no problem as all they need soil for now is to prop up the plants. Thus nearly half the population of the planet eats food produced with artificial fertilizer processed from petroleum.[19] The exponentially exploding population of civilization is out on the proverbial limb with a diet provided by a steadily declining, finite supply of petroleum.[20] Coal can provide those chemical fertilizers for a while longer but that too will eventually be exhausted and there are many minerals and other nutrients being lost that are not being replaced.

Erosion, desertification, toxification, and nonagricultural uses had consumed one-fifth of the world's arable land as we begin the 21st-Century. Another one-fifth will go by 2025. These figures are for arable land only and do not include the general erosion and degradation of lands all over the earth from human activities such as deforestation, overgrazing, fire and other results of injudicious human occupancy.[21]

If democratic control of society can be accomplished and human society can be agile enough, this situation can be turned around. Permaculture, a complex method of edible landscape design with a wide variety of perennial plants, can rebuild soils and slowly restore ecosystems while growing more food per acre than modern industrial agriculture.[22]

Bio-intensive gardening using particular varieties of plants, detailed by the Ecology Action research center at Willits, California, can feed one person on one thousand square feet of soil in perpetuity without robbing any other ecosystem of humus. All composting material is grown on that thousand square foot plot. There are hundreds of Permaculture projects around the world and groups have come from all corners of the world to learn these skills at workshops in Willits.[23]

Notes

[1] Herman E. Daly, *Steady-State Economics* (San Francisco: W.H. Freeman, 1977), pp. 6, 7, 17.

[2] Richard W. Franke, Barbara H. Chasin, "Power to the (Malayalee) People," *Z Magazine*, February 1998, pp. 16-20; Bill McKibben, "The Enigma of Kerala," *Utne Reader*, March/April, 1996, pp. 103-112; Arjun Makhijani, *From Global Capitalism to Economic Justice* (New York: Apex Press, 1992), pp. 133-34.

[3] Franke and Chasin, "Power to the (Malayalee) People," pp. 16-20; McKibben, "Enigma of Kerala," pp. 103-112; Harry Magdoff, "Are There Lessons To Be Learned?" *Monthly Review* (February 1991), p. 12; Richard W. Franke, Barbara H. Chasin, "Kerala State, India; Radical Reform as Development," *Monthly Review* (January 1991), pp. 1-23.

[4] Frances Moore Lappé, Rachel Schurman, Taking Population Seriously (San Francisco: Institute for Food and Development Policy, 1990), p. 55; James P. Grant, "Jumpstarting Development," *Foreign Policy* (Summer 1993), pp. 128-30.

[5] Jeremy Rifkin, *Entropy: Into the Greenhouse World*, (New York: Bantam Books, 1989), pp. 8-9; Robert Goodland, Herman E. Daly, Salah El Serafy, *Population, Technology, and Lifestyle* (Washington, D.C.: Island Press, 1992), pp. 8, 10-14.

[6] Lester R. Brown, *State of the World*, 1992 (New York: W.W. Norton, 1992), pp. 9-13; Goodland, Daly, and Serafy, *Population, Technology, and Lifestyle*, pp. 10-14.

[7] Sandi Brockway, *Macrocosm USA* (Cambria, CA: Macrocosm USA, 1992), p. 3; Goodland, Daly, and Serafy, *Population, Technology, and Lifestyle*, pp. 8, 10-14; Christian Parenti, "NASA's Assault on the Ozone Layer," *Lies of Our Times*, September 1993, p. 22.

[8] Jeremy Rifkin, *Biosphere Politics* (San Francisco: HarperCollins, 1992), pp. 73, 173.

[9] Rifkin, *Entropy*, pp. 119-20, 226.

[10] Ibid, p. 233.

[11] Ibid, pp. 59, 80-81, 143, 273; Goodland, Daly, and Serafy, *Population, Technology, and Lifestyle*, 27-28.

[12] Rifkin, *Entropy*, pp. 8-9, 59, 80-81, 119-20, 143, 233, 226, 273; *Biosphere Politics*, pp. 73, 173; Brown, *State of the World*, 1992, p. 9.

[13] William Greider, *One World, Ready or Not* (New York: Simon & Schuster, 1997), pp. 460-62, 465-67. Ecological tax reform, pollution taxes, or resource depletion taxes are essentially the same thing (Brown, Flavin, and Postel, *Saving the Planet*, Chapter 11). See also, Barry Commoner, *Making Peace With the Planet* (New York: Pantheon, 1990), especially pp. 47, 97; Jack Weatherford, *Indian Givers* (New York: Fawcett Columbine, 1988), Chapter 5.

[14] William H. Kötke, *The Final Empire: The Collapse of Civilization and the Seed of the Future* (Portland, OR: Arrow Point Press, 1993).

[15] George Börgstrom, *The Hungry Planet: The Modern World at the Edge of Famine*, (New York: Collier Books, 1972), p. 106.

[16] Erik P. Eckholm, *Losing Ground: Environmental Stress and World Food Prospects*, (New York: W.W. Norton, 1976), p. 94.

[17] Edward Hyams, *Soil and Civilization* (New York: Harper & Row, 1976), p. 69; David Attenborough, *The First Eden: The Mediterranean World and Man* (Boston: Little, Brown, 1987), p. 169; J.V. Thirgood, *Man and the Mediterranean Forest: A History of Resource Depletion* (New York: Academic Press, 1981), p. 62.

[18] William L. Thomas, Jr., Ed., *Man's Role in Changing Face of the Earth*, vol. 2 (Chicago, Ill: U. of Chicago Press, 1956), p. 510; David Sheridan, *Desertification of the United States* (U.S. Government Printing Office, #334-983: Council on Environmental Quality, 1981), p. 121.

[19] Jonathan Turk, Janet T. Wittes, Robert Wittes, Amos Turk, *Ecosystems, Energy, Population* (Toronto: W.B. Saunders, 1975), p. 123.

[20] William Robert Catton, *Overshoot: The Ecological Basis of Revolutionary Change* (Champaign, IL: University of Illinois Press, 1980).

[21] Norman Myers, General Ed., *Gaia: An Atlas of Planet Management* (Garden City, New York: Anchor Books, 1984), p. 40.

[22] Bill Mollison, *Permaculture: A Designers' Manual* (Tyalgum, Australia: Tagari, 1988).

[23] John Jeavons, *How to Grow More Vegetables than You Ever Thought Possible on Less Land than You Ever Imagined: A Primer on the Life Giving Biointensive Method of Organic Horticulture* (Berkeley, CA: Ten Speed Press, 1991).

21. The Political Structure of Sustainable World Development

Every country is part of a natural, easily outlined region for production and distribution. Unequal trade between economies on opposite sides of the earth, while ignoring the fact that every region in the world could both feed itself and produce its own needs, is economic insanity. This monstrous situation can only be because of politics, and bad politics at that. The world's engineers and progressive economists obviously were not consulted.

Adequate Resources and Markets for Efficient Economies

As a large population is essential for industries that require mass markets, progressive people have recognized and championed the integration and efficiency of large economic regions. These industries require a multitude of natural resources that are only available in specific regions of the earth. Engineers and economic planners can judge what countries form natural regional zones for efficient production and distribution.

Towards that goal, the Central American states formed the United Provinces on July 1, 1823, with a constitution based on that of the United States. This was only the first of over 25 such attempts at forming a viable united nation out of the fragmented Central American countries.[1] All Latin American countries could logically form 1-to-3 integrated regions that would support a balanced market economy. Though there are over a thousand languages throughout Africa, several efficient economic regions are conceivable. African nations have tried repeatedly to organize just such viable political and economic unions.[2]

The cultures of the Middle East have pride in centuries of grandeur under the Sumerian, Hittite, Phoenician, Assyrian, Egyptian, Babylonian, Mesopotamian, Persian, Islamic, and Ottoman empires. Time after time the social capital built by these great societies was destroyed as civilizations clashed. The rich cultural history, common language, and the bond of

Islamic religion would be a solid foundation on which to build community identity and a regionally interdependent economic infrastructure. Muslims have tried to do this by forming a "Moslem Brotherhood" and an "Arab League" that reach across those artificial borders. They continue to speak of one Arab nation consisting of a number of Arab states.[3] Egypt, the Sudan, and Yemen formed the United Arab Republic in 1958, were joined by Syria and Iraq in 1963, and then fragmented back into previously dictated political boundaries.

Africans are trying to establish an African Union (AU). Brunei, Indonesia, Malaysia, the Philippines, Singapore, and Thailand, with a market of 314-million consumers, have formed a regional bloc called ASEAN that, until the 1997-98 financial meltdown, was making rapid progress in developing their economies and markets.[4]

Small, fragmented, weak Developing World countries were designed by imperial powers of Europe specifically to keep them powerless. Their small political groupings and small economies prevented their development of autonomous strength. While regional organization and development must have been the dream of progressive thinkers in every dependent country, the dismembering of these regions before they could become viable nations has been the policy of all empires.

Witness the response of President James Monroe's secretary of state, John Quincy Adams, to the previously described attempt to form the United Provinces in Central America:

> Adams and Congress stalled until it was too late for the two delegates to attend. Even if they had arrived in time, Adams had placed the two under strict instructions not to join any kind of alliance, not to assume that Latin Americans could ever form a union of states, and not to in any way compromise the right of the United States to act unilaterally in the hemisphere when it suited Washington officials.[5]

After WWII, the nations of Africa were not only breaking free, they were coalescing into cooperative blocs. Forty years of massive destabilizations shattered those merging countries and their hopes. After the Cold War they are again speaking of economic cooperation but it will be years before those past externally supported struggles play themselves out and stable governments emerge.

A Political Framework for *Democratic-Cooperative-Capitalism*

If fully democratized, the political framework under which the necessary worldwide transfer of technology and tools can be carried out so that emerging nations can develop viable economies will have been established within the United Nations.[6] Although it must be restructured and fully democratized, this organization has long been working on these problems and has collected most of the necessary statistics. The representatives of many of these nations are already cooperating, and industrialization is their shared goal.

If the decision were made to provide industrial tools to the developing world, an agreement could readily be made between most countries within a region. As the first capital would go only to those that are amenable to a just society, there is no need to obtain the consent of every country. Though actually propaganda for public consumption as the West mobilized to destabilize the Soviet Union, these were the stated rules under which the Marshall Plan rebuilt Europe.

> Our policy was "directed not against any country or doctrine but against hunger, poverty, desperation and chaos. Its purpose should be the revival of a working economy in the world so as to permit the emergence of political and social conditions in which free institutions can exist." Any government that was willing to assist in the task of recovery would find full cooperation, but any government that maneuvered to block the recovery of others could not expect help from us. "Furthermore, governments, political parties, or groups which seek to perpetuate human misery in order to profit therefrom politically or otherwise will encounter the opposition of the United States."[7]

Europe has moved beyond that original rebuilding and is forming one cooperative unit of 500 million producers and consumers with one currency. With the proper support such as in the rebuilding of Europe, instead of destabilizations, Africa and Latin America could form economic unions more easily as they industrialize.

Human Rights and Equality of Rights

The developed world and Western cultures are far ahead of most (but not all) societies in human rights, equality of rights, rights for women, and separation of church and state necessary for a productive modern economy. But we must not forget that full rights include economic rights and the developed world is able to give its citizens many rights and a high standard of living because of the massive wealth siphoned from the weak undeveloped world to itself through inequalities of trade. Under these unequal trades, one society's good life and security is another society's impoverishment and insecurity.

As democracies of weak developing nations have been quickly and regularly overthrown by *imperial-centers-of-capital*, the struggles to maintain control, or regain control, of the destinies of embattled societies have required authoritarian governments. When pushed to the wall, a society will collapse or it may maintain a semblance of control by retreating into the politically impenetrable fundamentalist beliefs of religion where equality and rights have little consideration.

All that would change if the pressures to maintain a region as a supplier of basic commodities were replaced by a sincere philosophy, and sincere effort, to support sustainable development. Few governments would endure for long if they rejected an offer to industrialize just because the conditions required a democratic government that recognized its citizens' full rights. Leaders who were reluctant to surrender their dictatorial powers would, under these conditions, risk almost certain revolution. In any case, these dictators would have disappeared long ago were they not put in power and kept in power through the external support of imperial powers.[8]

Since the goal would be to win hearts and minds through democracy and development, continuing to support reactionary regimes would be self-defeating. Most insurrections are attempts to regain control of a people's own resources and destiny—in short, to gain economic freedom. If these desires for justice and rights were supported by the powerful, instead of denied, the world would quickly abandon war.

These insurrections could all be stopped dead in their tracks by honestly and effectively promoting democracy and capitalizing underdeveloped countries in trade for them giving up their weapons. This is what most are fighting for anyway. As production of armaments equaling several times the amount needed to produce industry for the world's impoverished would be eliminated, the cost would be nothing and there would be further substantial gains to the world in not having its social wealth destroyed by wars.

The United Nations overseeing peace in Namibia and Cambodia and the united military efforts to enforce a peace in Korea, the former Yugoslavia, and Iraq (even though they were actually re-imposing control by allied trading blocs maintaining access to cheap resources and valuable markets) have established the principle of a world body ensuring world peace.

If there is consideration of everyone's rights instead of primarily the rights of those culturally, religiously, or economically tied to outside powers (the lack of which is a fatal flaw in most peace efforts), this principle needs to be expanded to all nations so they can industrialize, feed themselves, live a respectable life, and start rebuilding their soils and ecosystems devastated by years of war and exploitation.

Security through Equality and Interdependence

As neo-mercantilist policies have been the cause of most wars, *spheres of influence, power vacuums, balances of power, preponderances of power, containments,* and *realpolitiks*, (all functioning under each *imperial-center-of-capital's Grand Strategy* in the *great game* of who will control the world's wealth) must be replaced by a guarantee of each society's security.

World trade should be restructured to provide *security through interdependence* as opposed to the current *insecurity through dependence.* Under guarantees of secure borders, the lower the level of weapons the more secure every nation will be. With all the world gaining rights and freedom, spheres of influence (which means little more than dominance over other societies) will disappear. Without dominant—and arbitrary—military power, there would then be no power vacuums, balance of power or containment struggles. As opposed to the current guarantees of war and oppression, realpolitiks, realist and moralist statecraft theory will mean peace, freedom, justice, and rights for all instead of immediate insecurity for some and eventual insecurity for all. National security would then be obtained through world security. It would no longer be "international politics in the national interest but national politics in the international interest."[9]

These ideas are not new. In 1899, the recognition of the destructive power of modern weapons led to the formation of a "convention for the pacific settlement of disputes which was adopted by 24 major states." And, after the horrors of WWI, the General Treaty for the Renunciation of Wars was formulated and signed by some of the major powers on August 27, 1928.[10] When a retired American five-star general laid out a plan to eliminate all the world's nuclear weapons in late 1996, he was joined within six months by over 20 military leaders from virtually all the major industrial countries.

Integrating Diverse Nationalities, Races, and Cultures

Countries with diverse nationalities, races, and cultures have special problems. Everyone should have equal access to jobs and capital and equal representation in government. Once the countries in a region are industrially integrated and markets are open to all, everyone's well-being will depend on cooperation. Such attainment of full rights, and the assurance of sanctions if war erupts, will eliminate most ethnic conflicts fought under religious banners—the former Yugoslavia was an outstanding example. Those diverse people were living cooperatively, peacefully, and broadly intermarrying until external powers allied with internal forces to expand their culture and wealth at the expense of Serbian Eastern Orthodox culture.[11]

The United Nations was specifically designed to be controlled by the *imperial-centers-of-capital.* Before it can effectively federalize the world it must become democratized along the lines of the World Constitution and Parliament Association Constitution, http://www.radford.edu/~peace/ippno/doc.html, and other groups pushing for federation of poor nations such as: Earth Federation, http:// old.jccc.net/~mfoster/rs/constitution.html; Commission on Global Governance, http://www.cgg.ch/; United Planetary Federation, http://www.upf.org/index.html; World Citizen Foundation, http://www.worldcitizen.org/; and The United Nations http://www.un.org/.

Notes

1 Walter Lefeber, *Inevitable Revolutions* (New York: W.W. Norton, 1984), pp. 24-27.

2 Organizations formed to further African unity are: AU (African Union); NEPAD (New Partnership for Africa's Development) OAU (Organization of African Unity); OAAU (Organization for African American Unity (founded by Frantz Fanon); OCAM (Organization Commune Africaine et Malagache); OERS (Organization of States Bordering the Senegal River); UDEAC (Customs Union of Central African States); OERM (Economic Organization of North Africa); EACM (East African Community and Common Market); CEAO (West African Economic Community); CEDEAO (The Economic Community of West African States). Francois N. Muyumba, Esther Atcherson, *Pan-Africanism and Cross-Cultural Understanding: A Reader* (Needham Heights, MA: Ginn Press, 1993), Chapter 3 by Andrew Conteh, Chapter 15 by Edmond J. Keller, and Chapter 19 by Bamidele A. Ojo; Cheikh Anta Diop, Black Africa, by Harold J. Salemson, trans. (Westport: Lawrence Hill, 1978), p. 1. In South America, there are Mercosur (Southern Cone Common Market), the Andean Pact, and many more.

3 Feroz, Ahmad, "Arab Nationalism, Radicalism, and the Specter of Neocolonialism," *Monthly Review* (February 1991): p. 32.

4 *Depth News*, Manila, Quoted by *World Press Review*, March 1991, p. 46.

5 Lefeber, *Inevitable Revolutions*, p. 24.

6 One is The United Nations Development Program (UNDP), 1 UN Plaza, New York, NY, 10017. *Human Development Report, 1991* (New York: Oxford University Press, 1991) addresses these needs and is only one of their many publications.

7 D. F. Fleming, *The Cold War and its Origins* (New York: Doubleday, 1961), p. 478; Walter Isaacson, Evan Thomas, *The Wise Men* (New York: Simon and Schuster, 1986), p. 414.

8 Sidney Lens, *Permanent War* (New York: Schocker Books, 1987), p. 27; John Stockwell, *The Praetorian Guard* (Boston: South End Press, 1991). See Chapter 7 of this work.

9 Anna Gyorgy, Trans., *Ecological Economics* (London: Zed Books, 1991), p. 7; read between the lines of Robert J. Art, Kenneth N Waltz's *The Use of Force: Military Power and International Politics* (New York: University Press of America, 1993) and read the treatises on diplomacy by authors listed therein.

10 William Preston Jr., Edward S. Herman, Herbert I. Schiller, *Hope and Folly* (Minneapolis: University of Minnesota Press, 1989), p. ix.

11 Michel Chossudovsky, "Dismantling Yugoslavia, Colonizing Bosnia," *CovertAction Quarterly* (Spring, 1996), pp. 31-37; Michael McClintock, *Instruments of Statecraft* (New York: Pantheon, 1992), pp. 71-82; Catherine Samaray, *Yugoslavia Dismembered* (New York: Monthly Review Press, 1995; Charles Lane, Theodore Sranger, Tom Post, "The Ghosts of Serbia," *Newsweek*, April 19, 1993, pp. 30-31; Dusko Doder, "Yugoslavia: New War, Old Hatreds," *Foreign Policy* (Summer 1993), pp. 4, 9-11, 18-19; Sean Gervasi, "Germany, U.S., and the Yugoslavian Crisis," *CovertAction Quarterly* (Winter 1992-93), pp. 41-45, 64-66; Thomas Kielinger, Max Otte, "Germany: The Presumed Power," *Foreign Policy* (Summer 1993), p. 55.

22. Equal Free Trade as opposed to Unequal Free Trade

With today's educated populations and communication systems, it is possible to calculate the waste of past centuries and the current waste, calculate the earth's sustainable development level, educate the world's citizens to these realities, design a program for sustainable world development and elimination of poverty, and reach those goals.

Regional and Local Self-sufficiency

> "A regime of global governance is needed in which world markets are managed so as to promote the cohesion of societies and the integrity of the states. Only a framework of global regulation—of currencies, capital movements, trade and environmental conservation—can enable the creativity of the world economy to be harnessed in the service of human needs."
> —John Gray, *False Dawn*, p. 199

The developed and developing countries should be designed to be as *regionally* self-sufficient as possible in food and industry. Industries that require large-scale economies should be regionally planned and integrated with all countries within a balanced trading area.

Markets would be free within regions (both developed and developing) but with managed trade between these unequal regions, with protections to be lowered in step with the equalizing of industrial technology, capital accumulation, and labor skills. Thus the labor and industrial capital in wealthy countries would be protected from destruction by the low labor costs of impoverished countries, and the industries and markets of the undeveloped world would be protected from the cheap production costs of the developed world. This requires the development of balanced (yet competitive) economies within currently undeveloped regions. The necessary capital can come both from the equalizing surcharge and radically simplified and more equitable methods of capital accumulation (subchapters "Accumulation of Capital Through *Democratic-Cooperative-Capitalism*," "Creation of Money," and "Investment" [Chapters 26 and 27]).

If wages paid in basic industry are equal to wages paid by the consumer of those products (Adam Smith's concept of labor retaining the value of what it produces), this will create initial buying power and the expenditure of those wages on consumer needs will produce more buying power (the economic multiplier and development of a market economy). Once the internal market economies of impoverished nations are developed and a skilled labor force trained, those countries should be integrated with, and enjoy free trade between, other developed regions using the maximum efficiencies (comparative advantage) of each region.

"What is needed is a global regulatory framework for multinational corporations—a set of common standards for labor rights, tax and wage rates, and environmental protection—as well as the means, both national and international, to enforce them."[1] Instead of policies that bring well-paid labor down to the wages of the lowest paid, equalizing managed trade would be raising the wages of the poorly paid to those of the better paid.

Once control is wrenched from corporate imperialists, individual countries should allow access to their markets only to corporations that are good citizens working for the betterment of all societies. For the right to sell within that market and prevent tax and labor bidding wars between communities, a corporation can be required to meet basic standards of behavior. The developed world and the Developing World

> [ought to reject any new trade agreements that do not include a meaningful social contract—rules that establish baseline standards for health, labor laws, working conditions, the environment, wages. The world economy needs a global minimum wage law—one that establishes a rising floor under the most impoverished workers in industrial employment.[2]

Developing Regions should be trading with Each Other

Whenever possible, countries in the underpaid developing world should be trading with each other. If trading countries pay roughly equal wages for production of the products traded, neither confiscates the wealth of the other and the efficiencies of trade can function honestly.

By trading with each other while building industry, developing nations with low-paid labor can develop their economies much more rapidly than when trading with a nation with high-paid labor. If labor is idle and the treasury empty (it always is in the dependent trading nation—that is the essence of a subtly-monopolized world economy), raw material or semi-processed goods can be bartered for industries (technology) as opposed to trading those resources for trinkets.

Regional Trading Currencies

A respected news weekly recognized that, "Under the Bretton Woods system, the Federal Reserve acted as the world's central bank. This gave America enormous leverage over economic policies of its principal trading partners."[a] No country is free when another country has such leverage over its entire economy.

Money is only the representative value resulting from combining resources (land), labor, and industrial capital. By peripheral nations using the currency of an imperial center as its trading currency, the imperial center can actually print money to own industry within those periphery countries. By forming regional trading blocs and printing their own trading currency, the Developing World has all four requirements for production, resources, labor, industrial capital, and finance capital. The wealth produced provides the value to back the created and circulating money.

The developing world need only form regional trading blocs, manage their own trading currency, and utilize their money-printing power to build industries and develop an efficient economic infrastructure (roads, railroads, harbors, etc). The building of the industries and economic infrastructure will provide buying power to consumers, and that buying power will be the engine to maintain economic development. By tying their currency values to a basket of commodities (see below) all nations can gain the freedom and advantages of their central bank creating money. Once economic development is advancing rapidly, the proper share of development funds will come from money flowing within the economy.

Each undeveloped region of Asia, Africa, or Latin America has at least one country that is quite well developed (India, Brazil, Argentina, Mexico, South Africa, South Korea, Taiwan, and Japan) that could serve as a center of development. China is large enough to develop industry and markets on its own. Each of those countries should be organized with their neighbors as one production/distribution region and balanced industrial capital should be distributed throughout each region. With managed trade equalizing wage discrepancies as the world's natural resources are converted to consumer products and thus monetized, the employment of workers in balanced industries producing for their own societies will develop regional buying power and markets and capitalize those values in those regions. Those regions will then have both natural and capitalized wealth.

It must be emphasized that when this capitalization is complete each country will have equal rights (within its region) to resources, industrial capital, and markets. Those rights automatically translate into job rights, buying power, and that nation's share of social wealth. Nations that are poorer in resources need to be assigned a higher level of industrial capital.

---

[a] People and nations all over the world hoard hard currency. Until those hoarded dollars, pounds, marks, euros, or yen are spent in their country of origin, they are interest-free loans to the powerful imperial centers. Money spent to purchase outside the imperial center may be a debit to the person purchasing but so long as that money circulates outside the imperial center the only cost to the money-creating nation is the cost of printing and accounting. An interest free loan properly invested will accumulate that value to the imperial center every 5-to-15-years.

But the regional average should still be that all-important ratio of approximately one unit of industrial capital to 30 units of social capital (see next chapter) and all capital should, on the average, be regionally and locally owned.

The Imperial Centers Understand Well the Importance of Equally-Paid Labor

The experienced imperial centers understand the need of equally-productive industry and equally paid labor well. When the relatively poor countries of Greece, Portugal, and Spain wanted to join the Common Market, the planners knew the low wages of those countries would drive down the wages of the rest of Europe. They therewith "implemented a 15-year plan which included massive transfers of direct aid, designed to accelerate development, raise wages, regularize safety and environmental standards, and improve living conditions in the poorer nations."[3] The American Revolution led this battle for world freedom:

> The Declaration of Independence sounded the first global proclamation of the fundamental equality of human beings and their consequent entitlements to "inalienable rights." The Bill of Rights made many of those rights enforceable, especially for white men; yet it also acknowledged, in the Ninth Amendment, that the initial enumeration of rights was by no means comprehensive. A century later, the Reconstruction Amendments expanded coverage to all citizens regardless of race; and in 1920 the Nineteenth Amendment extended full citizenship to women. Following the atrocities of World War II, Presidents Franklin Roosevelt and Harry Truman sought to extend the concept of human rights worldwide. With Eleanor Roosevelt as chief U.S. negotiator, the Universal Declaration of Human Rights was adopted without a dissenting vote by the United Nations General Assembly in 1948.[4]

Those universal human rights include economic rights which can only be obtained if the rights of labor are equal to the rights of capital:

> [With] the mobility of capital threaten[ing] to ratchet down living standards for the great majority; what is needed is a regulatory framework for multinational corporations—a set of common standards for labor rights, tax and wage rates, and environmental protection.... [All societies] need to be able to exert greater control over multinational corporate activity so that the human and natural resources they possess are not merely exploited for the benefit of others.... The United States ... could alter the terms of access to its markets that corporations (domestic and foreign) now enjoy.... In this way a more level playing field would emerge and multinational corporations would find it more difficult to ratchet down tax rates, public investment, wages, and environmental standards ... corporations could be induced to help realize, rather than undermine, national and community goals.... In the early 1960s, for instance, auto manufacturers wishing to sell cars in California were required to meet tough emission standards adopted by the state.[5]

Invisible Borders between the Imperial Center and the Periphery of Empire Disappear

Professor Lester Thurow addresses one-third of the world's productive capacity being now idle. A substantial amount of that industry being on the periphery of empire is a change from past economic crises. Just trying to survive, those industries on the periphery will be pouring products into the imperial centers. This accounted for America's great gain in wealth between 1992 and 2000. The steadily rising stock markets were creating wealthy people, thus creating buying power, and the masses in the imperial centers were receiving value (wealth) via those low import prices.

Market value has a relationship to use-value. Those cheap resource imports are manufactured into valuable consumer products and cheaply manufactured high-quality imports have value. If imported product costs drop by half (those low wages on the periphery for equally-productive work), either the trader banks more value, the consumers gain more value, or both. If better materials and technology doubles the useable life or productive use of a product, the value to the consumer doubles. (Note: The productivity of computers doubles every few years while their price has dropped over 50% the past five years while cars which seldom ran over 70,000 miles 40 years ago now are in use 200,000 to 300,000 miles.)

When stock market values on the periphery start dropping and import values to the imperial centers (the periphery's export values) keep dropping, the periphery of empire is losing value and buying power in both cases. But, so long as other values in the imperial centers (primarily real-estate) hold or increase, the values to borrow against, and thus the buying power, will hold. But if the stock markets in the imperial centers fall far enough, other values will plateau or start to fall and, at some point, the values to borrow against will not be there and buying power in those once-wealthy nations will start falling. As buying power has already shrunken rapidly on the periphery, the buying power to keep the world economy afloat will have shrunk drastically, prices will drop, and more of the world's productive capacity will have to close down.

The imperial centers can, and does, print money to provide buying power to their citizens and increase values. If commodity import prices to the imperial centers shrink, values will continue to be imported or produced in those imperial centers even as values continue to drop on the periphery. (Money creation power is seldom used to protect the periphery.) The balance between wealth in the imperial centers and wealth on the periphery can, within reason and depending upon the military power of the imperial centers, be held at either a high or low differential. Today it is being held at a high, and growing, differential. Poverty on the periphery is expanding while wealth in the imperial centers is, or at least was, still growing.

Siphoning from the periphery of empire to the imperial center at the rate of 25-to-1 through a 20% differential in pay for equally-productive labor will increase exponentially if currency values widen (Chapter 1). If that wealth differential continues to grow as the wealth of the periphery pours into the imperial center, or if the citizens on the periphery of empire figure out why it is that they are so poor while it is their natural resources and labor that are producing the wealth for the imperial centers, a flashpoint will have been reached.

These *invisible borders* created by subtle-monopoly legal structures established over the centuries to protect power and wealth can be proven by simple mental exercise: All wealth is processed from natural resources (by labor utilizing industrial capital) and most the world's resources are in the impoverished world. Pay labor on the periphery of empire the same for equally-productive work as labor within the *imperial-centers-of-capital*, permit them industrial capital (technology) to produce for themselves, allow them equal access to world markets, and soon all people will be equal as they build and produce for themselves and the world, not just producing for the wealthy world. Under *democratic-cooperative-capitalism* those *invisible borders* will have disappeared. The periphery of empire, previously a huge plantation system providing resources and labor to the *wealthy imperial-centers-of-capital*, will have gained control of their destiny. All people will have regained full rights to their share of the life-sustaining modern commons.

Returning Title to Natural Wealth to its Rightful Owners

Control at any one of several points (resources, technology, finance, markets, or figurehead governments) can gain effective control of a society's wealth, which is a prerogative of ownership. Those mines, oil fields, forests, and fields could, through equalization surcharges (properly called landrent), be returned to their rightful owners. The exposure of the current subtle monopolies protected by the Adam Smith philosophy and military force explains why the IMF/World Bank/GATT/NAFTA/WTO/ MAI/GATS/FTAA/Military colossus insists on destroying the power of governments and privatizing all social wealth. Only strong governments and firm policies can take the world's destiny out of the hands of the subtle monopolies of the *imperial-centers-of-capital.*

Tariffs to Equalize Equally-Productive but Unequally-Paid Labor

In neo-mercantilist world trade, one society's security is another society's insecurity. Where free trade as practiced by neo-mercantilists protected only the powerful wealthy world, the protection of both people and the environment starts with security for all people. Early tariffs were tolls for the right to cross or trade on land owned by lords and nobles. Such tariffs on exports confiscate a share of labor's wages and capital's profits in the exporting country, while tariffs on imports confiscate a share of the wages and profits of another country's labor and capital.

If the tariff is on imported oil or another commodity in which there is little labor or capital involved, that tariff is primarily a landrent tax (oil and other raw materials are land) confiscating the landrent of the exporting country. If the tariff is on a labor-intensive import item, that tariff is primarily confiscating labor values that properly belong to the exporting country. Landrent values and labor values of another society can be confiscated by importing undervalued commodities produced in dependent countries too weak to demand full landrent and labor values. That confiscation of weak societies' wealth can be eliminated by pricing raw materials relative to the cost of mining the world's poorer mineral deposits and harvesting from its poorer soils and applying surcharges to equalize equally-productive labor values.

Pricing Commodities relative to the Cost of Mining and Harvesting the World's Poorer Soils

Instead of mass privatizations that effectively transfer title to corporate imperialists, commodities should be priced relative to the cost of mining and logging (or substitute commodities) in the resource-scarce developed world. Labor values should be calculated, equalizing surcharges collected, and these funds used to pay for the needed renewable energy capitalization for the undeveloped, commodity-exporting countries. Through such incentives and disincentives, resources will be conserved, pollution reduced, and the environment protected.

A part of the surcharge on exported commodities—rebalancing the unequal pay for equally-productive labor and replacing the landrent historically going to the corrupt elite of impoverished nations—can be used to pay corporations (no longer corporate imperialists) for relinquishing subtle monopolization of industrial technology. There will be no debt trap. If industry and infrastructure are contracted to be built—as opposed to being funded by direct loans—there will be limited siphoning of wealth to Swiss bank accounts.

Currently the cost of minerals in the United States is only 1.7% of GNP and the cost of fuel only 2%.[6] This demonstrates that there is plenty of room to increase the price of minerals and carbon fuels to a level that the lower grade deposits in the developed world can be mined and renewable energy utilized. The recycling of minerals would then be profitable and renewable energy would be competitive.

With labor equally paid, initially through tariffs and resource depletion (landrent) surcharges balancing production costs, the world can then mine all deposits (rich and poor), maximize product life (because consumer products now appear expensive), and can recycle (because they are actually now cheaper) the consumed minerals, paper, plastic, and other materials. Though developing-world resources may appear higher priced under these rules, they are really cheaper. Far more people will be provided with the amenities of life (which is the proper measure of cost) even as the world's resources and ecosystems are protected.

Once resources are no longer wasted producing arms—and social efficiencies such as those outlined in the classics of Thorstein Veblen, Stuart Chase, Ralph Borsodi, this author's previous work, and many others documenting the enormous wasted labor and resources—are instituted, the developed nations can afford to use their poorer deposits, develop new technology, or trade (equally now) with those who have rich deposits.

Equalizing Managed-Trade

Regions must have balanced integration of their industries and markets. The European Economic Community provides the model and experience. Long before becoming serious about a common market and against the rules of laissez faire development Western Europe integrated its production of steel and coal.[7] With their borders guaranteed and resources integrated, once-dependent countries can stop worrying about being attacked and can concentrate on building the industrial tools, infrastructure, and social structure for a productive regional economy.

To develop the impoverished world to a sustainable level, we need to apply Friedrich List's philosophies for developing powerful nations to the development of the world's weak nations. If a country lacks natural resources, it should be permitted a higher level of industrial capital. This is what happened with the three miracle countries: Japan, Taiwan, and South Korea. With limited resources, they were given access to industrial technology, capital, and markets, they protected those industries and their home markets, and they became wealthy.

It is possible to turn "win-lose" or "lose-lose" trade wars into "win-win" equalizing managed trade. A wealthy importing country should pay an equalizing surcharge based upon equitable landrent and labor values on imports from the region which has lost title to its resources and whose labor is underpaid. Surcharges on trades between regions would be only relative to inequality of wage rates for equally-productive labor and to equalize costs between rich and poor deposits of natural resources.

Those surcharges should not go directly to the typically corrupt Developing World nation. They should go into a compensation/development/ecosystem protection fund to pay directly for developing a region's infrastructure, constructing Developing World industries, developing renewable energy resources, developing environmentally sound products, designing and implementing ecologically sustainable lifestyles, rebuilding soils, and cleaning up and revitalizing the world's ecosystems. Those surcharges should be lowered in step with industrialization and wage increases of the developing nation. Once roughly equal in technology and when labor is equally paid, surcharges would be eliminated and honest free trade would flow between those regions.

But yet remaining should be a resource depletion tax to fund ecologically sustainable lifestyles for rebuilding the soils, and for cleaning up and revitalizing the world's ecosystems. Those regions would now have free trade and the world's ecological health would be protected by what is essentially a worldwide landrent tax imposed upon depletable resources. As technological parity is being reached, the surcharge protecting labor values would be disappearing but the resource equalization landrent charges and ecosystem protection taxes would remain (they go by many names, resource depletion tax, ecological tax, et al., but they are all essentially a landrent tax.).

Under a world development plan that maintained regional competition between societies of roughly equal industrial development and wage rates, while managing trade between unequally developed societies, the destruction of viable industries and communities would cease even as competition within regions increased. With the social savings of capital protected from low-wage competition but maintaining efficient competition, prices would fall and living standards would rise dramatically.

Restoring the World's Soils and Ecosphere

Some scientists have concluded the only way to absorb increased carbon dioxide emissions, besides cutting back on fossil fuel burning, is to reforest the planet. In an experiment, a section of barren North Africa was fenced off from sheep and goats and planted to grass. That forage grew beautifully and stabilized the once-blowing sand. Grass grows in rich soils while, with even less rain, shrubs and trees grow in poor soils, so forests in suitable climates and soils will do well also. The Baltistan region of Pakistan went beyond those experiments and in parts of this desert region "there is a sea of green" where the local population has planted trees. If these impoverished people can be financed by a small Dutch aid program, the vast oil wealth of the Arab world can finance the restoration of Middle Eastern and North African soils. China, with its dense population and low per-capita income, plans to reforest 20% "of the entire land mass of the country"[8]

A cooperative effort by a team of scientists, agronomists, engineers, and doctors in Gaviotas, Columbia, took title to 25,000 acres of that nation's worst soils and started rapid restoration of those desolate areas. To their surprise, in the shade of planted trees a part of the Amazon forest that had been destroyed so long ago it had disappeared from social memory started rapidly sprouting upon those barren *Los Llanos* plains.[9] Moshe Alamaro, a graduate student at the Massachusetts Institute of Technology, perfected a method where 1-year-old trees are grown in biodegradable, aerodynamic, pointed cylinders containing the required moisture and nutrients and which plant themselves at the rate of 800,000 trees a day when dropped from airplanes.

Once wars in a region are abandoned and industrial capital provides consumer products and tools, these people can replant their grasslands and forests. The initial grasses can be seeded to hold down the soil and then ecological restoration teams can begin locating the grasses, forbs, and shrubs to complete the restoration of a region's natural ecology.[10]

With care, local and regional ecosystems can be restored and grazing can continue. However, this cannot be done using the present corporate-controlled agricultural system. The many different species of grazing animals (deer, elk, bighorn sheep, pronghorn antelope, bison, et al.) consume different species of grasses, forbs, bushes, and even trees. Therefore, a natural ecosystem is cropped evenly, is not damaged, and can produce more meat per acre than a system of pasturing cattle. In a recent study on the African Serengeti plains, "An untouched savanna [was found to be] capable of an annual production of twenty-four to thirty-seven tons of meat per square kilometer in the form of wild animals while the best pasture-cattle system in Africa can yield only eight tons of beef per square kilometer per year."[11] (Most prairies will have a much smaller differential) Eliminating native species destroys the balanced ecology and pasturing only cattle leads to overgrazing of the grasses that are holding down the soil upon which the entire ecosystem depends.[12] If a preponderance of tree and shrub species has not become extinct, the complete ecosystem of forests can also be restored. Using the new science of Ecoforestry, a new forest can be guided toward its maturation while being selectively harvested.[13]

With desertification threatening one-third of the planet and increasing global temperatures from increased carbon dioxide levels, forest restoration is of urgent concern.[14] Using soil-based materials for homes is many times cheaper and more efficient than lumber, so timber cutting can be reduced to a sustainable level while those forests are rebuilding. Homes of rammed earth, stone, straw bale, and fired adobe with a ceramic interior have been demonstrated to equal or surpass wood frame buildings in cost, structural strength, warmth, and safety.[15] The second most intensive consumer of forests is paper. As we discuss below, society can be even better informed through electronic databases than through printed matter. Society can do away with disposable diapers and other timber-wasting social habits or it can produce such items from hemp and kenaf.[16]

There are great economic benefits from forest restoration: expensive hydroelectric reservoirs do not silt up as quickly; there is less need for expensive filtration plants; floods are reduced; forest soil holds the moisture and grows more timber and shrubs; long-dead springs will come to life and currently dry stream beds will run year round; fish would return to those new streams; the retained water is expired back into the atmosphere and increases rainfall both upon that forest and on regions downwind; mushrooms, berries, medicinal herbs, and many other products and animals to enrich a society will increase; and, of equal importance, a reforested earth, along with other conservation measures, could pull carbon dioxide out of the air to stave off the potential of the feared runaway greenhouse effect.

Extinction of plant and animal species makes it impossible to rebuild the original ecosystems which logging, grazing, and burning have destroyed. Soils that once grew a rich forest ecosystem and are now eroded to bedrock cannot be rebuilt within any useful time frame. Soils eroded to subsoil can be planted to shrubbery and a few hardy trees, but will take many centuries to rebuild topsoil that will support flora and fauna similar to what once grew there.

However, where there is still some topsoil left, grasses take hold quickly, and—with controlled grazing—start the centuries-long job of rebuilding those soils. Replanting ponderosa pine forests where there is still soil will start rebuilding the soil immediately and they will mature enough in 50 to 100 years for selective harvesting. Douglas fir, redwood forests, and equatorial rain forests will also start building soils immediately and can be harvested very selectively as they grow, but they will require three to five-times longer to reach climax maturity.

An ecosystem rebuilding time-frame is measured in centuries yet nature starts building topsoil and repairing the ecosystem damage done by 5,000 years of abuse as soon as man stops mining those soils through harvesting the covering flora and fauna. Roadway cuts stayed barren for decades when left for nature to heal yet eco-scientists have learned to establish soil-building grasses and vegetation on those barren and rocky subsoils in 1-to-3 years. So establishing a viable soil-building ecosystem on most eroded soils is very practical. Once that first soil-stabilizing vegetation is established, eco-scientists can replant the species which once grew there and, so long as humans let that ecosystem rebuild and when rebuilt does not over-harvest, nature will do the rest.

The replanting of grasses and reforestation south of the Sahara would reverse the march of that desert, which is now moving south at the rate of 10 miles per year. Only by such protection of the environment can the future of these indigenous people, and all people, be protected. If those grasslands and forests are restored, this would soften regional temperatures and climates.

Conserving Hydrocarbon Fuels

Under an international program to conserve natural resources, promote the use of renewable fuels, and protect the ecosystem, the proper price of oil and coal should be assessed high enough to make wind, solar, and other renewable energy competitive and maintain the consumption rate of oil and coal at a level that would consume the world's oil and coal both in balance and within the ability of the earth to absorb the carbon dioxide and other pollutants produced. This can be accomplished through a resource depletion surcharge (note: oil, coal, minerals, forests—all natural resources—are land, and this is a landrent tax). Using up the world's oil in 50 years and moving to the coal fields when the oil fields are exhausted would only ensure waste of those precious fuels and, create further unbalanced world economies as well as increase the threat of the greenhouse effect.

These hydrocarbons are so valuable for fabrics, plastics, medicines, smelting of ores, and powering ships and airplanes that—long before they are exhausted—their price should be held above that of other fuels both to limit pollution and to conserve them far into the future. Equalization surcharges going into a development and ecosystem protection fund, title to their own resources, rights to the latest industrial technology, and elimination of arms purchases and wars will provide the necessary financial resources for the balanced industrialization of the developing world as well as for environmental cleanup, reforestation, replanting of grass, and other ecological protections throughout the world.

The Middle East and the Caspian Basin have possibly 80% of the world's oil reserves, but that is expected to be depleted in 50 years. That is a very short time. Those desert regions have the advantage of solar energy being cheaper than in most other areas of the world, and it is imperative that they, along with the rest of the world, develop a sustainable energy policy.

The industrial nations should agree to provide industrial capital and technology to peaceful Middle East nations. If they were to give up their arms under guarantees of peace, inviolable borders, and access to capital and markets, they could no longer waste their wealth on wars, nor would they want to. Before these cheap hydrocarbon fuels became scarce, the world would be accustomed to non-polluting solar, wind, tide, and geothermal energy. This would both protect the ecosystem and save those hydrocarbons for other much more valuable uses for future generations.

Even as light bulbs are being invented that require one-fourth the electricity—and similar efficiencies are being obtained for electric motors, refrigerators, and other equipment—electricity generated by windmills and solar energy through photovoltaic cells is becoming competitive with fossil-fuel-generated electricity. When a substantial share of electricity is generated by these relatively nonpolluting and limitless energy sources, the well-known efficiency gains of mass production will lower their costs, enabling society to make the decision to radically reduce consumption of fossil fuels. That decision can, and should, be made in the near future. Automakers plan to have cars fueled by hydrogen that emit no pollution on the market in the first decade of this Century. As hydrogen is one of the most plentiful elements on earth and mass-produced fuel-cell-powered cars are expected to be priced competitively with gas powered cars, the world does not have to abandon cars.

Build them Industries Instead of giving them money

With the record of corruption within impoverished countries, people will question giving them money. That can be handled by building their industry directly by contract, not giving money. To build a balanced economy, provide consumer buying power, and develop arteries of commerce that will absorb the production of these industries, contractors and labor in those countries should be used. Legitimacy and security of contracts is the basis of any sound economy. Engineers know what those costs should be and, if cost overruns start coming in, the contractor who has proven incapable should be replaced—just as any good contract would require.

Once the industry is built, shares should be issued to managers and workers. Shares should be paid for out of wages and profits and as that money is repaid it can be used for building social capital (homes, roads, libraries, et al.). The development of consumer buying power and arteries of commerce would require a protective period equalizing the pay of equally-productive labor between regions. Once the region is economically viable, with adequate social capital and local buying power, the industry would then be on its own to sink or swim. With workers owning a share of the industry, the potential of gains through good management, the certainty of loss through poor management, the ability to regulate their own wages to stay competitive, and all this within an organized plan to develop a balanced economy, one can safely say most will succeed.[17] When provided the industry, as opposed to the money to build industry, those people will have physical capital. The only profits to be made then are in production; there is no development money to intercept and send to a Swiss bank account.

With care taken to organize homes and markets around jobs, and computers and modern communication permitting much work to be performed at home, the transportation needs of a well-planned, secure, well-cared-for society could be but a fraction of that currently seen as necessary in the developed world. A trend toward smaller homes—such as are the norm in Europe—could be fostered, consuming much less of the Earth's stored capital (timber, minerals, and fossil fuels).

Notes

1 Gerald Epstein, "Mortgaging America," *World Policy Journal* (Winter 1990-91), especially pp. 37, 53.

2 William Greider, *Who Will Tell the People?* (New York: Simon and Schuster, 1992), pp. 402-03.

3 AFL-CIO Task Force Bulletin on Trade, 1992.

4 Andrew A. Reding, "Bolstering Democracy in the Americas," *World Policy Journal* (Summer 1992): 403.

5 Gerald Epstein, "Mortgaging America." *World Policy Journal* (Winter 1990-91), pp. 52-56; see also p. 47.

6 Herman E. Daly, *Steady-State Economics* (San Francisco: W.H. Freeman, 1977), p. 109. See also Brian Milani, *Designing the Green Economy: The Postindustrial Alternative to Corporate Globalization* (New York: Rowman & Littlefield, 2000).

7 Dean Acheson, *Present at the Creation* (New York: W.W. Norton, 1987), pp. 382-84.

8 Lester Thurow, *Head to Head: The Coming Economic Battle Among Japan, Europe, and America* (New York: William Morrow, 1992), p. 223; Jeremy Rifkin, *Entropy: Into the Greenhouse World* (New York: Bantam Books, 1989), p. 220.

9 Alan Weisman, "Nothing Wasted, Everything Gained," Mother Jones, March/April, 1998, pp. 56-59; Alan Weisman, *In Context* (No 42, 1995), pp. 6-8.

10 Stephanie Mills, In Service of the Wild: Restoring and Reinhabiting Damaged Land (Boston: Beacon Press, 1995); John J. Berger, Ed., Environmental Restoration: Science and Strategies for Restoring the Earth (Washington, DC: Island Press, 1990); William E. McClain, Illinois Prairie: Past and Future: A Restoration Guide (Springfield, IL: Illinois Department of Conservation, 1986)

11 Jonathan Turk et. al., *Ecosystems, Energy, Population* (Toronto: W.B Saunders Co., 1975).

12 William Kötke, *The Final Empire* (Portland, OR: Arrow Point Press, 1993), p. 36.

13 Alan Dregson, Duncan Taylor, editors, *Ecoforestry: The Art and Science of Sustainable Forest Use* (Gabriola Island, BC: New Society Publishers, 1997); Michael Pilarski, *Restoration Forestry: An International Guide to Sustainable Forestry Practices* (Durango, CO: Kivaki Press, 1994)

14 A Report by The International Institute for Environment and Development and The World Resources Institute, *World Resources 1987: An Assessment of the Resource Base That Supports the Global Economy* (New York: Basic Books, 1987), p. 289.

15 Michael Potts, *The Independent Home: Living Well with Power from the Sun, Wind, and Water* (Post Mills, VT: Chelsea Green, 1993); Athena Swentzell, *The Straw Bale House* (White River Junction, VT: Chelsea Green, 1994).

16 Atossa Soltani, Penelope Whitney, Ed.s, *Cut Waste, Not Trees* (San Francisco, CA: Rainforest Action Network, 1995); United States Department of Agriculture, *First Conference on Kenaf for Pulp: Proceedings* (Peoria, IL:USDA, 1968).

17 Roy Morrison, *We Build the Road as We Travel* (Philadelphia: New Society Publishers, 1991). Fawzy Mansour, Professor Emeritus of Political Economy at Ain Shams University, Cairo, Egypt, has a philosophy for Third World development quite similar to these last two chapters. Fawzy Mansour, "A Second Wave of National Liberation?" *Monthly Review* (February 1999), pp. 19-31.

23. A *Grand Strategy* for World Peace and Prosperity

> To hell with the [peace] dividend. The Pentagon can keep it. We want the principal.
>
> —David McReynolds, "The Words and the Will to Talk about Change"

Since WWII, the military expenditures of NATO and Warsaw Pact nations have consumed and/or forgone production of about four-times the value of everything manufactured and built in the United States (excluding clothes). Thus the wasted capital of the industrialized world during the Cold War is enough to have built homes, cars, and every other amenity of a modern country for 20% of the world or for 100% if a respectable, secure living were the goal as opposed to that of a consumer throwaway society:

> Without considering the full social cost to the American community, the combined Pentagon budgets of 1946—1981 represent a mass of resources equivalent to the cost of replacing just about all (ninety-four percent) of everything manmade in the United States [excluding the land but including every house, railroad, airplane, household appliance, etc.]. But when we take into account both the resources used by the military as well as the economic product forgone, then *we must appreciate the social cost of the military economy, 1946-1981, as amounting to about twice the "reproducible assets" of U.S. national wealth.* What has been forgone for American society is a quantity of material wealth sufficient to refurbish the United States, with an enormous surplus to spare.[1]

Almost $1-trillion a year was being spent on arms worldwide when the Soviets collapsed in 1990.[2] With the end of the Cold War, that annual cost dropped to $700-billion by 1998. The world has wasted over $2-trillion building arms since Professor Melman of Columbia University made these calculations.

An economy structured to eliminate subtle monopolies siphoning wealth to the powerful and creating fictional values would provide these societies with a quality living using a fraction of the per-capita resources and energy used in America. The two lifestyles are not even measurable. Some in the developed world have given up the "rat race," gone back to a quiet relaxed lifestyle, and prefer it. Depending on one's guidelines, the quality of life of a world society not based on an automobile/ throwaway economy could exceed U.S. standards. Witness the Indian state of Kerala: it is one of the poorer regions of India and may have that nation's highest average quality of life.[3]

A more just paradigm for the world requires a recognition of quiet days and evenings spent with the family watching TV, playing chess, and so forth while working two days per week.[4] Many recognize this would be a far higher quality of life than driving $40,000 cars and piloting $150,000 boats to the detriment of the entire world. Experts in the field judge, by avoiding a throwaway economy, a secure, quality living can be attained while consuming roughly 20% per-capita of what the United States currently consumes.[5]

Compounding Sustainable Industrial Development

At the close of the Cold War, the United States had $21-trillion worth of reproducible social capital and $1-trillion worth of industrial capital (1990 dollars). Subtracting military and other wasted industry leaves a ratio of approximately one unit of civilian industrial capital to 30 units of social capital.[6] At that ratio, the developed world would only have to provide to the developing world one-thirtieth their needed wealth, those all-important industrial tools with which they would produce their social capital.

Currently less then 50% of U.S. industrial capacity is producing for essential consumer needs.[a] The world's sustainable development level is 20% that of the U.S. throwaway economy. So rational planning would consider industrializing the developing world to 14% of the U.S. level. As in a balanced economy only 3.3% of a developed society's total wealth is industrial capital producing for the civilian economy, the developing world would still have to build the remaining 96.7% of wealth that is social capital.[b]

Roughly 20% of the world's population having attained the living standard of America's throwaway economy and another 40% the living

---

[a] Twenty percent is producing arms, 30% is idle, and we have yet to measure the waste of the current horribly inefficient monopoly system as addressed in this author's *Economic Democracy: A Blueprint for Global Peace and Prosperity.*

[b] We are calculating sustainable development at the level of technological efficiency of the year 2000. Paul Hawken, Amory Lovins, and L. Hunter Lovins, in there pathbreaking work Natural Capitalism: Creating the Next Industrial Revolution, point out that increased efficiencies of technology will eventually be able to produce "four, ten, or even a hundred times as much benefit from each unit of energy, water, materials, or anything else borrowed from the planet and consumed." (Paul Hawken, Natural Capitalism: Creating the Nest Industrial Revolution (New York: Little Brown and Company, 1999), p. 8. See also Brian Milani, Designing the Green Economy: The Postindustrial Alternative to Corporate Globalization (New York: Rowman & Littlefield, 2000).

standard of a bicycle/mass transit economy testifies to the feasibility of this thesis. The 60% of the world that is currently above poverty need only turn their minds to a quality lifestyle without waste and the remaining 40% of the world only needs the industrial technology and training to produce that same quality lifestyle. As unlikely a scenario as this is, the only other choices besides sustainable world development are the continued violence of fascist control of world resources and war and the struggles of suppressed people to gain their economic freedom.

World War II alone cost at least $10-trillion (1990 dollars), three-times enough to have industrialized the world at the current population level and six-times enough at the prewar population level.[7] The developing world and the developed world together have spent about $17-trillion on arms (converted to 1990 dollars) since WWII.[8] That is *five-times enough to have industrialized the developing world to a sustainable level over the past 50 years.* The $3.15-trillion needed for developing world industries would have left $13.85-trillion to provide training to run the machines and society; to install initial communications infrastructure to reach the populations with that training; to guarantee food until a country was able to produce its own; to search for, catalog, and develop resources; and for environmental protection.

Capitalizing the world would have been a much simpler job than waging all those wars, to say nothing of eliminating the reason for them. After all, under *democratic-cooperative-capitalism* there would have been the cooperation of those societies instead of their battles attempting to gain or retain their economic freedom. With the developing nations using these industrial tools, and production compounding (this is what compounding interest is supposed to do), they could have built their own social capital. The history of the last 75 years could then have been one of world peace, prosperity, and care for the soil, water, and air, instead of intrigues, trade wars, covert wars, cold wars, hot wars, dispossessions, poverty, and ecological destruction.

The World can be developed to a Sustainable Level and Poverty eliminated in Forty-Five Years

We have calculated that a society can be well cared for at 20% of the American consumption rate, or with as little as 14% of U.S. per-capita industrial capacity at the peak of the Cold War. As of that date (1990), the value of industrial tools stood at about $5,600 per person in the United States. (Homes, cars, roads, bridges, electric power, water systems, sewers, et al., are social capital. Steel mills, factories, and so forth are industrial tools.) By the above calculation, one would consider 14% of that—or under $900 industrial capacity per person—as adequate for an efficient, peaceful society.[a] Allowing 3.5-billion people without modern tools, $3.15-trillion of industrial capital is needed to develop the world to a sustainable level. That is 18.5% the amount spent on arms by the world since WWII.[9]

Assuming it would require 45 years for the developing world to be educated and to build social capital as it was being given industrial capital, and assuming a doubling of the developing world's population in that time span, it would require $6.3-trillion. That larger figure would be only $140-billion annually, or 14% of the $1-trillion spent on arms each year worldwide at the time of the Soviet collapse. That is only 28% of that spent by the West to win the Cold War (48% of that spent annually by the United States).[b]

Modern industries can spit out industrial tools just as fast as they can cars, refrigerators, airplanes, tanks, guns, or warships. (In all those unneeded tanks, guns, and warships there is more than enough steel to produce the industrial tools.) Since capital reproduces its value every 10 months, if one-forty-fifth of the required industrial capital were installed each year and used by the developing world to build social capital, by the 45th year of this mutual support policy of *democratic-cooperative-capitalism*, the entire world would be industrially and socially capitalized to a level that would provide a secure lifestyle for most of the world's citizens and within the capacity of the earth's resources and its ability to absorb waste.

This is not meant to outline either the exact methods or timetable for implementation. If engineers are authorized to proceed and are given access to productive capital, they can easily solve these problems. It is reasonable to assume the developing world can train workers, build the infrastructure (businesses, homes, roads, sewers, water, electricity, et al.), absorb this industrial capital, and produce the necessary social capital over a period of 45-to-50 years.

Society is a Social Machine producing its Needs

Industrial society is a machine; and every road, railroad, electric grid, water system, and sewer system et al., makes this machine more efficient. Newly industrializing countries cannot compete in world trade until such time as

---

[a] That is about $3,600 worth of industrial capital per family and $100,000 worth of social capital (1990).

[b] When one includes the National Security Agency, the CIA, and weapons programs carried out under the umbrella of the Atomic Energy Commission and Energy Department, the military budget was at least $350-billion (and rising to $450 billion), as opposed to the $292-billion official military budget we are using. Between $4-trillion and $5-trillion was spent on nuclear arms alone, mostly under cover of the Energy Department, since 1945 (Jonathan S. Landay, "Study Reveals U.S. Has Spent $4-Trillion on Nukes Since '45," *The Christian Science Monitor,* July 12, 1995, p. 3). See also David Moberg, "Cutting the U.S. Military: How Low Can We Go?" *In These Times,* February 12-18, 1992, p. 3; "U.S. Becomes Biggest Dealer of Arms in Worldwide Market," *The Spokesman Review,* October 15, 1992, p. A2; William D. Hartung, "Why Sell Arms?" *World Policy Journal* (Spring 1993), p. 57.

their internal communication, production, and transportation systems (a major part of society's social capital) are equal to those of the developed nations. Even conservative economists have calculated that in the United States—with its highly developed, but deteriorating, infrastructure—returns on such "public core investment would average 50-to-60% per year."[10] Investment in the infrastructure of a relatively undeveloped country would see far greater increases in efficiency, thus far greater profits to that society. The $170-billion (1990 dollars) Marshall Plan, with which the United States financed the reconstruction of Europe in five years, documents this plan's credibility.[11]

Once Industrialized, Industrial Production can be cut back

Let us assume a newly developing country produced a very good tractor and a full range of farm equipment. Because the useful life of most farm machinery is over 10 years, once its agriculture is capitalized less than 10% of normal production would provide replacements. There would be no place within its economy to sell 90% of what it could produce. If that production were exported that would destroy the machinery industry of another country. Capital will have destroyed capital.

The same principle holds true for capitalization of any economic sector of any society. When the home market is capitalized, the manufacturer must export or shut down much of the industry that produced those products. This is the primary reason capital looks for markets abroad. Certainly those industries can retool and enter another market, but their success in that market only means someone else must go out of business and again capital will have destroyed capital.

The Tragedy of the Commons

Like everything else standing in the way of *residual-feudal exclusive* title to nature's wealth, the common use of nature's wealth has been given a bad name. Periodically a researcher of economic history will run into the fable "The Tragedy of the Commons." This fable uses the example of pastures used in common as an inefficient economic, legal, and social structure. Each farmer has rights to pasture his cattle. To earn more money, self-interest dictates that some will turn more cattle onto that pasture than their allotment. The pasture is overgrazed, the soil erodes, and everyone loses.

The truth is the opposite of the fable. During the Great Depression, bankrupt farmers on the prairies of the American West were occasionally organized into "grazing districts" which are lands grazed in common. Each has an allotted number of cattle they can pasture and *any excess cattle are confiscated.* The fable ignores that these ranchers have equal rights and none have superior rights. The result, private land with unrestricted title are typically overgrazed as ranchers maximize their income by mining the topsoil through overgrazing while the soils of the commons, the grazing districts, are conserved.

Where did that fable come from? As addressed in Chapter 6, corporations today fund think-tanks to pour out *social-control beliefs* that protect their wealth and power. In the same manner the fable of the "Tragedy of the Commons" was promoted by the powerful centuries ago to justify the reduction of others rights and the increase in their rights through the privatization of the commons. The three centuries of the establishment of the British enclosure acts is only one of many examples of structuring inequality of rights into law through enclosure of the commons. The imposition of Adam Smith free trade philosophy, discussed in Chapter 3, is another example of inequality being structured into philosophy, custom, and law for the past 200 years. It was then, and still is today, a philosophy for continued enclosure of the commons. We will next address how, as opposed to the fable, a modern commons is many times more efficient than the current subtle-monopolization of nature's bounty.

Notes

[1] Seymour Melman, *Profits Without Production* (New York: Alfred A. Knopf, 1983), p. 151, emphasis added.

[2] Ruth Leger Sivard, *World Military and Social Expenditures* (Washington, D.C.: World Priorities).

[3] Richard W. Franke, Barbara H. Chasin, "Power to the (Malayalee) People," *Z Magazine,* February 1998, pp. 16-20; Bill McKibben, "The Enigma of Kerala," *Utne Reader,* March/April, 1996, pp. 103-112; Harry Magdoff, "Are There Lessons To Be Learned?" *Monthly Review* (February 1991): p. 12, analyzing Richard W. Franke, Barbara H. Chasin, "Kerala State, India: Radical Reform as Development," *Monthly Review* (January 1991), pp. 1-23.

[4] J.W. Smith, *The World's Wasted Wealth 2* (www.ied.info/cc.html: Institute for Economic Democracy, 1994).

[5] David C. Korten, *When Corporations Rule the World* (West Hartford, CT, Kumarian Press, 1995), p. 35; Jeremy Rifkin, *Entropy: Into the Greenhouse World* (New York: Bantam Books, 1989), p. 233; Richard J. Barnet, John Cavanagh, *Global Dreams: Imperial Corporations and the New World Order* (New York: Simon & Schuster, 1994), pp. 177-178.

[6] *Statistical Abstract of the U.S., 1990,* pp. 463, 734, charts 752, 1295 (check gross stock, total; value added by manufacture; gross book value of depreciable assets). These statistics demonstrate that each factory reproduces its value every ten months and that there is approximately $21 trillion worth of reproducible social capital and $1 trillion worth of industrial capital. Professor Seymour Melman, probably the leading authority on military waste; Mr. Greg Bishak, of the National Commission for Economic Conversion and Disarmament; and William Greider, *Who Will Tell the People?* (New York: Simon and Schuster, 1992), p. 370, judge U.S. industry wasted on arms at roughly 20%.

[7] Henry Wallace, *Towards World Peace* (Westport, CT: Greenwood Press, 1970), p. 12; Barry Bluestone and Irving Bluestone, *Negotiating the Future* (New York: Basic Books, 1992), pp. 33-34, 36.

[8] See endnote 6.

[9] Sivard, World Military and Social Expenditures.

[10] David Moberg, "Can Public Spending Rescue the Infrastructure? A Tale of Three Deficits," *In These Times,* February 13-19, 1991, p. 11.

[11] Lester Thurow, *Head to Head: The Coming Economic Battle Among Japan, Europe, and America* (New York: William Morrow, 1992), p. 94; Paul Kennedy, *The Rise and Fall of Great Powers* (New York: Random House, 1987), p. 360; *ABC News* and *NBC News,* June 4, 1987; Michael Barrat Brown, in *Fair Trade* (London: Zed Books, 1993), p. 96, puts the Marshal Plan at $200 billion in 1987 dollars.

Section B

Internal Trade

Economic Rights for all People

24. Adjusting *Residual-Feudal Exclusive* Property Rights Produces a Modern Land Commons

Before the advent of title to social wealth through industrial capital and finance capital all sustenance for life, and thus all wealth, was processed directly from land. Finance capital is the money symbol for industrial capital and these factories are only extremely efficient tools to process products from the land. So the subtle monopolization of finance capital and/or industrial capital is only an extension of the subtle monopolization of land. When wealth began to be produced by capital as well as land, powerful people undertook to lay claim to these instruments for the production of wealth just as historically they had laid claim to land.

The process of usurping rights through monopoly title to society's wealth takes many generations and leads to great wealth for a relative few and dispossession and poverty for many. This has a long way to go in the United States but the well-documented trend suggests that fewer and fewer own more and more. With the right to vote, and within the framework of America's ever-flexible Constitution, these rights can be reclaimed through restructuring law and custom to reclaim rights to the commons while protecting private ownership. To eliminate subtle monopolization and establishing a productive society, a modern land commons must be established through society collecting the landrent.

Land is subtly monopolized by the total tax structure of a nation. Before going on to their greater reward, almost every economist of high standing will say that Henry George's *Progress and Poverty*, describing the simplicity and justice of society collecting the landrent, outlines the most efficient and just tax structure.

Although this tax structure has been proposed by various highly respected people for 300 years, America's preeminent Henry George, is undoubtedly the leading economic philosopher on the subject. This chapter is his 1897 primary work—*Progress and Poverty*—condensed and simplified.[1]

The subtle monopolization of social wealth started centuries ago as the powerful structured superior rights into ownership of land. As British Prime Minister Winston Churchill said, land is " 'by far the greatest of monopolies—it is a perpetual monopoly, and it is the mother of all other forms of monopoly.' "[2] If you feel threatened by such a simple solution, keep in mind that when society collects its full due in a landrent tax all private property use-rights will be retained. Ownership of land for homes, businesses, and production will be both easier and cheaper. *Removal of subtle monopolization would not only increase your right to land and the profits from its productive use, it would ensure those rights.*

Land is Social Wealth

If a person were born with fully developed intelligence, physical ability, and judgment—but without social conditioning—one of the first confusing realities he or she would face is that all land belongs to someone else. Before one could legally stand, sit, lie down, or sleep, he or she would have to pay whoever owned that piece of land. This can be shown to be absurd by reflecting on the obvious: land, air, and water nurture all life and each living thing requires, and is surely entitled to, living space on this earth. No person produced any part of it, it was here when each was born, and its bounty is everybody's common right.

By observing title claims in action, earlier economic philosophers were able to deduce that the essential factor in creation of wealth was the appropriation of a useful part of nature by claiming exclusive private title and alienating all others from its use:

> The first man who, having enclosed a piece of ground, bethought himself as saying "this is mine," and found people simple enough to believe him, was the real founder of civil society. From how many crimes, wars, and murders, from how many horrors and misfortunes might not any one have saved mankind, by pulling up the stakes, or filling up the ditch, and crying to his fellows: "Beware of listening to this impostor; you are undone if you once forget that the fruits of the earth belong to us all, and the earth itself to nobody."[3]

Jean Jacques Rousseau, in *A Discourse on the Origins of Inequality*, was outlining the injustice of one person having unrestricted ownership of another's living space. This practice is only customary. It is part of social conditioning (*social-control paradigms* or beliefs) that all receive while growing up. Being thoroughly conditioned, and having never experienced or imagined anything else, few ever realize that under *exclusive* private ownership of land they do not have all their rights. Instead, the possibility of *eventually owning* one's piece of land is viewed as full rights. Being conscious of the not-so-distant past when common people did not have even this right, citizen's view and celebrate these limited rights as full rights.

Mark Twain recognized that appropriation of nature's gifts in unrestricted private title by one person means alienation and loss of rights for others. His article, "Archimedes," in Henry George's paper *The Standard*, July 27, 1889, describes how, if he owned the entire world, all the wealth of the world would be his and all the world's citizens would be his slaves.[4]

While one's lack of full rights is difficult to visualize when a person is accustomed to exclusive ownership to what nature provided free for all to use, it is easy to see if one uses a gift of nature, such as air, that has not yet been alienated from the commons. Air is one of nature's gifts and if a group could claim title to it (when windmills were invented, such efforts were made to claim title to the wind), each person would have to pay for the right to breathe just as now they have to pay for the right for a place to live.

One notes that water was still free long after land was fully claimed. As population density increased and water became scarce, it became profitable to claim exclusive title to water. Whenever those claims of ownership are encoded in law, water sources will develop high capitalized values and society will become accustomed to paying dearly for its drinking water. As one analyzes the primary monopolies of land, technology, money, and communications, it becomes apparent that *residual-feudal exclusive* title to a gift of nature creates unnecessary social costs. Instead of society paying non-producing monopolists, nature's bounty should be distributed to all a nation's citizens through the land tax structure, patent structure, or financial structure of private ownership within a modern commons.

Pride in Ownership must be maintained

Land is, unquestionably, social wealth. However, the right to one's space on this earth, the pride it returns to its owner, and the care normally given to one's personal property, are compelling reasons to keep most land under a *conditional* form of private ownership. If equal rights for all to a share of the production of land are acknowledged through society collecting the landrent, private ownership is socially efficient and fully justifiable. What is unjust is the unrestricted subtle monopolization of what nature freely produces on, above, and under, this land. It is necessary to keep private ownership of land and its benefits while eliminating subtle land monopolization and its unavoidable inequities.

The Feudal Origins of Land Titles

Societies have battled for title to land for millennia. One society's violent claim to land is another society's violent loss. Today's landowners are the descendants of the winners of the latest clashes of cultures.[5] After the collapse of the Roman Empire at the hands of the Germanic tribes, the common people regained their rights to the land, and the use of nature's wealth in common again developed a powerful following.[6] Their belief in freedom and natural rights resembles our belief in these principles today.

However, this reversion to social wealth in public ownership came under attack by powerful clans. Petr Kropotkin, that unique historian, describes the repression of these rights as the origin of the modern state: "Only wholesale massacres by the thousand could put a stop to this widely spread popular movement, and it was by the sword, the fire, and the rack that the young states secured their first and decisive victory over the masses of the people."[7] Those people were struggling against imposition of a legal structure which protected *exclusive* private title to land previously owned, and used, by all in common.

As described by Kropotkin, the medieval roots of our culture grimly parallel the massive slaughter in many developing world countries today. People in these countries are fighting to retain, or reclaim, their right to a fair share of the earth's resources—resources now owned by the cultural descendants of earlier violent thefts of land by feudal lords. The resemblance here is not a coincidence; current struggles are a continuation of that medieval battle over who shall have rights to nature's wealth and, as we will be demonstrating, today's land titles still have remnants of feudal exclusive property rights in them. However unjust, if a legal title to land or any other gift of nature can be established, those with unrestricted title can lay claim to the wealth produced by others.

In the 14th-Century, the sharing of social wealth in common was still practiced by local communities. But, tragically, that Century saw the beginning of a 300-year-effort by the aristocracy of Europe to erase all trace of communal rights. Kropotkin explains:

> The village communities were bereft of their folkmotes [community meetings], their courts and independent administration; their lands were confiscated. The guilds were spoilated of their possessions and liberties, and placed under the control, the fancy, and the bribery of the State's official. The cities were divested of their sovereignty, and the very springs of their inner life—the folkmote, the elected justices and administration, the sovereign parish and the sovereign guild—were annihilated; the State's functionary took possession of every link of what formerly was an organic whole. Under that fatal policy and the wars it engendered, whole regions, once populous and wealthy, were laid bare; rich cities became insignificant boroughs; the very roads which connected them with other cities became impracticable. Industry, art, and knowledge fell into decay.[8]

The efforts to alienate the individual from common use of the natural wealth of the land are documented in Britain by the nearly 4,000 enclosure acts passed between 1760 and 1844 that effectively gave legal sanction to this theft.[9] For the powerful to protect their title further, it was necessary to erase from social memory all traces of the earlier custom of social ownership of social wealth. Kropotkin points out that, "It was taught in the universities and from the pulpit that the institutions in which men formerly used to embody their needs of mutual support could not be tolerated in a properly organized State."[10] We hear those words yet today. A *social-control-paradigm* to protect a power-structure had been designed, put into law, and is now the legal structure we live under.

The classic descriptions of the evolution of capitalism explain how trade and industrial capital usurped the preeminent position of nobility with their historical title to all land. Yet in parts of Europe an elite social class still owns large tracts of land. As late as 1961, the Duke of Bedford, the Duke of Westminster, and the British Crown owned the most valuable sections of London, and large estates still abound throughout the countryside. In fact, at the turn of the 20th-Century,

> the English upper class consisted ... of around ten thousand people drawn almost entirely from a core of 1,500 families.... The aristocracy owned great estates and houses and works of art—but, above all, they owned land. Well over ninety percent of the acreage of Britain was theirs.[11]

Today's neo-liberal philosophies is an ongoing effort to prevent a rekindling of mutual support beliefs and social wealth held in common. Today we are taught, by those who parrot the original disinformation that, in an efficient economy, virtually all property should be privately owned with each individual a "free" bargaining agent. Henry George's and our disagreement with this *social-control paradigm* is that title to land, or any other gift of nature, should be *conditional* since no person built land and all are entitled to their share of nature's wealth. *Exclusive* title as opposed to *conditional* title is that remnant of feudal law which is the primary cause of today's inefficient economies creating a wealthy few and an impoverished many.

Private Ownership of Social Wealth moves to America

The powerful structured land ownership in America under the same rules as in Europe. The origins of "the manorial lords of the Hudson Valley" were huge landed estates "where the barons controlled completely the lives of their tenants." There were also huge estates in Virginia; one covered over 5-million acres and embraced 21 counties.[12] Such excessive greed contributed to the widespread dissatisfactions that fueled the American Revolution:

> Under Governor Benjamin Fletcher, three-quarters of the land in New York was granted to about thirty people. He gave a friend a half million acres for a token annual payment of 30 shillings. Under Lord Cornbury in the early 1700s one grant to a group of speculators was for two million acres.... In 1689, many of the grievances of the poor were mixed up in the farmers' revolt of Jacob Leisler and his group. Leisler was hanged, and the parceling out of huge estates continued.[13] [B]y 1698, New York had given thousands of acres to the Philipses, Van Cortlands, Van Rensselaers, Schuylers, Livingstons and Bayards; by 1754, Virginia had given almost three million acres to the Carters,

> Beverleys, and Pages—an early example of government "aid" to business men.[14]

Despite the egalitarian rhetoric of the American Revolution and an attempt to place a proclamation in the Constitution for a "common right of the whole nation to the whole of the land," the powerful looked out for their own interests by changing the wording of Locke's insightful phrase: "All men are entitled to life, liberty and land." This powerful statement that all could understand coming from a highly respected philosopher was a threat to those who subtly monopolized the land, so they restructured those words to "life, liberty and [the meaningless phrase] pursuit of happiness." The substitution in America's Constitution of phrases which would protect every person's rights to nature's wealth for phrases that protect only the *residual-feudal exclusive* rights of a few should alert one to check the meaning and purpose of all laws of all societies carefully.

Only portions of the huge estates described below were confiscated, and "speculation in western lands was one of the leading activities of capitalists in those days:"[15]

> Companies were formed in Europe and America to deal in Virginia lands, which were bought up in large tracts at the trifling cost of two cents per acre. This wholesale engrossment soon consumed practically all the most desirable lands and forced the home seeker to purchase from speculators or to settle as a squatter. [Moreover, observes Beard], as the settler sought to escape the speculator by moving westward, the frontier line of speculation advanced.[16]

Some of America's famous leaders were deeply involved:

> In the Ohio Valley a number of rich Virginia planter families, amongst whom were counted both the Lees and the Washingtons, had formed a land company and this, the Ohio Company, founded in 1748, was given a crown grant of half a million acres.[17] [And with] every member of the Georgia legislature but one [having] acquired a personal interest in the speculation schemes, [they sold thirty-five] "million acres to three ... land speculating companies for a total payment of less than $210,000.[18] [That is six-tenths of a cent per acre. Thus,] as the frontier was pushed back during the first half of the nineteenth century, land speculators working with banks [and corrupt legislators] stayed just ahead of new immigrants, buying up land cheap and then reselling it at high profits.[19]

Those who participated in these later land grabs knew well that the route to wealth lay in claiming *exclusive* title to land so that those who followed would have to buy it from them. Whether rented or sold at high capitalized values, a share of the wealth produced would be siphoned to the owners without expenditure of their labor.

Individuals, such as the butcher's son John Jacob Astor who had title to Manhattan Island, became immensely wealthy. Matthew Josephson, in *Robber Barons*, and Peter Lyon, in *To Hell in a Day Coach*, document the greatest land grab in history when the railroads, through control of state and federal governments, obtained unrestricted title to 183-million acres of land (9.3% of the land in the United States). By the turn of the century this included "more than one-third of Florida, one-fourth of North Dakota, Minnesota, and Washington and substantial chunks of 25 other states."[20]

> The state of Texas was the most generous of all: at one point they had actually given away about eight million more acres than they had in their power to bestow; as it finally turned out, they forked over to twelve railroad companies more than thirty-two million acres, which is more real estate than can be fitted inside the boundaries of the state of New York.[21]

Those to whom this land was parceled out had taken care to buy Congress and codify their exclusive title in legal statutes (inequality structured in law). The arrival of the railroads provided easy access to these lands and, as Henry George taught us, made them valuable. Instead of immigrants being allowed to choose land on a first-come-first-served basis and using its rental value to develop social infrastructure, the land-hungry poor were forced to buy the land from these profiteers. Land sales by speculators were contracts that siphoned a part of the future labor of those who bought the land to the speculator.

America's celebrated Homestead Act of 1862 came after most of the choice land had already been claimed by speculators. Some 600,000 pioneers received 80-million acres under this act, but this was less than half that allotted to the railroad barons, who were only the latest in a long line of profiteers. These new lords of the land thoroughly understood the legal mechanics of siphoning wealth produced by others to themselves. They knew that all the surplus land had to be owned before their land could have significant value, thus the Homestead Act was vital to their plans of attaining great wealth.

Saleable Land Titles permitted the Mobilization of Capital

Once land had been confiscated from the masses in the Middle Ages, it belonged permanently to the lord of that land and could only be lost through war. When English law changed to permit the sale of land, this created the foundation for modern capitalism. When an entrepreneur wished to speculate by building a factory or ship, land could be mortgaged for that venture. This provided a broader base of wealth to loan against than loaning against potential profits from monopoly trade rights issued to favored friends by royalty.

The privatization of land and resultant mobilization of capital was a key stage in the development of capitalism that expanded rights to more people. However, full rights were not attained for all. Left in place were subtle forms of land, capital, and finance capital monopolizations continually siphoning a large share of the wealth to those who escaped labor through *residual-feudal exclusive* title to what is properly social wealth (land and technology [money is a social technique]) and, through monopoly profits, title to what is properly the wealth of those whose labor produced it.

Slave labor has been a historic method to accumulate capital and pockets of slavery remain today. Export platforms in the Developing World that avoid taxes and pollution laws and pay 13-cents to 43-cents an hour for workers to produce items for sale in the developed world, where workers with the same qualifications are paid $6 to $10 an hour, is a simple capital accumulation scheme akin to slavery.

The forced acceptance of opium sales to China a century ago and the turn-a-round sales of drugs to the developed world today accumulates capital. Japan's and China's government accumulate capital through monopolization of a milder drug, cigarettes. Charging Japan's well-paid citizens triple the price for Japanese manufactures or food as the same item would cost in Europe or America was also little more than a capital accumulation scheme.

The "Robber Barons" of the late 19th and early 20th-Century accumulated capital at an unnecessarily great cost to America. That enormous cost was neither visible nor acknowledged because, even with massive destruction of natural wealth (timber, topsoil), the remaining resources could still provide a good living for the relatively small population. (The timber burned to clear the land could have provided a fine set of hardwood furniture for every family on earth.)

Through hard work, frugality and/or good fortune, a family owns a valuable piece of land. When the breadwinner's buying power decreases or ceases due to death, tracts of the land are sold off piecemeal to maintain the accustomed standard of living. All money from sales deposited within the banking system as savings become part of the nation's finance capital. Eventually all the tracts of land are sold, some of the money becomes accumulated capital, and the part spent to maintain the family, that also could have been accumulated capital if that person had worked for his or her living, becomes consumed capital.

Those smaller tracts of land that were sold off continue to gain in value and continue to be split into smaller tracts. Each time those tracts are sold or mortgaged, capital is either accumulated or consumed. John Jacob Astor's exclusive title to, and piecemeal sale of, Manhattan Island is probably America's leading example of wealth accumulation through continued land monopolization as tracts of land become smaller and smaller and their use-value rises higher and higher. The enormous values (potential capital) lying untouched and capital wasted through high living of heirs tells us there are better ways to accumulate capital.

Once a society is developed it requires only a simple adjustment in the law to attain full rights, freedom, and justice for all; society collecting the landrent. All other monopolies will fall once the principle of full rights, requiring everyone having equal rights to nature's wealth, is universally recognized and the "mother of all monopolies" (the private taxation of land) is eliminated. Once attaining full freedom and rights through society collecting landrent, each member of society will have attained their rights to land and the wealth produced by land.

Profound Thinkers Who Believed in Society Collecting the Landrent

The French Physiocrats were the originators of laissez faire—the philosophy of little government interference. They held as a cornerstone of their philosophy (appropriated from the work of John Locke, William Penn, Baruch Spinoza, and Richard Cantillon 50-to-100 years earlier) that society should collect the landrent. One of their most respected members, Mirabeau the Elder, held that this would increase social efficiency equal to the inventions of writing or money.

David Ricardo formulated the law of rent, which supports the logic of Mirabeau's statement. Put in simple terms, Ricardo's law of rent means that all income above that necessary to sustain labor will be claimed by the owners of the land without the expenditure of their labor. A subtle land monopolist retains ownership of land until some innovative entrepreneur sees its potential for more productive use. The high price demanded effectively siphons a part of the wealth produced by that entrepreneur and society's labor to the previous owner, the holder of that mortgage and sales contract.

It was Henry George who most clearly understood how Ricardo's law of rent siphoned society's surplus wealth to the owners of land and how that monopoly maintained itself through the ever-rising price of land. He outlined how wealth came directly from land and accrued to the owner; how all wealth above the survival needs of the hard-working people flowed to those with title to the land without expenditure of their labor; how these profits capitalized land values ever higher, perpetuating the flow of newly produced wealth to titleholders; how commercial successes were dependent on location and those profits too went largely to owners riding its value up to ever higher levels.

Adam Smith's statement that "every improvement in the circumstances of society raises rent" tells us he knew that title to land claims much of the wealth produced by the increased efficiencies of society.[22] The respected economist John Kenneth Galbraith, although questioning changing tax policy at this late date, accepted the justice of society collecting the landrent. In 1978, the conservative economist Milton Friedman stated, "In my opinion the least bad tax is the property tax on the unimproved value of land."[23]

Earlier philosophers who believed in the free enterprise philosophy of the Physiocrats—"society collecting the landrent"—include Thomas Paine, who is credited with proposing much of the Bill of Rights; William Penn, the founder of Pennsylvania; Herbert Spencer, the noted philosopher in his classic *Social Statics*; Thomas Sperry of the Newcastle Philosophical Society; and philosopher John Stuart Mill. These early economists were not radicals. They all "believed in the *sacredness* of private property, *particularly land*."[24]

The Robert Schalkenbach Foundation lists over 100 famous thinkers—including Confucius, Moses, Thomas Jefferson, Mark Twain, Henry Ford, John Maynard Keynes, Albert Einstein, President Eisenhower, and several popes—who recognized the principle that the natural product of the land belongs to all citizens, and lists various places in the modern world where these policies have been, at least in part, implemented.[25] In the late years of the 19th-Century and the early years of the 20th-Century, Henry George's policies had substantial influence and candidates for public office were being advised to take a stand for a landrent tax.[26]

But those who owed their fortunes to the structure of property rights and taxes were too well entrenched to be dislodged. Their fear of Henry George's philosophy motivated the funding of neo-liberal economics professors and politicians to prevent governments from adopting those policies, silenced the democratic dialogue begun by Henry George, and protected their vested monopoly interests.[27]

Just as corporations today fund professors and universities to produce studies that support their products or causes (the pay is good and one can find professors to produce studies to back up any cause), those who opposed Henry George's vision paid scholars to bend the truth and thus prevented people from insisting on their democratic rights.

Those corrupt scholars accomplished this feat by corrupting economic language and later academics unwittingly continue to teach that elite-protective philosophy. Classical economics clearly points out finance capital combines three elements of production—resources (land), labor, and industrial capital—to produce a nation's wealth. Biased neo-liberal economists combined land with industrial capital and left only industrial capital and labor as elements of production. Those redefined terms created an economic jargon, confused the public debate, and prevented the spreading of Henry George's concepts.[28]

Mason Gaffney's and Fred Harrison's analysis of the working papers of these professors leaves no doubt that they were specifically designing their philosophy to eliminate the threat of Henry George. This is a replay of Kropotkin's statement, "It was taught in the universities and from the pulpit that the institutions in which men formerly used to embody their needs of mutual support could not be tolerated in a properly organized State."[29]

Commercial Land

Visualize a trade in a primitive society with someone standing by collecting tribute for trading on a particular piece of ground. The landowner does no productive labor—he only monopolizes that land. Of course, to avoid paying tribute, that early trader only needed to move to another piece of land. Today that nearby land would also be claimed.

As Henry George taught us, the closer one approaches the center of commerce, the higher the price of land. Every transit line from the suburbs to a commercial district will raise commercial land values a calculable amount. This high value represents the cheapness and the quantity of trades within any population center and that saving (efficiency of trades) is recognized by the price business is willing to pay for that land.

Because rent lays claim to a large share of the wealth produced by commerce, the land values are very high in large population centers. Land values gradually lower as the distance from the center of population becomes greater and the trades become less frequent and more expensive. In a matter of minutes on that acre there would be millions of dollars' worth of trades in grain, diamonds, stocks, land, finance capital, or consumer products. A share of each trade is remitted to the landowner as rent: thus the high value of land within population centers.

It is not unusual for commercial land to be valued at 3, 4, or even 10-times the value of the buildings placed upon it.[30] Probably the highest priced acre in the world was in the center of Tokyo, valued, before values dropped over 75%, at $1.5-billion. The space of one footprint in Tokyo was valued at $8,000. The land area of the 23 wards of Tokyo was equal in monetary value to the entire land area of the United States. The land upon which the emperor's palace sat was valued at the price of all the land in California. All the land in tiny Japan was worth four-times as much as all the land in the huge United States. "In fact, the real estate value of Tokyo [in 1989] at $7.7-trillion [was] so high that, once collateralized and borrowed against (at 80% of [the then] current value), it could buy all the land in the United States for $3.7-trillion, and all the companies on the New York Stock Exchange, NASDAQ and several other exchanges for $2.6-trillion." Japanese business leaders "announced [in error] on American Television that a square meter of the Ginza [a part of Tokyo] was worth more than Seattle."[31]

To their disadvantage, businesses join subtle land monopolists in battling against increases in landrent taxes. If unnecessary government expenses were eliminated and landrent taxes were balanced to pay all government expenses, the cost of wages paid by business would lower by whatever amount of taxes were once paid by labor. Even more, there would be the additional savings of not having to keep track of sales, excise, and income taxes currently paid by both business and labor. Appropriate landrent taxes would roughly equal current interest or rent paid (or received) from land values and the current taxes paid on land.

Farm Land

David Ricardo makes the rather simple observation that the value of land will be lower as the quality lowers. (The quality of commercial land depends on population and accessibility for customers. The quality of farmland depends on rainfall, growing season, fertility, and accessibility to markets.) Once the quality is such that one can earn only the wages expended in production or distribution (at the margins), the land's value reaches zero. The economist's term "at the margins," then, represents the economic edge of profits. It also measures the edge of monopolies.

There is enough land in the United States to feed many times its current population. By exporting food to countries that—if their lands, resources, and trade were not subtly monopolized—could just as well feed themselves, by converting grain into high-priced fat, and by farming the public treasury, agriculture in the United States has made handsome profits and evaded Ricardo's law of rent. Unearned income (rent) from the subtle monopoly created by those laws is capitalized into, and maintains the value of, land. Under Ricardo's law of rent, but without sales to countries able to feed themselves or government supports (in America $31.2-billion average per year 1985-96[32]), the price of land would be almost zero while both the use-value and the monetized value of the rest of the world's farmland would be greater than ever.

Home Sites

In smaller cities of America, a typical $120,000 house will be on a $30,000 lot. In major population centers, it is not uncommon for a house to cost double, triple, or even 10-times that price. In Honolulu and parts of California, a comparable home would be $400,000 and in Washington, DC, it would be $800,000. As the labor and material prices of each of these homes are relatively equal, the price differential is the cost of land functioning under Ricardo's law of rent. The price of land accurately measures the landrent paid by producers of wealth to the subtle-monopoly landowners who did no work.

The powerbrokers took from the Physiocrats' free enterprise philosophy (or any other philosophy) only that which protected and further extended their wealth and power. As historically most members of legislative bodies were large landholders, naturally they did not accept that society should collect the landrent. If that were to happen, everyone would have immediate rights to their share of nature's wealth. The "divine rights" of private ownership of social wealth, which siphoned large amounts of wealth from those who produced to those who did not, would be converted to "conditional rights" where only those who produce are paid. The use-value of land is distributed instantly and without cost to all citizens through society collecting the landrent.

Take homes for an example: real estate taxes are currently levied mostly on the improvements and only in small part on the land. This tax structure is the key to subtle land monopolization. At 7% interest, the previously described $30,000 lot, if sold, would return $2,100 per year. The taxes on this typical home would also be $2,100. Removing all taxes on the house and placing them on the land (for a total of $4,200) and collecting the same tax ($2,100) on all equally-valued unused lots, would convert the current taxes to landrent taxes. That $2,100 in landrent paid to society instead of the absentee landlord reduces the price of house lots to zero.

There would be no increase in costs for homeowners. The amount once paid annually in interest would now be paid annually in a landrent tax. Even though the monetized value of the land disappears, its use-value actually increases. As land speculation would be eliminated, the purchase price would be only the value of labor and material that built the house. The initial capital required to purchase a home would drop to the cost of building the house or the depreciated value of an older home but the annual cost of owning that home would be only moderately less than under current monopoly rules. The former interest costs of land of a mortgaged home will have been converted to landrent taxes to pay for essential social services.

With essential social services paid from a landrent tax, all other taxes and the accounting and collection costs incurred can be eliminated, providing great savings to most individuals and society. Occasionally a city council person will become aware of the social efficiency of taxing unused land within their jurisdiction (if idle land is properly taxed it will quickly be put to use). But these alert local officials quickly find that the powerbrokers, frightened by Henry George's exposure of their centuries-old land monopolization scheme, have inserted restrictions into state constitutions and laws on local communities' ability to tax land.

Land held in unrestricted private ownership creates high capitalized land values. True free enterprise requires breaking that subtle monopoly through *exclusive* ownership; society should collect the rent. Distribution of land by capitalized value (price) would then be replaced by distribution of land by rental value paid to society. The net cost to the homeowner would be slightly lower (much lower if Mason Gaffney and Fred Harrison's estimation of 35% of national income being landrent is correct[33]) but there would be no subtle monopoly intercepting others' labor through private collection of rent on what nature provided.

Whoever is the better producer and is willing to work the land can easily outbid the incompetent, lazy, or absentee landowners and, with tax advantages eliminated, can also outbid corporate agriculture. Thus those who use land for production or distribution will, almost universally, have secure ownership of their land. The landrent would go to society to replace all other taxes and cover the costs of public services, the interest to the owners of capital (improvements, machinery, livestock, or inventory), and wages to the farmer, business owner, or entrepreneur.

Oil, copper, iron ore, and the like, while still in the ground, are land and can very properly be privately owned so long as society is paid the landrent. The world has adequate reserves of most of these minerals. It is only richer deposits and cheaper labor in the developing world which make their minerals more available. Under Adam Smith unequal free market philosophy, *the developed world's more expensive deposits are not mined until the undeveloped world's cheap deposits are exhausted.*

Developing land—clearing, drainage projects, shaping the land, irrigation dams, canals, and so forth—involving capital expenditures and labor requires special consideration. As development is one of the most productive uses of land and labor, anyone who invests in such improvements should be well paid. However, unconditional title to land development becomes exclusive title to the land. Once the investor is well reimbursed, the value of land improvements (not buildings) should be incorporated into the landrent.

The market has measured the rent value of that land. The landrent collected by society should equal that which is now collected both publicly (taxes) and privately (interest). The price spread between the choice sites and lower-valued sites should still be maintained through the landrent tax imposed. To accomplish this, the current private land tax (interest or rent) would be converted to a landrent tax that would be slightly lower than the former combination of taxes and land payments. With social costs covered by society collecting the landrent and with the former subtle land monopolists now working productively for their living, all other taxes could be eliminated.

If Society Collected the Landrent, all other Taxes could be eliminated

Except for schools and governing bodies, most public services authorized by law should not be supported by taxes. Directly provided services and their costs should be paid for through a user fee (tax) on gas, airplane tickets, harbor fees, and other use charges, thus ensuring that equal labor is exchanged for providing those services. In this sense, a gas tax to cover highway costs is really a user's fee for the labor required to build and maintain roads. This principal is recognized and accepted in gas taxes and in water, electricity, natural gas, garbage, airport, and postal charges.

Social Security, Railroad Retirement, Federal Employees Retirement, unemployment insurance, Medicare, and Medicaid, are—at this time—all improperly labeled as government expenses; they are actually paid-for insurance funds separate from expenses of running governments.[34] This is an accounting trick; President Lyndon Johnson added the retirement trust funds to the general budget to make the cost of the Vietnam War look smaller. According to Gore Vidal:

> In 1986 the gross revenue of the government was $794 billion. Of that amount, $294 billion was Social Security contributions, which should be subtracted from the National Security State. This leaves $500 billion. Of the $500 billion $286 billion went to defense; $12 billion to foreign arms to our client states; $8 billion to $9 billion to energy, which means, largely, nuclear weapons; $27 billion to veterans' benefits, the sad and constant reminder of the ongoing empire's recklessness; and finally, $142 billion to loans that were spent, over the past forty years, to keep the National Security State at war, hot or cold. So, of 1986's $500 billion in revenue, $475 billion was spent on National Security business.... Other Federal spending, incidentally, came to $177 billion ... which is about the size of the deficit, since only $358 billion was collected in taxes.[35]

Landrent will not sustain government waste and corporations feeding at the federal trough but will easily finance proper government services. In 1929, federal government expenditures were 1% of GNP—at the peak of the Cold War, they were approximately 24%.[36] David Stockman, a member of President Reagan's cabinet, calculated that after deducting bureaucratic waste and payments to

> law firms and lobbyists and trade associations in rows of shining office buildings along K Street in Washington; the consulting firms and contractors; the constituencies of special interests, from schoolteachers to construction workers, to failing businesses and multinational giants, all of whom came to Washington for money and legal protection against the perils of free competition ... that leaves seventeen cents for everything else that Washington does. The FBI and national parks, the county agents and the Foreign Service and the Weather Bureau—all the traditional operations of government—consumed only nine cents of each dollar. The remaining eight cents provided all the grants to state and local governments, for aiding handicapped children or building highways.[37]

The value of all land in the United States in 1990 was $3.7-trillion.[38] The current private tax (interest) at 6% converted to a landrent tax would bring in $222-billion. Former Budget Director David Stockman's calculation of only 9% of federal expenditure being for legitimate government business, applied to Gore Vidal's $500-billion in 1986 quoted above, leaves a proper cost of $45-billion to have run the federal government that year. Allowing

$50-billion for a rational defense budget and pointing all those feeding at the government trough back towards the free market that they claim is their ideal, leaves $127-billion plus the property taxes already being collected to run state governments. Serious Georgist scholars have calculated that in both the United States and Britain "the share of rent in the modern society, if the current system of taxation were abolished, would be [22-to-25%] of national income."[39] That is enough to fund local, state, and federal governments.

The payment of that landrent is, at first look, only slightly less costly than purchasing that land under current law. But a second look takes into consideration the elimination of all other taxes which, on balance, returns the cost of owning land to zero. Landrent has replaced all other taxes and all now have access to land. A landrent tax cannot be evaded and full rights to that part of the modern commons have been regained.

The accounting and collection costs of a landrent tax would be but a tiny percentage of the cost of collecting sales and income taxes. As all are paying landrent through the price of products, it will fall on each equally according to that individual's standard of living.

When necessary to regulate commerce, other taxes are proper but those funds should be returned to society through social services. For example, ecological taxes can support pollution-free energy development and resource conservation. The proper level of sin taxes (alcohol, tobacco, et al.) will lower disease through lowering consumption and the funds collected would offset health care costs incurred from such habits.

All farmers and business people know that machinery and inventory are relatively easy to obtain; it is the price of land that restricts ownership of farms and businesses. While land prices would drop to zero, use-values would remain the same. Actually it would increase. Commerce would flourish as businesspeople, farmers, and other entrepreneurs—all true producers—would be able to start business with only the capital necessary to buy buildings, machinery, and inventory.

Landrent being paid to society out of cash flow means only hardworking and talented people would own farms and businesses. The mechanism whereby excessive rights of absentee or incompetent landowners intercept the labor of others through unrestricted title to land would be replaced by society receiving the earnings from that social wealth. Labor costs to industries and businesses would be reduced by whatever taxes labor previously paid. The elimination of sales taxes, income taxes, and a large share of accounting costs would make replacing all taxes with landrent taxes a bargain for any business.

Although society would be enormously richer, the land would not have monetized (capitalized) value. Society collecting the landrent would create a modern land commons in which the wealth produced would be distributed relatively equally while retaining the efficiencies of private ownership.

Society, not the landowners, put that value there by increased population, roads, water, electricity, and sewers. The wealth collected through landrent should then be returned to the people through social services—schools, parks, other public facilities, and government. It must be emphasized that the landowner would retain all rights to his or her land except the right to retain unearned landrent.

An Opportunity to Restructure With Society Collecting the Landrent

China uses these tax principles extensively and continually updated literature from the Schalkenbach Foundation and various Henry George groups lists regions around the world where this tax reform is being studied and instituted.[40] Only a Henry George listserve or Internet search can keep up with those changes (Alanna Hartzok earthrts@pa.net.).

In spite of the many highly successful experiments around the world, the political barriers to this approach are normally unassailable—landowners have too much power in legislatures. But, just as Social Security, unemployment insurance, Railroad Retirement, and banking reforms were all enacted into law under crisis, there will be an opportunity to restructure if the world economy should again collapse. Land values would return to zero, and the search for answers will be paramount.

In a depression, characterized by inadequate income and collapsing values, ownership of bankrupt farms, homes, and businesses is normally relinquished to the counties in lieu of taxes. Almost all deposits and many loans are guaranteed by the U.S. government. In a collapse, the public will own the loan institutions and through them much of the land and capital. Even now, taxes diverted to support unnecessary agricultural production are all that keep the value of farmland from collapsing.

There are many poor producers in farming and business who are there only through inheritances, economic windfalls, or having bought land at depressed prices and having its value increase as society (not those landowners) increases in efficiency. With society collecting the landrent, those who produce from the land (be it farm, home, industry, or business) would be the owners. Interest income would go to capital (the owners of the buildings, machinery, livestock, or inventory), wages would go to those who worked (the farmer, industrialist, or businessperson), and landrent would go to society.

Absentee ownership of land (but not capital) would disappear. Production is the basis of all wealth and there would be only productive, well-paid people producing on that land. This is the efficiency gain equaling the invention of money or writing that the French Physiocrats recognized was possible if society collected the landrent. Virtually every citizen would own, and be receiving, a share of the use-value of the nation's land although that land would now have no monetary value.

Instant Restructuring to a Landrent Tax through Bonds

If a severe crisis transferred power from monopolists to the majority (a true democracy as we are outlining) laws for society collecting the landrent could be quickly passed. Landowners invested their money sincerely and should not in the process lose their equity. Homeowners and businesses would be instantly compensated through the efficiency increases and elimination of all other taxes. Farmers, large landowners, and landlords are only partially so compensated. Bonds can be issued to make up any losses. Retirement payments and minimum wage laws would have to be adjusted to compensate retirees and the low-paid.

The most important aspect of regaining rights to a modern land commons under *democratic-cooperative-capitalism* is that private ownership of land is retained, yet subtle land monopolists disappear, and the wealth created by land (not that created by labor and capital [stored labor]) is—through working less for a higher standard of living—instantly distributed to all without cost.

Private property rights, individualism, and competition are each strengthened through this relatively small change in the legal structure of property rights.

At every point in gain of rights there was no opportunity to reclaim common rights to the land. All powerful people had a stake in property retaining *residual-feudal unconditional* titles. With today's highly educated population those full rights can be reclaimed. All it takes is enough people to understand it.

Notes

1 All works of Henry George and many authors writing on him are available from the Robert Schalkenbach Foundation, 41 East 72nd St., NY, NY 10021 (212-988-1680), established for the purpose of keeping Henry George's philosophy alive.

2 Mason Gaffney and Fred Harrison, *The Corruption of Economics*, (London: Shepheard-Walwyn, 1994), pp. 13, 193.

3 Michael Parenti, *Power and the Powerless* (New York: St. Martin's Press 1978), pp. 184-85, quoting Jean Jacques Rousseau, "A Discourse on the Origins of Inequality," in The *Social Contract and Discourses* (New York: Dutton, 1950), pp. 234-85.

4 Henry George School (New York) website: *gopher://echonyc.com:70/11s/Cul/HGS.*

5 Henry George, *Progress and Poverty* (New York: Robert Schalkenbach Foundation, 1981), p. 342.

6 Petr Kropotkin, *Mutual Aid* (Boston: Porter Sargent, 1914), p. 225.

7 Ibid.

8 Ibid., p. 226.

9 Ibid., pp. 234-35.

---

[10] Ibid., p. 226. Read also George Renard's *Guilds in the Middle Ages* (New York: Augustus M. Kelley, 1968), Chapters 7, 8.

[11] Lewis Mumford, *The City in History* (New York: Harcourt Brace Jovanovich, 1961), p. 264; Angela Lambert, *Unquiet Souls* (New York: Harper and Row, 1984), p. 6.

[12] Charles A. Beard, *Economic Interpretation of the Constitution* (New York: Macmillan, 1941), p. 28; Howard Zinn, *A People's History of the United States* (New York: Harper Colophon Books, 1980), p. 48.

[13] Zinn, *People's History*, p. 48. See also Howard Zinn, *The Politics of History* (Chicago: University of Chicago Press, 1990), pp. 61-68.

[14] Herbert Aptheker, *The Colonial Era* (New York: International Publishers, 1966), pp. 37-38.

[15] Zinn, *People's History*, p. 83; Herbert Aptheker, *The American Revolution* (New York: International Publishers, 1985), p. 264, quoted in Beard, *Economic Interpretation*, p. 23; Petr Kropotkin, *The Great French Revolution* (New York: Black Rose Books, 1989), p. 143.

[16] Beard, *Economic Interpretation*, pp. 23, 27-28, quoting C.H. Ambler.

[17] Olwen Hufton, *Europe: Privilege and Protest* (Ithaca, NY: Cornell University Press, 1980), p. 113.

[18] Herbert Aptheker, *Early Years of the Republic* (New York: International Publishers, 1976), p. 125; Abraham Bishop, *Georgia Speculation Unveiled* (Readex Microprint Corporation, 1966), in forward.

[19] James Wessel, Mort Hartman, *Trading the Future* (San Francisco: Institute for Food and Development Policy, 1983), p. 14.

[20] Quoted by Peter Lyon, *To Hell in a Day Coach* (New York: J.B. Lippincott, 1968), p. 6. See also Edward Winslow Martin, *History of the Grange Movement* (New York: Burt Franklin, 1967); Joe E. Feagin, *Urban Real Estate Game* (Engelwood Cliffs, NJ: Prentice-Hall, Inc., 1983), pp. 57-58; speech by U.S. Representative Byron Dorgan, North Dakota, the statistics researched by his staff and quoted in *The North Dakota REC* (May 1984).

[21] Lyon, *To Hell in a Day Coach*, p. 6.

[22] Adam Smith, *The Wealth of Nations* (New York: Modern Library Edition, Random House, 1965), pp. 247, 647, 773-98.

[23] *101 Famous Thinkers on Owning Earth* (New York: Robert Schalkenbach Foundation); Durand Echeverria, *The Maupeou Revolution* (Baton Rouge: Louisiana University Press, 1985), p. 182; Guy Routh, *The Origin of Economic Ideas* (Dobbs Ferry, NY: Sheridan House, 1989), p. 62; John Kenneth Galbraith, *Economics in Perspective* (New York: Houghton Mifflin, 1987), Chapter 5, especially pp. 55, 168; Mark Blaug, *Great American Economists Before Keynes* (Atlantic Highlands, NJ: Humanities Press International, 1986), p. 86.

[24] Herbert Spencer, *Social Statics* (New York: Robert Schalkenbach Foundation, 1995 unabridged edition); Dan Nadudere, *The Political Economy of Imperialism* (London: Zed Books, 1977), p. 186; Phil Grant, *The Wonderful Wealth Machine* (New York: Devon-Adair, 1953), pp. 416, 434-38; Hufton, *Privilege and Protest*, p. 113 (emphasis added).

[25] 101 Famous Thinkers.

[26] Eugene M. Tobin, *Organize or Perish* (New York: Greenwood Press, 1986), pp. 14, 21, 56.

[27] Gaffney and Harrison, *Corruption of Economics.*

[28] Ibid.

[29] Kropotkin, *Mutual Aid*, p. 226. Read also George Renard's *Guilds in the Middle Ages* (New York: Augustus M. Kelley, 1968), Chapters 7, 8.

[30] Grant, *Wonderful Wealth Machine*, pp. 389-95.

[31] Paul Zane Pilzer, *Unlimited Wealth* (New York: Crown, 1990), p. 169; CBS, *60 Minutes*, October 25, 1987, *World Monitor*, July 17, 1990; Jim Impoco, Jack Egan, Douglas Pasternak, "The Tokyo Tidal Wave," *U.S. News and World Report*, September 17, 1990: p. 43; R. Taggart Murphy, *Weight of the Yen* (New York: WW Norton, 1996), pp. 195-200, 206, 212, 214, 218-19, 231, 244, 259; Chalmers Johnson, *Blowback: The Cost and Consequences of American Empire* (New York: Henry Holt & Company, 2000), p. 203; Edward W. Desmond, "Japan's Trillion-Dollar Hole," *Time*, April 8, 1996: p. 46; Edward W. Desmond, "The Failed

Miracle," *Time*, April 22, 1996: pp. 60-64. For a look at how these inflated land and stock prices intercept a nation's wealth read Kevin Phillips, *Politics of Rich and Poor*, pp. xii, 118, 122, 144, 150, 118. There are other estimates of total values in the United States; *The Statistical Abstract of the U.S., 1990*, pp. 463, 734 (charts 752, 1295) claims $21 trillion in reproducible value. To that would have to be added capitalized values and land values. Including land, economist Robert Samuelson claims just under $29 trillion (Robert Samuelson, "The Great Global Debtor," *Newsweek*, July 22, 1991: p. 40).

32 Government Accounting Office, *Letter Report*, October, 30, 1997: GAO/NSIAD-97-260.

33 Gaffney and Harrison, *Corruption of Economics*, p. 183.

34 Edward Boorstein, *What's Ahead?...The U.S. Economy* (New York: International Publishers, 1984), pp. 33-34.

35 Gore Vidal, "The National Security State: How To Take Back Our Country," *The Nation*, June 4, 1988, p. 782.

36 E.K. Hunt, Howard J. Sherman, *Economics* (New York: Harper and Row, 1990), p. 511.

37 William Greider, *The Education of David Stockman and Other Americans* (New York: New American Library, 1986), pp. 6, 17.

38 Samuelson, " Great Global Debtor," p. 40.

39 Gaffney and Harrison, *Corruption of Economics*, p. 183.

40 Geonomy Society, 30401 Navarro Ridge Road, Albion, CA 95410. See also the Henry George Foundation of America, 2000 Century Plaza, #238, Columbia, MD 21004; and the Robert Schalkenbach Foundation, 41 E. 72nd street, New York, NY 10021.

25. Restructuring *Residual-Feudal Exclusive* Patent Laws Produces a Modern Technology Commons

For centuries, as modern economies developed, the hidden hands of the alert and powerful were busy structuring laws and property rights to gain, or retain, title to wealth-producing sectors of the economy. Patent laws and stock markets were being subtly structured to monopolize technology.

That stock markets are crucial to raising investment capital in a modern economy is a myth. Most stock traders have no contact with new issues of stock and those who do are primarily taking an already established private company public. Most corporate investment needs are financed from profits, liberal depreciation schedules, and borrowing. As currently structured, investing in stock markets is primarily a bet on which corporation will most successfully expand its share of national and world markets. These are not investments in production per se.

Expanding markets means increased profits capitalized into the value of a company's stock and those capitalized values are claimed before those profits are banked. "Behind the abstraction known as 'the markets' lurks a set of institutions designed to maximize the wealth and power of the most privileged group of people in the world, the creditor-*rentier* class of the first world and their junior partners in the third."[1] Restructuring *residual-feudal exclusive* patent laws so that any person may use a patent by simply paying a royalty will erase those centuries of carefully crafted subtle-monopoly laws.

Under that simple legal change, the inventors would be well paid for their inventions and the price of consumer products would drop precipitously. Combining those social savings with free trade between equally developed regions and with managed trade between unequally developed regions, and dropping those protections in step with the harmonization of previously unequal economies, would protect both labor and capital worldwide. The masochistic destruction of jobs and capital under the current economic structure would be eliminated.

Labor should employ Capital

That capital is properly owned and employed by labor is recognized by no less an authority than Adam Smith. We again repeat the quote from his bible of capitalism *The Wealth of Nations*, "Produce is the natural wages of labor. Originally the whole belonged to the labourer. If this had continued all things would have become cheaper, though in appearance many things might have become dearer."[2] The "appearance of becoming dearer" is because each worker would have been fully paid. Things would have been cheaper because purchasing power of those fully-paid workers would have advanced in step with productive capacity and those who once made their living through claiming a share of others' labor would have to turn to productive labor. Those well-paid workers would have purchased more from other fully-paid workers and with that increased buying power others would produce more to take advantage of that market.

In short, purchasing power—which is so hard to generate under current subtle-monopoly rules—would have developed in step with the producing power of easily-built industrial technology. If monopolization could have been avoided, labor would have been fully paid and the world could have developed far more rapidly and without destructive wars.[a]

Let's assume that all industry suddenly increased 50% in efficiency. Half of the workforce would be unemployed and the owners of this new technology would rapidly claim all the wealth that previously went to those now unemployed. The wealth of the owners of technology—both actually and as a percentage of the nation's wealth—would increase dramatically, that of those still employed would remain the same, and those newly unemployed would be on welfare. It is only through steady expansion of distribution by unnecessary labor pulling a share of that siphoned wealth back as people search for a way to survive that society has avoided facing this reality.[3] An economy with 5% owners, 45% workers, and 50% welfare recipients is unthinkable in a country that claims equal rights for everybody.

If labor owned the capital it produced, then labor would employ—rather than be employed by—capital. Once subtly monopolized by exclusive title, capital's use *can be denied* to labor at any time, *and it will be denied* if no profit is made. The natural order of labor employing tools (capital) is reversed. If land and capital (both industrial and financial) were not subtly monopolized, land, labor, and capital could freely combine to produce social wealth, workers would receive their full wages from what they produced, and the owners of industry would receive full value for use

---

[a] This cannot happen until democracy is established. Theoretically we have democracy today. But that is only theoretical. We only have partial democracies with the potential of full democracies. Once those subtle monopolies are eliminated, a full democracy will emerge. Likewise if a crisis transposes into a full democracy the simple legal changes can be made to eliminate those subtle monopolies and establish efficient *democratic-cooperative-capitalism*.

of their capital. Elimination of the subtle monopolization of technology under current stock market and patent structures would also increase social efficiency equal to the invention of money or writing the French Physiocrats recognized was possible by elimination of land monopolization.

All nations and all people are stakeholders in a nation's economy and the world economy. No sector of the economy should have excessive rights (monopolization) structured in law. Just as with land, we are accustomed to wealthy people claiming ownership of the nation's capital. We are taught that this is the proper and most efficient social arrangement. Therefore we do not recognize the obvious: capital is social wealth. It is composed of all tools of production, it was produced by labor (capital is but stored labor), and all should be entitled to the opportunity of employing it, or being employed by it, and receiving a fair share of what is produced.

Capital, however, is often more productive under private ownership and, when this is so, private ownership is justified. In such cases, entrepreneurs, whose special talents lead to increased production, could properly buy this capital from those who produced it. A substantial share of society's capital has been justly claimed in this manner. Capital that is obtained by means other than trading useful labor (physical, innovative, or special talent) is an unjust interception of the production of others.

That which is more efficient under social ownership belongs to all society, with all citizens receiving the profits. For example, no profits are directly distributed from the increased wealth produced by highways, airports, harbors, or post offices. But the wealth that society is able to produce and distribute through the *common use* of these natural monopolies is many times more than a normal interest charge on their construction cost. Just as the use-value of land in a modern commons is distributed instantly and without cost, those profits under *democratic-cooperative-capitalism* are distributed instantly, silently, and efficiently through cheaper production/distribution costs and no wealth will have been claimed by subtle monopolization.

Social capital,[a] "real" private capital, and "fictitious" capital are all currently lumped together and collectively treated as private capital. Ownership of capital is considered proof that it was justly earned, and that the owner deserves compensation for its use. Below we are distinguishing between social, private, and fictitious capital. Once identified, the proper owners can claim their capital and the profits it produces. Fictitious capital can be eliminated altogether.

---

[a] "Social capital," as used here, refers to the physical products of labor that benefits all such as roads, schools, airports, harbors, et al. The term is also used by some scholars to refer to the unquantified, but real, value of social interconnections that aid the functioning of society, typically meaning a higher education level.

Efficient Socially-Owned Capital

The basic difference between what is properly social capital and private capital is that everybody uses social capital. It forms a natural monopoly, while proper private capital is used only to produce products or services for specific needs of specific people. Capital that is required for society's basic infrastructure (which is by its nature a monopoly and used by all citizens) cannot justly be bought and sold as private property. It is properly part of a modern commons through a modern legal/social structure, *democratic-cooperative-capitalism*. This includes not only highways, airports, harbors, and post offices, but also railroads, electric power systems, community water systems, and banking and communications infrastructure. Most will recognize that this natural monopoly infrastructure should belong to all society.

Although such facilities and services are publicly held in most Western nations, U.S. citizens are unaccustomed to railroads, electric power systems, banking, and communications being socially owned. These are nothing less than natural monopolies, and all claims of efficiency under private ownership are a rhetorical cover (a *social-control paradigm*) to hide the siphoning of the fruits of others' labor to those who hold title to those natural monopoly economic crossroads.[4]

This siphoning of wealth is shown in the privately-owned electric power monopolies. Almost 24% of the America is served by consumer-owned electric utilities (13.4% are publicly owned, 10.2% are rural cooperatives). Privately-owned companies charge 42.5% more for electricity than those that are publicly owned. Yet, since they serve population centers with the highest density of customers per mile, privately-owned electricity costs should be lower. The difference in electricity costs between privately-owned and publicly-owned electric companies is even greater than these statistics show. The publicly-owned utilities provide enough profits for some of those communities to build swimming pools, stadiums, and parks.[5]

Matthew Josephson's classic *Robber Barons*, Peter Lyon's even more profound *To Hell in a Day Coach*, and Edward Winslow Martin's *History of the Grange Movement* cover how the American railroads were built at public expense. As much as half the funds collected for building them were pocketed and over 9% of the land in the United States was deeded to these railroads. The pocketing of those funds, claiming title to these natural monopolies, and being deeded that land were little more than thefts of public wealth. Martin describes the building of the Union Pacific Railroad as perhaps the most flagrant example but the pattern was typical:

> Who then was Crédit Mobilier? It was but another name for the Pacific Railroad ring. The members were in Congress; they were trustees for the bondholders; they were directors, they were stockholders, they were contractors; in Washington they voted subsidies, in New York they received

> them, upon the plains they expended them, and in the Crédit Mobilier they divided them. Ever-shifting characters, they were ubiquitous—now engineering a bill, and now a bridge—they received money into one hand as a corporation, and paid into the other as a contractor. As stockholders they owned the road, as mortgagees they had a lien upon it, as directors they contracted for its construction, and as members of Crédit Mobilier they built it.... Reduced to plain English, the story of the Crédit Mobilier is simply this: The men entrusted with the management of the Pacific road made a bargain with themselves to build the road for a sum equal to about twice its actual cost, and pocketed the profits, which have been estimated at about thirty millions of dollars—this immense sum coming out of the taxpayers of the United States.[6]

"By 1870 the states alone had given $228,500,000 in cash, while another $300,000,000 had been paid over by counties and municipalities." Of course those millions of 19th-Century dollars would be hundreds of billions in inflated 21st-Century dollars. In the process of building those railroads, promoters skimmed off possibly one-half of this public investment and stockholders' capital, while simultaneously claiming 9.3% of the nation's land through land grants.[7] Josephson's description of them as robber barons is quite accurate.

With enforced privatizations through imposition of Reaganism/ Thatcherism (the first heavy promoters of this philosophy) on the developing world and the collapsed former Soviet Union, social wealth was being placed under *exclusive* private ownership in the 1990s at a rate that makes America's robber barons of the late 19th and early 20th-Century look like country bumpkins. Those defeated nations were paid pennies on the dollar to give up title to their natural wealth, their banks, and their limited industrial capital. The masses, of course, have little to say. In many cases, if not most, one member of these less than honest groups (to put it mildly) would be signing as government agent and another was the buyer.

Obviously there is no savings to society from the private ownership of a natural monopoly such as railroads, electricity, post offices, power systems, sewers, water systems, et al. And, as shown in the following chapters, the true cost of banking and communications, when properly structured under a public authority and used in common, would be only pennies per dollar of current costs.

Basic infrastructure (roads, water, electricity, et al.) is integral to a nation. *Society is a machine*; even though these basic facilities do not directly produce anything, an industrial society cannot function without them. They are an integral part of production and are just as important to social efficiency as modern factories.

To demonstrate this, compare the labor costs of a society with an undeveloped infrastructure to those of a society with a developed infrastructure. Vacation to any wilderness park, hike for a day, and calculate how efficient virtually any economic activity, such as sending and receiving mail, would be from that spot. In the 18th-Century, a letter traveling by U.S. mail from New York to Virginia (400 miles) took four to eight weeks and cost 60-cents a page.[8] Today it is 37-cents (possibly equal to less then a penny 200 years ago) for several pages anywhere in the nation and that letter normally arrives within 1-to-3 days. When China built a road into the almost inaccessible Tibet, the price of a box of matches dropped from one sheep to two pounds of wool.[9]

Efficient Privately-Owned Capital

Commercial activities producing for variable individual needs rather than everybody's needs are properly privately owned. As has been demonstrated in the former Soviet Union, the thousands of personal preferences (homes, clothes, furniture, jewelry, hobbies, recreational activities, et al.) cannot be provided efficiently by a public authority. Such personal needs can only be assessed by perceptive and talented individuals close enough to recognize and fulfill those needs. The capital to provide such services is more productive under private ownership. Unlike claiming the production of labor through subtle monopolization of land, capital, and finance capital, this increased productivity produces the wealth with which entrepreneurs pay the producers of that capital.

Most of the construction and production for basic social infrastructure operated under public authority is quite properly provided by tens of thousands of privately-owned industries. This free-enterprise, privately-owned capital can, under contract, accommodate the needs of public institutions while also making available diverse consumer products and services. We see this every day in contracts to build roads, haul mail, and so forth.

Fictitious Capital

Few economists agree on exactly what constitutes capital. Most include all wealth that produces a profit (titles, stocks, bonds, et al.). But, although the wealth this paper represents has a firm claim on part of society's income, much of it was banked, skimmed off, and resurfaced in another investment. The skimmed off share of that first certificate of investment is properly defined as *fictitious capital.* Bonds used to construct harbors, deepen riverbeds, and build railroads represent true capital. That which was pocketed and reinvested elsewhere is, since it ends up with two claims against the same dollar, only 50% productive.

In the previous example of building the Union Pacific Railroad, half the money was used to build; the other half was pocketed and reinvested elsewhere. The share of those certificates that was not productively used, yet had a claim on social production, was fraudulent. This fictitious capital may represent wealth to the owner, but it is not wealth to society. It is a certificate of ownership for capital that was paid for by others and that siphons wealth produced by others to an owner who has produced nothing.

The total capital underlying a debt instrument must pay profits to security holders at face value of those securities even though only a part of it actually built that industry. That share of those debt instruments that did not produce productive capital, social or private, is fictitious capital.

There are three physical foundations to production—land, labor, and capital. Land commands rent, labor is paid wages, and honest interest can only be for the productive use of true capital. Subtle patent monopolies capitalize stock values far above tangible values and those high values demand profits. It is through those excess profits that the production of others' labor is siphoned from those who produce to those who produced nothing. All capital that demands payment greater than the labor value of services provided society is properly labeled "*fictitious capital*."

Invention, a Social Process

> There is no isolated, self-sufficing individual. All production is, in fact, a production in and by the help of the community, and all wealth is such only in society. Within the human period of the race development, it is safe to say, no individual has fallen into industrial isolation, so as to produce any one useful article by his own independent effort alone. Even where there is no mechanical co-operation, men are always guided by the experience of others.
> —Thorstein Veblen

These words from one of America's eminent philosophers are well spoken. The long march of technology leading up to the present sophisticated level is based upon thousands of earlier discoveries—fire, smelting, the wheel, lathe, and screw—and untold millions of improvements on those basic innovations.[10] Many primitive, but revolutionary, technologies were discovered by Asian and Arab societies. Greek, Roman, and other cultures improved upon these methods, which were, in turn, used by later Western cultures. Invention is a social process built upon the insights of others. Stuart Chase's list of such contributions of 5000 years ago barely touches the subject:

> The generic Egyptian of 3,000 B.C., though unacquainted with iron, was an expert metallurgist in the less refractory metals. He could smelt them, draw them into wire, beat them into sheets, cast them into molds, emboss, chase, engrave, inlay, and enamel them. He had invented the lathe and the potter's wheel and could glaze and enamel earthenware. He was an expert woodworker, joiner and carver. He was an admirable sculptor, draftsman and painter. He was, and is, the world's mightiest architect in stone. He made sea-going ships. He had devised the loom, and knew how to weave cotton to such a fineness that we can only distinguish it from silk by the microscope. His

> language was rich, and he engrossed it in the handsomest system of written characters ever produced. He made excellent paper, and upon it beautiful literature was written.... He had invented most of the hand tools now in existence.... He had worked out the rudiments of astronomy and mathematics.[11]

There were also wedges, drills, wheels, pulleys, and gears—all were necessary before modern machines were possible. There had to be countless earlier inventions, back to the control of fire, before the Egyptians could have reached even that level of technology.

Not only does every modern invention rest on millions of insights going back to antiquity, its development requires thousands of people with special talents. For example, a British scientist's accidental discovery of penicillin has benefited almost every person in modern civilization. More people worked to develop and produce this antibiotic for the wounded in WWII than worked on the atomic bomb, and they were all funded with public money. Yet the drug was patented by an American who recognized that, if he could obtain that patent, he would have a subtle monopoly with a capitalized value that would siphon vast wealth to himself even though he had neither created nor produced anything.[12]

Every innovation is a part of nature. Just like land, oil, coal, iron ore, or any of nature's wealth, if something is to be discovered it had to have been there all the time. As technology is a part of nature, everybody should share its fruits. Inventions not only use the insights of millions of people throughout history and prehistory, they require the support and skills of millions of present workers as well. Stuart Chase estimated that at least 5,000 people were involved in contributing data to the writing of his book and these had millions of others to thank for their knowledge.

These people provided tools, materials, and services: pencils, paper, graphite, rubber, lead, typewriters, telephones, cars, electricity, typing, printing presses, book distribution, banking, and so forth. The people directly involved in Chase's education required educators, authors of textbooks, and their educators, ad infinitum. Every one of these consumer items required the labor and skills of thousands of people, some in distant parts of the world (such as producers of rubber or tin). Though the labor charge of some of these is infinitesimal, each is real and definite. Collectively they accumulate a substantial, though incalculable, value.[13]

While the contribution of any one person to the pool of social knowledge is truly small, the wealth diverted to those who own the patents to social knowledge can be substantial. It has been estimated that, if the developing world were capitalized to the level of the developed world, the royalty claims would be $1-trillion a year. These royalties would normally be going to people who "own" these efficient technologies but neither invented anything nor labored productively for this income. They are commercial chokepoints and the subtle monopolization of these tools of production (technology) permits huge overcharges that siphon an excessive share of the world's wealth to owners of patents. Those huge overcharges create excessive stock market values.

Inventors rarely receive much reward for their discoveries and innovations. The few who are compensated receive but a small share of the tribute charged by those who own this social wealth. That a small number of powerful people subtly monopolize inventions—and ever afterwards siphon to themselves the wealth produced by others—defies both decency and justice. This was well known to prominent inventors and industrialists such as Thomas A. Edison and Henry Ford. Both "agreed that all patent laws should be repealed since they benefit the manufacturer and not the inventor."[14]

We disagree with patent laws being repealed. They should be redesigned to be a part of a modern commons within *democratic-cooperative-capitalism* in which any person can use that technology by simply paying a royalty.

Capitalizing Actual and Fictitious Values

Inventions are a "more or less costless store of knowledge [that] is captured by monopoly capital and protected in order to make it secret and a 'rare and scarce commodity,' for sale at monopoly price[s]. So far as inventions are concerned a price is put on them *not because they are scarce* but *in order to make them scarce* to those who want to use them."[15]

The patent structure capitalizes value far above tangible values and, through those excess profits and without expenditure of their labor, intercepts wealth produced by others. Where inventions once went unchanged for decades or even centuries, many, if not most, patents are now obsolete before their 17-year life expires. By the time a key patent has run out, newer patents are able to boost efficiency yet more. As many of the earlier technologies are still essential to production, the owners of the latest patents control both the latest technologies and the support technologies in which the patents have run out. Honda's exclusive ownership of patents on the stratified charge engine, even though the basic principles for this crucial technology were invented 100 years ago, makes this all quite evident.

Corporations are in such powerful bargaining positions that only occasionally will a new invention pose a threat to them. As corporate control of other critical patents limits the inventor's options, these patents are bought for a fraction of their true value, or they are patented around and the inventor receives nothing. Controlling markets is integral to controlling patents:

> Any move by the neo-colonial state to revoke the patent law as a defensive measure would have very limited results since the market belongs to the monopolies. This becomes quite clear when it is realized that the other

> markets to which such products would be exported would still have such legislation protecting the same patents, and the transnational corporation would be in a position to require compliance. The mere ownership without the actual know-how which is guarded by the monopoly at headquarters would be useless. This is the whole point about monopoly. The world imperialist monopoly market would not exist if such a system of market control were not in operation.[16]

We view the inventions of 400 to 1100 years ago as primitive, yet in their time these simple inventions could produce—with less labor—both more and better products. Someone powerful enough to control these new techniques could trade one day's work for two, three, five, ten or as many days' production of other people's labor as the efficiency of his invention and political power allowed.

For example, the invention of the windmill was extremely valuable. If it could be monopolized, its owners could siphon to themselves the production of large amounts of others' labor. This potential created a dispute between the nobles, priests, and emperor "as to which one the wind belonged."[17]A 17th-Century French patent granted such a right to selected owners of windmills.[18]

However hard they tried, claiming ownership of the wind was quite difficult. But not so with other technology, the water mill, first used in Europe during the 10th-Century, permitted one worker to replace as many as 10 others. A stone planer eliminated seven workers out of eight. One worker with an Owens bottle machine could do the work of 18 hand blowers.[19] Modern technology has created even greater efficiency gains. Many credit the steam engine with the greatest single increase in productive efficiency, but Stuart Chase cites a study by C.M. Ripley of work costing $230 done by hand labor that would cost only $5 using electric power.[20] Modern electric furnaces and continuous casting have brought the direct labor expended in the steel industry down to only 1.8 hours per ton of steel produced.[21] So long as the production of others' labor could be claimed through a patent on any technology, that income potential is capitalized into the stock value of that industry.

The owner of that first water mill was able to trade his single day's work, grinding grain, for seven days' labor of a woodworker or blacksmith. In effect he was paid for seven days while working one. The owner of a patented stone planer would likely gain five days' value for only one of his own. Any person lucky enough to own a patented Owens bottle machine could probably have claimed 12 days' pay for each day's labor. If the manufacturer in Ripley's study had been able to patent that efficiency, he would have claimed title to the process. He could then have lowered his prices and still charged 20-to-30-times the labor value in his product. However, just like claiming ownership of the wind, it would be difficult to claim exclusive title to electricity, which accounts for the drop in costs in Ripley's study.

Royalties originated from Royalty conferring Monopoly Trading Rights

That the owners of patents are entitled to *royalties* exposes the feudal origin of the term. Patent rights to land and inventions were conferred upon favorites by kings and queens, with the understanding that the person so favored would share the earnings—royalties. In short, the origin of patents is indistinguishable from the paying of bribes for the privilege of doing business. Such bribes were the precursors of today's patent royalties.[22] *Exclusive* title to patents, as opposed to *conditional* title, is the *remnant of feudal patent law* that must be eliminated to attain full rights for all to the benefits of ever-more efficient technology.

The Foundation of Law is Military Power

The foundation of most law is power, largely expressed through military strength. Long before governments protected patents, they were protected by violence. "The struggle against rural trading and against rural handicrafts lasted at least seven or eight hundred years.... All through the fourteenth Century regular armed expeditions were sent out against all the villages in the neighborhood and looms or fulling-vats were broken or carried away."[23]Those early claims to technology, enforced by violence, were the forerunners of today's industrial patents. Those who would control technology have just become more sophisticated. They encode these exclusive rights in legal titles. Today, being accustomed to it and unaware of society's loss, we accept this as normal.

The growing efficiency of textile machinery started the Industrial Revolution. Primitive looms were improved upon by inventions such as Kay's flying shuttle, Hargreave's spinning jenny, Crompton's "mule," and the power loom. Between 1773 and 1795, the labor time to process 100 pounds of cotton went from 50,000 hours to 300 hours, an efficiency gain of 16,666%.[24] That efficiency gain within a time-span of only 22 years exposes how the owners of these technologies quickly dominated world trade. Quite simply, the technology was not shared. It was subtly monopolized through restricting the rights of production to the owners of patents.

The widespread use of machine weaving came about only because the technology was copied and the patents ignored. That 16,666% gain in 22 years is dwarfed by 150 power looms in Formosa weaving 24 hours a day under the watchful eyes of only one agile female operator on roller skates.[25] This is a gain of hundreds of thousands, if not millions, of times in efficiency. The labor component in the price of a yard of cloth produced by modern industry is small. This includes the labor to smelt the ore and fabricate the machines which is stored in that capital.

The economically powerful will say they are not claiming the production of anyone else's labor, as there is hardly any labor involved. But this is exactly how wealth is siphoned to those who subtly monopolize the tools of production. The price charged for those products is far above the cost of production and others are forced to trade large amounts of their labor for what was produced with a small amount of labor.

All society is denied the full benefit of cheap industrial goods when labor is charged more than they are paid to produce that product. If a product requires one hour's labor to produce and distribute, and then sells for three hours' labor value, it effectively siphons away the value produced by two hours of labor. (If that production is traded to country where equally-productive labor is paid one-third as much it siphons away nine hours of labor. [Chapter 1]) Standard economics and accounting do not measure this overcharge because it shows up in stock prices far beyond intrinsic value and in a market restricted to higher-priced labor. If that cloth were priced relative to the price paid labor to produce it (including fair interest for the stored labor value represented by that machinery) then it would be priced within reach of the world's low-paid labor.

A bushel of wheat required three hours to produce in 1830 but only 10 minutes in 1900.[26] A call to Montana State University in Bozeman revealed that in 1986 it took only 3.2 minutes of labor to produce one bushel of dryland Montana wheat. Other crops have similar efficiency gains.

Railroad labor per ton-mile is roughly only 3% that required only 50 years ago, and that 2,500% efficiency gain is dwarfed by the 4-million percent gain in transportation efficiency over the horse and wagon only 170 years ago.

The public did receive a large share of the labor savings in textiles, agriculture, transportation, and other technologies. With the common people's newly won rights (the U.S. Constitution and Bill of Rights), and with the enormously wealthy and sparsely inhabited lands of the Americas, the gains were just too great for the powerful to claim them all. However, due to the failure to build the buying power of developing world labor in step with the productivity of capital, there is much more production forgone and wasted than that which society so gratefully receives.

Patent laws evolved specifically to claim title to the gains of technology. With multiple patents—occasionally with only one key patent and control of markets—the owners of technology siphon to themselves large amounts of the production of others' labor.

Ownership of a key technology, the telephone, was Bell Telephone's advantage when that subtle monopoly was established. (Inventions not controlled by Bell, such as the dial phone, were suppressed for many years.)

The telegraph and telephone reduced communication costs by an amount comparable to the savings created by new technology in textiles and transportation. These efficiency gains of technology, protected by patents, produced the subtle monopoly profits that established Bell Telephone, a corporation larger than any in textiles or transportation.

Henry Ford's assembly line was a milestone in industrial technology that rapidly picked up the pace of the Industrial Revolution:

> The factory is not a new tool but an organization of production that eliminates the periods of idleness in the use of tools, machines, and human beings that are characteristic of agrarian and artisan production. In the artisan's shop the saw, chisel, file, and so forth are idle while the hammer is being used. In the factory all the tools are simultaneously in use in the hands of specialized workers; production is "in line" rather than "in series." But production in line requires a large scale of total output before it becomes feasible. The division of labor is limited by the extent of the market, as Adam Smith told us. But transportation, urbanization, and international trade provided a market of sufficient scale.[27]

During 1913 alone, the time required to assemble an automobile dropped from 728 minutes to 93. Until that year, the wage rate averaged $2.50 for a 10-hour day. Ford doubled the daily wages of his workers and reduced their hours from ten to eight, all while lowering the price of his cars.[28] This was unheard of in those times and drew much criticism from business and the press.

What Ford knew, and others did not, was that the profits were so large that with that 800% efficiency gain the wages could have been increased to almost $20 per day. Ford was strongly opposed by his managers and other investors. Had it not been for the influence of Emerson, it appears that the claim on others' wealth made possible through the innovation of the assembly line might have been much higher and lasted for a much longer time.

Attempts were made to subtly monopolize the emerging auto industry. George Baldwin Seldon, a lawyer specializing in patents, understood that, as the law was structured, patents laid claim to wealth produced by others. In 1899,

> he set his mind to working out the precise legal definition and wording of a patent that would give him the sole right to license and charge royalties on future automobile development in America.... Seldon had gone into partnership with a group of Wall Street investors who saw their chance to cut themselves in on the profits of the growing American car industry.[29]

The near success of Seldon and his partners in patenting the automobile illustrates the basic injustice of the current patent structure. Neither Seldon nor these investors had anything to do with the invention of automobiles. The first ones had been built in Europe 14 years earlier and virtually hundreds of auto companies were already in existence. Yet, if anyone had succeeded in patenting the process of building automobiles, every purchaser of an automobile would have had a part of the production of his or her labor siphoned to the owners of that patent who had invented nothing and had did no work.

Seldon's attempt at patenting the principle of the automobile is being successfully accomplished today in the patenting of processes. Corporations are being formed to patent embryo transfers, gene splicing, other advanced medical procedures, even title to human genes and genes of plants domesticated by primitive societies thousands of years ago. Any doctor who wishes to use these new procedures and any who grow a patented plant has to obtain a license and pay a royalty.[30]

The current race to patent human genes clearly outlines the subtly-monopoly cost of patent laws. There are thousands of human genes that directly affect human health. As patent laws now stand, some corporation is going to have a patent on (own) each gene. Let us say that there are 300 genes to be studied in a standard gene test and the royalty to be paid to each patent holder only $1. If a couple wishes to test themselves for defective genes before conception or their unborn child shortly after conception, the cost would be $300 (60 minutes, July 29, 2001, suggested the possibility of $1,000 royalties).

This added tax, though common to medical equipment and drugs, has not previously been added to the cost of an operation or food crops. If ownership of procedures and food plants had been established years ago, every bill for an operation and the cost for every plate of food would have had royalties added. Only those licensed by the patent holder could perform operations or raise crops and the added charges would siphon wealth to whoever owned the patent rights. Every future improvement in patented surgical procedures or improved crop strains would also be patented and, as technological improvement is ongoing, the patents subtle monopoly would never run out. Thus Microsoft's tens of billions of dollars of software overcharges all built from purchasing DOS for $3,000 and patenting it. The cost to society can be imagined if each producer or service provider had to pay a patent holder for the use of fire, wheels, wedges, levers, and gears. Inversely, the savings are evident in their free use because they are not patented (subtly monopolized).

There is one recent and remarkable exception to this rule. In parts of Africa, "as many as sixty percent of the people over age fifty-five are partly or completely blind" from becoming infected with a parasitic worm. Possibly 18-million people are affected. The pharmaceutical corporation Merck and Company owned the patent on a drug (*Ivermectin*) used to kill worms in animals. In October 1987, Merck announced they would provide this drug free of charge for Africans afflicted with this parasite. The company chairman, Dr. P. Roy Vagelos, noted, "It became apparent that people in need were unable to purchase it."[31] Here the loss to society from exclusive title was so obvious and devastating that these corporate executives made a moral decision to save the sight of millions of people. The cost to them was negligible; the gain to society was beyond measure.

An intense battle was fought over life saving drugs for AIDS victims. These drugs can be produced for a tiny fraction of the monopoly prices currently asked. Even at that fractional price few in the impoverished world can afford those life-saving drugs and at the monopoly price almost no one can afford them. Rather than face a court, drug companies have agreed to lower prices for Aids victims in Africa.

There is a loss to society from exclusive control of any technology, but it is usually not as obvious as in these dramatic examples, where the patent rules of exclusive use were abandoned. This example demonstrates the original morality of the medical industry when "*to patent an essential medicine was considered morally indefensible.*"[32] It is also morally indefensible for other inventions crucial to society. The previously mentioned Gaviotas community—which is regenerating the primeval Amazon forest of Colombia's barren Los Llanos plains while building a model community, using modern production methods to live off the land—does not believe in patenting technology. Its inventions—such as a cheap, 100-pound, windmill-driven water pump and cost-free, maintenance-free air conditioning—are spreading throughout Latin America.[33]

Innovation and technology thus create large reductions in labor costs in all segments of the economy. Most are more modest than the previous examples, but reductions of 90% are common and "from 1945 to 1970, the average increase in efficiency output per hour was 34-to-40% per decade"[34] Such savings do not exert the immediate shock to the economy that these numbers suggest. It takes time to retool industries and these corporations are in no hurry to destroy the value of their old production and distribution complexes.

Such overcharges cannot exist if labor is fully paid for their work. It only appears proper because people are accustomed to a subsistence wage for most labor, equally accustomed to all increased profits going to owners and management, and unaware of how rapidly that technology would spread around the world if capital were accumulated along the guidelines in this treatise (technology shared, and labor fully and equally paid under *democratic-cooperative-capitalism*). Under those restructured social rules, workers would have buying power, technology would be regionally available to produce desired products and the capital will have been accumulated to finance it all simply through the creation of money (next chapter), through deposit of a part of all interest going into a socially-owned capital accumulation fund (next chapter), or through the developing world being fully paid for their resources and labor (Chapters 22 and 23).

A Nation's Wealth is Measured by, and Siphoned to Titleholders through, Capitalized Values

Shares in corporations are sold with the price based on how profitable they are expected to be—their capitalized value. This idea proved to be a real bonanza. Where conservative business people typically estimated the capitalized value of the company at 10-times the yearly profit, the stock markets—anticipating future increases in profits—capitalized these values far higher, frequently 20-to-30-times annual profits and occasionally even more. It is not uncommon for the price of stock going public (called IPOs, initial price offerings) to jump 500% the first week. As these higher values claim a greater share of a nation's loans (created money), this is a capital accumulation bonanza. But the rapid movement of this accumulated capital from the hands of one speculator to another can do as much, or more, harm than it does good. Witness the current financial collapse of Southeast Asia, The Great Depression of the 1930s, the collapse of the stock market bubble in 2000, and other such collapses throughout history.

All in one stroke, an individual or group could lay claim to the efficiency of a technology through capitalizing its value and selling shares to other investors. This siphoning of the production of others' labor—through the mechanism of capitalized values—concentrated wealth in the hands of a few, accumulated capital, and gave capitalism its name.

Through carefully structured laws, the hidden hand of the wealthy kept claiming an ever-larger share of this wealth. Labor, just as naturally, tried to retain or reclaim what they produced. The rights gained in the American Revolution and enshrined in its Constitution, and the natural justice of those rights, eventually increased the power and income of labor. This and the expansion of unnecessary labor led to more people retaining a greater share of society's wealth.[35] With these savings more broadly distributed, there evolved the present diversified markets to sell shares in industry and concentrate money capital.

Most of the wealth measured by capitalized values is claimed by the primary subtle monopolizations of land, patents (technology), and finance capital. If these excessive rights of property were replaced by the rights of society to collect the landrent (a modern land commons), the right for any person to use any technology through paying a reasonable royalty (a modern technology commons) and productive labor were fully paid, all society would be wealthier even though monetized (capitalized) wealth would be lower. The excessive charges of subtle monopolization create high capitalized values. By removing these subtle monopolizations and paying labor fully for what it produces, measured values would equal the value of the labor and capital (stored labor) that produced that wealth.

The Financial Structure to Harvest the Profits of Subtly-Monopolized Patents

The battle for corporate ownership is centered in the stock market. Millions of hours are spent by speculators (they call themselves investors) trying to figure out which company is going to increase its capitalized value. The game is calculating profits that will translate into capitalized value. It is viewed as a simple method of keeping score. But claiming the production of others' labor—through profits from shares in the nation's industry as technology continually replaces labor—is the underlying theme. Values that were once claimed by labor are now claimed by the shareowners of the new industrial technology.

Innovators, investors, and underwriters of hot new companies will print enough stock to absorb any foreseeable fictitious value. (Market psychology and speculation [also laddering, run an Internet search] may inflate these values higher yet, and the lucky or astute small investor may gain wealth.) This process takes place in all companies where the owners become aware of the potential of capitalization to produce instant wealth. The alert tap into this wealth-siphoning process encoded into law by their predecessors.

Securities analyst and investment fund manager George J.W. Goodman, under the pseudonym Adam Smith, outlined the magic of capitalizing this unearned income. He christened this stock, and titled his book, *Supermoney*. He proves that this stock is in reality a "Supercurrency":

> In 1972 we have a good example of Supercurrency. The Levitz brothers ... were furniture retailers whose company netted $60,000 or so a year. Then the company noticed that sales were terrific when they ran the year-end clearance sale from the warehouse: furniture right in the carton, cash on the barrelhead, 20 percent off. The idea was successful, they added more warehouses, and the company went public—in fact, superpublic. At one point, it was selling for seventeen times its book value.... [They] banked $33-million of public money for their stock, and still held $300-million worth.... Now when they want to pay grocery bills [buy a boat, a summer home, travel abroad or whatever], they peel off some of the [$333-million], as much as the market can stand. They have moved into the Supercurrency class.[36]

Goodman's example of "Supercurrency" is just another way of describing capitalization of fictitious values. There is the successful company, the underwriters, the innovation of a cheaper production or distribution system, and investors clamoring for shares in this innovative company, and—at 17-times tangible assets—94% of the stock value is a fictitious monopolized value. The stock market abounds in examples of much higher fictitious capitalized values. The 1998-99 Internet stocks which had never turned a profit yet were valued at hundreds of billions of dollars were recent examples as were the disappearance of those values over the next two years.

The overcharge to maintain that assumed value is the interception of the production of others' labor.

If that illusory value cannot be sustained, then the wealth of the purchaser of that stock at that illusory value will disappear. While these fortunes were made through title claims to technology (those values being based on efficiencies of technology), the Federal Reserve calculated that 25% of U.S. citizens in 1974, increasing to 54% in 1988, had no net assets.[37] Lester Thurow explains that this impoverishment of many while wealth is accumulated by a lucky few is due to "the process of capitalizing disequilibrium" (distortions of trade—and thus distortions of values—either internal or external) and that "patient savings and reinvestment has little or nothing" to do with generating large fortunes.[38] Thurow concludes that

> at any moment in time, the highly skewed distribution of wealth is the product of two approximately equal factors—instant fortunes and inherited wealth. Inherited fortunes, however, were themselves created in a process of instant wealth in an earlier generation. *These instant fortunes occur because new long-term disequilibriums (sic) in the real capital market are capitalized in the financial markets....* Those who are lucky and end up owning the stocks that are capitalized at high multiples win large fortunes in the random walk. Once fortunes are created, they are husbanded, augmented, and passed on, not because of "homo economicus" [economic man] desires to store up future consumption but because of desires for power within the family, economy, or society.[39]

Of course, the small fortunes accumulated by the upper middle class are from these same disequilibria in the value of land and capital. Except by violence or trickery, how else can wealth beyond what one produces be accumulated? The income demanded by these fictitious values is a private tax upon the rest of society, and quite accurately labeled *air.* "By reducing air to vendability, scarcity could be capitalized. Business would be richer—and every man, woman and child in the country would be poorer."[40]

A study of the market over a full boom and bust cycle will find these fictitious values developing in most stocks. The reasons given may be many but the underlying cause is clear: the steady rise in the nation's efficiency is captured by, and mirrored in, stock and land values. Every speculator dreams of becoming wealthy by owning some of these stocks or land. The powerful and cunning, with better than even odds, buy and sell in rhythm with the inflation and deflation of stock and land prices to lay claim to much of this new wealth.

Those who win the gamble on who will own the world's land and industrial and distributive technology are freed from the necessity of laboring for their living. This is not a contradiction. Their speculative efforts are certainly labor. However, when unnecessary, that labor is fictitious, and such earnings are winnings of bets.

Capitalizing values is necessary to decide the sale price of a business. However, not only should everyone involved receive proper compensation for his or her labor, innovations, and risk; society should receive its share. Society not only provided tens of thousands of necessary preceding innovations; it also provided the schools, skills, tools, labor, markets, and infrastructure. Nature provided the resources, including the inventions that were waiting to be discovered. To monopolize technology, however subtly, is to deny others full rights to its use even when independently invented.

There is a necessity for a stock market. It has, however, gone far beyond its proper function of providing capital to industries through the sale of stock. That the stock market's primary purpose today is financing the nation's business is pure fiction; trades in the stock market have little to do with capital investment:

> Buying a stock from a broker does not add one red cent to the corporate treasury and provides no investment capital except if the stock is newly issued. But new issues by major corporations are fairly rare because issuing new stock dilutes equity and depresses stock prices. As a result, the bulk of shares now traded on the stock markets were issued twenty or fifty years ago. Since then the shares have passed through many hands, and their prices have fluctuated over a wide range. Yet all these transactions have been strictly between the buyers and sellers of stocks, aided and abetted by stockbrokers trying to eke out a modest living.... [S]peculators are not really interested in the company whose stock they temporarily own. They want to take their profits and get out. They are not investing in the proper sense of the word; they are simply gambling. Ownership of corporations has become largely a game of chance in which the individual players try to guess what the other players will do.[41]

Market Bubbles and Crashes

Speculators are unaware that their gains are unearned. If the market wipes them out, they feel they have lost earnings when actually it was just the odds of the gamble and their turn to lose. Like the casinos they are, the stock markets are primarily a mechanism for the redistribution of wealth, not its production. It is a gambling game in which the rest of society's members are spectators—spectators who continually have their share of the nation's increased wealth thrown on the table of a game of chance they are not playing.

The danger of gambling with the nation's wealth was addressed by *Business Week's* 1987 cover story, "Playing with Fire":

> By stoking a persuasive desire to beat the game, innovation and deregulation have tilted the axis of the financial system away from investment toward speculation. The U.S. has evolved into what Lord Keynes might have called a "casino society"—a nation obsessively devoted to high-stakes financial maneuvering as a shortcut to wealth.... "Speculators may do no harm as

> bubbles on a steady stream of enterprise. But the position is serious when enterprise becomes the bubble on a whirlpool of speculation. When the capital development of a country becomes a byproduct of the activities of a casino, the job is likely to be ill-done."[42]

What is normally spoken of as a market "bubble" is only the claiming of wealth produced by others through rights of ownership that have gotten out of hand. History is replete with examples. Charles Mackay, in *Extraordinary Popular Delusions and the Madness of Crowds*, describes the tulip craze that broke out in Europe in the 17th-Century. Before that particular insanity dissipated, one particular tulip bulb cost "two lasts of wheat, four lasts of rye, four fat oxen, eight fat swine, twelve fat sheep, two hogsheads of wine, four tuns of butter, one thousand lbs. of cheese, a complete bed, a suit of clothes and a silver drinking cup."[43]

One wonders at the variety of commodities traded for that one flower bulb, but their total value of 2,500 florins serves as a guideline to the money value paid for other bulbs. During this period, prices ranged from 2,000 florins for an inferior bulb to 5,500 florins for the choicest varieties. "Many persons were known to invest a fortune of 100,000 florins in the purchase of 40 roots."[44] Although tulips are not stocks, the principle is the same.

At the turn of the 18th-Century, John Law implemented a plan to sell stock in enterprises in the Mississippi wilderness to pay off the huge debt of the French government. Though this scheme was seriously flawed, Law's banking reforms were quite sound and the French economy prospered. The plan went awry when the money rolled in. Those selling paper were so busy getting rich they neglected to invest in production anywhere; they merely reinvested in more paper. In a speculative frenzy, fortunes changed hands as people sold, and then bought back, nothing but paper.

The stock in this Mississippi scheme had no value because there was no investment and thus no production. Law's scheme seemed like such an effortless way to get rich that it caught the attention of cunning financiers in England. (Of course, the English also had to do something to protect their capital fleeing to France to buy into Law's Mississippi scheme.) Although Spain controlled most of South America, and the English had limited trade rights within it, stock companies were set up to trade within this territory. Visions of wealth stirred up a speculative fever, and companies were formed for very unlikely endeavors. Soon, so many joined the game that it got out of hand and the government had to call a halt to new issues. The intention of most of these promoters can be summed up by one audacious proposal. This promoter touted "a company for carrying on an undertaking of great advantage, but nobody to know what it is."[45]

Since the organizers of these companies had no intention of producing anything, their capital was 100% fictitious. Proof that this capital was not real was given when the speculative bubble collapsed. There were no tangible assets, production, or services to back the value of the stock; there was only the transferring of wealth from the naive to the cunning or lucky.

When wild speculation breaks loose, there is no relationship between value and price. Even when the stock market behaves normally, there are always stocks whose prices defy logic. This activity can only be attributed to crowd psychology, as described by Mackay, although sly promoters pull strings at every opportunity.[a]

Options, Futures, and other Derivatives are Gambling Chips in a Worldwide Casino

The markets for stocks, bonds, commodities, futures, options, currencies, mortgages, money markets, in fact virtually every exchange market anywhere in the world, are now one huge market. Options or futures are only the buyer betting the stock will go up and the seller that it will go down; neither has a stake in that stock beyond the gamble. Options and futures may appear to have a legitimate purpose in takeover schemes, but when purchased by those attempting the takeover, they are not even gambles. The psychology of the market almost guarantees that the stock price will rise. This increase in valuation provides the money for takeovers.

The historic speculations in options, futures, and other simple bets are dwarfed by the derivative markets of the late 20th-Century, which evolved both to reduce risk and to bypass the market's margin limitations. Long-Term Capital Management's bankruptcy crisis in 1998 uncovered the unsettling reality that this small hedge fund with a capital base of only $2-billion had over $1-trillion in bets in the derivatives markets, betting primarily on the Russian Ruble. This was a margin of only 0.02% and many of the estimated 400 other hedge funds would have similar slim margins bet on similarly volatile currencies.[46] "Corporations have become chips in a casino game, played for high stakes by people who produce nothing, invent nothing, grow nothing and service nothing. The market is now a game in itself."[47] Capitalized fictitious values are also like chips on a poker table; they finance the game. But, unlike chips, when the game is over these deflated stocks cannot be traded in for full value.

The markets are a high stakes, *low risk* (except at the peak of a bubble) gambling casino where these overcapitalized values are distributed. Everyone recognizes the high stakes. The unacknowledged low risk is due to the constantly increasing value of the nation's capital accruing to stockowners. This increase in value is due to the capitalized value of the

---

[a] Before the Great Depression the price earnings ratio reached 19-to-1. The world is watching to see if the price earnings ratio of 30-to-1 will become the next crash. This time around the market dropped 40% the first three years of the market slide. The first two years of the collapse before the Great Depression the market dropped 25%.

production of labor claimed by the owners of increasingly efficient technology. Due to exposés of fraud in the commodities and futures markets, farmers became aware of this fact and some have clamored for the closing down of the nonproductive futures markets.[48]

Just as selling short and other trading practices developed in the early established markets as a form of harvesting profits, sharp traders have leveraged world markets with stock and currency options, futures on options (options on options), futures on interest rates, warrants (a form of option), and thousands of other similar subdivisions of value called "derivatives":

> Futures contracts on interest rates did not exist in 1971.... Today there are outstanding contracts for $3-trillion worth of them, a little more than half of the gross national product of the United States.... The market for tradable options has grown from essentially zero in 1973—the year the Chicago Board Options Exchange opened for the first time—to a market where more than $170-billion changes hands each day. One hundred and seventy billion is enough money to build 1.7-million average homes.... Eight hundred billion dollars ... is exchanged each day in the world's currency markets.... Every three days a sum of money passes through the fiber-optic network under the pitted streets of New York equal to the total output for one year of all of America's companies and all its workforce. And every two weeks the annual product of the world passes through the network of New York.... Sums of similar magnitude pass through the streets of Tokyo, London, Frankfurt, Chicago, and Hong Kong.... [This] "financial economy" is somewhere between twenty and fifty times larger than the real economy. It is not the economy of trade but of speculation. Its commerce is in financial instruments [paper][49].

Since Joel Kurtzman wrote the above, daily currency exchanges are $1.5-trillion a day ($547-trillion a year) or over 55-times that needed to finance the $10-trillion per year needed for world foreign trade and foreign investment each year. It has been estimated that a healthy economy requires 2-to-$3 speculated for every $1 that runs the real economy.[50] Allowing a multiple of the high figure, $3, means $30-trillion per year moving through the money markets will run the world economy and $517-trillion is needless speculation which puts the world at risk even as it transfers massive sums from producers to speculators.

Strip away all the hype and derivatives are simply bets on the direction of a particular market. With personal computers able to track stocks, bonds, commodities, futures, options, et al. in virtually any of these markets worldwide, there are massive gyrations of values as speculators buy and sell these packaged paper symbols of wealth.[51] Just as the formation of the stock market and the manipulation of stock values became the primary mechanism through which robber barons appropriated the industrial wealth of America and laid the base for America's financial aristocracy, a new breed of robber barons are harvesting fortunes running the markets of the world up and down. A fresh crop of bright people have placed themselves between the world's savers and its producers and consumers to intercept the new wealth produced by the increased efficiencies of technology. As these speculators produced nothing and thus had nothing to trade of value, that wealth can only have come from true producers.

While the world economy staggered and labor's share of wealth declined, the world market in paper symbols of wealth missed a few beats: the U.S. stock market collapse of October 19, 1987 (from which it recovered), the savings and loan and banking crisis in the United States in 1990 (now recovered),[52] the collapse of the Tokyo stock and land markets (not yet recovered), the 1997-2003 financial meltdown of 40% of the world, all on the periphery of *imperial-centers-of-capital* (the jury is still out on their recovery), and the current 2000-2003 40% stock value collapse. Insecurity forced capital to flee back to its imperial centers, forcing those markets to new highs, then new lows, and they continued rising and falling as speculators jockeyed for position and/or fled for safer havens which now (March 2003) too seem risky.

We have yet to see if the enormous sums of accumulated capital in the *imperial-centers-of-capital* will bid the limited available stocks back to atmospheric heights and then crash, whether it will be used to build even more industrial capacity to service a shrunken world consumer market and crash from that excess capacity, whether a fascist financial and military fix will protect the current monopolizers of capital, or whether the tigers on the periphery can be restarted. Though those tigers may rise above their current lows, that they can regain their previous vigor is doubtful. The intense competition of surplus productive capacity that goes with a reduction in world buying power makes capital accumulation very difficult.

Bringing the World's Markets under Control

Buying and selling investments is the legitimate purpose of stock markets; any activity beyond that is gambling. Eliminating subtle monopolization through slight changes in the law and establishing the modern land, technology, patent, and money commons we are advocating will eliminate those speculations. In "Inflation, Deflation, and Constant Value: Creating Honest Money," in the next chapter, we demonstrate how easy it would be to stabilize commodity prices by tying currency values to commodity values. Stable prices would eliminate all need for derivatives and all purpose of market speculation. Once the markets were stabilized by tying the world's money to commodity markets, speculation in commodities and markets would disappear. Those of speculative nature would now invest in the beating heart of capitalism, entrepreneurial speculation.

Restructuring Patent Laws

> I know of no original product invention, not even electric shavers or heating pads, made by any of the giant laboratories or corporations, with the possible exception of the household garbage grinder.... The record of the giants is one of moving in, buying out and absorbing the smaller creators. —T. K. Quinn, *Giant Business: Threat to Democracy*

Quinn was later informed that the garbage disposal was also an appropriated idea.[53]

The importance of societies retaining and furthering technical knowledge is demonstrated by China having the basic knowledge required for an industrial revolution at least 800 years before Europe invented and used these technologies. A millennium ago the Chinese were producing massive amounts of iron and steel. They had invented the compass and rudders for large ships. They had paper, movable type, and the printing press. They built suspension bridges. They had matches, wheelbarrows, wheeled metal plows, mechanical seeders, horse collars, rotary threshing machines and a drill to tap into natural gas. They knew the decimal system, negative numbers, and the concept of zero. And they once knew how to produce primary tools of world conquest, gunpowder, cannon, and large ships.[54] But most of that technological knowledge was forgotten because the Chinese lacked an ideological and legal system of title to, and use of, intellectual property rights.

Inventions and innovations are the cornerstones of prosperity. To establish them in social memory and reward the inventors and innovators, those technologies must be used and those inventors and innovators must be well paid.[55] It is necessary to reward both those who had the original innovative ideas and those who put those ideas to work.

The present policy of restricting access to technology should be changed to one of easy access with proper compensation for inventors, developers, and producers while returning the maximum savings to society. Old patents should be left intact. New patents should be available for all to use with but one stipulation: "royalties will be paid to the patent holder." This does not reduce anyone's rights. Many holders of older patents will see financial advantages to the new system and will transfer to the new patent structure. After 17 years, the last of the older patents will have expired and the subtle monopolization of technology, and its overcharge to society, will disappear.

All patents should be required to be recorded in simple, easily understood language. People with knowledge of production and distribution needs could then browse through these patents and spot those that might be useful. (Many patents are now filed in deliberately obscure language to delay any possible use by competitors.[56]) To analyze and catalog these inventions and innovations would require an extensive "national network of regional assistance centers" for the orderly registration of patents.

When the expense and risk involved in product development and market penetration are greater than those associated with invention, these efforts should receive the largest share of the patent royalties. Once a product is brought to market, a *development patent* would be established by filing with the regional patent office. Development patent holders would be entitled to royalties, but all would be free to use the innovation after filing notice of their use.

Under this mutual support structure, new inventions would be available for all to use. The inventors, developers, and producers would be adequately paid for their ideas, capital, labor, and risk. Society would be paid through low-priced products and services. This is all within the framework of the American and most other Constitutions.

With everybody having the right to use these innovations, the overcharges for fictitious capital and fictitious wages of the present patent system would be eliminated. This would do away with the current policy of industries buying up and shelving patents that threaten to destroy the value of obsolete industrial capital. Every producer would have a right to their use:

> There are countless numbers of patents which, if in operation, would much cheapen the articles they could produce, but they are intentionally shelved to prevent competition. Concerns operating under old inventions for which they have expended great sums to erect plants [and] buy up these new and cheaper methods to prevent competitors from getting hold of them. They then tuck them away in their safes never to be used.[57]

"Technical knowledge in a functional society would be free." Without it,

> new inventions may not only be suppressed, they may be pre-suppressed. A concern may get patents on a whole series of processes in order to tie up the field for the next generation or more.... If scientific advance could be kept free and accessible, with proper reward for the inventor duly secured—a large amount of labor power which now trades on the processes of patenting and mystification—lawyers, "fixers," patent clerks and the like, would be released to useful service, a large amount of duplicated scientific research would be saved, and above all the way cleared to let society benefit at once and directly in the new discovery.[58]

Producers would register all patents used in their production process. This registration would include where patented technology is being used and the gross sales of products or services using this technology. Royalties, predetermined by volume on a sliding scale, would then be distributed to the patent holders.

Full Rights to use any Technology is more efficient and Pays Inventors Better

The patent system could be far simpler and administration costs lowered to almost nothing by evaluating the value of a patent, paying inventors and developers its capitalized value, and placing their innovations in the public domain (a modern commons). The inventor and/or developer would have instant wealth with which to develop more inventions, all would be free to use the inventions, and there would be no cost for accounting or for disbursing royalties. The patent's value will be instantly capitalized with the inventor the gainer, instead of the current complex process of capitalization of monopoly values through the stock market. Most inventors would want their inventions to have maximum use and opt for instant cash and free use by all. Inventions not recognized as valuable, a frequent occurrence, would be proved by developers who would then file development patents and both inventor and developer would be paid.

Because producers can use the most efficient technology to remain competitive, businesses and communities would no longer have to shut down because their market was overwhelmed by a competitor with a patent monopoly (capital destroying capital). With all traces of feudal monopoly rights restructured to *democratic-cooperative-capitalism* the world's communities and businesses would be quite secure even as they gained the maximum benefits from the newest technologies.

Competitive Monopolies, Developmentally Mature Technology, and Standardization

A vast range of intellectual pursuits is required to develop the tens of thousands of inventions involved in the manufacture of most consumer products. The most efficient way to develop new inventions or techniques is through competition. Inventors must be free to invent and develop products as they see fit. There is, however, a time when a technology becomes developmentally mature. At that time, society should consider standardization, a common practice in industry.

Once standardized, development and production costs will drop to a fraction of those for competitive monopolies. Automobiles are a good example. There were at least 502 automobile companies formed in the United States between 1900 and 1908. There has been a great rationalization of this industry and only three U.S. manufacturers are left.

Labor expended in production and distribution of automobiles could be reduced even further through more standardization. In early November 1998, airline companies had concluded they could reduce costs 20% through standardizing passenger jets. Carrying this rationalization of production to its unavoidable conclusion would create a corporate, centrally planned, privately-owned economy.

The cost of research and development for the first color TV was $125-million. The development of high-definition TV will require several billions. A new generation of computers in 1985 required $750-million. The development of these many incompatible computer systems was necessary to sort out which technology would be the most efficient. But there comes a time when a decision must be made as to when society will be served by standardizing technology. The cost of research, development, consumer education, manufacturing, and distribution of several incompatible technologies is roughly the cost of developing one technology multiplied by the number of incompatible technologies.

The moment society decided to develop one primary computer hardware/software technology and language, it would be impossible to bring to market an incompatible computer. All producers would then expend their efforts on developing and producing compatible hardware and software. The cost of computers and communications would drop precipitously and their uses expand exponentially. Every major computer user is frustrated by the many incompatible languages and software. If most keystrokes or symbols were standardized to mean the same thing in all software, education time and costs would drop even as proficiency increased. These savings would permit generous compensation to the nation's creative talent and risk-takers.

The efficiencies of computer/software compatibility will be here shortly and then a further market shakeout will come with a few large producers and distributors remaining. In fact, the monopolizers of computer technology should be looking closely at the Linux operating system available for free on the Internet that is capturing a continually increasing share of the market. Once enough free software has been created to work with it, and that will be soon, the developing world will surely use that operating system. Thus China, South Africa, and a few other nations have decided to use Linux operating systems. It could swiftly take over and wipe out much of the developed-world's current monopolized market.

Again, the most important aspect of regaining rights to a modern commons is that private ownership is retained, yet subtle monopolists disappear, and the wealth created by nature (not that created by labor and capital [stored labor]) is—while working less for a higher standard of living—instantly distributed to all. Distribution of wealth under *democratic-cooperative-capitalism* would be through fully productive labor, fully productive capital, and the instant and costless distribution of use-value within a modern commons.

Full and equal rights means none would be in poverty. GNP and the average workweek would fall by half even as average living standards rise. Those reductions in waste and gains in living standards measure the wasted labor, wasted capital, and wasted resources within a subtly monopolized economy. Economic efficiency gains from the relatively small change in property rights to establish a modern technology commons (under *democratic-cooperative-capitalism*) would equal the invention of electricity.

We next address how to increase access to finance capital for the talented and motivated and lower the cost for all citizens.

Notes

1 Doug Henwood, *Wall Street* (New York: Verso, 1997), p. 7.

2 Adam Smith, *Wealth of Nations* (New York: Random House, 1965), p. 64.

3 J.W. Smith, *The World's Wasted Wealth 2* (www.ied.info/cc.html: Institute for Economic Democracy, 1994).

4 John D. Donahue, *The Privatization Decision:* (New York: Basic Books, 1989).

5 *Public Power Directory and Statistics for 1983* (Washington, DC: American Public Power Association, 1983); Jeanie Kilmer, "Public Power Costs Less." *Public Power Magazine*, May/June 1985, pp. 28-31; the late Montana Senator Lee Metcalf and Vic Reinemer, *Overcharge* (New York: David McKay, 1967).

6 Edward Winslow Martin, *History of the Grange Movement* (New York: Burt Franklin, 1967), pp. 62, 70.

7 Matthew Josephson, *Robber Barons* (New York: Harcourt Brace Jovanovich, 1962), p. 92; Joe E. Feagin, *The Urban RealEstate Game* (Englewood Cliffs, NJ: Prentice-Hall, 1983), pp. 57-8; Peter Lyon, *To Hell in a Day Coach* (New York: J.B. Lippincott, 1968), p. 6; see also Martin, *Grange Movement.*

8 Wilfred Owen, *Strategy for Mobility* (Westport, CT: Greenwood Press, 1978), p. 23.

9 John Prados, *The Presidents' Secret Wars* (New York: William Morrow, 1986), p. 152.

10 Lewis Mumford, *Pentagon of Power* (New York: Harcourt Brace Jovanovich, 1964), pp. 134, 139; Stuart Chase, *Men and Machines* (New York: Macmillan, 1929), Chapters 3-4.

11 Chase, *Men and Machines*, pp. 42-43.

12 PBS, *Nova* (September 2, 1986).

13 Stuart Chase, *The Economy of Abundance* (New York: Macmillan, 1934), Chapter 8.

14 Phil Grant, *The Wonderful Wealth Machine* (New York: Devon-Adair Co., 1953), pp. 301-06.

15 Dan Nadudere, *The Political Economy of Imperialism* (London: Zed Books, 1977), p. 251, quoting in part from E. Penrose, *The International Patent System,* 1951, p. 29.

16 Ibid, pp. 186, 255.

17 Karl Marx, *Capital* (New York: International Publishers, 1967), volume 1, p. 375, footnote 2.

18 Nadudere, *Political Economy of Imperialism*, p. 38, quoting Leo Huberman, Man's Worldly Goods, pp. 128-29.

19 Lewis Mumford, *Technics and Civilization* (New York: Harcourt Brace Jovanovich, 1963), pp. 227-28, 438. Read also Nadudere, *Political Economy of Imperialism*, pp. 51-55.

20 Chase, *Economy of Abundance*, p. 166.

21 Lester Thurow, *Head to Head: The Coming Economic Battle Among Japan, Europe, and America* (New York: William Morrow, 1992), p. 187.

22 Grant, Wonderful Wealth Machine, pp. 301-306.

23 Karl Polanyi, *The Great Transformation* (Boston: Beacon Press, 1957), p. 277, quoting from Pirenne, *Medieval Cities*, p. 211.

24 Marx, Capital, volume 1, pp. 372-74, 428, 435, 562; Eric R. Wolf, *Europe and the People Without History* (Berkeley: University of California Press, 1982), pp. 273-74, 279.

25 Richard Barnet, *The Lean Years* (New York: Simon and Schuster, 1980), p. 260. Besides the ownership of patents, Third World development requires the control of resources and markets as outlined in this author's *The World's Wasted Wealth 2*, Part 2.

26 Howard Zinn, *A People's History of the United States* (New York: Harper Colophon Books, 1980), p. 277.

27 Herman E. Daly and John B. Cobb, Jr., *For the Common Good* (Boston: Beacon Press, 1989), p. 11.

28 Robert Lacey, *Ford* (New York: Ballantine Books, 1986), pp. 118-40; also Juliet Schor, *The Overworked American* (New York: Basic Books, 1991), p. 61.

29 Lacey, Ford, pp. 105-06; Brian Tokar, *Redesigning Life? The Worldwide Challenge to Genetic Engineering* (London: Zed Books, 2001).

30 Tokar, *Redesigning Life?;* Stanley Wohl, Medical-Industrial Complex (New York: Harmony Books, 1984), pp. 69-71; Ivan Illich, *Medical Nemesis* (New York: Bantam Books, 1979), p. 245.

31 Stephen Budiansky, "An Act of Vision for the Developing World," *U.S. News and World Report* (November 2, 1987), p. 14.

32 Jean-Pierre Berlan, "The Commodification of Life," *Monthly Review* (December 1989), p. 24.

33 Alan Weisman, "Columbia's Modern City," *In Context*, No. 42, 1995, pp. 6-8; Los Angeles Times Sunday Magazine, September 25, 1994.

34 E.K. Hunt, Howard Sherman, *Economics* (New York: Harper and Row, 1990), p. 166.

35 Smith, *World's Wasted Wealth 2.*

36 "Adam Smith" (George J. W. Goodman), *Supermoney* (New York: Random House, 1972), pp. 21-22.

37 Lester C. Thurow, *Generating Inequality* (New York: Basic Books, 1975), p. 14; "Worker's State," *The Nation* (September 19, 1988), pp. 187-88.

38 Thurow, Generating Inequality, p. 149.

39 Ibid, p. 154, (emphasis added).

40 Chase, Economy of Abundance, p. 165.

41 Rolf H. Wild, *Management by Compulsion* (Boston: Houghton Mifflin, 1978), pp. 92, 94-95.

42 Anthony Banco, "Playing With Fire," *Business Week* (September 16, 1987), p. 78, quoting Keynes.

43 Charles Mackay, Extraordinary *Delusions and Madness of Crowds* (New York: Farrar, Straus and Giroux, 1932), pp. 90-97.

44 Ibid, pp. 1-45; Lester Thurow, *The Future of Capitalism: How Today's Economic Forces Shape Tomorrow's World* (England: Penguin Books, 1996), p. 221; John Train, *Famous Financial Fiascoes* (New York: Clarkson N. Potter, 1985), pp. 33-41, 108-89.

45 Mackay, *Delusions*, pp. 46-88; see also Train, *Fiascoes*, pp. 88-95; Charles P. Kindleberger, *Manias, Panics, and Crashes* (New York: Basic Books, 1978), pp. 220-21.

46 Peter Gowan, *The Global Gamble*: (New York: verso, 1999), pp. 95-98. 118-123.

47 1987 presidential hopeful Representative Richard A. Gephardt of Missouri, in a speech to the Securities Industry Institute of the Wharton School of Business; Haynes Johnson, " 'Teflon' 80s Bear Striking Resemblance to 'Giddy' 20s," *The Missoulian*, March 25, 1987, reprinted from *The Washington Post.*

48 Paul Richter, "Commodity Marts Face Fraud Fallout," *Los Angeles Times*, July 4, 1989, p. A2.

49 Kurtzman, *Death of Money*, pp. 12, 17, 77, 128; see also pp. 39, 65, 64-65, 236.

50 Lester Thurow, *Building Wealth: The New Rules for Individuals, Companies and Nations in a knowledge Based Economy* (New York: HarperCollins, 2000), p. 67; William Tabb, *The Amoral Elephant: Globalization and the Struggle for Global Justice in the Twenty-First Century* (New York: Monthly Review Press, 2001), p.83. Richard C. Longworth, *Global Squeeze: The Coming Crisis of First-World Nations* (Chicago: Contemporary Books, 1999), pp. 7, 256; Gowan, *The Global Gamble.*

51 What Joel Kurtzman, economist and business editor for the New York Times, calls "images of labor, wisdom, and wealth" (Kurtzman, *Death of Money*, p. 161).

52 Kurtzman, *Death of Money*, pp. 73, 96, 99, 113, 117, 120-21, 196, 228.

53 Paul A. Baran, Paul M. Sweezy, *Monopoly Capital* (New York: Monthly Review Press, 1968), p. 49, quoted from T. K. Quinn, *Giant Business*: (New York: Exposition Press, 1954), p. 117.

54 Lester Thurow, *The Future of Capitalism: How Today's Economic Forces Shape Tomorrow's World* (England: Penguin Books, 1996, p. 15; Lester Thurow, *Building Wealth: The New Rules for Individuals, Companies, and Nations in a knowledge-Based Economy* (New York: HarperCollins, 2000), pp. 85, 102.

55 Michael Goldhaber, *Reinventing Technology* (New York: Routledge & Kegan Paul, 1986), p. 185.

56 Ibid, pp. 185, 197.

57 Stuart Chase, *The Tragedy of Waste* (New York: Macmillan, 1925), pp. 204-205.

58 Ibid,

26. A Modern Money Commons

Money is the mirror image of a modern economy and many people instinctively point to financiers as the source of society's problems. Yet one has to research deeply to get beneath the *social-control-paradigms* which protect the subtle monopolization of money and finance capital.[1]

From Barter to Commodity Money

Before the widespread use of money, trading involved the simplest form of commercial transaction, barter. Barter is the exchange of two or more products of roughly equal value. This limits most trading to persons possessing equally valuable items. Eventually cattle, tobacco, salt, tea, blankets, skins, and other items were used as a form of money. Such commodities were the most desirable because they were durable, portable, readily exchangeable, and had the most recognizable common measure of value.

Products intended for consumption typically have one to three owners on their way from producer to consumer. Those that are used as money may have dozens or even hundreds of owners. Whether a product is used for exchange or consumption distinguishes it as money or a commodity. The products listed above were imperfect as a medium of exchange, and their limited usefulness limited trade. They created problems of storage, transportation, protection, and not everyone could use these commodities.

From Commodity Money to Coins of Precious Metal

Only highly desirable, useful items could become money. No one would accept a piece of paper, brass, or copper in trade for what he or she had worked so hard to produce. Such a trade would effectively rob one of hard-earned wealth.

Gold and silver have been highly esteemed and accepted as money in most cultures. The first known coin, the shekel, was minted in "the temples of Sumer about 5,000 years ago," and coins of measured value have been routinely minted from precious metals ever since.[2] Except for scarcity values, the labor required to produce a given amount of gold, silver, or precious stones was roughly equal to the labor required to produce any other item that this treasure could buy. As accustomed as we are to viewing gold as money, it is still commodity money: desirable, useful, and requiring roughly equal labor to produce.

Inequality of money values is only inequality of exchanged labor values. Often when rulers became strapped for cash (usually because of war), they resorted to debasing their currency by lowering the gold or silver content and replacing it with inexpensive metals such as copper. The labor value represented by these debased coins was less than the labor value of the items purchased. Assuming the labor cost of gold was 300-times that of copper, each day's production of copper substituted and traded as gold would confiscate the value of 300 days of labor spent producing useful items. It was the universally recognized value of pure precious metals that became the first readily acceptable money.[3]

With gold (or any precious metal) divisible into units of measurable value, a trade could be made for any product. This convenience fueled world trade, for it was only with handy universally accepted money that commerce could flourish. However, as these precious metals had to be located, mined, delivered, stored, and protected before society could have money, trades were still clumsy.

From Gold, to Gold-Backed Paper Money, to Paper Money

The use of gold as money was handicapped by its weight, bulk, and the need for protection against debasement. These problems were eventually eliminated by printing paper money that could be redeemed for a stated amount of gold or silver (the gold standard). As this paper money was backed by gold, there remained the complication of finding, mining, smelting, and storing this valuable commodity.

The next step in the evolution of money was the use of pure paper money. (Paper money was almost universally resorted to in revolutions, although it usually had little value once the banking systems returned to the gold standard.) Benjamin Franklin had proposed paper money, and, while it was used less successfully in the New England colonies, it was used productively in the middle colonies in promoting production and commerce while controlling deflation. The powerful of Britain recognized the threat to their control of trade and outlawed the printing of money in the colonies. This effectively dictated control of commerce and who would profit, and was a contributory cause of the American Revolution.[4]

World Wars I and II weakened the old imperial nations, eroding the subtle monopoly of the gold standard.[5] As most of their gold had been traded for war materiel, these countries had to keep printing money to rebuild their shattered cities and industrial plants. To return to money backed by gold would have been to leave their economies at the mercy of U.S. bankers. Thus the subtle monopoly of the gold standard was partially broken in these countries. The arms race that followed WWII almost totally eliminated gold-backed money as nations continued to print money wastefully for war.

Once freed from its bondage to gold, paper money *represented* rather than possessed value. Printed at little cost, it could be traded for as much wealth as its stated value. Society now required only one finished product to make a trade. Those who sold their labor in the form of these products received in return the paper symbols of value and needed only save this money until they wished to buy products produced by others. Paper money, used productively and not backed by gold, was true money.

From Paper Money, to Checkbook Money, to Money as a Blip on a Computer Screen

As simple and light as paper money was, it was still too clumsy for most trades. Most of these units of value called money were deposited in a bank (just as gold had been) and trades were then consummated with checks. These were more efficient than cash, because each check was a symbol that the signer had produced, saved, or borrowed that much wealth, and that its money form, safely deposited in the bank, was now being traded for equal value in other products or services. Most family, business, corporate, and international trades are done with these symbols of deposited savings—checks, drafts, notes, bills of exchange, and the like.

Commodity money (hides, tobacco, et al.) had dozens, possibly hundreds, of owners before this trading medium returned to its status as a commodity to be consumed. Gold (still commodity money) retained the status of money much longer and had thousands of owners. Gold-backed paper money traded more conveniently and had many tens of thousands of owners. Reserve deposit money, traded by check—via bank debits and credits—can have an endless number of owners, as this representation of value keeps moving from owner to owner. Modern computer money (still reserve deposit money) is but a blip on magnetic tape or disk that can be instantly debited from one account and credited to another. Though tied closely to checkbook money, this is the ultimate in efficient money.

Paper money and checks are familiar to everybody. Even a child learns quickly what they are and how to use them. When most of the historical and ideological mystiques are eliminated, money is easy to understand. The banking system collects all production (symbolized by money), completes society's trades through debits and credits, lends the surplus production (savings) to those who—at any particular moment—have capital or consumer needs greater than their savings, and—through borrowing from the Federal Reserve to expand their reserves and increase their loan capacity—creates more money for an expanding economy. Money is no more complicated than this.

What makes money appear mysterious is that the powerful have always controlled it. Its secrets are protected by governments, bankers, and subtle finance monopolists of every shade trying to siphon to themselves others' wealth. The process is quite simple. In a trade, symbolized by money, the actual value of products or services, bought or sold, could be higher or lower than its actual labor value (higher priced or lower priced). The production of labor may be claimed either by underpaying for labor, by overcharging for products or services, or both. To make this clear, we will quote our own words from our opening chapter:

> In direct trades between countries, wealth accumulation potential compounds in step with the pay differential for equally-productive labor. If the pay differential is 5, the difference in wealth accumulation potential is 25-to-1. If the pay differential is 10, the wealth accumulation advantage is 100-to-1. If the pay differential is 20, the wealth accumulation advantage is 400-to-1. If the pay differential is 40, the wealth accumulation advantage is 1,600-to-1. If the pay differential is 60 (the pay differential between the defeated Russia and the victorious America, 23-cents an hour against $14 an hour), the wealth accumulation advantage is 3,600-to-1.

Credit or Trust Money

People accept money because they trust that the value represented can be replaced by equal value in another commodity or service. Credit (pure trust) is both the oldest and most modern currency. When credit is given, nothing is received for the item of value except a promise. Each month, families and businesses are provided with products or services (value) and then billed. This is a procedure based on trust. Cash money is also based on the trust that it can be redeemed for equal value.

If money is controlled with equality and honesty, there is trust. Money then exchanges freely and is easily understood. We are describing money and banking in the everyday language that would apply if the remaining flaws in money's creation and control were eliminated.

The Different Meanings of Money

Money is correctly referred to as a unit of accounting, savings, stored value, a measure of value, a standard of value, a receipt for value, a system of accounting, a deferred payment, a transferable claim, a lien against future production, an IOU, and an information medium. At a fundamental level, money represents the value of the final product of combining the elements of production—land, industrial capital, and labor. In a properly structured society, money represents the value of labor, profits on stored labor (capital), and a share of the costs of running society represented by landrent being paid to society as outlined in the above chapter on land.

To the layperson, money is normally explained as a medium of exchange. This is true. However, a medium of exchange implies equality and it is precisely the *inequality of exchanges* that is the greatest problem. To understand these inequalities, we must have a better explanation of money.

Money is a Contract against another Person's Labor

Money is first, and foremost, a contract against another person's labor. Except for land or scarcity items, value is properly a measure of the time and quality of labor spent producing a product or service. If the difference between the payment received for productive labor and the price paid by the consumer for a product or service is greater than fair value for expediting that trade, either the producer was underpaid, the final consumer was overcharged, or both. When intermediaries underpay producers or overcharge consumers, they are siphoning away the production of the labors of one or the other, or both. This process is seen in the notorious and once common practice of forced shopping at the company store. The underpaid workers' meager wages were further reduced by their compulsory purchase of overpriced merchandise.[6]

Savings implies that something has been produced and not consumed. But even if a commodity is produced for consumption, it is properly understood as capital until sold to the final consumer. It then becomes his or her wealth for consumption (some commodities, such as a meal, are consumed in minutes and some, such as homes, are consumed in decades or even centuries) and is no longer capital. Products are sold, production expenses are paid, any surplus is deposited in a bank, and that deposit is credited at the Federal Reserve to expand the depositing bank's reserves. Banks lend these reserves to others for investment or consumption. The savings (stored labor) has become money capital. The parties who labored to create or distribute these products are only lending their surplus production in its money form with the promise to be paid interest for what their stored labor produced. Interest is the money form of wealth produced by that stored labor (capital).

Money Productively Contracting Labor

Because money is always controlled by those who rule, revolutionaries resort to printing money to finance their insurrections. As opposed to wars to control trade, successful revolutionary wars, like those of the United States, France, the Soviet Union, and China, were fought for freedom, were productive expenditures of labor, and all were fought with paper money.[7]

Every battle for freedom requires large expenditures. Most labor is donated by those directly involved, but much of the weaponry, clothing, food, and medicine must be paid for with money. Money is thus a tool for mobilizing society's labor to produce great things—in this case freedom.

Examples of money properly employing labor are seen every day in farming, in the creation of consumer products, and in the building of homes, roads, schools, shopping centers, and factories. The rebuilding of Europe after WWII was a productive use of labor employed by U.S. capital, as was the industrialization of Japan, Taiwan, and South Korea. However, as most of this book exposes, the politics of their capital development would point more to the powerful protecting their interests than to meeting humanitarian needs.

Money Unproductively Contracting Labor

An efficient economy requires only $3 of speculation money for every $1 invested in the real economy and currency speculation for financing world trade alone is 55-times the real economy. The massive profits from this unnecessary speculation are a charge against other stakeholders within the world economy.

To use one's own *earned* money for speculation is properly one's privilege. But borrowing society's money capital for speculating on land, gold, silver, commodities, already issued stock, or currency, is an attempt to intercept social production by speculating with society's savings; there is no intent to produce.

The use of society's savings for corporate takeovers usually is a battle between the powerful for control. Whether the takeover is successful or not, these unproductive uses of social capital continually milk money from the economy. All this unnecessary activity diverts money capital from its true purpose, production and distribution. More appropriately, massive speculation beyond that needed for an efficient economy is an exercise in social insanity. By taking the easy way out, society is being irresponsible.

An even more nonproductive use of money occurs when labor is contracted to destroy others' capital (war), or to work at endeavors from which neither the present generation nor its descendants will benefit (see *Cooperative Capitalism: A Blueprint for Global Peace and Prosperity* by this author). In 1800, Robert Owen, manager of a family textile mill in Scotland, began his famous social experiment of paying workers well, giving them decent housing, educating their children, and doing all this profitably. He calculated that this community of 2,500 persons (workers and families) was producing as much as a community of 600,000 did less than 50 years before.

Owen wondered where the wealth from such a large increase in efficiency was going. He concluded it was being consumed by the petty wars continually fought by aristocracy.[8] The mill workers were being underpaid for their work, the customers were being overcharged for their cloth, and the production of their labor, in its money form, was being siphoned away and used to contract materiel and labor for war. Labor was being paid to fight because this generated the greatest rewards for those who controlled the use of money. This was wasteful to the rest of society; nothing useful was produced when that confiscated wealth was spent, and much of what existed was destroyed.

In the 15th-Century, "about 70% of Spanish revenues and around two-thirds of the revenues of other European countries" were employed in these wars.[9] Most of this revenue was siphoned away from a country's own citizens. The treasure pillaged from the Americas was but a small share of the wealth destroyed in European wars:

> Until the flow of American silver brought massive additional revenues to the Spanish crown (roughly from the 1560s to the late 1630s), the Habsburg war effort principally rested upon the backs of Castilian peasants and merchants; and even at its height, the royal income from sources in the New World was only about one-quarter to one-third of that derived from Castile and its six million inhabitants.[10]

The powerful today are wasting massive wealth battling over the world's wealth, identical to Robert Owen's analysis 200 years ago.

There must be Money before Wealth

In a modern economy, credit money (trust) must be available. People would not produce beyond their immediate needs unless they knew they could safely lend that production (savings) and reclaim it when needed. Just like a powerful train or modern roads, money expedites the transfer of commodities between producers and consumers. Because it represents a set value of labor, a person can trade that value for equal value of any of the millions of items or services produced by other people.

If there are not enough savings to fully employ resources, labor, and capital, it is a simple matter to create more money. So long as money contracts labor to produce needed products, the value represented by that money (the item or service produced) is real. First printed to contract labor for increased production of wealth, this money continues through the economy employing more labor for the needs of whoever passes it along the economic chain, or it is lent to others to finance their needs. Once an economy is fully employed and in balance, there is a continual circulation of these contracts against labor we call money, and there is no need to print more.

If there is to be trust in money, and if the financial machinery of a society is to function smoothly, there must be fair pay for productive labor. But with land, industrial capital (technology), and money capital subtly monopolized and thus claiming an excessive share of the wealth produced, labor is underpaid. Much of those excess profits are spent on siphoning more wealth away from the weak, graft spent for that same purpose, extravagant lifestyles, and wars to protect it all.

Allowing for protection of the environment and conservation of resources, if the best possible living standard for every person were society's goal, resources, labor, and industrial capital would be used to capacity through efficient contracting of all labor for true production. As technology improves and social efficiency increases, the decision will eventually have to be made that living standards are adequate at the current production level or that resources are inadequate to employ more labor. Working hours should then be reduced in step with that gain in efficiency without lowering living standards.

Here subtle monopolization becomes highly visible. Let us assume that society wrenched control of government from the powerful. Society could then print the necessary money to employ the idle labor and resources to produce the amenities of life many people are currently unable to obtain. Those who control land, capital, money capital, and fictitious capital would immediately protest that they have the capacity to produce for these needs. This would be true. However—within subtly-monopolized economies—unearned rent, unearned profits, and the fictitious wages of wasted labor siphon away at least 60% of productive labor's efforts without having produced anything of value to trade. This creates unnecessarily high costs, leaves the underpaid and unemployed with insufficient money to contract for their needs, and assures that industrial capital will produce at some small fraction of capacity. If each person were productively employed, the average hours worked per week for the same standard of living would shrink by half or more.[11]

For those who look at every progressive recommendation as communist, remember that communism had as one of its specific goals the elimination of money. This philosophy considers money an indispensable tool as society maximizes money's efficiency as any businessperson would his or her tools.

Learning the Secret of Bank-Created Money

The secret of creating money was first learned by goldsmiths. Others' gold was deposited with them for safekeeping. Goldsmiths learned that deposits were usually left for a substantial period and they could safely make loans in the form of receipts for gold. These receipts circulated as money with the gold remaining on deposit. On balance, loans were paid off faster than the gold was reclaimed. Therefore, loans could be issued for several times the amount on deposit and loans of several times the value of the deposited gold became "created" money.[12]

Whenever Rothschild or other early bankers loaned 10 certificates of gold at 10% interest, for every unit of gold they owned or held for safekeeping, each year their personal net worth would increase equal to all gold on deposit. When a banking system used gold or goldbacked currency as money, its creation of money was identical to that of the goldsmiths.

One hundred years ago, a prudent bank with $1-million in gold that decided to maintain its reserves at 10% could print $10-million in banknotes and loan them all that same day and $9-million of that would be bank-created money. Viewing the banking system as one bank, which any one-currency banking system is, a bank today with $1-million in reserves and a 10% reserve requirement could initially make only $900,000 in loans. But, as the money kept circulating back, it could loan 90% of each new reserve deposit and eventually would loan out $10-million, the same as the prudent banker 100 years ago. Assuming a sound economy and *prudent bankers*, the money created in a modern economy—as it circulates within the economy productively contracting land, labor, and industrial capital—is backed by the wealth produced.

The 13 American colonies printed money to fight the Revolutionary War but this power of government to create money was not used by the United States again in any great measure until President Lincoln printed greenbacks to finance the Civil War. As soon as the Civil War was over, the U.S. government ceased creating money and started pulling those greenbacks out of the economy. This destruction of money caused bankruptcies to soar for the first 10 postwar years as wealth was again consolidated within the hands of entrenched wealth.[13] There was no need for those bankruptcies. If those greenbacks had been allowed to stand, and so long as there were unemployed resources and labor and consumer needs, that money would have continued to circulate freely within the economy, combining labor and industrial capital with America's immense natural wealth, creating even more wealth.

While conservative banks were reining in loans, a post-Civil War level of $33.60 of gold or gold-backed currency in reserve for every $100 on deposit dropping to $1 in gold for each created dollar (as it was gold-backed, it was bank-created money) by 1913 hid the fact that greedy bankers loaned 20 to 50-times their reserves or even more. Banks pooled funds to cover runs on banks but runs on weak banks would spill over into runs on strong banks. With their depositors' money loaned out operating the economy, thus not immediately collectable (illiquid), perfectly sound banks would go under and bankrupt many farms and businesses with them.

Primary-Created Money and Circulation-Created Money

Bankers substantially resolved their liquidity problems in 1913 through the establishment of the Federal Reserve System.[14] Since that act, U.S. banks that were members of the Federal Reserve System could not loan above a set multiple of their reserves. The reserve requirement of state chartered nonmember banks varied for the next 67 years, some requiring no reserves. In 1980, all U.S. banks were brought under the Federal Reserve System and, ever since, creation of money has been regulated by the Federal Reserve, not private banks.

Ever since all banks were brought under the reserve requirements of the Federal Reserve, it has been the circulation of money proper that creates most money, not the banks themselves. Money already created by the U.S. Treasury or the Federal Reserve is only assisted by banks in its circulation and creation of more money, just as every other person through whose hands that money passes assists in money circulation and money creation. A bank cannot credit a customer's account unless that bank is already credited with those funds in its account at the Federal Reserve. In short, the first, or primary, money in the historic circulation of money is first created by the Federal Reserve or Treasury (government) through crediting a bank's reserves without debiting anyone's funds. When those credited reserves (primary-created money) are loaned out, spent, and returned to a bank to be credited to their reserves and again loaned out, that is circulation-created money. Some excess profits are made by banks in the money creation process but only on the wide difference between the interest rate paid the Federal Reserve and that charged the customer.

If a bank credits a borrower's account with $10,000, we are taught this is the creation of money by private banks. But that is not so. That private bank must have 110% that much money credited to it in its reserve account at the Fed before that loan could be made. Not one cent will have been created except to the extent the borrower—and others into whose hands the money circulates—spends that money and that then is circulation-created money, not bank-created money. Under a reserve system, only when a banking system is viewed as one bank does a bank create money.[a] If the receiver of what is commonly referred to as "bank-created money" puts it under the mattress instead of depositing it into a reserve account, the money creation process stops. But as soon as that person spends that money or deposits it into a reserve account, the money continues to circulate and create more money each time it changes hands.

[a] A hint as to how enormously efficient a banking system could be if it was controlled directly by society for maximizing the gains to all stakeholders as opposed designed to maximize profits for a few

So each person spending money is every bit as important in the creation of circulation money as the banks which credit their borrowers' accounts with 90% of their reserves. In fact, one could argue that the spenders of that money are more important. That money could be spent several times as cash, be counted each time, and, until someone deposits it in a bank from which it is loaned, there is no need to deduct any part for reserves.

The Fed's Open Market Operations hide the Simplicity of Money Creation

To maintain the mystery of how simple money creation really could be, bankers conceived the devious Open Market Operations of the Fed. The interest on Treasury securities owned by the Fed being returned to the U.S. Treasury leaves no other conclusion than that this money was surreptitiously created under cover of the Fed. The expansion or contraction of treasury notes owned by the public either creates or destroys money. Reserves are increased through the U.S. Treasury selling bonds to the Fed and the Fed crediting the treasury with those funds but not debited from any other account. The Fed is "printing" the money to buy those bonds. The Treasury was thus spending what appeared to be money borrowed from the Fed but, since both are arms of the government (see below), this was actually money it had printed itself.[15]

When all the books are balanced, any money printed and spent for government purposes or used to purchase treasuries on the open market, both expanding the money supply and neither debited from another reserve account, is primary-created money. That money is deposited into the receiver's account in a private bank and credited at the Federal Reserve to that bank from which, under current reserve requirements, 90% can be loaned out. Private borrowers would spend that loaned to them and those moneys would circulate within the economy and be deposited back into some bank's reserve account.

Each time the Fed transfers reserves from one bank's reserve account to another bank's reserve account (via cashed checks), 90% of those transferred reserves can be loaned out. Once the limit of money creation through circulation of money is reached, any further increase in the money supply requires either the Treasury openly printing more money for government expenditures, private banks borrowing from the Federal Reserve to increase their reserves (created money), or the Federal Reserve creating money when purchasing treasury bonds in the market (again created money).[16] (The Canadian banking system has had no reserve requirement for several years, so Canadian banks do create money.)

The purchasing of treasury bonds on the open market is the Fed's primary money creation tool but, when one analyzes that the final owner of those treasuries, or goods and services from that created money is the American people, all three methods of creating money function the same. A Treasury check is cashed, the banking system returns the check to the Fed for clearing and the Fed credits the bank in which that check was deposited with an increase in reserves equal to the face value of the check. However, no reserve account is debited as it is with private checks presented to the Federal Reserve for clearance; it is primary-created money of which typically 90% can be loaned out. The loaned money is spent and is deposited back into some bank's reserves, 90% of those reserves are again loaned out, and this money-creation circulation continues until the money is too small an amount to consider.

The interest paid by the U.S. Treasury on Fed-purchased T-bills goes to the Fed, which annually returns all that plus a part of other profits (currency trading, priced services to banks, et al.) to the Treasury. Thus in 1994 the Fed received $19.247-billion from the U.S. Treasury as interest on bonds and paid to the Treasury $20.470-billion, or $1.223-billion more than it received in interest.

That the Fed is privately owned is all a shell game. The unpaid principal and interest on those Fed-purchased, and thus government-owned, bonds are simply credits and debits on the Fed's and Treasury's books. Both are government agencies and when interest is paid to the Fed by the Treasury it, plus other profits, are promptly returned to the Treasury, thus proving there never was a debt to the Fed. Those Fed-held Treasury bonds are a charade. The Treasury could have openly created that money and bought back those treasuries, just as was done surreptitiously by the Fed. But this would have made the simplicity of non-debt-created money visible to all and maintaining that secret is the whole purpose of the charade.

Member banks only technically own the Fed. If they really owned it, they would be receiving the interest on bonds owned by the Fed. In 1994, as discussed above, member banks received $212-million in dividends and $283-million for their mysterious "surplus fund," which only means the government should have received $20.965-billion instead of $20.470-billion.

Those Fed buildings were built with created money, operation costs are paid for by charges to banks, the Fed reports to Congress, and the payment of 97% of the profits of the Fed to the Treasury is proof that bankers know well that the Fed is an appendage to the treasury and both are arms of the federal government.

Under the fiction of ownership, bankers do control Fed policy. That they do not have the courage to distribute amongst themselves the profits from those Fed-owned bonds proves they know they do not own the Fed. That part of the national debt owed to the Federal Reserve can be eliminated by simply writing it off. After all, one cannot owe money to oneself. The only sense in which private banks own the Federal Reserve is that it is they who receive most of the interest on that created money. This is accomplished through the rate spread between the interest paid the Fed and that charged the consumer.

A growing economy requires more money, which banks obtain by selling government bonds to the Federal Reserve.[17] To pay for these treasuries, when the Fed's check comes back to itself for clearing, the Fed simply credits the selling bank with that number of dollars without debiting from any reserve account; it is primary-created money. That primary-created money is deposited into the reserves of the bank which sold those bonds and that bank can now make new loans at whatever multiple is dictated by reserve requirements; that multiple of the original created money is circulation-created money.

When loans are being repaid faster than money is borrowed, the money disappears from an economy by that same multiple. The produced wealth has been consumed or becomes storage of real wealth owned by those who produced more than they consumed.

In a steady state economy, money is being destroyed (by consumption and depreciation) as fast as it is created or, if you prefer, created as fast as it is destroyed. To put it another way, consumption and production are in balance.

Whether used for fighting wars, building social infrastructure, expanding industry, or providing services, primary-created money is continually circulating. Each time this money changes hands between a depositor in a reserve account and a borrower from those reserve accounts, it is used either to create value or purchase value. Each change of hands between saver and borrower is counted. This, we are taught, is the classic creation of money by banks. However, when checks are presented to a bank for deposit into one reserve account or for payment of that loan, the funds are deducted from another bank's reserve account. The original primary-created monies, the reserve accounts, do not increase as money circulates; one's credits are always another's debits.

It is the counting of that money each time it changes hands that gives the appearance of more money. If one had been using a diamond (commodity money) as money, it too would have gone from hand to hand, that value would have been counted each time as an increase in the money supply, but one could see that—when that circulation began, throughout its circulation, and when that circulation was complete—there was at all times only the same number of diamonds.

So a bank making a loan based on reserves does not create money. Money circulation itself creates money. For the first loan of a classical circulation of money to have been made from a reserve account, the primary funds had to have been created by government printing money for social infrastructure or services, or by the Fed printing money through purchasing treasuries. A lowering of reserve requirements creates money and an elimination of all reserves transfers the right of money creation to private banks and, if other limitations are not established, eliminates all limits on the creation of money.

If an economy is stable, savings within the circulation of money, in the form of continual crediting and debiting of reserve deposits, will continue to operate the economy. Although the speed of circulation has some bearing on quantity of money, an expansion of an economy typically will require the creation of more money.

Money is destroyed when it is deposited in a bank and not loaned back out. Pay off all debts and all that is left is circulating currency. When reserve deposit money quits circulating, money disappears from the economy even if vast pools of reserve deposits (potential circulating money) have built up. The moribund Japanese economy with trillions of dollars in savings on the books, as addressed above, is a prime example. If equity prices in Japan continue to fall, the fiction of trillions of dollars on the books will be exposed. If the economy turns around and those equities rise, those savings will be valid.[a]

It is a matter of semantics. One can claim the money creation process starts at any point. A person is creating money if he or she writes a check without funds in the bank. He or she must then earn that money (we assume honestly through productive labor) and depositing it in the bank before the check comes in. The bank only balances the reserve deposits and loans. Assuming the earnings from that productive labor are in cash and it is deposited in the bank just before the check is presented for payment, no bank has made any loan and no one's reserve deposits are lowered, but money has been created.

All borrowers (consumers of the moment) are borrowing the deposits of all producers (savers of the moment). (One may be borrowing from oneself, either from a checking account or out of pocket, and expecting to replenish the bank account or pocket change [both are savings]). The banking system keeps an account of these trades between people. Many are equal trades—in a month or year, most people earn roughly what they spend—but the unequal trades (more produced [earned] than spent, or

---

[a] Bankers know all this and successfully lobby bailouts for their larger troubled banks. Japan is right and Western banking rules are wrong. The world should take note of this inadvertent example of protection of both banks and people that banking rules need changing to protect all stakeholders, not just bankers. A banking system structured as per this chapter should never face these crises that our current speculative-structured banks face every day.

By accounting rules, most Japanese banks have been broke for years. By those same rules, if Japan had closed those banks that would have destroyed what was left of its land and stock values, wiped out those trillions in savings, forced the sale of property in American and American bonds, and not only collapsed the Japanese economy but would have collapsed the world economy. Witness the violent 1987 collapse of the American stock market when Japan started selling American bonds (Richard C. Longworth, *Global Squeeze: The Coming Crisis of First-World Nations* [Chicago: Contemporary Books, 1999], pp. 22, 53).

more consumed [spent] than earned) are balanced by lending and borrowing deposited savings residing in banks' reserve accounts.

Some believe that it is by producing value that money is created. Commodities are produced and offered for sale, money is borrowed to buy them, and—on balance—the money received by the producer goes right back to the bank and essentially finances the sale of what was produced. Others hold that it is the offering of money that motivates production of wealth. The first argument is more accurate in describing the early use of money and the second is more typical of a modern economy.

As described throughout this author's *The World's Wasted Wealth 2* and the *Cooperative Capitalism: A Blueprint for Global Peace and Prosperity* and the classics of Veblen, Chase, Borsodi, and others, it is possible to be paid but not produce value. If the purchasers think they are receiving value, in the current monetary system that is tantamount to real value. However, if money contracted only productive labor and full value were paid for that labor, money would represent a more realistic value and would become a symbol of actual wealth. Money would then be only a tool, a symbol for the trade of productive labor.

Under conditions of equal rights (when each person is fairly paid for his or her genuinely productive work), money lent combines land, labor, and industrial capital to produce full value in needed goods and services. A society can be fully productive only if each of its citizens are fully productive. Neither money nor the economy can become truly efficient until all nonproductive siphoning of wealth through unequal trades in value, as opposed to producing and trading equal value, is eliminated. Likewise, every contracting of labor for nonproductive use must, on final analysis, be paid for by appropriating value from other stakeholders' productive labor.

A Money Commons structured to protect the Rights of All

People unproductively attached to the arteries of commerce, either for making a living or making fortunes, see only their momentary self-interest and will not permit the necessary legal and social changes to eliminate those wasted labors. Because of the *social-control-paradigms* created by think-tanks supported by the power-structure and perpetuated through the university system and the media (see Chapter 6), only under extreme crisis can change be imposed upon them. For the sake of precision and clarity, and recognizing that only small changes are likely and then only under severe crisis, we will be outlining a fully reconstructed banking system.

Let's assume that an economically viable, highly-educated population emigrates and starts up a new economy in virgin territory and was planning to manage it honestly, equally, and efficiently. There are no labor-created values in this virgin territory but this population brings with them basic industrial tools and has the knowledge to run an economy and create a new nation. These modern Pilgrims arrive with the papers already prepared to establish a Treasury to create money, a Federal Reserve to keep account of this new nation's trades through debiting and crediting between bank reserves, and private bankers to provide a place to deposit savings from which loans are made for both production and consumption.

The Treasury is empowered to create money for combining their industrial tools (industrial capital) and labor with the plentiful resources to produce the necessities of life, basic infrastructure, homes, businesses, consumer products, and more industrial tools. The primary-created money that created that wealth is deposited into reserve deposits where 90% is loaned out, circulated within the community, returned as new reserve deposits, and 90% is continually loaned out again.

This primary-created money, and the circulation of that money creating more money, financed cutting and sawing timber, mining ore, smelting ore, producing machine tools, building shoe and textile factories, building factories to produce consumer durables, building retail outlets, and so forth. Of course, to make the function of money and banking visible, we have theoretically shrunk several generations of building industrial and social capital into a few cycles of the creation and circulation of money.

So long as there is surplus labor, unused resources, and a social need not cared for through the current circulation of money, a nation's treasury can properly create (print) more primary-created money. A society can design the proper balance between money creation and money destruction. The proper balance between wealth creation and wealth destruction (consumption) will mirror that proper money balance. Economists can easily calculate any surplus buying power that may occasionally develop. An increase in the discount rate will soak up that surplus buying power and a decrease will expand the money supply.

Efficient money under a banking system as a part of the modern commons (under *democratic-cooperative-capitalism)* will be so productive it will quickly strip the earth's resources. Thus the creation of money must be planned within the earth's resource capacity and its ability to absorb society's wastes without ecological destruction. In a nation's early development stage—so long as there are surplus labor, resources, and industry—primary money can be created to build schools, roads, railroads, electric power, sewer systems, and post offices. All such infrastructure is properly a part of the modern commons and makes society far more efficient and the wealth created backs the new money. This productive wealth provides the backing for the money created to produce it and the commodities and services produced are the wealth that both backs and absorbs the circulating money operating those industries and services.

When primary-created money is spent for development, society owns what is built or has a mortgage against that created wealth. To the extent an economy needs an increase in the money supply, federal, state, and local needs and basic infrastructure (roads, railroads, schools, et al.) could be financed by Treasury-created money and there would be no debt. To the extent there are unemployed workers, unused resources, unused industrial capital, and unmet human needs—and taking into consideration the capacity of the earth to recycle wastes to protect resources, ecology, and environment for future generations—it is only necessary for a nation's treasury to create the money to employ that labor, utilize those resources, and meet those needs.

Instead of almost exclusively lending against equity, bankers would need to be knowledgeable about community needs and lend appropriately for those needs. Each region and each community should have equal rights to a nation's (or the world's) savings and equal rights to created money.

So long as an economy is expanding productively, and providing value to be purchased by this newly created money, there is no need to tax the public for constructing public buildings or providing services. However, if there are no idle resources or labor to expand wealth production, creation of money will create inflation. If there is not to be an expansion of wealth production, public construction and operation of governments must then come out of taxes.

Note how close banking already is to a modern money commons: Through a "Revolving Reserve Account," total deposits and loans of each individual bank should be accounted for just as they are now through banks debiting and crediting customer accounts and the Fed debiting and crediting bank reserves. Reserve requirements should be regulated just as now. Banks should be collectors and loaners of the nation's savings, just as now. All loan institutions should be brought under reserve requirements. All money loaned above the revolving reserves would be created by the Treasury Department (just as now except the accounting of Treasury-created money is buried in a fictional debt of the Treasury to the Fed).[18]

The Fed can lower margin requirements where loan needs are high (poorer regions which need development, regions of natural disaster, et al.) and raise margin requirements in booming sectors of the economy. (That would be primarily the "paper" sector—stocks, derivatives, currency speculations, commodities, and bonds, which each should have the pure speculative aspect [95% of current stock, commodity, and currency market activities], but not the entrepreneurial speculative aspect [the 5% actually investing in the real economy], eliminated.) The affluent sectors of the economy awash in funds are thus rebalanced with the undeveloped sectors deprived of finance capital.

With banking rights held in common, there would be *local rights to finance capital.* Each region and each bank would have "rights" to, and pay interest on, its share of created money and savings, but only the national treasury could create primary money. The creation of money would be by a formula established by law and, adjustable to the deficits or surpluses of a region, automatically distributed. There would be neither control by an elite nor control by politics. It would be a formula of regional, local, and individual rights to created money and savings. The sucking of regional money to money-center banks to be used for speculation would disappear.

The success of local currencies proves that regions, localities, and individuals are denied their full rights to finance capital. But local scrip is not legal tender, not universally accepted, and thus limited in circulation. With banks attuned to take care of those needs, each locality would, in the form of rights to finance capital, effectively have its local currency and, because it is legal tender and can be spent anywhere, it would be much more efficient than current, enormously labor intensive, local currency schemes, LET Systems, Ithica Hours, Time Dollars, et al.[a]

Honest money, such as we are proposing in the modern commons, is efficient locally, nationally, and internationally. Efficient means they are instantly acceptable anywhere and accounting costs are infinitesimal. The money itself is the accounting system and those accounting costs are reduced to a fraction of the accounting costs under subtle monopolization.

The Populists of the late 19th-Century studied banking reform and their agenda

> became a sourcebook for political reforms spanning the next fifty years: a progressive income tax; federal regulation of railroads, communications, and other corporations; legal rights for labor unions; government price stabilization and credit programs for farmers.... The populist plan would essentially employ the full faith and credit of the United States government directly to assist the "producing classes" who needed financing for their enterprises. In effect, the government would *circumvent the bankers and provide credit straight to the users.... The government would provide "money at cost," instead of money lent by merchants and bankers at thirty-five or fifty or a hundred per cent interest.*[19]

There have been many reforms since those days of blatant extortion by the owners of finance capital, but "the money-creation system that Congress adopted in 1913 [and reformed during the Great Depression] ... preserved the private banking system as the intermediary that controlled the distribution of new money and credit."[20]

That current exorbitant interest rates are unnecessary was demonstrated by early Scottish bankers, whose thrift is so well known that even today a person careful with his or her money is called "Scotch." In the 19th-Century, the universal practice of Scottish banks was to set interest on loans between 1-and-2% above that paid depositors. Their innovative practices are still considered a model of banking stability.[21] With the proper banking

---

[a] An Internet search will locate these local currencies and more. Tom Greco, *Understanding and creating Alternatives to Legal Tender* (White River JCT, VT: Chelsea Green Publishing, 2001) will bring one up to date on local currencies worldwide.

service charge having been well established at 1-to-2% for small-volume banking using expensive hand accounting, 1% would be a proper service charge for large-volume banking using inexpensive computerized accounting.

During the stable years following WWII, the real rate of interest in the United States (allowing for inflation) hovered between that 1-and-2%. Previously, the normal world rate had been 2-to-3%.[22] Although the real rate of interest in the United States during what were considered the best years the world economy has ever known was under 2%, we will allow the highest long-term average real rate of interest, 3%, as a fair rate. With subtle monopolization and the waste it engenders eliminated, with workers fully paid for their fully productive labor, and with true interest at the high end of historical norms, both capital (stored labor) and current labor would be well paid. People would save and those savings would be available for productive investments.

There need be nothing more than checking accounts paying, by law, 3% interest. Each person's checking and savings would be the same account. Interest rate controls would eliminate money market instruments and the attendant wasted labor competing for deposits. Detractors may decry this as a loss of their rights. But the only right lost is that of the powerful to intercept the production of others' labor, especially those pure gamblers whose wagers in the world market casinos amount to at least 50-times the investment, labor, commodity, bond, and loan activity in the real economy.

In a banking system, total debits and credits will balance (withdrawals equaling deposits). With a fully integrated banking system, any deviation from that balance could be quickly corrected by loan policy. The visible flow of funds would be the economic pulse of the nation. Any unexplained deficit in one bank could be immediately looked into while normal deficits are balanced by others' normal surpluses. Increasing or decreasing the interest rate for consumer credit and/or decreasing or increasing it for investment in productive capital would balance the economy.

As a tool under a banking authority (under community control), money can fine-tune an economy to the maximum capacity of resources and labor. It must be emphasized that such a truly efficient society (*democratic-cooperative-capitalism*) could quickly consume the world's resources and pollute the environment. The needs of a society must be balanced with conservation of these resources and protection of the environment. This can be done only with social policy firmly under social control—not under corporate, finance monopoly control.

To provide an adequate living standard for all people and still protect the world's resources and environment, a balance between a respectable living standard and the capacity of the earth's resources and ecosystem would have to be reached. Assuming centers of capital could no longer siphon the world's wealth to themselves and then waste it battling over that wealth, societies could then progress calmly. To prevent inflation, an empowered Treasury/Federal Reserve could both restrict creation of money and/or increase interest rates. Energy taxes (really landrent taxes) can be quickly raised to pull surplus money out of an economy or lowered to put more money into the economy. To prevent inflation, interest and/or energy taxes and/or transaction taxes flowing to the Treasury/Fed could be increased where that money would be destroyed by virtue of not loaning it back out. To prevent deflation, an empowered Treasury need only lower interest rates and/or create more money.

The opportunity to restructure could happen by default. In all banking crises in all countries, massive public funds are infused into the banking system to stabilize it. Under the rules of capitalism, those whose money are invested own, and make decisions on, that property."[23]

As Eastern Europe and the former Soviet Union have demonstrated, restructuring any society is painful. But restructuring to honest banking after a financial crisis will stabilize, not destabilize, an economy. As one integrated banking system, all loan institutions, including money markets, should be subject to reserve requirements and regulated interest. In short, all banks operate as one bank. The regulated interest rate on savings should be a real rate of 3%, which, as typically the bank rate paid on savings is less than the rate of inflation, is much more than most of the world's banks are now paying.

Even with a nation's Treasury Department as the only creator of money, countries cannot control their finance markets except by coordinated action of the major currency nations. To prevent flight of capital, all major countries would have to act simultaneously to bring money markets under control.

Most countries' banks are publicly owned and currencies in the world banking system cannot escape even from a private banking system such as in America. Whenever a serious policy dispute erupts between any country (Iran, Iraq, Cuba, North Korea) and the United States, their dollar accounts throughout the world are frozen. Every trade financed by money capital of any currency that moves between two banks just creates a change in bank reserves at the central bank for that currency. If that central bank does not honor a transaction in its currency through suspending targeted banks' access to their reserves, those banks have lost access to their currency and no money can change hands. As we write this (November 2001), President George Bush is threatening to suspend rights of disbursing or accepting dollars for any bank in the world that does not cooperate in the search for those who are funding terrorist attacks on America. The U.S. central bank (the Federal Reserve) can control dollars anywhere in the world. Theoretically other countries can control their currencies but this is true only of countries that are economically powerful. The power to discount currencies of weak nations gives powerful nations effective control over other nations' currency values and thus control over their ability to create money.

With coordinated action to bring the world's money markets within a banking system with required reserves and regulated interest, bidding for a nation's savings—and other subtle methods of finance monopolization—can be eliminated. Nothing is more important for a nation's economy than productive use of its investment funds, and nothing is more important to the world economy than the stability of currency and commodity markets.

Inflation, Deflation, and Constant Value: Creating Honest Money

Eliminating inflation and deflation and maintaining a constant-value currency while expanding the money supply to finance true production and distribution are as simple as, and an extension of, the obsolete gold standard. A banking authority need only tie its money to the value of "a basket of 30 or more of the most commonly used commodities—gold, wheat, soybeans, rice, steel, copper, et al."[24] The uncontrolled money markets can be brought within the banking system by law and required to deposit reserves with the Federal Reserve. To establish this stable-value money, a nation's treasury/federal reserve could use a part of the reserves to buy commodity contracts and would be the official arbitrageur for those contracts. As this use only replaces previous users of these same reserves, this does not reduce the money supply (reserves) operating the real economy. Ralph Borsodi, economist and lifetime promoter of a banking authority issuing money backed by a broad base of commodities, sums it up:

> The essential difference [between speculation and arbitrage in commodity and currency markets] is that the arbitrageur buys and sells [contracts of different maturity dates] simultaneously [on different markets] while the speculator buys and sells at different times. The effect of arbitrage on price movements is to stabilize them; the effect of speculation is to intensify them. If arbitrage were to be conducted on a large enough and wide enough scale, speculation would become less and less enticing. But perhaps even more than this, if it were to be promoted and practiced by an independent international agency such as the bank-of-issue I am calling for on the magnitude this would make possible, it would stabilize prices to such a degree that stabilization as a serious problem would disappear. Stabilization would make speculation peripheral instead of central in the determination of the prices of basic commodities of the world.-[25]

It is not necessary to wait for a nation to establish honest money. Any international bank could do so by establishing a commodity market database, updating it continuously by computer, and agreeing to debit and credit trades in a constant value backed by this "basket of commodities." In the currency markets, with the value of this new money indexed to, and backed by, those commodities, other currencies would adjust their value to this constant value and those currency values too would be updated continuously. With the risk of loss eliminated, the contracts of international traders would be tied to constant-value accounts and they would accept payments and make payments at that constant value.

Commodity-basket contracts would be purchased with these reserve deposits. When a demand was made on that account, the bank would convert the money to the currency demanded using its commodity basket value, pay the demand, and debit the account. The natural function of the market pays owners of those contracts and, rather than interest on loans, normal holding profits would be made on commodity contracts. As currently commodity contracts require funding, there would be no increase in demand for finance capital. Financing would only shift from speculation financing to stability financing.

Once enough constant-value accounts were established, incoming and outgoing money would roughly balance. As the purpose is to maintain the broad average of values, the bank commodities traders would do no speculating. They would be selling contracts approaching their delivery dates and buying new ones of later delivery dates. The security provided by this constant-value money would be so attractive that it would drain money from other banks and money markets, which would have to follow suit or lose deposits. "We will have Gresham's law operating in reverse; good money will be driving bad money out of circulation."[26]

With the pattern established, commodity markets would establish contracts for this basket of commodities and update its value continuously. It would be most economical to include the maximum amount of commodities in one basket, and all countries, banks, and markets could index their money to this same standard. If done properly, there would be one international currency. Any bank in any country could then buy these commodity-basket contracts to back constant-value reserve deposits and sell them to debit demands against those reserve deposits.[a]

In the currency markets, the value of any currency relative to that stable money would be available to everyone at all times. The more banks and countries that backed their money with these commodity-basket contracts, the fewer funds they would need to keep in reserve to protect their money. If all countries tied their currencies to these stable values, world trades would match currency transfers and all would have a secure international currency that could be redeemed by simply spending it in the marketplace.

---

[a] If it was national policy, the central bank could keep those reserves invested in contracts. Inflation and deflation can also be eliminated, and thus a stable value currency created, by indexing wages and contracts to the price changes of a broad basket of commodities.

The "national character of currencies would be of no consequence, they would be but different tokens representing the same commodities."[27] Their value would be ensured and could be realized simply by being spent.

With speculation eliminated, the value of all contracts, and thus the money required to fund them, would equal the value of all commodities in transit and storage. So long as market speculation was eliminated through commodity contracts backing a nation's money, all money would retain its value relative to those commodity contracts.

If producers and buyers organized into respective trade associations that continually analyzed world supply and demand, this would not eliminate the producers' opportunity as sellers to maximize their prices or as buyers the right to minimize prices.[28] That would still be subject to supply and demand.

Because banks could not protect against counterfeiting, they would issue credits but could not print currency. But with computers to verify a customer through thumb prints, infrared thermogram palm images, artery, vein, eye pattern, and signature scanning (procedures now in use), a check on a constant-value account would be equal to currency. This would attract world traders looking for secure currency and other countries would have to follow suit or lose finance capital. As it can protect against counterfeiting, any nation that desired stable money values could print a constant-value currency and protect it with commodity-basket contracts. This currency would not only be of high value to world traders, world travelers desiring constant-value currency would flock to its use.

Money "cannot be stabilized unless trade is stable."[29] Assuming the shenanigans—selling short, futures on options, and other "derivative products" designed within the worldwide market casino to accelerate the siphoning of wealth from the weak and innocent to the powerful and sophisticated—were eliminated, each country would produce commodities equal to the contracts sold by its farms, firms, and industries. The more waste that is eliminated and replaced by true production and efficient distribution, the more commodity contracts a country can sell, the more of others' commodities it can buy, and the wealthier it will be. Assuming subtle monopolizations were eliminated, all had access to capital and markets, and these newly capitalized countries formed trade associations to sell their commodities and labor at fair market prices (meaning elimination of the massive wage differentials between equally-productive labor worldwide), each currency would be valued and backed by its nation's production. Understanding and implementing this process would be the best method of minimizing waste, maximizing production, protecting a nation's wealth, and organizing a peaceful, wealthy world.

To depositors who kept an adequate bank balance, credit cards could be issued in this constant-value money. A part of these funds would be invested in constant-value commodity-basket contracts. Once constant-value money was widely used, countries could no longer debase their currency by printing money for nonproductive purposes. It would be immediately discounted in the markets, citizens would flock to the constant-value money, and nothing would be gained (meaning their citizens' wealth could not be arbitrarily siphoned away by inflation induced by their government). Neither could external powers siphon away the wealth of weak nations through discounting their currency and thus deflating its value. (To pull in more deposits and thus strengthen their currencies, developing nations should sell their U.S. or euro treasuries in which their reserves are now invested and invest in a broad basket of commodities.)

"When for a time in the 1970s the price of copper was held fairly steady many dealers went out of business. There was nothing to speculate on in that market"[30] With stable constant values, individuals not using those commodities or currencies in their businesses would no longer borrow society's finance capital to speculate in commodity markets, nor would they do so with their own cash. Protected by constant-value money backed by the world's commodities, true producers would not need to speculate. Speculation in commodity and currency markets would cease and the funds of both speculators and true producers would be available for true investment. Commodity prices, thus consumer prices, would decrease by whatever amount was once siphoned away by these gamblers and confidence in constant-value money would increase efficiencies in international trade, creating even more values. Individual commodities could suffer temporary losses in value but average values would remain stable and those stabilized values would virtually eliminate world economic collapses.

During the adjustment to a balanced economy with honest money, losses by one group and gains by others through inflation or deflation could be eliminated by indexing reserve deposits and loans to commodity-basket values. Of course, by that indexing (assuming wages were included), a country would be placing its currency on a commodity-basket standard and responsible law would require that the printing of money could not exceed any increase in a nation's commodity or service production.[31]

Any printing of money for nonproductive purposes would be offset by corresponding changes in currency values. Once all commodity contracts were owned by businesses dealing in those commodities and by the world's treasuries/central reserve banks, the world will have achieved honest money. Therefore, if ever commodity-basket backed money were started anyplace, it could eventually force honest money on the world.

By tying money to commodities one has only gained a part of full trade rights. Equality in commodity trades requires weak countries being equally paid for their labor and resources. When equally and fully paid and—assuming quality management, access to markets, access to technology, etc—poor nations can immediately start accumulating wealth.

Accumulation of Capital through *Democratic-Cooperative-Capitalism*

Powerful bankers thousands of miles away have no concept of local needs and no loyalty to local people. Farmers, homeowners, and small businesses are strapped for finance capital with their locally produced wealth siphoned thousands of miles away and lent to stock speculators, merger and takeover artists, currency speculators, and other gamblers in the worldwide market casino.

It will be a simple matter to calculate finance capital needs and assign a loan surcharge to all loans to go into a socially-owned capital accumulation fund kept in, and loaned from, local banks. Capital needs of each region, state, county, and community could be calculated. So long as there are surplus labor and resources and real value is to be produced, finance capital can be obtained through printing money (primary-created money). But once the capital accumulation fund is established, it will largely replenish itself through loan repayments and interest rates high enough to cover loan losses.

A quick analysis of the simplicity of a socially-owned capital accumulation fund makes it clear that capital accumulated in the past through monopolization has gone for many other things besides society's finance capital needs, primarily for extravagant living.

Every alert entrepreneur knows that the big profits end up with those who call the tune with their money. With a socially-owned capital accumulation fund, instead of capital accumulation through subtle monopolies, citizen with sound ideas, but no capital, would have the opportunity to realize the profits from their abilities and accumulate capital in their own names. Wealth, now accumulated by true producers, would quickly diffuse itself broadly and relatively equally throughout the population.

Just as each individual has rights, regions and communities should have rights to their share of a nation's finance capital. By outlawing the borrowing of social funds for speculation in the worldwide gambling casino (but not outlawing borrowing for new speculative enterprises), and giving each community or region rights to capital, a national banking authority could guide lending into productive channels throughout the nation. An international authority could guide capital to productive channels and needy regions worldwide. Regional authorities could lend productively within their region, and local authorities within their locality. A nation's banking system would then be structured for the maximum support of all its citizens, and the needs of other countries would be receiving attention. Society could set a minimum housing standard and eventually reach that goal; innovative businesses should have high priority, but a society could give equal priority to ecological protection, farms, homes, schools, roads, parks, public buildings, or whatever investment would maximize that society's well-being.

Assuming they had access to voters through reserved TV channels as advocated in the next chapter and were elected to a single 10-to-12 year term, regional directors could be freed of political pressures. These directors could oversee their region's financial rights, while local directors could oversee state, county, and community funding rights. A national director should be little more than an umpire overseeing the equitable sharing of the nation's finance capital as outlined in law or, better yet, the Constitution. If those rights of access to capital were coupled with the elimination of unnecessary labor, with the remaining productive jobs shared, and if equally-productive work were equally paid, there would be equality relative to one's ability and energy expended.

Consumer credit (within limits) should be a right instantly available, just as it has been pioneered by computerized credit cards. Using infrared thermogram palm images, artery, vein, eye pattern, and thumb print and signature scanning (procedures now in use), along with a credit check, the risk will be small. Each person's right to credit would be tempered by being subject to standards much as they are now, and the local credit union—now an integrated member of the banking system operating as one bank—would be in a position to know a member's creditworthiness. Local bankers should best know the needs of society and the creditworthiness of those who borrow to build and produce for that society. If not, they should not be bankers.

The economies of all prosperous nations are dynamic due to the hopes and dreams of its citizens. These hopes are the motivation for the millions of small businesses springing up. The economic health of a nation requires that those with ideas, talents, and energy have access to finance capital. With rights to credit, a nation's talented can bring together land, labor, capital, and technology at the right time and in the right place to fulfill society's needs. If there is a shortage of finance capital for productive use, and the resources are available and can be used without destroying the environment, a nation's treasury can quickly create the money to increase the reserves of the private banking system.

Only individuals operating under free enterprise and competition can develop the millions of ideas necessary for the progress of science, industry, and society. In order for citizens to fulfill these visions and provide their special expertise, it is necessary that they have access to credit. With entrepreneurs having rights to finance capital and banking personnel trained to be generous, yet careful, innovation in production by business and industry (productive speculation) would be unhampered.

Credit is now rationed by the simple method of checking track records, and lending up to a certain percentage of the borrower's equity—a great rule for monopolists. "Loans are made in a very impersonal way—

everything depends on 'track record,' and if you don't have a 'track record' [or equity], as most young people do not—you can forget it."[32] Access to investment capital should be a right based on productive merit as well as collateralized equity. Thus credit for productive people in their first ventures would be easier to obtain. With employees of the banking authority trained to be alert to productive investment requests, these loans would be quite simple. When a loan request was received, an evaluation would be made of its potential productive and financial success. If it looked reasonable, the loan would be approved. This is precisely how loans in America were made for the first 15-to-20 years after WWII. After the boom years were over, banks reverted to primarily loans against equity.

With the elimination of capitalized values in land, monopolized capital, and "fictitious capital" under *democratic-cooperative-capitalism* there will not be these artificial values against which to lend. But neither will money capital be needed to purchase these fictitious values. Smaller loans will be backed by a smaller, but more secure, true value. A loan would, of course, require financial accountability by the borrower just as it does now.

With initial capital promised from the regional capital accumulation fund, an entrepreneur could issue stock for the rest of his or her financial needs and this primary bank loan would be secure. With elimination of subtle communication monopolies (addressed next), those who buy this stock will be investing risk capital directly into production rather than having to go through finance monopolies that will claim most of the physical and intellectual labors involved in the endeavor.

It is not necessary to lend strictly to owners who would then hire workers. Those with insight need only prepare a prospectus describing the product or service, market potential, profit expected, financial requirement, and labor needs. The loan institution would study the proposal and—assuming the ideas were sound and beneficial to the community—would approve the loan. Workers would study the prospectus, and agree to 10-to-20% of their wages being deducted to buy 60 to 80% of the stock.

With workers owning a share of an industry and a share of their wages being used to pay off the loan as we have suggested earlier, the owners of this capital would be true producers. Society would receive useful products or services and the nation's savers and national treasury would be fully paid for their finance capital.

With these triple benefits to society, bankers should be taught to pay close attention to requests for investment credits; they are the sinews of capitalism. Most workers would stay on the job, but, once the new business was secure and their new stock had capitalized value, the talented ones would search out another prospectus, help develop another business, train more workers, gain more capitalized value, and move on again. Labor would be both mobile and highly productive just as capital is now and the most productive of those workers would be the accumulators of capital.

This would be mobilization of labor without the dispossession that has been so typical of past capitalization processes. Labor would have the same rights to gains in efficiencies of technology as investors now have. The talented would be in high demand by the developers of industry.

Besides collateral protection, there are three flows of money that make those loans secure—landrent, profits, and a share of wages. Society's collection of landrent could, and should, permit it to accept a larger share of the risks of new entrepreneurs. Every success increases the use-value, and thus the rental value, of that land. The risk of uncollateralized investment loans could also be offset by a surcharge on the interest to go into an insurance fund. With these restructured borrowing rights, many more people would qualify for investment capital than under equity loans. If successful, they and their workers would, through the shares purchased, own that capital honestly, as opposed to the current custom of capitalizing values through subtle monopolization of social wealth.

Those searching for a higher return—and confident they have found good investments—could directly employ their capital. Those with the opportunity to lend their savings at a higher rate would be free to do so. But they could no longer obtain high profits by simple tribute for the use of subtly monopolized capital. Those who once bid for money market funds would now have to compete for loans on their projects' productive merits. This would eliminate pure speculation with social funds while retaining that right with personal funds.

Once restructured, a society will have to address the increased efficiencies and technology's massive reduction of labor needs. They must then reduce labor time and share the productive jobs. If this is not done, new monopolizers will emerge.

A socially-owned capital accumulation fund within a modern financial commons will eliminate the centers of power created through monopoly capital accumulation which have historically controlled governments and maintained the worldwide wealth-siphoning system and its inevitable wars.

Japan operated just such a capital accumulation fund and utilized it with a vengeance to reach its current position on world trade. We do not suggest a nation's international trade capital accumulation fund be that aggressive but it would be great protection against others' predatory trade practices.

(The subchapters "If Society Collected Landrent, All Other Taxes Could Be Eliminated," "Creation of Money" [this chapter] and "Investment and job Opportunities" [Chapter 27] support this subchapter.)

Negative Interest

Throughout the expansion and stable stages of business cycles, most property and business owners clearly recognized that a steady inflation rate increased their property values faster than the interest costs on money borrowed. Entrepreneurs recognized that this negative interest carried them through the early tough years until their business matured and this had a lot to do with establishing a productive economy.

Where slightly negative interest rates were the rule during the early and middle stages of an economic cycle, supernegative interest rates were the rule in bubble phases of economic cycles. When those bubbles collapsed, loans then carried superpositive interest rates with all the destructive forces a theoretician would expect.

Negative interest can function well on the investment side of the ledger of an economy but not on the savings side as promoted by classic negative interest theorists. Money saved is properly only a symbol for produced wealth. In a modern economy, where capital accumulation depends upon the individual savings of millions of people, there would be inadequate investment money if savings decreased in value each year as promoted by classic negative interest theorists.[a]

The Simplicity of Paying Taxes through Taxing the Circulation of Money

In countries where a landrent tax is not feasible due to the political power of property owners, there is another option for eliminating inequitable taxes and improving the efficiency of economies. In both 1988 and 1998 a *transaction tax* on the circulation of money (a user fee) was proposed to the American congress which sent it to the Congressional Research Service of the Library of Congress for study where it was found it quite feasible. A tax of only 1/20 of 1% (.0005) upon the $550-trillion that passed through America's Federal Reserve in 1998 would have brought in more than the $2.3-trillion collected by both Federal and State taxes that year. Not only would this have relieved every citizen of personally paying those taxes, it would have relieved each one of many days work of keeping those records, of all the money paid to tax accountants and attorneys, of the cost of all tax cases in the courts, of the cost of legislative battles over tax law, and on and on. Certainly millions of lawyers, accountants, judges, federal and state lobbyists, all the secretaries and support workers, those who maintain those offices and furnish their supplies and all those people will have to find productive work. But that is a saving to every productively employed person and is just what creating an efficient economy is all about.[b]

---

[a] We are fully aware that this is not the classical interpretation of negative interest. But we feel the classical interpretation fails when it comes to savings while this interpretation remains valid.

[b] This paragraph supports our previous work, J.W. Smith, *The World's Wasted Wealth: Save Our Wealth and Save Our Environment*, (www.ied.info/cc.html: The Institute for Economic Democracy, 1994) and *Cooperative Capitalism: A Blueprint for Global Peace and Prosperity* (www.ied.info/cc.html. The Institute for Economic Democracy, 2003) outlines how 50% of

Money: A Measure of Productive Labor Value

Citizens judge the value of most commodities by imperfect memory and comparison. Witness our exposure in the next chapter of unnecessary costs built into the price of products and services. Our earlier research, documenting distribution through unnecessary labor, outlines even greater unnecessary costs.[33] Using money to contract only for productive employment would give a true measure of labor value to every product and service. It is the responsibility of the leaders of society to maintain an honest relationship between the compensation paid capital and labor to produce and distribute commodities and services, and the price charged the consumer.

This philosophy—first proposed by the founders of free-enterprise philosophy, the French Physiocrats—can become reality only by eliminating the unearned share of income from private landrent, monopolized technology, fictitious capital, and fictitious wages. All inflate costs and siphon to non-producers the wealth created by truly productive labor. This does not limit a person's right to contract out his or her labor, or to contract for others' labor. It eliminates the nonproductive element of contracts siphoning away the labor of others. If the labor value of wealth is protected from inflated fictional values, the value of the symbol of wealth (money) will be stable. The public will then much more accurately judge values and society will function efficiently and equitably.

With proper control of society's money we could have full employment, stable prices, low interest rates, and stable exchange rates. If this could be managed, there would be no inflation, deflation, recessions, or depressions (except from natural disasters or war). How to achieve a peaceful and just society is no secret; what is required simply conflicts with the privileges of powerful people.

Again, the most important aspect of regaining rights to a modern money commons is that private ownership is retained, yet subtle money monopolists disappear, and the wealth created by the efficiencies of money (not that created by labor and capital [stored labor]) is—through working less for a higher standard of living—instantly and without cost distributed to all. Distribution of wealth would be through fully productive labor and fully productive capital. Full and equal rights under *democratic-cooperative-capitalism* means none would be in poverty.

The economic efficiency gains for society through elimination of subtle monopolization and establishing a modern land, technology, and financial

---

all work in America is unnecessary except as a system of distribution. Tax lawyer John A. Newman proposed this transaction tax on the circulation of money to the American Congress in 1988 and Paul Bottis (*http://www.taxmoney-notpeople.com* and *http://www.madashellclub.com*) is continually proposing it to the those legislators today.

commons would equal the invention of money, the printing press, and electricity. Under that reclaiming of the modern commons under *democratic-cooperative-capitalism* a quality lifestyle is possible working only 2-to-3 days per week.

The efficiencies of subtle-monopoly capitalism we have heard about for generations are fictions protecting the monopolization of wealth and power. It is the arteries of commerce running through these unproductive subtle monopolies and the battles over monopolization of resources and the *wealth-producing-process* that wastes enormous amounts of labor, resources, and capital. Many are forced to the margins of the flow of commerce and some are excluded altogether.

The expansion of full private property rights, individualism, and competition to all people under *democratic-cooperative-capitalism* brings all within the economic system, eliminates that waste, and creates an efficient, productive, peaceful society. With work time halved and free time doubled, the arts (music, sculptors, painting, singing, et al.) will expand exponentially.

Notes

1 William F. Hixson, *It's Your Money* (Toronto, Canada: COMER, 1997); T. R. Thoren, R. F. Warner, *The Truth in Money Book* (Chagrin
Falls, Ohio : *Truth in Money*, 1994).

2 Joel Kurtzman, *The Death of Money* (New York: Simon and Schuster, 1993), p. 11.

3 William Greider, *Secrets of the Temple* (New York: Simon and Schuster, 1987), p. 335.

4 John Kenneth Galbraith, *Money* (Boston: Houghton Mifflin, 1976), pp. 62-70.

5 Ibid, pp. 167-78; Greider, *Secrets of the Temple*, pp. 228, 282.

6 *Philip S. Foner, From Colonial Times to the Founding of the American Federation of Labor (New York: International Publishers, 1947), p. 67.*

7 *S. P. Breckinridge, Legal Tender (New York: Greenwood Press, 1969), Chapter 7; Galbraith, Money, pp. 72-75.*

8 *Carl Cohen, Editor, Communism, Fascism, Democracy (New York: Random House, 1962), pp. 13-14; Paul Kennedy, The Rise and Fall of Great Powers (New York: Random House, 1987), p. 53.*

9 *Galbraith,* Money, *pp. 18-19.*

10 *Paul Kennedy,* The Rise and Fall of the Great Powers. *New York: Random House, 1987,p. 53.*

11 J.W. Smith, *The World's Wasted Wealth 2* (www.ied.info/cc.html: Institute for Economic Democracy, 1994).

12 E.K. Hunt, Howard J. Sherman, *Economics* (New York: Harper and Row, 1990), pp. 491-93, 505-508.

13 Thoren and Warner, *Truth in Money,* pp. 120-24.

14 William F. Hixson, Triumph of the Bankers: Money and Banking in the Eighteenth and Nineteenth Centuries (Westport, Conn: Praeger, 1993), Chapter 23; Hixon, It's Your Money, Chapter 5.

15 Hixon, *It's Your Money*, Chapters 5, 6.

16 Ibid

17 Greider, *Secrets of the Temple*, pp. 61-62.

18 Hixson, *It's Your Money,* Chapters 5, 6.

19 Greider, "Annals of Finance," *The New Yorker,* November 16, 1987, pp. 72, 78, emphasis added.

20 Ibid, pp. 72, 78.

21 George Tucker, *The Theory of Money and Banks Investigated* (New York: Greenwood Press, 1968), pp. 219, 255.

---

[22] Michael Moffitt, *The World's Money* (New York: Simon and Schuster, 1983) p. 197; John H. Makin, *The Global Debt Crisis* (New York: Basic Books, 1984), p. 162.

[23] Greider, *Secrets of the Temple*, p. 630; Christian Miller, "Wall Street's Fondest Dream: The Insanity of Privatizing Social Security," *Dollars and Sense*, November/December 1998, pp. 30-35; Edward S. Herman, "The Assault on Social Security," *Z Magazine*, November 1995, pp. 30-35; Bernstein, Merton C., Joan Brodshaug Bernstein, Social Security: The System that Works (New York: Basic Books, 1988).

[24] Ralph Borsodi, *Inflation* (E. F. Schumacher Society, Box 76 RD 3, Great Barrington, MA 01230, 1989). See also Irving Fisher's work in the 1930s; Arjun Makhijani, *From Global Capitalism to Economic Justice* (New York: Apex Press, 1992), pp. 121-27, appendix; Michael Barratt Brown, *Fair Trade* (London: Zed Books, 1993), especially pp. 53-63, 150; Kurtzman, *Death of Money*, p. 236.

[25] Borsodi, *Inflation*, p. 73.

[26] Ibid, p. 8.

[27] Ibid.

[28] Brown, *Fair Trade*, especially pp. 53-63, 150.

[29] William Greider, "The Money Question," *World Policy Journal* (Fall, 1988), p. 608.

[30] Brown, Fair Trade, p. 56.

[31] Julian Schuman, *China: An Uncensored Look* (Sagaponack, NY: Second Chance Press, 1979), pp. 49-50, 160.

[32] Robert Swann, *The Need for Local Currencies* (Great Barrington, MA, E.F. Schumacher Society, 1990), p. 6.

[33] Smith, The World's Wasted Wealth 2.

27. A Modern Information Commons

The technology is at hand to educate a population for as little as 5-to-15% of what is considered normal today. Here the Developing World has the opportunity to make an end run around wealthy nations. Restructuring in the developed world is prevented because information is monopolized by the financial power of the three primary subtle monopolies, land, technology, and finance capital. To open the channels of communication to the masses as suggested herein is to open the door for the slight legal changes necessary for emerging nations to avoid those monopolies.

Control of information controls people (albeit without their realization), which in turn protects these subtle monopolies. This process ensures that the distribution of wealth will remain in the same channels going to approximately the same people. Wealth will circulate among a predetermined group of people as they each intercept a part of social production. These *social-control-paradigms* are kept firmly in place through subtle monopolization of the communications industry. And it requires no conspiracy. Each one does just what you or I would do: they fiercely protect the source of their livelihood and their opportunities to gain wealth.

The Television Industry's Capitalized Value

Commercial television makes so much money doing its worst, it can't afford to do its best.

—Harry F. Waters and Janet Huck, "*The Future of Television*"

Communication is considered cheap. Yet it is possible to make long-distance contacts for a fraction of current costs. By 1967, scientists had determined they could build a satellite powerful enough to broadcast directly to home television sets. This satellite would simultaneously handle transoceanic phone calls for about a penny a minute and slightly higher phone call charges would easily cover the cost of TV satellite transmissions.[1] However, *U.S. News & World Report* predicted at the time that, "The big decision will be made by statesmen and politicians, not by scientists."[2] This was prophetic. By 2002, the total communications traffic of America was handled on less than 5% of the installed, privately owned, fiber-optic/satellite communication system.

The enormous waste of industrial capital is obvious. With hundreds of TV channels available to every home piggybacking on telephone satellites, and assuming the pennies per person were paid for by all society under a modern communication commons, monopolization of the TV broadcast spectra will be eliminated. Of course, democratic access to the masses over cheap airways for any group who could build a broadcasting station at a cost of a few-hundred-thousand-dollars was not acceptable to the powerful who controlled the communications airways. Those few hundred thousand dollars in tangible construction costs per station would be converted to hundreds of millions of dollars of capitalized value if monopolized.

Politicians were influenced not only by owners of regional broadcasting and cable television stations, but by major corporations who wanted to manipulate consumers' buying choices. These interests were so successfully protected that direct broadcast never became a reality until signal scrambling/unscrambling technology maintaining the established monopolies was developed.[3]

In 1973, "television stations in major markets earn[ed] 90-to 100-percent return[s] on tangible investments annually."[4] A TV station in Tampa, Florida, which had been bought in 1979 for an already inflated $17.6-million, sold six years later for $197.5-million. The average price of all TV stations doubled between 1982 and 1984, yet one year later they were still earning 40-to-60% profits. In major markets, a typical station and license worth $10-million in 1959 was worth $400 to $500-million by 1987.[5]

The true dimension of this interception of wealth through not-so-subtly monopolized technology can be gauged by "one major-market PBS broadcasting station ... cost[ing] $1.5-million" in 1987.[6] That $1.5-million actual construction cost as opposed to the $400-million to $500-million capitalized value the market placed on these stations accurately measures the fictitious capital and its interception of the production of others' labor. The conservative periodical *U.S. News & World Report* recognized this when they headlined:

> Who Will Control TV? This Battle Has It All—Power, Money, Politics. On the Outcome Rides the Future of America's Most Pervasive Medium and the Programs It Brings into Homes.... Wall Street has discovered that ownership of TV stations is tantamount to running a money machine that churns out profits in good times and bad.[7]

The Public paid for Satellite Development

The American public paid for satellite development, and corporate ownership of this technology, is corporate socialism at its best. During the 1950s and 1960s, the U.S. public paid $24-billion (about $300-billion in inflated 2003 dollars) to develop satellite communications.[8] The cost of building and launching the first satellites was less than $100-million each or under $1.9-billion for the 19 satellites in use in 1989. There were then about 900 television stations in the United States. Given that $1.5-million would establish a PBS station in a metropolitan area, and allowing a generous initial cost of $5-million per station, the total tangible costs of the 900 TV stations then in use would be $4.5-billion. The entire system in use in 1989 could have been constructed for $6.4-billion. That is about $52 per U.S. family, a 3% addition to the $160-billion they had already paid.

For an understanding of the U.S. communication overcapacity, consider the Syncom satellite, designed by Hughes Aircraft Company in 1961, alone could "handle twenty-two times the [then] existing volume of long-distance telephone service in the United States."[9] By 1998, far more powerful multipurpose satellites with total capacity of many times any anticipated use were being launched, several hundred commercial communications satellites were in orbit, and 1,554 commercial and educational TV stations were licensed for use.

The rapid increase in technological efficiency multiplied the capacity of the communications systems. The changeover from analog to digital signals multiplied communications capacity several times over with relatively little investment.[10] Then technological breakthroughs squeezed a further 10-times the bandwidths used by these communications satellites. This was the foundation of the much-discussed gift when these added spectra were essentially given to communication corporations in 1998. Not only were there far more bandwidths available than necessary, each TV station was then able to split its assigned spectrum into six channels.

Thus, with minimal investment, technological breakthroughs provided a capacity gain of 100-times or more on the already orbiting satellites. The latest fiber-optic lines have a capacity 4-million-times the old copper lines. If there were enough traffic to use this capacity, the value of those systems would be multiplied many times their already obscene capitalized values with almost no investment. Communication charges are dropping rapidly but, due to those technology advances, less than 5% of current capacity is utilized and it is paying for that overcapacity that prevents costs from dropping even further. Established as a modern communication commons, it is actually possible for a nation, or the world, to establish a communications system where everyone can talk to anyone anywhere in the world for the penny per minute first calculated.

A Totally Integrated Communications System

Using local computerized switching terminals, each servicing several city blocks, these fiber-optic lines are capable of transmitting those hundreds of TV channels described above and phone service to every properly wired home. Where homes are widely separated, those same channels can be received by direct broadcast. Upon electronic command from a home TV set, any channel on any satellite can be instantly routed to that home.

It is estimated that replacing the old copper lines and switching equipment to fiber-optic lines and computerized switching systems cost about $1,000 per business and home. The United States has about 100-million of these consumer communications terminals replacing telephones, at a cost of about $120-billion.[11] The immense capacity of satellite communication for long-distance, point-to-point, and point-to-multipoint communications, and the equally large capacity of fiber-optics for point-to-point and local service (under 400 miles), can be combined with compatible computerized telephones, personal computers, software, database supercomputers, laser recorders, and high-resolution picture tubes to form a totally integrated communications system.[a]

With this technology, communication is practically instantaneous. Information is stored in databank computers and, when specific information is requested, it is sent out with an automatically encoded route code. This "packet switch" (the almost instantaneously transmitted information signal) can find its way in split seconds through many switching terminals, satellites, and trunk lines to a requesting communications terminal where it can be stored in an electronic buffer of a computerized telephone, laser recorder, or computer.

With fully compatible computers and software and all producers having access to technology, the above home equipment and databanks should have cost the United States possibly another $250-billion. A totally integrated communications system within a modern communication commons should have cost Americans about $370-billion. However, in the battle for market share under subtly-monopolized technology, several times this amount has been spent. A communication commons within *democratic-cooperative-capitalism* would be fully operational with less than 10% the investment of the current subtle-monopoly system.

Though this equipment may be expensive initially, it has such a large capacity that even long distance will be inexpensive per unit of information transferred. This will create great savings in other segments of the economy—predominantly in distribution, as here the major costs are in obtaining information. Only if this technology is monopolized will it be beyond the reach of the ordinary person.

A communications system designed to care for all citizens' needs, used in common, and operated by a publicly mandated authority would be even more accessible than highways. Such easily accessible communications lines would permit consumers to bypass the intermediaries currently claiming the production of their labors. But those people must live too. The only way

[a] To calculate the cost today, so long as inflation continues, double these figures every 10 years.

economies can avoid enormous waste in distribution (or an economic collapse) is to share the remaining productive jobs.[a]

Communication eliminates Intermediaries and reduces Trading Costs

Thorstein Veblen's and Stuart Chase's estimation[12] that labor in the retail industry in the 1920s could be reduced over 50% is being proven by Wal-Mart Stores. It is establishing superstores 10-to-30 miles apart, buying directly from manufacturers, and distributing directly to those superstores. As Wal-Mart sells consumer products for less than individual stores can purchase them, small-town retail stores are closing down all over America.[13] As efficient as Wal-Mart appears, using modern communications technology to bypass retailers altogether for moderate to higher-priced items offers even greater savings.

The difference between manufacturing cost and the consumer price measures the major cost of most products—distribution. Typically, manufacturing costs are under 20% of the final selling price of a consumer product.[14] With mail-order shipping charges from 2-to-5% of retail price, no one would pay intermediaries 3-to-5-times the production cost if it were feasible to study the products on the Internet, contact the producer, buy the item, and have it shipped directly. With today's communications system, one need only transport oneself to and from one's job (or perform that job right at home on a computer and over phone lines) to produce one's share of the nation's wealth and then search for, and order electronically, one's share of what others produce. This would substantially reduce the 1.9 people distributing for every one currently producing.

Shopping requires information and middlemen are primarily in the information business. With an integrated communications system employing the latest technology, it would be possible for producers and consumers to trade directly and cheaply again, just as those first trade's did thousands of years ago. The subtle monopolization of distribution, now exploited by an army of intermediaries, would be largely eliminated.

Dell Computers pioneering this sales technique for computers forced others to do the same. Trades over the Internet, directly between the manufacturer and consumer increased 80% a year up to 1998 to 3% of all sales and exceeds 6% today. Those sales increases will continue to expand and direct trades for middle-priced to expensive items will be the norm by the first quarter to the middle of this Century.

---

[a] J.W. Smith, *The World's Wasted Wealth: Save Our Wealth, Save Our Environment* (www.ied.info/cc.html, The Institute for Economic Democracy, 1994) and *Cooperative Capitalism: A Blueprint for Global Peace and Prosperity* (www.ied.info/cc.html. The Institute for Economic Democracy, 2003.) addresses how it is already possible to reduce the workweek by 50% or more.

Currently America has 10 square feet of retail floor space for each shopper and, with four stores opening for each one being closed, they are headed towards 12 square feet. For comparison, Britain has only two square feet per shopper. That surplus retail floor space can only mean higher costs even as Internet shopping is rapidly lowering costs to a fraction of the current costs. A great shakeout of the retail industry will take place.

The savings to the developing world through establishing direct trades between consumer and producer will be enormous. The buildings and support infrastructure for at least 30% and possibly 60% of what the developed world considers necessary for distribution do not have to be built.

Bill Gates, who accumulated $60-billion (April 1999) because he understood communications technology better than most, said, "The information highway isn't quite right. A metaphor that comes closer to describing a lot of the activities that will take place is the ultimate market."[15] This chapter is an outline of that "ultimate market."

Big-ticket, Infrequently-Purchased Items

Autos, appliances, furniture, farm equipment, industrial equipment, and major tools are all big-ticket, infrequently-purchased items whose buying requires accurate information but not the promotional/persuasive advertising that hammers at us incessantly. We trust and get information from direct experience and we make the most important decisions by observing products in daily use. In a modern communications commons, customers would make purchase decisions by dialing an index of different manufacturers of the particular product in which they are interested.

This index would have basic information about all the manufacturers of that product required to make an informed decision—energy efficiency, noise level, hours of useful life, price, and other features. (Note the pressure this would put on manufacturers to make the most efficient products and stand out in this all-important master index.) From this master index, the consumer would choose brands and models from moving pictures of that item in use. A computerized telephone would dial the product databank, request the information, and receive it in an audio-video electronic buffer, laser recorder, or computer—all in seconds.

Buyers would, at their leisure, study engineering specifications, styling, and actual use of the product on their television or computer. Once a decision was made, they would only need to punch in the code for the desired order—model, color, and accessories—and a databank computer would instantly note the closest distribution point where that item was available. If one was not available at a distribution center close by, buyers would choose delivery from the factory.

The bank account number, thumbprint, eye-scan, thermogram palm images, and signature of an Internet shopper would be verified by a master computer and that account instantly debited. If a credit line had been established at the local credit union or bank and recorded in an integrated computer, credit needs would be handled simultaneously. The entire process need not involve advertising, sales, or banking labor, and would greatly reduce storage and transportation labor.

Product guarantees, maintenance, and repairs would be taken care of by local private enterprise under standardized guarantees. The secret of successful direct trades between manufacturer and consumer over the Internet, and the resultant elimination of distribution intermediaries, will be guaranteed high-quality products.

From the initial information request to the completion of a trade, the communication arteries would only be in use for a few seconds. There would be tens of thousands of simultaneous communications. Both seller and buyer would save time and labor, as verbal explanations and mailing of information are largely eliminated. The current time-consuming exchange of information would be handled in split seconds.

This automatic and instantaneous transfer of massive amounts of information would mean an infinitesimal labor and capital cost per communication. This would conserve millions of acres of trees and eliminate tens of thousands of jobs currently manufacturing paper, producing brochures, and distributing that information, including salespersons and a large percent of the labor servicing and maintaining retail establishments as well as the retail establishments themselves.

Every qualified producer would enjoy the right to place his or her product or service in the databank and pay the charges (a percentage of gross sales) out of cash flow. In place of millions of dollars up front to advertise through the present openly monopolized newspaper, radio, and TV system, there would be only a small charge for entering the product information in a retail database computer. To eliminate clogging the databanks with useless information of producers no longer in business, regular payments would be required to retain the privilege of selling through this integrated communications network.

This would break the subtle monopolization of our production and distribution system by wealthy corporations. Currently only those with large financial backing can pay the monopoly charges of the media and gain access to the public; all others are financially excluded. Starting up a truly productive industry would become quite simple. A new company's advertising would have full billing alongside that of major entrenched producers. A few wealthy corporations would no longer decide, through promotional/persuasive advertising, what the public wants or what is good for them. Consumers would have easy access to all choices.

Several large corporations have established just such databanks. They are, however, individual databanks for each corporation without that all-important master index used in common and thus are an extension of monopolization.[16] Without that master index, individual databases will be relatively hard to find and that one crucial aspect, the ability to compare, would be lost. Harbor freight's 80% price reduction on moderate-priced and high-priced tools (addressed on page 204) proves this consumer product price reduction in a modern commons is possible.

Inexpensive, Small, Frequently-Traded Items

The markup on perishable groceries is about 100% while the markup on small nonperishable consumer durables is several hundred percent. There is a competitive sales monopoly at work in the latter. Taking full advantage of modern communications would remove all purchases above an intermediate price range out of the wasteful, duplicated retail outlets. Simultaneously, the consumers' choices would be increased by access to these products through databanks.

If traded directly between distant producers and consumers, individual shipping and handling costs would be too high for most small, frequently purchased items. Thus groceries, household supplies, cosmetics, knickknacks and most small, inexpensive consumer items would be most efficiently distributed through the present retail outlets. The breakeven point would be in the lower range of the intermediate-priced occasionally purchased items.

Even now companies in Japan are attempting to establish computer grocery shopping. "A housewife can switch on her personal computer and scan the list of goods available for sale.... The order will be delivered strictly on time."[17]

Offices at home are a continually expanding phenomenon. This reduces traffic and requires fewer expensive buildings on valuable land. Such plans are in line with our suggestions and the savings are quite apparent.

Wholesalers of small-ticket consumer items would keep the quality and price of all products posted in a databank computer. Purchasing agents would periodically analyze this information. Once initial trust had been established, a retailer would check those updated bulletin boards for the best buys. This would eliminate the need for many jobbers and other salespeople.

Shopping as a Social Event entails a Cost

Shopping is recreation for many people and a status symbol for others. Direct communication between producers and consumers would change society's psychological profile. If enough people decided they wished to do their shopping socially and expensively, that would be their choice. They would have no trouble finding merchants to accommodate them. To compensate for the additional labor, the products would cost more. The added unit costs would be properly accounted for under socializing and recreation (like Tupperware or Avon), or social status (like Tiffanys). The majority would surely choose to save their money by using the most direct and least labor-intensive (cheapest) method of completing a trade. As direct trades would be only for intermediate to big-ticket items, this would in no way impinge on local coffeehouse-type trades where socializing is the primary activity.

A Modern Communications Commons Doubling Distribution Efficiency

When a manufacturer produces a product, it is normally ready to use, and customers already understand the use for which it was designed. All that is missing for potential consumers is complete information on where the best quality product is available at the lowest possible price. In the United States, once direct contact is established between producer and consumer, it would only require roughly 100,000 railroaders, possibly 1-million truckers (down from 1991's 1.3-million), and a system of organized freight terminals to distribute the nation's production. It would be quite simply a freight postal system just as with Christmas packages today. The item would be delivered just as United Parcel Service or the Post Office does today or consumers would receive notices of the arrivals of their purchases and pick them up at the local freight terminal.

As it requires a central dispatching office, most truck freight is handled by moderate to large trucking companies. They may either own all their trucks or sublease from independent truckers who own and drive their own rigs. There are normally several trucking companies in any moderate-size city, each complete with loading docks, storage capacity, dispatching equipment, and staff.

Even without an efficient modern communications commons in place, the following shipping pattern is forming:

(1) Shippers are punching into their communications terminal the information on loads to be shipped;

(2) independent truckers with laptop computers are dialing a computer programmed for dispatching all loads;

(3) the trucker punches in his or her location and freight preferences and where he or she would like to deliver the next load;

(4) the computer instantly shows where the loads are, the type of freight, the required pickup and delivery times, the rate per mile, et al.;

(5) the trucker chooses a load, informs the computer, and records his or her identification number;

(6) and the computer records the acceptance, removes that load from the databank, provides a contract number to the trucker, and informs the shipper.

Minimal dispatching costs will eventually reduce freight charges, recording and billing are handled automatically by computer and only a few intermediaries are necessary. There is no need for duplicated dispatching services, loading docks, storage facilities, equipment, and personnel. This does not restrict any trucker or company from signing contracts outside the national computerized dispatching system. It does, however, break the competitive monopoly created by the minimum capital requirements for a trucking company. Each independent trucker is on an equal footing with corporate trucking companies.

When producers and consumers trade through a communications commons operated by public authority, just as they now transport over publicly maintained transportation commons, costs drop precipitously. The competitive monopolies of retail outlets for intermediate-to high-priced products will eventually be eliminated. The nation's freight will quickly settle into flow patterns and be moved as regularly as mail by the cheapest combination of rail, truck, ship, and plane.

It might take a consumer from one day (small items) to a week (large items) to receive a purchase, but, at possibly 1/2 the price, they are well paid for this wait. The actual transit time of products between producer and consumer would be a fraction of that currently taken through jobbers, wholesalers and retailers.

Manufacturers' on-time delivery of parts to the factory that greatly reduces storage and finance capital costs will have been expanded to on-time shipping to consumers. Instead of time spent in warehouses and retail stores, the products are immediately packaged and addressed and go directly from the factory to the truck which takes it to a distribution point near the customer. Local delivery will deliver to the home or office. On-time delivery of finished products would eliminate most wholesale storage and retail buildings, as well as use of heat, electricity, inventory, stocking clerks, sales clerks, maintenance workers, building repairs, security, and so on.

Those within the retail system who formerly bought, stored, and sold these products are available to engage in productive labor. Society will eventually attain an undreamed-of efficiency. Over 50% of these intermediaries between producer and consumer will eventually be eliminated and, assuming society was alert and restructured labor's working hours, all would be free to share the remaining productive work and each need work only 2-to-3 days per week.

The present communications infrastructure is already capable of handling this long-distance information transmission and the distribution efficiency we are discussing requires only the establishment of databanks for public use, just as we now use highways. The only way this can happen without a total collapse of economies is if fully-productive jobs are shared equally so as to expand buying power in step with increased productive capacity.

If the world's citizens had equality and opportunity instead of daily battles for survival feeding on the fringes of these massive subtle monopolies, family trauma would decline rapidly, fewer children would be abused and neglected, prisons would shrink, more than 80% of the insurance industry would disappear even as society was better insured, the medical and law industries would shrink to a fraction of their present size even as those needs were better cared for, the arts will expand rapidly to utilize the free time, other nations would produce their own food and developed world agriculture would shrink accordingly even as the world's citizens were more secure, equities markets would shrink to a tiny fraction of today's trades, the arms industry would disappear, and on and on. The world is far richer than we realize; currently much of our wealth is wasted. [a]

Once those productive jobs were shared, the average workweek reduced, and labor fully paid, the small amount of time necessary to labor for one's share of the nation's wealth would be the proper measure of the price of products and services. Our previous research concluded that an efficient economy using modern technology of production and distribution could reduce its labor time by well over 50%.[18] That potential reduction in costs through elimination of unnecessary labor and fully paying labor is the meaning of Adam Smith's little-noticed insightful statement, "If produce had remained the natural wages of labor, all things would have become cheaper, though in appearance many things might have become dearer."

Trades should still pay for "Free" TV

As most families watch TV and all purchase products, the fairest source of funds is to collect them through consumer purchases, just as advertisers do now. Companies will have paid for advertising products or services through paying for listing on indexes and databases within society's integrated communications system. Producers using this service need only calculate the price markup necessary to cover a communications surcharge on gross revenues.

---

[a] These are the conclusions of *Cooperative Capitalism: A Blueprint for Global Peace and Prosperity*, this author's research on the inefficiency of the subtly-monopolized American economy.

There is such a surplus of communication channels to carry TV and phone conversations simultaneously that there would be little need for additional equipment. With the elimination of monopolization of the airwaves as described above, the TV transmission charges would be minimal, and most of the funds collected would go toward programming and entertainers. All producers would have access to every consumer. Impulse buying would be greatly reduced, creating more savings for society. When people wanted or needed something, they would buy it without being pressured.

Reserving TV Time for New Products

While innovations on a familiar product would be readily presented to the public through a databank, totally new products are expensive to market. Innovators would require special access to the public. To complement other methods of familiarization, some TV channels should be specifically reserved to promote such innovations. Novelty buffs comprise a large segment of the population, and there are few of us who do not have some interest. A program demonstrating these creations would be quite popular.

An undeveloped society needs promotional/persuasive advertising to alert a population to the standard of living possible with developed capital. There must be demand before the industries and distribution arteries can be established. However, once the production/distribution infrastructure is in place with society energized to produce and accustomed to that standard of living, promotional/persuasive advertising becomes wasteful. Rather than titillate the consumer with thousands of toys to be played with and discarded, it would be much more socially efficient to abandon promotional/persuasive advertising and permit people to advance to a higher intellectual, social, and cultural level.

The low cost of reaching the shopper through a databank gives society these opportunities The maximum average living standard within the capabilities of the earth's resources and ecosystem can be calculated. Society could, and should, use those proven promotional/persuasive methods to educate people about eliminating the waste of the current distribution systems. Shoppers would decide what products they want by observing them in use or scanning the databanks. Any item that is truly useful will become a common household item. There would be fewer nonessential products sold and those resources currently wasted on titillating toys would be diverted to producing for the world's needy. In short, just as many in the developed world have already abandoned the "conspicuous consumption" lifestyle, a rational lifestyle would be made popular. Once a rational lifestyle was established, peer pressure would tend to encourage it.

If people are so dull that a society with a respectable living standard cannot function without promotional/persuasive advertising (which we do not believe), society would analyze advertising for essential and nonessential products for the desired standard of living. After all, many items (cigarettes, alcohol, and chemical-laden processed foods) lower the quality of life, spending social funds on their promotion is economic insanity. Even when spent by private industry, advertising for cigarettes and alcohol are still social funds. Those costs are recovered in the sales price. The public pays the bill for the debasement of their lives.

The same holds true for nonessential, resource-consuming, and environment-polluting lifestyles. Driving a $60,000 automobile while others are driving $20,000 cars may draw admiration today, but if society were taught that this was at the expense of humankind's survival it would incur broad disapproval. The resources saved and pollution prevented by that refocused social mindset would be substantial, and essential to the survival of thousands of species, to humankind's quality of life, and most probably to our survival.

When radio first came on the scene, plans for public education were sidetracked by commercial interests. When cable television arrived with its potential for hundreds of channels, idealistic planners again tried to establish an education medium. Powerful interests again subverted the public interest and monopolized these valuable media for commercial interests. The chance for society to become truly informed was lost. When CBS's brilliant scientist, Peter Karl Goldmark, was proposing just such uses for TV as we are outlining, CBS was so worried about his plan that it offered him $75,000 a year to do nothing (which he turned down).[19]

Rather than being radical, the following suggestions are similar to the original plans for radio and cable television and are only one of the many ways these hundreds of TV channels could be organized.

Music, Sports, Movies, and Game Shows

Music, sports, movies, and game shows have an established market and draw large audiences. Fifteen to 20 channels should be reserved for each of these interests. Only pennies per viewer, paid painlessly through consumer purchases, would bring in millions per broadcast to the investors, stars, directors, managers, and support labor. There would be adequate channels to guarantee all promising entertainers the opportunity to present their shows for a probationary period. If successful, as shown by automatic computer recording of viewer interest, their shows would be made permanent.

With communication channels now open there would no longer be monopolization through high-priced promotion. With these equal rights, it would be talent that counted. There would be many more able people investing, designing, producing, and starring in many more shows. Along with more time to enjoy TV, viewer choices would rise, and the truly talented artists would be well paid for their efforts. All would have a reasonable opportunity to prove their abilities.

A formula of gradually reduced pay per million viewing hours as a show increased in popularity would compensate performers relative to their popularity, little different than now. If the industry were designed for access to the public for new performers, monopoly control of entertainment industries would disappear, along with the interception of others' labor that their substantial income represents.

Investment and Job Opportunities

Several TV channels should be reserved for direct communication between those offering investment opportunities and investors looking for those opportunities. As everyone with savings would have common access to this investment information stored in databanks, the subtle money monopolists would be totally bypassed. Individual investors would put their risk capital in innovations that went unrecognized by regular loan institutions. If the entrepreneurs' insights and talents were truly productive, investors would receive much higher than average returns. However, if their claims to insight were not valid, they would not be able to hide behind the protective shield of subtle monopolization.

An entrepreneur who had obtained community approval and initial investment capital from the bank (nothing new; they need both now) would deposit a prospectus in a databank. Investors would study the various investment plans, buy shares in the most promising ventures, and have their accounts automatically debited—all without intermediaries.

Talented workers would look over prospectuses, which would include labor needs and incentives, and, if they saw where their talents would be used productively and profitably (and assuming they had fulfilled their contract to train a replacement), they could transfer to that new job. Labor would be mobile and free (not dispossessed as in a reserve labor force), with rights to their share of the efficiency gains of technology. (in a modern industrial society, each worker would work only 2-to-3 days per week. See the work of Charles Fourier 180 years ago and Thorstein Veblen, Bertrand Russell, Lewis Mumford, Stuart Chase, Upton Sinclair, and Ralph Borsodi in the first half of the 20th-Century. Late-20th-Century writers describing the same phenomenon are Juliet Schor, Seymour Melman—Samuel Bowles, David Gordon, and Thomas Weiskopf—Jeremy Rifkin, Andre Gorz, Hans-Peter Martin and Harold Schumann, numerous European authors, and this author's *The World's Wasted Wealth 2* and *Cooperative Capitalism: A Blueprint for Global Peace and Prosperity*.)

If a replacement were not immediately available, other workers at the factory could double their pay by working four days a week, or triple it by working six days. Strict rules, however, would have to be followed. To permit doubling up on established jobs would appropriate the labor rights of others and subvert the entire economy. The unemployed would be denied their rights to a share of social production while those working excessive hours would have more than their share.

For their risk, the original innovators and investors would receive the initial higher profits plus the increased values of a successful company. Through sharing in the profits, workers and management who bought stock through deductions of 10-to-20% of their wages would be well compensated. The profit potential would maximize their desire to maximize efficiency and provide incentive to look for new industries to develop and again share in the profits.

Assuming society had eliminated subtle patent monopolies as discussed above, others would quickly analyze and duplicate the innovative production or distribution process; prices would fall to just that required to compensate the innovators, labor, and capital. Through low priced products, society would be well compensated. The reduction in the price of consumer products will match the lower income of fewer days work so wage rates would stay the same.

If a communications commons within *democratic-cooperative-capitalism* reduced production and distribution costs 60% and adequate compensation to the innovators was 10%, the public would quickly benefit by a 50% reduction in the price of consumer products. Through the reduced income of a shorter workweek matching the reduction in living costs there would be no loss in living standards. Societies which decided to forego a throwaway society and opt for fuel-cell-car/bicycle economy and other efficient transportation systems would provide a quality lifestyle with even less labor.

The subchapters "Creation of Money," and "Accumulation of Capital through *Democratic-Cooperative-Capitalism*" (Chapter 26) are integral to this subchapter.

Education

Since the desire to emulate is the basis of all learning, educating children can be quite simple. Children want the approval of their parents and other members of society. They love to excel and desire equality with their peers. They are curious and, if not discouraged, love to learn. The present educational system puts too many barriers in their way; "half of all gifted children float through school with average or worse grades, never realizing their potential ... almost 20 percent will drop out."[20]

There are many reasons: a child may be timid and terrified of school, an inferiority complex may prevent a student from functioning, or excessive pressure to do well may be daunting. The school district may have obsolete books and teaching aids; the school may be understaffed so students don't get the individual attention they need. Local peer groups (gangs) may replace parents and teachers as role models. Parents may not be involved enough in their child's learning. Or the curriculum may be so slow it is boring. With elimination of these and other barriers, many currently with low grades will blossom right along with their peers.

Schools are a commons but they need to be restructured to a modern commons.[a] With 40-to-60 TV channels reserved for education, every subject now taught at elementary, secondary, college, and university level would reach every home free of charge.[b] Each subject would have several teachers and be broadcast at various hours of the day. The competition would be intense for the teaching positions on such programs and, once picked, these best educators in the nation would be well paid. Each taped course would be edited for maximum clarity, simplicity, and comprehension. Reasoning is quite natural and nothing can beat a good educator whose taped lectures anticipate, and are carefully structured to answer, most questions. With all society having access, the fictions and omissions of history (especially omissions) would be challenged, researched, and corrected.

With their lessons on tape, these high-quality educators would be spending less time teaching than any one of the tens of thousands of teachers they replaced. They would concentrate on studying their own and others' lectures for ways to improve. Modeling is the most potent teacher of all and these great teachers would be great role models.

The minimum equipment required for each student would be a TV set, while the local education system would provide workbooks to match the TV lessons. As these lessons would be in a databank accessible through the integrated communications system, a VCR would also be desirable. With recorders and societal incentives, students would tape the lessons and study when they had the free time and were emotionally ready. They could replay the lessons as many times as necessary for maximum comprehension.

So long as a student maintained an adequate grade average, a share of the money society saved on maintaining the present school system could be paid to each child's family. Allowing, of course, for each child's ability, it would be logical to pay this incentive for each subject and on an average of all subjects. This would be high motivation for families to restructure their time for home education. With spending money earned for each subject, motivated students would zip through many subjects. Developing nations

---

[a] Workers in the developed world are tied to the enormously wasteful arteries of commerce of subtle-monopoly capitalism. Thus they cannot change. But, as addressed next, the developing world is not locked in and thus they have the opportunity to establish an efficient *democratic-cooperative-capitalism* and leapfrog the developed world.

[b] Representative Ron Wyden of Oregon and Senator Edward Kennedy introduced bills which "would require the dedication of an entire channel on the new public-TV satellite to instructional shows aimed at preschoolers and elementary-school children" (Miriam Horn, "Can the Boob Tube Finally Get Serious," *U.S. News & World Report,* August 24, 1992, p. 61).

do not have to deconstruct an entrenched, expensive educational system and their citizen's motivation for education is high so there would be no need for incentive pay. But they would have high incentive to utilize their current classrooms as administrative and testing stations and educate their populations, children and adults, through satellite television.

With the 2-to-3 day workweek possible in a developed country, there would be adequate time for parents to stay home and monitor their children's learning. With rapport between parent and child, intelligent children would cover a current year's education in as little as four months. The most intelligent and motivated would have the knowledge of Ph.D.s at an age when they would normally be in their middle university classes—which, incidentally, would eliminate another monopoly.

Actually those students would have a much broader education than most Ph.D.s. Currently most doctoral studies are very narrow in focus. Without breadth of education, the answers to the world's problems will not be found. Conversely, if universities emphasized graduate degrees that covered a broad spectrum of disciplines instead of narrow fields, answers would be found relatively quickly. Through free TV studies, students would have that broad education. This is proven by over 1-million American children already being successfully home schooled, doing well in universities, and their numbers are growing 15% a year, all without government support.[21]

Students would not be pressured to follow the teaching of any one professor. Other professors might have a different view on history or society and, if that student were really interested, he or she would listen to many views. Judgments would be made while still young and idealistic. All this would be gained while enjoying the irreplaceable quality time between parent and child. Some talented students who do not have parental support would find a surrogate family by immersing themselves in education.

Private or public day-care education centers would be operated for the few who could not function under, or who were unable to arrange for, home self-education. Those who were intellectually capable but who failed to maintain a minimum average would lose their incentive funds and would be required to attend these specially structured classes.

The compensations and identity received by siblings and friends for successful home schooling would be noticed by younger children and would provide motivation to avoid the formal school setting.

This is quite conservative. A first-grader would be proud to go shopping with earnings and it is hard to visualize many children being irresponsible toward their education if it meant losing both their freedom of choice and their spending money. They would quickly learn responsibility when it meant both financial and emotional rewards. Once in operation, society would quickly become accustomed to such a system and the need for brick and mortar schools would be minimal.

Children can be just as easily culturally trained to quality as they can to trash. All society would gain from more positive cultural training, so it would be logical to eliminate the senseless violence in today's children's programs. At the least, quality children's programs could be assigned a block of channels so conscientious parents could maximize their children's intellectual and moral growth.

Incentive funds, as a right, would in no way impinge on others' rights. Those rights could only be exercised by obtaining a set grade average. Citizens without children already pay taxes to support schools and home education would save society far more than the cost of these incentive funds. In fact, those funds cost nothing; they go right back to the people from whom they came. Over time, society would become accustomed to this and such incentives would be looked upon as normal as wages.

Older students would soon learn to structure their flexible education time around their job. There need not be a sharp cutoff between school years and entering the workforce. The options of both pursuing education for a career and earning one's living would be increased. Instead of a division between students and workers, the two would overlap until the young adults opted for a career.

Motivated children, youths, young adults, and adults would obtain most of their education at home and at their own pace. Curious children with a desire to learn, which is most of them, would find the field wide open. Left to their own devices, they would quickly learn that it was their time and labor that were being conserved by dedication and attention to the subjects being taught.

Many talented children's potential, now lost through boredom and diversion to socially undesirable activities, would be salvaged. The brightest would probably attain a 12th grade education in less than eight years, the middle level in 10, and with these motivations even the slower group, which currently sets the pace of a classroom, would learn more quickly. There would be adequate resources and time to give special support to those who are unable to cope for various reasons. This would not only conserve society's labor, it would economize students' energy and time. This potential was shown by an experiment with interactive videos that reduced learning time while increasing comprehension 30%.[22]

Having watched great videos on The Learning Channel, The History Channel, The Arts and Entertainment Channel, The Discovery Channel, public broadcasting channels, CNN, and an occasional program on other stations, we conclude that the statement, "A picture is worth a thousand words," should be changed to; "One documentary is worth a million words." The best of those documentaries combines the wisdom of many researchers developed by many lifetimes of study. All viewers will absorb that knowledge at some level. Avid reading will seldom bring one close to the understanding gained from a well-researched 1-hour documentary. The gain for the slower and less avid readers could only be of much greater dimension. As opposed to being bored and discouraged, students will enjoy their education.

A central testing facility would be maintained that would issue scholastic level certificates and incentive funds. These achievement tests would be designed to educate children to compete with the best in the world. This would quickly equip all nations to compete in world trade.[23] Since credentials are crucial for obtaining good jobs, all would have access to their scores, the right to analyze their wrong answers, and the right to retake tests.

Classes that require hands-on learning would be held in a classroom setting just as now, along with supporting taped programs. Millions who dreamed of additional education would find it freely available in what was previously their idle time.

As no one's knowledge is complete, every curriculum would be subject to review and correction. The Great Saint-Mihiel battle of WWI that never happened (see final chapter) and other examples of fraudulent history addressed throughout this book are not exceptions. Distorted history is the norm and such failures to tell the full truth seriously retards democratic development. Correct and full knowledge of such events is critical to society planning its future.

Every day we learn something new or reinforce what we already know. To waste huge amounts of resources and to inflict enormous violence, injustice, and poverty as we have been documenting—while continually affirming nice-sounding slogans about efficiency, justice, and compassion—seriously limits true knowledge. Redesigning society to produce and distribute efficiently would give children a better cultural education. Likewise with the centuries of proto-mercantilism, mercantilism, neo-mercantilism, corporate imperialism, and the wars they engendered as societies battled over the world's resources and the *wealth-producing-process.* An education fully exposing the causes of this waste and violence would provide a much firmer foundation for the further evolution of society towards its stated goals of peace, justice and freedom from want.

It is not possible to get every student to enjoy learning for its own sake. If given a choice, most people would choose to do things that best support their need for identity and security, which for many is obtained in work, sports, and hobbies rather than in intellectual pursuits. There will be those who, though unable to compete across the board scholastically, will take great interest and do well in one field. These suggestions would give the maximum incentive to learn in the fields of one's choice.

Schools, as now structured, do perform a babysitting function. But, if that is the criterion, society should be aware that the potential of many children is lost and that babysitting is what they are paying for, not education. One must also be aware that early industrialists hoped that "the elementary school could be used to break the labouring classes into those habits of work discipline now necessary for factory production...."Putting little children to work at school for very long hours at very dull subjects was seen as a positive virtue, for it made them 'habituated, not to say naturalized, to labour and fatigue.' "[24]

Inspired Teachers for every Student

People feel insecure at any suggestion of fundamental change in their social institutions and most are closely attached to the institutions of education. But, in the current school structure, where is that all-important role model if the student has a poor, mediocre, or burned-out teacher? Under the system proposed here there would be many great teachers, each teaching his or her deepest beliefs, and their videotaped lectures would be freely available for all.

Students watching those videotaped lectures would judge for themselves what was closest to the truth. By eliminating the current monopoly on education (in the soft sciences—economics, political science, finance, some social studies, and, believe it or not, history—what passes for education is, unwittingly, really programming [propaganda]), production of low-quality lectures would be the exception.

Certainly, good hands-on teachers are wonderful, but how can they hold enthusiasm with 25 or 30 children to teach? Is not honest interaction quite impossible with even half that number? Would not the best possible teacher, backed up by professional graphics, be able to put on an enthusiastic performance and that enthusiasm be there forever on videotape? With an inspired teacher and professional graphics, even a slow student could learn more than in a crowded and socially isolated classroom. And why slow the others? Not being in direct competition, would not that slow or timid student have a better chance of not developing an inferiority complex, and thus do better?

Parents interacting closely with their Children's Education

With their increased free time, motivated parents would enjoy watching their children learn and answering their questions. Children would ask an interested parent many more questions than they would a teacher. Would not that motivated parent go into deeper detail than the teacher who has so little time to spare for individual attention? Students too timid to function freely in class would function confidently in a home setting. In the upper grades, motivated parents would share the experience and learn with their children.

Better Institutions for Socialization

Socialization is of high importance but the elimination of this function of schools would free both timid and slower students for concentration on their studies. Youth social clubs would spring up and children would sign up voluntarily as opposed to the requirement to attend school. When children join a social club by choice, they would be bound by the rules of social courtesy, not classroom discipline, and would mix, relate, and learn social graces at a faster pace than in a school setting. Parents would automatically seek such groups to replace the baby-sitting function of schools. With so much free time, the arts (music, dance, sculptors, singing, painting, and many other skills) would expand rapidly.

Maintaining Curiosity, Creativity, and Love of Learning

Education freely available to all in their free time would bypass that greatest of all destroyers of curiosity and creativity, the straitjacketing of children into conformity. We cannot count on a great teacher in every classroom. We cannot count on even half being good. Witness Massachusetts, a state with much higher quality schools than the average, in 1998 over half the teachers failed state qualification tests. There are over 15,000 educational experiments yearly. Some show dramatic improvements in education scores. Yet the overall average of scores does not improve. Either these better teaching methods are not spreading to other schools or those schools do not have motivated teachers. Why not combine modern technology with the students' abilities and desires and trade the constraints of the current system for the opportunity of a full and enjoyable education?

Certainly one can point to great teachers and the gains for their lucky students. But there would be no loss to those children in this proposed educational structure. Instead, the number of children educated to their maximum potential would increase by a factor of two or three, or more. With easy access to classes in their spare time, many adults would gain an education. Those who have a burning desire for another profession can gain credentials for their desired career even if finances are limited. Potentially great artists would now have the opportunity to discover their talents—painters, poets, writers, singers, sculptors, ad infinitum?

There are undoubtedly many latent Einsteins currently spending their lives in drudgery who would educate themselves and have their genius suddenly blossom for all the world to see and enjoy in the form of a book, a song, a new theory, an invention. A large percentage of society educating itself to a much higher level would develop an even more efficient and productive society while protecting the environment and natural resources.

Once Borderline Teachable Graduating at the Top of Their Class

Inspirational teachers and programs have proven they can parent impoverished children with damaged psyches into becoming successful citizens. One such teacher is Ms. Marva Collins in Chicago. She worked among her students, rather than from her desk. Each time one did well she would put her hand under his or her chin, lift the child's eyes to hers, and say, "you are brilliant," or give some other sincere compliment. Minority children in her class deemed borderline teachable graduated from the university at the top of their class, and went on to become professors, lawyers, and other successful professionals. Failures were almost nonexistent.

Charles Murray, in his infamous book *The Bell Curve*, cited Ms. Collin's program specifically, pointing out that such programs could not possibly improve academic achievement or cognitive functioning. Having documented Ms. Collins successes 20 years earlier, *Sixty Minutes* went back after Murray's book came out and checked on those 33 children. Those students were the roaring successes described above and thoroughly proved Murray's thesis was racist nonsense supported by corporate hard-right think-tank money as outlined in Chapter 6.[25]

While restructuring to a just society, such programs would be used to salvage such at-risk children. But, once all have equal access to a society's benefits and opportunities, most will be good parents and, through modern technology, most children can be well educated.

Culture and Recreational Learning

Fine arts and recreational learning programs, such as are produced by public broadcasting stations (and increasingly by for-profit shows), are enjoyable to people and add to their knowledge. Fifteen to 20 TV channels would be reserved for these high-quality shows. The social benefits of learning while relaxing are self-evident. Popular educational talk shows and good recreational, educational TV command a loyal audience.

Most of these shows, however, are on public broadcasting stations outside the system of collecting costs through advertising. They depend on grants and donations. One live commercial show can easily exceed one PBS station's yearly cost for all of its taped shows.[26] With their fair share of TV funds coming to them through a restructured advertising medium still financed by sales as described above, the present financial struggles of those who broadcast quality programs would be eliminated. This income would permit expansion of these stations as the rental costs of their taped shows would be minuscule compared to the original productions.

Minority Cultures

Five to 10 TV channels would be reserved for ethnic minorities. They are now inadequately represented and participate in national culture only to a limited extent. With these new rights, they would quickly develop outstanding media and political personalities to articulate essential issues and challenge the social-control-paradigms that protect power-structures and keep them in bondage. With their own communications channels, equal access to land and jobs, and the right to retain what their labors produce, members of minorities would share the nation's work and its wealth and participate in national decision making. Every citizen might at last attain and exercise the full rights of equal citizenship.

New methods of distribution and governing skills that contribute to social efficiency are as much a matter of invention as mechanical devices. Among the cultural and educational programs would be one or more channels reserved for introducing and demonstrating innovations and inventions. Alert, imaginative minds would relate their special expertise to other machines, production processes, distribution methods, and social policies, and along with new products would devise simpler methods of manufacturing, distributing, and governing.

Foreign Cultures

Guaranteeing representation of their views should apply also to foreign cultures. When the vulnerable are not present to defend themselves, *managers-of-state*, seeking followers for aggressive intent, can portray them as enemies. Eight-to-12 channels should be reserved for their views. With all sides presenting their views, society would be hard-pressed to falsely accuse others. It would be equally difficult for *managers-of-state* to hide their aggressive intentions as they create enemies to justify their wars.

By mutual agreement there should be reciprocal presentations of cultural programs between countries to provide cross-cultural information. Broadcast standards would limit propaganda. Beamed to every home, programs would show people throughout the world at work and at play. People would begin to appreciate—and thus respect—both what we have in common and what is distinctly different. There would be intense pressure to extend full rights globally once the world's impoverished whose representatives would be able to explain how they are kept in poverty by the siphoning of their wealth to centers of capital. The careful documenting of the waste and inefficiencies of corporate mercantilism would result in laws that would quickly rein in their excess power.

Local Television

Most local TV stations now pick up national programs from satellites and rebroadcast them to local viewers. Though their primary purpose is to transmit local shows and events, with a totally integrated system, these stations would broadcast nationally when a local event was of national interest. Local stations would be a source of community information and culture—ideally a medium for citizens to share ideas and experiences with each other. Local elections and community development would have complete coverage. There would be adequate time to broadcast local sports, concerts, plays, parades, and community information forums on a broad range of issues. Meetings of governing bodies, normally open to the public by law, would be beamed over local TV.

Talented local people would have their chance at national exposure without the time, expense, and risk of leaving their local area and the security it provides.

Elections

Many leaders are so busy leading their constituents down the path of confiscation of the wealth of the weak that they have, or take, little time for a sincere research of innovative ideas. In fact, politics as now contrived is hardly amenable to new ideas. As explained in "Suppressing Freedom of Thought in a Democracy" (Chapter 6) society is kept to the right of the political spectrum and elite-protective, *social-control-paradigms* keep political rhetoric within *permitted-parameters-of-debate.* To move outside those parameters is political and social suicide.

To break that control of information by the powerful, 10-to-20 reserved TV channels would be needed for serious leaders to present their views. Please consider the final chapter "Media to Empower the Powerless" as an integral part of this chapter. There we describe how to break the chains placed upon the minds of the masses. Once those chains are removed, leaders sincerely promoting the rights of all people can come to the fore.

With politicians having access to the public through reserved TV channels, there would be no need to spend private funds for elections. Such money makes the recipient beholden to that supporter. Private funding should be prohibited by law. Massive numbers of unused channels are available. Putting them to use by law would cost almost nothing. With those running for office having free access to the public and elections becoming commonsense debates of the issues, the advantage would be with those who were most knowledgeable and articulate. Politicians want to be just as honest as anyone else and with free access to the voters taking campaign funds would be a severe handicap.

Without a crisis, few of the above reforms can become social policy. However, power may eventually shift to permit the claiming of these rights. During a crisis such as the Great Depression everyone would be looking for answers and the masses can reclaim their rights to communication channels and with those rights more rights will be reclaimed. Past *social-control rhetoric* will then be exposed.

Homes as Low-Budget TV Stations

New communications technology is being invented so fast and becoming so cheap that the economically powerful are having a hard time controlling it. Local TV stations can now be almost as cheap as their radio counterparts. Low-power TV transmitters (LPTV) are available that can transmit up to 15 miles. As the new millennium rolls in there will be over 2,000 licensed in America. The U.S. government pays about 75% of the roughly $90,000 start-up costs for each station:[27]

> The FCC awarded the first 23 licenses for LPTV stations in September 1983 by drawing the names of applicants from the same plexiglass barrel used by Selective Service officials to pick draft registration numbers during the Vietnam War. One can only hope that the second drawing bodes better for activists than the first. Chances are that it will. Eight of the first 23 licenses went to minority firms. Both the lottery method and the sheer number of potential stations seem to favor greater access by radicals and reformers to LPTV than to standard TV, where the purchase price of a station in a major metropolitan area can run into tens of millions of dollars. Low-power television should increase access to the airwaves by minorities, women, political activists, environmentalists, workers, and other elements of the broad, loose coalition of the disenfranchised that has, of necessity, invented alternative media.[28]

These stations should be established with bylaws limiting them to ownership and control by the community. If not, whenever they develop an audience, monopolists would offer such a price for them that few would survive to provide alternative information to the nation.

Corporations have discovered they can target specialty markets with radio ads and, as the profits climb, the price of radio stations soars.[29] There are no more channels available and low-income groups have lost many opportunities for inexpensive communication:

> Doing without information is tantamount to being excluded from the democratic process. Still it is this principle that now is being introduced across the informational spectrum—from pay TV, to 'deregulated' telephone services, to charges for on-line data bank services, to the disappearance of modestly priced government and academic information.... The *kind and character* of the information that will be sought, produced and disseminated will be determined, if the market criteria prevail, by the most powerful bidders in the information market place—the conglomerates and the transnational companies.... In this process] Americans are forever being congratulated by

> their leaders for being the beneficiaries of the most technologically advanced, complex, expensive, and adaptable communications facilities and processes in the world. This notwithstanding, and this is the paradox, people in the United States may be amongst the globe's least knowledgeable in comprehending the sentiments and changes of recent decades in the international arena. Despite thousands of daily newspapers, hundreds of magazines, innumerable television channels, omnipresent radio, and instantaneous information delivery systems, Americans are sealed off surprisingly well from divergent outside (or even domestic) opinion.... There is a demonstrable inability to recognize, but much less empathize with, a huge have-not world.[30]

Professor Herbert Schiller explains how Americans are "sealed off" from the realities of the have-not world:

> How many movies did [corporate America] make about the labor movement? After all, America is made up of people who work. Where is the history of these people? Where's the day-in day-out history of the African American population? Where's the day-in and day-out history of women? Not just one program. Where's the whole history of the people? Where's the history of protest movements in America? Can you imagine the kind of material that could come from American protest movements? The entertainment people are always saying that they don't have enough dramatic material. Who are they kidding?[31]

We can only hope that communication becomes just like the windmill, steam engine, and electricity—so cheap that the powerful will lose control. It is then that the weak may claim their full rights.

This may happen. In Springfield, Illinois, a blind 31-year-old black man, M'Banna Kantako, became fed up because nothing in the media addressed the problems of blacks. He set up a one-watt radio transmitter the size of a toaster that covers a diameter of two miles. Just as government attacks on George Seldes's weekly *In Fact* were ignored 40 years ago, local media ignored the Federal Communications Commission's attempts to shut Kantako's station down. It is not hard to understand why. If the local media alerted the local people to the suppression of a competitor, many more would check out what Kantako had to say. Thus, "Not one has defended Kantako's right of access to the airwaves. Not one has defended the right to the free flow of information that we selectively demand of certain other countries.... Not one has mentioned the pro-democracy potentials of Kantako's model."[32]

There is also a little-known "deep dish" TV network in operation providing alternative news. It has aired programs on the Persian Gulf War. It has beamed a program called "Behind Censorship" directly to individual PBS stations and individuals with dish antennas. Its views were so at odds with the rhetoric pouring out of the media some felt the Public Broadcasting System would be forced to censor these documentaries.[33]

Many documentaries are addressing in a low key some of the frauds of the Cold War. Although, in the U.S., American terrorism is largely untouched, other Western assassinations are being lightly addressed; one actually pointed out that, after the assassination of Trotsky, the Soviet Union established a policy of no assassinations outside their borders and broke that rule only once. Covert actions are heavily sanitized but they are occasionally covered. One documentary actually discussed that archives of the former Soviet Union demonstrate the Soviet Union did not exercise monolithic control over other nations within its sphere of influence, but instead they were frustrated at times by the policies of their satellites. Such information is, of course, a total antithesis of propaganda during the Cold War.

The format proposed here—each interest group presenting its views within the same forum—would avoid fragmentation or control by powerful groups. When on the same platform with those who were emotionally well-balanced and conceptually sound those with far-out concepts would be recognized for the demagogues they are and would be ignored by most. It is to the benefit of all to restructure to a socially-managed communications system that maximizes individuality and competition.

With each person having to work only two to three days per week for a quality living, those with artistic abilities and dreams will have time to study and hone their skills. Music, painting, sculpturing, sports, writing, inventions—virtually every skill and the enjoyment of those arts—will expand exponentially.

GNP and the average workweek would fall by possibly half even as average living standards rise. Those reductions measure the wasted labor, wasted capital, and wasted resources under unrestricted private title to nature's wealth. The money no longer flows through those low-productivity monopolies to provide a high living to those not producing.

Notes

[1] Joseph C. Goulden, *Monopoly*, (New York: Pocket Books, 1970), p. 96; Robert McChesney, Editor, *Capitalism and the Information Age: The Political Economy of the Global Communication Revolution* (New York: Monthly Review Press, 1998); Robert McChesney, *Corporate Media and the Threat to Democracy*, (New York: Seven Stories Press, 1997).

[2] Robert McChesney and Edward S. Herman, *The Global Media: The Missionaries of Global Capitalism* (Washington, DC: Cassell, 1997).

[3] Ben Bagdikian, *Media Monopoly* (Boston: Beacon Press, 1987), pp. 138-40, 148, 229. Herman, McChesney, and Herman, *The Global Media.*

[4] Mark Green, *The Other Government* (New York: W.W. Norton, 1978), p. 222.

[5] Bernard D. Nossiter, "The F.C.C.'s Big Giveaway Show," *The Nation*, October 26, 1985, p. 403; PBS, McNeil/Lehrer News Hour, March 21, 1987, Alvin P. Sanoff, Clemens P. Work, Manuel Schiffres, Kenneth Walsh, Linda K. Lanier, Ronald A. Taylor, Robert J. Morse, "Who Will Control TV," *U.S. News and World Report* (May 13, 1985), p. 60; the 40-to-60% profits were reported on *CBS News*, March 25, 1985.

[6] John Stromnes, "Rural Montana Gets Taste of Public TV," *The Missoulian*, October 8, 1987, p. 9. Stromnes' source is Dan Tone from University of Nevada at Reno.

[7] Sanoff, "Who Will Control TV," p. 60.

[8] Goulden, *Monopoly*, p. 110.

[9] Ibid, p. 104.

[10] "Firm Claims Breakthrough in High-Definition Television," *The Spokesman-Review*, July 13, 1989, p. A9.

[11] Bill Gates, "The Road Ahead," *Newsweek,* November 27, 1995, p. 61.

[12] Thorstein Veblen, *Engineers and the Price System*, New York: B.W. Huebsch, 1921, p. 110; Stuart Chase, *Tragedy of Waste* (New York: Macmillan, 1925), p. 222, quoting Thorstein Veblen; Lester Thurow, *Head to Head: The Coming Economic Battle Among Japan, Europe, and America* (New York: William Morrow, 1992), p. 49.

[13] Veblen, *Engineers and the Price System*, p. 110; Chase, *Tragedy of Waste*, p. 222; Thurow, *Head to Head*, p. 49; CBS, *60 Minutes*, September 2, 1995.

[14] Paul Zane Pilzer, *Unlimited Wealth* (New York: Crown, 1990), p. 44.

[15] Steven Levy, "Bills New Vision," *Newsweek*, November 27, 1995, p. 68.

[16] William J. Cook, "Reach Out and Touch Everyone," *U.S. News and World Report* (October 10, 1988), pp. 49-50.

[17] Ivan Ladanov and Vladimar Pronnikov, "Craftsmen and Electronics," *New Times*, no. 47 (November 1988), pp. 24-25.

[18] J.W. Smith, *The World's Wasted Wealth 2* (www.ied.info/cc.html: Institute for Economic Democracy, 1994).

[19] Bagdikian, *Media Monopoly*, 1987, pp. 138-40, 148, 229; William Manchester, *The Glory and the Dream* (New York: Bantam Books, 1988), p. 975.

[20] Anne Windishar, "Expert: 20% of Gifted Kids Drop Out," *Spokane Chronicle*, January 7, 1988, p. B7.

[21] Rebecca Winters, "From Home to Harvard," *Time*, September 11, 2000, p. 55.

[22] *CNN News*, May 24, 1988.

[23] Thurow, *Head to Head*, pp. 273-79, especially p. 278.

[24] Juliet Schor, *The Overworked American* (New York: Basic Books, 1991), p. 61.

[25] *60 Minutes*, September 24, 1995; Herrnstein, Richard J., and Charles Murray. *The Bell Curve: Intelligence and Class Structure in American Life* (New York: Free Press, 1994), p. 399.

[26] Salt Lake City's PBS station, $1 million per year rented all tapes.

[27] *Broadcasting and Cablecasting Yearbook*; Stromnes, p. 9.

[28] David Armstrong, *Trumpet to Arms* (Boston: South End Press, 1981), p. 340.

[29] "The Rush To Gulp US Radio Stations," *Christian Science Monitor*, May 7, 1996, p. 18. The title of this article says it well.

[30] Herbert I. Schiller, *Information and the Crisis Economy* (Boston: Oxford University Press, 1986), pp. 109, 122.

[31] Herbert Schiller (Interview), "The Information Highway: Paving Over the Public," *Z Magazine*, March, 1994, pp. 46-50. See also Peggy Norton, "Independent Radio's Problems and Prospects," *Z Magazine*, March, 1990, pp. 51-57.

[32] Mike Townsend, "Microwatt Revolution," *Lies of Our Times*, January 1991.

[33] Dan Cohen, "Deep Dish: Outsiders on Public TV," *The Guardian*, May 6, 1992, p. 19.

28. Media to Empower the Powerless

The thoughts of society are controlled for the benefit and protection of the powerful through funding of think-tanks, biased professors, and universities—most unaware of their own biases—by foundations, corporations and intelligence services; through covert establishment of supportive (hard right) media with public (intelligence service) funds; and through world events being run through intelligence services' wordsmiths who restructure them to the desired view of the world (Chapter 6). If a country needs to be brought under control (Iran, Libya, Cuba, Yugoslavia, et al.—countries which have killed very few of their citizens), there will be loud rhetoric of human rights abuses, state terrorism, or of a particularly vicious dictator. When a country is needed as an ally (Syngman Rhee in South Korea, Suharto in Indonesia, Somoza in Nicaragua, all of whom killed tens of thousands, even hundreds of thousands, of their own citizens), one will hear only a rhetoric of authoritative governments.

These created views of the world are put out while massive slaughters by covertly supported dictators are totally ignored, downgraded, or blamed on others. Thus the public is not aware that many violent events—planned, financed, armed, and guided by powerful nations' intelligence services—even happened.

Sincere but unwitting professors and equally sincere and unaware writers and reporters, not realizing how this massive fraudulent information was planted, have put out articles and books by the thousands based on this badly tainted and frequently totally false information, and continue to do so.

Thousands of novels produced to entertain the masses are based on this created view of the world and all are making a lot of money producing as both serious education and entertainment propaganda nonsense for the masses.

Some Frauds of History

The battle of Saint-Mihiel is recorded in virtually every history book as the turning point of WWI. Five hundred and fifty thousand Allied troops were supposedly involved and tens of thousands of Germans captured. Yet no such battle occurred. "There was not one German soldier or one German gun within forty or fifty miles." One "blundering war correspondent," as George Seldes called himself, and "two United States Army artists 'captured' the town," hours before the Allied army arrived.[1]

What became written history was the timed press releases the army had prepared in advance—a clear example of the creation of *social-control-paradigms*. The same was true of much of the first months of the Korean War. Until the Chinese joined North Korea, it was a war of U.S. military press releases.

Certainly there were some hard battles in the Korean War. But, as we documented above, many battles describing "hordes of North Koreans" never happened, and horrendous naval and aerial assaults against defenseless North Korean civilians designed to prevent the North Koreans from accepting a peace settlement were excluded from the news and from history.[2] (Western leaders were programming the world so they could arm and fight covert wars, overt wars, and their Cold War.) The same is true of much else in history.

The turning over of many European governments to fascism during the Great Depression when the entrenched power-structures were threatened with the loss of that power through the vote (known only to a few in-depth researchers) is one example of history that needs to be addressed in popular literature.[3] With the masses unaware of how democratic solutions were avoided in that crisis, the potential for a replay if democracy again threatens to break out is high.

The improperly named Spanish Civil War took place in the one country in which the powerful did permit a truly democratic election and the alliance of aristocracy and wealth lost control of the government. The fascists used foreign military power to take back Spain. Analyzing that history makes it evident that fascism is an arm of the world's wealthy powerbrokers and the wars they start are either to protect their monopoly powers or decide among themselves over who will establish the rules of unequal trade (World Wars I and II).

With government information services, intelligence services, and think-tank press releases; with foundation, corporate, and intelligence service funding of the propaganda process; and with negligible resources among the impoverished, the politically weak, or motivated researchers, the beliefs of the world stay to the right of the political spectrum. There is no left and no functioning middle. There is only a right and an extreme right, which, because there is no true left or true middle, are viewed by the people as a political right and a political left.

Restructuring the Media to cover the Full Political Spectrum

Instead of only the agenda of the *managers-of-state* and the powerful being supported and promoted by these carefully crafted interpretations of national and international events, newspapers, magazines, TV, and radio should provide the spokespeople for the groups or societies under assault (the true middle and the true left) with equal space and time to present their side. It does not even have to be done by law. One conscientious publisher or broadcaster can do it.

60 Minutes is the most popular news documentary on TV, even if it does not present with balance the controversial views of the world we are describing. Similar newspapers, news magazines, TV programs, or radio stations that expanded the horizons of their audiences through laying the carefully crafted, propagandized view of events side by side with articulate spokespersons for peace, freedom, justice, rights, and majority rule for all in the world, would soon be in high demand nationwide, especially if they simultaneously explained the propaganda process that has historically kept the masses under control.

The rules would be very basic: all exposures of human rights abuses would be encouraged but no one would be permitted to put out propaganda or promote hatred of another group or society. Of course this would mean that the State Department, intelligence agencies, and their spokespersons (ambassadors and other government agencies) would have to abandon their propaganda. No public institution that preaches peace, freedom, justice, rights, and majority rule can stand if exposed that they are really behind policies of inequality, injustice, violence, and terror.

Subtle, But Explosive, one-liners would alert the Masses

Concerning politics, economics, some sociology, history, and money—all soft disciplines—the world is primarily programmed (propagandized), not educated. Some of what we are addressing is available in select classes in the university system, but in very narrow fields attended by a very small percentage of students. The proof is visible by simply talking to people. Not only are few aware of the distortions of reality by *managers-of-state* that this book has addressed in depth, they will be upset at, and disbelieve, any suggestion they were not fully informed.

Occasionally a one-line snapshot of true history is shown, but not with a big enough picture to alert the masses. A vitriolic report on Russia's Boris

Yeltsin's statement discussed earlier that, "The Russians may have American prisoners over there yet" was followed by such a one-sentence statement, "There were over 730 American Airmen shot down over the Soviet Union during the Cold War." Those vitriolic statements were meaningless; the real story was that last sentence. If analyzed, along with the knowledge that no Soviet planes were carrying out acts of war across the borders of Western nations, that sentence in all media as opposed to one medium-sized newspaper would blow away some of the fog created by the propaganda of the Cold War that is the lens through which the masses view the world.

As I write this a guest professor/author on Fox news was able to quickly slip in the reality that 200,000 Iraqi's were killed in the Gulf War, another 1-million were killed by the embargo, and it appeared the slaughter may be worse this time. The newscaster's facial expression made it obvious he was aware of this history and his quick change of subject demonstrated that this was unintended information.

Whenever discussing the dictator Suharto of Indonesia it would only be necessary to add, "Indonesia's democratically elected Sukarno was overthrown on the second attempt by the CIA, which resulted in the slaughter of between 500,000 and 1-million civilians." The public would be instantly alerted, demand to know the facts, and such covert actions would cease. Especially if that sentence was followed by a second: "Between 12-million and 15-million people have been violently slaughtered by such covert and overt actions and the United States has been the primary promoter and supporter of such destabilizations." Instead, the masses hear volumes of injustices done by others. These injustices are primarily manufactured by the CIA, or other intelligence agencies, and described in government press releases as reality.

When Argentina is in the news surely an alert anchor could point out that, "Roughly 500 of Argentina's disappeared were pregnant women who were imprisoned to term, gave birth by cesarean section, were drugged and loaded on a nightly flight of death over the Atlantic Ocean, and their babies were adopted into military families." Perhaps another day he or she could slip in, "This slaughter of mostly innocents was well known to the government and, through their confessions to their priests, the church." We say mostly innocents because they were only speaking up for their rights and most were totally nonviolent.

A news report on Iranian terrorism followed by the sentence, "The Iranians are angry over America's Operation Ajax, which overthrew their democracy and reestablished the dictatorship of the Shah," would alert citizens to take a closer look at other violent events around the world.

Whenever a news release comes over the wire about slaughter in Latin America by insurgents such as in the 1970s and 1980s, almost certainly intelligence service and/or State Department press releases, the local reporter only needs to add one line: "U.S. intelligence established and supported death squads during the Cold War which killed thousands of peaceful prospective leaders (the potential Gandhis and Martin Luther Kings) of those countries." Sources should be given so the reader can quickly check on these facts. This would quickly alert the masses to the reality that these were suppressions of the same freedoms Americans fought for in 1776 and the War of 1812.

The media, as all people, are conscientious and if they knew how the news was controlled, and if they knew the true history, they would keep slipping in those little one-liners that would expose the propaganda.

Putting the West's state-sponsored terrorism alongside any other terrorism or human rights abuses would quickly demonstrate who has created the most terror and insecurity throughout the world. Once alerted by the exposure of how propaganda works in a "free" society, the people would easily spot these intelligence agency creations and, because it would mean defeat at election time, propaganda would cease. Their integrity at stake, universities would weed out compliant professors who take intelligence service or corporate money to produce fraudulent research, the corporate funded think-tanks generating most of this disinformation would disappear, and the media would become the responsible reporters of news they want to be.

The Developing World can Leapfrog Decades in the Development Process

As they are in a race against the time when their populations will overwhelm them, each region should be given the communications systems (radio and direct broadcast satellite TV) to reach all their people with the message of:

(1) how to gain control of their land and grow and consume high-calorie crops with the proper proportions of the nine essential amino acids for the body to produce its own protein; as both serious education and entertainment; as both serious education and entertainment; as both serious education and entertainment;

(2) how to industrialize their regions, develop a balanced economy, and create buying power;

(3) the population levels their resources will support while protecting the ecosystem;

(4) how Italy, Japan, Germany, China, Sri Lanka, Colombia, Chile, Burma, Cuba, and the Indian state of Kerala slowed their population growths;

(5) achieving large gains from limiting, and especially reducing, their populations;

(6) and how in all industrialized nations a rapid reduction in births took place automatically in step with the gains in quality of life and security.

As citizens will buy their own TV sets, for the cost of producing the documentaries, establishing the satellite TV system, providing workbooks, and establishing testing stations, all Developing World children of all ages would have access to all grades of education, including a masters or doctorate, for a fraction of the cost in the developed world. Satellite broadcasts will cover entire continents and all those countries can share the setup and operational costs.

Education would start on any subject as soon as the education documentaries were filmed. Students or communities able to finance TVs, work tables, notebooks, slates, and other necessities would start their formal education immediately. Those with access to a TV but too poor to afford the other basics, would develop keen enough memories to pass tests, just as their ancestors handed down the wisdom of the ages by memorized stories.

This restructured educational system will be an advantage over the developed world. Developed-world education bureaucracies are locked into the current expensive structure so thoroughly that it will be impossible to uproot them. Not only can the Developing World be educated for from 5-to-15% the cost of the developed world, if they can avoid those imposed beliefs, they can be much better educated.

Think what the Developing World could do if they could avoid propaganda masquerading as an honest education, which is the reason the developed world will go to any length to prevent the dependent world from gaining control of its information systems. To lose control of the world's information systems is to lose control of the imposed beliefs that in turn would eliminate control of the periphery of empire.

Politicians speaking to, and listening to, the People

The purpose of McCarthyism was to lock academics, the media, and all opinion makers inside the *permitted-parameters-of-debate* of the Cold War. Although it destroyed the lives of thousands of conscientious people, it worked brilliantly and is still a powerful force today. It is only because we are so totally immersed in it, and thus consider it customary and normal, that we are unaware of the true hold of this massive *social-control-paradigm.*

William Greider, in *Who Will Tell the People?*, explains how the big guns of those *social-control paradigms* work. The leaders of Congress know well the rough outline of laws that will be passed. What the public hears is a thunderous rhetoric within narrow parameters to the right of the political spectrum, jockeying for position with the voters. Except for corporations which fund the elections, the public is essentially un-represented and decisions are made far from the public arena. We badly need a book that explains this process within governments as thoroughly as we hope we have explained it on the national and world scene.

Politics, as now contrived, is hardly amenable to new ideas. Society is kept to the right of the political spectrum and *social-control beliefs* keep political rhetoric within those *permitted-parameters-of-debate.* To move outside these parameters is political and social suicide.

Assuming there is no economic crisis, an ideologically programmed population is guaranteed to vote in support of the social policy the current power-structure shrilly promotes; there are no choices outside those parameters. To move to what is a true middle position is to be instantly attacked as liberal, socialist, heretical, un-American, or even Communist—the reductionist clichés of the *social-control paradigm*, the Cold War, in effect since 1960. Therefore, few knowledgeable leaders can freely say what they believe. They avoid all in-depth analysis and commitments.

These politicians should not be too heavily criticized for their evasions. To admit openly that the Soviet military threat was not real, to recognize that mercantilist principles still dominated world trade, to acknowledge the ongoing suppressions of developing nations' attempts to gain control of their destiny or to promote truly progressive social policies would cost them their political life.

If a conscientious politician suggested even moderate plans to restructure any of the wasteful segments of the economy we have been outlining, the big guns of the many subtle monopolies would, through cranking up the rhetoric of the operative *social-control-paradigm*, collectively and immediately sink their political ships.

Ten to 20 reserved TV channels would be needed for serious leaders to present their views. Serious, in this instance, means having a substantial segment of the population to represent—corporations, business people, farmers (all now over represented), women (have just gained representation), labor (represented but unwittingly supporting suppression of other labor worldwide [the purpose of the propaganda process]), minorities, the poor, conservationists, peace groups, and others (these last four are currently essentially without representation in the government or the media [they do have representation on the margins in academia]).

If there is anywhere politicians must be, it is in the spotlight. Those not attending these in-depth background discussions would be relinquishing their claim to leadership. With authorities such as those cited throughout this book invited to these forums, it would be difficult to duck the issues. There would just be too many questions.

Only when all have the opportunity to present their views and challenge *social-control rhetoric*, or even make it counterproductive, can there be true democracy. Those who presented a consistent and accurate view of reality, and promoted a policy for the maximum good of the people, would gather a loyal following.

Most of the public would not watch these in-depth discussions, but those who did would gain from the knowledge of these experts. Interested people would make value judgments on the history leading to the present problems, study the different solutions that were presented, and analyze the intelligence and integrity of the leaders proposing these solutions. It is these interested people and their opinions that guide the thinking of the nation.

These opinion makers (intellectuals, leaders, and the news media) would watch the information forums to inform themselves and, in turn, inform the public. To do less would leave one uninformed and lose one's followers. With elections structured for candidates to prove their mettle—like the famous Lincoln-Douglas debates—the now-informed citizens would be enabled to make responsible voting decisions.

Understanding economics becomes easy when we realize that the classical economists were protecting wealth and power. They consistently insisted that labor should be paid just enough to reproduce itself and that all wealth produced by increased efficiencies of technology should go to capital even as they ignored that this primitive accumulation of capital went first and foremost to grand castles and high living.[a]

As the common people fought for equal rights, the power-structure protected itself by trumpeting each gain of rights as full and equal rights. But those excess rights of capital promoted by classical economists have never been fully set aside, the full and equal rights promoted by a minority of philosophers has never been attained, and it is this lack of full rights which creates the poverty and violence of today's world.

Provide equal rights through the suggested slight changes in the structure of property rights eliminates the current unacknowledged subtle land, technology, and money monopolies that are the essence of today's economy. Without cost and without waste use-values are distributed to all. The quality of life rises rapidly even as the hours of required labor and the GDP drop precipitously. The drop in GDP measures the previously wasted labor, capital, and resources of a subtly monopolized economy. The GDP then rises as people utilize their new free time to develop their many artistic talents or to simply socialize with friends.

Under a modern commons within *democratic-cooperative-capitalism* the just rights of private property are fully protected, individualism and competition are strengthened, and money no longer flows through subtle monopolies to the interceptors of wealth. Society's production is instead—through the mechanism of equal pay for equally-productive labor distributed to the producers of that wealth. Through equal sharing of productive jobs, each

---

[a] Michael Perelman, *The Invention of Capitalism: Classical Political Economy and the Secret History of Primitive Accumulation* (London: Duke University Press, 2000), especially p. 91: Thomas C. Patterson, *Inventing Western Civilization* (New York: Monthly Review Press, 1997). There were a few exceptions. Gerard Winstanley in the 16th century, Jean Jacques Rousseau in the 17th century, Johann Herder in the 18th century, and Karl Marx in the 19th century spoke to the rights of labor (Perelman, *The Invention of Capitalism*, Chapter 3).

will have a just claim to their proper share and there will be no severe poverty. Under those rules of equality, the need for massive military forces and their attendant massive slaughters disappear.

Those owning and working within the superstructure of those subtle monopolies are the world's brightest and most talented. That is why they reached for and attained those positions and they will unanimously dispute their redundancy even as a few of them finance and guide the enormous propaganda process which protects their excess rights. The gains to society will be enormous when under a system of full and equal rights with a sharing of productive jobs these talented and brilliant people will be producing wealth instead of intercepting wealth.

This is an opportune moment to stake a claim to the moral high ground, share the enormous productivity of technology, eliminate most poverty, protect the world's ecosystems, and gain the respect and loyalty of the world. Any nation, or group of nations, which leads the world down that path to world peace and prosperity will go down in history as a moral and conscientious society which led the world to peace and prosperity.

Compassion, good judgment, and very possibly even the survival of humankind, require that the world trading system be restructured from the current corporate imperialism, with its violence, poverty, and despoiling of environments, to a caring *democratic-cooperative-capitalism* with a minimum level of violence and poverty and a rebuilding of the ecosystems so crucial for the survival of all life. In the words of John Maynard Keynes, "Ultimately, mankind would be freed of the morbid love of money to confront the deeper questions of human existence—how to live wisely and agreeably and well."[4]

Turning Weapons into Consumer Products

If the world's *managers-of-state* were to abandon the interception of wealth through corporate mercantilist control of technology and trade, guarantee secure borders, industrialize impoverished societies, collect and destroy their weapons, and reduce the weapons of the super-powers in step with world disarmament, global peace could become a very real possibility.

If there were no arms among the disaffected, and an *honest* international body was overseeing peace, hostilities and minor clashes might develop, but wars would be impossible. With weapons adequate only for internal security, with borders guaranteed, and with honesty in sharing the fruits of nature and technology, societies would give up the losses from conflict for the gains from cooperation.

As stated previously, President Woodrow Wilson knew all this. His trusted political confidant, Edward Mandell House, studied the European secret agreements to divide the Ottoman Empire and

> was dismayed by their contents.... [He told the British Foreign Secretary, Lord Balfour], "It is all bad.... They are making it a breeding place for future war."... [A]board ship enroute to the peace conference in 1919, [President] Wilson told his associates that "I am convinced that if this peace is not made on the highest principles of justice, it will be swept away by the peoples of the world in less than a generation. If it is any other sort of peace then I shall want to run away and hide ... for there will follow not mere conflict but cataclysm."[5]

President Wilson fought for those goals even when he was severely ill with a stroke. But the political forces arrayed against him were too great and he failed to get the United States to join and lead the League of Nations in gaining and guaranteeing rights for all. President Franklin D. Roosevelt repeatedly tried to abandon the imposed inequalities of trade that created so much of the world's conflict. His "attempt to replace aggression with international understanding had failed in China and Spain. Undaunted, he wrote [Britain's] Prime Minister Neville Chamberlain proposing a great conference at which treaties would be altered without resorting to force and all nations assured access to raw materials. Chamberlain declined."[6]

Although he was at first carried along by the nation's cold warriors, President John F. Kennedy also spoke about peace and justice for the world. Just weeks before he was assassinated he spoke of a strategy for peace: "Not a *Pox Americana* enforced on the world by American weapons of war ... not merely peace for Americans, but peace for all men; not merely in our time but peace for all time."[7]

Knowing that the enormous productivity of capital can produce a respectable lifestyle for all assures that most of the developing world will accept disarmament as the price of capitalization. Those elusive goals of capitalization and peace are what progressive developing world leaders have been fighting for anyway. In 1950, conservative Senators Brine McMahon and Millard Tydings "made dramatic speeches in the Senate ... moral crusade for peace" and a $50-billion ($300-billion 1990 dollars) "global Marshall Plan" financed by the United States and augmented by an undertaking by all nations to put two-thirds of their armament expenditures to "constructive ends."[8]

An Offer the Impoverished World cannot refuse

In plain and unambiguous language, this should be the offer of the powerful industrialized nations to the world: the cancellation of all unjust debts; the conversion of industrial capital once producing arms to production of industrial tools for the Developing World; a fully democratized United Nations to oversee the balanced and peaceful capitalization of the Developing World; the borders of *all* countries to be guaranteed; the newly democratized United Nations given the authority, soldiers, and the arms to back up that guarantee; and a worldwide embargo to go into effect automatically against any country that attacks or subverts another country.

Due to those major powers' addiction to living cheaply off other societies and the potential for cheating, perhaps earlier international efforts for sustained world peace were premature. However, with TV and radio soon to be present in most homes worldwide, it is possible for the entire world to have a basic understanding of the problems (people must be told the problems honestly instead of propagandized) and satellites can spot any major arms production or troop movement anywhere in the world.

The major powers could disarm in step with the disarmament of the world and could turn the industry currently wasted on arms production towards capitalizing the undeveloped world, rebuilding the world's soils, and protecting the ecosystem. The same expansion of industrial and trade rights to the entire world as is intended to be extended only to allies within the current trading bloc would eliminate the need for military waste and free that productive capacity, resources, and labor for sustainable development of the world.

Whoever firmly establishes disarmament and expands it to developing world industrialization will go down in history as one of the world's greatest leaders, far exceeding the reputations of Presidents George Washington, Abraham Lincoln, Franklin Roosevelt, or India's Mahatma Gandhi. Once other nations declare their willingness to disarm and place their security in the hands of a fully democratized United Nations, the developed nations will be hard-pressed to find excuses not to utilize their surplus productive capacity to provide those all-important industrial tools to the Developing World.

Since most arms are normally used either to repress a country's own population or for external powers to provide support for a faction within a country, the foregoing guarantee should extend to the protection of existing democratic governments from internal overthrow by force. But there also must be guarantees of free elections, constitutional governments, freedom of speech, freedom of religion, and separation of church and state. A fully democratized United Nations should have the authority to oversee the disarming of belligerents, the establishment of democracies, and the holding of free elections in any country torn by revolution. Once those countries are disarmed legitimate leaders can be elected.

The World Can, and Will, Disarm

Under the guarantees against both internal and external aggression described, and with promises of capitalization and the sharing of markets and resources, the military weapons of developing states—above those needed for normal police duty—should be collected and destroyed.

Once the rest of the world is disarmed, and all are therefore safe from attack, the weapons of mass destruction can be destroyed and adequate conventional weapons can be transferred to a world body to oversee peace. With destruction of the weapons of war and equal rights to capital, resources, and trade, all societies could eventually produce for, and provide equal rights for, all their citizens.

As a condition of receiving capital, emerging nations would have to agree to permit inspection of any factory suspected of weapons production. The only way this can happen is if the dominant powers—and that now means only the United States and its allies—recognize the potential for peace and take the lead in disarming and capitalizing the world.

Powerful Nations will not willingly give up Their Superior Rights

Powerful nations respond only to another equal power. However, just laying out the simplicity of eliminating poverty by full and equal rights for all severely weakens these mighty powers. It remains for all weak nations of a region to ally together for the power to gain their freedom. With that power they can negotiate to trade resources for technology and they can negotiate for equality of pay for equally-productive work. To not do so is to stay in poverty and watch their natural wealth become someone else's manufactured and capitalized wealth.

With political rights you are politically free but may still be ill-fed, ill-clothed, and poorly housed. Provide equal economic rights for all people through efficient and productive *democratic-cooperative-capitalism* and all people can be well-fed, well-clothed, and live in a respectable home.

Certainly those powerful nations will manufacture excuses as they always have (the leaders of these new breaks for freedom are killers, dictators, and terrorists) and send in the military to suppress these allied breaks for freedom. But, if these newly allied nations firmly hold their ground; a few hundreds of millions will no longer be able to preach peace, freedom, justice, rights, and majority rule while simultaneously using their military to suppress those very same rights for billions of people.

Mahatma Gandhi of India showed that to the world. When the people of India stood up together, refused to fight, but also refused to accept British rule, the British had to leave. All wealth comes from natural resources and those resources are primarily in the impoverished world. If the developing world refuses to work those mines, cut those forests, pump that oil, drive those trucks, or load those ships, (just as the followers of Gandhi did) the powerful nations will have no choice except to negotiate in good faith.[a] This war of words is a war they cannot win if we seriously engage them in that battle. The truth is too simple and too obvious

But before people can organize they must fully understand why they are poor while others are rich. Our research provides those simple reasons why and also maps the road out of poverty. *Democratic-cooperative-capitalism* is that road.

Notes

1 George Seldes, *Even The Gods Can't Change History* (Secaucus, N.J: Lyle Stuart, 1976), p. 16.

2 I.F. Stone, *The Hidden History of the Korean War* (Boston: Little Brown, 1952). See Chapter seven in this work for a synopsis.

3 John Gray, *False Dawn* (New York: The Free Press, 1998), pp. 196, 211; Karl Polanyi, *The Great Transformation* (Boston: Beacon Press, 1957), Chapter 20, especially p. 38.

4 William Greider, *Secrets of the Temple* (New York: Simon and Schuster, 1987), pp. 173-74.

5 David Fromkin, *A Peace to End All Peace* (New York: Avon Books, 1989), pp. 257, 262.

6 William Manchester, *The Glory and the Dream*, Bantam (New York: Bantam Books, 1975), p. 178.

7 Ibid, pp. 989-90.

8 Dean Acheson, *Present at the Creation* (New York: W.W. Norton, 1987), p. 377.

---

[a] Germany's industrial sector was occupied by France after WWII. When German labor refused to work, France was forced to abandon the occupation.

Conclusion: Guidelines for World Development

(1) Developing nations must ally together so as to negotiate equally with the allied imperial centers.

(2) Equal pay for equally-productive work to provide roughly equal buying power relative to the talents and energy expended to all who are employed.

(3) Sharing those productive jobs would melt the invisible economic borders which currently guide the wealth into the hands of only the adequately paid. Each employable person now need work only two to three days per week.

(4) Elimination of the subtle monopolizations of land, technology, finance capital, and information (Part IV) will restructure to *democratic-cooperative-capitalism* and increase economic and social efficiency equal to the invention of Money, the printing press, and electricity.

(5) And addressing population issues and sustainable development so that the earth has the capacity to provide resources for all and the environment to absorb wastes. With the most Catholic country in the world, Italy, having a birth rate per family of 1.29, Germany 1.51, and Japan 1.53—far below replacement levels leading the way—other regions adjusting population to the capacity of the earth's resources and environment is an attainable goal.

There are 15 subsidiary guidelines to reach those goals:

(1) The wealthy world must (as per Chapter 23) turn their war industries towards producing industrial technology for any nation or region of the world that agrees to eliminate terrorism, that agrees to reduce their military to a level that provides internal security but leaves no offensive capabilities, and that agrees to provide full political and economic rights to all its citizens—including women and minorities. These rights to include: a constitutional government, democratic elections, freedom of speech,

freedom of religion, and separation of religion and state. As this is exactly what most destabilized emerging nations were in the process of constructing, agreement on these conditions for developmental aid will be quickly accepted. Industries and access to markets would go only to those who agreed to these conditions. The authoritative dictatorships that the *imperial-centers-of-capital* have placed in power and kept in power throughout the world for two centuries will quickly melt away once that sincere offer is made.

(2) All military weapons beyond that necessary for internal security should be turned over to a fully democratized United Nations and destroyed. In trade, the powerful nations will assign their military forces to that democratized United Nations which would guarantee the borders of all nations. All weapons of mass destruction in all nations should be destroyed.

(3) A fully democratized United Nations should be chartered with the responsibility to oversee world peace and all nations should agree to place a worldwide embargo against any nation which attacks or subverts any other nation—or against any nation which attempts to retain or build its own military capacity to wage war.

(4) Any honest accounting would show the wealthy world in enormous debt to the Developing World through centuries of imperialism, slavery, and structural exploitation designed to create indebtedness through *plunder-by-trade*. Thus all unjust Third Word debts should be cancelled.

(5) Markets should be free between regions of equal development and equal pay. Trade between countries and regions unequally paid for equally-productive labor should be managed to prevent the continued *plunder-by-trade* as outlined in Chapters 1 and 2.

(6) To take control of their destiny, regions should establish their own central bank and trading currencies as per Chapter 26.

(7) The level playing field so crucial to efficient economics should be leveled upwards. Through equalizing surcharges minerals and other resources in the low-paid countries should be priced relative to mining or harvesting of those same resources or substitute commodities in the well-paid developed world. Labor values should be calculated and equalizing surcharges collected on exports of mined, harvested, and manufactured products as per Chapters 22 and 23.

(8) Funds collected from these equalizing surcharges (tariffs) on international trade should go towards building industries and economic infrastructure in the lower-paid regions and for renewable energy capitalization, developing environmentally sound products, designing and implementing ecologically sustainable lifestyles, rebuilding soils, and cleaning up and revitalizing the ecosystems of both the developing and developed world. Protections should be lowered in step with the equalizing of industrial technology, capital accumulation, and labor skills.

With the cost of minerals in the United States at 1.7% of GNP and the cost of fuel 2%, economies can handle those equalization surcharges.[1]

Through those same surcharges (or call then resource depletion taxes), the price of minerals and carbon fuels in the developing world should be increased to a level near that of the lower grade deposits in the developed world. The recycling of minerals would then be profitable and renewable energy would be competitive. The consumption of the world's oil and coal will be slower, pollution pressures will be lower, and all countries will develop faster.

Once equalizing surcharges are established, the entire world will be able to develop to a sustainable level and poverty will be largely eliminated. What appears more expensive to the few in the affluent developed world is really far cheaper to the billions in the entire world.

(9) To prevent diversion of funds, money should not be distributed directly to developing nations or regions. Fulfillment of contract is the essence of a successful economy. Any industry or infrastructure built with developing world money or with equalizing surcharge funds should be built by contract and the contractors paid from those funds. However, since they now have the tools of production and access to technology, contactors and labor within those regions would be utilized.

(10) Once nations or regions are roughly equal in technology and labor roughly equally paid, surcharges should be eliminated and fair and honest free trade will flow between nations and between regions. We will have turned "win-lose" and "lose-lose" trade wars into "win-win" equalizing managed fair trade and from there into honest and equal free trade.

(11) There should be a balance between industry and resources. A nation or region short on resources should be allotted a higher level of industrialization. (Japan provides the ideal example.) Once all nations and regions are roughly equal in world trade, equalizing surcharges on resources should metamorphose into a resource depletion tax to fund rebuilding soils and revitalizing the world's ecosystems.

(12) As has already been successfully tested, one-year-old trees in biodegradable, aerodynamic, pointed cylinders can be planted at the rate of 800,000 trees a day per plane. Newly planted grass grows beautifully in North Africa when fenced off from goats. Technology has been developed to grow extensive ground cover in 1-to-3 years on steep, barren, infertile road cuts. The technology is here to reforest and regenerate the earth and a resource depletion tax is the proper source of funds.[2]

(13) Patent laws should be restructured, as per Chapter 25, to pay inventors well yet technology is available for use by all. Destruction of industries and communities through industries moving offshore would cease—even as competition between and within regions increased. Prices would fall and living standards would rise rapidly.

(14) To protect everyone's rights and freedom, the world's intelligence services should remain operative and alert. As opposed to being the planners of most of the world's most violent acts of terrorism, these

agencies should be mandated to cooperate in preventing terrorist attacks or wars anywhere in the world. As opposed to today's demanding job of suppressing breaks for freedom, that mandated change alone will eliminate most terrorism and all wars.

(15) The buying power for a healthy economy comes from wages paid to productive labor. Those earnings are spent for family needs and that money is spent again and again as it is passed from hand to hand to purchase necessary food, fiber, shelter, and services. Thus care must be taken by both the developed and developing world for each region (not small or medium sized nations) to produce most of their own food and consumer products and provide most of their own services.

Restructuring to true rights and freedom for all in the world as addressed in these rules for peaceful world development, and all people having some control of their own destiny, will eliminate most violence in this world.

With the wealthy developed world sincerely promoting equality in world trade through relinquishing their monopoly on resources, technology, and finance capital, and with that newly-produced wealth relatively equally shared in the developing regions through equality in wages and equal access to jobs, poverty will quickly be alleviated and violence will subside.

A Practical Approach for Poor Nations and regions to Develop

Lets us design an emerging nation development plan utilizing cheap broadly-available resources. Europe has cheap, fireproof, rammed-earth homes over 300 years old. Most regions have massive numbers of unemployed labor and can, working within a modern commons, build high-quality, rammed-earth homes with fired (ceramic) interiors cheaply. (Some regions will use other building materials stone, straw bale, wood, et al. (run a Google Internet search).

A university would bring in experts to train the first homebuilders. These newly-trained experts would train others on the job. The experts would be paid but the worker's pay would be their training as master homebuilders. Assuming five workers to a crew, every three houses built would train five more experts, expanding the homebuilding project exponentially. Industries would be built to produce the doors, windows, plumbing, carpets, roofs, ceilings, and furniture and those industries would expand exponentially along with the home building.

Though these homes will be built cheaply they have full use-value. As the project matured labor building some of those homes would be paid. In other homes the master builder would be paid to train more volunteer workers. These newly-trained volunteers can build more homes utilizing more volunteers. They would build homes for themselves, family, and friends. Thus they are paid indirectly but are well-paid.

As real value is being produced, money can be created by that nation or region up to the value of those homes, businesses and inventory. This provides the money to build the industries, regional businesses, and inventory necessary to service that developing community.

Simultaneous with building homes a country or region must develop a prosperous agriculture. Farms, equipment, and the food produced have value and, as it is locally produced, money can be created for that development. All resources should be processed into high value-added products both for regional consumption and export. As economic activity increases and community values rise, buying power increases to purchase that production.

So long as countries or regions are utilizing local resources, money can be created to build industries and infrastructure. This would include building their own TV and computer industries and providing a free education via satellite. A development region can be expanded to include an oil-producing region.

But soon that country or region will need technology and industries that are firmly under the control of the imperial centers. It is at this point that regions must ally together to negotiate equally with the imperial centers to trade access to resources for access to technology. To not ally together would be to see the wealth created transferred to those imperial centers via unequal pay for equally-productive labor, resources purchased below full value, and the resulting inevitable debt traps.

These are Historic Moments

We all know the fable of the king whose tailor promised him clothes made of gold, could not create the gold thread, dressed him in invisible gold clothes, the whole kingdom marveled at his beautiful gold clothes, and it took a child to see the truth and say, "The king has no clothes."

For 50 years these *imperial-centers-of-capital* have dressed themselves in the fine clothes of peace, freedom, justice, rights, and majority rule. Throughout those same 50 years *policies-of-state* of that empire has been anything but peace, freedom, justice, rights, and majority rule.

These are historic moments. If a further world economic collapse cannot be stopped and the empire's armies are busy hopping all over the globe keeping all countries in line, the empire will stand exposed. America's decapitation of the leadership of Iraq to gain control of world oil prices while 65% to 85% of the citizens of virtually every country in the world except America and Israel said no means that many leaders, new and old, will be standing up. Many will see their freedom is also at risk and say the obvious, "This empire is not for peace, freedom, justice, rights, or majority rule. This empire is for maintaining control of our resources and the *wealth-producing-process*."

When that can be said on the evening news—as news anchor Walter Cronkite shaking his head essentially said about the Vietnam War forced the powerbrokers to make peace—people will in unison see that this empire has no clothes.

If we do not stand up and speak openly about the obvious, the world may not break free. Those are the two options: freedom for all or the mighty military of the imperial centers controlling the world's resources, controlling the *wealth-producing-process*, and imposing poverty on weak nations. That is not necessary, eliminate the waste of that control process (in both internal economies and in world trade) and there is enough on this earth for everybody.

---

1 Herman E. Daly, *Steady-State Economics* (San Francisco: W.H. Freeman, 1977), p. 109. See also Brian Milani, *Designing the Green Economy: The Postindustrial Alternative to Corporate Globalization* (New York: Rowman & Littlefield, 2000).

2 Alan Weisman, "Nothing Wasted, Everything Gained," *Mother Jones* (March/April, 1998), pp. 56-59; William Kötke, *The Final Empire* (Portland, OR: Arrow Point Press, 1993), p. 36; Stephanie Mills, *In Service of the Wild: Restoring and Reinhabiting Damaged Land* (Boston: Beacon Press, 1995); John J. Berger, Ed., *Environmental Restoration: Science and Strategies for Restoring the Earth* (Washington, DC: Island Press, 1990); William E. McClain, *Illinois Prairie: Past and Future: A Restoration Guide* (Springfield, IL: Illinois Department of Conservation, 1986); Jonathan Turk et. al., *Ecosystems, Energy, Population* (Toronto: W.B. Saunders Co., 1975); Alan Dregson, Duncan Taylor, editors, *Ecoforestry: The Art and Science of Sustainable Forest Use* (Gabriola Island, BC: New Society Publishers, 1997); Michael Pilarski, *Restoration Forestry: An International Guide to Sustainable Forestry Practices* (Durango, CO: Kivaki Press, 1994); *A Report by The International Institute for Environment and Development and The World Resources Institute, World Resources 1987: An Assessment of the Resource Base That Supports the Global Economy* (New York: Basic Books, 1987), p. 289; Alan Weisman, "Columbia's Modern City," *In Context* (No 42, 1995), pp. 6-8; Lester Thurow, *Head to Head: The Coming Economic Battle Among Japan, Europe, and America* (New York: William Morrow, 1992), p. 223; Jeremy Rifkin, *Entropy: Into the Greenhouse World* (New York: Bantam Books, 1989), p. 220.

Appendix I. Expansion and Contraction of Cultures

There is a deeper psychological reason for world violence than claiming of wealth. Humans, like all creatures, struggle for space on this earth. That struggle causes the borders of cultures over the centuries to expand and contract like an accordion. The primary considerations that dictated the winners, and thus decided who expanded their culture, were new technologies and resources.

The award-winning physiologist Jared Diamond outlines how the domestication of the horse by Proto-Indo-Europeans (PIE) between 3,000 and 5,000 years ago permitted Indo-Europeans to combine their greater mobility with new technologies such as the wheel, metallurgy, and the plow to form an economic/military package with which Indo-European speaking people steamrolled their way across the world and today subdivisions of the Indo-European language are spoken by half the people of the world.

> For thousands of years [after the domestication of the horse], the military value of horses continued to improve with inventions ranging from metal bits and horse-drawn battle chariots around 2000 BC. to the horseshoes, stirrups, and saddles of later cavalry. While most of these advances didn't originate in the steppes, steppe people were still the ones who profited the most, because they had more pasture and hence more horses.... Speakers of Proto-Indo-European merely happened to be in the right place at the right time to put together a useful package of technology. Through that stroke of luck, theirs was the mother tongue whose daughter languages came to be spoken by half the world today.[1]

Within that major cultural expansion were many mini-steamrollings as different subdivisions of Indo-European culture (Spain, Britain, Holland, Portugal, Germany, Italy, et al.) struggled for wealth, power, and territory. At times the losers were decimated and the gene pool of the winners expanded. At other times the losers absorbed the winners and their gene pool expanded as they carried the cultural steamroller forward. The language differentiated in different regions but the basic Indo-European language and culture, on an ever-widening language/cultural base, continued its expansion. Its greatest expansion was the colonization of the world in the past 500 years.

Where primitive cultures were typically pushed off the face of the earth (Indians throughout the Americas and island cultures throughout the world), Western culture has advanced (we hope) to where genocide is no longer acceptable. But those battles between cultures go on in the form of battles over control of resources and world trade, the cornerstones of wealth production and wealth distribution. The winners of these latest struggles and their allies are, as always, wealthy and the losers are, again as usual, impoverished.

Many early societies, such as the American Indians, were very democratic. But these people did not have immunity to diseases common to Europe and Asia. Populations collapsed to a fraction of their previous levels, and entire tribal subdivisions in these regions disappeared. Over 95% of the native populations of the Americas were exterminated in what was undoubtedly the greatest genocide in history.

The Indians on the Caribbean islands were hunted down with dogs and given the choice of accepting the white man's religion and being choked to death or not accepting and having both hands cut off and turned loose. The natives of Tasmania were similarly hunted down with dogs and eliminated. These genocides, when recorded at all, are recorded only in little-known archives. Military commanders would record their assaults on native populations as defensive battles of an on-going war with the natives as the aggressors, not as a military offensive that burned their villages, destroyed their crops, and slaughtered innocent women and children.

Death from disease is frequently addressed; even the distribution of blankets infected with smallpox to decimate the Indian population is occasionally mentioned. But the destruction of a culture's food supply and the destruction of the economic structure which provided food, clothing, and shelter, the resultant sickness and deaths, and the fact that populations not having some immunity to smallpox (the world's greatest killer) suffered a 75% mortality rate—and thus that the giving of those infected blankets was a key part of planned mass genocide—are not mentioned in polite history.

The paying of bounties for Indians, with a special premium for Indian boy scalps by the American colonies starting in 1641 and reaffirmed through enacting those same laws in the states of New York, Massachusetts, Virginia, Pennsylvania, Connecticut, Georgia, Indiana, Kentucky, Texas, California, Oregon, North Dakota, South Dakota, Colorado, and Arizona (an incomplete list), just as was done with wolves and coyotes, is such obvious state murder of innocents that only the bravest researchers dare put it in print. A reading of our sources will conclude that this description of Indian genocide throughout both the Americas is very conservative. Entire tribes by the dozens if not hundreds were wiped off the face of the earth.[a]

Of course, all that gets recorded in American history is that the Indians were savages who scalped people, not that they were largely a friendly, pacifist people willing to share with these strangers, whose government structure provided the model for the U.S. government and whose scalping were only copying that which was being done to them. When you take a close look at history, it is a history of survival of the meanest. Violent cultures overwhelm gentle cultures and commit massive genocide then write history depicting those gentle people as savages and themselves as gentle benevolent people.

A study of the slave trade will arrive at the same conclusion; the violent cultures of Christians and Muslims were enslaving and impoverishing gentle cultures for centuries. Very safely kept out of history books is that Hitler's plans for extermination of what he felt were inferior races were developed from his admiration of America's laws and policies for extermination of Indians and enslavement of blacks.[b] Of course, Hitler knew of the Genocides of the Americas because, like all cultures, his culture could write

---

[a] For societies with superior technology and superior weapons "steamrolling" many American Indian tribes into to extinction, read: Ward Churchhill, *A Little Matter of Genocide: Holocaust and Denial in the Americas, 1492 to the Present* (San Francisco: City Lights Books, 1997); Austin Murphy, *The Triumph of Evil: The Reality of the USA's Cold War Victory* (Florence, Italy: European Press Academic Publishers, 2000), Introduction; B. Cook, "Hitler's Extermination Policy and the American Indian," *Indian Historian* 6, Summer 1973), pp. 48-49; Koning, Hans, *The Conquest of America: How the Indian Nations Lost Their Continent* (New York: Monthly Review Press, 1993); Kirkpatrick Sale, *The Conquest of Paradise* (New York: Alfred A. Knopf, 1991); D. Stannard, *American Holocaust* (Oxford: Oxford University Press, 1992); R. Thornton, *American Indian Holocaust and Survival* (Norman: University of Oklahoma Press, 1987); Ronald Wright, *Stolen Continents: The Americas Through Indian Eyes* (New York: Houghton Mifflin, 1992). See also: H. Chittenden, *The American Fur Trade of the Far West* (New York: Francis P. Harper, 1902); Churchhill, Ward, *Indians Are Us.*(Monroe: Common Courage Press, 1994); A. Domenech, *Deserts of North America* (London: Longman, Green, Longman, and Roberts, 1860); R. Downes, *Council Fires* (Pittsburgh: University of Pittsburgh Press, 1940); Jack D. Forbes, *The Indian in America's Past* (Englewood Cliffs, NJ: Prentice Hall, 1964); D. Grinde, "Cherokee Removal and American Politics." *Indian Historian* 8, Winter 1975, pp. 33-42; A. Jaimes, *The State of Native America* (Boston: South End Press, 1992); F. Jennings, *The Invasion of America* (Chapel Hill: University of North Carolina Press, 1975); C. Larsen, "In the Wake of Columbus: Native Population Biology in the Postcontact Americas." *American Journal of Physical Anthropology* 54, 1994, Supplement 19, pp. 109-154; P. Marks, *In a Barren Land* (New York: William Morrow and Company, 1998); C. Meister, "Demographic Consequences of Euro-American Contact on Selected American Indian Populations and their Relationship to the Demographic Transition" *Ethnohistory* 23, 1976, pp. 161-172; H. Merriam, "The Indian Population of California." *American Anthropologist* 7, 1905, pp. 594-606; V. Miller, "Whatever Happened to the Yuki?" *Indian Historian* 8, Fall 1975, pp. 6-12; F. Waters, *Book of the Hopi* (New York: Penguin, 1977); Jack Weatherford, *Indian Givers: How the Indians of the Americas Transformed the World* (New York: Ballantine, 1988).

[b] Upon learning about Hitler copying America's policies of genocide, I immediately wondered if this is why I could never locate a copy of Hitler's *Mein Kampf* that was not abridged. An empire would not want a book with such explosive history in its libraries.

the honest history of another culture while studiously ignoring the injustices of their own.

The collapse of the civilizations of the losers in these "clashes of cultures" can be seen today as the population of the collapsed Russian economy shrinks by 800,000-per-year.[2] As Russians "theoretically" still have control of their land and resources and they have not been subject to germ warfare or bounties for their scalps, their defeat was not nearly as total as that of the native populations of the Americas, Africa, and Australia. Islands were especially vulnerable to their natives being erased off the face of the earth.

The violent suppression of rights, theft of wealth, and claiming of land rights on the periphery of empire is as old as history. As this is being written, Sixty Minutes presents a documentary on Britain shipping 10,000 temporarily abandoned children to Australia over a period of 30 years, telling them they were orphans. Only on arriving in Australia did they find out the Church and State had collaborated to send these children half way around the world to populate the land to keep it away from the "Asian hordes." Only 40-to-50 years later did they find out their parents had been alive all along.[3]

Notes

1 Jared Diamond, The Third Chimpanzee: The Evolution and Future of the Human Animal (New York: HarperCollins, 1992), pp. 272-73 and Guns, Germs, and Steel: The Fate of Human Societies (New York: W.W. Norton, 1999).

2 *60 Minutes,* May, 19, 1996.

3 *60 Minutes*, February, 3, 2002

Bibliography

ABurish, Said K. *A Brutal Friendship: The West and the Arab Elite.* New York: St Martin's Press, 1997.

Acheson, Dean. *Present at the Creation.* New York: W.W. Norton, 1987.

Ackland, L. *Credibility Gap: A Digest of The Pentagon Papers.* Philadelphia, PA: The National Literature Service. 1972.

Adams, J. *Secret Armies.* New York: The Atlantic Monthly Press 1987.

Addison, Charles G. *The Knights Templar.* London: Longman, Brown, Green, and Longman, 1842.

AFL-CIO Task Force on Trade bulletin, 1992.

"Ag Export Value Projected to Climb." *Great Falls Tribune* (March 5, 1992).

Agee, Philip. "Tracking Covert Actions into the Future." *Covert Action Information Bulletin* (Fall 1992).

_____. *Inside the Company: CIA Diary.* New York: Bantam Books, 1975.

_____. and Louis Wolf, *Dirty Work.* London: Zed Books, 1978.

"Ag Exports Projected to Climb." AP, *Great Falls Tribune* (March 5, 1992).

Ahmad, Feroz. "Arab Nationalism, Radicalism, and the Specter of Neocolonialism." Monthly Review (February 1991).

Alexander, Yonah and Michael S. Swetnam. *Osama Bin Laden's al-Queda: Profile of a Terrorist Network.* Ardsley NY: Transnational Publishers, 2001.

Allen, Terry. "In GATT They Trust." *Covert Action Information Bulletin* 40 (Spring, 1992).

Altvater, Elmar, Kurt Hubner, Jochen Lorentzen, Raul Rojas,. *The Poverty of Nations.* New Jersey: Zed Books, 1991.

Alvord, Clarence Walworth. *The Mississippi Valley in British Politics: A Study of Trade, Land Speculation, and Experiments in Imperialism Culminating in the American Revolution.* New York: Russell & Russell, 1959.

Ambrose, S.E. *Ike's Spies.* Garden City, New York: Doubleday . 1981.

Ameringer, C.D. *U.S. Foreign Intelligence.* Lexington, MA: Lexington Books, 1990.

Andrew, C. *For the President's Eyes Only: Secret Intelligence and the American Presidency From Washington To Bush.* New York: HarperCollins Publishers 1995.

Anta Diop, Cheikh. *Black Africa.* Translated by Harold J. Salemson. Westport: Lawrence Hill, 1978.

Aptheker, Herbert. *The American Revolution.* New York: International Publishers, 1985.

_____. *The Colonial Era.* 2nd ed. New York: International Publishers, 1966.

_____. *Early Years of the Republic.* New York: International Publishers, 1976.

Arévalo, Juan José. *Anti-Kommunism in Latin America.* New York: Lyle Stuart, 1963.

Armstrong, David. *Trumpet to Arms.* Boston: South End Press, 1981.

Arnove, Anthony. *Iraq Under Siege: The Deadly Impact of Sanctions and War.* South End Press: Cambridge, 2002.

Arrighi, Giovanni. *The Long Twentieth Century.* New York: Verso, 2000.

Art, Robert J. and Kenneth N. Waltz. *The Use of Force: Military Power and International Politics.* New York: University Press of America, 1993.

Attenborough, David. *The First Eden: The Mediterranean World and Man.* Boston: Little, Brown, 1987.

Avirgan, Tony, M. Honey, editors, *Lapenca: On Trial in Costa Rica.* San Jose, CA: Editorial Porvenir. 1987.

Bagdikian, Ben. *Media Monopoly.* Boston: Beacon Press, 1987.

Bairoch, Paul. *Economics and World History: Myths and Paradoxes.* Chicago: University of Chicago Press, 1993.

_____. *Cities and Economic Development From the Dawn of History to the* Present. Chicago: University of Chicago Press, 1988.

Baker, Dean. "Job Drain." *The Nation* (July 12, 1993).

Bamford, James. *Body of Secrets: Anatomy of the Ultra-Secret National Security Agency.* New York: Doubleday, 2001.

Banco, Anthony. "Playing With Fire." *Business Week* (September 16, 1987).

The Banneker Center's Corporate Welfare Shame Links. Http://www.progress.org/banneker/cw.html.

Baran, Paul A., and Paul M. Sweezy. *Monopoly Capital.* London: Monthly Review Press, 1968.

Barck, Oscar Theodore, Jr. and Hugh Talmage Lefler. *Colonial America,* 2nd ed. New York: Macmillan, 1968.

Barnett, Correli. *The Collapse of British Power.* New York: Morrow, 1971.

Barnet, Richard. *The Lean Years.* New York: Simon and Schuster, 1980._

_____. *The Alliance.* New York: Simon and Schuster, 1983.

_____. *The Rockets' Red Glare*: War, Politics and American Presidency. New York: Simon and Schuster, 1983.

_____. "Lords of the Global Economy." *The Nation* (December 19, 1994).

_____. and John Cavanagh. *Global Dreams: Imperial Corporations and the New World Order.* New York: Simon and Schuster, 1994.

Barr, Cameron W. "Making the Financial Architecture More Crisis Proof." *The Christian Science Monitor* (March 3, 1999).

Bartlett, Alan F. *Machiavellian Economics*. England: Schumacher, 1987.

Barlett, Donald L., James B. Steele. America: *What Went Wrong?*. Kansas City: Andrews and McMeel, 1992.

_____. "Fantasy Island and Other Perfectly Legal Ways that Big companies Manage to avoid Billions in Federal Taxes." *Time* (November 16, 1998).

_____. "Paying a Price for Polluters." *Time* (November 23, 1998).

_____. "The Empire of Pigs." *Time* (November 30, 1998).

Beard, Charles A. *An Economic Interpretation of the Constitution.* New York: Macmillan Publishing Co, 1941.

Beaud, Michel. *A History of Capitalism, 1500 to 1980*. New York: Monthly Review Press, 1983.

Beeching, Jack. *The Chinese Opium Wars*. New York: Harcourt Brace Jovanovich, 1975.

Bello, W. *U.S. Sponsored Low Intensity Conflict in the Philippines.* San Francisco: Institute for Food and Development Policy (December, 1987).

_____. *Dark Victory: The United States and Global Poverty.* San Francisco: Institute for Food and Development Policy, 1999.

Bemis, Samuel Flagg. *A Diplomatic History of the United States*. New York: Henry Holt, 1936.

Bennet, David H. *The Party of Fear*. Chapel Hill: University of North Carolina Press, 1988.

Bentley, Michael. *Politics Without Democracy*. London: Fontana Paperbacks, 1984.

Bergen, Peter L. *Holy War Inc.: Inside the Secret World of Osama Bin Laden.* New York: Simon & Schuster, 2001.

Berger, John J., ed. *Environmental Restoration: Science and Strategies for Restoring the Earth.* Washington, DC: Island Press, 1990

Berlan, Jean-Pierre. "*The Commodification of Life*." Monthly Review (December 1989).

Bernstein, Carl. "The Holy Alliance." *Time Magazine* (February 24, 1992).

Bernstein, Merton C., Joan Brodshaug Bernstein. *Social Security: The System That Works*. New York: Basic Books, 1988.

"Big Lie Exposed," *Workers World*, April 12, 2001.

Bishop, Abraham. *Georgia Speculation Unveiled*. Readex Microprint Corporation, 1966.

Blackstock, Nelson. Cointelpro: *The FBI's Secret War on Political Freedom.* New York: Anchor Foundation, 1988.

Blaufarb, D.S. *The Counterinsurgency Era: U.S. Doctrine and Performance 1950 To Present.* New York: The Free Press, 1977.

Blaug, Mark. *Great American Economists Before Keynes*. Atlantic Highlands, NJ: Humanities Press International, 1986.

Bluestone, Barry, Irving Bluestone. *Negotiating the Future*. New York: Basic Books, 1992.

Blum, William. Rogue State: *A Guide to the World's Only Super Power.* Monroe, ME: Common Courage Press, 2000.

_____. The CIA: *A Forgotten History*. New Jersey: Zed Books Ltd., 1986.

_____. Killing Hope: *U.S. Military Interventions Since World War II.* Monroe, Me: Common Courage Press, 1995.

Bond, Gordon C. *The Grand Expedition*. Athens: University of Georgia Press, 1979.

Bonner, R. *Waltzing With A Dictator*. New York: Times Books 1987.

Bonvie, Linda, Bill Bonvie, Donna Gates. "*Stevia: The Natural Sweetener That Frightens Nutrasweet*, Earth Island Journal (Winter 1997-98).

"Bookworld," *Washington Post* (April 14, 1994, from McGehee *CIABASE*, Box 5022, Herndon, VA 22070, http://come.to/CIABASE/.

Boorstein, Edward. *What's Ahead? - - - The U.S. Economy*. New York: International Publishers, 1984.

Boorstin, Daniel J. "History's Hidden Turning Points." *U.S. News & World Report* (April 22, 1991).

Börgstrom, George. *The Hungry Planet: The Modern World at the Edge of Famine.* New York: Collier Books, 1972,

Borosage, R.L., Marks, J. editors. *The CIA File*. New York: Grossman Publishers, 1976.

Borsodi, Ralph. *Inflation*. Great Barrington, MA: E.F. Schumacher Society, 1989.

Bortzutzky, Silvia. "The Chicago Boys, Social Security and Welfare in Chile", The Radical Right and the Welfare State: An International Assessment of International Social Policy and Welfare, Howard Glennerster, James Midgley, ed. Lanham, MD: *Barnes and Noble*, 1991.

Breckenfield, Gurney. "Higher Taxes That Promote Development." *Fortune* (August 8, 1983).

Breckinridge, S. P. *Legal Tender.* New York: Greenwood Press, 1969.
Bridge, F.R., *The Habsburg Monarchy.* New York: St. Martin's Press, 1990.
Broadcasting and Cablecasting Yearbook.
Brockway, Sandi. *Macrocosm USA.* Cambria, CA: Macrocosm USA, Inc., 1992.
Brody, Reed. *Contra Terror in Nicaragua: Report of a Fact Finding Mission*: September 1984-January 1985. Boston: South End Press, 1985.
Brown, George E. Jr., William J. Goold, John Cavanagh. "Making Trade Fair." *World Policy Journal* (Spring, 1992).
Brown, Lester R. *State of the World.* New York: W.W. Norton, 1998.
_____. Christopher Flavin, and Sandra Postel. *Saving the Planet.* New York: W.W. Norton, 1991.
Brown, Michael Barratt. *Fair Trade.* London: Zed Books, 1993.
Brown, Walt. *Treachery in Dallas.* New York: Carroll & Graf, 1995.
Browne, Lewis. *Stranger Than Fiction: A Short History of the Jews.* New York: Macmillan, 1925.
Budiansky, Stephen. "An Act of Vision for the Third World." *U.S. News & World Report* (November 2, 1987).
"Buffalo Battalion—South Africa's Black Mercenaries." *Covert Action Information Bulletin* (July/August 1981).
Bulletin from the AFL-CIO Task Force on Trade (1992).
Bulletin Of Concerned Asian Scholars. Boulder, CO.
Bunzl, John, *The Simultaneous Policy: An Insider's Guide to Saving Humanity and the Planet.* London: New European Publications 2002.
Burgoon, Brian. "NAFTA Thoughts." Dollars and Sense. (September/October 1995).
Burman, Edward. *The Inquisition: Hammer of Heresy.* New York: Dorset Press, 1992.
Burnes, James. *The Knights Templar. London*: Paybe and Foss, 1840.
Buzgalin, Alexander, Andrei Kolganov. *Bloody October in Moscow: Political Repression in the Name of Reform.* New York: Monthly Review Press, 1994.
Cagan, Joanna, Neil DeMause. *Field of Schemes.* Monroe Maine: Common Courage Press, 1998.
Caldwell, M. Editor *Ten Years Military Terror Indonesia.* Nottingham: Spokesmen Books, no date.
Calloni, Stella. "The Horror Archives of Operation Condor." *CovertAction Quarterly* 50 (Fall 1994).
Carey, Alex. Tak*ing the Risk out of Democracy; Corporate Propaganda versus Freedom and Liberty.* Chicago: University of Illinois Press, 1995.
Carsten, F. L. *Britain and the Weimar Republic.* New York: Schocken Books, 1984.
_____. *The Rise of Fascism.* Berkeley: University of California Press, 1982.
Castro, Fidel. *Nothing Can Stop the Course of History.* New York: Pathfinder Press, 1986.
_____. *Capitalism in Crisis: Globalization and World Politics Today.* New York: Ocean Press, 2000.
Catton, William Robert. Overshoot: *The Ecological Basis of Revolutionary Change* Champaign, IL: University of Illinois Press, 1980.
Caute, David. *The Great Fear.* New York: Simon and Schuster, 1978.
Cavanagh, John. "Review of The Rise and Fall of Economic Liberalism: The Making of the Economic Gulag." *Monthly Review* (May 1997).
_____. Ed. *Trading Freedom.* San Francisco: The Institute for Food and Development Policy, 1992.
CBS News
Chamberlain, E. R. *The Fall of the House of Borgia.* New York: Dorset Press, 1987.
Chamorro, E., "Packaging the Contras: A case of CIA Disinformation." *Monograph Series Number 2.* New York: Institute For Media Analysis, 1987.
"Change." *Railway Age* (November 1984).
Chase, Stuart. *The Economy of Abundance.* New York: The Macmillan Company, 1934.
_____. *Men and Machines.* New York: The Macmillan Company, 1929.
_____. *The Tragedy of Waste.* New York: The Macmillan Company, 1925.
Chavkin, Samuel. *The Murder of Chile.* New York: Everest House, 1982.
Li, Cheng. *Rediscover China: Dynamics and Dilemmas of Reform.* Oxford: Rowman and Littlefield, 1997.
Chester, E.T. *Covert Network: Progressives, the International Rescue Committee, and the CIA.* New York: M.E. Sharpe, 1995.
Chien, Arnold J. "Tanzanian Tales." *Lies of Our Times* (January 1991).
"China Maneuvering Around Quotas to Market Textiles to United States." *The Spokesman-Review* (January 10, 1989).
Chinweizu. "Debt Trap Peonage." *Monthly Review* (November 1985).
Chittenden, H. *The American Fur Trade of the Far West.* New York: Francis P. Harper, 1902.
Chomsky, Noam. "Enduring Truths: Changing Markets." *CovertAction Quarterly* (Spring 1996).
_____. *The Culture of Terrorism.* Boston: South End Press, 1988.
_____. *Deterring Democracy.* New York: Verso, 1992.
_____. *Year 501: The Conquest Continues.* Boston: South End Press, 1993.

_____. *The Prosperous Few and the Restless Many*. Berkeley: Odonian Press, 1993.

_____. *On Power and Ideology*, South End Press, 1990.

Chossudovsky, Michel. "United States War Machine: Revving the Engines of World Warr III, *CovertAction Quarterly* (Fall 2002).

_____. "Dismantling Yugoslavia, Colonizing Bosnia." *CovertAction Quarterly* (Spring, 1996).

_____. *The Globalization of Poverty: Impacts of IMF and World Bank Reforms*. London: Zed Books, 1997.

_____. *War and Globalization: The Truth behind September 11*. Centre for Research on Globalization, 2002)

Choucri, Nazli, and Robert C. North. *Nations in Conflict*. San Francisco: W. H. Freeman, 1974.

Church Committee Report. *Congressional Record*. 1975-76.

Churchhill, Ward. *Cointelpro Papers : Documents from the FBI's Secret Wars Against Domestic Dissent*. South End Press, 1990.

_____. *Indians Are Us*. Monroe: Common Courage Press, 1994.

_____. *A* Little Matter of Genocide: Holocaust and Denial in the Americas, 1492 to the Present. San Francisco: City Lights Books, 1997.

_____. Agents of Repression : The FBI's Secret Wars Against the Black Panther Party and the American Indian Movement. Boston South End Press, 1989.

The Christian Science Monitor (December 4, 1997).

Clairmont, Frederic F. *The Rise and Fall of Economic* Liberalism.. Goa India: The Other India Press, 1996.

Clark, Ramsey. *Hidden Agenda: U.S./NATO Takeover of Yugoslavia*, New York: International action Center, 2002.

Clarridge, Duane R. *A Spy for all Seasons: My Life in the CIA*.. New York: Scribner, 1997.

Cline, R.S. *Secrets, Spies, and Scholars*. Washington, DC: Acropolis Books, 1976.

CNN Frontline (November 18, 1991).

CNN Headline News (June 28, 1990).

Cockburn, Alexander. "Beat the Devil." *The Nation* (March 6, 1989).

_____. and Jeffrey St. Clair. *Whiteout: The CIA, Drugs and the Press*. New York: Verso, 1998.

Codevilla, Angelo. *Informing Statecraft*. New York: The Free Press, 1992.

Cohen, Carl, ed. *Communism, Fascism, Democracy*. New York: Random House, 1962.

Cohen, Dan. "Deep Dish: Outsiders on Public TV." *The Guardian* (May 6, 1992).

Cohen, Stephen. *Failed Crusade: America and the Tragedy of Post-Communist Russia*. New York: W.W. Norton, 2000.

Colby, Gerard, Charlotte Dennett. *Thy Will Be Done: The Conquest of the Amazon: Nelson Rockefeller and Evangelism in the Age of Oil*. New York: Harper Collins, 1995.

_____. Du Pont: *Behind the Nylon Curtain*. Englewood Cliffs, N.J.: Prentice-Hall, 1974.

Colby, William. *Honorable Men*. New York: Simon and Schuster, 1978.

Coleman, Peter. *Liberal Conspiracy*. London: Collier Macmillan, 1989.

Collmer, Kathy. "Guess Who's Coming to Dinner?" *Utne Reader* (July/August, 1992).

Collon, Michel. *Liars Poker: The Great Powers, Yugoslavia and the Wars of the future*. New York:: International action Center, 2002

Committee of Concerned Asian Scholars, The Indochina Story: A Fully Documented Account. New York: Pantheon Books, 1970.

Commoner, Barry. *Making Peace With the Planet*. New York: Pantheon, 1990.

Commons, John R. *Legal Foundations of Capitalism*. London: Transaction Publishers, 1995.

_____. *Institutional Economics*. London: Transaction Publishers, 1995.

Conboy, K., J. Morrison. *Shadow War: The CIA's Secret War in* Laos. Boulder, CO: Paladin Press, 1995.

Condliffe, J. B. *The Commerce of Nations*. New York: Norton, 1950.

Constantino, R., L.R. Constantino. *The Philippines: The Continuing Past*. Quezon City, Philippines: The Foundation for Nationalist Studies, 1978.

Cook, B. *The Declassified Eisenhower*. Garden City, NY: Doubleday, 1981.

_____--, "Hitler's Extermination Policy and the American Indian." *Indian Historian* 6, Summer 1973.

Cook, Don. *Forging the Alliance*. London: Seeker and Warburg, 1989.

Cook, William J. "Reach Out and Touch Everyone." *U.S. News & World Report* (October 10, 1988).

Cooley, John K. *Unholy Wars: Afghanistan, America, and International Terrorism*, 2nd edition. London: Pluto Press, 2000.

Cooper, Marc. Chile and the End of Pinochet." *The Nation* (February 26, 2001

Cooper, Mathew, Dorian Friedman. "The Rich in America." *U.S. News & World Report* (November 18, 1991).

Cooper, Mathew. "Give Trade a Chance." *U.S. News & World Report* (February 14, 1994).

Copeland, M. *Beyond Cloak and Dagger*. New York: Pinnacle Books, 1975.

Cordovez, D, S.S. Harrison, *Out of Afghanistan: The Inside Story of the Soviet Withdrawal*. New York: Oxford University Press, 1995.

Corn, D. *Blond Ghost: Ted Shackley and the CIA's Crusades*. New York: Simon and Schuster, 1994.

Corn, David, Jefferson Morley. "Beltway Bandits." *The Nation* (April 9, 1988).

Corwin, Julie, Douglas Stranglin, Suzanne Possehl, Jeff Trimble. "The Looting of Russia." *U.S. News & World Report* (March 7, 1994).

"The Costs of War." *The Nation* (December 24, 1990).

Counterspy (All issues).

CovertAction Quarterly (All Issues).

Cottin, Heather. "George Soros, Imperial Wizard: Master-Builder of the New Bribe Sector, Systematically Bilking the World" *CovertAction Quarterly* (Fall 2002).

Covington, Sally. "Right Thinking, Big Grants, and Long Term Strategy: How Conservative Philanthropies and Think Tanks Transform U.S. Policy." *CovertAction Quarterly* (Winter 1998).

Crowther, Samuel. *America Self-Contained.* Garden City, N.Y.: Doubleday, Doran & Co., 1933.

Curry, Richard O. *An Uncertain Future: Thought Control and Repression During the Reagan-Bush Era.* Los Angeles: First Amendment Foundation, 1992.

Currey, C.B. Edward Lansdale: *The Unquiet American.* Boston: Houghton Mifflin Company, 1988.

Daly, Herman E. *Steady-State Economics.* San Francisco: W.H. Freeman 1977.

_____. John B. Cobb Jr. *For the Common Good.* Boston: Beacon Press, 1989.

_____. Salah El Serafy, editors. *Population, Technology, and Lifestyle.* Washington DC: Island Press, 1992.

Danaher, Kevin, Editor. *50 Years Is Enough: The Case Against the World Bank and the International Monetary Fund.* Boston: South End Press, 1995.

Das, Bhagirath Lal. *WTO: The Doha Agenda: The New Negotiations on World Trade.* London: Zed Books, 2003, and his many other books.

Daraul, Arkon. A History of Secret Societies. Secaucus, NJ: Citadel Press, 1961.

David, Arie E. The Strategy of Treaty Termination. New Haven: Yale University Press, 1975.

DeForest, O., Chanoff, D. *Slow Burn.* New York: Simon and Schuster, 1990.

Dentzer, Susan. "The Coming Global Boom." *U.S. News & World Report* (July 16, 1990).

Depth News, Manila, Quoted by *World Press Review* (March 1991).

De Rosa, Peter. *Vicars of Christ: The Dark Side of the Papacy.* New York: Crown Publishers, 1988.

Desmond, Edward W. "Japan's Trillion-Dollar Hole." *Time* (April 8, 1996).

_____. "The Failed Miracle." *Time* (April 22, 1996).

Diamond, Jared. *Guns, Germs, and Steel: The Fates of Human Societies.* New York: W.W. Norton, 1999.

_____. *The Third Chimpanzee: The Evolution and Future of the Human Animal.* New York: HarperCollins, 1992.

DiEugenio, James and Lisa Pease. *The Assassinations: Probe Magazine on JFK, MLK, RFK, and Malcolm X.* Los Angeles: Feral House, 2003.

Dinges, John, Saul Landau. *Assassination on Embassy Row.* New York: Pantheon Books, 1980.

Dobbowski, Michael N., Isodor Wallimann. *Radical Perspectives on the Rise of Fascism in Germany.* New York: Monthly Review Press, 1989.

Dobson, John M. *Two Centuries of Tariffs: The Background and Emergence of the U.S. International Trade Commission.* Washington DC: U.S. International Trade Commission, 1976.

Doder, Dusko. "Yugoslavia: New War, Old Hatreds." *Foreign Policy* (Summer 1993).

Domenech, A. *Deserts of North America.* London: Longman, Green, Longman, and Roberts, 1860.

Donahue, John D. *The Privatization Decision: Public Ends and Private Means.* New York: Basic Books, 1989.

Donner, Frank J. *The Age of Surveillance: The Aims and Methods of America's Political Intelligence System.* New York: Random House, 1981.

Dorgan, Byron, Senator. *The North Dakota REC* (May 1984).

Douglas-Hamilton, James. *Motive For a Mission: The Story Behind Rudolf Hess's Flight to Britain.* New York: Paragon House, 1979.

Douthwaite, Richard. "Community Money." *Yes* (Spring 1999).

Downes, R. *Council Fires.* Pittsburgh: University of Pittsburgh Press, 1940.

Downing, John. *Radical Media.* Boston: South End Press, 1984.

Dregson, Alan, Duncan Taylor, Editors. *Ecoforestry: The Art and Science of Sustainable Forest Use.* Gabriola Island, BC: New Society Publishers, 1997

Drucker, Peter. *The New Realities.* New York: Harper & Row, 1989.

Echeverria, Durand. *The Maupeou Revolution: A Study in the History of Libertarianism.* Baton Rouge: Louisiana State University Press, 1985.

Eckholm, Erik P. *Losing Ground: Environmental Stress and World Food Prospects.* New York: W.W. Norton, 1976.

Eckes, Alfred E., Jr. *Opening America's Markets: U.S. Foreign Trade Policy Since 1776.* Chapel Hill: University of North Carolina Press, 1995.

Elkington, John, *Cannibals With Forks.* Gabriola Island, B.C.: New Society Publishers, 1998.

Emerson, S. *Secret Warriors.* New York: G.P. Putnam, 1988.

Endicott, Stephen, Edward Hagerman. *The United States and Biological Warfare: Secrets from the Early Cold War and Korea.* Bloomington, IN: Indiana University Press, 1998.

Epstein, Gerald. "Mortgaging America." *World Policy Journal* (Winter 1990-91).

Epstein, Jack. "Dickens Revisited," *The Christian Science Monitor* (August 24, 1995).

_____. "Argentina's 'Dirty War' Laundry May Get a Public Airing," *The Christian Science Monitor* (December 4, 1997).

Erdman, Andrew. "The Billionaires." *Fortune* (September 10, 1990).

Erickson, J. *The Road to Berlin.* New Haven: Yale University Press, 1983.

Etzold, Thomas H., John Lewis Gaddis. *Containment: Documents On American Policy and Strategy*, 1945-50. New York: Columbia University Press, 1978.

Fallows, James. "How the World Works." *The Atlantic Monthly* (December 1993).

Faux, Jeff. "The Austerity Trap and the Growth Alternative." *World Policy Journal* (Summer 1988).

Feagin, Joe E. *The Urban Real Estate Game.* Engelewood Cliffs, NJ: Prentice-Hall, 1983.

Feffer, John. "The Browning of Russia." *CovertAction Quarterly* (Spring 1996).

Felix, David. "Latin America's Debt Crisis." *World Policy Journal* (Fall 1990).

Fingleton, Eamonn. *In Praise of Hard Industries: Why Manufacturing, not the Information Economy, is the Key to Future Prosperity.* New York: Houghton Mifflin, 1999.

"Firm Claims Breakthrough in High-Definition Television." *The Spokesman-Review* (July 13, 1989).

Fisher, Fritz. *Germany's Aims in the First World War.* New York: W. W. Norton, 1967.

"Five Ways Out," *Time* (November 30, 1998).

Flaherty, Patrick. "Behind Shatalinomics: Politics of Privatization," *Guardian* (October 10, 1990).

Fleming, D. F. *The Cold War and Its Origins.* 2 vol. New York: Doubleday, 1961.

Flexner, James Thomas. *George Washington: The Forge of Experience.* Boston: Little Brown and Co., 1965.

Foner, Philip S. *Labor and World War I.* New York: International Publishers, 1987.

_____. *Abraham Lincoln: Selections From His Writings.* New York: International Publishers, 1944.

_____. *From Colonial Times to the Founding of the American Federation of Labor.* New York: International Publishers, 1947.

_____. *From the Founding of the A.F. of L. to the Emergence of American Imperialism.* New York: International Publishers, 1982.

Forbes, Jack D. *The Indian in America's Past.* Englewood Cliffs, NJ: Prentice Hall, 1964.

Ford, Peter. "Regime Change: A Look at Washington's Methods and Degrees of Success in Dislodging Foreign Leaders," *The Christian Science Monitor*, January 27, 2003,

Francis, David R. "Debt riddled Russia to Ask for Forgiveness." *The Christian Science Monitor* (April 5, 1999).

Franke, Richard W. Barbara H. Chasin. "Power to the Malayalee People." *Z Magazine* (February 1998).

_____. "Kerala State, India: Radical Reform as Development." *Monthly Review* (January 1991).

Frazer, Phillip. "Dirty Tricks Down Under." *Mother Jones* (February/March 1984).

Frazier, H., ed. *Uncloaking the CIA.* New York: The Free Press, 1978.

Freeland, Chrystia. *Sale of the Century: Russia's Wild Ride From Communism to Capitalism*, New York: Crown Publishers, 2000.

Freemantle, B. *CIA.* New York: Stein and Day, 1983.

Fresia, Jerry. *Toward an American Revolution: Exposing the Constitution and Other Illusions.* Boston, South End Press, 1988.

Fromkin, David. *A Peace To End All Peace.* New York: Avon Books, 1989.

Furiati, Claudia. *ZR Rifle: The Plot to Kill Kennedy and Castro.* Melbourne: Ocean Press, 1994.

Gaffney, Mason, Fred Harrison. *The Corruption of Economics: With The Development of Democracy, Mind Control Became the Urgent* Need: Neo-Classical Economics Was the Tool. London: Shepheard-Walwyn, 1994.

Galbraith, John Kenneth. *Economics in Perspective.* New York: Houghton Mifflin, 1987.

_____. *Money.* New York: Houghton Mifflin, 1976.

_____. "Which Capitalism for Eastern Europe." *Harpers* (April 1990).

_____. and Stanislav Menshikov. *Capitalism, Communism, and Coexistence.* Boston: Houghton Mifflin Company, 1988.

Galeano, Eduardo. *Guatemala: Occupied Country.* New York: Monthly Review Press, 1969.

Gardner, Lloyd C. *Safe for Democracy. New York*: Oxford University Press, 1984.

Garrison, Jim. *On the Trail of the Assassins.* New York: Sheridan Square Press, 1988.

Garvin, G. *Everybody Has His Own Gringo: The CIA and the Contras.* New York: Brassey's,1992.

Garwood, Darrell. *Under Cover: Thirty-Five Years of CIA Deception.* New York: Grove Press, 1985.

Gates, Bill. "The Road Ahead." *Newsweek* (November 27, 1995).

Geonomy Society, 30401 Navarro Ridge Rd, Albion, CA 95410 .

George, Henry. *Progress and Poverty.* New York: Robert Schalkenbach Foundation,1981.

George, Susan. *The Lugano Report: On Preserving Capital in the Twenty-First Century*. Sterling, VA: Pluto Press, 1999.

_____. *Ill Fares the Land*. Washington, DC: Institute for Policy Studies, 1984.

_____. *A Fate Worse Than Debt*. Rev. New York: Grove Weidenfeld, 1990.

_____. *How the Other Half Dies*. Montclair, NJ: Allen Osmun, 1977.

_____. *The Debt Boomerang*. San Francisco: Westview Press, 1992.

_____. and Fabrizio Sabelli. *Faith and Credit*. San Francisco: Westview Press, 1994.

Gervasi, Sean. "Germany, U.S., and the Yugoslavian Crisis." *CovertAction Quarterly* (Winter 1992-93).

Gervasi, S., Wong, S. "The Reagan Doctrine and The Destabilization Of Southern Africa" April 1990. Unpublished paper from McGehee

Gettleman, M., J. Franklin, M. Young, B. Franklin, *Vietnam and America: The Most Comprehensive Documented History Of The Vietnam War*. New York: Grove Press, 1995.

Gibbs, D., *The Political Economy of Third World Intervention: Mines, Money and U.S. Policy in the Congo Crisis*. Chicago, IL: The University of Chicago Press, 1991.

Gill, Stephen. The Geopolitics of the Asian Crisis." *Monthly Review* (March 1999).

Gill, William J. *Trade Wars Against America: A History of United States Trade and Monetary Policy*. New York: Praeger, 1990.

Gleijeses, P. *Shattered Hope: The Guatemalan Revolution and the United States, 1944-1954*. Princeton, New Jersey, Princeton University Press, 1991.

Gohari, M.J. *The Taliban: Ascent to Power*. New York: Oxford University Press, 2000.

Goldhaber, Michael. *Reinventing Technology*. New York: Routledge & Kegan Paul, 1986.

Goldsmith, Edward. *The Future of Progress: Reflections on Environment and Development*. Berkeley: International Society for Ecology and Culture, 1995.

Goodland, Robert, Herman E. Daly, Salah El Serafy, editors. *Population, Technology, and Lifestyle*. Washington DC: Island Press, 1992.

Goodman, David. "Political Spy Trial in Pretoria." *In These Times* (September 19-25, 1984).

Goodson, Larry P. *Afghanistan's Endless War: State failure, Regional Politics, and the Rise of the Taliban*. Seattle: University of Washington Press, 2001.

Goodspeed, D. J. *The German Wars*. New York: Bonanza Books, 1985.

Gorbachev, Mikhail. *Perestroika*. New York: Harper & Row, 1987.

Gordon, John Steele. *Hamilton's Blessing: The Extraordinary Life and Times of Our National Debt*. New York: Walker and Co., 1997.

Gorz, André. *Ecology as Politics*. Boston: South End Press, 1980.

_____. *Paths to Paradise: On the Liberation From Work*. Boston: South End Press, 1985.

Goulden, Joseph C. *Monopoly*. New York: Pocket Books, 1970.

Government Accounting office, *Letter Report*, GAO/NSIAD-97-260. (October, 30, 1997). Gowan, Peter. "Old Medicine in New Bottles." *World Policy Journal* (Winter 1991-92).

Grant, James P. "Jumpstarting Development." *Foreign Policy* (Summer 1993).

Grant, Phil. *The Wonderful Wealth Machine*. New York: Devon-Adair, 1953.

Gray, John. *False Dawn*. New York: The New Press, 1998.

Greco, Tom. *Understanding and creating Alternatives to Legal Tender*. White River JCT, VT: Chelsea Green Publishing, 2001.

Green, Duncan. *Silent Revolution*. London: Cassel, 1995.

Green, Hardy. "Income Erosion: Economic Landslides." *In These Times* (November 14-20, 1990).

Green, Larry. "Subsidies: Half of '87 Farm Income to Come from Government." *Los Angeles Times*, reprinted in *The Missoulian* (October 25, 1987).

Green, Mark. *The Other Government*. Rev. New York: W.W. Norton, Inc., 1978.

Greenberg, Michael. *British Trade and the Opening of China 1800-1842*. New York: Monthly Review Press, reprint of 1951 edition.

Greider, William. *One World Ready or Not*. New York: Simon and Schuster, 1997.

_____."Annals of Finance." The New Yorker, (November 9, 1987; Nov. 16, 1987; November 23, 1987).

_____. *The Education of David Stockman and Other Americans*. New York: New American Library, 1986.

_____. "The Money Question." *World Policy Journal* (Fall 1988).

_____. *Secrets of the Temple*. New York: Simon and Schuster, 1987.

_____. *Who Will Tell the People?* New York: Simon and Schuster, 1992.

Grinde, D. "Cherokee Removal and American Politics." *Indian Historian 8* (Winter 1975), 33-42.

Griswold, Deirdre. "Marxism, Reformism and Anarchism: Lessons from a Steel Mill in Slovakia." *Workers World* (December 14, 2000).

Groden Robert J., Harrison Edward Livingstone. *High Treason: The Assassination of President John F. Kennedy and New Evidence of Conspiracy*. New York: Berkeley Books, 1990.

Grose, Peter. *Gentleman Spy : The Life of Allen Dulles*. Boston: University of Massachusetts Press, 1996.

Gross, Bertram. "Rethinking Full Employment." *The Nation* (January 17, 1987).

Grosser, Paul E., and Edwin G. Halperin, *Anti-Semitism: Causes and Effects.* New York: Philosophical Library, 1983.
Grun, Bernard. *Timetables of American History.* New York: Simon and Schuster, 1979.
Gueye, Ousseynu. "Let African Farmers Compete." World Press Review (October 2002).
Guma, Greg. "Cracks in the Covert Iceberg." *Toward Freedom* (May 1998).
Gunson, P., A. Thompson, G. Chamberlain. *The Dictionary of Contemporary Politics of South America.* New York: Routledge, 1989.
Gup, Ted, *The Book of Honor: Covert Lives and Classified Deaths at the CIA.* New York: Doubleday, 2000.
Gyorgy, Anna, trans. *Practical Program for Global Reform.* London: Atlantic Highlands, N.J.: Zed Books, 1992
_____. *Ecological Economics.* London: Zed Books, 1991.
Hahnel, Robin. "Capitalist Globalism in Crisis." *Z Magazine* (March 1999).
Hall, Ivan P. *Cartels of the Mind: Japan's Intellectual Closed Shop.* New York: WW Norton, 1998.
Hancock, Graham. *Lords of Poverty.* New York: Atlantic Monthly Press, 1989.
Hartmann, Betsy, James K. Boyce. *Needless Hunger: Voices from a Bangladesh Village.* Rev. San Francisco, CA: Institute for Food and Development Policy, 1982.
Hartung, William D. "Why Sell Arms?" *World Policy Journal* (Spring 1993).
Hawken, Paul, Amory Lovins, L. Hunter Lovins. *Natural Capitalism: Creating the Next Industrial Revolution.* New York: Little Brown and Company, 1999.
Hatal, William H. Richard J. Verey. "Recognizing the 'Third Way.' *The Christian Science Monitor* (March 3, 1999).
Heckscher, Eli F. *Mercantilism*, 2 vol. New York: The Macmillan Company, 1955.
Heidenry, D. *Theirs Was the Kingdom: Lila and Dewitt Wallace the Story of the Reader's Digest.* New York: W.W. Norton, 1993.
Heilig, Bruno. "Why The German Republic Fell:"
gopher://echonyc.com:70/00/Cul/HGS/germecon.
Henry George Foundation of America, 2000 Century Plaza, #238, Columbia, MD. 21004
Henry George School. New York: gopher://echonyc.com:70/11s/Cul/HGS.
Henwood, Doug. *Wall Street.* New York: Verso, 1997.
_____. "Clinton and the Austerity Cops." *The Nation* (November 23, 1992).
_____. "The U.S. Economy: The Enemy Within." *Covert Action* (Summer 1992).
Herman, Edward S. *The Real Terror Network.* Boston: South End Press, 1982.
_____. "The Assault on Social Security." *Z Magazine* (November 1995).
_____. and Noam Chomsky. *Manufacturing Consent: The Political Economy of the Mass Media.* New York: Pantheon, 1988.
_____. and F. Broadhead. *Demonstration Elections: U.S. Staged Elections in the Dominican Republic, Vietnam, and El Salvador*, Boston: South End Press, 1984 .
_____. and Gerry O'Sullivan. *The Terrorism Industry.* New York: Pantheon Books, 1989.
Herrnstein, Richard J., and Charles Murray. *The Bell Curve: Intelligence and Class Structure in American Life.* New York: Free Press, 1994.
Hersh, Burton. *The Old Boys: The American Elite and the Origins of the CIA.* New York: Charles Scribner's Sons, 1992.
Heuvel, Katrina vanden. Editorial, *The Nation* (August 10-17, 1998).
"High Court: This Property Is Condemned," *Newsweek* (June 11, 1984).
Hightower, Jim. "NAFTA, We Don't Hafta." *Utne Reader* (July/August 1993).
Hillkirk, John. "Users' Aim: 1 Language in All Computers." *USA Today* (June 7, 1988).
Hinckle, Warren, William Turner. *The Fish Is Red: The Story of the Secret War Against Castro.* New York: Harper & Row, 1981.
_____. *Deadly Secrets: The CIA-Mafia War Against Castro and The Assassination of J.F.K.* New York: Thunder Mouth Press, 1992.
Hines, Colin, Tim Lang. Jerry Mander, Edward Goldsmith, eds. *The Case Against the Global Economy and For A Turn Toward the Local.* San Francisco: Sierra Club, 1996.
Hitchens, Christopher. *The Trial of Henry Kissinger.* New York: Verso, 2001.
Hixson, William F. *It's Your Money.* Toronto, Canada: 1997.
_____. *Triumph of the Bankers: Money and Banking in the Eighteenth and Nineteenth Centuries.* Westport, Conn.: Praeger, 1993.
Hizak, Shlomo. *Building or Breaking: What Does a Jew Think When A Christian Says "I Love You"?* San Diego: Jerusalem Center for Biblical Studies and Research, 1985.
Hofstadter, Richard. *The Paranoid Style in American Politics.* Chicago: University of Chicago Press, 1979.
Horn, Miriam. "Can the Boob Tube Finally Get Serious." *U.S. News & World Report* (August 24, 1992).
Howarth, Stephen. *Knights Templar.* New York: Dorset Press, 1982.
Hufton, Olwen. Europe: *Privilege and Protest.* Ithaca, NY: Cornell University Press, 1980.

Human Development Report, 1991. New York: Oxford University Press, 1991.

"Hunger as a Weapon." *Food First Action Alert*. Institute for Food and Development Policy, undated.

Hunt, E. K., Howard J. Sherman. *Economics*. New York: Harper & Row, 1990.

Hunt, H.J. *Undercover: Memoirs of an American Secret Agent*. New York: Berkeley Publishing, 1974.

Huntington, Samuel P. *The Clash of Civilizations*. New York: Simon and Schuster, 1996.

Hyam, Ronald. *Britain's Imperial Century, 1815 - 1914: A Study of Empire and Expansion*. London: B. T. Batsford, 1976.

Hyams, Edward. *Soil and Civilization*. New York: Harper & Row, 1976.

Impoco, Jim, Jack Egan, Douglas Pasternak. "The Tokyo Tidal Wave." *U.S. News & World Report* (September 17, 1990).

"In Fact." *The Nation,* (March 25, 1996).

Irwin, Douglas A. *Against the Tide: An Intellectual History of Free Trade*. Princeton, N.J.: Princeton University Press, 1996.

Isaacson, Walter, and Evan Thomas, *The Wise Men*. New York: Simon and Schuster, 1986.

Jackson, Brooks. *Honest Graft: Big Money and the American Political Process*. New York: Alfred A Knopf, 1988.

Jacobs, Dan. *The Brutality of Nations*. New York: Alfred A. Knopf, 1987.

Jai-eui, Lee. *Kwangju Diary: Beyond Death, Beyond the Darkness of Age*. Los Angeles: University of California, 1999.

Jaimes, A. *The State of Native America*. Boston: South End Press, 1992.

Jayko, Margaret. *FBI on Trial: The Victory in the Socialist Workers Party Suit against Government Spying*. New York: Pathfinder Press, 1989.

Jeavons, John. *How to Grow More Vegetables Than You Ever Thought Possible On Less Land Than You Ever Imagined: A Primer On The Life Giving Biointensive Method Of Organic* Horticulture. Berkeley, CA: Ten Speed Press, 1991.

Jeffreys-Jones, R. *The CIA & American Democracy*. New Haven CT: Yale University Press, 1989.

Jennings, F. *The Invasion of America*. Chapel Hill: University of North Carolina Press, 1975.

Jensen, Derrick, *A Language Older Than Words*. New York: Context Books, 2000

Johnson, Chalmers. *Blowback: The Costs and Consequences of the American Empire*. New York: Henry Holt & Company, 2000.

Johnson, Emory R. *History of Domestic and Foreign Commerce of the United States. Washington* DC: Carnegie Institute of Washington, 1915.

Johnson, Haynes. "Teflon 80s Bear Striking Resemblance to 'Giddy' 20s." *The Missoulian* (March 25, 1987).

Johnson, Loch .K. *America's Secret Power*. New York: Oxford University Press, 1989.

Johnstone, Diane. "GATTastrophe: Free-Trade Ideology Versus Planetary Survival." *In These Times*. (December 19-25, 1990).

Jonas, Susanne. *The Battle for Guatemala: Rebels, Death Squads, and U.S. Power*. San Francisco: Westview Press, 1991.

Josephson, Matthew. *Robber Barons*. New York: Harcourt Brace Jovanovich, 1962.

Joynt, Carey B., and Percy E. Corbett. *Theory and Reality in World Politics*. Pittsburgh: University of Pittsburgh Press, 1978.

Jukes, Jeffrey. *Stalingrad at the Turning Point*. New York: Ballantine Books, 1968.

Kadane, Kathy. *States News Service* and Ralph McGehee's *http://come.to/CIABASE/*.

Kagarlitsky, Boris. *Square Wheels: How Russian Democracy Got Derailed*. New York: Monthly Review Press, 1994.

Kahin, G.M., J.W. Lewis, *United States in Vietnam*. New York: Dell Publishing Company. 1969.

Kahin, McT. *Subversion as Foreign Policy: The Secret Eisenhower and Dulles Debacle in Indonesia*. New York: New Press. 1995.

Kaku, Michio and Daniel Axelrod. *To Win A Nuclear War*. Boston: South End Press, 1987.

Kaplan, D. *Fires of the Dragon: Politics, Murder and the Kuomintang*. NY: Atheneum, 1992.

Karmatz, Laura, Alisha Labi, Joan Levinstein, Special Report, "States at War," *Time* (November 9, 1998).

Karnow, S. *In Our Image: America's Empire In The Philippines*. New York: Random House, 1989.

Kaslow, Amy. "The Price of Low-Cost Clothes: US Jobs." *The Christian Science Monitor* (August 20, 1995).

Kelley, Sean. *America's Tyrant: The CIA and Mobutu of Zaire*. (Washington DC: American University Press, 1993),

Kendall, Don. "Meat-eaters Consuming Less Fat." *The Missoulian* (February 4, 1987).

———. "U.S Farmers Look to the developing world." *The Spokesman-Review* (January 5, 1988).

Kennedy, Paul. *The Rise and Fall of the Great Powers*. New York: Random House, 1987.

Kernaghan, Charles. "Sweatshop Blues." *Dollars and Sense* (March/April, 1999).

Kessler, R. *Inside The CIA: Revealing The Secrets Of The World's Most Powerful Spy Agency*. New York: Pocket Books, 1992.

Ketchum, Richard M., ed. *The American Heritage Book of the Revolution.* New York: American Heritage Publishing, 1971.

Kettle, Michael. *The Allies and the Russian Collapse.* Minneapolis: University of Minnesota Press, 1981.

Khan, Sadruddin Aga, Editor. *Policing the Global Economy: Why, How and for Whom.* Cameron Bay Publishers, 1998.

Kielinger, Thomas, Max Otte. "Germany: The Presumed Power." *Foreign Policy* (Summer 1993).

Kindleberger, Charles P. *Manias, Panics, and Crashes.* New York: Basic Books, Inc., 1978.

King, Martin Luther, Junior, *The Black Panthers Speak.* Da Capo Press, 1995.

Kinzer, Stephen. *Bitter Fruit.* New York: Anchor Press/Doubleday, 1984.

Klare, Michael T. *Resource Wars: The New Landscape of Global Conflict.* New York: Henry Holt and Company, 2001.

____, P. Kornbluh. *Low Intensity Warfare.* New York: Pantheon Books, 1988.

Klein, Naomi. *No Logo.* New York: Random House, 1999.

Knightley, Philip. *The First Casualty.* New York: Harcourt Brace Jovanovich, Publishers, 1975.

Kohn, Stephen M. *American Political Prisoners: Prosecution under the Espionage and Sedition Acts.* Westport: Praeger Publishers, 1994.

Kolko, Gabriel. *The Politics of War.* New York: Pantheon, 1990.

Komisar, Lucy. "Documented Complicity: Newly Released Files Set the Record Straight on U.S. Support for Pinochet." *The Progressive* (September, 1999).

Koning, Hans. *The Conquest of America: How the Indian Nations Lost Their Continent.* New York: Monthly Review Press, 1993.

Kornblush, Peter. *Nicaragua, The Price of Intervention: Reagan's War Against the Sandinistas.* Washington DC: Institute for Policy Studies, 1987.

Kornblush, P., M. Byrne. *The Iran-Contra Scandal: The Declassified History.* New York: A National Security Archive Documents Reader, The New Press. 1993.

Korten, David. *When Corporations Rule the World.* West Hartford, CT: Kumarian Press and San Francisco: Berret-Koehler, 1995

Kötke, William H. *The Final Empire: The Collapse of Civilization and the Seed of the Future.* Portland, OR: Arrow Point Press, 1993.

Kotz, David. "Russia in Shock: How Capitalist 'Shock Therapy' is Destroying Russia's Economy." *Dollars and Sense* (June 1993).

Kraus, Michael. *The United States to 1865.* Ann Arbor: University of Michigan Press, 1959.

Kropotkin, Petr. *Mutual Aid.* Boston: Porter Sargent Publishers Inc., 1914.

_____. *The Great French Revolution.* New York: Black Rose Books, 1989.

_____. *The State.* London: Freedom Press, 1987.

Kurtzman, Joel. *The Death of Money.* New York: Simon and Schuster, 1993.

_____. *The Decline and Crash of the American Economy.* New York: W.W. Norton, 1988.

Kwitny, Jonathan. *The Crimes of Patriots.* New York: W.W. Norton, 1987.

_____. *Endless Enemies: The Making of an Unfriendly World.* New York: Congdon & Weed, 1984.

Labeviere, Richard. *Dollars for Terror: The United States and Iran.* New York: Algora Publishing, 2000.

Lacey, Robert. *Ford.* New York: Ballantine Books, 1986.

Ladanov, Ivan, Vladimar Pronnikov. "Craftsmen and Electronics." *New Times* 47 (November 1988).

Lambert, Angela. *Unquiet Souls.* New York: Harper & Row, 1984.

Landau, Saul, and Sarah Anderson. "Autumn of the Autocrat." *CovertAction Quarterly* 64 (Spring 1998),

_____. "Moscow Rules Moss's Mind." *CovertAction Quarterly* 16 (Summer 1985).

_____. "Opus Die: Secret Order Vies for Power." *CovertAction Quarterly* 18 (Winter 1983).

Landay, Jonathan S. "Study Reveals U.S. Has Spent $4 Trillion on Nukes Since '45." *The Christian Science Monitor* (July 12, 1995).

Landis, F.S. *Psychological Warfare and Media Operations in Chile 1970-1973.* Doctoral dissertation, University of Illinois, 1975.

Lane, Charles, Theodore Stanger, Tom Post. "The Ghosts of Serbia." *Newsweek* (April 19, 1993).

Lane, Mark. *Plausible Denial: Was the CIA Involved in the Assassination of JFK?* New York: Thunder Mouth Press, 1991.

Lansdale, E.G. *In the Midst of Wars.* New York: Harper & Row, 1972.

Lappé, Frances Moore. *Diet for a Small Planet.* Rev. New York: Ballantine Books, 1978.

_____. . *World Hunger: Twelve Myths.* New York: Grove Press: 1998.

_____. and Joseph Collins. *Food First: Beyond the Myth of* Scarcity. Rev. New York: Ballantine Books, 1979.

_____. and Rachel Schurman. *Taking Population Seriously.* San Francisco: Institute for Food and Development Policy, 1990.

_____. and Anna Lappé, *Hope's Edge: The Next Diet for a Small Planet.* New York: Penguin Putman, 2002.

Larsen, C. "In the Wake of Columbus: Native Population Biology in the Postcontact Americas." *American Journal of Physical Anthropology* 54 (1994, Supplement 19), 109-154.
Layne, Christopher. "Rethinking American Grand Strategy." *World Policy Journal* (Summer 1998).
Lea, Henry Charles. *The Inquisition of the Middle Ages.* New York: Citidel Press, 1954.
Lee, Dwight E. *Europe's Crucial Years.* Hanover, NH: Clark University Press, 1974.
Lee, Martin A. and Norman Solomon. *Unreliable Sources: A Guide to Detecting Bias in the news.* New York: Carol Publishing, 1990.
Lefeber, Walter. *Inevitable Revolutions.* New York: W.W. Norton, 1984.
Leigh, David. *The Wilson Plot.* New York: Pantheon, 1988.
Lens, Sidney. *Permanent War.* New York: Schocken Books, 1987.
Levant, V. *Quiet Complicity: Canadian Involvement In The Vietnam* War. Toronto, Canada: Between the Lines, 1986.
Levy, Steven. "Bills New Vision." *Newsweek* (November 27, 1995).
Lewis, Hunter, Donald Allison. *The Real Cold War.* New York: Coward, McCann, and Geoghegan, 1982.
Lilliston, Ben. "Shredding 'the Ecologist." *The Progressive* (February 1999).
Lindsey, Hal. *The Road to the Holocaust.* New York: Bantam Books, 1989.
Lippmann, Walter. *Public Opinion.* New York: Simon & Schuster, 1949.
List, Friedrich. *The National System of Political Economy.* Fairfield, NJ: Augustus M. Kelley, 1977.
Litvinoff, Barnet. *The Burning Bush.* New York: E.P. Dutton, 1988.
Livingston, Harrison Edward. *Killing the Truth: Deceit and Deception in the JFK Case.* New York: Carroll & Graf, 1993.
Loftus, John. *The Belarus Secret.* New York: Alfred A. Knopf, 1982.
Lohbeck, K. *Holy War, Unholy Victory: Eyewitness to the CIA's Secret War in Afghanistan.* Washington DC: Regnery Gateway, 1993,
Logan, John A. *The Great Conspiracy: Its Origin and History, 1732-1775.* New York: A.R Hart & Co., 1886.
Longworth, Richard C. *Global Squeeze: The Coming Crisis of First-World Nations.* Chicago: Contemporary Books, 1999.
"Low Cholesterol Beef Produced on State Ranches." *The Missoulian* (October 15, 1986).
Lyon, Peter. *To Hell in a Day Coach.* New York: J. B. Lippincott Company, 1968.
MacDonald, William, ed. *Documentary Source Book of American History, 1606-1926*, 3rd ed.. New York: MacMillan, 1926.
Mackay, Charles. *Extraordinary Delusions and Madness of Crowds.* 2nd. ed. New York: Farrar Straus and Giroux, 1932.
Mackay, Neil. "Bush Planned Iraq 'Regime Change' Before Coming President." *The Sunday Herald* (Scotland), September 15, 2002. MacKenzie, Angus, *Secrets: The CIA's War at Home.* Berkeley: University of California Press, 1997.
Madsen, Wayne. "Crypto Ag: The NSA's Trojan Whore?" *CovertAction Quarterly* (Winter 1998).
Magdoff, Harry. "A Note on the Communist Manifesto." *Monthly Review*, (May 1998).
_____. "Are There Lessons To Be Learned?" *Monthly Review* (February 1991).
_____. and Paul M. Sweezy. *Stagnation and the Financial Explosion.* New York: Monthly Review Press (1987).
Makhijani, Arjun. *From Global Capitalism to Economic Justice.* New York: Apex Press, 1992.
Makin, John H. *The Global Debt Crisis.* New York: Basic Books, 1984.
Malkin, Lawrence. *The National Debt.* New York: Henry Holt, 1988.
Manchester, William. *The Glory and The Dream.* New York: Bantam Books, 1988.
Mander, Jerry, Edward Goldsmith. *The Case Against the Global Economy.* San Francisco: Sierra Club Books, 1996.
Mann, Jim. "China's Response to U.S.: Slow, Slow." *Los Angeles Times* (October 28, 1998).
Mansoor, Feisal, "The Health of Nations," *Lanka Monthly Digest* (December 2000).
Mansour, Fawzy "A Second Wave of National Liberation?" *Monthly Review* (February 1999).
Manz. Beatriz .*Refugees of A Hidden War: The Aftermath of Counterinsurgency in Guatemala.* New York: State University of New York, 1988.
Marchetti, Victor, John D. Marks. *The CIA and the Cult of Intelligence.* New York: Knopf 1974; Dell Publishing, 1980.
Marcuse, Peter. "Letter from the German Democratic Republic." *Monthly Review* (July/August 1990).
"Mark Twain on Henry George" at gopher://echonyc.com:70/00/Cul/HGS/archimed
Marks, P. *In a Barren Land.* New York: William Morrow and Company, 1998.
Marrs, Jim. *Crossfire: The Plot That Killed Kennedy.* New York: Carroll and Graf, 1989.
Marshall, J., P.D. Scott, J. Hunter. *The Iran-Contra Connection.* Boston, MA: South End Press, 1987.
"Marshall Plan for Creditors and Speculators." *Economic Reform*" (January 1999).
Martin, D. *Wilderness of Mirrors.* New York: Harper and Row, 1980.
Martin, Edward Winslow. *History of the Grange Movement.* New York: Burt Franklin, 1967.

Martin, Hans-Peter and Harold Schuman. *The Global Trap: Globalization & the Assault on Democracy and Prosperity*. London: Zed Books, 1997.
Marton, Kati. *The Polk Conspiracy: Murder and Cover Up in the Case of CBS News Correspondent George Polk*. New York: Farrar, Staus & Giroux, 1990.
Marx, Karl. *Capital*, 3 vols. edited by Frederick Douglas. New York: International Publishers, 1967.
Mayer, Milton. *They Thought They Were Free*. Chicago, University of Chicago Press, 1955.
Mayers, David. *George Kennan*. New York: Oxford University Press, 1988.
Maynes, Charles William, "A New Strategy for Old Foes and New Friends." *World Policy Journal*, (Summer 2000).
McCann, T. *An American Company: The Tragedy of United Fruit*. New York: Crown Publishers, 1976.
McChesney, Robert. *Corporate Media and the Threat to Democracy*. New York: Seven Stories Press, 1997.
_____. ed. *Capitalism and the Information Age: The Political Economy of the Global Communication* Revolution. New York: Monthly Review Press, 1998.
_____. and Edward S. Herman. T*he Global Media: The Missionaries of Global Capitalism*. Washington, D. C.: Cassell, 1997.
McClain, William E. *Illinois Prairie: Past and Future: A Restoration* Guide. Springfield, IL: Illinois Department of Conservation, 1986.
McClintock, Michael. *Instruments of Statecraft: U.S. Guerrilla Warfare, Counter Insurgency, and Counter Terrorism* 1940-1990. New York: Pantheon, 1992.
_____. *The American Connection: State Terror and Popular Resistance in Guatemala*. London: Zed Books, 1985.
_____. *The American Connection: State Terror and Popular Resistance in El Salvador*. London: Zed Books, 1985.
McGehee, Ralph W. *Deadly Deceits*. New York: Sheridan Square Press, 1983.
_____. *CIABASE*, Box 5022, Herndon, VA 22070; http://come.to/CIABASE/.
McGehee, Ralph. "The Indonesia File." *The Nation* (Sept. 24, 1990).
McIntyre, Robert S. "The Populist Tax Act of 1989." *The Nation* (April 2, 1988).
McKibben, Bill. "The Enigma of Kerala." *Utne Reader* (Mar/April 1996).
McNeill, William H. *The Pursuit of Power*. Chicago: University of Chicago Press, 1982.
McReynolds, David. "The Words and the Will to Talk About Change." *The Progressive* (March 28, 1991).
Mead, Walter Russell. "After Hegemony." *New Perspective Quarterly*, (1987).
_____. "American Economic Policy in the Antemillenial Era." *World Policy Journal*, (Summer 1989).
_____. "The Bush Administration and the New World Order." *World Policy Journal* (Summer 1991).
_____. *Mortal Splendor*. Boston: Houghton Mifflin Company, 1987.
_____. "Saul Among the Prophets." *World Policy Journal*, (Summer 1991).
Medvedev, Roy. "Parallels Inappropriate." *New Times* (July 1989).
Meister, C. "Demographic Consequences of Euro-American Contact on Selected American Indian Populations and their Relationship to the Demographic Transition." *Ethnohistory* 23 (1976), 161-172.
Melman, Seymour. *Profits Without Production*. New York: Alfred A. Knopf, 1983.
Merriam, H. "The Indian Population of California." *American Anthropologist* 7 (1905), 594-606.
Metcalf, Lee, Vic Reinemer. *Overcharge*. New York: David McKay, 1967.
Milani, Brian. *Designing the Green Economy: The Postindustrial Alternative to Corporate Globalization*. New York: Rowman & Littlefield, 2000.
Miller, Christian, "Wall Street's Fondest Dream: The Insanity of Privatizing Social Security," *Dollars and Sense* (November/December 1998).
Miller, John C. *Origins of the American Revolution*. Boston: Little Brown and Co., 1943.
Miller, N. *Spying for America*. New York: Paragon House, 1989.
Miller, V. "Whatever Happened to the Yuki?" *Indian Historian* 8 (Fall 1975), 6-12.
Mills, Stephanie. *In Service of the Wild: Restoring and Reinhabiting Damaged Land*. Boston: Beacon Press, 1995.
Minnick, Wendell. *Spies and Provocateurs: A Worldwide Encyclopedia of Persons Conducting Espionage and Covert Action, 1946-1991*. Jefferson, North Carolina: McFarland,1992.
Minter, W. *Apartheid's Contras: An Inquiry into the Roots of War in Angola and Mozambique*. London, England. ZED Books, 1994.
Mirow, Kurt Rudolph, Harry Maurer. *Webs of Power*. Boston: Houghton Mifflin Company, 1982.
Moberg, David. "Cutting the U.S. Military: How Low Can We Go?" *In These Times* (February 12-18, 1992).
_____. "Can Public Spending Rescue the Infrastructure: A Tale of Three Deficits." *In These Times* (February 13-19, 1991).
Moffitt, Michael. "Shocks, Deadlocks, and Scorched Earth: Reaganomics and the Decline of U.S. Hegemony." *World Policy Journal* (Fall 1987).
_____. *The World's Money*. New York: Simon and Schuster, 1983.
Mohammad, Yousai, M. Adkin. *The Beartrap: Afghanistan's Untold Story*. London, England: Leo Cooper, 1992.
Mollison, Bill. *Permaculture: A Designers' Manual*. Tyalgum, Australia: Tagari Pub., 1988.

Monbiot, George. "A Discreet Deal in the Pipeline" The Guardian (15 February 2001).
Moore, David W. *The Super Pollsters: How they Measure and Manipulate Public Opinion in America.* New York: Four Walls Eight Windows, 1992.
Morison, Samuel Eliot and Henry Steele Commanger, *Growth of the American Republic*, 5th ed. New York: W.W. Norton, 1959.
Morgan, Dan and David B Ottaway. "In Iraqi Oil Scenario, Oil is Key Issue: U.S. Drillers Eye Huge Petroleum Pool." *Washington Post*, September 14, 2002.
Morrison, Roy. *We Build the Road as We Travel.* Philadelphia: New Society Publishers, 1991.
Mumford, Lewis. *The City in History.* New York: Harcourt Brace Jovanovich, 1961.
_____. *Pentagon of Power.* New York: Harcourt Brace Jovanovich, 1964, 1970.
_____. *Technics and Civilization.* New York: Harcourt Brace Jovanovich, 1963.
_____. *Technics and Human Development.* New York: Harcourt Brace Jovanovich, 1967.
Murphy, Austin. *The Triumph of Evil: The Reality of the USA's Cold War Victory.* Italy: European Press Academic Publishing, 2000.
Murphy, R. Taggart. *The Weight of The Yen.* New York: W.W. Norton, 1996.
Muyumba, Francois N., Esther Atcherson. *Pan-Africanism and Cross-Cultural Understanding: A Reader.* Needham Heights, MA: Ginn Press, 1993.
Myers, Norman, General Editor. *Gaia: An Atlas of Planet Management* Garden City, New York: Anchor Books, 1984.
Nadudere, Dan. *The Political Economy of Imperialism.* London: Zed Books, 1977.
Nair, K. *Devil and His Dart: How the CIA is Plotting in The Third World.* New Delhi: Sterling Publishers, 1986.
Namier, Sir Lewis and John Brooke, *Charles Townsend.* New York: St. Martin's Press, 1964.
Narton, Kati. *The Polk Conspiracy: Murder and Cover-up in the case of Correspondent George Polk.* New York: Farrar, Straus, and Giroux, 1990.
National Endowment for Democracy, *Annual Report.*
National Geographic TV (August 23, 1987).
Neilson, Francis. *How Diplomats Make War.* New York: Robert Schalkenbach Foundation, 1984.
"New Financial Architecture Crumbles." *Economic Reform* (March 1999).
Newman, Richard J, "A Kosovo Numbers Game," *U.S. News & World Report* (July 12, 1999).
Noakes, J., G. Pridham, editors. *Nazism 1919 - 1945.* 2 vols. New York: Schocken Books, 1988.
Norton, Peggy. "Independent Radio's Problems and Prospects." *Z Magazine* (March, 1990).
Nossiter, Bernard D. "The F.C.C.'s Big Giveaway Show." *The Nation* (October 26, 1985).
Nova. PBS (September 2, 1986).
Oberman, Heiko A. *The Roots of Anti-Semitism.* Philadelphia: Fortress Press, 1984.
Omestat, Thomas. "Addicted to Sanctions." *U.S. News & World Report* (June 15, 1998).
101 Famous Thinkers on Owning Earth, New York: Robert Schalkenbach Foundation, no date.
O'Toole, G.J.A. *Honorable Treachery.* New York: Atlantic Monthly Press, 1991.
Owen, Wilfred. *Strategy for Mobility.* Westport, CT: Greenwood Press, 1978.
Palast, Greg. *The Best Democracy that Money can buy: The Truth about Corporate Cons, Globalization, and High-finance Fraudsters.* London: Penguin Books, 2003.
Parakal, P.V. *Secret Wars Of CIA.* New Delhi: Sterling Publishers Private Limited, 1984.
Parenti, Christian. "Nasa's Assault on the Ozone Layer." *Lies of Our Times* (September 1993).
Parenti, Michael. *Power and the Powerless.* New York: St. Martin's Press, 1978.
_____. *History as Mystery.* San Francisco: City Light Books, 1999.
_____. *To Kill a Nation.* New York: Verso, 2000.
_____. *Inventing Reality: The Politics of the Mass Media.* New York: St Martins's Press, 1986.
Parnas, David Lorge. "Con: Dayton's a Step Back—Way back," *Peace* (March/April 1996).
Pastor, Robert A., Ed. *A Century's Journey: How the Great Powers Shape the World.* New York: Basic Books, 1999.
Patterson, Charles. *Anti-Semitism: The Road to the Holocaust and Beyond.* New York: Walker, 1982.
Patterson, Thomas. *Inventing Western Civilization.* New York: Cornerstone Books, 1997.
Pauly, David, Rich Thomas, and Judith Evans,. "The Dirty Little Debt Secret." *Newsweek* (April 17, 1989).
Pearson, Hugh. *The Shadow of the Panther: Huey Newton and the Price of Black Power in America.* Perseus Press, 1995.
Pentagon Papers: *The Defense Department History of United States Decision Making on Vietnam*, Senator Mike Gravel Ed. Boston: Beacon Press, 1971.
Pepper, William F. *An Act of State: The Execution of Martin Luther King.* New York: Verso, 2003.
Perleman, Michael. *The Invention of Capitalism: Classical Political Economy and the Secret History of Primitive Accumulation.* London: Duke University Press, 2000.
Peterson, Scott . "In War, Some Facts Less Factual." *The Christian Science Monitor September 6, 2002.*

Peterzell, J. *Reagan's Secret Wars*, CNSS Report 108. Washington, DC: Center for National Security Studies, 1984.
Petras, James. "Argentina: Between Disintegration & Revolution." *CovertAction Quarterly* (Fall 2002).
_____. "Latin America's Free Market Paves the Road to Recession." *In These Times* (February 13-19).
_____. and Henry Veltmeyer, "Latin America at the End of the Millennium," *Monthly review* (July/August 1999).
Phillips, D.A. *The Night Watch*. New York: Atheneum, 1977.
Phillips, Kevin. *Boiling Point: Democrats, Republicans, and the Decline of Middle Class Prosperity*. New York: Random House, 1993.
_____. *The Politics of Rich and Poor*. New York: Random House, 1990.
Pilarski, Michael. *Restoration Forestry: An International Guide to Sustainable Forestry Practices*. Durango, CO: Kivaki Press, 1994.
Pilzer, Paul Zane. *Unlimited Wealth*. New York: Crown Publishing, 1990.
Pirenne, Henri. *Economic and social history of medieval Europe*. New York: Harcourt, Brace, 1937.
Pike Committee Report. *Congressional Record* (1975-76)
Pitt, William Rivers with Scott Ritter. *War on Iraq*. New York: Context Books, 2002.
Polanyi, Karl. *The Great Transformation*. Boston: Beacon Press, 1957.
Poole, Fred, Max Vanzi. *Revolution in the Philippines: The United States in A Hall of Cracked Mirrors*. New York: McGraw-Hill, 1984.
Pool, James, Suzanne Pool. *Who Financed Hitler?* New York: The Dial Press, 1978.
Porter, G. "The politics of counterinsurgency in the Philippines: Military and Political Options." *Philippine Studies Occasional Paper No. 9*. Honolulu: University of Hawaii, Center for Philippine Studies (1987).
Potts, Michael. *The Independent Home: Living Well with Power from the Sun, Wind, and Water*. Post Mills, VT: Chelsea Green Pub. Co., 1993.
Powell, Bill. "Iraq, We Win, Then What." *Fortune* (November 25, 2003).
Powers, T. *The Man Who Kept The Secrets*. New York: Alfred A. Knopf, 1979.
Prados, John. *The Presidents' Secret Wars*. New York: William Morrow, 1986.
_____. *The Presidents Secret Wars, revised*. Warwick: Elephant Paperbacks, 1996.
_____. Prados, John. *The Hidden History of the Vietnam War*. Chicago: Elephant Paperbacks, 1995.
_____. *Keepers Of The Keys A History Of The National Security Council From Truman To Bush*. New York: William Morrow, 1991.
Prager, Dennis. *Why the Jews: The Reason for Antisemitism*. New York: Simon and Schuster, 1983.
Preston, William, Jr., Edward S. Herman, Herbert I. Schiller, *Hope and Folly*. Minneapolis: University of Minnesota Press, 1989.
"Proud Russia on Its Knees." *U.S. News & World Report* (February 8, 1999).
Prouty, L.F. JFK: *The CIA, Vietnam, and the Plot to Assassinate John F. Kennedy*. New York: Birch Lane Press, 1992.
_____. *The Secret Team*. Englewood Cliffs, NJ: Prentice-Hall, 1973.
Public Power Directory and Statistics for 1983. Washington, DC: American Public Power Association, 1983.
Quigley, John. *The Ruses for War: American Interventionism Since World War II*. Buffalo: Prometheus Books, 1992.
Quinn, T. K. *Giant Business: Threat to Democracy. 3rd. ed.* New York: Exposition Press, 1954.
Raanes, Tuva. "A Divine Country All on Its Own." *World Press Review*, October 2002.
Raghavan, Chakravarthi. *Recolonization: GATT, the Uruguay Round & the Developing World*. London: Zed Books, 1990.
Rai Milan. *War Plan Iraq*. London: Verso Press, 2002.
Ranelagh, John. *The Agency: The Rise and Decline of the CIA*. New York: Simon and Schuster, 1986.
Ratner Michael. "The Pinochet Principle: Who's Next?" *CovertAction Quarterly 66* (Winter 1999)
Rayack, Elton, *Not So Free to Choose: The Political Economy of Milton Friedman and Ronald Reagan*. Westport, Conn: Praeger, 1986.
Re *Latin America Magazine*, August, 1974,
Reding, Andrew A. "Bolstering Democracy in The Americas." *World Policy Journal* (Summer 1992).
Reed, John. *The Education of John Reed*. New York: International Publishers, 1955.
Renard, George. *Guilds of the Middle Ages*. New York: Augustus M. Kelly, 1968.
A Report by The International Institute for Environment and Development and The World Resources Institute,
World Resources (1987): An Assessment of the Resource Base That Supports the Global Economy. New York: Basic Books, 1987.
Rich, Bruce. "Conservation Woes at the World Bank." *The Nation* (January 23, 1989).
Richard, David. *Stevia Rebaudiana: Nature's Sweet Secret*. Bloomingdale, IL: Vital Health, 1999.
Richelson, J. *American Espionage and The Soviet Target*. New York: William Morrow, 1987.
_____. *The U.S. Intelligence Community*. Cambridge, MA: Ballinger Publishing Company, 1985.

Richter, Paul. "Commodity Marts Face Fraud Fallout." *Los Angeles Times*, Quoted in the Missoulian (July 4, 1987).

Ridenour, R. Back Fire: *The CIA's Biggest Burn.* Havana, Cuba: José Marti Publishing House, 1991.

Rifkin, Jeremy. *Beyond Beef.* New York: Dutton, 1992.

_____. "Beyond Beef." *Utne Reader* (March/April 1992).

_____. *Biosphere Politics.* San Francisco: HarperCollins, 1992.

_____. *Entropy: Into the Greenhouse World.* Rev. ed. New York: Bantam Books, 1989.

Robert Schalkenbach Foundation, 41 E. 72nd Streets, New York, NY 10021.

Roberts, J.M. *The Triumph of the West.* London: British Broadcasting Company, 1985.

Robbins, C. The Ravens: *The Men Who Flew In America's Secret War.* New York: Crown Publishers, 1987.

Robinson, Linda. "America's Secret Armies," *U.S. News & World Report* (November 4, 2002).

_____. "What didn't we do to get rid of Castro." *U.S. News & World Report* (October 26, 98).

Robinson, William I. *A Faustian Bargain: U.S. Intervention in the Nicaraguan Elections and American Foreign Policy in the Post-Cold War Era.* Boulder, CO: Westview Press, 1992.

Rodman, Peter. *More Precious Than Peace.* New York: Charles Scribner & Sons, 1994.

Rojas, Raul. *The Poverty of Nations.* New Jersey: Zed Books, 1991.

Roosevelt, Kermit. *Countercoup: The Struggle for the Control Of Iran.* New York: McGraw-Hill, 1979.

Rositzke, H. *The CIA's Secret Operations.* New York: Thomas Y. Crowell Company, 1977.

Ross, Michael. "Yeltsin: POWs 'Summarily Executed.'" *The Spokesman Review* (November 12, 1992).

Rousseau, Jean Jacques. *"A Discourse on the Origins of Inequality." The Social Contract and Discourses.* New York: Dutton, 1950.

Routh, Guy. *The Origin of Economic Ideas.* Dobbs Ferry, NY: Sheridan House, 1989.

Rubenstein, Richard L. *Approaches to Auschwitz: The Holocaust and Its Legacy.* Atlanta: John Knox Press, 1987.

_____. *The Age of Triage.* Boston: Beacon Press, 1983.

Ruether, Rosemary. *Faith and Fratricide: The Theological Roots of Anti-Semitism* New York: Seabury Press, 1974.

"Rural Montana Gets Taste of Public TV." *The Missoulian* (October 8, 1987).

"The Rush To Gulp US Radio Stations." *The Christian Science Monitor* (May 7, 1996).

Rzheshevsky, Oleg. *World War II: Myths and the Realities. Moscow, U.S. USSR*: Progress Publishers, 1984.

Sachar, Abram L. *A History of the Jews.* New York: Knopf, 1965.

Sale, Kirkpatrick. *The Conquest of Paradise.* New York: Alfred A. Knopf, 1991.

Samaray, Catherine. *Yugoslavia Dismembered.* New York: Monthly Review Press, 1995.

Sampson, Anthony. *The Midas Touch.* New York: Truman Talley Books/Plume, 1991.

_____. *The Money Lenders.* New York: Penguin Books, 1981.

Samuelson, Robert. "The Great Global Debtor." *Newsweek* (July 22, 1991).

Saunders, Frances Stoner. *The Cultural Cold War: The CIA and the World of Arts and Letters.* New York: The Free Press, 1999.

Sanders, Jerry W. "The Prospects for 'Democratic Engagement'." *World Policy Journal* (Summer 1992).

Sandford, R.R. *The Murder of Allende.* A. Conrad, translator, New York: Harper & Row, 1975.

Sanoff, Alvin P., et al. "Who Will Control TV." *U.S. News & World Report* (May 13, 1985).

Sayre, Nora. *Running Time: Films of the Cold War.* New York: Dial Press, 1980.

Scheer, Christopher. "Illegals Made Slaves to Fashion." *The Nation* (September 11, 1995).

Schiller, Herbert I. *Information and the Crisis Economy.* Boston: Oxford University Press, 1986.

_____. *Communications and Cultural Domination.* White Plains, NY: M. E. Sharp, Inc., 1976.

_____. "The Information Superhighway: Paving over the Public." *Z Magazine* (March 1994).

_____. *Mind Managers.* Boston: Beacon Press, 1973.

Schirmer, Daniel B. and Stephen Rosskamm Shalom. *The Philippines Reader: A History of Colonialism, Dictatorship, and Resistance.* Boston: South End Press, 1987.

Schlesinger, Stephen. "The CIA Censor's History." *The Nation* (September 7, 1997).

Schlosstein, Steven. *Trade War.* New York: Congdon and Weed, 1984.

Schor, Juliet B. "Workers of the World Unwind." *Technology Review* (November/December 1991).

_____. *The Overworked American.* Basic Books, 1991.

Schrecker, Ellen. *No Ivory Tower: McCarthyism in the Universities.* New York: Oxford University Press, 1986.

Schuman, Julian. *China: an Uncensored Look.* Sagaponack, NY : Second Chance Press, 1979.

Scott, P.D. "Exporting military-economic development: America and the overthrow of Sukarno, 1965-67." In M. Caldwell, editor. *Ten Years Military Terror Indonesia.* Nottingham: Spokesmen Books.

Seldes, George. *Even the Gods Can't Change History.* Secaucus, NJ: Lyle Stuart, Inc., 1976.

_____. *Never Tire of Protesting.* New York: Lyle Stuart, 1968.

_____. "The Roman Church and Franco." *The Human Quest* (March/April 1994).

Seneker, Harold. "The World's Billionaires." *Forbes* (October 5, 1987).

Sergeyev, F.F. *Chile: CIA Big Business*, L. Bobrov, translator. Moscow, USSR: Progress Publishers, 1981.

"Set in Concrete." *The Economist.* (June 3, 1995).
Shalom, Stephan Rosskamm. "Bullets, Gas, and The Bomb." *Z Magazine* (February 1991).
_____. *Imperial Alibis.* Boston: South End Press, 1993.
Sheehan, N. *A Bright Shining Lie.* New York: Random House, 1988.
Sheridan, David. *Desertification of the United States.* Washington DC: U.S. Government Printing Office, #334-983: Council on Environmental Quality, 1981.
Shiva, Vananda. *Biopiracy: The Plunder of Nature and Knowledge.* Boston: South End Press, 1997.
_____. *Stolen Harvest: The Hijacking of the Global Food Supply.* Boston: South End Press, 2000.
Shoup, L., W. Minter. *Imperial Brain Trust: The Council on Foreign Relations & United States Foreign Policy.* New York: Monthly Review Press, 1977.
Simon, Jean-Marie. Guatemala: *Eternal Spring Eternal Tyranny.* New York: W.W. Norton, 1988.
Simpson, Christopher. *Blowback.* New York: Weidenfeld & Nicolson, 1988.
Sipols, Vilnis. *The Road to Great Victory.* Moscow, USSR: Progress Publishers, 1985.
Sivard, Ruth Leger. *World Military and Social Expenditures.* Washington, DC: World Priorities, published Annually, all issues.
60 Minutes (CBS). April 20, 1987; October 25, 1987; September 2, 1995; May 19, 1996.
Skidmore, Thomas, Peter Smith, "*The Pinochet Regime*", *In Modern Latin America, 2nd ed.*. New York: Oxford University Press, 1989.
Sklar, Holly, *Washington's War On Nicaragua.* Boston: South End Press, 1988.
Smith, Adam. *The Wealth of Nations.* New York: Random House, 1965.
"Smith, Adam" (George J.W. Goodman). *Supermoney.* New York: Random House, 1972.
_____. *Nightly Business Report, PBS* (June 17, 1987).
Smith, J. Allen. *The Spirit of American Government: A Study of the Constitution: Its Origin, Influence and Relation to Democracy*, New York: Macmillan, 1907.
Smith, J.W. *WHY?: The Deeper History* Behind the September 11th, Terrorist Attack on America. updated and expanded 2nd edition. www.ied.info/cc.html: The Institute for Economic Democracy, 2003.
_____. *Cooperative Capitalism: A Blueprint for Global Peace and Prosperity.* www.ied.info/cc.html. The Institute for Economic Democracy, 2003.
_____. *The World's Wasted Wealth 2.* The Institute for Economic Democracy, www.ied.info/cc.html. The Institute for Economic Democracy, 1994.
Smith, Mathew. *Say Goodbye to America: The Sensational and Untold Story Behind the Assassination of John F. Kennedy.* London: Mainstream Publishing, 2001.
Snepp, Frank. *Decent Interval.* New York: Random House, 1977.
Soltani, Atossa, Penelope Whitney, Editors. *Cut Waste, Not Trees.* San Francisco, CA: Rainforest Action Network, 1995.
Spencer, Herbert. *Social Statics.* Robert Schalkenbach Foundation, 1850 unabridged ed.
Stannard, D. *American Holocaust.* Oxford: Oxford University Press, 1992.
Stauber, John and Sheldon Ramption. *Toxic Sludge is Good for You: Lies, Damn Lies and the Public Relations Industry.* Monroe, ME: Common Courage Press, 1995.
"States' Right: Hawaii's Land Reform Upheld." *Time* (June 11, 1984).
Statistical Abstract of the United States. Washington DC: U.S. Government Printing Office, 1990, 1992.
Stelzer, Gus. *The Nightmare of Camelot: An Exposé of the Free Trade Trojan Horse.* Seattle, Wash.: PB publishing, 1994.
Stephanson, Anders. *Kennan and the Art of Foreign Policy.* Cambridge: Harvard University Press, 1989.
Stiglitz, Joseph. *Globalization and its Discontents* New York: WW Norton, 2002
Stigum, Marcia. *Money Markets.* Homewood, IL: Dow Jones-Irwin, 1978.
Stockwell, John. *In Search of Enemies.* New York: W. W. Norton, 1978.
_____. *The Praetorian Guard.* Boston: South End Press, 1991.
Stone, I.F. *The Hidden History of the Korean War.* Boston: Little, Brown, 1952.
_____. *Polemics and Prophecy.* Boston: Little Brown, 1970.
Stone, Oliver. *Movie JFK.*
Strange, Susan. *The Retreat of the State: The Diffusion of Power in the Global Economy*, Cambridge, UK: Cambridge Studies in International Relations number 49, 1998.
Stromnes, John. "Rural Montana Gets Taste of Public TV." *The Missoulian* (October 8, 1987).
Summers, Anthony. *Conspiracy.* New York: Paragon House, 1989.
Swann, Robert. *The Need for Local Currencies.* Great Barrington, MA: E.F. Schumacher Society, 1990.
Swearingen, M. Wesley. *FBI Secrets : An Agent's Exposé.* Boston: South End Press, 1995.
Swentzell, Athena. *The Straw Bale House.* White River Junction, VT: Chelsea Green Pub. Co., 1994..
Synan, Edward A. *The Pope and the Jews in the Middle Ages.* New York: Macmillan, 1965.
Tabb, William. *The Amoral Elephant: Globalization and the Struggle for Global Justice in the Twenty-First Century.* New York: Monthly Review Press, 2001.

Taheri, Amir. *Nest of Spies: America's Journey to Disaster in Iran.* New York: Pantheon Books, 1988.

Taylor, Edmond. *The Fall of the Dynasties: The fall of the Old Order, 1905-1922.* New York: Dorset Press, 1989.

Thirgood, J.V. *Man and the Mediterranean Forest: A History of Resource Depletion.* New York: Academic Press, 1981.

Thomas, E. The *Very Best Men: Four Who Dared: The Early Years of the CIA..* New York: Simon & Schuster, 1995.

Thomas, Peter D.J. *The Townshend Duties Crisis: The Second Phase of the American Revolution, 1776-1773.* Oxford: Clarendon Press, 1987.

Thomas, Rich. "From Russia, With Chips," *Newsweek* (August 6, 1990).

Thomas, William L. Jr., Ed. *Man's Role In Changing The Face Of The Earth,* 2 vols. Chicago, Ill: U. of Chicago Press, 1956.

Thompson, D., R. Larson. *Where Were You Brother?* London: War on Want Publishers 1978.

Thompson, E. P., Dan Smith. Protest and Survive. New York: *Monthly Review Press,* 1981.

Thoren, Theodore R., Richard F. Warner. *The Truth in Money.* Chagrin Falls, Ohio: Truth in Money Publishers, 1994.

Thornton, R. *American Indian Holocaust and Survival.* Norman: University of Oklahoma Press, 1987.

"Three Musketeers, The." *Time.* (February 15, 1996).

Thurow, Lester C. *Head to Head: The Coming Economic Battle Among Japan, Europe, and America.* New York: William Morrow, 1992.

_____. "Falling Wages, Failing Policy." *Dollars and Sense* (September/October 1996).

_____. "The Crusade That is Killing Prosperity." *The American Prospect* (March/April 1996).

_____. *Dangerous Currents.* New York: Random House, 1983.

_____. *Generating Inequality.* New York: Basic Books, 1975.

_____. "Investing in America's Future." *Economic Policy Institute, C-Span Transcript.* (October 21, 1991).

_____. *The Future of Capitalism: How Today's Economic Forces Shape Tomorrow's* World. England, Penguin Books, 1996.

_____. Thurow, Lester, *Building Wealth: The New Rules for Individuals, Companies and Nations in a knowledge Based Economy.* New York: HarperCollins, 2000.

Tobin, Eugene *M. Organize or Perish. New York: Greenwood Press, 1986.*

Tokar, Brian. Redesigning Life? The Worldwide Challenge to Genetic Engineering. London: Zed Books, 2001.

"Top 1% Own More Than Bottom 90%," *The Des Moines Register* (April 21, 1992).

Townsend, Mike. "Microwatt Revolution." *Lies of Our Times* (January 1991).

Train, John. *Famous Financial Fiascoes.* New York: Clarkson N. Potter,1985.

Treverton, G. *Covert Action: The Limits of Intervention in the Post-War World.* New York: Basic Books, 1987.

Tuchman, Barbara. *The March of Folly.* New York: Alfred A. Knopf, 1984.

Tucker, George. *The Theory of Money and Banks Investigated.* New York: Greenwood Press, 1968.

Tucker, Robert W. "The Triumph of Wilsonianism." *World Policy Journal* (Winter 1993/94).

Turk, Jonathan, Janet T. Wittes, Robert Wittes, Amos Turk. *Ecosystems, Energy, Population.* Toronto: W.B. Saunders Co., 1975.

Turner, Stansfield. *Secrecy and Democracy: The CIA in Transition.* Boston: Houghton Mifflin Company, 1985.

"TV Direct From Satellite to Your Home—It Could Be Soon." *U.S. News & World Report* (June 26, 1967).

Twentieth Century Fund. *The Need to Know: The Report of The Twentieth Century Fund Task Force on Covert Action and American Democracy.* New York: The Twentieth Century Fund Press, 1992.

Tynan, Judy. "Farm Credit System's Transfers Face Trial." *The Spokesman-Review* (December 31, 1986).

United Nations Commission on the Truth in El Salvador. *From Madness To Hope: The 12-Year War In El Salvador.* U.N. Security Council (1993).

United Nations Human Development Report. 1991, 1998.

United Nations Truth Commission on Guatemala. *U.N Security Council* (1995, 1999).

"U.S. Becomes Biggest Dealer of Arms in Worldwide Market." *The Spokesman Review* (October 15, 1992).

United States Department of Agriculture, *First Conference on Kenaf for Pulp: Proceedings.* Peoria, IL: USDA, 1968.

Uribe, A. *The Black Book of American Intervention in Chile.* Boston, MA: Beacon Press, 1975.

Valentine, Douglas. *The Phoenix Program.* New York: William Morrow, 1990.

Vandenberg, Arthur Hendrick. *The Greatest American.* New York: G.P. Putman's and Sons, 1921

Vanek, Jaroslav. *The Labor Managed Economy.* London: Cornell University Press, 1977.

Veblen, Thorstein. *Engineers and the Price System.* New York: B. W. Huebsch, Inc., 1921.

_____. *Essays in Our Changing Order.* New York: The Viking Press, 1934.

_____. *The Vested Interests.* New York: B. W. Huebsch Inc., 1919.

Vidal, Gore. "The National Security State: How To Take Back Our Country." *The Nation* (June 4, 1988).
Volkman, Ernest, Blaine Baggett. *Secret Intelligence*. New York: Doubleday, 1989.
Volman, Dennis. "Salvador Death Squads: A CIA Connection?" *The Christian Science Monitor* (May 8, 1984).
Wachtel, Howard M. "Labor's Stake in WTO." *The American Prospect* (March/April 1998).
_____. "The Global Funny Money Game." The Nation (December 26, 1987).
_____. *Money Mandarins*. New York: Pantheon Books, 1986.
_____. *The Politics of International Money*. Amsterdam: Transnational Institute, 1987.
Wallace, Henry. *Towards World Peace*. Westport, CT: Greenwood Press, 1970.
Wallerstein, Immanuel. *The Origin of the Modern World System*. 2 vol. New York: Academic Press, 1974.
Walter, Ingo. *The Secret Money Market*. New York: HarperCollins, 1990.
Waters, F. *Book of the Hopi*. New York: Penguin, 1977.
Waters, Mary-Alice. *The Rise and Fall of the Nicaraguan Revolution*. New York: New International, 1994.
Watson, B., S. Watson, G. Hopple. *United States Intelligence: An Encyclopedia*. New York: Garland Publishing, 1990.
Watt, Donald Cameron. *How War Came: The Immediate Origins of the Second World War*. New York: Pantheon Books, 1989.
Weatherford, Jack. *Indian Givers*. New York: Fawcett Columbine, 1988.
Wedel, Janine R. "The Harvard Boys Do Russia," *The Nation* (June 1, 1998).
Weiner, T. *Blank Check: The Pentagon's Black Budget*. New York: Warners Books, 1990.
Weir Fred. "Brain Drain." *In These Times* (December 14, 1992).
_____. "Interview: Fred Weir in Russia." *CovertAction Quarterly* (Summer 1993).
Weisbrot, Mark. "The Mirage of Progress." *The American Prospect,* supplement (Winter 2002), pp. A10-A123.
Weisman, Alan. "Columbia's Modern City." *In Context* 42 (1995).
_____. Nothing Wasted, Everything Gained:." *Mother Jones* (March/April, 1998).
Weissman, Steve. *The Trojan Horse*. Rev. ed. Palo Alto: Ramparts Press, 1975.
Wessel, James, Mort Hartman. *Trading the Future*. San Francisco: Institute for Food and Policy Development, 1983.
West, Nigel. *Games of Intelligence*. New York: Crown Publishers, 1989.
Westerfield, H. B. editor. *Inside CIA's Private World: Declassified Articles from the Agency's Internal Journal 1955-1992*. New Haven CT. Yale University Press, 1995.
Wiener, Don. "Will GATT Negotiators Trade Away the Future." *In These Times* (February 12-18, 1992).
Wild, Rolf H. *Management by Compulsion*. Boston: Houghton Mifflin Company, 1978.
Willan, Philip. *Puppetmasters: The Political Use of Terrorism in Italy*. London: Constable, 1991.
Williams, Eric. *From Columbus to Castro*. New York: Vintage Books, 1984.
Williams, William Appleman. *The Contours of American History*. New York: W.W. Norton, 1988.
_____. *Empire as a Way of Life*. Oxford: Oxford University Press, 1980.
_____. *The Tragedy of American Diplomacy*. New York: W. W. Norton, 1988.
Williamson, Samuel Jr. *The Politics of Grand Strategy*. London: Ashfield Press, 1969.
Willis, Henry Parker, and B.H. Beckhart. *Foreign banking systems*. New York, Henry Holt, 1929.
Wilson, Edward O. *Life On Earth*. Stamford, Conn: Sinauer Associates, 1973.
_____. Life: Cells, *Organisms,Populations*. Sunderland, MA: Sinauer Associates, 1977.
_____. *In Search of Nature*. Washington, DC: Island Press, 1996.
Wilson, Edward O., Charles J. Lumsden. *Genes, Mind, and Culture: The Coevolutionary Process*. Cambridge, MA: Harvard University Press, 1981.
_____. *Promethean Fire: Reflections On the Origin of Mind*. Cambridge, MA: Harvard University Press, 1983.
Wilson, Edward O., Robert H. MacArthur. The Theory of Island Biogeography. Princeton, N.J.: Princeton University Press, 1967.
Windishar, Anne. "Expert: 20% of Gifted Kids Drop Out." *Spokane Chronicle* (January 7, 1988).
Winks, Robin W. *Cloak & Gown: Scholars in the Secret War, 1939-1961*. New York: Quill, 1987.
Wise, David, Thomas B. Ross. *The Espionage Establishment*. New York: Bantam Books, 1978.
Wittner, Lawrence. *American Intervention in Greece*. New York: Columbia University Press, 1982.
Wright, Robin. *Sacred Rage: The Wrath of Militant Islam*. New York: Simon & Schuster, 1985.
Wright, Ronald. *Stolen Continents: The Americas Through Indian Eyes*. New York: Houghton Miflin, 1992.
Wolf, Eric R. *Europe and the People Without History*. Berkeley: University of California Press, 1982.
Wolf, Louis. "Inaccuracy in Media: Accuracy in Media Rewrites the News and History. *CovertAction Quarterly* 21 (Spring 1984).
Woodhouse, C.M. *The Rise and Fall of the Greek Colonels*. New York: Franklin Watts, 1985.
"Workers' State." Editorial in *The Nation* (September 19, 1988).
World Monitor. July 17, 1990.

World Resources. Report by the International Institute for Environment and Development and The World Resources Institute (1987).

Wu, Harry. "A Prisoner's Journey." *Newsweek* (September 23, 1991).

Wu Yi, "China-US Trade Balances: An objective Evaluation." *Beijing Review* (June 10-16, 1996).

Wyden, P. *Bay Of Pigs The Untold Story.* New York: Simon and Schuster, 1979.

Yallop, David A., *In God's Name.* New York: Bantaam Books, 1984.

Yochelson, John. "China's Boom Creates a U.S. Trade Dilemma." *The Christian Science Monitor* (March 1, 1994).

Young, M. *The Vietnam Wars 1945-1990.* New York: HarpersCollins, 1991.

Zeagler, Jean. *Switzerland Exposed.* New York: Allison & Busby, 1981.

Zinn, Howard. *A People's History of the United States.* New York: Harper Colophon Books, 1980.

_____. *The Politics of History.* Chicago: University of Illinois Press, 1990.

_____. *The Twentieth Century.* New York: Harper & Row, 1984.

Zuckerman, Mortimer B. "Where Have the Good Jobs Gone" *U.S. News & World Report* (July 31, 1995).

Index

ABOUT THE AUTHOR

With a Ph.D. in political economics, J.W. Smith has written broadly and lectured widely at conferences around the world. This is the 3rd edition of his 4th book on the causes and cures of world poverty.

J.W. Smith not only takes a different view from most economists his deep research pushes dense and impossible to understand neoliberal economics off the table and replaces it with sensible economics that we can all understand. As he says, "neoliberal economics makes sense only within borders of an empire. As soon as one steps outside those borders they make no sense at all. How could it? It is designed to lay claim to the wealth of the periphery of empire?"

Smith's 20 years of deep study of economic history builds a new school of thought. Where else do you read how wealth accumulation increases or decreases exponentially with the differential in pay between equally productive labor? That evolving from plunder by raids to plunder by trade became the signature of "civilized" nations? That Adam Smith free trade was specifically designed to entrench this system of laying claim to others wealth? Or that no nation ever developed under that philosophy? The exposure of these realities provide a new foundation upon which to understand the world.

That understanding of economic history leads us to Smith's explanation of how Western "democracies" evolved from feudalism and today's property rights laws retain the essentials of those feudal exclusive rights to nature's bounty. The concept these monopoly rights which exclude the weak from their rightful share follows naturally.

Smith provides the historic foundation to understand how Western "democracies" evolved from feudalism, that property rights still retain feudal exclusive rights to nature's bounty, and that it is these monopoly rights excluding the weak from their rightful share as the powerful continue the privatization of the commons that impoverishes so many people.

Smith looked deeply under the blanket of imposed belief systems protecting the power structure and its stolen wealth and concluded the debris of custom and law are the barriers preventing Western societies from evolving into peaceful and far more productive societies.

Smith's explanation of how the elimination of those monopolies through expanding individual rights and competition through a modern commons increasing economic efficiency equal to the invention of money, writing, and electricity providing all with a quality life working only two to three days per week; all while protecting the earth's resources and ecosphere, provides a ray of light on what we must do for a peaceful and prosperous world.

Many have, or sense, these fundamentals of poverty already; they just have not learned how to articulate them. A quick read of Smith's research will provide the articulation tools to go head to head with those imposing the very philosophy which is creating their poverty. That is a debate the powerbrokers and their negotiators cannot win once the masses and their negotiators are armed with the simple tools of truth.

Being fully free is having full and equal economic rights. If the world's poor share this knowledge among themselves, and especially if Developing World universities accept the job of informing the masses, no amount of propaganda and bluster can stop the world from gaining their full rights and rising out of poverty.

There is no left in the Western political system, only a right and an extreme right and that nation is moving further right all the time. This thesis is not to the left, it is in the middle. We are not proposing government ownership of industry as socialism does. We are proposing restructuring private property rights to provide full and equal rights to all and maximize the efficiencies of the *wealth-producing-process*. The solid logic and the enormous gains possible under *democratic-cooperative-capitalism* permits the so-called left (really the middle) to regain their voice.

Share your unique understanding through your books. If all this were to happen, this knowledge will sweep across the world and not even the powerful nation's *Mighty Wurlitzer* could stop it. The truth is too simple and too sensible. People are good. Prove to philosophers and negotiators in the wealthy world that poverty can be relatively quickly eliminated and many will recognize they have been misinformed and support you.

Form study groups to look deeply into every aspect of why there is poverty and how to eliminate it. Professors, organize your peers and students to study this in depth.

If you wish to join, or financially support, one of our groups, please do so through a check to addresses at the web sites below or paying a membership fee through PayPal and simultaneously emailing us your name and address. That payment and email will automatically register you as a member. Go to www.ied.info/resources.html or www.ied.info/cc.html for further updates. Please join us:

The Institute for Cooperative Capitalism

1st World, $30 Students/3rd World $10

Creating a blueprint for global peace and prosperity

www.paypal.com/, account: cc@ccus.info

www.ccus.info/

The Institute for Economic Democracy

1st World, $30 Students/3rd World $10
Sustainable development research: peace and prosperity for all
www.paypal.com/, account: ied@ied.info
www.ied.info/

Global Literacy Outreach

1st World, $30 Students/3rd World $10
Illuminating the darkness of illiteracy
www.paypal.com/, account: glo@gloliteracy.org
www.gloliteracy.org/

International Philosophers for Peace

1st World, $30 Students/3rd World $10
Developing a just social, economic, & political basis for peace and human well-being
www.paypal.com/, account: ippno@ippno.org
wwwippno.org/

Action Institute for Literacy and Human Resource Development

1st World, $30 Students/3rd World $10
Education through Project Learning Communities (PLC)
www.paypal.com/, account: plc@ailahurd.org
www.ailahurd.org/

The Hour Money Institute for Global Harmony

1st World, $30 Students/3rd World $10
Dedicated to establishing an hour of work as the money unit worldwide
www.paypal.com/, hourmoney@hourmoney.org
wwwhourmoney.org/

Network On Democracy Over Empire

1st World, $30 Students/3rd World $10
Dedicated to egalitarian democracies replacing the global imperial system
www.paypal.com/, accounts: wdavis@kent.edu
wwwaltedavis.info/

Global Issues (www.globalissues.org)

A very active supporter but does not take donations at this time

Rights are available for publishing in your region, in English or translations, www.ied.info/cc.html.

ied@ied.info

A special price to groups for books in bulk as a money-earning/ educational project, www.ied.info/cc.html.

ied@ied.info

We are available to present these concepts to your class or group. There is the potential that this can be handled at no cost to you, www.ied.info/cc.html.

ied@ied.info